THIRD EDITION

COMPUTER SYSTEM ARCHITECTURE

M. Morris Mano

California State University
Los Angeles

PRENTICE HALL, ENGLEWOOD CLIFFS, NEW JERSEY 07632

Library of Congress Cataloging-in-Publication Data

Mano, M. Morris
    Computer system architecture / M. Morris Mano. -- 3rd ed.
        p.   cm.
    Includes index.
    ISBN 0-13-175563-3
    1. Computer architecture.   I. Title.
QA76.9.A73M36   1993
004.2'2--dc20   92-12094
                                                       CIP

Acquisitions editor: *Pete Janzow*
Production editor: *Jennifer Wenzel*
Designer: *Sheree Goodman*
Copy editor: *Barbara Zeiders*
Cover designer: *Bass & Goldman, Inc.*

Prepress buyer: *Linda Behrens*
Manufacturing buyer: *David Dickey*
Supplements editor: *Alice Dworkin*
Editorial assistant: *Phyllis Morgan*

© 1993, 1982, 1976 by Prentice-Hall, Inc.
A Paramount Communications Company
Englewood Cliffs, New Jersey 07632

The author and publisher of this book have used their best efforts in preparing this book. These efforts include the development, research, and testing of the theories and programs to determine their effectiveness. The author and publisher make no warranty of any kind, expressed or implied, with regard to these programs or the documentation contained in this book. The author and publisher shall not be liable in any event for incidental or consequential damages in connection with, or arising out of, the furnishing, performance, or use of these programs.

ISBN   0-13-175563-3

Prentice-Hall International (UK) Limited, *London*
Prentice-Hall of Australia Pty. Limited, *Sydney*
Prentice-Hall Canada Inc., *Toronto*
Prentice-Hall Hispanoamericana, S.A., *Mexico*
Prentice-Hall of India Private Limited, *New Delhi*
Prentice-Hall of Japan, Inc., *Japan*
Simon & Schuster Asia Pte. Ltd., *Singapore*
Editora Prentice-Hall do Brasil, Ltda., *Rio de Janeiro*

Contents

CHAPTER FOUR

Register Transfer and Microoperations   93

CHAPTER FIVE

Basic Computer Organization and Design   123

CHAPTER SIX

Programming the Basic Computer   173

CHAPTER SEVEN

Microprogrammed Control   213

Input-Output Organization   381

CHAPTER TWELVE

Memory Organization   445

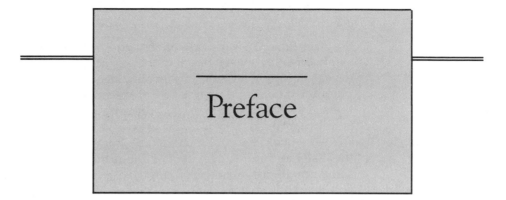

Preface

This book deals with computer architecture as well as computer organization and design. Computer architecture is concerned with the structure and behavior of the various functional modules of the computer and how they interact to provide the processing needs of the user. Computer organization is concerned with the way the hardware components are connected together to form a computer system. Computer design is concerned with the development of the hardware for the computer taking into consideration a given set of specifications.

The book provides the basic knowledge necessary to understand the hardware operation of digital computers and covers the three subjects associated with computer hardware. Chapters 1 through 4 present the various digital components used in the organization and design of digital computers. Chapters 5 through 7 show the detailed steps that a designer must go through in order to design an elementary basic computer. Chapters 8 through 10 deal with the organization and architecture of the central processing unit. Chapters 11 and 12 present the organization and architecture of input-output and memory. Chapter 13 introduces the concept of multiprocessing. The plan of the book is to present the simpler material first and introduce the more advanced subjects later. Thus, the first seven chapters cover material needed for the basic understanding of computer organization, design, and programming of a simple digital computer. The last six chapters present the organization and architecture of the separate functional units of the digital computer with an emphasis on more advanced topics.

The material in the third edition is organized in the same manner as in the second edition and many of the features remain the same. The third edition, however, offers several improvements over the second edition. All chapters except two (6 and 10) have been completely revised to bring the material up to date and to clarify the presentation. Two new chapters were added: chapter 9 on pipeline and vector processing, and chapter 13 on multiprocessors. Two sections deal with the reduced instruction set computer (RISC). Chapter 5 has been revised completely to simplify and clarify the design of the basic computer. New problems have been formulated for eleven of the thirteen chapters.

The physical organization of a particular computer including its registers, the data flow, the microoperations, and control functions can be described symbolically by means of a hardware description language. In this book we develop a simple register transfer language and use it to specify various computer operations in a concise and precise manner. The relation of the register transfer language to the hardware organization and design of digital computers is fully explained.

The book does not assume prior knowledge of computer hardware and the material can be understood without the need of prerequisites. However, some experience in assembly language programming with a microcomputer will make the material easier to understand. Chapters 1 through 3 can be skipped if the reader is familiar with digital logic design.

The following is a brief description of the subjects that are covered in each chapter with an emphasis on the revisions that were made in the third edition.

Chapter 1 introduces the fundamental knowledge needed for the design of digital systems constructed with individual gates and flip-flops. It covers Boolean algebra, combinational circuits, and sequential circuits. This provides the necessary background for understanding the digital circuits to be presented.

Chapter 2 explains in detail the logical operation of the most common standard digital components. It includes decoders, multiplexers, registers, counters, and memories. These digital components are used as building blocks for the design of larger units in the chapters that follow.

Chapter 3 shows how the various data types found in digital computers are represented in binary form in computer registers. Emphasis is on the representation of numbers employed in arithmetic operations, and on the binary coding of symbols used in data processing.

Chapter 4 introduces a register transfer language and shows how it is used to express microoperations in symbolic form. Symbols are defined for arithmetic, logic, and shift microoperations. A composite arithmetic logic shift unit is developed to show the hardware design of the most common microoperations.

Chapter 5 presents the organization and design of a basic digital computer. Although the computer is simple compared to commercial computers, it nevertheless encompasses enough functional capabilities to demonstrate the power of a stored program general purpose device. Register transfer language is used to describe the internal operation of the computer and to specify the requirements for its design. The basic computer uses the same set of instructions as in the second edition but its hardware organization and design has been completely revised. By going through the detailed steps of the design presented in this chapter, the student will be able to understand the inner workings of digital computers.

Chapter 6 utilizes the twenty five instructions of the basic computer to illustrate techniques used in assembly language programming. Programming examples are presented for a number of data processing tasks. The relationship between binary programs and symbolic code is explained by examples. The basic operations of an assembler are presented to show the translation from symbolic code to an equivalent binary program.

Chapter 7 introduces the concept of microprogramming. A specific micro-programmed control unit is developed to show by example how to write microcode for a typical set of instructions. The design of the control unit is carried-out in detail including the hardware for the microprogram sequencer.

Chapter 8 deals with the central processing unit (CPU). An execution unit with common buses and an arithmetic logic unit is developed to show the general register organization of a typical CPU. The operation of a memory stack is explained and some of its applications are demonstrated. Various instruction formats are illustrated together with a variety of addressing modes. The most common instructions found in computers are enumerated with an explanation of their function. The last section introduces the reduced instruction set computer (RISC) concept and discusses its characteristics and advantages.

Chapter 9 on pipeline and vector processing is a new chapter in the third edition. (The material on arithmetic operations from the second edition has been moved to Chapter 10.) The concept of pipelining is explained and the way it can speed-up processing is illustrated with several examples. Both arithmetic and instruction pipeline is considered. It is shown how RISC processors can achieve single-cycle instruction execution by using an efficient instruction pipeline together with the delayed load and delayed branch techniques. Vector processing is introduced and examples are shown of floating-point operations using pipeline procedures.

Chapter 10 presents arithmetic algorithms for addition, subtraction, multiplication, and division and shows the procedures for implementing them with digital hardware. Procedures are developed for signed-magnitude and signed-2's complement fixed-point numbers, for floating-point binary numbers, and for binary coded decimal (BCD) numbers. The algorithms are presented by means of flowcharts that use the register transfer language to specify the sequence of microoperations and control decisions required for their implementation.

Chapter 11 discusses the techniques that computers use to communicate with input and output devices. Interface units are presented to show the way that the processor interacts with external peripherals. The procedure for asynchronous transfer of either parallel or serial data is explained. Four modes of transfer are discussed: programmed I/O, interrupt initiated transfer, direct memory access, and the use of input-output processors. Specific examples illustrate procedures for serial data transmission.

Chapter 12 introduces the concept of memory hierarchy, composed of cache memory, main memory, and auxiliary memory such as magnetic disks. The organization and operation of associative memories is explained in detail. The concept of memory management is introduced through the presentation of the hardware requirements for a cache memory and a virtual memory system.

Chapter 13 presents the basic characteristics of mutiprocessors. Various interconnection structures are presented. The need for interprocessor arbitration, communication, and synchronization is discussed. The cache coherence problem is explained together with some possible solutions.

Every chapter includes a set of problems and a list of references. Some of the problems serve as exercises for the material covered in the chapter. Others are of a more advanced nature and are intended to provide practice in solving problems associated with computer hardware architecture and design. A solutions manual is available for the instructor from the publisher.

The book is suitable for a course in computer hardware systems in an electrical engineering, computer engineering, or computer science department. Parts of the book can be used in a variety of ways: as a first course in computer hardware by covering Chapters 1 through 7; as a course in computer organization and design with previous knowledge of digital logic design by reviewing Chapter 4 and then covering chapters 5 through 13; as a course in computer organization and architecture that covers the five functional units of digital computers including control (Chapter 7), processing unit (Chapters 8 and 9), arithmetic operations (Chapter 10), input-output (Chapter 11), and memory (Chapter 12). The book is also suitable for self-study by engineers and scientists who need to acquire the basic knowledge of computer hardware architecture.

Acknowledgments

My thanks goes to those who reviewed the text: particularly Professor Thomas L. Casavant of the University of Iowa; Professor Murray R. Berkowitz of George Mason University; Professor Cem Ersoy of Brooklyn Polytechnic University; Professor Upkar Varshney of the University of Missouri, Kansas City; Professor Karan Watson of Texas A&M University, and Professor Scott F. Midkiff of the Virginia Polytechnic Institute.

M. Morris Mano

CHAPTER ONE

Digital Logic Circuits

IN THIS CHAPTER

1-1   Digital Computers

digital

The digital computer is a digital system that performs various computational tasks. The word *digital* implies that the information in the computer is represented by variables that take a limited number of discrete values. These values are processed internally by components that can maintain a limited number of discrete states. The decimal digits 0, 1, 2, . . . , 9, for example, provide 10 discrete values. The first electronic digital computers, developed in the late 1940s, were used primarily for numerical computations. In this case the discrete elements are the digits. From this application the term *digital computer* has emerged. In practice, digital computers function more reliably if only two states are used. Because of the physical restriction of components, and because human logic tends to be binary (i.e., true-or-false, yes-or-no statements), digital components that are constrained to take discrete values are further constrained to take only two values and are said to be *binary*.

bit

Digital computers use the binary number system, which has two digits: 0 and 1. A binary digit is called a *bit*. Information is represented in digital computers in groups of bits. By using various coding techniques, groups of bits can be made to represent not only binary numbers but also other discrete

1

symbols, such as decimal digits or letters of the alphabet. By judicious use of binary arrangements and by using various coding techniques, the groups of bits are used to develop complete sets of instructions for performing various types of computations.

In contrast to the common decimal numbers that employ the base 10 system, binary numbers use a base 2 system with two digits: 0 and 1. The decimal equivalent of a binary number can be found by expanding it into a power series with a base of 2. For example, the binary number 1001011 represents a quantity that can be converted to a decimal number by multiplying each bit by the base 2 raised to an integer power as follows:

$$1 \times 2^6 + 0 \times 2^5 + 0 \times 2^4 + 1 \times 2^3 + 0 \times 2^2 + 1 \times 2^1 + 1 \times 2^0 = 75$$

The seven bits 1001011 represent a binary number whose decimal equivalent is 75. However, this same group of seven bits represents the letter K when used in conjunction with a binary code for the letters of the alphabet. It may also represent a control code for specifying some decision logic in a particular digital computer. In other words, groups of bits in a digital computer are used to represent many different things. This is similar to the concept that the same letters of an alphabet are used to construct different languages, such as English and French.

A computer system is sometimes subdivided into two functional entities: hardware and software. The hardware of the computer consists of all the electronic components and electromechanical devices that comprise the physical entity of the device. Computer software consists of the instructions and data that the computer manipulates to perform various data-processing tasks.

program   A sequence of instructions for the computer is called a *program*. The data that are manipulated by the program constitute the *data base*.

A computer system is composed of its hardware and the system software available for its use. The system software of a computer consists of a collection of programs whose purpose is to make more effective use of the computer. The programs included in a systems software package are referred to as the *operating system*. They are distinguished from application programs written by the user for the purpose of solving particular problems. For example, a high-level language program written by a user to solve particular data-processing needs is an application program, but the compiler that translates the high-level language program to machine language is a system program. The customer who buys a computer system would need, in addition to the hardware, any available software needed for effective operation of the computer. The system software is an indispensable part of a total computer system. Its function is to compensate for the differences that exist between user needs and the capability of the hardware.

computer hardware   The hardware of the computer is usually divided into three major parts, as shown in Fig. 1-1. The central processing unit (CPU) contains an arithmetic

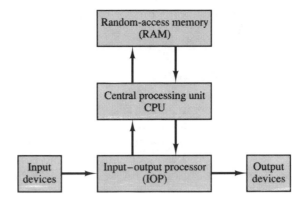

Figure 1-1 Block diagram of a digital computer.

and logic unit for manipulating data, a number of registers for storing data, and control circuits for fetching and executing instructions. The memory of a computer contains storage for instructions and data. It is called a random-access memory (RAM) because the CPU can access any location in memory at random and retrieve the binary information within a fixed interval of time. The input and output processor (IOP) contains electronic circuits for communicating and controlling the transfer of information between the computer and the outside world. The input and output devices connected to the computer include keyboards, printers, terminals, magnetic disk drives, and other communication devices.

This book provides the basic knowledge necessary to understand the hardware operations of a computer system. The subject is sometimes considered from three different points of view, depending on the interest of the investigator. When dealing with computer hardware it is customary to distinguish between what is referred to as computer organization, computer design, and computer architecture.

computer organization   *Computer organization* is concerned with the way the hardware components operate and the way they are connected together to form the computer system. The various components are assumed to be in place and the task is to investigate the organizational structure to verify that the computer parts operate as intended.

computer design   *Computer design* is concerned with the hardware design of the computer. Once the computer specifications are formulated, it is the task of the designer to develop hardware for the system. Computer design is concerned with the determination of what hardware should be used and how the parts should be connected. This aspect of computer hardware is sometimes referred to as *computer implementation*.

computer architecture   *Computer architecture* is concerned with the structure and behavior of the computer as seen by the user. It includes the information formats, the instruction set, and techniques for addressing memory. The architectural design of a computer system is concerned with the specifications of the various functional modules, such as processors and memories, and structuring them together into a computer system.

The book deals with all three subjects associated with computer hardware. In Chapters 1 through 4 we present the various digital components used in the organization and design of computer systems. Chapters 5 through 7 cover the steps that a designer must go through to design and program an elementary digital computer. Chapters 8 and 9 deal with the architecture of the central processing unit. In Chapters 11 and 12 we present the organization and architecture of the input–output processor and the memory unit.

1-2   Logic Gates

Binary information is represented in digital computers by physical quantities called *signals*. Electrical signals such as voltages exist throughout the computer in either one of two recognizable states. The two states represent a binary variable that can be equal to 1 or 0. For example, a particular digital computer may employ a signal of 3 volts to represent binary 1 and 0.5 volt to represent binary 0. The input terminals of digital circuits accept binary signals of 3 and 0.5 volts and the circuits respond at the output terminals with signals of 3 and 0.5 volts to represent binary input and output corresponding to 1 and 0, respectively.

Binary logic deals with binary variables and with operations that assume a logical meaning. It is used to describe, in algebraic or tabular form, the manipulation and processing of binary information. The manipulation of bi-

gates

nary information is done by logic circuits called *gates*. Gates are blocks of hardware that produce signals of binary 1 or 0 when input logic requirements are satisfied. A variety of logic gates are commonly used in digital computer systems. Each gate has a distinct graphic symbol and its operation can be described by means of an algebraic expression. The input–output relationship of the binary variables for each gate can be represented in tabular form by a *truth table*.

The names, graphic symbols, algebraic functions, and truth tables of eight logic gates are listed in Fig. 1-2. Each gate has one or two binary input variables designated by A and B and one binary output variable designated by

AND

x. The AND gate produces the AND logic function: that is, the output is 1 if input A and input B are both equal to 1; otherwise, the output is 0. These conditions are also specified in the truth table for the AND gate. The table shows that output x is 1 only when both input A and input B are 1. The algebraic operation symbol of the AND function is the same as the multiplication symbol of ordinary arithmetic. We can either use a dot between the variables or

Name	Graphic symbol	Algebraic function	Truth table
AND	 A, B → x	$x = A \cdot B$ or $x = AB$	A B | x 0 0 | 0 0 1 | 0 1 0 | 0 1 1 | 1
OR	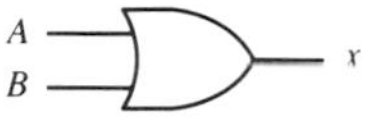 A, B → x	$x = A + B$	A B | x 0 0 | 0 0 1 | 1 1 0 | 1 1 1 | 1
Inverter	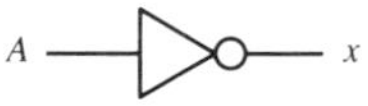 A → x	$x = A'$	A | x 0 | 1 1 | 0
Buffer	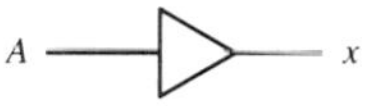 A → x	$x = A$	A | x 0 | 0 1 | 1
NAND	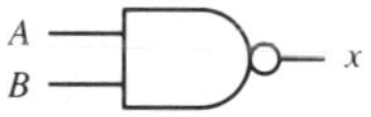 A, B → x	$x = (AB)'$	A B | x 0 0 | 1 0 1 | 1 1 0 | 1 1 1 | 0
NOR	 A, B → x	$x = (A + B)'$	A B | x 0 0 | 1 0 1 | 0 1 0 | 0 1 1 | 0
Exclusive-OR (XOR)	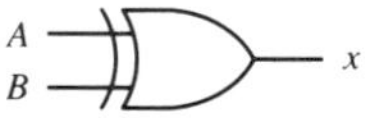 A, B → x	$x = A \oplus B$ or $x = A'B + AB'$	A B | x 0 0 | 0 0 1 | 1 1 0 | 1 1 1 | 0
Exclusive-NOR or equivalence	 A, B → x	$x = (A \oplus B)'$ or $x = A'B' + AB$	A B | x 0 0 | 1 0 1 | 0 1 0 | 0 1 1 | 1

Figure 1-2 Digital logic gates.

5

concatenate the variables without an operation symbol between them. AND gates may have more than two inputs, and by definition, the output is 1 if and only if all inputs are 1.

OR

The OR gate produces the inclusive-OR function; that is, the output is 1 if input A or input B or both inputs are 1; otherwise, the output is 0. The algebraic symbol of the OR function is +, similar to arithmetic addition. OR gates may have more than two inputs, and by definition, the output is 1 if any input is 1.

inverter

The inverter circuit inverts the logic sense of a binary signal. It produces the NOT, or complement, function. The algebraic symbol used for the logic complement is either a prime or a bar over the variable symbol. In this book we use a prime for the logic complement of a binary variable, while a bar over the letter is reserved for designating a complement microoperation as defined in Chap. 4.

The small circle in the output of the graphic symbol of an inverter designates a logic complement. A triangle symbol by itself designates a buffer circuit. A buffer does not produce any particular logic function since the binary value of the output is the same as the binary value of the input. This circuit is used merely for power amplification. For example, a buffer that uses 3 volts for binary 1 will produce an output of 3 volts when its input is 3 volts. However, the amount of electrical power needed at the input of the buffer is much less than the power produced at the output of the buffer. The main purpose of the buffer is to drive other gates that require a large amount of power.

NAND

The NAND function is the complement of the AND function, as indicated by the graphic symbol, which consists of an AND graphic symbol followed by a small circle. The designation NAND is derived from the abbreviation of NOT-AND. The NOR gate is the complement of the OR gate and uses an OR graphic symbol followed by a small circle. Both NAND and NOR gates may have more than two inputs, and the output is always the complement of the AND or OR function, respectively.

NOR

exclusive-OR

The exclusive-OR gate has a graphic symbol similar to the OR gate except for the additional curved line on the input side. The output of this gate is 1 if any input is 1 but excludes the combination when both inputs are 1. The exclusive-OR function has its own algebraic symbol or can be expressed in terms of AND, OR, and complement operations as shown in Fig. 1-2. The exclusive-NOR is the complement of the exclusive-OR, as indicated by the small circle in the graphic symbol. The output of this gate is 1 only if both inputs are equal to 1 or both inputs are equal to 0. A more fitting name for the exclusive-OR operation would be an odd function; that is, its output is 1 if an odd number of inputs are 1. Thus in a three-input exclusive-OR (odd) function, the output is 1 if only one input is 1 or if all three inputs are 1. The exclusive-OR and exclusive-NOR gates are commonly available with two inputs, and only seldom are they found with three or more inputs.

1-3   Boolean Algebra

Boolean function

Boolean algebra is an algebra that deals with binary variables and logic operations. The variables are designated by letters such as A, B, x, and y. The three basic logic operations are AND, OR, and complement. A Boolean function can be expressed algebraically with binary variables, the logic operation symbols, parentheses, and equal sign. For a given value of the variables, the Boolean function can be either 1 or 0. Consider, for example, the Boolean function

$$F = x + y'z$$

truth table

The function F is equal to 1 if x is 1 or if both y' and z are equal to 1; F is equal to 0 otherwise. But saying that $y' = 1$ is equivalent to saying that $y = 0$ since y' is the complement of y. Therefore, we may say that F is equal to 1 if $x = 1$ or if $yz = 01$. The relationship between a function and its binary variables can be represented in a truth table. To represent a function in a truth table we need a list of the 2^n combinations of the n binary variables. As shown in Fig. 1-3(a), there are eight possible distinct combinations for assigning bits to the three variables x, y, and z. The function F is equal to 1 for those combinations where $x = 1$ or $yz = 01$; it is equal to 0 for all other combinations.

logic diagram

A Boolean function can be transformed from an algebraic expression into a logic diagram composed of AND, OR, and inverter gates. The logic diagram for F is shown in Fig. 1-3(b). There is an inverter for input y to generate its complement y'. There is an AND gate for the term $y'z$, and an OR gate is used to combine the two terms. In a logic diagram, the variables of the function are taken to be the inputs of the circuit, and the variable symbol of the function is taken as the output of the circuit.

The purpose of Boolean algebra is to facilitate the analysis and design of digital circuits. It provides a convenient tool to:

1. Express in algebraic form a truth table relationship between binary variables.

Figure 1-3   Truth table and logic diagram for $F = x + y'z$.

x	y	z	F
0	0	0	0
0	0	1	1
0	1	0	0
0	1	1	0
1	0	0	1
1	0	1	1
1	1	0	1
1	1	1	1

(a) Truth table

(b) Logic diagram

2. Express in algebraic form the input–output relationship of logic diagrams.

3. Find simpler circuits for the same function.

Boolean expression

A Boolean function specified by a truth table can be expressed algebraically in many different ways. By manipulating a Boolean expression according to Boolean algebra rules, one may obtain a simpler expression that will require fewer gates. To see how this is done, we must first study the manipulative capabilities of Boolean algebra.

Table 1-1 lists the most basic identities of Boolean algebra. All the identities in the table can be proven by means of truth tables. The first eight identities show the basic relationship between a single variable and itself, or in conjunction with the binary constants 1 and 0. The next five identities (9 through 13) are similar to ordinary algebra. Identity 14 does not apply in ordinary algebra but is very useful in manipulating Boolean expressions. Identities 15 and 16 are called DeMorgan's theorems and are discussed below. The last identity states that if a variable is complemented twice, one obtains the original value of the variable.

TABLE 1-1 Basic Identities of Boolean Algebra

(1) $x + 0 = x$	(2) $x \cdot 0 = 0$
(3) $x + 1 = 1$	(4) $x \cdot 1 = x$
(5) $x + x = x$	(6) $x \cdot x = x$
(7) $x + x' = 1$	(8) $x \cdot x' = 0$
(9) $x + y = y + x$	(10) $xy = yx$
(11) $x + (y + z) = (x + y) + z$	(12) $x(yz) = (xy)z$
(13) $x(y + z) = xy + xz$	(14) $x + yz = (x + y)(x + z)$
(15) $(x + y)' = x'y'$	(16) $(xy)' = x' + y'$
(17) $(x')' = x$	

The identities listed in the table apply to single variables or to Boolean functions expressed in terms of binary variables. For example, consider the following Boolean algebra expression:

$$AB' + C'D + AB' + C'D$$

By letting $x = AB' + C'D$ the expression can be written as $x + x$. From identity 5 in Table 1-1 we find that $x + x = x$. Thus the expression can be reduced to only two terms:

$$AB' + C'D + A'B + C'D = AB' + C'D$$

DeMorgan's theorem

DeMorgan's theorem is very important in dealing with NOR and NAND gates. It states that a NOR gate that performs the $(x + y)'$ function is equivalent to the function $x'y'$. Similarly, a NAND function can be expressed by either $(xy)'$ or $(x' + y')$. For this reason the NOR and NAND gates have two distinct graphic symbols, as shown in Figs. 1-4 and 1-5. Instead of representing a NOR gate with an OR graphic symbol followed by a circle, we can represent it by an AND graphic symbol preceded by circles in all inputs. The invert-AND symbol for the NOR gate follows from DeMorgan's theorem and from the convention that small circles denote complementation. Similarly, the NAND gate has two distinct symbols, as shown in Fig. 1-5.

To see how Boolean algebra manipulation is used to simplify digital circuits, consider the logic diagram of Fig. 1-6(a). The output of the circuit can be expressed algebraically as follows:

$$F = ABC + ABC' + A'C$$

Each term corresponds to one AND gate, and the OR gate forms the logical sum of the three terms. Two inverters are needed to complement A' and C'. The expression can be simplified using Boolean algebra.

$$F = ABC + ABC' + A'C = AB(C + C') + A'C$$
$$= AB + A'C$$

Note that $(C + C')' = 1$ by identity 7 and $AB \cdot 1 = AB$ by identity 4 in Table 1-1.

The logic diagram of the simplified expression is drawn in Fig. 1-6(b). It requires only four gates rather than the six gates used in the circuit of Fig. 1-6(a). The two circuits are equivalent and produce the same truth table relationship between inputs A, B, C and output F.

Figure 1-4 Two graphic symbols for NOR gate.

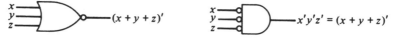

(a) OR-invert	(b) invert-AND

Figure 1-5 Two graphic symbols for NAND gate.

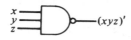
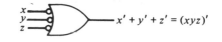

(a) AND-invert	(b) invert-OR

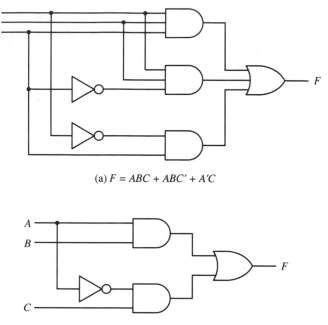

(a) $F = ABC + ABC' + A'C$

(B) $F = AB + A'C$

Figure 1-6   Two logic diagrams for the same Boolean function.

Complement of a Function

The complement of a function F when expressed in a truth table is obtained by interchanging 1's and 0's in the values of F in the truth table. When the function is expressed in algebraic form, the complement of the function can be derived by means of DeMorgan's theorem. The general form of DeMorgan's theorem can be expressed as follows:

$$(x_1 + x_2 + x_3 + \cdots + x_n)' = x_1' x_2' x_3' \cdots x_n'$$

$$(x_1 x_2 x_3 \cdots x_n)' = x_1' + x_2' + x_3' + \cdots + x_n'$$

From the general DeMorgan's theorem we can derive a simple procedure for obtaining the complement of an algebraic expression. This is done by changing all OR operations to AND operations and all AND operations to OR operations and then complementing each individual letter variable. As an example, consider the following expression and its complement:

$$F = AB + C'D' + B'D$$

$$F' = (A' + B')(C + D)(B + D')$$

The complement expression is obtained by interchanging AND and OR operations and complementing each individual variable. Note that the complement of C' is C.

1-4   Map Simplification

The complexity of the logic diagram that implements a Boolean function is related directly to the complexity of the algebraic expression from which the function is implemented. The truth table representation of a function is unique, but the function can appear in many different forms when expressed algebraically. The expression may be simplified using the basic relations of Boolean algebra. However, this procedure is sometimes difficult because it lacks specific rules for predicting each succeeding step in the manipulative process. The map method provides a simple, straightforward procedure for simplifying Boolean expressions. This method may be regarded as a pictorial arrangement of the truth table which allows an easy interpretation for choosing the minimum number of terms needed to express the function algebraically. The map method is also known as the Karnaugh map or K-map.

minterm
Each combination of the variables in a truth table is called a minterm. For example, the truth table of Fig. 1-3 contains eight minterms. When expressed in a truth table a function of n variables will have 2^n minterms, equivalent to the 2^n binary numbers obtained from n bits. A Boolean function is equal to 1 for some minterms and to 0 for others. The information contained in a truth table may be expressed in compact form by listing the decimal equivalent of those minterms that produce a 1 for the function. For example, the truth table of Fig. 1-3 can be expressed as follows:

$$F(x, y, z) = \Sigma\ (1, 4, 5, 6, 7)$$

The letters in parentheses list the binary variables in the order that they appear in the truth table. The symbol Σ stands for the sum of the minterms that follow in parentheses. The minterms that produce 1 for the function are listed in their decimal equivalent. The minterms missing from the list are the ones that produce 0 for the function.

The map is a diagram made up of squares, with each square representing one minterm. The squares corresponding to minterms that produce 1 for the function are marked by a 1 and the others are marked by a 0 or are left empty. By recognizing various patterns and combining squares marked by 1's in the map, it is possible to derive alternative algebraic expressions for the function, from which the most convenient may be selected.

The maps for functions of two, three, and four variables are shown in Fig. 1-7. The number of squares in a map of n variables is 2^n. The 2^n minterms are listed by an equivalent decimal number for easy reference. The minterm

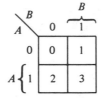

(a) Two-variable map

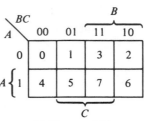

(b) Three-variable map

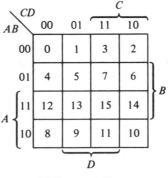

(c) Four-variable map

Figure 1-7 Maps for two-, three-, and four-variable functions.

numbers are assigned in an orderly arrangement such that adjacent squares represent minterms that differ by only one variable. The variable names are listed across both sides of the diagonal line in the corner of the map. The 0's and 1's marked along each row and each column designate the value of the variables. Each variable under brackets contains half of the squares in the map where that variable appears unprimed. The variable appears with a prime (complemented) in the remaining half of the squares.

The minterm represented by a square is determined from the binary assignments of the variables along the left and top edges in the map. For example, minterm 5 in the three-variable map is 101 in binary, which may be obtained from the 1 in the second row concatenated with the 01 of the second column. This minterm represents a value for the binary variables A, B, and C, with A and C being unprimed and B being primed (i.e., $AB'C$). On the other hand, minterm 5 in the four-variable map represents a minterm for four variables. The binary number contains the four bits 0101, and the corresponding term it represents is $A'BC'D$.

adjacent squares   Minterms of adjacent squares in the map are identical except for one variable, which appears complemented in one square and uncomplemented in the adjacent square. According to this definition of adjacency, the squares at the extreme ends of the same horizontal row are also to be considered adjacent. The same applies to the top and bottom squares of a column. As a result, the four corner squares of a map must also be considered to be adjacent.

A Boolean function represented by a truth table is plotted into the map by inserting 1's in those squares where the function is 1. The squares containing 1's are combined in groups of adjacent squares. These groups must contain a number of squares that is an integral power of 2. Groups of combined adjacent squares may share one or more squares with one or more groups. Each group of squares represents an algebraic term, and the OR of those terms gives the simplified algebraic expression for the function. The following examples show the use of the map for simplifying Boolean functions.

In the first example we will simplify the Boolean function

$$F(A, B, C) = \Sigma \ (3, 4, 6, 7)$$

The three-variable map for this function is shown in Fig. 1-8. There are four squares marked with 1's, one for each minterm that produces 1 for the function. These squares belong to minterms 3, 4, 6, and 7 and are recognized from Fig. 1-7(b). Two adjacent squares are combined in the third column. This column belongs to both B and C and produces the term BC. The remaining two squares with 1's in the two corners of the second row are adjacent and belong to row A and the two columns of C', so they produce the term AC'. The simplified algebraic expression for the function is the OR of the two terms:

$$F = BC + AC'$$

The second example simplifies the following Boolean function:

$$F(A, B, C) = \Sigma \ (0, 2, 4, 5, 6)$$

The five minterms are marked with 1's in the corresponding squares of the three-variable map shown in Fig. 1-9. The four squares in the first and fourth columns are adjacent and represent the term C'. The remaining square marked with a 1 belongs to minterm 5 and can be combined with the square of minterm 4 to produce the term AB'. The simplified function is

$$F = C' + AB'$$

Figure 1-8 Map for $F(A, B, C) = \Sigma \ (3,4,6,7)$.

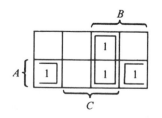

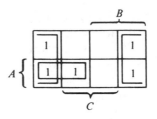

Figure 1-9 Map for $F(A, B, C) = \Sigma (0,2,4,5,6)$.

The third example needs a four-variable map.

$$F(A, B, C, D) = \Sigma (0, 1, 2, 6, 8, 9, 10)$$

The area in the map covered by this four-variable function consists of the squares marked with 1's in Fig. 1-10. The function contains 1's in the four corners that, when taken as a group, give the term $B'D'$. This is possible because these four squares are adjacent when the map is considered with top and bottom or left and right edges touching. The two 1's on the left of the top row are combined with the two 1's on the left of the bottom row to give the term $B'C'$. The remaining 1 in the square of minterm 6 is combined with minterm 2 to give the term $A'CD'$. The simplified function is

$$F = B'D' + B'C' + A'CD'$$

Product-of-Sums Simplification
The Boolean expressions derived from the maps in the preceding examples were expressed in sum-of-products form. The product terms are AND terms and the sum denotes the ORing of these terms. It is sometimes convenient to obtain the algebraic expression for the function in a product-of-sums form. The

Figure 1-10 Map for $F(A, B, C, D) = \Sigma (0,1,2,6,8,9,10)$.

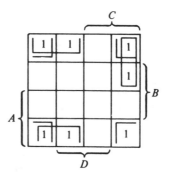

sums are OR terms and the product denotes the ANDing of these terms. With a minor modification, a product-of-sums form can be obtained from a map.

The procedure for obtaining a product-of-sums expression follows from the basic properties of Boolean algebra. The 1's in the map represent the minterms that produce 1 for the function. The squares not marked by 1 represent the minterms that produce 0 for the function. If we mark the empty squares with 0's and combine them into groups of adjacent squares, we obtain the complement of the function, F'. Taking the complement of F' produces an expression for F in product-of-sums form. The best way to show this is by example.

We wish to simplify the following Boolean function in both sum-of-products form and product-of-sums form:

$$F(A, B, C, D) = \Sigma\ (0, 1, 2, 5, 8, 9, 10)$$

The 1's marked in the map of Fig. 1-11 represent the minterms that produce a 1 for the function. The squares marked with 0's represent the minterms not included in F and therefore denote the complement of F. Combining the squares with 1's gives the simplified function in sum-of-products form:

$$F = B'D' + B'C' + A'C'D$$

If the squares marked with 0's are combined, as shown in the diagram, we obtain the simplified complemented function:

$$F' = AB + CD + BD'$$

Taking the complement of F', we obtain the simplified function in product-of-sums form:

$$F = (A' + B')(C' + D')(B' + D)$$

Figure 1-11   Map for $F(A, B, C, D) = \Sigma\ (0,1,2,5,8,9,10)$.

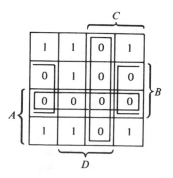

The logic diagrams of the two simplified expressions are shown in Fig. 1-12. The sum-of-products expression is implemented in Fig. 1-12(a) with a group of AND gates, one for each AND term. The outputs of the AND gates are connected to the inputs of a single OR gate. The same function is implemented in Fig. 1-12(b) in product-of-sums form with a group of OR gates, one for each OR term. The outputs of the OR gates are connected to the inputs of a single AND gate. In each case it is assumed that the input variables are directly available in their complement, so inverters are not included. The pattern established in Fig. 1-12 is the general form by which any Boolean function is implemented when expressed in one of the standard forms. AND gates are connected to a single OR gate when in sum-of-products form. OR gates are connected to a single AND gate when in product-of-sums form.

NAND implementation

A sum-of-products expression can be implemented with NAND gates as shown in Fig. 1-13(a). Note that the second NAND gate is drawn with the graphic symbol of Fig. 1-5(b). There are three lines in the diagram with small circles at both ends. Two circles in the same line designate double complementation, and since $(x')' = x$, the two circles can be removed and the resulting diagram is equivalent to the one shown in Fig. 1-12(a). Similarly, a product-of-sums expression can be implemented with NOR gates as shown in Fig. 1-13(b). The second NOR gate is drawn with the graphic symbol of Fig. 1-4(b). Again the two circles on both sides of each line may be removed, and the diagram so obtained is equivalent to the one shown in Fig. 1-12(b).

NOR implementation

Don't-Care Conditions

The 1's and 0's in the map represent the minterms that make the function equal to 1 or 0. There are occasions when it does not matter if the function produces 0 or 1 for a given minterm. Since the function may be either 0 or 1, we say that we don't care what the function output is to be for this minterm. Minterms that may produce either 0 or 1 for the function are said to be don't-care conditions and are marked with an × in the map. These don't-care conditions can be used to provide further simplification of the algebraic expression.

don't-care conditions

Figure 1-12 Logic diagrams with AND and OR gates.

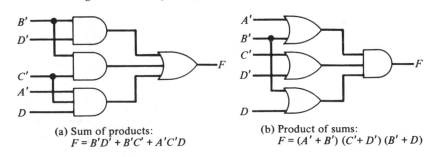

(a) Sum of products:
$F = B'D' + B'C' + A'C'D$

(b) Product of sums:
$F = (A' + B')(C' + D')(B' + D)$

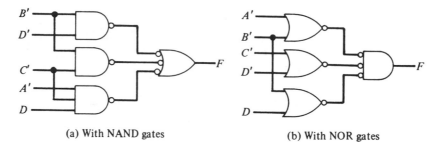

(a) With NAND gates   (b) With NOR gates

Figure 1-13   Logic diagrams with NAND or NOR gates.

When choosing adjacent squares for the function in the map, the ×'s may be assumed to be either 0 or 1, whichever gives the simplest expression. In addition, an × need not be used at all if it does not contribute to the simplification of the function. In each case, the choice depends only on the simplification that can be achieved. As an example, consider the following Boolean function together with the don't-care minterms:

$$F(A, B, C) = \Sigma \ (0, 2, 6)$$

$$d(A, B, C) = \Sigma \ (1, 3, 5)$$

The minterms listed with F produce a 1 for the function. The don't-care min terms listed with d may produce either a 0 or a 1 for the function. The remaining minterms, 4 and 7, produce a 0 for the function. The map is shown in Fig. 1-14. The minterms of F are marked with 1's, those of d are marked with ×'s, and the remaining squares are marked with 0's. The 1's and ×'s are combined in any convenient manner so as to enclose the maximum number of adjacent squares. It is not necessary to include all or any of the ×'s, but all the 1's must be included. By including the don't-care minterms 1 and 3 with the 1's in the first row we obtain the term A'. The remaining 1 for minterm 6 is combined with minterm 2 to obtain the term BC'. The simplified expression is

$$F = A' + BC'$$

Note that don't-care minterm 5 was not included because it does not contribute to the simplification of the expression. Note also that if don't-care minterms 1 and 3 were not included with the 1's, the simplified expression for F would have been

$$F = A'C' + BC'$$

This would require two AND gates and an OR gate, as compared to the expression obtained previously, which requires only one AND and one OR gate.

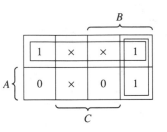

Figure 1-14   Example of map with don't-care conditions.

The function is determined completely once the ×'s are assigned to the 1's or 0's in the map. Thus the expression

$$F = A' + BC'$$

represents the Boolean function

$$F(A, B, C) = \Sigma \, (0, 1, 2, 3, 6)$$

It consists of the original minterms 0, 2, and 6 and the don't-care minterms 1 and 3. Minterm 5 is not included in the function. Since minterms 1, 3, and 5 were specified as being don't-care conditions, we have chosen minterms 1 and 3 to produce a 1 and minterm 5 to produce a 0. This was chosen because this assignment produces the simplest Boolean expression.

1-5   Combinational Circuits

block diagram

A combinational circuit is a connected arrangement of logic gates with a set of inputs and outputs. At any given time, the binary values of the outputs are a function of the binary combination of the inputs. A block diagram of a combinational circuit is shown in Fig. 1-15. The n binary input variables come from an external source, the m binary output variables go to an external destination, and in between there is an interconnection of logic gates. A combinational circuit transforms binary information from the given input data to the required output data. Combinational circuits are employed in digital computers for generating binary control decisions and for providing digital components required for data processing.

A combinational circuit can be described by a truth table showing the binary relationship between the n input variables and the m output variables. The truth table lists the corresponding output binary values for each of the 2^n input combinations. A combinational circuit can also be specified with m Boolean functions, one for each output variable. Each output function is expressed in terms of the n input variables.

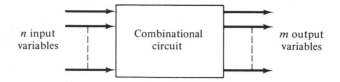

Figure 1-15 Block diagram of a combinational circuit.

analysis
The analysis of a combinational circuit starts with a given logic circuit diagram and culminates with a set of Boolean functions or a truth table. If the digital circuit is accompanied by a verbal explanation of its function, the Boolean functions or the truth table is sufficient for verification. If the function of the circuit is under investigation, it is necessary to interpret the operation of the circuit from the derived Boolean functions or the truth table. The success of such investigation is enhanced if one has experience and familiarity with digital circuits. The ability to correlate a truth table or a set of Boolean functions with an information-processing task is an art that one acquires with experience.

design
The design of combinational circuits starts from the verbal outline of the problem and ends in a logic circuit diagram. The procedure involves the following steps:

1. The problem is stated.
2. The input and output variables are assigned letter symbols.
3. The truth table that defines the relationship between inputs and outputs is derived.
4. The simplified Boolean functions for each output are obtained.
5. The logic diagram is drawn.

To demonstrate the design of combinational circuits, we present two examples of simple arithmetic circuits. These circuits serve as basic building blocks for the construction of more complicated arithmetic circuits.

Half-Adder

The most basic digital arithmetic circuit is the addition of two binary digits. A combinational circuit that performs the arithmetic addition of two bits is called a half-adder. One that performs the addition of three bits (two significant bits and a previous carry) is called a full-adder. The name of the former stems from the fact that two half-adders are needed to implement a full-adder.

The input variables of a half-adder are called the augend and addend bits. The output variables the sum and carry. It is necessary to specify two output variables because the sum of $1 + 1$ is binary 10, which has two digits. We assign symbols x and y to the two input variables, and S (for sum) and C

x	y	C	S
0	0	0	0
0	1	0	1
1	0	0	1
1	1	1	0

(a) Truth table

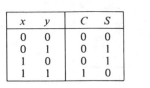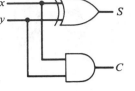

(b) Logic diagram

Figure 1-16   Half-adder.

(for carry) to the two output variables. The truth table for the half-adder is shown in Fig. 1-16(a). The C output is 0 unless both inputs are 1. The S output represents the least significant bit of the sum. The Boolean functions for the two outputs can be obtained directly from the truth table:

$$S = x'y + xy' = x \oplus y$$

$$C = xy$$

The logic diagram is shown in Fig. 1-16(b). It consists of an exclusive-OR gate and an AND gate.

Full-Adder

A full-adder is a combinational circuit that forms the arithmetic sum of three input bits. It consists of three inputs and two outputs. Two of the input variables, denoted by x and y, represent the two significant bits to be added. The third input, z, represents the carry from the previous lower significant position. Two outputs are necessary because the arithmetic sum of three binary digits ranges in value from 0 to 3, and binary 2 or 3 needs two digits. The two outputs are designated by the symbols S (for sum) and C (for carry). The binary variable S gives the value of the least significant bit of the sum. The binary variable C gives the output carry. The truth table of the full-adder is shown in Table 1-2. The eight rows under the input variables designate all possible combinations that the binary variables may have. The value of the output variables are determined from the arithmetic sum of the input bits. When all input bits are 0, the output is 0. The S output is equal to 1 when only one input is equal to 1 or when all three inputs are equal to 1. The C output has a carry of 1 if two or three inputs are equal to 1.

The maps of Fig. 1-17 are used to find algebraic expressions for the two output variables. The 1's in the squares for the maps of S and C are determined directly from the minterms in the truth table. The squares with 1's for the S output do not combine in groups of adjacent squares. But since the output is 1 when an odd number of inputs are 1, S is an odd function and represents

TABLE 1-2 Truth Table for Full-Adder

Inputs			Outputs	
x	y	z	C	S
0	0	0	0	0
0	0	1	0	1
0	1	0	0	1
0	1	1	1	0
1	0	0	0	1
1	0	1	1	0
1	1	0	1	0
1	1	1	1	1

the exclusive-OR relation of the variables (see the discussion at the end of Sec. 1-2). The squares with 1's for the C output may be combined in a variety of ways. One possible expression for C is

$$C = xy + (x'y + xy')z$$

Realizing that $x'y + xy' = x \oplus y$ and including the expression for output S, we obtain the two Boolean expressions for the full-adder:

$$S = x \oplus y \oplus z$$
$$C = xy + (x \oplus y)z$$

The logic diagram of the full-adder is drawn in Fig. 1-18. Note that the full-adder circuit consists of two half-adders and an OR gate. When used in subsequent chapters, the full-adder (FA) will be designated by a block diagram as shown in Fig. 1-18(b).

Figure 1-17   Maps for full-adder.

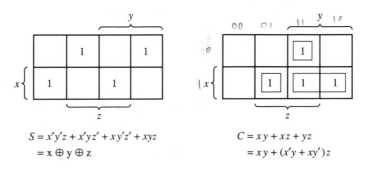

$$S = x'y'z + x'yz' + xy'z' + xyz$$
$$= x \oplus y \oplus z$$

$$C = xy + xz + yz$$
$$= xy + (x'y + xy')z$$

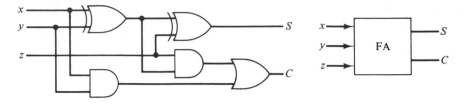

(a) Logic diagram (b) Block diagram

Figure 1-18 Full-adder circuit.

1-6 Flip-Flops

The digital circuits considered thus far have been combinational, where the outputs at any given time are entirely dependent on the inputs that are present at that time. Although every digital system is likely to have a combinational circuit, most systems encountered in practice also include storage elements, which require that the system be described in terms of sequential circuits. The most common type of sequential circuit is the synchronous type. Synchronous sequential circuits employ signals that affect the storage elements only at discrete instants of time. Synchronization is achieved by a timing device called a clock pulse generator that produces a periodic train of *clock pulses*. The clock pulses are distributed throughout the system in such a way that storage elements are affected only with the arrival of the synchronization pulse. Clocked synchronous sequential circuits are the type most frequently encountered in practice. They seldom manifest instability problems and their timing is easily broken down into independent discrete steps, each of which may be considered separately.

clocked sequential circuit

The storage elements employed in clocked sequential circuits are called flip-flops. A flip-flop is a binary cell capable of storing one bit of information. It has two outputs, one for the normal value and one for the complement value of the bit stored in it. A flip-flop maintains a binary state until directed by a clock pulse to switch states. The difference among various types of flip-flops is in the number of inputs they possess and in the manner in which the inputs affect the binary state. The most common types of flip-flops are presented below.

SR Flip-Flop

The graphic symbol of the *SR* flip-flop is shown in Fig. 1-19(a). It has three inputs, labeled S (for set), R (for reset), and C (for clock). It has an output Q and sometimes the flip-flop has a complemented output, which is indicated with a small circle at the other output terminal. There is an arrowhead-shaped symbol in front of the letter C to designate a *dynamic input*. The dynamic

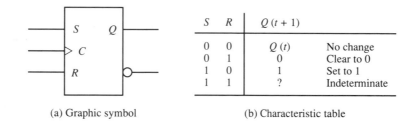

S	R	Q (t + 1)	
0	0	Q (t)	No change
0	1	0	Clear to 0
1	0	1	Set to 1
1	1	?	Indeterminate

(a) Graphic symbol   (b) Characteristic table

Figure 1-19   SR flip-flop.

indicator symbol denotes the fact that the flip-flop responds to a positive transition (from 0 to 1) of the input clock signal.

The operation of the SR flip-flop is as follows. If there is no signal at the clock input C, the output of the circuit cannot change irrespective of the values at inputs S and R. Only when the clock signal changes from 0 to 1 can the output be affected according to the values in inputs S and R. If $S = 1$ and $R = 0$ when C changes from 0 to 1, output Q is set to 1. If $S = 0$ and $R = 1$ when C changes from 0 to 1, output Q is cleared to 0. If both S and R are 0 during the clock transition, the output does not change. When both S and R are equal to 1, the output is unpredictable and may go to either 0 or 1, depending on internal timing delays that occur within the circuit.

The characteristic table shown in Fig. 1-19(b) summarizes the operation of the SR flip-flop in tabular form. The S and R columns give the binary values of the two inputs. $Q(t)$ is the binary state of the Q output at a given time (referred to as *present state*). $Q(t + 1)$ is the binary state of the Q output after the occurrence of a clock transition (referred to as *next state*). If $S = R = 0$, a clock transition produces no change of state [i.e., $Q(t + 1) = Q(t)$]. If $S = 0$ and $R = 1$, the flip-flop goes to the 0 (clear) state. If $S = 1$ and $R = 0$, the flip-flop goes to the 1 (set) state. The SR flip-flop should not be pulsed when $S = R = 1$ since it produces an indeterminate next state. This indeterminate condition makes the SR flip-flop difficult to manage and therefore it is seldom used in practice.

D Flip-Flop

The D (data) flip-flop is a slight modification of the SR flip-flop. An SR flip-flop is converted to a D flip-flop by inserting an inverter between S and R and assigning the symbol D to the single input. The D input is sampled during the occurrence of a clock transition from 0 to 1. If $D = 1$, the output of the flip-flop goes to the 1 state, but if $D = 0$, the output of the flip-flop goes to the 0 state.

The graphic symbol and characteristic table of the D flip-flop are shown in Fig. 1-20. From the characteristic table we note that the next state $Q(t + 1)$

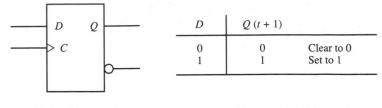

D	$Q(t+1)$	
0	0	Clear to 0
1	1	Set to 1

(a) Graphic symbol   (b) Characteristic table

Figure 1-20 D flip-flop.

is determined from the D input. The relationship can be expressed by a characteristic equation:

$$Q(t + 1) = D$$

This means that the Q output of the flip-flop receives its value from the D input every time that the clock signal goes through a transition from 0 to 1.

Note that no input condition exists that will leave the state of the D flip-flop unchanged. Although a D flip-flop has the advantage of having only one input (excluding C), it has the disadvantage that its characteristic table does not have a "no change" condition $Q(t + 1) = Q(t)$. The "no change" condition can be accomplished either by disabling the clock signal or by feeding the output back into the input, so that clock pulses keep the state of the flip-flop unchanged.

JK Flip-Flop

A *JK* flip-flop is a refinement of the *SR* flip-flop in that the indeterminate condition of the *SR* type is defined in the *JK* type. Inputs *J* and *K* behave like inputs *S* and *R* to set and clear the flip-flop, respectively. When inputs *J* and *K* are both equal to 1, a clock transition switches the outputs of the flip-flop to their complement state.

The graphic symbol and characteristic table of the *JK* flip-flop are shown in Fig. 1-21. The *J* input is equivalent to the *S* (set) input of the *SR* flip-flop, and the *K* input is equivalent to the *R* (clear) input. Instead of the indeterminate condition, the *JK* flip-flop has a complement condition $Q(t + 1) = Q'(t)$ when both *J* and *K* are equal to 1.

T Flip-Flop

Another type of flip-flop found in textbooks is the *T* (toggle) flip-flop. This flip-flop, shown in Fig. 1-22, is obtained from a *JK* type when inputs *J* and *K* are connected to provide a single input designated by *T*. The *T* flip-flop

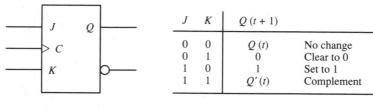

J	K	Q (t + 1)	
0	0	Q (t)	No change
0	1	0	Clear to 0
1	0	1	Set to 1
1	1	Q' (t)	Complement

(a) Graphic symbol   (b) Characteristic table

Figure 1-21   JK flip-flop.

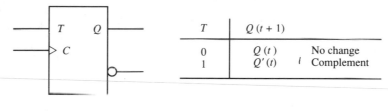

T	Q (t + 1)	
0	Q (t)	No change
1	Q' (t)	Complement

(a) Graphic symbol   (b) Characteristic table

Figure 1-22   T flip-flop.

therefore has only two conditions. When $T = 0$ ($J = K = 0$) a clock transition does not change the state of the flip-flop. When $T = 1$ ($J = K = 1$) a clock transition complements the state of the flip-flop. These conditions can be expressed by a characteristic equation:

$$Q(t + 1) = Q(t) \oplus T$$

Edge-Triggered Flip-Flops

The most common type of flip-flop used to synchronize the state change during a clock pulse transition is the edge-triggered flip-flop. In this type of flip-flop, output transitions occur at a specific level of the clock pulse. When the pulse input level exceeds this threshold level, the inputs are locked out so that the flip-flop is unresponsive to further changes in inputs until the clock pulse returns to 0 and another pulse occurs. Some edge-triggered flip-flops cause a transition on the rising edge of the clock signal (positive-edge transition), and others cause a transition on the falling edge (negative-edge transition).

clock pulses   Figure 1-23(a) shows the clock pulse signal in a positive-edge-triggered D flip-flop. The value in the D input is transferred to the Q output when the clock makes a positive transition. The output cannot change when the clock is in the 1 level, in the 0 level, or in a transition from the 1 level to the 0 level.

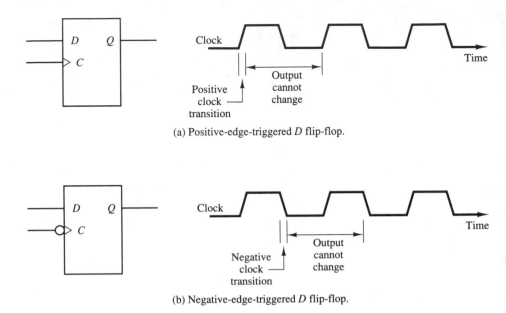

(a) Positive-edge-triggered D flip-flop.

(b) Negative-edge-triggered D flip-flop.

Figure 1-23 Edge-triggered flip-flop.

The effective positive clock transition includes a minimum time called the *setup time* in which the D input must remain at a constant value before the transition, and a definite time called the *hold time* in which the D input must not change after the positive transition. The effective positive transition is usually a very small fraction of the total period of the clock pulse.

Figure 1-23(b) shows the corresponding graphic symbol and timing diagram for a negative-edge-triggered D flip-flop. The graphic symbol includes a negation small circle in front of the dynamic indicator at the C input. This denotes a negative-edge-triggered behavior. In this case the flip-flop responds to a transition from the 1 level to the 0 level of the clock signal.

master-slave flip-flop

Another type of flip-flop used in some systems is the master-slave flip-flop. This type of circuit consists of two flip-flops. The first is the master, which responds to the positive level of the clock, and the second is the slave, which responds to the negative level of the clock. The result is that the output changes during the 1-to-0 transition of the clock signal. The trend is away from the use of master-slave flip-flops and toward edge-triggered flip-flops.

Flip-flops available in integrated circuit packages will sometimes provide special input terminals for setting or clearing the flip-flop asynchronously. These inputs are usually called "preset" and "clear." They affect the flip-flop on a negative level of the input signal without the need of a clock pulse. These inputs are useful for bringing the flip-flops to an initial state prior to its clocked operation.

Excitation Tables

The characteristic tables of flip-flops specify the next state when the inputs and the present state are known. During the design of sequential circuits we usually know the required transition from present state to next state and wish to find the flip-flop input conditions that will cause the required transition. For this reason we need a table that lists the required input combinations for a given change of state. Such a table is called a flip-flop excitation table.

Table 1-3 lists the excitation tables for the four types of flip-flops. Each table consists of two columns, $Q(t)$ and $Q(t + 1)$, and a column for each input to show how the required transition is achieved. There are four possible transitions from present state $Q(t)$ to next state $Q(t + 1)$. The required input conditions for each of these transitions are derived from the information available in the characteristic tables. The symbol $\times$ in the tables represents a don't-care condition; that is, it does not matter whether the input to the flip-flop is 0 or 1.

TABLE 1-3 Excitation Table for Four Flip-Flops

$Q(t)$	$Q(t + 1)$	S	R	$Q(t)$	$Q(t + 1)$	D
	SR flip-flop				D flip-flop	
0	0	0	$\times$	0	0	0
0	1	1	0	0	1	1
1	0	0	1	1	0	0
1	1	$\times$	0	1	1	1

$Q(t)$	$Q(t + 1)$	J	K	$Q(t)$	$Q(t + 1)$	T
	JK flip-flop				T flip-flop	
0	0	0	$\times$	0	0	0
0	1	1	$\times$	0	1	1
1	0	$\times$	1	1	0	1
1	1	$\times$	0	1	1	0

The reason for the don't-care conditions in the excitation tables is that there are two ways of achieving the required transition. For example, in a JK flip-flop, a transition from present state of 0 to a next state of 0 can be achieved by having inputs J and K equal to 0 (to obtain no change) or by letting $J = 0$ and $K = 1$ to clear the flip-flop (although it is already cleared). In both cases J must be 0, but K is 0 in the first case and 1 in the second. Since the required transition will occur in either case, we mark the K input with a don't-care $\times$

and let the designer choose either 0 or 1 for the *K* input, whichever is more convenient.

1-7 Sequential Circuits

A sequential circuit is an interconnection of flip-flops and gates. The gates by themselves constitute a combinational circuit, but when included with the flip-flops, the overall circuit is classified as a sequential circuit. The block diagram of a clocked sequential circuit is shown in Fig. 1-24. It consists of a combinational circuit and a number of clocked flip-flops. In general, any number or type of flip-flops may be included. As shown in the diagram, the combinational circuit block receives binary signals from external inputs and from the outputs of flip-flops. The outputs of the combinational circuit go to external outputs and to inputs of flip-flops. The gates in the combinational circuit determine the binary value to be stored in the flip-flops after each clock transition. The outputs of flip-flops, in turn, are applied to the combinational circuit inputs and determine the circuit's behavior. This process demonstrates that the external outputs of a sequential circuit are functions of both external inputs and the present state of the flip-flops. Moreover, the next state of flip-flops is also a function of their present state and external inputs. Thus a sequential circuit is specified by a time sequence of external inputs, external outputs, and internal flip-flop binary states.

Flip-Flop Input Equations

An example of a sequential circuit is shown in Fig. 1-25. It has one input variable *x*, one output variable *y*, and two clocked *D* flip-flops. The AND gates, OR gates, and inverter form the combinational logic part of the circuit. The interconnections among the gates in the combinational circuit can be specified by a set of Boolean expressions. The part of the combinational circuit that generates the inputs to flip-flops are described by a set of Boolean expressions called flip-flop input equations. We adopt the convention of using the flip-flop input symbol to denote the input equation variable name and a subscript to

input equation

Figure 1-24 Block diagram of a clocked synchronous sequential circuit.

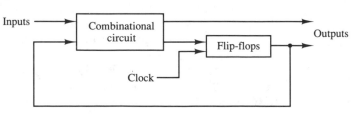

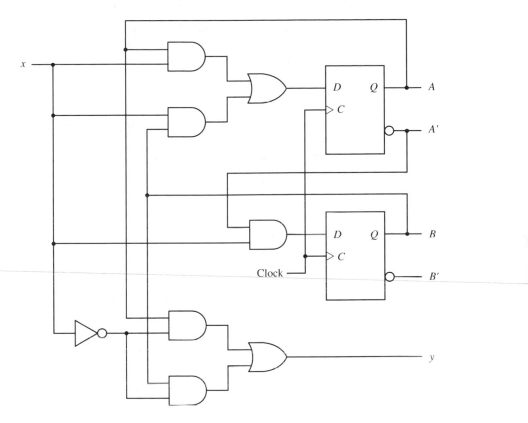

Figure 1-25   Example of a sequential circuit.

designate the symbol chosen for the output of the flip-flop. Thus, in Fig. 1-25, we have two input equations, designated D_A and D_B. The first letter in each symbol denotes the D input of a D flip-flop. The subscript letter is the symbol name of the flip-flop. The input equations are Boolean functions for flip-flop input variables and can be derived by inspection of the circuit. Since the output of the OR gate is connected to the D input of flip-flop A, we write the first input equation as

$$D_A = Ax + Bx$$

where A and B are the outputs of the two flip-flops and x is the external input. The second input equation is derived from the single AND gate whose output is connected to the D input of flip-flop B:

$$D_B = A'x$$

The sequential circuit also has an external output, which is a function of the input variable and the state of the flip-flops. This output can be specified algebraically by the expression

$$y = Ax' + Bx'$$

From this example we note that a flip-flop input equation is a Boolean expression for a combinational circuit. The subscripted variable is a binary variable name for the output of a combinational circuit. This output is always connected to a flip-flop input.

State Table

The behavior of a sequential circuit is determined from the inputs, the outputs, and the state of its flip-flops. Both the outputs and the next state are a function of the inputs and the present state. A sequential circuit is specified by a state table that relates outputs and next states as a function of inputs and present states. In clocked sequential circuits, the transition from present state to next state is activated by the presence of a clock signal.

The state table for the circuit of Fig. 1-25 is shown in Table 1-4. The table consists of four sections, labeled *present state, input, next state,* and *output*. The

present state

next state

present-state section shows the states of flip-flops A and B at any given time t. The input section gives a value of x for each possible present state. The next-state section shows the states of the flip-flops one clock period later at time $t + 1$. The output section gives the value of y for each present state and input condition.

The derivation of a state table consists of first listing all possible binary combinations of present state and inputs. In this case we have eight binary combinations from 000 to 111. The next-state values are then determined from the logic diagram or from the input equations. The input equation for flip-flop A is

$$D_A = Ax + Bx$$

The next-state value of a each flip-flop is equal to its D input value in the present state. The transition from present state to next state occurs after application of a clock signal. Therefore, the next state of A is equal to 1 when the present state and input values satisfy the conditions $Ax = 1$ or $Bx = 1$, which makes D_A equal 1. This is shown in the state table with three 1's under the column for next state of A. Similarly, the input equation for flip-flop B is

$$D_B = A'x$$

The next state of B in the state table is equal to 1 when the present state of A is 0 and input x is equal to 1. The output column is derived from the output equation

$$y = Ax' + Bx'$$

TABLE 1-4 State Table for Circuit of Fig. 1-25

Present state		Input	Next state		Output
A	B	x	A	B	y
0	0	0	0	0	0
0	0	1	0	1	0
0	1	0	0	0	1
0	1	1	1	1	0
1	0	0	0	0	1
1	0	1	1	0	0
1	1	0	0	0	1
1	1	1	1	0	0

state table

The state table of any sequential circuit is obtained by the procedure used in this example. In general, a sequential circuit with m flip-flops, n input variables, and p output variables will contain m columns for present state, n columns for inputs, m columns for next state, and p columns for outputs. The present state and input columns are combined and under them we list the 2^{m+n} binary combinations from 0 through $2^{m+n} - 1$. The next-state and output columns are functions of the present state and input values and are derived directly from the circuit or the Boolean equations that describe the circuit.

State Diagram

state diagram

The information available in a state table can be represented graphically in a state diagram. In this type of diagram, a state is represented by a circle, and the transition between states is indicated by directed lines connecting the circles. The state diagram of the sequential circuit of Fig. 1-25 is shown in Fig. 1-26. The state diagram provides the same information as the state table and is obtained directly from Table 1-4. The binary number inside each circle identifies the state of the flip-flops. The directed lines are labeled with two binary numbers separated by a slash. The input value during the present state is labeled first and the number after the slash gives the output during the present state. For example, the directed line from state 00 to 01 is labeled 1/0, meaning that when the sequential circuit is in the present state 00 and the input

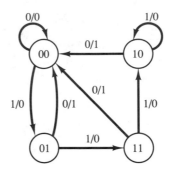

Figure 1-26   State diagrams of sequential circuit.

is 1, the output is 0. After a clock transition, the circuit goes to the next state 01. The same clock transition may change the input value. If the input changes to 0, the output becomes 1, but if the input remains at 1, the output stays at 0. This information is obtained from the state diagram along the two directed lines emanating from the circle representing state 01. A directed line connecting a circle with itself indicates that no change of state occurs.

There is no difference between a state table and a state diagram except in the manner of representation. The state table is easier to derive from a given logic diagram and the state diagram follows directly from the state table. The state diagram gives a pictorial view of state transitions and is the form suitable for human interpretation of the circuit operation. For example, the state diagram of Fig. 1-26 clearly shows that starting from state 00, the output is 0 as long as the input stays at 1. The first 0 input after a string of 1's gives an output of 1 and transfers the circuit back to the initial state 00.

Design Example

The procedure for designing sequential circuits will be demonstrated by a specific example. The design procedure consists of first translating the circuit specifications into a state diagram. The state diagram is then converted into a state table. From the state table we obtain the information for obtaining the logic circuit diagram.

We wish to design a clocked sequential circuit that goes through a sequence of repeated binary states 00, 01, 10, and 11 when an external input x is equal to 1. The state of the circuit remains unchanged when $x = 0$. This type *binary counter* of circuit is called a 2-bit binary counter because the state sequence is identical to the count sequence of two binary digits. Input x is the control variable that specifies when the count should proceed.

The binary counter needs two flip-flops to represent the two bits. The state diagram for the sequential circuit is shown in Fig. 1-27. The diagram is drawn to show that the states of the circuit follow the binary count as long as

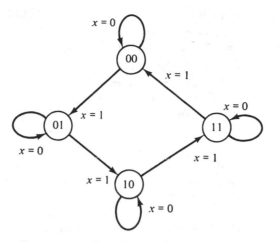

Figure 1-27   State diagram for binary counter.

$x = 1$. The state following 11 is 00, which causes the count to be repeated. If $x = 0$, the state of the circuit remains unchanged. This sequential circuit has no external outputs, and therefore only the input value is labeled in the diagram. The state of the flip-flops is considered as the outputs of the counter.

We have already assigned the symbol x to the input variable. We now assign the symbols A and B to the two flip-flop outputs. The next state of A and B, as a function of the present state and input x, can be transferred from the state diagram into a state table. The first five columns of Table 1-5 constitute the state table. The entries for this table are obtained directly from the state diagram.

excitation table   The excitation table of a sequential circuit is an extension of the state table. This extension consists of a list of flip-flop input excitations that will cause the

TABLE 1-5 Excitation Table for Binary Counter

Present state		Input	Next state		Flip-flop inputs			
A	B	x	A	B	J_A	K_A	J_B	K_B
0	0	0	0	0	0	×	0	×
0	0	1	0	1	0	×	1	×
0	1	0	0	1	0	×	×	0
0	1	1	1	0	1	×	×	1
1	0	0	1	0	×	0	0	×
1	0	1	1	1	×	0	1	×
1	1	0	1	1	×	0	×	0
1	1	1	0	0	×	1	×	1

required state transitions. The flip-flop input conditions are a function of the type of flip-flop used. If we employ JK flip-flops, we need columns for the J and K inputs of each flip-flop. We denote the inputs of flip-flop A by J_A and K_A, and those of flip-flop B by J_B and K_B.

The excitation table for the JK flip-flop specified in Table 1-3 is now used to derive the excitation table of the sequential circuit. For example, in the first row of Table 1-5, we have a transition for flip-flop A from 0 in the present state to 0 in the next state. In Table 1-3 we find that a transition of states from $Q(t) = 0$ to $Q(t + 1) = 0$ in a JK flip-flop requires that input $J = 0$ and input $K = \times$. So 0 and $\times$ are copied in the first row under J_A and K_A, respectively. Since the first row also shows a transition for flip-flop B from 0 in the present state to 0 in the next state, 0 and $\times$ are copied in the first row under J_B and K_B. The second row of Table 1-5 shows a transition for flip-flop B from 0 in the present state to 1 in the next state. From Table 1-3 we find that a transition from $Q(t) = 0$ to $Q(t + 1) = 1$ requires that input $J = 1$ and input $K = \times$. So 1 and $\times$ are copied in the second row under J_B and K_B, respectively. This process is continued for each row of the table and for each flip-flop, with the input conditions as specified in Table 1-3 being copied into the proper row of the particular flip-flop being considered.

Let us now consider the information available in an excitation table such as Table 1-5. We know that a sequential circuit consists of a number of flip-flops and a combinational circuit. From the block diagram of Fig. 1-24, we note that the outputs of the combinational circuit must go to the four flip-flop inputs J_A, K_A, J_B, and K_B. The inputs to the combinational circuit are the external input x and the present-state values of flip-flops A and B. Moreover, the Boolean functions that specify a combinational circuit are derived from a truth table that shows the input–output relationship of the circuit. The entries that list the combinational circuit inputs are specified under the "present state" and "input" columns in the excitation table. The combinational circuit outputs are specified under the "flip-flop inputs" columns. Thus an excitation table transforms a state diagram to a truth table needed for the design of the combinational circuit part of the sequential circuit.

The simplified Boolean functions for the combinational circuit can now be derived. The inputs are the variables A, B, and x. The outputs are the variables J_A, K_A, J_B, and K_B. The information from the excitation table is transferred into the maps of Fig. 1-28, where the four simplified flip-flop input equations are derived:

$$J_A = Bx \qquad K_A = Bx$$
$$J_B = x \qquad K_B = x$$

The logic diagram is drawn in Fig. 1-29 and consists of two JK flip-flops and an AND gate. Note that inputs J and K determine the next state of the counter when a clock signal occurs. If both J and K are equal to 0, a clock signal will

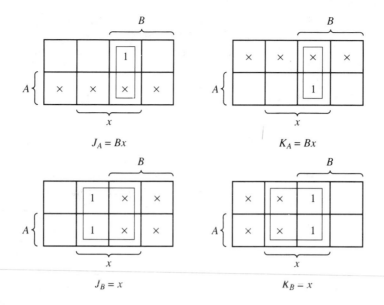

$$J_A = Bx$$

$$K_A = Bx$$

$$J_B = x$$

$$K_B = x$$

Figure 1-28 Maps for combinational circuit of counter.

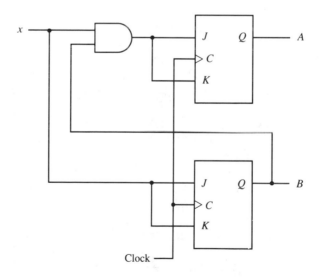

Figure 1-29 Logic diagram of a 2-bit binary counter.

have no effect; that is, the state of the flip-flops will not change. Thus when $x = 0$, all four inputs of the flip-flops are equal to 0 and the state of the flip-flops remains unchanged even though clock pulses are applied continuously.

Design Procedure

The design of sequential circuits follows the outline described in the preceding example. The behavior of the circuit is first formulated in a state diagram. The number of flip-flops needed for the circuit is determined from the number of bits listed within the circles of the state diagram. The number of inputs for the circuit is specified along the directed lines between the circles. We then assign letters to designate all flip-flops and input and output variables and proceed to obtain the state table.

For m flip-flops and n inputs, the state table will consist of m columns for the present state, n columns for the inputs, and m columns for the next state. The number of rows in the table will be up to 2^{m+n}, one row for each binary combination of present state and inputs. For each row we list the next state as specified by the state diagram. Next, the flip-flop type to be used in the circuit is chosen. The state table is then extended into an excitation table by including columns for each input of each flip-flop. The excitation table for the type of flip-flop in use can be found in Table 1-3. From the information available in this table and by inspecting present state-to-next state transitions in the state table, we obtain the information for the flop-flop input conditions in the excitation table.

The truth table for the combinational circuit part of the sequential circuit is available in the excitation table. The present-state and input columns constitute the inputs in the truth table. The flip-flop input conditions constitute the outputs in the truth table. By means of map simplification we obtain a set of flip-flop input equations for the combinational circuit. Each flip-flop input equation specifies a logic diagram whose output must be connected to one of the flip-flop inputs. The combinational circuit so obtained, together with the flip-flops, constitutes the sequential circuit.

The outputs of flip-flops are often considered to be part of the outputs of the sequential circuit. However, the combinational circuit may also contain external outputs. In such a case the Boolean functions for the external outputs are derived from the state table by combinational circuit design techniques.

A set of flip-flop input equations specifies a sequential circuit in algebraic form. The procedure for obtaining the logic diagram from a set of flip-flop input equations is a straightforward process. First draw the flip-flops and label all their inputs and outputs. Then draw the combinational circuit from the Boolean expressions given by the flip-flop input equations. Finally, connect outputs of flip-flops to inputs in the combinational circuit and outputs of the combinational circuit to flip-flop inputs.

PROBLEMS

1-1. Determine by means of a truth table the validity of DeMorgan's theorem for three variables: $(ABC)' = A' + B' + C'$.

1-2. List the truth table of a three-variable exclusive-OR (odd) function: $x = A \oplus B \oplus C$.

1-3. Simplify the following expressions using Boolean algebra.
   a. $A + AB$
   b. $AB + AB'$
   c. $A'BC + AC$
   d. $A'B + ABC' + ABC$

1-4. Simplify the following expressions using Boolean algebra.
   a. $AB + A(CD + CD')$
   b. $(BC' + A'D)(AB' + CD')$

1-5. Using DeMorgan's theorem, show that:
   a. $(A + B)'(A' + B')' - 0$
   b. $A + A'B + A'B' = 1$

1-6. Given the Boolean expression $F = x'y + xyz'$:
   a. Derive an algebraic expression for the complement F'.
   b. Show that $F \cdot F' = 0$.
   c. Show that $F + F' = 1$.

1-7. Given the Boolean function

$$F = xy'z + x'y'z + xyz$$

   a. List the truth table of the function.
   b. Draw the logic diagram using the original Boolean expression.
   c. Simplify the algebraic expression using Boolean algebra.
   d. List the truth table of the function from the simplified expression and show that it is the same as the truth table in part (a).
   e. Draw the logic diagram from the simplified expression and compare the total number of gates with the diagram of part (b).

1-8. Simplify the following Boolean functions using three-variable maps.
   a. $F(x, y, z) = \Sigma (0, 1, 5, 7)$
   b. $F(x, y, z) = \Sigma (1, 2, 3, 6, 7)$
   c. $F(x, y, z) = \Sigma (3, 5, 6, 7)$
   d. $F(A, B, C) = \Sigma (0, 2, 3, 4. 6)$

1-9. Simplify the following Boolean functions using four-variable maps.
   a. $F(A, B, C, D) = \Sigma (4, 6, 7, 15)$
   b. $F(A, B, C, D) = \Sigma (3, 7, 11, 13, 14, 15)$
   c. $F(A, B, C, D) = \Sigma (0, 1, 2, 4, 5, 7, 11, 15)$
   d. $F(A, B, C, D) = \Sigma (0, 2, 4, 5, 6, 7, 8, 10, 13, 15)$

1-10. Simplify the following expressions in (1) sum-of-products form and (2) product-of-sums form.

a. $x'z' + y'z' + yz' + xy$

b. $AC' + B'D + A'CD + ABCD$

1-11. Simplify the following Boolean function in sum-of-products form by means of a four-variable map. Draw the logic diagram with (a) AND-OR gates; (b) NAND gates.

$$F(A, B, C, D) = \Sigma\ (0, 2, 8, 9, 10, 11, 14, 15)$$

1-12. Simplify the following Boolean function in product-of-sums form by means of a four-variable map. Draw the logic diagram with (a) OR-AND gates; (b) NOR gates.

$$F(w, x, y, z) = \Sigma\ (2, 3, 4, 5, 6, 7, 11, 14, 15)$$

1-13. Simplify the Boolean function F together with the don't-care conditions d in (1) sum-of-products form and (2) product-of-sums form.

$$F(w, x, y, z) = \Sigma\ (0, 1, 2, 3, 7, 8, 10)$$

$$d(w, x, y, z) = \Sigma\ (5, 6, 11, 15)$$

1-14. Using Table 1-2, derive the Boolean expression for the S (sum) output of the full-adder in sum-of-products form. Then by algebraic manipulation show that S can be expressed as the exclusive-OR of the three input variables.

$$S = x \oplus y \oplus z$$

1-15. A majority function is generated in a combinational circuit when the output is equal to 1 if the input variables have more 1's than 0's. The output is 0 otherwise. Design a three-input majority function.

1-16. Design a combinational circuit with three inputs x, y, z and three outputs A, B, C. When the binary input is 0, 1, 2, or 3, the binary output is one greater than the input. When the binary input is 4, 5, 6, or 7, the binary output is one less than the input.

1-17. Show that a JK flip-flop can be converted to a D flip-flop with an inverter between the J and K inputs.

1-18. Using the information from the characteristic table of the JK flip-flop listed in Fig. 1-21(b), derive the excitation table for the JK flip-flop and compare your answer with Table 1-3.

1-19. A sequential circuit has two D flip-flops A and B, two inputs x and y, and one output z. The flip-flop input equations and the circuit output are as follows:

$$D_A = x'y + xA$$

$$D_B = x'B + xA$$

$$z = B$$

    a. Draw the logic diagram of the circuit.

    b. Tabulate the state table.

1-20. Design a 2-bit count-down counter. This is a sequential circuit with two flip-flops and one input x. When $x = 0$, the state of the flip-flops does not change. When $x = 1$, the state sequence is 11, 10, 01, 00, 11, and repeat.

1-21. Design a sequential circuit with two JK flip-flops A and B and two inputs E and x. If $E = 0$, the circuit remains in the same state regardless of the value of x. When $E = 1$ and $x = 1$, the circuit goes through the state transitions from 00 to 01 to 10 to 11 back to 00, and repeat. When $E = 1$ and $x = 0$, the circuit goes through the state transitions from 00 to 11 to 10 to 01 back to 00, and repeat.

REFERENCES

1. Hill, F. J., and G. R. Peterson, *Introduction to Switching Theory and Logical Design*, 3rd ed. New York: John Wiley, 1981.

2. Mano, M. M., *Digital Design*, 2nd ed. Englewood Cliffs, NJ: Prentice Hall, 1991.

3. Roth, C. H., *Fundamentals of Logic Design*, 3rd ed. St. Paul, MN: West Publishing, 1985.

4. Sandige, R. S., *Modern Digital Design*. New York: McGraw-Hill, 1990.

5. Shiva, S. G., *Introduction to Logic Design*. Glenview, IL: Scott, Foresman, 1988.

6. Wakerly, J. F., *Digital Design Principles and Practices*. Englewood Cliffs, NJ: Prentice Hall, 1990.

7. Ward, S. A., and R. H. Halstead, Jr., *Computation Structures*. Cambridge, MA: MIT Press, 1990.

CHAPTER TWO

Digital Components

IN THIS CHAPTER

2-1   Integrated Circuits

IC

Digital circuits are constructed with integrated circuits. An integrated circuit (abbreviated IC) is a small silicon semiconductor crystal, called a *chip*, containing the electronic components for the digital gates. The various gates are interconnected inside the chip to form the required circuit. The chip is mounted in a ceramic or plastic container, and connections are welded by thin gold wires to external pins to form the integrated circuit. The number of pins may range from 14 in a small IC package to 100 or more in a larger package. Each IC has a numeric designation printed on the surface of the package for identification. Each vendor publishes a data book or catalog that contains the exact description and all the necessary information about the ICs that it manufactures.

As the technology of ICs has improved, the number of gates that can be put in a single chip has increased considerably. The differentiation between those chips that have a few internal gates and those having hundreds or thousands of gates is made by a customary reference to a package as being either a small-, medium-, or large-scale integration device.

SSI

Small-scale integration (SSI) devices contain several independent gates in a single package. The inputs and outputs of the gates are connected directly

41

to the pins in the package. The number of gates is usually less than 10 and is limited by the number of pins available in the IC.

MSI

Medium-scale integration (MSI) devices have a complexity of approximately 10 to 200 gates in a single package. They usually perform specific elementary digital functions such as decoders, adders, and registers.

LSI

Large-scale integration (LSI) devices contain between 200 and a few thousand gates in a single package. They include digital systems, such as processors, memory chips, and programmable modules.

VLSI

Very-large-scale integration (VLSI) devices contain thousands of gates within a single package. Examples are large memory arrays and complex microcomputer chips. Because of their small size and low cost, VLSI devices have revolutionized the computer system design technology, giving designers the capability to create structures that previously were not economical.

Digital integrated circuits are classified not only by their logic operation but also by the specific circuit technology to which they belong. The circuit technology is referred to as a *digital logic family*. Each logic family has its own basic electronic circuit upon which more complex digital circuits and functions are developed. The basic circuit in each technology is either a NAND, a NOR, or an inverter gate. The electronic components that are employed in the construction of the basic circuit are usually used for the name of the technology. Many different logic families of integrated circuits have been introduced commercially. The following are the most popular.

TTL	Transistor-transistor logic
ECL	Emitter-coupled logic
MOS	Metal-oxide semiconductor
CMOS	Complementary metal-oxide semiconductor

TTL is a widespread logic family that has been in operation for many years and is considered as standard. ECL has an advantage in systems requiring high-speed operation. MOS is suitable for circuits that need high component density, and CMOS is preferable in systems requiring low power consumption.

TTL

The transistor-transistor logic family was an evolution of a previous technology that used diodes and transistors for the basic NAND gate. This technology was called DTL, for "diode-transistor logic." Later the diodes were replaced by transistors to improve the circuit operation and the name of the logic family was changed to "transistor-transistor logic." This is the reason for mentioning the word "transistor" twice. There are several variations of the TTL family besides the standard TTL, such as high-speed TTL, low-power TTL, Schottky TTL, low-power Schottky TTL, and advanced Schottky TTL. The power supply voltage for TTL circuits is 5 volts, and the two logic levels are approximately 0 and 3.5 volts.

ECL

The emitter-coupled logic (ECL) family provides the highest-speed digital circuits in integrated form. ECL is used in systems such as supercomputers and signal processors where high speed is essential. The transistors in ECL gates operate in a nonsaturated state, a condition that allows the achievement of propagation delays of 1 to 2 nanoseconds.

MOS

The metal-oxide semiconductor (MOS) is a unipolar transistor that depends on the flow of only one type of carrier, which may be electrons (n-channel) or holes (p-channel). This is in contrast to the bipolar transistor used in TTL and ECL gates, where both carriers exist during normal operation. A p-channel MOS is referred to as PMOS and an n-channel as NMOS. NMOS is the one that is commonly used in circuits with only one type of MOS

CMOS

transistor. The complementary MOS (CMOS) technology uses PMOS and NMOS transistors connected in a complementary fashion in all circuits. The most important advantages of CMOS over bipolar are the high packing density of circuits, a simpler processing technique during fabrication, and a more economical operation because of low power consumption.

Because of their many advantages, integrated circuits are used exclusively to provide various digital components needed in the design of computer systems. To understand the organization and design of digital computers it is very important to be familiar with the various components encountered in integrated circuits. For this reason, the most basic components are introduced in this chapter with an explanation of their logical properties. These components provide a catalog of elementary digital functional units commonly used as basic building blocks in the design of digital computers.

2-2 Decoders

Discrete quantities of information are represented in digital computers with binary codes. A binary code of n bits is capable of representing up to 2^n distinct elements of the coded information. A decoder is a combinational circuit that converts binary information from the n coded inputs to a maximum of 2^n unique outputs. If the n-bit coded information has unused bit combinations, the decoder may have less than 2^n outputs.

decoder

The decoders presented in this section are called n-to-m-line decoders, where $m \leq 2^n$. Their purpose is to generate the 2^n (or fewer) binary combinations of the n input variables. A decoder has n inputs and m outputs and is also referred to as an $n \times m$ decoder.

The logic diagram of a 3-to-8-line decoder is shown in Fig. 2-1. The three data inputs, A_0, A_1, and A_2, are decoded into eight outputs, each output

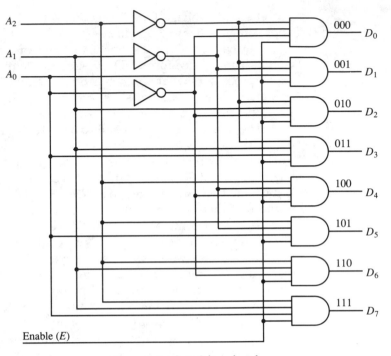

Figure 2-1   3-to-8-line decoder.

representing one of the combinations of the three binary input variables. The three inverters provide the complement of the inputs, and each of the eight AND gates generates one of the binary combination. A particular application of this decoder is a binary-to-octal conversion. The input variables represent a binary number and the outputs represent the eight digits of the octal number system. However, a 3-to-8-line decoder can be used for decoding any 3-bit code to provide eight outputs, one for each combination of the binary code.

Enable input   Commercial decoders include one or more enable inputs to control the operation of the circuit. The decoder of Fig. 2-1 has one enable input, E. The decoder is enabled when E is equal to 1 and disabled when E is equal to 0.

The operation of the decoder can be clarified using the truth table listed in Table 2-1. When the enable input E is equal to 0, all the outputs are equal to 0 regardless of the values of the other three data inputs. The three $\times$'s in the table designate don't-care conditions. When the enable input is equal to 1, the decoder operates in a normal fashion. For each possible input combination, there are seven outputs that are equal to 0 and only one that is equal to 1. The output variable whose value is equal to 1 represents the octal number equivalent of the binary number that is available in the input data lines.

TABLE 2-1 Truth Table for 3-to-8-Line Decoder

Enable	Inputs			Outputs							
E	A_2	A_1	A_0	D_7	D_6	D_5	D_4	D_3	D_2	D_1	D_0
0	$\times$	$\times$	$\times$	0	0	0	0	0	0	0	0
1	0	0	0	0	0	0	0	0	0	0	1
1	0	0	1	0	0	0	0	0	0	1	0
1	0	1	0	0	0	0	0	0	1	0	0
1	0	1	1	0	0	0	0	1	0	0	0
1	1	0	0	0	0	0	1	0	0	0	0
1	1	0	1	0	0	1	0	0	0	0	0
1	1	1	0	0	1	0	0	0	0	0	0
1	1	1	1	1	0	0	0	0	0	0	0

NAND Gate Decoder

Some decoders are constructed with NAND instead of AND gates. Since a NAND gate produces the AND operation with an inverted output, it becomes more economical to generate the decoder outputs in their complement form. A 2-to-4-line decoder with an enable input constructed with NAND gates is shown in Fig. 2-2. The circuit operates with complemented outputs and a complemented enable input E. The decoder is enabled when E is equal to 0. As indicated by the truth table, only one output is equal to 0 at any given time; the other three outputs are equal to 1. The output whose value is equal to 0 represents the equivalent binary number in inputs A_1 and A_0. The circuit is disabled when E is equal to 1, regardless of the values of the other two inputs.

Figure 2-2 2-to-4-line decoder with NAND gates.

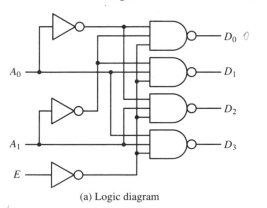

E	A_1	A_0	D_0	D_1	D_2	D_3
0	0	0	0	1	1	1
0	0	1	1	0	1	1
0	1	0	1	1	0	1
0	1	1	1	1	1	0
1	$\times$	$\times$	1	1	1	1

(a) Logic diagram   (b) Truth table

When the circuit is disabled, none of the outputs are selected and all outputs are equal to 1. In general, a decoder may operate with complemented or uncomplemented outputs. The enable input may be activated with a 0 or with a 1 signal level. Some decoders have two or more enable inputs that must satisfy a given logic condition in order to enable the circuit.

Decoder Expansion

There are occasions when a certain-size decoder is needed but only smaller sizes are available. When this occurs it is possible to combine two or more decoders with enable inputs to form a larger decoder. Thus if a 6-to-64-line decoder is needed, it is possible to construct it with four 4-to-16-line decoders.

Figure 2-3 shows how decoders with enable inputs can be connected to form a larger decoder. Two 2-to-4-line decoders are combined to achieve a 3-to-8-line decoder. The two least significant bits of the input are connected to both decoders. The most significant bit is connected to the enable input of one decoder and through an inverter to the enable input of the other decoder. It is assumed that each decoder is enabled when its E input is equal to 1. When E is equal to 0, the decoder is disabled and all its outputs are in the 0 level. When $A_2 = 0$, the upper decoder is enabled and the lower is disabled. The lower decoder outputs become inactive with all outputs at 0. The outputs of the upper decoder generate outputs D_0 through D_3, depending on the values of A_1 and A_0 (while $A_2 = 0$). When $A_2 = 1$, the lower decoder is enabled and the upper is disabled. The lower decoder output generates the binary equivalent D_4 through D_7 since these binary numbers have a 1 in the A_2 position.

Figure 2-3 A 3×8 decoder constructed with two 2×4 decoders.

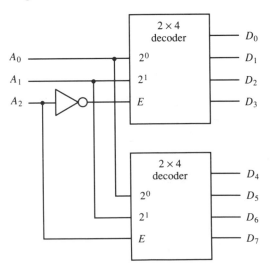

The example demonstrates the usefulness of the enable input in decoders or any other combinational logic component. Enable inputs are a convenient feature for interconnecting two or more circuits for the purpose of expanding the digital component into a similar function but with more inputs and outputs.

Encoders

An encoder is a digital circuit that performs the inverse operation of a decoder. An encoder has 2^n (or less) input lines and n output lines. The output lines generate the binary code corresponding to the input value. An example of an encoder is the octal-to-binary encoder, whose truth table is given in Table 2-2. It has eight inputs, one for each of the octal digits, and three outputs that generate the corresponding binary number. It is assumed that only one input has a value of 1 at any given time; otherwise, the circuit has no meaning.

TABLE 2-2 Truth Table for Octal-to-Binary Encoder

Inputs								Outputs		
D_7	D_6	D_5	D_4	D_3	D_2	D_1	D_0	A_2	A_1	A_0
0	0	0	0	0	0	0	1	0	0	0
0	0	0	0	0	0	1	0	0	0	1
0	0	0	0	0	1	0	0	0	1	0
0	0	0	0	1	0	0	0	0	1	1
0	0	0	1	0	0	0	0	1	0	0
0	0	1	0	0	0	0	0	1	0	1
0	1	0	0	0	0	0	0	1	1	0
1	0	0	0	0	0	0	0	1	1	1

The encoder can be implemented with OR gates whose inputs are determined directly from the truth table. Output $A_0 = 1$ if the input octal digit is 1 or 3 or 5 or 7. Similar conditions apply for the other two outputs. These conditions can be expressed by the following Boolean functions:

$$A_0 = D_1 + D_3 + D_5 + D_7$$

$$A_1 = D_2 + D_3 + D_6 + D_7$$

$$A_2 = D_4 + D_5 + D_6 + D_7$$

The encoder can be implemented with three OR gates.

2-3   Multiplexers

multiplexer

A multiplexer is a combinational circuit that receives binary information from one of 2^n input data lines and directs it to a single output line. The selection of a particular input data line for the output is determined by a set of selection inputs. A 2^n-to-1 multiplexer has 2^n input data lines and n input selection lines whose bit combinations determine which input data are selected for the output.

A 4-to-1-line multiplexer is shown in Fig. 2-4. Each of the four data inputs I_0 through I_3 is applied to one input of an AND gate. The two selection inputs S_1 and S_0 are decoded to select a particular AND gate. The outputs of the AND gates are applied to a single OR gate to provide the single output. To demonstrate the circuit operation, consider the case when $S_1 S_0 = 10$. The AND gate associated with input I_2 has two of its inputs equal to 1. The third input of the gate is connected to I_2. The other three AND gates have at least one input equal to 0, which makes their outputs equal to 0. The OR gate output is now equal to the value of I_2, thus providing a path from the selected input to the output.

The 4-to-1 line multiplexer of Fig. 2-4 has six inputs and one output. A truth table describing the circuit needs 64 rows since six input variables can have 2^6 binary combinations. This is an excessively long table and will not be shown here. A more convenient way to describe the operation of multiplexers is by means of a function table. The function table for the multiplexer is shown in Table 2-3. The table demonstrates the relationship between the four data inputs and the single output as a function of the selection inputs S_1 and S_0.

Figure 2-4   4-to-1-line multiplexer.

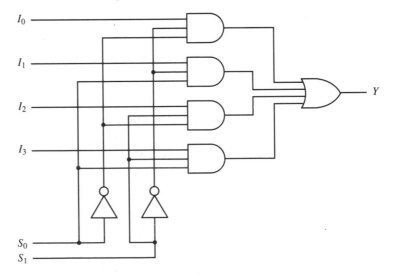

data selector

When the selection inputs are equal to 00, output Y is equal to input I_0. When the selection inputs are equal to 01, input I_1 has a path to output Y, and similarly for the other two combinations. The multiplexer is also called a *data selector*, since it selects one of many data inputs and steers the binary information to the output.

TABLE 2-3 Function Table for 4-to-1-Line Multiplexer

Select		Output
S_1	S_0	Y
0	0	I_0
0	1	I_1
1	0	I_2
1	1	I_3

The AND gates and inverters in the multiplexer resemble a decoder circuit, and indeed they decode the input selection lines. In general, a 2^n-to-1-line multiplexer is constructed from an n-to-2^n decoder by adding to it 2^n input lines, one from each data input. The size of the multiplexer is specified by the number 2^n of its data inputs and the single output. It is then implied that it also contains n input selection lines. The multiplexer is often abbreviated as MUX.

As in decoders, multiplexers may have an enable input to control the operation of the unit. When the enable input is in the inactive state, the outputs are disabled, and when it is in the active state, the circuit functions as a normal multiplexer. The enable input is useful for expanding two or more multiplexers to a multiplexer with a larger number of inputs.

In some cases two or more multiplexers are enclosed within a single integrated circuit package. The selection and the enable inputs in multiple-unit construction are usually common to all multiplexers. As an illustration, the block diagram of a quadruple 2-to-1-line multiplexer is shown in Fig. 2-5. The circuit has four multiplexers, each capable of selecting one of two input lines. Output Y_0 can be selected to come from either input A_0 or B_0. Similarly, output Y_1 may have the value of A_1 or B_1, and so on. One input selection line S selects one of the lines in each of the four multiplexers. The enable input E must be active for normal operation. Although the circuit contains four multiplexers, we can also think of it as a circuit that selects one of two 4-bit data lines. As shown in the function table, the unit is enabled when $E = 1$. Then, if $S = 0$, the four A inputs have a path to the four outputs. On the other hand, if $S = 1$, the four B inputs are applied to the outputs. The outputs have all 0's when $E = 0$, regardless of the values of S.

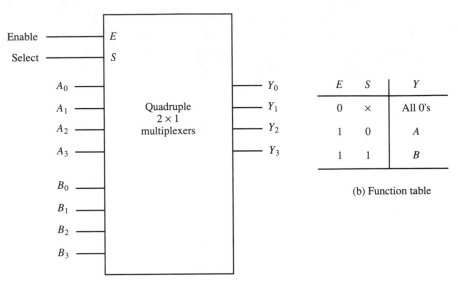

(a) Block diagram

E	S	Y
0	×	All 0's
1	0	A
1	1	B

(b) Function table

Figure 2-5   Quadruple 2-to-1 line multiplexers.

2-4   Registers

A register is a group of flip-flops with each flip-flop capable of storing one bit of information. An n-bit register has a group of n flip-flops and is capable of storing any binary information of n bits. In addition to the flip-flops, a register may have combinational gates that perform certain data-processing tasks. In its broadest definition, a register consists of a group of flip-flops and gates that effect their transition. The flip-flops hold the binary information and the gates control when and how new information is transferred into the register.

Various types of registers are available commercially. The simplest register is one that consists only of flip-flops, with no external gates. Figure 2-6 shows such a register constructed with four D flip-flops. The common clock input triggers all flip-flops on the rising edge of each pulse, and the binary data available at the four inputs are transferred into the 4-bit register. The four outputs can be sampled at any time to obtain the binary information stored in the register. The *clear* input goes to a special terminal in each flip-flop. When this input goes to 0, all flip-flops are reset asynchronously. The clear input is useful for clearing the register to all 0's prior to its clocked operation. The clear input must be maintained at logic 1 during normal clocked operation. Note that the clock signal enables the D input but that the clear input is independent of the clock.

register load   The transfer of new information into a register is referred to as *loading* the register. If all the bits of the register are loaded simultaneously with a common

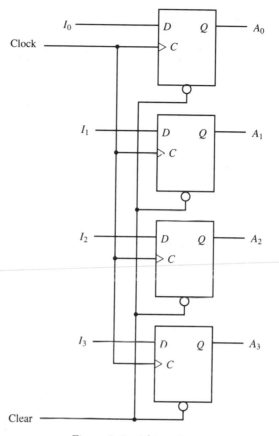

Figure 2-6 4-bit register

clock pulse transition, we say that the loading is done in parallel. A clock transition applied to the C inputs of the register of Fig. 2-6 will load all four inputs I_0 through I_3 in parallel. In this configuration, the clock must be inhibited from the circuit if the content of the register must be left unchanged.

Register with Parallel Load

Most digital systems have a master clock generator that supplies a continuous train of clock pulses. The clock pulses are applied to all flip-flops and registers in the system. The master clock acts like a pump that supplies a constant beat to all parts of the system. A separate control signal must be used to decide which specific clock pulse will have an effect on a particular register.

A 4-bit register with a load control input that is directed through gates and into the D inputs is shown in Fig. 2-7. The C inputs receive clock pulses at all times. The buffer gate in the clock input reduces the power requirement

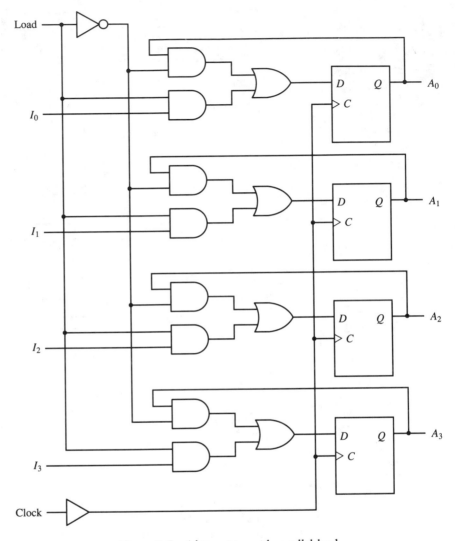

Figure 2-7   4-bit register with parallel load.

from the clock generator. Less power is required when the clock is connected to only one input gate instead of the power consumption that four inputs would have required if the buffer were not used.

The load input in the register determines the action to be taken with each clock pulse. When the load input is 1, the data in the four inputs are transferred into the register with the next positive transition of a clock pulse. When the load input is 0, the data inputs are inhibited and the D inputs of the flip-flops are connected to their outputs. The feedback connection from output to input is necessary because the D flip-flop does not have a "no change" condition.

With each clock pulse, the D input determines the next state of the output. To leave the output unchanged, it is necessary to make the D input equal to the present value of the output.

Note that the clock pulses are applied to the C inputs at all times. The load input determines whether the next pulse will accept new information or leave the information in the register intact. The transfer of information from the inputs into the register is done simultaneously with all four bits during a single pulse transition.

2-5 Shift Registers

A register capable of shifting its binary information in one or both directions is called a shift register. The logical configuration of a shift register consists of a chain of flip-flops in cascade, with the output of one flip-flop connected to the input of the next flip-flop. All flip-flops receive common clock pulses that initiate the shift from one stage to the next.

serial input

The simplest possible shift register is one that uses only flip-flops, as shown in Fig. 2-8. The output of a given flip-flop is connected to the D input of the flip-flop at its right. The clock is common to all flip-flops. The *serial input* determines what goes into the leftmost position during the shift. The *serial output* is taken from the output of the rightmost flip-flop.

Sometimes it is necessary to control the shift so that it occurs with certain clock pulses but not with others. This can be done by inhibiting the clock from the input of the register if we do not want it to shift. When the shift register of Fig 2-8 is used, the shift can be controlled by connecting the clock to the input of an AND gate, and a second input of the AND gate can then control the shift by inhibiting the clock. However, it is also possible to provide extra circuits to control the shift operation through the D inputs of the flip-flops rather than the clock input.

Bidirectional Shift Register with Parallel Load

A register capable of shifting in one direction only is called a unidirectional shift register. A register that can shift in both directions is called a bidirectional shift register. Some shift registers provide the necessary input and output terminals

Figure 2-8 4-bit shift register.

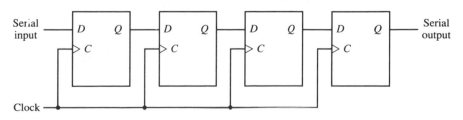

for parallel transfer. The most general shift register has all the capabilities listed below. Others may have some of these capabilities, with at least one shift operation.

1. An input for clock pulses to synchronize all operations.
2. A shift-right operation and a serial input line associated with the shift-right.
3. A shift-left operation and a serial input line associated with the shift-left.
4. A parallel load operation and n input lines associated with the parallel transfer.
5. n parallel output lines.
6. A control state that leaves the information in the register unchanged even though clock pulses are applied continuously.

A 4-bit bidirectional shift register with parallel load is shown in Fig. 2-9. Each stage consists of a D flip-flop and a 4×1 multiplexer. The two selection inputs S_1 and S_0 select one of the multiplexer data inputs for the D flip-flop. The selection lines control the mode of operation of the register according to the function table shown in Table 2-4. When the mode control $S_1S_0 = 00$, data input 0 of each multiplexer is selected. This condition forms a path from the output of each flip-flop into the input of the same flip-flop. The next clock transition transfers into each flip-flop the binary value it held previously, and no change of state occurs. When $S_1S_0 = 01$, the terminal marked 1 in each multiplexer has a path to the D input of the corresponding flip-flop. This causes a shift-right operation, with the serial input data transferred into flip-flop A_0 and the content of each flip-flop A_{i-1} transferred into flip-flop A_i for $i = 1, 2, 3$. When $S_1S_0 = 10$ a shift-left operation results, with the other serial input data going into flip-flop A_3 and the content of flip-flop A_{i+1} transferred into flip-flop A_i for $i = 0, 1, 2$. When $S_1S_0 = 11$, the binary information from each input I_0 through I_3 is transferred into the corresponding flip-flop, resulting in a parallel load operation. Note that the way the diagram is drawn, the shift-right operation shifts the contents of the register in the down direction while the shift left operation causes the contents of the register to shift in the upward direction.

TABLE 2-4 Function Table for Register of Fig. 2-9

Mode control		Register operation
S_1	S_0	
0	0	No change
0	1	Shift right (down)
1	0	Shift left (up)
1	1	Parallel load

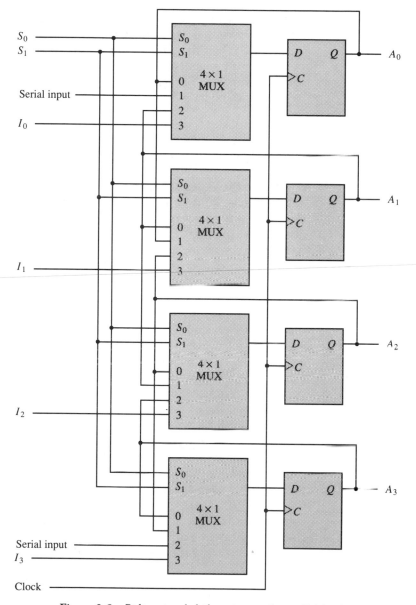

Figure 2-9 Bidirectional shift register with parallel load.

Shift registers are often used to interface digital systems situated remotely from each other. For example, suppose that it is necessary to transmit an n-bit quantity between two points. If the distance between the source and the destination is too far, it will be expensive to use n lines to transmit the n bits in parallel. It may be more economical to use a single line and transmit the information serially one bit at a time. The transmitter loads the n-bit data in parallel into a shift register and then transmits the data from the serial output line. The receiver accepts the data serially into a shift register through its serial input line. When the entire n bits are accumulated they can be taken from the outputs of the register in parallel. Thus the transmitter performs a parallel-to-serial conversion of data and the receiver converts the incoming serial data back to parallel data transfer.

2-6   Binary Counters

A register that goes through a predetermined sequence of states upon the application of input pulses is called a counter. The input pulses may be clock pulses or may originate from an external source. They may occur at uniform intervals of time or at random. Counters are found in almost all equipment containing digital logic. They are used for counting the number of occurrences of an event and are useful for generating timing signals to control the sequence of operations in digital computers.

Of the various sequences a counter may follow, the straight binary sequence is the simplest and most straightforward. A counter that follows the binary number sequence is called a binary counter. An n-bit binary counter is a register of n flip-flops and associated gates that follows a sequence of states according to the binary count of n bits, from 0 to $2^n - 1$. The design of binary counters can be carried out by the procedure outlined in Sec. 1-7 for sequential circuits. A simpler alternative design procedure may be carried out from a direct inspection of the sequence of states that the register must undergo to achieve a straight binary count.

Going through a sequence of binary numbers such as 0000, 0001, 0010, 0011, and so on, we note that the lower-order bit is complemented after every count and every other bit is complemented from one count to the next if and only if all its lower-order bits are equal to 1. For example, the binary count from 0111 (7) to 1000 (8) is obtained by (a) complementing the low-order bit, (b) complementing the second-order bit because the first bit of 0111 is 1, (c) complementing the third-order bit because the first two bits of 0111 are 1's, and (d) complementing the fourth-order bit because the first three bits of 0111 are all 1's.

A counter circuit will usually employ flip-flops with complementing capabilities. Both T and JK flip-flops have this property. Remember that a JK flip-flop is complemented if both its J and K inputs are 1 and the clock goes through a positive transition. The output of the flip-flop does not change if $J = K = 0$. In addition, the counter may be controlled with an enable input that turns the counter on or off without removing the clock signal from the flip-flops.

Synchronous binary counters have a regular pattern, as can be seen from the 4-bit binary counter shown in Fig. 2-10. The C inputs of all flip-flops receive the common clock. If the count enable is 0, all J and K inputs are maintained

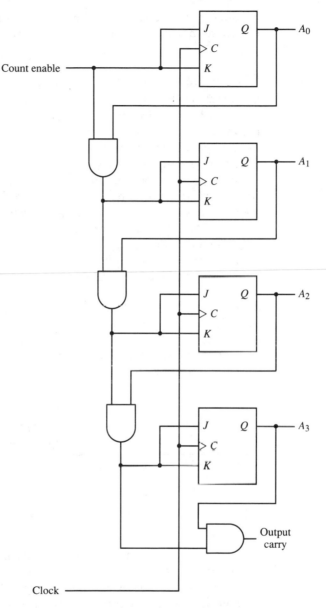

Figure 2-10 4-bit synchronous binary counter.

at 0 and the output of the counter does not change. The first stage A_0 is complemented when the counter is enabled and the clock goes through a positive transition. Each of the other three flip-flops are complemented when all previous least significant flip-flops are equal to 1 and the count is enabled. The chain of AND gates generate the required logic for the J and K inputs. The output carry can be used to extend the counter to more stages, with each stage having an additional flip-flop and an AND gate.

Binary Counter with Parallel Load

Counters employed in digital systems quite often require a parallel load capability for transferring an initial binary number prior to the count operation. Figure 2-11 shows the logic diagram of a binary counter that has a parallel load capability and can also be cleared to 0 synchronous with the clock. When equal to 1, the clear input sets all the K inputs to 1, thus clearing all flip-flops with the next clock transition. The input load control when equal to 1, disables the count operation and causes a transfer of data from the four parallel inputs into the four flip-flops (provided that the clear input is 0). If the clear and load inputs are both 0 and the increment input is 1, the circuit operates as a binary counter.

The operation of the circuit is summarized in Table 2-5. With the clear, load, and increment inputs all at 0, the outputs do not change even when pulses are applied to the C terminals. If the clear and load inputs are maintained at logic 0, the increment input controls the operation of the counter and the outputs change to the next binary count for each positive transition of the clock. The input data are loaded into the flip-flops when the load control input is equal to 1 provided that the clear is disabled, but the increment input can be 0 or 1. The register is cleared to 0 with the clear control regardless of the values in the load and increment inputs.

TABLE 2-5 Function Table for the Register of Fig. 2-11

Clock	Clear	Load	Increment	Operation
↑	0	0	0	No change
↑	0	0	1	Increment count by 1
↑	0	1	×	Load inputs I_0 through I_3
↑	1	×	×	Clear outputs to 0

Counters with parallel load are very useful in the design of digital computers. In subsequent chapters we refer to them as registers with load and

increment   increment operations. The *increment* operation adds one to the content of a register. By enabling the count input during one clock period, the content of the register can be incremented by one.

2-7 Memory Unit

A memory unit is a collection of storage cells together with associated circuits needed to transfer information in and out of storage. The memory stores binary

word   information in groups of bits called *words*. A word in memory is an entity of

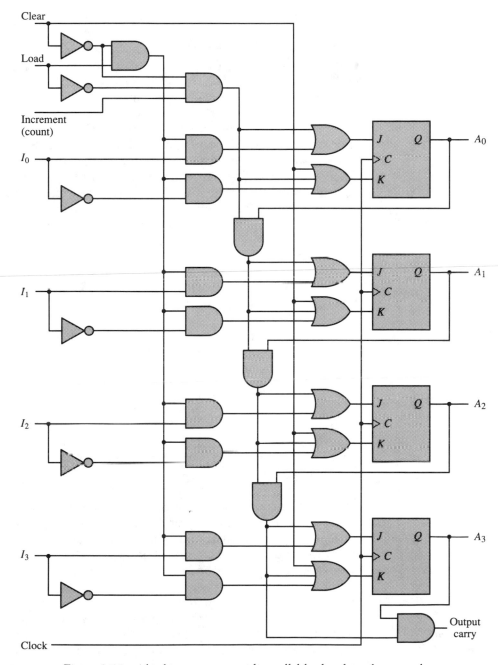

Figure 2-11   4-bit binary counter with parallel load and synchronous clear.

bits that move in and out of storage as a unit. A memory word is a group of 1's and 0's and may represent a number, an instruction code, one or more alphanumeric characters, or any other binary-coded information. A group of eight bits is called a *byte*. Most computer memories use words whose number of bits is a multiple of 8. Thus a 16-bit word contains two bytes, and a 32-bit word is made up of four bytes. The capacity of memories in commercial computers is usually stated as the total number of bytes that can be stored.

byte

The internal structure of a memory unit is specified by the number of words it contains and the number of bits in each word. Special input lines called address lines select one particular word. Each word in memory is assigned an identification number, called an address, starting from 0 and continuing with 1, 2, 3, up to $2^k - 1$ where k is the number of address lines. The selection of a specific word inside the memory is done by applying the k-bit binary address to the address lines. A decoder inside the memory accepts this address and opens the paths needed to select the bits of the specified word. Computer memories may range from 1024 words, requiring an address of 10 bits, to 2^{32} words, requiring 32 address bits. It is customary to refer to the number of words (or bytes) in a memory with one of the letters K (kilo), M (mega), or G (giga). K is equal to 2^{10}, M is equal to 2^{20}, and G is equal to 2^{30}. Thus $64K = 2^{16}$, $2M = 2^{21}$, and $4G = 2^{32}$.

Two major types of memories are used in computer systems: random-access memory (RAM) and read-only memory (ROM).

Random-Access Memory

RAM

In random-access memory (RAM) the memory cells can be accessed for information transfer from any desired random location. That is, the process of locating a word in memory is the same and requires an equal amount of time no matter where the cells are located physically in memory: thus the name "random access."

Communication between a memory and its environment is achieved through data input and output lines, address selection lines, and control lines that specify the direction of transfer. A block diagram of a RAM unit is shown in Fig. 2-12. The n data input lines provide the information to be stored in memory, and the n data output lines supply the information coming out of memory. The k address lines provide a binary number of k bits that specify a particular word chosen among the 2^k available inside the memory. The two control inputs specify the direction of transfer desired.

write and read operations

The two operations that a random-access memory can perform are the write and read operations. The write signal specifies a transfer-in operation and the read signal specifies a transfer-out operation. On accepting one of these control signals, the internal circuits inside the memory provide the desired function. The steps that must be taken for the purpose of transferring a new word to be stored into memory are as follows:

1. Apply the binary address of the desired word into the address lines.

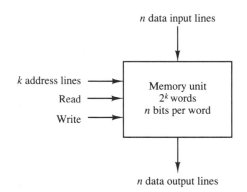

Figure 2-12   Block diagram of random access memory (RAM).

2. Apply the data bits that must be stored in memory into the data input lines.

3. Activate the *write* input.

The memory unit will then take the bits presently available in the input data lines and store them in the word specified by the address lines.

The steps that must be taken for the purpose of transferring a stored word out of memory are as follows:

1. Apply the binary address of the desired word into the address lines.

2. Activate the *read* input.

The memory unit will then take the bits from the word that has been selected by the address and apply them into the output data lines. The content of the selected word does not change after reading.

Read-Only Memory

ROM

As the name implies, a read-only memory (ROM) is a memory unit that performs the read operation only; it does not have a write capability. This implies that the binary information stored in a ROM is made permanent during the hardware production of the unit and cannot be altered by writing different words into it. Whereas a RAM is a general-purpose device whose contents can be altered during the computational process, a ROM is restricted to reading words that are permanently stored within the unit. The binary information to be stored, specified by the designer, is then embedded in the unit to form the required interconnection pattern. ROMs come with special internal electronic fuses that can be "programmed" for a specific configuration. Once the pattern is established, it stays within the unit even when power is turned off and on again.

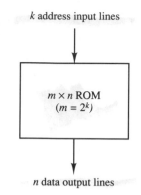

k address input lines

$m \times n$ ROM
$(m = 2^k)$

n data output lines

Figure 2-13 Block diagram of read only memory (ROM).

An $m \times n$ ROM is an array of binary cells organized into m words of n bits each. As shown in the block diagram of Fig. 2-13, a ROM has k address input lines to select one of $2^k = m$ words of memory, and n output lines, one for each bit of the word. An integrated circuit ROM may also have one or more enable inputs for expanding a number of packages into a ROM with larger capacity.

The ROM does not need a read-control line since at any given time, the output lines automatically provide the n bits of the word selected by the address value. Because the outputs are a function of only the present inputs (the address lines), a ROM is classified as a combinational circuit. In fact, a ROM is constructed internally with decoders and a set of OR gates. There is no need for providing storage capabilities as in a RAM, since the values of the bits in the ROM are permanently fixed.

ROMs find a wide range of applications in the design of digital systems. Basically, a ROM generates an input–output relation specified by a truth table. As such, it can implement any combinational circuit with k inputs and n outputs. When employed in a computer system as a memory unit, the ROM is used for storing fixed programs that are not to be altered and for tables of constants that are not subject to change. ROM is also employed in the design of control units for digital computers. As such, they are used to store coded information that represents the sequence of internal control variables needed for enabling the various operations in the computer. A control unit that utilizes a ROM to store binary control information is called a microprogrammed control unit. This subject is dicsussed in more detail in Chapter 7.

Types of ROMs

The required paths in a ROM may be programmed in three different ways. The first, *mask programming*, is done by the semiconductor company during the last fabrication process of the unit. The procedure for fabricating a ROM requires that the customer fill out the truth table that he or she wishes the ROM to satisfy. The truth table may be submitted in a special form provided by the manufacturer or in a specified format on a computer output medium. The manufacturer makes the corresponding mask for the paths to produce the 1's and 0's according to the customer's truth table. This procedure is costly because the vendor charges the customer a special fee for custom masking the particular ROM. For this reason, mask programming is economical only if a large quantity of the same ROM configuration is to be ordered.

PROM

For small quantities it is more economical to use a second type of ROM called a *programmable read-only memory* or PROM. When ordered, PROM units contain all the fuses intact, giving all 1's in the bits of the stored words. The fuses in the PROM are blown by application of current pulses through the output terminals for each address. A blown fuse defines a binary 0 state, and an intact fuse gives a binary 1 state. This allows users to program PROMs in their own laboratories to achieve the desired relationship between input addresses and stored words. Special instruments called *PROM programmers* are available commercially to facilitate this procedure. In any case, all procedures for programming ROMs are hardware procedures even though the word "programming" is used.

The hardware procedure for programming ROMs or PROMs is irreversible, and once programmed, the fixed pattern is permanent and cannot be altered. Once a bit pattern has been established, the unit must be discarded if the bit pattern is to be changed. A third type of ROM available is called *erasable PROM* or EPROM. The EPROM can be restructured to the initial value even though its fuses have been blown previously. When the EPROM is placed under a special ultraviolet light for a given period of time, the shortwave radiation discharges the internal gates that serve as fuses. After erasure, the EPROM returns to its initial state and can be reprogrammed to a new set of words. Certain PROMs can be erased with electrical signals instead of ultravi-

EEPROM

olet light. These PROMs are called *electrically erasable PROM* or EEPROM.

PROBLEMS

2-1. TTL SSI come mostly in 14-pin IC packages. Two pins are reserved for power supply and the other pins are used for input and output terminals. How many circuits are included in one such package if it contains the following type of circuits? (a) Inverters; (b) two-input exclusive-OR gates; (c) three-input OR gates; (d) four-input AND gates; (e) five-input NOR gates; (f) eight-input NAND gates; (g) clocked *JK* flip-flops with asynchronous clear.

2-2. MSI chips perform elementary digital functions such as decoders, multiplexers, registers, and counters. The following are TTL-type integrated circuits that provide such functions. Find their description in a data book and compare them with the corresponding component presented in this chapter.

> **a.** IC type 74155 dual 2-to-4-line decoders.
> **b.** IC type 74157 quadruple 2-to-1-line multiplexers.
> **c.** IC type 74194 4-bit bidirectional shift register with parallel load.
> **d.** IC type 74163 4-bit binary counter with parallel load and synchronous clear.

2-3. Construct a 5-to-32-line decoder with four 3-to-8-line decoders with enable and one 2-to-4-line decoder. Use block diagrams similar to Fig. 2-3.

2-4. Draw the logic diagram of a 2-to-4-line decoder with only NOR gates. Include an enable input.

2-5. Modify the decoder of Fig. 2-2 so that the circuit is enabled when $E = 1$ and disabled when $E = 0$. List the modified truth table.

2-6. Draw the logic diagram of an eight-input, three-output encoder whose truth table is given in Table 2-2. What is the output when all the inputs are equal to 0? What is the output when only input D_0 is equal to 0? Establish a procedure that will distinguish between these two cases.

2-7. Construct a 16-to-1-line multiplexer with two 8-to-1-line multiplexers and one 2-to-1-line multiplexer. Use block diagrams for the three multiplexers.

2-8. Draw the block diagram of a dual 4-to-1-line multiplexers and explain its operation by means of a function table.

2-9. Include a two-input AND gate with the register of Fig. 2-6 and connect the gate output to the clock inputs of all the flip-flops. One input of the AND gate receives the clock pulses from the clock pulse generator. The other input of the AND gate provides a parallel load control. Explain the operation of the modified register.

2-10. What is the purpose of the buffer gate in the clock input of the register of Fig. 2-7?

2-11. Include a synchronous clear capability to the register with parallel load of Fig. 2-7.

2-12. The content of a 4-bit register is initially 1101. The register is shifted six times to the right with the serial input being 101101. What is the content of the register after each shift?

2-13. What is the difference between serial and parallel transfer? Using a shift register with parallel load, explain how to convert serial input data to parallel output and parallel input data to serial output.

2-14. A ring counter is a shift register as in Fig. 2-8 with the serial output connected to the serial input. Starting from an initial state of 1000, list the sequence of states of the four flip-flops after each shift.

2-15. The 4-bit bidirectional shift register with parallel load shown in Fig. 2-9 is enclosed within one IC package.
  a. Draw a block diagram of the IC showing all inputs and outputs. Include two pins for power supply.
  b. Draw a block diagram using two ICs to produce an 8-bit bidirectional shift register with parallel load.

2-16. How many flip-flops will be complemented in a 10-bit binary counter to reach the next count after (a) 1001100111; (b) 0011111111?

2-17.   Show the connections between four 4-bit binary counters with parallel load (Fig. 2-11) to produce a 16-bit binary counter with parallel load. Use a block diagram for each 4-bit counter.

2-18.   Show how the binary counter with parallel load of Fig. 2-11 can be made to operate as a divide-by-N counter (i.e., a counter that counts from 0000 to N-and back to 0000). Specifically show the circuit for a divide-by-10 counter using the counter of Fig. 2-11 and an external AND gate.

2-19.   The following memory units are specified by the number of words times the number of bits per word. How many address lines and input–output data lines are needed in each case? (a) 2K $\times$ 16; (b) 64K $\times$ 8; (c) 16M $\times$ 32; (d) 4G $\times$ 64.

2-20.   Specify the number of bytes that can be stored in the memories listed in Prob. 2-19.

2-21.   How many 128 $\times$ 8 memory chips are needed to provide a memory capacity of 4096 $\times$ 16?

2-22.   Given a 32 $\times$ 8 ROM chip with an enable input, show the external connections necessary to construct a 128 $\times$ 8 ROM with four chips and a decoder.

2-23.   A ROM chip of 4096 $\times$ 8 bits has two enable inputs and operates from a 5-volt power supply. How many pins are needed for the integrated circuit package? Draw a block diagram and label all input and output terminals in the ROM.

REFERENCES

1. Hill, F. J., and G. R. Peterson, *Introduction to Switching Theory and Logical Design*, 3rd ed. New York: John Wiley, 1981.

2. Mano, M. M., *Digital Design*, 2nd ed. Englewood Cliffs, NJ: Prentice Hall, 1991.

3. Roth, C. H., *Fundamentals of Logic Design*, 3rd ed. St. Paul, MN: West Publishing, 1985.

4. Sandige, R. S., *Modern Digital Design*. New York: McGraw-Hill, 1990.

5. Shiva, S. G., *Introduction to Logic Design*. Glenview, Il: Scott, Foresman, 1988.

6. Wakerly, J. F., *Digital Design Principles and Practices*. Englewood Cliffs, NJ: Prentice Hall, 1990.

7. Ward, S. A., and R. H. Halstead, Jr., *Computation Structures*. Cambridge, MA: MIT Press, 1990.

CHAPTER THREE

Data Representation

IN THIS CHAPTER

3-1   Data Types

Binary information in digital computers is stored in memory or processor registers. Registers contain either data or control information. Control information is a bit or a group of bits used to specify the sequence of command signals needed for manipulation of the data in other registers. Data are numbers and other binary-coded information that are operated on to achieve required computational results. In this chapter we present the most common types of data found in digital computers and show how the various data types are represented in binary-coded form in computer registers.

The data types found in the registers of digital computers may be classified as being one of the following categories: (1) numbers used in arithmetic computations, (2) letters of the alphabet used in data processing, and (3) other discrete symbols used for specific purposes. All types of data, except binary numbers, are represented in computer registers in binary-coded form. This is because registers are made up of flip-flops and flip-flops are two-state devices that can store only 1's and 0's. The binary number system is the most natural system to use in a digital computer. But sometimes it is convenient to employ different number systems, especially the decimal number system, since it is used by people to perform arithmetic computations.

Number Systems

radix

A number system of *base*, or *radix*, r is a system that uses distinct symbols for r digits. Numbers are represented by a string of digit symbols. To determine the quantity that the number represents, it is necessary to multiply each digit by an integer power of r and then form the sum of all weighted digits. For example, the decimal number system in everyday use employs the radix 10 system. The 10 symbols are 0, 1, 2, 3, 4, 5, 6, 7, 8, and 9. The string of digits 724.5 is interpreted to represent the quantity

decimal

$$7 \times 10^2 + 2 \times 10^1 + 4 \times 10^0 + 5 \times 10^{-1}$$

that is, 7 hundreds, plus 2 tens, plus 4 units, plus 5 tenths. Every decimal number can be similarly interpreted to find the quantity it represents.

binary

The *binary* number system uses the radix 2. The two digit symbols used are 0 and 1. The string of digits 101101 is interpreted to represent the quantity

$$1 \times 2^5 + 0 \times 2^4 + 1 \times 2^3 + 1 \times 2^2 + 0 \times 2^1 + 1 \times 2^0 = 45$$

To distinguish between different radix numbers, the digits will be enclosed in parentheses and the radix of the number inserted as a subscript. For example, to show the equality between decimal and binary forty-five we will write $(101101)_2 = (45)_{10}$.

octal
hexademical

Besides the decimal and binary number systems, the *octal* (radix 8) and *hexadecimal* (radix 16) are important in digital computer work. The eight symbols of the octal system are 0, 1, 2, 3, 4, 5, 6, and 7. The 16 symbols of the hexadecimal system are 0, 1, 2, 3, 4, 5, 6, 7, 8, 9, A, B, C, D, E, and F. The last six symbols are, unfortunately, identical to the letters of the alphabet and can cause confusion at times. However, this is the convention that has been adopted. When used to represent hexadecimal digits, the symbols A, B, C, D, E, F correspond to the decimal numbers 10, 11, 12, 13, 14, 15, respectively.

A number in radix r can be converted to the familiar decimal system by forming the sum of the weighted digits. For example, octal 736.4 is converted to decimal as follows:

$$(736.4)_8 = 7 \times 8^2 + 3 \times 8^1 + 6 \times 8^0 + 4 \times 8^{-1}$$
$$= 7 \times 64 + 3 \times 8 + 6 \times 1 + 4/8 = (478.5)_{10}$$

The equivalent decimal number of hexadecimal F3 is obtained from the following calculation:

$$(F3)_{16} = F \times 16 + 3 = 15 \times 16 + 3 = (243)_{10}$$

conversion

Conversion from decimal to its equivalent representation in the radix r system is carried out by separating the number into its *integer* and *fraction* parts and converting each part separately. The conversion of a decimal integer into a base r representation is done by successive divisions by r and accumulation of the remainders. The conversion of a decimal fraction to radix r representation is accomplished by successive multiplications by r and accumulation of the integer digits so obtained. Figure 3-1 demonstrates these procedures.

The conversion of decimal 41.6875 into binary is done by first separating the number into its integer part 41 and fraction part .6875. The integer part is converted by dividing 41 by $r = 2$ to give an integer quotient of 20 and a remainder of 1. The quotient is again divided by 2 to give a new quotient and remainder. This process is repeated until the integer quotient becomes 0. The coefficients of the binary number are obtained from the remainders with the first remainder giving the low-order bit of the converted binary number.

The fraction part is converted by multiplying it by $r = 2$ to give an integer and a fraction. The new fraction (*without* the integer) is multiplied again by 2 to give a new integer and a new fraction. This process is repeated until the fraction part becomes zero or until the number of digits obtained gives the required accuracy. The coefficients of the binary fraction are obtained from the integer digits with the first integer computed being the digit to be placed next to the binary point. Finally, the two parts are combined to give the total required conversion.

Octal and Hexadecimal Numbers

The conversion from and to binary, octal, and hexadecimal representation plays an important part in digital computers. Since $2^3 = 8$ and $2^4 = 16$, each octal digit corresponds to three binary digits and each hexadecimal digit corresponds to four binary digits. The conversion from binary to octal is easily accomplished by partitioning the binary number into groups of three bits each. The corresponding octal digit is then assigned to each group of bits and the string of digits so obtained gives the octal equivalent of the binary number. Consider, for example, a 16-bit register. Physically, one may think of the

Figure 3-1   Conversion of decimal 41.6875 into binary.

Integer = 41		Fraction = 0.6875
41		0.6875
20	1	$\underline{\qquad\times\ 2}$
10	0	1.3750
5	0	$\underline{\qquad\times\ 2}$
2	1	0.7500
1	0	$\underline{\qquad\times\ 2}$
0	1	1.5000
		$\underline{\qquad\times\ 2}$
		1.0000

$$(41)_{10} = (101001)_2 \qquad (0.6875)_{10} = (0.1011)_2$$

$$(41.6875)_{10} = (101001.1011)_2$$

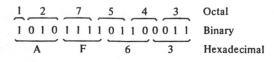

Figure 3-2 Binary, octal, and hexadecimal conversion.

register as composed of 16 binary storage cells, with each cell capable of holding either a 1 or a 0. Suppose that the bit configuration stored in the register is as shown in Fig. 3-2. Since a binary number consists of a string of 1's and 0's, the 16-bit register can be used to store any binary number from 0 to $2^{16} - 1$. For the particular example shown, the binary number stored in the register is the equivalent of decimal 44899. Starting from the low-order bit, we partition the register into groups of three bits each (the sixteenth bit remains in a group by itself). Each group of three bits is assigned its octal equivalent and placed on top of the register. The string of octal digits so obtained represents the octal equivalent of the binary number.

Conversion from binary to hexadecimal is similar except that the bits are divided into groups of four. The corresponding hexadecimal digit for each group of four bits is written as shown below the register of Fig. 3-2. The string of hexadecimal digits so obtained represents the hexadecimal equivalent of the binary number. The corresponding octal digit for each group of three bits is easily remembered after studying the first eight entries listed in Table 3-1. The correspondence between a hexadecimal digit and its equivalent 4-bit code can be found in the first 16 entries of Table 3-2.

TABLE 3-1 Binary-Coded Octal Numbers

Octal number	Binary-coded octal	Decimal equivalent	
0	000	0	↑
1	001	1	
2	010	2	Code
3	011	3	for one
4	100	4	octal
5	101	5	digit
6	110	6	
7	111	7	↓
10	001 000	8	
11	001 001	9	
12	001 010	10	
24	010 100	20	
62	110 010	50	
143	001 100 011	99	
370	011 111 000	248	

Table 3-1 lists a few octal numbers and their representation in registers in binary-coded form. The binary code is obtained by the procedure explained above. Each octal digit is assigned a 3-bit code as specified by the entries of the first eight digits in the table. Similarly, Table 3-2 lists a few hexadecimal numbers and their representation in registers in binary-coded form. Here the binary code is obtained by assigning to each hexadecimal digit the 4-bit code listed in the first 16 entries of the table.

Comparing the binary-coded octal and hexadecimal numbers with their binary number equivalent we find that the bit combination in all three representations is exactly the same. For example, decimal 99, when converted to binary, becomes 1100011. The binary-coded octal equivalent of decimal 99 is 001 100 011 and the binary-coded hexadecimal of decimal 99 is 0110 0011. If we neglect the leading zeros in these three binary representations, we find that their bit combination is identical. This should be so because of the straightforward conversion that exists between binary numbers and octal or hexadecimal. The point of all this is that a string of 1's and 0's stored in a register could represent a binary number, but this same string of bits may be interpreted as holding an octal number in binary-coded form (if we divide the bits in groups of three) or as holding a hexadecimal number in binary-coded form (if we divide the bits in groups of four).

TABLE 3-2 Binary-Coded Hexadecimal Numbers

Hexadecimal number	Binary-coded hexadecimal	Decimal equivalent	
0	0000	0	
1	0001	1	
2	0010	2	
3	0011	3	
4	0100	4	
5	0101	5	
6	0110	6	Code
7	0111	7	for one
8	1000	8	hexadecimal
9	1001	9	digit
A	1010	10	
B	1011	11	
C	1100	12	
D	1101	13	
E	1110	14	
F	1111	15	
14	0001 0100	20	
32	0011 0010	50	
63	0110 0011	99	
F8	1111 1000	248	

The registers in a digital computer contain many bits. Specifying the content of registers by their binary values will require a long string of binary digits. It is more convenient to specify content of registers by their octal or hexadecimal equivalent. The number of digits is reduced by one-third in the octal designation and by one-fourth in the hexadecimal designation. For example, the binary number 1111 1111 1111 has 12 digits. It can be expressed in octals as 7777 (four digits) or in hexadecimal as FFF (three digits). Computer manuals invariably choose either the octal or the hexadecimal designation for specifying contents of registers.

Decimal Representation

The binary number system is the most natural system for a computer, but people are accustomed to the decimal system. One way to solve this conflict is to convert all input decimal numbers into binary numbers, let the computer perform all arithmetic operations in binary and then convert the binary results back to decimal for the human user to understand. However, it is also possible for the computer to perform arithmetic operations directly with decimal numbers provided they are placed in registers in a coded form. Decimal numbers enter the computer usually as binary-coded alphanumeric characters. These codes, introduced later, may contain from six to eight bits for each decimal digit. When decimal numbers are used for internal arithmetic computations, they are converted to a binary code with four bits per digit.

binary code

A binary code is a group of n bits that assume up to 2^n distinct combinations of 1's and 0's with each combination representing one element of the set that is being coded. For example, a set of four elements can be coded by a 2-bit code with each element assigned one of the following bit combinations; 00, 01, 10, or 11. A set of eight elements requires a 3-bit code, a set of 16 elements requires a 4-bit code, and so on. A binary code will have some unassigned bit combinations if the number of elements in the set is not a multiple power of 2. The 10 decimal digits form such a set. A binary code that distinguishes among 10 elements must contain at least four bits, but six combinations will remain unassigned. Numerous different codes can be obtained by arranging four bits in 10 distinct combinations. The bit assignment most commonly used for the decimal digits is the straight binary assignment listed in the first 10 entries of Table 3-3. This particular code is called *binary-coded decimal* and is

BCD

commonly referred to by its abbreviation BCD. Other decimal codes are sometimes used and a few of them are given in Sec. 3-5.

It is very important to understand the difference between the *conversion* of decimal numbers into binary and the *binary coding* of decimal numbers. For example, when *converted* to a binary number, the decimal number 99 is represented by the string of bits 1100011, but when represented in BCD, it becomes 1001 1001. The *only* difference between a decimal number represented by the familiar digit symbols 0, 1, 2, . . . , 9 and the BCD symbols 0001, 0010, . . . , 1001 is in the symbols used to represent the digits—the number itself is exactly the

TABLE 3-3 Binary-Coded Decimal (BCD) Numbers

Decimal number	Binary-coded decimal (BCD) number	
0	0000	↑
1	0001	
2	0010	
3	0011	Code
4	0100	for one
5	0101	decimal
6	0110	digit
7	0111	
8	1000	
9	1001	↓
10	0001 0000	
20	0010 0000	
50	0101 0000	
99	1001 1001	
248	0010 0100 1000	

same. A few decimal numbers and their representation in BCD are listed in Table 3-3.

Alphanumeric Representation

Many applications of digital computers require the handling of data that consist not only of numbers, but also of the letters of the alphabet and certain

character

special characters. An *alphanumeric character set* is a set of elements that includes the 10 decimal digits, the 26 letters of the alphabet and a number of special characters, such as $, +, and =. Such a set contains between 32 and 64 elements (if only uppercase letters are included) or between 64 and 128 (if both uppercase and lowercase letters are included). In the first case, the binary code will require six bits and in the second case, seven bits. The standard alphanumeric binary

ASCII

code is the ASCII (American Standard Code for Information Interchange), which uses seven bits to code 128 characters. The binary code for the uppercase letters, the decimal digits, and a few special characters is listed in Table 3-4. Note that the decimal digits in ASCII can be converted to BCD by removing the three high-order bits, 011. A complete list of ASCII characters is provided in Table 11-1.

Binary codes play an important part in digital computer operations. The codes must be in binary because registers can only hold binary information. One must realize that binary codes merely change the symbols, not the meaning of the discrete elements they represent. The operations specified for digital

TABLE 3-4 American Standard Code for Information Interchange (ASCII)

Character	Binary code	Character	Binary code
A	100 0001	0	011 0000
B	100 0010	1	011 0001
C	100 0011	2	011 0010
D	100 0100	3	011 0011
E	100 0101	4	011 0100
F	100 0110	5	011 0101
G	100 0111	6	011 0110
H	100 1000	7	011 0111
I	100 1001	8	011 1000
J	100 1010	9	011 1001
K	100 1011		
L	100 1100		
M	100 1101	space	010 0000
N	100 1110	.	010 1110
O	100 1111	(	010 1000
P	101 0000	+	010 1011
Q	101 0001	$	010 0100
R	101 0010	*	010 1010
S	101 0011	)	010 1001
T	101 0100	−	010 1101
U	101 0101	/	010 1111
V	101 0110	,	010 1100
W	101 0111	=	011 1101
X	101 1000		
Y	101 1001		
Z	101 1010		

computers must take into consideration the meaning of the bits stored in registers so that operations are performed on operands of the same type. In inspecting the bits of a computer register at random, one is likely to find that it represents some type of coded information rather than a binary number.

Binary codes can be formulated for any set of discrete elements such as the musical notes and chess pieces and their positions on the chessboard. Binary codes are also used to formulate instructions that specify control information for the computer. This chapter is concerned with *data* representation. Instruction codes are discussed in Chap. 5.

3-2 Complements

Complements are used in digital computers for simplifying the subtraction operation and for logical manipulation. There are two types of complements for each base r system: the r's complement and the $(r - 1)$'s complement.

When the value of the base r is substituted in the name, the two types are referred to as the 2's and 1's complement for binary numbers and the 10's and 9's complement for decimal numbers.

$(r - 1)$'s Complement

9's complement

Given a number N in base r having n digits, the $(r - 1)$'s complement of N is defined as $(r^n - 1) - N$. For decimal numbers $r = 10$ and $r - 1 = 9$, so the 9's complement of N is $(10^n - 1) - N$. Now, 10^n represents a number that consists of a single 1 followed by n 0's. $10^n - 1$ is a number represented by n 9's. For example, with $n = 4$ we have $10^4 = 10000$ and $10^4 - 1 = 9999$. It follows that the 9's complement of a decimal number is obtained by subtracting each digit from 9. For example, the 9's complement of 546700 is $999999 - 546700 = 453299$ and the 9's complement of 12389 is $99999 - 12389 = 87610$.

1's complement

For binary numbers, $r = 2$ and $r - 1 = 1$, so the 1's complement of N is $(2^n - 1) - N$. Again, 2^n is represented by a binary number that consists of a 1 followed by n 0's. $2^n - 1$ is a binary number represented by n 1's. For example, with $n = 4$, we have $2^4 = (10000)_2$ and $2^4 - 1 = (1111)_2$. Thus the 1's complement of a binary number is obtained by subtracting each digit from 1. However, the subtraction of a binary digit from 1 causes the bit to change from 0 to 1 or from 1 to 0. Therefore, the 1's complement of a binary number is formed by changing 1's into 0's and 0's into 1's. For example, the 1's complement of 1011001 is 0100110 and the 1's complement of 0001111 is 1110000.

The $(r - 1)$'s complement of octal or hexadecimal numbers are obtained by subtracting each digit from 7 or F (decimal 15) respectively.

$(r's)$ Complement

10's complement

The r's complement of an n-digit number N in base r is defined as $r^n - N$ for $N \neq 0$ and 0 for $N = 0$. Comparing with the $(r - 1)$'s complement, we note that the r's complement is obtained by adding 1 to the $(r - 1)$'s complement since $r^n - N = [(r^n - 1) - N] + 1$. Thus the 10's complement of the decimal 2389 is $7610 + 1 = 7611$ and is obtained by adding 1 to the 9's complement value. The 2's complement of binary 101100 is $010011 + 1 = 010100$ and is obtained by adding 1 to the 1's complement value.

2's complement

Since 10^n is a number represented by a 1 followed by n 0's, then $10^n - N$, which is the 10's complement of N, can be formed also be leaving all least significant 0's unchanged, subtracting the first nonzero least significant digit from 10, and then subtracting all higher significant digits from 9. The 10's complement of 246700 is 753300 and is obtained by leaving the two zeros unchanged, subtracting 7 from 10, and subtracting the other three digits from 9. Similarly, the 2's complement can be formed by leaving all least significant 0's and the first 1 unchanged, and then replacing 1's by 0's and 0's by 1's in all other higher significant bits. The 2's complement of 1101100 is 0010100 and is obtained by leaving the two low-order 0's and the first 1 unchanged, and then replacing 1's by 0's and 0's by 1's in the other four most significant bits.

In the definitions above it was assumed that the numbers do not have a radix point. If the original number N contains a radix point, it should be removed temporarily to form the r's or $(r-1)$'s complement. The radix point is then restored to the complemented number in the same relative position. It is also worth mentioning that the complement of the complement restores the number to its original value. The r's complement of N is $r^n - N$. The complement of the complement is $r^n - (r^n - N) = N$ giving back the original number.

Subtraction of Unsigned Numbers

The direct method of subtraction taught in elementary schools uses the borrow concept. In this method we borrow a 1 from a higher significant position when the minuend digit is smaller than the corresponding subtrahend digit. This seems to be easiest when people perform subtraction with paper and pencil. When subtraction is implemented with digital hardware, this method is found to be less efficient than the method that uses complements.

subtraction

The subtraction of two n-digit unsigned numbers $M - N (N \neq 0)$ in base r can be done as follows:

1. Add the minuend M to the r's complement of the subtrahend N. This performs $M + (r^n - N) = M - N + r^n$.

end carry

2. If $M \geq N$, the sum will produce an end carry r^n which is discarded, and what is left is the result $M - N$.

3. If $M < N$, the sum does not produce an end carry and is equal to $r^n - (N - M)$, which is the r's complement of $(N - M)$. To obtain the answer in a familiar form, take the r's complement of the sum and place a negative sign in front.

Consider, for example, the subtraction $72532 - 13250 = 59282$. The 10's complement of 13250 is 86750. Therefore:

$$
\begin{aligned}
M &= 72532 \\
\text{10's complement of } N &= +86750 \\
\text{Sum} &= 159282 \\
\text{Discard end carry } 10^5 &= -100000 \\
\text{Answer} &= 59282
\end{aligned}
$$

Now consider an example with $M < N$. The subtraction $13250 - 72532$ produces negative 59282. Using the procedure with complements, we have

$$
\begin{aligned}
M &= 13250 \\
\text{10's complement of } N &= +27468 \\
\text{Sum} &= 40718
\end{aligned}
$$

There is no end carry

Answer is negative 59282 = 10's complement of 40718

     Since we are dealing with unsigned numbers, there is really no way to get an unsigned result for the second example. When working with paper and pencil, we recognize that the answer must be changed to a signed negative number. When subtracting with complements, the negative answer is recognized by the absence of the end carry and the complemented result.

     Subtraction with complements is done with binary numbers in a similar manner using the same procedure outlined above. Using the two binary numbers $X = 1010100$ and $Y = 1000011$, we perform the subtraction $X - Y$ and $Y - X$ using 2's complements:

$$
\begin{array}{rr}
X = & 1010100 \\
\text{2's complement of } Y = & +0111101 \\ \hline
\text{Sum} = & 10010001 \\
\text{Discard end carry } 2^7 = & -10000000 \\ \hline
\text{Answer: } X - Y = & 0010001 \\
\end{array}
$$

$$
\begin{array}{rr}
Y = & 1000011 \\
\text{2's complement of } X = & +0101100 \\ \hline
\text{Sum} = & 1101111 \\
\end{array}
$$

There is no end carry

Answer is negative 0010001 = 2's complement of 1101111

3-3 Fixed-Point Representation

Positive integers, including zero, can be represented as unsigned numbers. However, to represent negative integers, we need a notation for negative values. In ordinary arithmetic, a negative number is indicated by a minus sign and a positive number by a plus sign. Because of hardware limitations, computers must represent everything with 1's and 0's, including the sign of a number. As a consequence, it is customary to represent the sign with a bit placed in the leftmost position of the number. The convention is to make the sign bit equal to 0 for positive and to 1 for negative.

binary point   In addition to the sign, a number may have a binary (or decimal) point. The position of the binary point is needed to represent fractions, integers, or mixed integer–fraction numbers. The representation of the binary point in a register is complicated by the fact that it is characterized by a position in the register. There are two ways of specifying the position of the binary point in a register: by giving it a fixed position or by employing a floating-point representation. The fixed-point method assumes that the binary point is always fixed in one position. The two positions most widely used are (1) a binary point in the extreme left of the register to make the stored number a fraction, and (2) a binary point in the extreme right of the register to make the stored number an integer. In either case, the binary point is not actually present, but its presence is assumed from the fact that the number stored in the register is treated as a fraction or as an integer. The floating-point representation uses a second register to store a number that designates the position of the decimal point in the first register. Floating-point representation is discussed further in the next section.

Integer Representation

signed numbers

When an integer binary number is positive, the sign is represented by 0 and the magnitude by a positive binary number. When the number is negative, the sign is represented by 1 but the rest of the number may be represented in one of three possible ways:

1. Signed-magnitude representation
2. Signed-1's complement representation
3. Signed 2's complement representation

The signed-magnitude representation of a negative number consists of the magnitude and a negative sign. In the other two representations, the negative number is represented in either the 1's or 2's complement of its positive value. As an example, consider the signed number 14 stored in an 8-bit register. +14 is represented by a sign bit of 0 in the leftmost position followed by the binary equivalent of 14: 00001110. Note that each of the eight bits of the register must have a value and therefore 0's must be inserted in the most significant positions following the sign bit. Although there is only one way to represent +14, there are three different ways to represent −14 with eight bits.

In signed-magnitude representation	1 0001110
In signed-1's complement representation	1 1110001
In signed-2's complement representation	1 1110010

The signed-magnitude representation of −14 is obtained from +14 by complementing only the sign bit. The signed-1's complement representation of −14 is obtained by complementing all the bits of +14, including the sign bit. The signed-2's complement representation is obtained by taking the 2's complement of the positive number, including its sign bit.

The signed-magnitude system is used in ordinary arithmetic but is awkward when employed in computer arithmetic. Therefore, the signed-complement is normally used. The 1's complement imposes difficulties because it has two representations of 0 (+0 and −0). It is seldom used for arithmetic operations except in some older computers. The 1's complement is useful as a logical operation since the change of 1 to 0 or 0 to 1 is equivalent to a logical complement operation. The following discussion of signed binary arithmetic deals exclusively with the signed-2's complement representation of negative numbers.

Arithmetic Addition

The addition of two numbers in the signed-magnitude system follows the rules of ordinary arithmetic. If the signs are the same, we add the two magnitudes and give the sum the common sign. If the signs are different, we subtract the smaller magnitude from the larger and give the result the sign of the larger magnitude. For example, (+25) + (−37) = −(37 − 25) = −12 and is done by subtracting the smaller magnitude 25 from the larger magnitude 37 and using the sign of 37 for the sign of the result. This is a process that requires the comparison of the signs and the magnitudes and then performing either addition or subtraction. (The procedure for adding binary numbers in signed-magnitude representation is described in Sec. 10-2.) By contrast, the rule for adding numbers in the signed-2's complement system does not require a comparison or subtraction, only addition and complementation. The procedure is very simple and can be stated as follows: Add the two numbers, including their sign bits, and discard any carry out of the sign (leftmost) bit position. Numerical examples for addition are shown below. Note that negative numbers must initially be in 2's complement and that if the sum obtained after the addition is negative, it is in 2's complement form.

2's complement addition

+6	00000110		−6	11111010
+13	00001101		+13	00001101
+19	00010011		+7	00000111

+6	00000110		−6	11111010
−13	11110011		−13	11110011
−7	11111001		−19	11101101

In each of the four cases, the operation performed is always addition, including the sign bits. Any carry out of the sign bit position is discarded, and negative results are automatically in 2's complement form.

The complement form of representing negative numbers is unfamiliar to people used to the signed-magnitude system. To determine the value of a negative number when in signed-2's complement, it is necessary to convert it to a positive number to place it in a more familiar form. For example, the signed binary number 11111001 is negative because the leftmost bit is 1. Its 2's complement is 00000111, which is the binary equivalent of +7. We therefore recognize the original negative number to be equal to −7.

Arithmetic Subtraction

Subtraction of two signed binary numbers when negative numbers are in 2's complement form is very simple and can be stated as follows: Take the 2's complement of the subtrahend (including the sign bit) and add it to the minuend (including the sign bit). A carry out of the sign bit position is discarded.

This procedure stems from the fact that a subtraction operation can be changed to an addition operation if the sign of the subtrahend is changed. This is demonstrated by the following relationship:

$$(\pm A) - (+B) = (\pm A) + (-B)$$

$$(\pm A) - (-B) = (\pm A) + (+B)$$

But changing a positive number to a negative number is easily done by taking its 2's complement. The reverse is also true because the complement of a negative number in complement form produces the equivalent positive number. Consider the subtraction of $(-6) - (-13) = +7$. In binary with eight bits this is written as $11111010 - 11110011$. The subtraction is changed to addition by taking the 2's complement of the subtrahend (-13) to give $(+13)$. In binary this is $11111010 + 00001101 = 100000111$. Removing the end carry, we obtain the correct answer 00000111 $(+7)$.

It is worth noting that binary numbers in the signed-2's complement system are added and subtracted by the same basic addition and subtraction rules as unsigned numbers. Therefore, computers need only one common hardware circuit to handle both types of arithmetic. The user or programmer must interpret the results of such addition or subtraction differently depending on whether it is assumed that the numbers are signed or unsigned.

Overflow

When two numbers of n digits each are added and the sum occupies $n + 1$ digits, we say that an overflow occurred. When the addition is performed with paper and pencil, an overflow is not a problem since there is no limit to the width of the page to write down the sum. An overflow is a problem in digital computers because the width of registers is finite. A result that contains $n + 1$ bits cannot be accommodated in a register with a standard length of n bits. For this reason, many computers detect the occurrence of an overflow, and when it occurs, a corresponding flip-flop is set which can then be checked by the user.

The detection of an overflow after the addition of two binary numbers depends on whether the numbers are considered to be signed or unsigned. When two unsigned numbers are added, an overflow is detected from the end carry out of the most significant position. In the case of signed numbers, the leftmost bit always represents the sign, and negative numbers are in 2's complement form. When two signed numbers are added, the sign bit is treated as part of the number and the end carry does not indicate an overflow.

An overflow cannot occur after an addition if one number is positive and the other is negative, since adding a positive number to a negative number produces a result that is smaller than the larger of the two original numbers. An overflow may occur if the two numbers added are both positive or both negative. To see how this can happen, consider the following example. Two signed binary numbers, +70 and +80, are stored in two 8-bit registers. The range of numbers that each register can accommodate is from binary +127 to binary −128. Since the sum of the two numbers is +150, it exceeds the capacity of the 8-bit register. This is true if the numbers are both positive or both negative. The two additions in binary are shown below together with the last two carries.

```
        carries: 0 1                 carries: 1 0
          +70   0 1000110              −70   1 0111010
          +80   0 1010000              −80   1 0110000
         +150   1 0010110             −150   0 1101010
```

Note that the 8-bit result that should have been positive has a negative sign bit and the 8-bit result that should have been negative has a positive sign bit. If, however, the carry out of the sign bit position is taken as the sign bit of the result, the 9-bit answer so obtained will be correct. Since the answer cannot be accommodated within 8 bits, we say that an overflow occurred.

overflow detection   An overflow condition can be detected by observing the carry into the sign bit position and the carry out of the sign bit position. If these two carries are not equal, an overflow condition is produced. This is indicated in the examples where the two carries are explicitly shown. If the two carries are applied to an exclusive-OR gate, an overflow will be detected when the output of the gate is equal to 1.

Decimal Fixed-Point Representation

The representation of decimal numbers in registers is a function of the binary code used to represent a decimal digit. A 4-bit decimal code requires four flip-flops for each decimal digit. The representation of 4385 in BCD requires 16 flip-flops, four flip-flops for each digit. The number will be represented in a register with 16 flip-flops as follows:

$$0100 \quad 0011 \quad 1000 \quad 0101$$

By representing numbers in decimal we are wasting a considerable amount of storage space since the number of bits needed to store a decimal number in a binary code is greater than the number of bits needed for its equivalent binary representation. Also, the circuits required to perform decimal arithmetic are more complex. However, there are some advantages in the use of decimal representation because computer input and output data are generated by people who use the decimal system. Some applications, such as business data processing, require small amounts of arithmetic computations compared to the amount required for input and output of decimal data. For this reason, some computers and all electronic calculators perform arithmetic operations directly with the decimal data (in a binary code) and thus eliminate the need for conversion to binary and back to decimal. Some computer systems have hardware for arithmetic calculations with both binary and decimal data.

The representation of signed decimal numbers in BCD is similar to the representation of signed numbers in binary. We can either use the familiar signed-magnitude system or the signed-complement system. The sign of a decimal number is usually represented with four bits to conform with the 4-bit code of the decimal digits. It is customary to designate a plus with four 0's and a minus with the BCD equivalent of 9, which is 1001.

The signed-magnitude system is difficult to use with computers. The signed-complement system can be either the 9's or the 10's complement, but the 10's complement is the one most often used. To obtain the 10's complement of a BCD number, we first take the 9's complement and then add one to the least significant digit. The 9's complement is calculated from the subtraction of each digit from 9.

The procedures developed for the signed-2's complement system apply also to the signed-10's complement system for decimal numbers. Addition is done by adding all digits, including the sign digit, and discarding the end carry. Obviously, this assumes that all negative numbers are in 10's complement form. Consider the addition $(+375) + (-240) = +135$ done in the signed-10's complement system.

$$
\begin{array}{ll}
0\ 375 & (0000\ 0011\ 0111\ 0101)_{BCD} \\
+9\ 760 & (1001\ 0111\ 0110\ 0000)_{BCD} \\
\hline
0\ 135 & (0000\ 0001\ 0011\ 0101)_{BCD}
\end{array}
$$

The 9 in the leftmost position of the second number indicates that the number is negative. 9760 is the 10's complement of 0240. The two numbers are added and the end carry is discarded to obtain +135. Of course, the decimal numbers inside the computer must be in BCD, including the sign digits. The addition is done with BCD adders (see Fig. 10-18).

The subtraction of decimal numbers either unsigned or in the signed-10's complement system is the same as in the binary case. Take the 10's complement of the subtrahend and add it to the minuend. Many computers have special hardware to perform arithmetic calculations directly with decimal numbers in BCD. The user of the computer can specify by programmed instructions that the arithmetic operations be performed with decimal numbers directly without having to convert them to binary.

3-4 Floating-Point Representation

mantissa

exponent

The floating-point representation of a number has two parts. The first part represents a signed, fixed-point number called the mantissa. The second part designates the position of the decimal (or binary) point and is called the exponent. The fixed-point mantissa may be a fraction or an integer. For example, the decimal number +6132.789 is represented in floating-point with a fraction and an exponent as follows:

Fraction	Exponent
+0.6132789	+04

The value of the exponent indicates that the actual position of the decimal point is four positions to the right of the indicated decimal point in the fraction. This representation is equivalent to the scientific notation $+0.6132789 \times 10^{+4}$.

Floating-point is always interpreted to represent a number in the following form:

$$m \times r^e$$

Only the mantissa m and the exponent e are physically represented in the register (including their signs). The radix r and the radix-point position of the mantissa are always assumed. The circuits that manipulate the floating-point numbers in registers conform with these two assumptions in order to provide the correct computational results.

A floating-point binary number is represented in a similar manner except that it uses base 2 for the exponent. For example, the binary number +1001.11 is represented with an 8 bit fraction and 6-bit exponent as follows:

Fraction	Exponent
01001110	000100

fraction

The fraction has a 0 in the leftmost position to denote positive. The binary point of the fraction follows the sign bit but is not shown in the register. The exponent has the equivalent binary number +4. The floating-point number is equivalent to

$$m \times 2^e = +(.1001110)_2 \times 2^{+4}$$

normalization

A floating-point number is said to be *normalized* if the most significant digit of the mantissa is nonzero. For example, the decimal number 350 is normalized but 00035 is not. Regardless of where the position of the radix point is assumed to be in the mantissa, the number is normalized only if its leftmost digit is nonzero. For example, the 8-bit binary number 00011010 is not normalized because of the three leading 0's. The number can be normalized by shifting it three positions to the left and discarding the leading 0's to obtain 11010000. The three shifts multiply the number by $2^3 = 8$. To keep the same value for the floating-point number, the exponent must be subtracted by 3. Normalized numbers provide the maximum possible precision for the floating-point number. A zero cannot be normalized because it does not have a nonzero digit. It is usually represented in floating-point by all 0's in the mantissa and exponent.

Arithmetic operations with floating-point numbers are more complicated than arithmetic operations with fixed-point numbers and their execution takes longer and requires more complex hardware. However, floating-point representation is a must for scientific computations because of the scaling problems involved with fixed-point computations. Many computers and all electronic calculators have the built-in capability of performing floating-point arithmetic operations. Computers that do not have hardware for floating-point computations have a set of subroutines to help the user program scientific problems with floating-point numbers. Arithmetic operations with floating-point numbers are discussed in Sec. 10-5.

3-5 Other Binary Codes

In previous sections we introduced the most common types of binary-coded data found in digital computers. Other binary codes for decimal numbers and alphanumeric characters are sometimes used. Digital computers also employ other binary codes for special applications. A few additional binary codes encountered in digital computers are presented in this section.

Gray Code

Gray code

Digital systems can process data in discrete form only. Many physical systems supply continuous output data. The data must be converted into digital form before they can be used by a digital computer. Continuous, or analog, information is converted into digital form by means of an analog-to-digital converter. The reflected binary or *Gray code*, shown in Table 3-5, is sometimes used for the converted digital data. The advantage of the Gray code over straight binary numbers is that the Gray code changes by only one bit as it sequences from one number to the next. In other words, the change from any number to the next in sequence is recognized by a change of only one bit from 0 to 1 or from 1 to 0. A typical application of the Gray code occurs when the analog data are represented by the continuous change of a shaft position. The shaft is partitioned into segments with each segment assigned a number. If adjacent segments are made to correspond to adjacent Gray code numbers, ambiguity is reduced when the shaft position is in the line that separates any two segments.

Gray code counters are sometimes used to provide the timing sequences

TABLE 3-5 4-Bit Gray Code

Binary code	Decimal equivalent	Binary code	Decimal equivalent
0000	0	1100	8
0001	1	1101	9
0011	2	1111	10
0010	3	1110	11
0110	4	1010	12
0111	5	1011	13
0101	6	1001	14
0100	7	1000	15

that control the operations in a digital system. A Gray code counter is a counter whose flip-flops go through a sequence of states as specified in Table 3-5. Gray code counters remove the ambiguity during the change from one state of the counter to the next because only one bit can change during the state transition.

Other Decimal Codes

Binary codes for decimal digits require a minimum of four bits. Numerous different codes can be formulated by arranging four or more bits in 10 distinct possible combinations. A few possibilities are shown in Table 3-6.

TABLE 3-6 Four Different Binary Codes for the Decimal Digit

Decimal digit	BCD 8421	2421	Excess-3	Excess-3 gray
0	0000	0000	0011	0010
1	0001	0001	0100	0110
2	0010	0010	0101	0111
3	0011	0011	0110	0101
4	0100	0100	0111	0100
5	0101	1011	1000	1100
6	0110	1100	1001	1101
7	0111	1101	1010	1111
8	1000	1110	1011	1110
9	1001	1111	1100	1010
	1010	0101	0000	0000
Unused	1011	0110	0001	0001
bit	1100	0111	0010	0011
combi-	1101	1000	1101	1000
nations	1110	1001	1110	1001
	1111	1010	1111	1011

The BCD (binary-coded decimal) has been introduced before. It uses a straight assignment of the binary equivalent of the digit. The six unused bit combinations listed have no meaning when BCD is used, just as the letter H has no meaning when decimal digit symbols are written down. For example, saying that 1001 1110 is a decimal number in BCD is like saying that 9H is a decimal number in the conventional symbol designation. Both cases contain an invalid symbol and therefore designate a meaningless number.

One disadvantage of using BCD is the difficulty encountered when the 9's complement of the number is to be computed. On the other hand, the 9's complement is easily obtained with the 2421 and the excess-3 codes listed in Table 3-6. These two codes have a self-complementing property which means that the 9's complement of a decimal number, when represented in one of these codes, is easily obtained by changing 1's to 0's and 0's to 1's. This property is useful when arithmetic operations are done in signed-complement representation.

self-complementing

weighted code

The 2421 is an example of a *weighted code*. In a weighted code, the bits are multiplied by the weights indicated and the sum of the weighted bits gives the decimal digit. For example, the bit combination 1101, when weighted by the respective digits 2421, gives the decimal equivalent of $2 \times 1 + 4 \times 1 + 2 \times 0 + 1 + 1 = 7$. The BCD code can be assigned the weights 8421 and for this reason it is sometimes called the 8421 code.

excess-3 code

The excess-3 code is a decimal code that has been used in older computers. This is an unweighted code. Its binary code assignment is obtained from the corresponding BCD equivalent binary number after the addition of binary 3 (0011).

From Table 3-5 we note that the Gray code is not suited for a decimal code if we were to choose the first 10 entries in the table. This is because the transition from 9 back to 0 involves a change of three bits (from 1101 to 0000). To overcome this difficulty, we choose the 10 numbers starting from the third entry 0010 up to the twelfth entry 1010. Now the transition from 1010 to 0010 involves a change of only one bit. Since the code has been shifted up three numbers, it is called the excess-3 Gray. This code is listed with the other decimal codes in Table 3-6.

Other Alphanumeric Codes

The ASCII code (Table 3-4) is the standard code commonly used for the transmission of binary information. Each character is represented by a 7-bit code and usually an eighth bit is inserted for parity (see Sec. 3-6). The code consists of 128 characters. Ninety-five characters represent *graphic symbols* that include upper- and lowercase letters, numerals zero to nine, punctuation marks, and special symbols. Twenty-three characters represent *format effectors*, which are functional characters for controlling the layout of printing or display devices such as carriage return, line feed, horizontal tabulation, and back space. The other 10 characters are used to direct the data communication flow and report its status.

EBCDIC

Another alphanumeric (sometimes called *alphameric*) code used in IBM equipment is the EBCDIC (Extended BCD Interchange Code). It uses eight bits for each character (and a ninth bit for parity). EBCDIC has the same character symbols as ASCII but the bit assignment to characters is different.

When alphanumeric characters are used internally in a computer for data processing (not for transmission purposes) it is more convenient to use a 6-bit code to represent 64 characters. A 6-bit code can specify the 26 uppercase letters of the alphabet, numerals zero to nine, and up to 28 special characters. This set of characters is usually sufficient for data-processing purposes. Using fewer bits to code characters has the advantage of reducing the memory space needed to store large quantities of alphanumeric data.

3-6 Error Detection Codes

Binary information transmitted through some form of communication medium is subject to external noise that could change bits from 1 to 0, and vice versa. An error detection code is a binary code that detects digital errors during transmission. The detected errors cannot be corrected but their presence is indicated. The usual procedure is to observe the frequency of errors. If errors occur infrequently at random, the particular erroneous information is transmitted again. If the error occurs too often, the system is checked for malfunction.

parity bit

The most common error detection code used is the *parity bit*. A parity bit is an extra bit included with a binary message to make the total number of 1's either odd or even. A message of three bits and two possible parity bits is shown in Table 3-7. The $P(\text{odd})$ bit is chosen in such a way as to make the sum of 1's (in all four bits) odd. The $P(\text{even})$ bit is chosen to make the sum of all 1's even. In either case, the sum is taken over the message and the P bit. In any particular application, one or the other type of parity will be adopted. The even-parity scheme has the disadvantage of having a bit combination of all 0's, while in the odd parity there is always one bit (of the four bits that constitute the message and P) that is 1. Note that the $P(\text{odd})$ is the complement of the $P(\text{even})$.

parity generator

During transfer of information from one location to another, the parity bit is handled as follows. At the sending end, the message (in this case three bits) is applied to a *parity generator*, where the required parity bit is generated. The message, including the parity bit, is transmitted to its destination. At the receiving end, all the incoming bits (in this case, four) are applied to a *parity checker* that checks the proper parity adopted (odd or even). An error is detected if the checked parity does not conform to the adopted parity. The parity method detects the presence of one, three, or any odd number of errors. An even number of errors is not detected.

parity checker

TABLE 3-7 Parity Bit Generation

Message xyz	P(odd)	P(even)
000	1	0
001	0	1
010	0	1
011	1	0
100	0	1
101	1	0
110	1	0
111	0	1

odd function

Parity generator and checker networks are logic circuits constructed with exclusive-OR functions. This is because, as mentioned in Sec. 1-2, the exclusive-OR function of three or more variables is by definition an odd function. An odd function is a logic function whose value is binary 1 if, and only if, an odd number of variables are equal to 1. According to this definition, the P(even) function is the exclusive-OR of x, y, and z because it is equal to 1 when either one or all three of the variables are equal to 1 (Table 3-7). The P(odd) function is the complement of the P(even) function.

As an example, consider a 3-bit message to be transmitted with an odd parity bit. At the sending end, the odd-parity bit is generated by a parity

Figure 3-3   Error detection with odd parity bit.

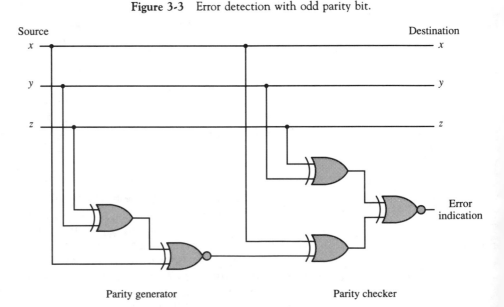

generator circuit. As shown in Fig. 3-3, this circuit consists of one exclusive-OR and one exclusive-NOR gate. Since $P(even)$ is the exclusive-OR of x, y, z, and $P(odd)$ is the complement of $P(even)$, it is necessary to employ an exclusive-NOR gate for the needed complementation. The message and the odd-parity bit are transmitted to their destination where they are applied to a parity checker. An error has occurred during transmission if the parity of the four bits received is even, since the binary information transmitted was originally odd. The output of the parity checker would be 1 when an error occurs, that is, when the number of 1's in the four inputs is even. Since the exclusive-OR function of the four inputs is an odd function, we again need to complement the output by using an exclusive-NOR gate.

It is worth noting that the parity generator can use the same circuit as the parity checker if the fourth input is permanently held at a logic-0 value. The advantage of this is that the same circuit can be used for both parity generation and parity checking.

It is evident from the example above that even-parity generators and checkers can be implemented with exclusive-OR functions. Odd-parity networks need an exclusive-NOR at the output to complement the function.

PROBLEMS

3-1. Convert the following binary numbers to decimal: 101110; 1110101; and 110110100.

3-2. Convert the following numbers with the indicated bases to decimal: $(12121)_3$; $(4310)_5$; $(50)_7$; and $(198)_{12}$.

3-3. Convert the following decimal numbers to binary: 1231; 673; and 1998.

3-4. Convert the following decimal numbers to the bases indicated.
   a. 7562 to octal
   b. 1938 to hexadecimal
   c. 175 to binary

3-5. Convert the hexadecimal number F3A7C2 to binary and octal.

3-6. What is the radix of the numbers if the solution to the quadratic equation $x^2 - 10x + 31 = 0$ is $x = 5$ and $x = 8$?

3-7. Show the value of all bits of a 12-bit register that hold the number equivalent to decimal 215 in (a) binary; (b) binary-coded octal; (c) binary-coded hexadecimal; (d) binary-coded decimal (BCD).

3-8. Show the bit configuration of a 24-bit register when its content represents the decimal equivalent of 295: (a) in binary; (b) in BCD; (c) in ASCII using eight bits with even parity.

3-9. Write your name in ASCII using an 8-bit code with the leftmost bit always 0. Include a space between names and a period after a middle initial.

3-10.   Decode the following ASCII code:

1001010 1001111 1001000 1001110 0100000 1000100 1001111 1000101

3-11.   Obtain the 9's complement of the following eight-digit decimal numbers: 12349876; 00980100; 90009951; and 00000000.

3-12.   Obtain the 10's complement of the following six-digit decimal numbers: 123900; 090657; 100000; and 000000.

3-13.   Obtain the 1's and 2's complements of the following eight-digit binary numbers: 10101110; 10000001; 10000000; 00000001; and 00000000.

3-14.   Perform the subtraction with the following unsigned decimal numbers by taking the 10's complement of the subtrahend.
a. 5250 − 1321   **b.** 1753 − 8640
c. 20 − 100   **d.** 1200 − 250

3-15.   Perform the subtraction with the following unsigned binary numbers by taking the 2's complement of the subtrahend.
a. 11010 − 10000   **b.** 11010 − 1101
c. 100 − 110000   **d.** 1010100 − 1010100

3-16.   Perform the arithmetic operations $(+42) + (-13)$ and $(-42) - (-13)$ in binary using signed-2's complement representation for negative numbers.

3-17.   Perform the arithmetic operations $(+70) + (+80)$ and $(-70) + (-80)$ with binary numbers in signed-2's complement representation. Use eight bits to accommodate each number together with its sign. Show that overflow occurs in both cases, that the last two carries are unequal, and that there is a sign reversal.

3-18.   Perform the following arithmetic operations with the decimal numbers using signed-10's complement representation for negative numbers.
a. $(-638) + (+785)$
b. $(-638) - (+185)$

3-19.   A 36-bit floating-point binary number has eight bits plus sign for the exponent and 26 bits plus sign for the mantissa. The mantissa is a normalized fraction. Numbers in the mantissa and exponent are in signed-magnitude representation. What are the largest and smallest positive quantities that can be represented, excluding zero?

3-20.   Represent the number $(+46.5)_{10}$ as a floating-point binary number with 24 bits. The normalized fraction mantissa has 16 bits and the exponent has 8 bits.

3-21.   The Gray code is sometimes called a reflected code because the bit values are reflected on both sides of any 2^n value. For example, as shown in Table 3-5, the values of the three low-order bits are reflected over a line drawn between 7 and 8. Using this property of the Gray code, obtain:
a. The Gray code numbers for 16 through 31 as a continuation of Table 3-5.
b. The excess-3 Gray code for decimals 10 to 19 as a continuation of the list in Table 3-6.

3-22.   Represent decimal number 8620 in (a) BCD; (b) excess-3 code; (c) 2421 code; (d) as a binary number.

3-23. List the 10 BCD digits with an even parity in the leftmost position (total of five bits per digit). Repeat with an odd-parity bit.

3-24. Represent decimal 3984 in the 2421 code of Table 3-6. Complement all bits of the coded number and show that the result is the 9's complement of 3984 in the 2421 code.

3-25. Show that the exclusive-OR function $x = A \oplus B \oplus C \oplus D$ is an odd function. One way to show this is to obtain the truth table for $y = A \oplus B$ and for $z = C \oplus D$ and then formulate the truth table for $x = y \oplus z$. Show that $x = 1$ only when the total number of 1's in A, B, C, and D is odd.

3-26. Derive the circuits for a 3-bit parity generator and 4-bit parity checker using an even-parity bit. (The circuits of Fig. 3-3 use odd parity.)

REFERENCES

1. Hill, F. J., and G. R. Peterson, *Introduction to Switching Theory and Logical Design*, 3rd ed. New York: John Wiley, 1981.

2. Langholz, G., J. Francioni, and A. Kandel, *Elements of Computer Organization*. Englewood Cliffs, NJ: Prentice Hall, 1989.

3. Lewin, M. H., *Logic Design and Computer Organization*. Reading, MA: Addison-Wesley, 1983.

4. Mano, M. M., *Digital Design*, 2nd ed. Englewood Cliffs, NJ: Prentice Hall, 1991.

5. Roth, C. H., *Fundamentals of Logic Design*, 3rd ed. St. Paul, MN: West Publishing, 1985.

6. Sandige, R. S., *Modern Digital Design*. New York: McGraw-Hill, 1990.

7. Shiva, S. G., *Introduction to Logic Design*. Glenview, Il: Scott, Foresman, 1988.

8. Tomek, I., *Introduction to Computer Organization*. Rockville, MD: Computer Science Press, 1981.

9. Wakerly, J. F., *Microcomputer Architecture and Programming*. New York: John Wiley, 1981.

10. Ward, S. A., and R. H. Halstead, Jr., *Computation Structures*. Cambridge, MA: MIT Press, 1990.

CHAPTER FOUR

Register Transfer and Microoperations

IN THIS CHAPTER

4-1 Register Transfer Language

A digital system is an interconnection of digital hardware modules that accomplish a specific information-processing task. Digital systems vary in size and complexity from a few integrated circuits to a complex of interconnected and interacting digital computers. Digital system design invariably uses a modular approach. The modules are constructed from such digital components as registers, decoders, arithmetic elements, and control logic. The various modules are interconnected with common data and control paths to form a digital computer system.

microoperation

Digital modules are best defined by the registers they contain and the operations that are performed on the data stored in them. The operations executed on data stored in registers are called microoperations. A microoperation is an elementary operation performed on the information stored in one or more registers. The result of the operation may replace the previous binary information of a register or may be transferred to another register. Examples of microoperations are shift, count, clear, and load. Some of the digital components introduced in Chap. 2 are registers that implement microoperations. For example, a counter with parallel load is capable of performing the microoperations increment and load. A bidirectional shift register is capable of performing the shift right and shift left microoperations.

The internal hardware organization of a digital computer is best defined by specifying:

1. The set of registers it contains and their function.
2. The sequence of microoperations performed on the binary information stored in the registers.
3. The control that initiates the sequence of microoperations.

It is possible to specify the sequence of microoperations in a computer by explaining every operation in words, but this procedure usually involves a lengthy descriptive explanation. It is more convenient to adopt a suitable symbology to describe the sequence of transfers between registers and the various arithmetic and logic microoperations associated with the transfers. The use of symbols instead of a narrative explanation provides an organized and concise manner for listing the microoperation sequences in registers and the control functions that initiate them.

register transfer language

The symbolic notation used to describe the microoperation transfers among registers is called a register transfer language. The term "register transfer" implies the availability of hardware logic circuits that can perform a stated microoperation and transfer the result of the operation to the same or another register. The word "language" is borrowed from programmers, who apply this term to programming languages. A programming language is a procedure for writing symbols to specify a given computational process. Similarly, a natural language such as English is a system for writing symbols and combining them into words and sentences for the purpose of communication between people. A register transfer language is a system for expressing in symbolic form the microoperation sequences among the registers of a digital module. It is a convenient tool for describing the internal organization of digital computers in concise and precise manner. It can also be used to facilitate the design process of digital systems.

The register transfer language adopted here is believed to be as simple as possible, so it should not take very long to memorize. We will proceed to define symbols for various types of microoperations, and at the same time, describe associated hardware that can implement the stated microoperations. The symbolic designation introduced in this chapter will be utilized in subsequent chapters to specify the register transfers, the microoperations, and the control functions that describe the internal hardware organization of digital computers. Other symbology in use can easily be learned once this language has become familiar, for most of the differences between register transfer languages consist of variations in detail rather than in overall purpose.

4-2   Register Transfer

registers
Computer registers are designated by capital letters (sometimes followed by numerals) to denote the function of the register. For example, the register that holds an address for the memory unit is usually called a memory address register and is designated by the name *MAR*. Other designations for registers are *PC* (for program counter), *IR* (for instruction register, and *R1* (for processor register). The individual flip-flops in an n-bit register are numbered in sequence from 0 through $n - 1$, starting from 0 in the rightmost position and increasing the numbers toward the left. Figure 4-1 shows the representation of registers in block diagram form. The most common way to represent a register is by a rectangular box with the name of the register inside, as in Fig. 4-1(a). The individual bits can be distinguished as in (b). The numbering of bits in a 16-bit register can be marked on top of the box as shown in (c). A 16-bit register is partitioned into two parts in (d). Bits 0 through 7 are assigned the symbol L (for low byte) and bits 8 through 15 are assigned the symbol H (for high byte). The name of the 16-bit register is *PC*. The symbol $PC(0-7)$ or $PC(L)$ refers to the low-order byte and $PC(8-15)$ or $PC(H)$ to the high-order byte.

register transfer
Information transfer from one register to another is designated in symbolic form by means of a replacement operator. The statement

$$R2 \leftarrow R1$$

denotes a transfer of the content of register $R1$ into register $R2$. It designates a replacement of the content of $R2$ by the content of $R1$. By definition, the content of the source register $R1$ does not change after the transfer.

A statement that specifies a register transfer implies that circuits are available from the outputs of the source register to the inputs of the destination register and that the destination register has a parallel load capability. Nor-

Figure 4-1   Block diagram of register.

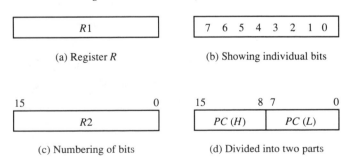

$R1$	7 6 5 4 3 2 1 0
(a) Register R	(b) Showing individual bits

15 0	15 8 7 0
$R2$	$PC\ (H)$ | $PC\ (L)$
(c) Numbering of bits	(d) Divided into two parts

mally, we want the transfer to occur only under a predetermined control condition. This can be shown by means of an *if-then* statement.

$$\text{If } (P = 1) \text{ then } (R2 \leftarrow R1)$$

control function

where P is a control signal generated in the control section. It is sometimes convenient to separate the control variables from the register transfer operation by specifying a *control function*. A control function is a Boolean variable that is equal to 1 or 0. The control function is included in the statement as follows:

$$P: \quad R2 \leftarrow R1$$

The control condition is terminated with a colon. It symbolizes the requirement that the transfer operation be executed by the hardware only if $P = 1$.

Every statement written in a register transfer notation implies a hardware construction for implementing the transfer. Figure 4-2 shows the block diagram that depicts the transfer from $R1$ to $R2$. The n outputs of register $R1$ are connected to the n inputs of register $R2$. The letter n will be used to indicate any number of bits for the register. It will be replaced by an actual number when the length of the register is known. Register $R2$ has a load input that is activated by the control variable P. It is assumed that the control variable is synchronized with the same clock as the one applied to the register. As shown

Figure 4-2 Transfer from $R1$ to $R2$ when $P = 1$.

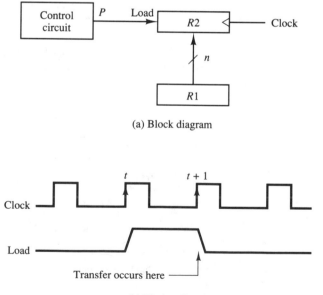

(a) Block diagram

(b) Timing diagram

in the timing diagram, P is activated in the control section by the rising edge of a clock pulse at time t. The next positive transition of the clock at time $t + 1$ finds the load input active and the data inputs of $R2$ are then loaded into the register in parallel. P may go back to 0 at time $t + 1$; otherwise, the transfer will occur with every clock pulse transition while P remains active.

Note that the clock is not included as a variable in the register transfer statements. It is assumed that all transfers occur during a clock edge transition. Even though the control condition such as P becomes active just after time t, the actual transfer does not occur until the register is triggered by the next positive transition of the clock at time $t + 1$.

The basic symbols of the register transfer notation are listed in Table 4-1. Registers are denoted by capital letters, and numerals may follow the letters. Parentheses are used to denote a part of a register by specifying the range of bits or by giving a symbol name to a portion of a register. The arrow denotes a transfer of information and the direction of transfer. A comma is used to separate two or more operations that are executed at the same time. The statement

$$T: \quad R2 \leftarrow R1, \quad R1 \leftarrow R2$$

denotes an operation that exchanges the contents of two registers during one common clock pulse provided that $T = 1$. This simultaneous operation is possible with registers that have edge-triggered flip-flops.

TABLE 4-1 Basic Symbols for Register Transfers

Symbol	Description	Examples
Letters (and numerals)	Denotes a register	MAR, $R2$
Parentheses ( )	Denotes a part of a register	$R2(0–7)$, $R2(L)$
Arrow ←	Denotes transfer of information	$R2 \leftarrow R1$
Comma ,	Separates two microoperations	$R2 \leftarrow R1, R1 \leftarrow R2$

4-3 Bus and Memory Transfers

common bus

A typical digital computer has many registers, and paths must be provided to transfer information from one register to another. The number of wires will be excessive if separate lines are used between each register and all other registers in the system. A more efficient scheme for transferring information between registers in a multiple-register configuration is a common bus system. A bus structure consists of a set of common lines, one for each bit of a register, through which binary information is transferred one at a time. Control signals determine which register is selected by the bus during each particular register transfer.

One way of constructing a common bus system is with multiplexers. The multiplexers select the source register whose binary information is then placed on the bus. The construction of a bus system for four registers is shown in Fig. 4-3. Each register has four bits, numbered 0 through 3. The bus consists of four 4×1 multiplexers each having four data inputs, 0 through 3, and two selection inputs, S_1 and S_0. In order not to complicate the diagram with 16 lines crossing each other, we use labels to show the connections from the outputs of the registers to the inputs of the multiplexers. For example, output 1 of register A is connected to input 0 of MUX 1 because this input is labeled A_1. The diagram shows that the bits in the same significant position in each register are connected to the data inputs of one multiplexer to form one line of the bus. Thus MUX 0 multiplexes the four 0 bits of the registers, MUX 1 multiplexes the four 1 bits of the registers, and similarly for the other two bits.

Figure 4-3   Bus system for four registers.

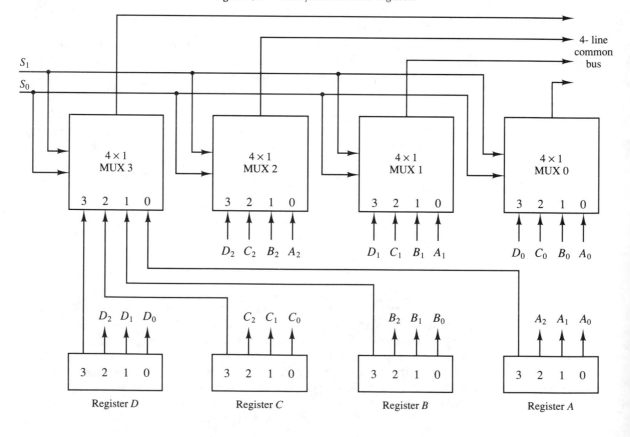

bus selection

The two selection lines S_1 and S_0 are connected to the selection inputs of all four multiplexers. The selection lines choose the four bits of one register and transfer them into the four-line common bus. When $S_1S_0 = 00$, the 0 data inputs of all four multiplexers are selected and applied to the outputs that form the bus. This causes the bus lines to receive the content of register A since the outputs of this register are connected to the 0 data inputs of the multiplexers. Similarly, register B is selected if $S_1S_0 = 01$, and so on. Table 4-2 shows the register that is selected by the bus for each of the four possible binary value of the selection lines.

TABLE 4-2 Function Table for Bus of Fig. 4-3

S_1	S_0	Register selected
0	0	A
0	1	B
1	0	C
1	1	D

In general, a bus system will multiplex k registers of n bits each to produce an n-line common bus. The number of multiplexers needed to construct the bus is equal to n, the number of bits in each register. The size of each multiplexer must be $k \times 1$ since it multiplexes k data lines. For example, a common bus for eight registers of 16 bits each requires 16 multiplexers, one for each line in the bus. Each multiplexer must have eight data input lines and three selection lines to multiplex one significant bit in the eight registers.

The transfer of information from a bus into one of many destination registers can be accomplished by connecting the bus lines to the inputs of all destination registers and activating the load control of the particular destination register selected. The symbolic statement for a bus transfer may mention the bus or its presence may be implied in the statement. When the bus is includes in the statement, the register transfer is symbolized as follows:

$$BUS \leftarrow C, \quad R1 \leftarrow BUS$$

The content of register C is placed on the bus, and the content of the bus is loaded into register $R1$ by activating its load control input. If the bus is known to exist in the system, it may be convenient just to show the direct transfer.

$$R1 \leftarrow C$$

From this statement the designer knows which control signals must be activated to produce the transfer through the bus.

Three-State Bus Buffers

three-state gate

A bus system can be constructed with three-state gates instead of multiplexers. A three-state gate is a digital circuit that exhibits three states. Two of the states are signals equivalent to logic 1 and 0 as in a conventional gate. The third state

high-impedance

is a *high-impedance state*. The high-impedance state behaves like an open circuit, which means that the output is disconnected and does not have a logic signif-

buffer

icance. Three-state gates may perform any conventional logic, such as AND or NAND. However, the one most commonly used in the design of a bus system is the buffer gate.

The graphic symbol of a three-state buffer gate is shown in Fig. 4-4. It is distinguished from a normal buffer by having both a normal input and a control input. The control input determines the output state. When the control input is equal to 1, the output is enabled and the gate behaves like any conventional buffer, with the output equal to the normal input. When the control input is 0, the output is disabled and the gate goes to a high-impedance state, regardless of the value in the normal input. The high-impedance state of a three-state gate provides a special feature not available in other gates. Because of this feature, a large number of three-state gate outputs can be connected with wires to form a common bus line without endangering loading effects.

bus system

The construction of a bus system with three-state buffers is demonstrated in Fig. 4-5. The outputs of four buffers are connected together to form a single bus line. (It must be realized that this type of connection cannot be done with gates that do not have three-state outputs.) The control inputs to the buffers determine which of the four normal inputs will communicate with the bus line. No more than one buffer may be in the active state at any given time. The connected buffers must be controlled so that only one three-state buffer has access to the bus line while all other buffers are maintained in a high-impedance state.

One way to ensure that no more than one control input is active at any given time is to use a decoder, as shown in the diagram. When the enable input of the decoder is 0, all of its four outputs are 0, and the bus line is in a high-impedance state because all four buffers are disabled. When the enable input is active, one of the three-state buffers will be active, depending on the binary value in the select inputs of the decoder. Careful investigation will reveal that Fig. 4-5 is another way of constructing a 4×1 multiplexer since the circuit can replace the multiplexer in Fig. 4-3.

To construct a common bus for four registers of n bits each using three-

Figure 4-4 Graphic symbols for three-state buffer.

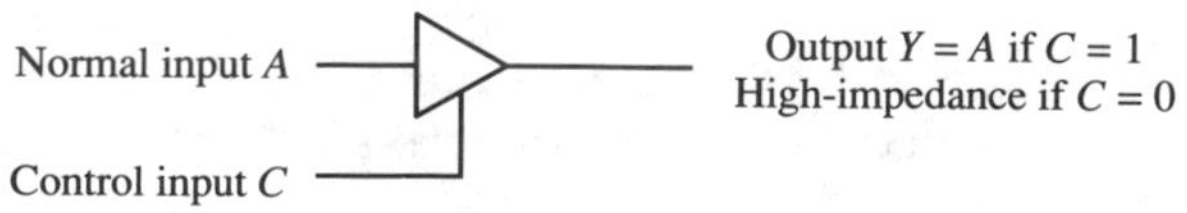

Normal input A ————▷———— Output $Y = A$ if $C = 1$
                                High-impedance if $C = 0$

Control input C ————

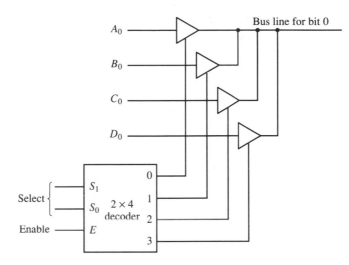

Figure 4-5 Bus line with three state-buffers.

state buffers, we need n circuits with four buffers in each as shown in Fig. 4-5. Each group of four buffers receives one significant bit from the four registers. Each common output produces one of the lines for the common bus for a total of n lines. Only one decoder is necessary to select between the four registers.

Memory Transfer

The operation of a memory unit was described in Sec. 2-7. The transfer of information from a memory word to the outside environment is called a *read* operation. The transfer of new information to be stored into the memory is called a *write* operation. A memory word will be symbolized by the letter M. The particular memory word among the many available is selected by the memory address during the transfer. It is necessary to specify the address of M when writing memory transfer operations. This will be done by enclosing the address in square brackets following the letter M.

Consider a memory unit that receives the address from a register, called the address register, symbolized by AR. The data are transferred to another *memory read* register, called the data register, symbolized by DR. The read operation can be stated as follows:

$$\text{Read:} \quad DR \leftarrow M[AR]$$

This causes a transfer of information into DR from the memory word M selected by the address in AR.

memory write   The write operation transfers the content of a data register to a memory word M selected by the address. Assume that the input data are in register $R1$

and the address is in AR. The write operation can be stated symbolically as follows:

$$\text{Write:} \quad M[AR] \leftarrow R1$$

This causes a transfer of information from $R1$ into the memory word M selected by the address in AR.

4-4   Arithmetic Microoperations

A microoperation is an elementary operation performed with the data stored in registers. The microoperations most often encountered in digital computers are classified into four categories:

1. Register transfer microoperations transfer binary information from one register to another.
2. Arithmetic microoperations perform arithmetic operations on numeric data stored in registers.
3. Logic microoperations perform bit manipulation operations on non-numeric data stored in registers.
4. Shift microoperations perform shift operations on data stored in registers.

The register transfer microoperation was introduced in Sec. 4-2. This type of microoperation does not change the information content when the binary information moves from the source register to the destination register. The other three types of microoperations change the information content during the transfer. In this section we introduce a set of arithmetic microoperations. In the next two sections we present the logic and shift microoperations.

The basic arithmetic microoperations are addition, subtraction, increment, decrement, and shift. Arithmetic shifts are explained later in conjunction with the shift microoperations. The arithmetic microoperation defined by the statement

$$R3 \leftarrow R1 + R2$$

add microoperation

specifies an *add* microoperation. It states that the contents of register $R1$ are added to the contents of register $R2$ and the sum transferred to register $R3$. To implement this statement with hardware we need three registers and the digital component that performs the addition operation. The other basic arithmetic microoperations are listed in Table 4-3. Subtraction is most often implemented through complementation and addition. Instead of using the minus operator, we can specify the subtraction by the following statement:

subtract microoperation

$$R3 \leftarrow R1 + \overline{R2} + 1$$

$\overline{R2}$ is the symbol for the 1's complement of $R2$. Adding 1 to the 1's complement produces the 2's complement. Adding the contents of $R1$ to the 2's complement of $R2$ is equivalent to $R1 - R2$.

TABLE 4-3 Arithmetic Microoperations

Symbolic designation	Description
$R3 \leftarrow R1 + R2$	Contents of $R1$ plus $R2$ transferred to $R3$
$R3 \leftarrow R1 - R2$	Contents of $R1$ minus $R2$ transferred to $R3$
$R2 \leftarrow \overline{R2}$	Complement the contents of $R2$ (1's complement)
$R2 \leftarrow \overline{R2} + 1$	2's complement the contents of $R2$ (negate)
$R3 \leftarrow R1 + \overline{R2} + 1$	$R1$ plus the 2's complement of $R2$ (subtraction)
$R1 \leftarrow R1 + 1$	Increment the contents of $R1$ by one
$R1 \leftarrow R1 - 1$	Decrement the contents of $R1$ by one

The increment and decrement microoperations are symbolized by plus-one and minus-one operations, respectively. These microoperations are implemented with a combinational circuit or with a binary up-down counter.

The arithmetic operations of multiply and divide are not listed in Table 4-3. These two operations are valid arithmetic operations but are not included in the basic set of microoperations. The only place where these operations can be considered as microoperations is in a digital system, where they are implemented by means of a combinational circuit. In such a case, the signals that perform these operations propagate through gates, and the result of the operation can be transferred into a destination register by a clock pulse as soon as the output signal propagates through the combinational circuit. In most computers, the multiplication operation is implemented with a sequence of add and shift microoperations. Division is implemented with a sequence of subtract and shift microoperations. To specify the hardware in such a case requires a list of statements that use the basic microoperations of add, subtract, and shift (see Chapter 10).

Binary Adder

To implement the add microoperation with hardware, we need the registers that hold the data and the digital component that performs the arithmetic addition. The digital circuit that forms the arithmetic sum of two bits and a previous carry is called a full-adder (see Fig. 1-17). The digital circuit that generates the arithmetic sum of two binary numbers of any length is called a *binary adder*. The binary adder is constructed with full-adder circuits con-

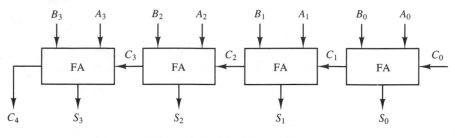

Figure 4-6 4-bit binary adder.

full-adder

nected in cascade, with the output carry from one full-adder connected to the input carry of the next full-adder. Figure 4-6 shows the interconnections of four full-adders (FA) to provide a 4-bit binary adder. The augend bits of A and the addend bits of B are designated by subscript numbers from right to left, with subscript 0 denoting the low-order bit. The carries are connected in a chain through the full-adders. The input carry to the binary adder is C_0 and the output carry is C_4. The S outputs of the full-adders generate the required sum bits.

An n-bit binary adder requires n full-adders. The output carry from each full-adder is connected to the input carry of the next-high-order full-adder. The n data bits for the A inputs come from one register (such as $R1$), and the n data bits for the B inputs come from another register (such as $R2$). The sum can be transferred to a third register or to one of the source registers ($R1$ or $R2$), replacing its previous content.

Binary Adder-Subtractor

The subtraction of binary numbers can be done most conveniently by means of complements as discussed in Sec. 3-2. Remember that the subtraction $A - B$ can be done by taking the 2's complement of B and adding it to A. The 2's complement can be obtained by taking the 1's complement and adding one to the least significant pair of bits. The 1's complement can be implemented with inverters and a one can be added to the sum through the input carry.

The addition and subtraction operations can be combined into one common circuit by including an exclusive-OR gate with each full-adder. A 4-bit *adder-subtractor* circuit is shown in Fig. 4-7. The mode input M controls the operation. When $M = 0$ the circuit is an adder and when $M = 1$ the circuit becomes a subtractor. Each exclusive-OR gate receives input M and one of the inputs of B. When $M = 0$, we have $B \oplus 0 = B$. The full-adders receive the value of B, the input carry is 0, and the circuit performs A plus B. When $M = 1$, we have $B \oplus 1 = B'$ and $C_0 = 1$. The B inputs are all complemented and a 1 is added through the input carry. The circuit performs the operation A plus the

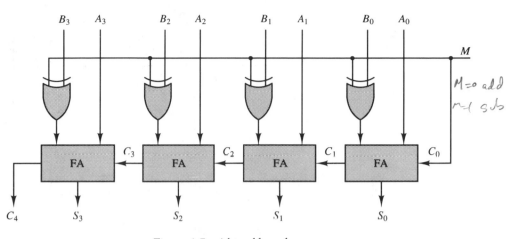

M=o add
r-1 sub

Figure 4-7   4-bit adder-subtractor.

2's complement of B. For unsigned numbers, this gives $A - B$ if $A \geq B$ or the 2's complement of $(B - A)$ if $A < B$. For signed numbers, the result is $A - B$ provided that there is no overflow.

Binary Incrementer

The increment microoperation adds one to a number in a register. For example, if a 4-bit register has a binary value 0110, it will go to 0111 after it is incremented. This microoperation is easily implemented with a binary counter (see Fig. 2-10). Every time the count enable is active, the clock pulse transition increments the content of the register by one. There may be occasions when the increment microoperation must be done with a combinational circuit independent of a particular register. This can be accomplished by means of half-adders (see Fig. 1-16) connected in cascade.

incrementer

The diagram of a 4-bit combinational circuit incrementer is shown in Fig. 4-8. One of the inputs to the least significant half-adder (HA) is connected to logic-1 and the other input is connected to the least significant bit of the number to be incremented. The output carry from one half-adder is connected to one of the inputs of the next-higher-order half-adder. The circuit receives the four bits from A_0 through A_3, adds one to it, and generates the incremented output in S_0 through S_3. The output carry C_4 will be 1 only after incrementing binary 1111. This also causes outputs S_0 through S_3 to go to 0.

The circuit of Fig. 4-8 can be extended to an n-bit binary incrementer by extending the diagram to include n half-adders. The least significant bit must have one input connected to logic-1. The other inputs receive the number to be incremented or the carry from the previous stage.

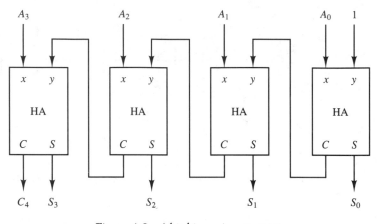

Figure 4-8 4-bit binary incrementer.

Arithmetic Circuit

arithmetic circuit

The arithmetic microoperations listed in Table 4-3 can be implemented in one composite arithmetic circuit. The basic component of an arithmetic circuit is the parallel adder. By controlling the data inputs to the adder, it is possible to obtain different types of arithmetic operations.

The diagram of a 4-bit arithmetic circuit is shown in Fig. 4-9. It has four full-adder circuits that constitute the 4-bit adder and four multiplexers for choosing different operations. There are two 4-bit inputs A and B and a 4-bit output D. The four inputs from A go directly to the X inputs of the binary adder. Each of the four inputs from B are connected to the data inputs of the multiplexers. The multiplexers data inputs also receive the complement of B. The other two data inputs are connected to logic-0 and logic-1. Logic-0 is a fixed voltage value (0 volts for TTL integrated circuits) and the logic-1 signal can be generated through an inverter whose input is 0. The four multiplexers are

input carry

controlled by two selection inputs, S_1 and S_0. The input carry C_{in} goes to the carry input of the FA in the least significant position. The other carries are connected from one stage to the next.

The output of the binary adder is calculated from the following arithmetic sum:

$$D = A + Y + C_{in}$$

where A is the 4-bit binary number at the X inputs and Y is the 4-bit binary number at the Y inputs of the binary adder. C_{in} is the input carry, which can be equal to 0 or 1. Note that the symbol + in the equation above denotes an arithmetic plus. By controlling the value of Y with the two selection inputs S_1 and S_0 and making C_{in} equal to 0 or 1, it is possible to generate the eight arithmetic microoperations listed in Table 4-4.

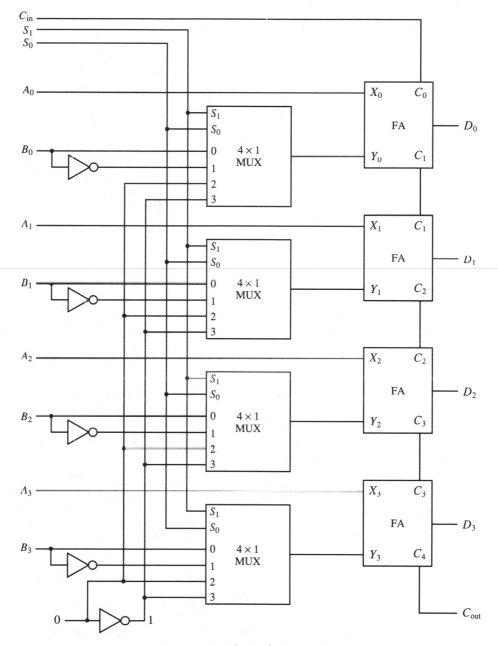

Figure 4-9   4-bit arithmetic circuit.

TABLE 4-4 Arithmetic Circuit Function Table

Select			Input	Output	
S_1	S_0	C_{in}	Y	$D = A + Y + C_{in}$	Microoperation
0	0	0	B	$D = A + B$	Add
0	0	1	B	$D = A + B + 1$	Add with carry
0	1	0	$\bar{B}$	$D = A + \bar{B}$	Subtract with borrow
0	1	1	$\bar{B}$	$D = A + \bar{B} + 1$	Subtract
1	0	0	0	$D = A$	Transfer A
1	0	1	0	$D = A + 1$	Increment A
1	1	0	1	$D = A - 1$	Decrement A
1	1	1	1	$D = A$	Transfer A

addition

When $S_1 S_0 = 00$, the value of B is applied to the Y inputs of the adder. If $C_{in} = 0$, the output $D = A + B$. If $C_{in} = 1$, output $D = A + B + 1$. Both cases perform the add microoperation with or without adding the input carry.

subtraction

When $S_1 S_0 = 01$, the complement of B is applied to the Y inputs of the adder. If $C_{in} = 1$, then $D = A + \bar{B} + 1$. This produces A plus the 2's complement of B, which is equivalent to a subtraction of $A - B$. When $C_{in} = 0$, then $D = A + \bar{B}$. This is equivalent to a subtract with borrow, that is, $A - B - 1$.

When $S_1 S_0 = 10$, the inputs from B are neglected, and instead, all 0's are inserted into the Y inputs. The output becomes $D = A + 0 + C_{in}$. This gives $D = A$ when $C_{in} = 0$ and $D = A + 1$ when $C_{in} = 1$. In the first case we have a direct transfer from input A to output D. In the second case, the value of A

increment

is incremented by 1.

decrement

When $S_1 S_0 = 11$, all 1's are inserted into the Y inputs of the adder to produce the decrement operation $D = A - 1$ when $C_{in} = 0$. This is because a number with all 1's is equal to the 2's complement of 1 (the 2's complement of binary 0001 is 1111). Adding a number A to the 2's complement of 1 produces $F = A + $ 2's complement of $1 = A - 1$. When $C_{in} = 1$, then $D = A - 1 + 1 = A$, which causes a direct transfer from input A to output D. Note that the microoperation $D = A$ is generated twice, so there are only seven distinct microoperations in the arithmetic circuit.

4-5 Logic Microoperations

Logic microoperations specify binary operations for strings of bits stored in registers. These operations consider each bit of the register separately and treat them as binary variables. For example, the exclusive-OR microoperation with the contents of two registers $R1$ and $R2$ is symbolized by the statement

$$P: \quad R1 \leftarrow R1 \oplus R2$$

It specifies a logic microoperation to be executed on the individual bits of the registers provided that the control variable $P = 1$. As a numerical example, assume that each register has four bits. Let the content of $R1$ be 1010 and the content of $R2$ be 1100. The exclusive-OR microoperation stated above symbolizes the following logic computation:

$$
\begin{array}{ll}
1010 & \text{Content of } R1 \\
\underline{1100} & \text{Content of } R2 \\
0110 & \text{Content of } R1 \text{ after } P = 1
\end{array}
$$

The content of $R1$, after the execution of the microoperation, is equal to the bit-by-bit exclusive-OR operation on pairs of bits in $R2$ and previous values of $R1$. The logic microoperations are seldom used in scientific computations, but they are very useful for bit manipulation of binary data and for making logical decisions.

special symbols

Special symbols will be adopted for the logic microoperations OR, AND, and complement, to distinguish them from the corresponding symbols used to express Boolean functions. The symbol $\vee$ will be used to denote an OR microoperation and the symbol $\wedge$ to denote an AND microoperation. The complement microoperation is the same as the 1's complement and uses a bar on top of the symbol that denotes the register name. By using different symbols, it will be possible to differentiate between a logic microoperation and a control (or Boolean) function. Another reason for adopting two sets of symbols is to be able to distinguish the symbol $+$, when used to symbolize an arithmetic plus, from a logic OR operation. Although the $+$ symbol has two meanings, it will be possible to distinguish between them by noting where the symbol occurs. When the symbol $+$ occurs in a microoperation, it will denote an arithmetic plus. When it occurs in a control (or Boolean) function, it will denote an OR operation. We will never use it to symbolize an OR microoperation. For example, in the statement

$$P + Q: \quad R1 \leftarrow R2 + R3, \quad R4 \leftarrow R5 \vee R6$$

the $+$ between P and Q is an OR operation between two binary variables of a control function. The $+$ between $R2$ and $R3$ specifies an add microoperation. The OR microoperation is designated by the symbol $\vee$ between registers $R5$ and $R6$.

List of Logic Microoperations

There are 16 different logic operations that can be performed with two binary variables. They can be determined from all possible truth tables obtained with two binary variables as shown in Table 4-5. In this table, each of the 16 columns F_0 through F_{15} represents a truth table of one possible Boolean function for the

TABLE 4-5 Truth Tables for 16 Functions of Two Variables

x	y	F_0	F_1	F_2	F_3	F_4	F_5	F_6	F_7	F_8	F_9	F_{10}	F_{11}	F_{12}	F_{13}	F_{14}	F_{15}
0	0	0	0	0	0	0	0	0	0	1	1	1	1	1	1	1	1
0	1	0	0	0	0	1	1	1	1	0	0	0	0	1	1	1	1
1	0	0	0	1	1	0	0	1	1	0	0	1	1	0	0	1	1
1	1	0	1	0	1	0	1	0	1	0	1	0	1	0	1	0	1

two variables x and y. Note that the functions are determined from the 16 binary combinations that can be assigned to F.

The 16 Boolean functions of two variables x and y are expressed in algebraic form in the first column of Table 4-6. The 16 logic microoperations are derived from these functions by replacing variable x by the binary content of register A and variable y by the binary content of register B. It is important to realize that the Boolean functions listed in the first column of Table 4-6 represent a relationship between two binary variables x and y. The logic microoperations listed in the second column represent a relationship between the binary content of two registers A and B. Each bit of the register is treated as a binary variable and the microoperation is performed on the string of bits stored in the registers.

TABLE 4-6 Sixteen Logic Microoperations

Boolean function	Microoperation	Name
$F_0 = 0$	$F \leftarrow 0$	Clear
$F_1 = xy$	$F \leftarrow A \wedge B$	AND
$F_2 = xy'$	$F \leftarrow A \wedge \overline{B}$	
$F_3 = x$	$F \leftarrow A$	Transfer A
$F_4 = x'y$	$F \leftarrow \overline{A} \wedge B$	
$F_5 = y$	$F \leftarrow B$	Transfer B
$F_6 = x \oplus y$	$F \leftarrow A \oplus B$	Exclusive-OR
$F_7 = x + y$	$F \leftarrow A \vee B$	OR
$F_8 = (x + y)'$	$F \leftarrow \overline{A \vee B}$	NOR
$F_9 = (x \oplus y)'$	$F \leftarrow \overline{A \oplus B}$	Exclusive-NOR
$F_{10} = y'$	$F \leftarrow \overline{B}$	Complement B
$F_{11} = x + y'$	$F \leftarrow A \vee \overline{B}$	
$F_{12} = x'$	$F \leftarrow \overline{A}$	Complement A
$F_{13} = x' + y$	$F \leftarrow \overline{A} \vee B$	
$F_{14} = (xy)'$	$F \leftarrow \overline{A \wedge B}$	NAND
$F_{15} = 1$	$F \leftarrow$ all 1's	Set to all 1's

Hardware Implementation

The hardware implementation of logic microoperations requires that logic gates be inserted for each bit or pair of bits in the registers to perform the required logic function. Although there are 16 logic microoperations, most computers use only four—AND, OR, XOR (exclusive-OR), and complement—from which all others can be derived.

logic circuit

Figure 4-10 shows one stage of a circuit that generates the four basic logic microoperations. It consists of four gates and a multiplexer. Each of the four logic operations is generated through a gate that performs the required logic. The outputs of the gates are applied to the data inputs of the multiplexer. The two selection inputs S_1 and S_0 choose one of the data inputs of the multiplexer and direct its value to the output. The diagram shows one typical stage with subscript i. For a logic circuit with n bits, the diagram must be repeated n times for $i = 0, 1, 2, \ldots, n - 1$. The selection variables are applied to all stages. The function table in Fig. 4-10(b) lists the logic microoperations obtained for each combination of the selection variables.

Some Applications

Logic microoperations are very useful for manipulating individual bits or a portion of a word stored in a register. They can be used to change bit values, delete a group of bits, or insert new bit values into a register. The following examples show how the bits of one register (designated by A) are manipulated

Figure 4-10 One stage of logic circuit.

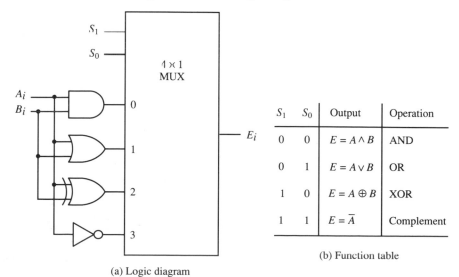

S_1	S_0	Output	Operation
0	0	$E = A \wedge B$	AND
0	1	$E = A \vee B$	OR
1	0	$E = A \oplus B$	XOR
1	1	$E = \overline{A}$	Complement

(b) Function table

(a) Logic diagram

by logic microoperations as a function of the bits of another register (designated by *B*). In a typical application, register *A* is a processor register and the bits of register *B* constitute a logic operand extracted from memory and placed in register *B*.

selective-set

The *selective-set* operation sets to 1 the bits in register *A* where there are corresponding 1's in register *B*. It does not affect bit positions that have 0's in *B*. The following numerical example clarifies this operation:

$$
\begin{array}{ll}
1010 & A \text{ before} \\
\underline{1100} & B \text{ (logic operand)} \\
1110 & A \text{ after}
\end{array}
$$

The two leftmost bits of *B* are 1's, so the corresponding bits of *A* are set to 1. One of these two bits was already set and the other has been changed from 0 to 1. The two bits of *A* with corresponding 0's in *B* remain unchanged. The example above serves as a truth table since it has all four possible combinations of two binary variables. From the truth table we note that the bits of *A* after the operation are obtained from the logic-OR operation of bits in *B* and previous values of *A*. Therefore, the OR microoperation can be used to selectively set bits of a register.

selective-complement

The *selective-complement* operation complements bits in *A* where there are corresponding 1's in *B*. It does not affect bit positions that have 0's in *B*. For example:

$$
\begin{array}{ll}
1010 & A \text{ before} \\
\underline{1100} & B \text{ (logic operand)} \\
0110 & A \text{ after}
\end{array}
$$

Again the two leftmost bits of *B* are 1's, so the corresponding bits of *A* are complemented. This example again can serve as a truth table from which one can deduce that the selective-complement operation is just an exclusive-OR microoperation. Therefore, the exclusive-OR microoperation can be used to selectively complement bits of a register.

selective-clear

The *selective-clear* operation clears to 0 the bits in *A* only where there are corresponding 1's in *B*. For example:

$$
\begin{array}{ll}
1010 & A \text{ before} \\
\underline{1100} & B \text{ (logic operand)} \\
0010 & A \text{ after}
\end{array}
$$

Again the two leftmost bits of *B* are 1's, so the corresponding bits of *A* are cleared to 0. One can deduce that the Boolean operation performed on the individual bits is *AB'*. The corresponding logic microoperation is

$$
A \leftarrow A \wedge \overline{B}
$$

The *mask* operation is similar to the selective-clear operation except that the bits of A are cleared only where there are corresponding 0's in B. The mask operation is an AND micro operation as seen from the following numerical example:

$$
\begin{array}{ll}
1010 & A \text{ before} \\
\underline{1100} & B \text{ (logic operand)} \\
1000 & A \text{ after masking}
\end{array}
$$

The two rightmost bits of A are cleared because the corresponding bits of B are 0's. The two leftmost bits are left unchanged because the corresponding bits of B are 1's. The mask operation is more convenient to use than the selective-clear operation because most computers provide an AND instruction, and few provide an instruction that executes the microoperation for selective-clear.

The *insert* operation inserts a new value into a group of bits. This is done by first masking the bits and then ORing them with the required value. For example, suppose that an A register contains eight bits, 0110 1010. To replace the four leftmost bits by the value 1001 we first mask the four unwanted bits:

$$
\begin{array}{ll}
0110 \ 1010 & A \text{ before} \\
\underline{0000 \ 1111} & B \text{ (mask)} \\
0000 \ 1010 & A \text{ after masking}
\end{array}
$$

and then insert the new value:

$$
\begin{array}{ll}
0000 \ 1010 & A \text{ before} \\
\underline{1001 \ 0000} & B \text{ (insert)} \\
1001 \ 1010 & A \text{ after insertion}
\end{array}
$$

The mask operation is an AND microoperation and the insert operation is an OR microoperation.

The *clear* operation compares the words in A and B and produces an all 0's result if the two numbers are equal. This operation is achieved by an exclusive-OR microoperation as shown by the following example:

$$
\begin{array}{ll}
1010 & A \\
\underline{1010} & B \\
0000 & A \leftarrow A \oplus B
\end{array}
$$

When A and B are equal, the two corresponding bits are either both 0 or both 1. In either case the exclusive-OR operation produces a 0. The all-0's result is then checked to determine if the two numbers were equal.

4-6 Shift Microoperations

Shift microoperations are used for serial transfer of data. They are also used in conjunction with arithmetic, logic, and other data-processing operations. The contents of a register can be shifted to the left or the right. At the same time that the bits are shifted, the first flip-flop receives its binary information from the serial input. During a shift-left operation the serial input transfers a bit into the rightmost position. During a shift-right operation the serial input transfers a bit into the leftmost position. The information transferred through the serial input determines the type of shift. There are three types of shifts: logical, circular, and arithmetic.

logical shift

A *logical* shift is one that transfers 0 through the serial input. We will adopt the symbols *shl* and *shr* for logical shift-left and shift-right microoperations. For example:

$$R1 \leftarrow \text{shl } R1$$

$$R2 \leftarrow \text{shr } R2$$

are two microoperations that specify a 1-bit shift to the left of the content of register $R1$ and a 1-bit shift to the right of the content of register $R2$. The register symbol must be the same on both sides of the arrow. The bit transferred to the end position through the serial input is assumed to be 0 during a logical shift.

circular shift

The *circular* shift (also known as a *rotate* operation) circulates the bits of the register around the two ends without loss of information. This is accomplished by connecting the serial output of the shift register to its serial input. We will use the symbols *cil* and *cir* for the circular shift left and right, respectively. The symbolic notation for the shift microoperations is shown in Table 4-7.

TABLE 4-7 Shift Microoperations

Symbolic designation	Description
$R \leftarrow \text{shl } R$	Shift-left register R
$R \leftarrow \text{shr } R$	Shift-right register R
$R \leftarrow \text{cil } R$	Circular shift-left register R
$R \leftarrow \text{cir } R$	Circular shift-right register R
$R \leftarrow \text{ashl } R$	Arithmetic shift-left R
$R \leftarrow \text{ashr } R$	Arithmetic shift-right R

arithmetic shift

An *arithmetic* shift is a microoperation that shifts a signed binary number to the left or right. An arithmetic shift-left multiplies a signed binary number by 2. An arithmetic shift-right divides the number by 2. Arithmetic shifts must leave the sign bit unchanged because the sign of the number remains the same

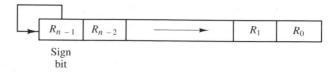

Figure 4-11   Arithmetic shift right.

when it is multiplied or divided by 2. The leftmost bit in a register holds the sign bit, and the remaining bits hold the number. The sign bit is 0 for positive and 1 for negative. Negative numbers are in 2's complement form. Figure 4-11 shows a typical register of n bits. Bit R_{n-1} in the leftmost position holds the sign bit. R_{n-2} is the most significant bit of the number and R_0 is the least significant bit. The arithmetic shift-right leaves the sign bit unchanged and shifts the number (including the sign bit) to the right. Thus R_{n-1} remains the same, R_{n-2} receives the bit from R_{n-1}, and so on for the other bits in the register. The bit in R_0 is lost.

The arithmetic shift-left inserts a 0 into R_0, and shifts all other bits to the left. The initial bit of R_{n-1} is lost and replaced by the bit from R_{n-2}. A sign reversal occurs if the bit in R_{n-1} changes in value after the shift. This happens if the multiplication by 2 causes an overflow. An overflow occurs after an arithmetic shift left if initially, before the shift, R_{n-1} is not equal to R_{n-2}. An overflow flip-flop V_s can be used to detect an arithmetic shift-left overflow.

$$V_s = R_{n-1} \oplus R_{n-2}$$

If $V_s = 0$, there is no overflow, but if $V_s = 1$, there is an overflow and a sign reversal after the shift. V_s must be transferred into the overflow flip-flop with the same clock pulse that shifts the register.

Hardware Implementation

A possible choice for a shift unit would be a bidirectional shift register with parallel load (see Fig. 2-9). Information can be transferred to the register in parallel and then shifted to the right or left. In this type of configuration, a clock pulse is needed for loading the data into the register, and another pulse is needed to initiate the shift. In a processor unit with many registers it is more efficient to implement the shift operation with a combinational circuit. In this way the content of a register that has to be shifted is first placed onto a common bus whose output is connected to the combinational shifter, and the shifted number is then loaded back into the register. This requires only one clock pulse for loading the shifted value into the register.

shifter   A combinational circuit shifter can be constructed with multiplexers as shown in Fig. 4-12. The 4-bit shifter has four data inputs, A_0 through A_3, and four data outputs, H_0 through H_3. There are two serial inputs, one for shift left

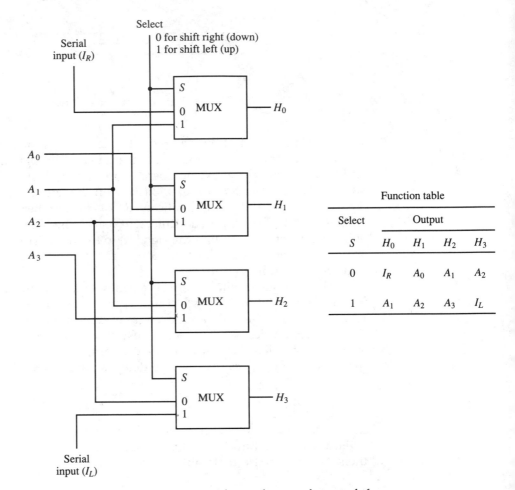

Figure 4-12   4-bit combinational circuit shifter.

(I_L) and the other for shift right (I_L). When the selection input $S = 0$, the input data are shifted right (down in the diagram). When $S = 1$, the input data are shifted left (up in the diagram). The function table in Fig. 4-12 shows which input goes to each output after the shift. A shifter with n data inputs and outputs requires n multiplexers. The two serial inputs can be controlled by another multiplexer to provide the three possible types of shifts.

4-7   Arithmetic Logic Shift Unit

Instead of having individual registers performing the microoperations directly, computer systems employ a number of storage registers connected to a common operational unit called an arithmetic logic unit, abbreviated ALU. To

ALU

perform a microoperation, the contents of specified registers are placed in the inputs of the common ALU. The ALU performs an operation and the result of the operation is then transferred to a destination register. The ALU is a combinational circuit so that the entire register transfer operation from the source registers through the ALU and into the destination register can be performed during one clock pulse period. The shift microoperations are often performed in a separate unit, but sometimes the shift unit is made part of the overall ALU.

The arithmetic, logic, and shift circuits introduced in previous sections can be combined into one ALU with common selection variables. One stage of an arithmetic logic shift unit is shown in Fig. 4-13. The subscript i designates a typical stage. Inputs A_i and B_i are applied to both the arithmetic and logic

Figure 4-13   One stage of arithmetic logic shift unit.

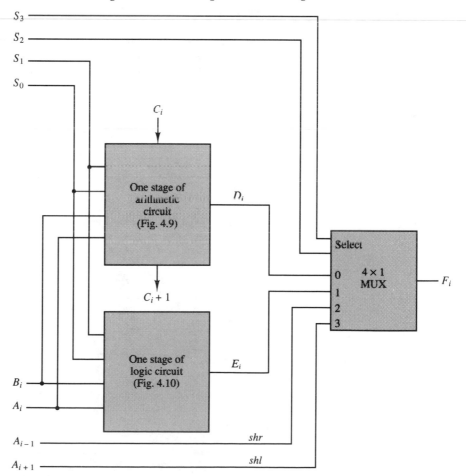

units. A particular microoperation is selected with inputs S_1 and S_0. A 4×1 multiplexer at the output chooses between an arithmetic output in E_i and a logic output in H_i. The data in the multiplexer are selected with inputs S_3 and S_2. The other two data inputs to the multiplexer receive inputs A_{i-1} for the shift-right operation and A_{i+1} for the shift-left operation. Note that the diagram shows just one typical stage. The circuit of Fig. 4-13 must be repeated n times for an n-bit ALU. The output carry C_{i+1} of a given arithmetic stage must be connected to the input carry C_i of the next stage in sequence. The input carry to the first stage is the input carry C_{in}, which provides a selection variable for the arithmetic operations.

The circuit whose one stage is specified in Fig. 4-13 provides eight arithmetic operation, four logic operations, and two shift operations. Each operation is selected with the five variables S_3, S_2, S_1, S_0, and C_{in}. The input carry C_{in} is used for selecting an arithmetic operation only.

Table 4-8 lists the 14 operations of the ALU. The first eight are arithmetic operations (see Table 4-4) and are selected with $S_3 S_2 = 00$. The next four are logic operations (see Fig. 4-10) and are selected with $S_3 S_2 = 01$. The input carry has no effect during the logic operations and is marked with don't-care $\times$'s. The last two operations are shift operations and are selected with $S_3 S_2 = 10$ and 11. The other three selection inputs have no effect on the shift.

TABLE 4-8 Function Table for Arithmetic Logic Shift Unit

Operation select						
S_3	S_2	S_1	S_0	C_{in}	Operation	Function
0	0	0	0	0	$F = A$	Transfer A
0	0	0	0	1	$F = A + 1$	Increment A
0	0	0	1	0	$F = A + B$	Addition
0	0	0	1	1	$F = A + B + 1$	Add with carry
0	0	1	0	0	$F = A + \overline{B}$	Subtract with borrow
0	0	1	0	1	$F = A + \overline{B} + 1$	Subtraction
0	0	1	1	0	$F = A - 1$	Decrement A
0	0	1	1	1	$F = A$	Transfer A
0	1	0	0	$\times$	$F = A \wedge B$	AND
0	1	0	1	$\times$	$F = A \vee B$	OR
0	1	1	0	$\times$	$F = A \oplus B$	XOR
0	1	1	1	$\times$	$F = \overline{A}$	Complement A
1	0	$\times$	$\times$	$\times$	$F = \text{shr } A$	Shift right A into F
1	1	$\times$	$\times$	$\times$	$F = \text{shl } A$	Shift left A into F

=== PROBLEMS ===

4-1. Show the block diagram of the hardware (similar to Fig. 4-2a) that implements the following register transfer statement:

$$yT_2: \quad R2 \leftarrow R1, \quad R1 \leftarrow R2$$

4-2. The outputs of four registers, $R0$, $R1$, $R2$, and $R3$, are connected through 4-to-1-line multiplexers to the inputs of a fifth register, $R5$. Each register is eight bits long. The required transfers are dictated by four timing variables T_0 through T_3 as follows:

$$T_0: \quad R5 \leftarrow R0$$
$$T_1: \quad R5 \leftarrow R1$$
$$T_2: \quad R5 \leftarrow R2$$
$$T_3: \quad R5 \leftarrow R3$$

The timing variables are mutually exclusive, which means that only one variable is equal to 1 at any given time, while the other three are equal to 0. Draw a block diagram showing the hardware implementation of the register transfers. Include the connections necessary from the four timing variables to the selection inputs of the multiplexers and to the load input of register $R5$.

4-3. Represent the following conditional control statement by two register transfer statements with control functions.

$$\text{If } (P = 1) \text{ then } (R1 \leftarrow R2) \text{ else if } (Q = 1) \text{ then } (R1 \leftarrow R3)$$

4-4. What has to be done to the bus system of Fig. 4-3 to be able to transfer information from any register to any other register? Specifically, show the connections that must be included to provide a path from the outputs of register C to the inputs of register A.

4-5. Draw a diagram of a bus system similar to the one shown in Fig. 4-3, but use three-state buffers and a decoder instead of the multiplexers.

4-6. A digital computer has a common bus system for 16 registers of 32 bits each. The bus is constructed with multiplexers.
 a. How many selection inputs are there in each multiplexer?
 b. What size of multiplexers are needed?
 c. How many multiplexers are there in the bus?

4-7. The following transfer statements specify a memory. Explain the memory operation in each case.
 a. $R2 \leftarrow M[AR]$
 b. $M[AR] \leftarrow R3$
 c. $R5 \leftarrow M[R5]$

4-8.   Draw the block diagram for the hardware that implements the following statements:

$$x + yz:\quad AR \leftarrow AR + BR$$

where AR and BR are two n-bit registers and x, y, and z are control variables. Include the logic gates for the control function. (Remember that the symbol + designates an OR operation in a control or Boolean function but that it represents an arithmetic plus in a microoperation.)

4-9.   Show the hardware that implements the following statement. Include the logic gates for the control function and a block diagram for the binary counter with a count enable input.

$$xyT_0 + T_1 + y'T_2:\quad AR \leftarrow AR + 1$$

4-10.   Consider the following register transfer statements for two 4-bit registers $R1$ and $R2$.

$$xT:\quad R1 \leftarrow R1 + R2$$
$$x'T:\quad R1 \leftarrow R2$$

Every time that variable $T = 1$, either the content of $R2$ is added to the content of $R1$ if $x = 1$, or the content of $R2$ is transferred to $R1$ if $x = 0$. Draw a diagram showing the hardware implementation of the two statements. Use block diagrams for the two 4-bit registers, a 4-bit adder, and a quadruple 2-to-1-line multiplexer that selects the inputs to $R1$. In the diagram, show how the control variables x and T select the inputs of the multiplexer and the load input of register $R1$.

4-11.   Using a 4-bit counter with parallel load as in Fig. 2-11 and a 4-bit adder as in Fig. 4-6, draw a block diagram that shows how to implement the following statements:

$$x:\quad R1 \leftarrow R1 + R2 \qquad \text{Add } R2 \text{ to } R1$$
$$x'y:\quad R1 \leftarrow R1 + 1 \qquad \text{Increment } R1$$

where $R1$ is a counter with parallel load and $R2$ is a 4-bit register.

4-12.   The adder-subtractor circuit of Fig. 4-7 has the following values for input mode M and data inputs A and B. In each case, determine the values of the outputs: S_3, S_2, S_1, S_0, and C_4.

	M	A	B
a.	0	0111	0110
b.	0	1000	1001
c.	1	1100	1000
d.	1	0101	1010
e.	1	0000	0001

4-13. Design a 4-bit combinational circuit decrementer using four full-adder circuits.

4-14. Assume that the 4-bit arithmetic circuit of Fig. 4-9 is enclosed in one IC package. Show the connections among two such ICs to form an 8-bit arithmetic circuit.

4-15. Design an arithmetic circuit with one selection variable S and two n-bit data inputs A and B. The circuit generates the following four arithmetic operations in conjunction with the input carry C_{in}. Draw the logic diagram for the first two stages.

S	$C_{in} = 0$	$C_{in} = 1$
0	$D = A + B$ (add)	$D = A + 1$ (increment)
1	$D = A - 1$ (decrement)	$D = A + \overline{B} + 1$ (subtract)

4-16. Derive a combinational circuit that selects and generates any of the 16 logic functions listed in Table 4-5.

4-17. Design a digital circuit that performs the four logic operations of exclusive-OR, exclusive-NOR, NOR, and NAND. Use two selection variables. Show the logic diagram of one typical stage.

4-18. Register A holds the 8-bit binary 11011001. Determine the B operand and the logic microoperation to be performed in order to change the value in A to:
a. 01101101
b. 11111101

4-19. The 8-bit registers AR, BR, CR, and DR initially have the following values:

$$AR = 11110010$$
$$BR = 11111111$$
$$CR = 10111001$$
$$DR = 11101010$$

Determine the 8-bit values in each register after the execution of the following sequence of microoperations.

$AR \leftarrow AR + BR$	Add BR to AR
$CR \leftarrow CR \wedge DR, BR \leftarrow BR + 1$	AND DR to CR, increment BR
$AR \leftarrow AR - CR$	Subtract CR from AR

4-20. An 8-bit register contains the binary value 10011100. What is the register value after an arithmetic shift right? Starting from the initial number 10011100, determine the register value after an arithmetic shift left, and state whether there is an overflow.

4-21. Starting from an initial value of $R = 11011101$, determine the sequence of binary values in R after a logical shift-left, followed by a circular shift-right, followed by a logical shift-right and a circular shift-left.

4-22. What is the value of output H in Fig. 4-12 if input A is 1001, $S = 1$, $I_R = 1$, and $I_L = 0$?

4-23. What is wrong with the following register transfer statements?
 a. xT: $AR \leftarrow \overline{AR}$, $AR \leftarrow 0$
 b. yT: $R1 \leftarrow R2$, $R1 \leftarrow R3$
 c. zT: $PC \leftarrow AR$, $PC \leftarrow PC + 1$

REFERENCES

1. Bell, C. G., J. C. Mudge, and J. E. McNamara, *Computer Engineering.* Bedford, MA: Digital Press, 1980.

2. Booth, T. L., *Introduction to Computer Engineering*, 3rd ed. New York: John Wiley, 1984.

3. Hays, J. F., *Computer Architecture and Organization*, 2nd ed. New York: McGraw-Hill, 1988.

4. Hill, F. J., and G. R. Peterson, *Digital Systems: Hardware Organization and Design*, 3rd ed. New York: John Wiley, 1987.

5. Mano, M. M., *Computer Engineering: Hardware Design.* Englewood Cliffs, NJ: Prentice Hall, 1988.

6. Patterson, D. A., and J. L. Hennessy, *Computer Architecture: A Quantitative Approach.* San Mateo, CA: Morgan Kaufmann Publishers, 1990.

7. Prosser, F. P., and D. E. Winkel, *The Art of Digital Design*, 2nd ed. Englewood Cliffs, NJ: Prentice Hall, 1987.

8. Sandige, R. S., *Modern Digital Design.* New York: McGraw-Hill, 1990.

9. Shiva, S. G., *Computer Design and Architecture*, 2nd ed. New York: HarperCollins Publishers, 1991.

10. Tomek, I., *Introduction to Computer Organization.* Rockville, MD: Computer Science Press, 1981.

11. Ward, S. A., and R.H. Halstead, Jr., *Computation Structures.* Cambridge, MA: MIT Press, 1990.

CHAPTER FIVE

Basic Computer Organization and Design

IN THIS CHAPTER

5-1   Instruction Codes

In this chapter we introduce a basic computer and show how its operation can be specified with register transfer statements. The organization of the computer is defined by its internal registers, the timing and control structure, and the set of instructions that it uses. The design of the computer is then carried out in detail. Although the basic computer presented in this chapter is very small compared to commercial computers, it has the advantage of being simple enough so we can demonstrate the design process without too many complications.

The internal organization of a digital system is defined by the sequence of microoperations it performs on data stored in its registers. The general-purpose digital computer is capable of executing various microoperations and, in addition, can be instructed as to what specific sequence of operations it must perform. The user of a computer can control the process by means of a program. A program is a set of instructions that specify the operations, operands, and the sequence by which processing has to occur. The data-processing task may be altered by specifying a new program with different instructions or specifying the same instructions with different data.

A computer instruction is a binary code that specifies a sequence of microoperations for the computer. Instruction codes together with data are stored in memory. The computer reads each instruction from memory and places it in a control register. The control then interprets the binary code of the instruction and proceeds to execute it by issuing a sequence of microoperations. Every computer has its own unique instruction set. The ability to store and execute instructions, the stored program concept, is the most important property of a general-purpose computer.

instruction code

An instruction code is a group of bits that instruct the computer to perform a specific operation. It is usually divided into parts, each having its own particular interpretation. The most basic part of an instruction code is its

operation code

operation part. The operation code of an instruction is a group of bits that define such operations as add, subtract, multiply, shift, and complement. The number of bits required for the operation code of an instruction depends on the total number of operations available in the computer. The operation code must consist of at least n bits for a given 2^n (or less) distinct operations. As an illustration, consider a computer with 64 distinct operations, one of them being an ADD operation. The operation code consists of six bits, with a bit configuration 110010 assigned to the ADD operation. When this operation code is decoded in the control unit, the computer issues control signals to read an operand from memory and add the operand to a processor register.

At this point we must recognize the relationship between a computer operation and a microoperation. An operation is part of an instruction stored in computer memory. It is a binary code that tells the computer to perform a specific operation. The control unit receives the instruction from memory and interprets the operation code bits. It then issues a sequence of control signals to initiate microoperations in internal computer registers. For every operation code, the control issues a sequence of microoperations needed for the hardware implementation of the specified operation. For this reason, an operation code is sometimes called a macrooperation because it specifies a set of microoperations.

The operation part of an instruction code specifies the operation to be performed. This operation must be performed on some data stored in processor registers or in memory. An instruction code must therefore specify not only the operation but also the registers or the memory words where the operands are to be found, as well as the register or memory word where the result is to be stored. Memory words can be specified in instruction codes by their address. Processor registers can be specified by assigning to the instruction another binary code of k bits that specifies one of 2^k registers. There are many variations for arranging the binary code of instructions, and each computer has its own particular instruction code format. Instruction code formats are conceived by computer designers who specify the architecture of the computer. In this chapter we choose a particular instruction code to explain the basic organization and design of digital computers.

Stored Program Organization

The simplest way to organize a computer is to have one processor register and an instruction code format with two parts. The first part specifies the operation to be performed and the second specifies an address. The memory address tells the control where to find an operand in memory. This operand is read from memory and used as the data to be operated on together with the data stored in the processor register.

opcode

Figure 5-1 depicts this type of organization. Instructions are stored in one section of memory and data in another. For a memory unit with 4096 words we need 12 bits to specify an address since $2^{12} = 4096$. If we store each instruction code in one 16-bit memory word, we have available four bits for the operation code (abbreviated opcode) to specify one out of 16 possible operations, and 12 bits to specify the address of an operand. The control reads a 16-bit instruction from the program portion of memory. It uses the 12-bit address part of the instruction to read a 16-bit operand from the data portion of memory. It then executes the operation specified by the operation code.

Figure 5-1 Stored program organization.

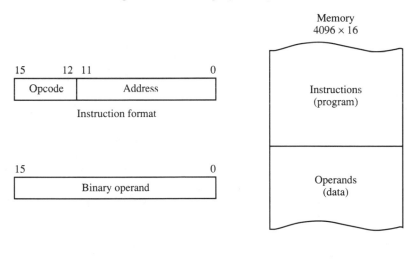

accumulator (AC)

Computers that have a single-processor register usually assign to it the name accumulator and label it *AC*. The operation is performed with the memory operand and the content of *AC*.

If an operation in an instruction code does not need an operand from memory, the rest of the bits in the instruction can be used for other purposes. For example, operations such as clear *AC*, complement *AC*, and increment *AC* operate on data stored in the *AC* register. They do not need an operand from memory. For these types of operations, the second part of the instruction code (bits 0 through 11) is not needed for specifying a memory address and can be used to specify other operations for the computer.

Indirect Address

immediate instruction

It is sometimes convenient to use the address bits of an instruction code not as an address but as the actual operand. When the second part of an instruction code specifies an operand, the instruction is said to have an immediate operand. When the second part specifies the address of an operand, the instruction is said to have a direct address. This is in contrast to a third possibility called indirect address, where the bits in the second part of the instruction designate an address of a memory word in which the address of the operand is found. One bit of the instruction code can be used to distinguish between a direct and an indirect address.

As an illustration of this configuration, consider the instruction code format shown in Fig. 5-2(a). It consists of a 3-bit operation code, a 12-bit address, and an indirect address mode bit designated by *I*. The mode bit is 0 for a direct address and 1 for an indirect address. A direct address instruction is shown in Fig. 5-2(b). It is placed in address 22 in memory. The *I* bit is 0, so the instruction is recognized as a direct address instruction. The opcode specifies an ADD instruction, and the address part is the binary equivalent of 457. The control finds the operand in memory at address 457 and adds it to the content of *AC*. The instruction in address 35 shown in Fig. 5-2(c) has a mode bit *I* = 1. Therefore, it is recognized as an indirect address instruction. The address part is the binary equivalent of 300. The control goes to address 300 to find the address of the operand. The address of the operand in this case is 1350. The operand found in address 1350 is then added to the content of *AC*. The indirect address instruction needs two references to memory to fetch an operand. The first reference is needed to read the address of the operand; the

effective address

second is for the operand itself. We define the *effective address* to be the address of the operand in a computation-type instruction or the target address in a branch-type instruction. Thus the effective address in the instruction of Fig. 5-2(b) is 457 and in the instruction of Fig 5-2(c) is 1350.

The direct and indirect addressing modes are used in the computer presented in this chapter. The memory word that holds the address of the operand in an indirect address instruction is used as a pointer to an array of

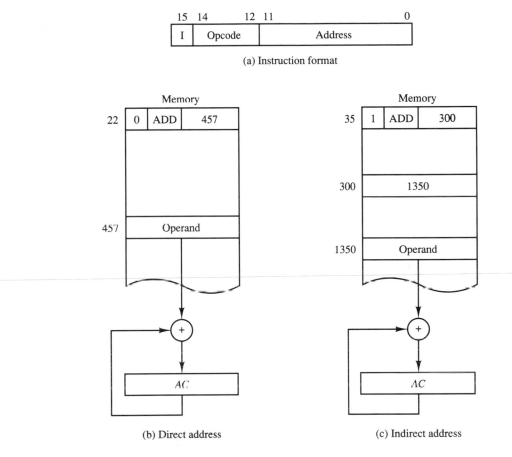

(a) Instruction format

(b) Direct address

(c) Indirect address

Figure 5-2 Demonstration of direct and indirect address.

data. The pointer could be placed in a processor register instead of memory as done in commercial computers.

5-2 Computer Registers

Computer instructions are normally stored in consecutive memory locations and are executed sequentially one at a time. The control reads an instruction from a specific address in memory and executes it. It then continues by reading the next instruction in sequence and executes it, and so on. This type of instruction sequencing needs a counter to calculate the address of the next instruction after execution of the current instruction is completed. It is also necessary to provide a register in the control unit for storing the instruction code after it is read from memory. The computer needs processor registers for manipulating data and a register for holding a memory address. These requirements dictate the register configuration shown in Fig. 5-3. The registers are also listed in Table 5-1 together with a brief description of their function and the number of bits that they contain.

The memory unit has a capacity of 4096 words and each word contains 16 bits. Twelve bits of an instruction word are needed to specify the address of an operand. This leaves three bits for the operation part of the instruction and a bit to specify a direct or indirect address. The data register (DR) holds the operand read from memory. The accumulator (AC) register is a general-purpose processing register. The instruction read from memory is placed in the instruction register (IR). The temporary register (TR) is used for holding temporary data during the processing.

TABLE 5-1 List of Registers for the Basic Computer

Register symbol	Number of bits	Register name	Function
DR	16	Data register	Holds memory operand
AR	12	Address register	Holds address for memory
AC	16	Accumulator	Processor register
IR	16	Instruction register	Holds instruction code
PC	12	Program counter	Holds address of instruction
TR	16	Temporary register	Holds temporary data
INPR	8	Input register	Holds input character
OUTR	8	Output register	Holds output character

program counter (PC)

The memory address register (AR) has 12 bits since this is the width of a memory address. The program counter (PC) also has 12 bits and it holds the address of the next instruction to be read from memory after the current instruction is executed. The PC goes through a counting sequence and causes the computer to read sequential instructions previously stored in memory. Instruction words are read and executed in sequence unless a branch instruction is encountered. A branch instruction calls for a transfer to a nonconsecutive instruction in the program. The address part of a branch instruction is transferred to PC to become the address of the next instruction. To read an instruction, the content of PC is taken as the address for memory and a memory read cycle is initiated. PC is then incremented by one, so it holds the address of the next instruction in sequence.

Two registers are used for input and output. The input register (INPR) receives an 8-bit character from an input device. The output register (OUTR) holds an 8-bit character for an output device.

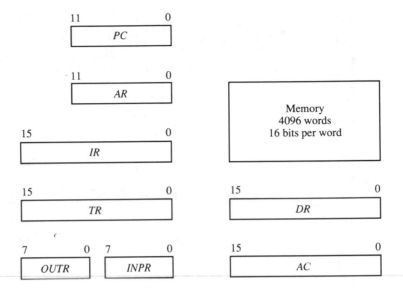

Figure 5-3 Basic computer registers and memory.

Common Bus System

The basic computer has eight registers, a memory unit, and a control unit (to be presented in Sec. 5-4). Paths must be provided to transfer information from one register to another and between memory and registers. The number of wires will be excessive if connections are made between the outputs of each register and the inputs of the other registers. A more efficient scheme for transferring information in a system with many registers is to use a common bus. We have shown in Sec. 4-3 how to construct a bus system using multiplexers or three-state buffer gates. The connection of the registers and memory of the basic computer to a common bus system is shown in Fig. 5-4.

The outputs of seven registers and memory are connected to the common bus. The specific output that is selected for the bus lines at any given time is determined from the binary value of the selection variables S_2, S_1, and S_0. The number along each output shows the decimal equivalent of the required binary selection. For example, the number along the output of DR is 3. The 16-bit outputs of DR are placed on the bus lines when $S_2S_1S_0 = 011$ since this is the binary value of decimal 3. The lines from the common bus are connected to the inputs of each register and the data inputs of the memory. The particular *load (LD)* register whose LD (load) input is enabled receives the data from the bus during the next clock pulse transition. The memory receives the contents of the bus when its write input is activated. The memory places its 16-bit output onto the bus when the read input is activated and $S_2S_1S_0 = 111$.

Four registers, DR, AC, IR, and TR, have 16 bits each. Two registers, AR

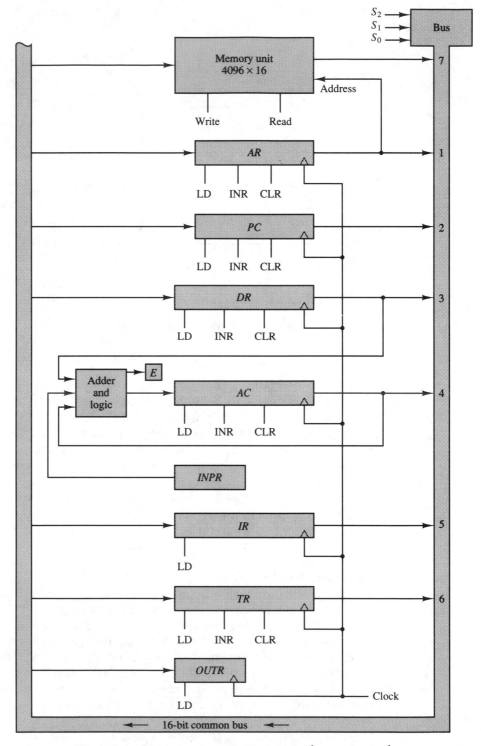

Figure 5-4 Basic computer registers connected to a common bus.

and *PC*, have 12 bits each since they hold a memory address. When the contents of *AR* or *PC* are applied to the 16-bit common bus, the four most significant bits are set to 0's. When *AR* or *PC* receive information from the bus, only the 12 least significant bits are transferred into the register.

The input register *INPR* and the output register *OUTR* have 8 bits each and communicate with the eight least significant bits in the bus. *INPR* is connected to provide information to the bus but *OUTR* can only receive information from the bus. This is because *INPR* receives a character from an input device which is then transferred to *AC*. *OUTR* receives a character from *AC* and delivers it to an output device. There is no transfer from *OUTR* to any of the other registers.

The 16 lines of the common bus receive information from six registers and the memory unit. The bus lines are connected to the inputs of six registers and the memory. Five registers have three control inputs: LD (load), INR (increment), and CLR (clear). This type of register is equivalent to a binary counter with parallel load and synchronous clear similar to the one shown in Fig. 2-11. The increment operation is achieved by enabling the count input of the counter. Two registers have only a LD input. This type of register is shown in Fig. 2-7.

memory address

The input data and output data of the memory are connected to the common bus, but the memory address is connected to *AR*. Therefore, *AR* must always be used to specify a memory address. By using a single register for the address, we eliminate the need for an address bus that would have been needed otherwise. The content of any register can be specified for the memory data input during a write operation. Similarly, any register can receive the data from memory after a read operation except *AC*.

The 16 inputs of *AC* come from an adder and logic circuit. This circuit has three sets of inputs. One set of 16-bit inputs come from the outputs of *AC*. They are used to implement register microoperations such as complement *AC* and shift *AC*. Another set of 16-bit inputs come from the data register *DR*. The inputs from *DR* and *AC* are used for arithmetic and logic microoperations, such as add *DR* to *AC* or AND *DR* to *AC*. The result of an addition is transferred to *AC* and the end carry-out of the addition is transferred to flip-flop *E* (extended *AC* bit). A third set of 8-bit inputs come from the input register *INPR*. The operation of *INPR* and *OUTR* is explained in Sec. 5-7.

Note that the content of any register can be applied onto the bus and an operation can be performed in the adder and logic circuit during the same clock cycle. The clock transition at the end of the cycle transfers the content of the bus into the designated destination register and the output of the adder and logic circuit into *AC*. For example, the two microoperations

$$DR \leftarrow AC \quad \text{and} \quad AC \leftarrow DR$$

can be executed at the same time. This can be done by placing the content of *AC* on the bus (with $S_2S_1S_0 = 100$), enabling the LD (load) input of *DR*, transferring the content of *DR* through the adder and logic circuit into *AC*, and enabling the LD (load) input of *AC*, all during the same clock cycle. The two transfers occur upon the arrival of the clock pulse transition at the end of the clock cycle.

5-3 Computer Instructions

Instruction format

The basic computer has three instruction code formats, as shown in Fig. 5-5. Each format has 16 bits. The operation code (opcode) part of the instruction contains three bits and the meaning of the remaining 13 bits depends on the operation code encountered. A memory-reference instruction uses 12 bits to specify an address and one bit to specify the addressing mode *I*. *I* is equal to 0 for direct address and to 1 for indirect address (see Fig. 5-2). The register-reference instructions are recognized by the operation code 111 with a 0 in the leftmost bit (bit 15) of the instruction. A register-reference instruction specifies an operation on or a test of the *AC* register. An operand from memory is not needed; therefore, the other 12 bits are used to specify the operation or test to be executed. Similarly, an input–output instruction does not need a reference to memory and is recognized by the operation code 111 with a 1 in the leftmost bit of the instruction. The remaining 12 bits are used to specify the type of input–output operation or test performed.

The type of instruction is recognized by the computer control from the four bits in positions 12 through 15 of the instruction. If the three opcode bits in positions 12 though 14 are not equal to 111, the instruction is a memory-reference type and the bit in position 15 is taken as the addressing mode *I*. If the 3-bit opcode is equal to 111, control then inspects the bit in position 15. If this bit is 0, the

Figure 5-5 Basic computer instruction formats.

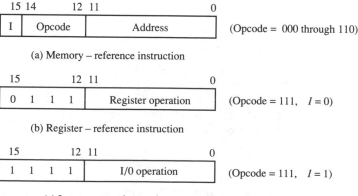

(a) Memory – reference instruction

(b) Register – reference instruction

(c) Input – output instruction

instruction is a register-reference type. If the bit is 1, the instruction is an input–output type. Note that the bit in position 15 of the instruction code is designated by the symbol *I* but is not used as a mode bit when the operation code is equal to 111.

Only three bits of the instruction are used for the operation code. It may seem that the computer is restricted to a maximum of eight distinct operations. However, since register-reference and input–output instructions use the remaining 12 bits as part of the operation code, the total number of instructions can exceed eight. In fact, the total number of instructions chosen for the basic computer is equal to 25.

The instructions for the computer are listed in Table 5-2. The symbol designation is a three-letter word and represents an abbreviation intended for

TABLE 5-2 Basic Computer Instructions

	Hexadecimal code		
Symbol	$I = 0$	$I = 1$	Description
AND	0xxx	8xxx	AND memory word to *AC*
ADD	1xxx	9xxx	Add memory word to *AC*
LDA	2xxx	Axxx	Load memory word to *AC*
STA	3xxx	Bxxx	Store content of *AC* in memory
BUN	4xxx	Cxxx	Branch unconditionally
BSA	5xxx	Dxxx	Branch and save return address
ISZ	6xxx	Exxx	Increment and skip if zero
CLA		7800	Clear *AC*
CLE		7400	Clear *E*
CMA		7200	Complement *AC*
CME		7100	Complement *E*
CIR		7080	Circulate right *AC* and *E*
CIL		7040	Circulate left *AC* and *E*
INC		7020	Increment *AC*
SPA		7010	Skip next instruction if *AC* positive
SNA		7008	Skip next instruction if *AC* negative
SZA		7004	Skip next instruction if *AC* zero
SZE		7002	Skip next instruction if *E* is 0
HLT		7001	Halt computer
INP		F800	Input character to *AC*
OUT		F400	Output character from *AC*
SKI		F200	Skip on input flag
SKO		F100	Skip on output flag
ION		F080	Interrupt on
IOF		F040	Interrupt off

hexadecimal code programmers and users. The hexadecimal code is equal to the equivalent hexadecimal number of the binary code used for the instruction. By using the hexadecimal equivalent we reduced the 16 bits of an instruction code to four digits with each hexadecimal digit being equivalent to four bits. A memory-reference instruction has an address part of 12 bits. The address part is denoted by three x's and stand for the three hexadecimal digits corresponding to the 12-bit address. The last bit of the instruction is designated by the symbol I. When $I = 0$, the last four bits of an instruction have a hexadecimal digit equivalent from 0 to 6 since the last bit is 0. When $I = 1$, the hexadecimal digit equivalent of the last four bits of the instruction ranges from 8 to E since the last bit is 1.

Register-reference instructions use 16 bits to specify an operation. The leftmost four bits are always 0111, which is equivalent to hexadecimal 7. The other three hexadecimal digits give the binary equivalent of the remaining 12 bits. The input–output instructions also use all 16 bits to specify an operation. The last four bits are always 1111, equivalent to hexadecimal F.

Instruction Set Completeness

Before investigating the operations performed by the instructions, let us discuss the type of instructions that must be included in a computer. A computer should have a set of instructions so that the user can construct machine language programs to evaluate any function that is known to be computable. The set of instructions are said to be complete if the computer includes a sufficient number of instructions in each of the following categories:

1. Arithmetic, logical, and shift instructions
2. Instructions for moving information to and from memory and processor registers
3. Program control instructions together with instructions that check status conditions
4. Input and output instructions

Arithmetic, logical, and shift instructions provide computational capabilities for processing the type of data that the user may wish to employ. The bulk of the binary information in a digital computer is stored in memory, but all computations are done in processor registers. Therefore, the user must have the capability of moving information between these two units. Decision-making capabilities are an important aspect of digital computers. For example, two numbers can be compared, and if the first is greater than the second, it may be necessary to proceed differently than if the second is greater than the first. Program control instructions such as branch instructions are used to change the sequence in which the program is executed. Input and output instructions are needed for communication between the computer and the user. Programs and data must be transferred into memory and results of computations must be transferred back to the user.

The instructions listed in Table 5-2 constitute a minimum set that provides all the capabilities mentioned above. There is one arithmetic instruction, ADD, and two related instructions, complement AC(CMA) and increment AC(INC). With these three instructions we can add and subtract binary numbers when negative numbers are in signed-2's complement representation. The circulate instructions, CIR and CIL, can be used for arithmetic shifts as well as any other type of shifts desired. Multiplication and division can be performed using addition, subtraction, and shifting. There are three logic operations: AND, complement AC(CMA), and clear AC(CLA). The AND and complement provide a NAND operation. It can be shown that with the NAND operation it is possible to implement all the other logic operations with two variables (listed in Table 4-6). Moving information from memory to AC is accomplished with the load AC(LDA) instruction. Storing information from AC into memory is done with the store AC(STA) instruction. The branch instructions BUN, BSA, and ISZ, together with the four skip instructions, provide capabilities for program control and checking of status conditions. The input (INP) and output (OUT) instructions cause information to be transferred between the computer and external devices.

Although the set of instructions for the basic computer is complete, it is not efficient because frequently used operations are not performed rapidly. An efficient set of instructions will include such instructions as subtract, multiply, OR, and exclusive-OR. These operations must be programmed in the basic computer. The programs are presented in Chap. 6 together with other programming examples for the basic computer. By using a limited number of instructions it is possible to show the detailed logic design of the computer. A more complete set of instructions would have made the design too complex. In this way we can demonstrate the basic principles of computer organization and design without going into excessive complex details. In Chap. 8 we present a complete list of computer instructions that are included in most commercial computers.

The function of each instruction listed in Table 5-2 and the microoperations needed for their execution are presented in Secs. 5-5 through 5-7. We delay this discussion because we must first consider the control unit and understand its internal organization.

5-4 Timing and Control

clock pulses

The timing for all registers in the basic computer is controlled by a master clock generator. The clock pulses are applied to all flip-flops and registers in the system, including the flip-flops and registers in the control unit. The clock pulses do not change the state of a register unless the register is enabled by a control signal. The control signals are generated in the control unit and provide control inputs for the multiplexers in the common bus, control inputs in processor registers, and microoperations for the accumulator.

hardwired control

There are two major types of control organization: hardwired control and microprogrammed control. In the hardwired organization, the control logic is implemented with gates, flip-flops, decoders, and other digital circuits. It has the advantage that it can be optimized to produce a fast mode of operation. In the microprogrammed organization, the control information is stored in a control memory. The control memory is programmed to initiate the required sequence of microoperations. A hardwired control, as the name implies, re-quires changes in the wiring among the various components if the design has

microprogrammed control

to be modified or changed. In the microprogrammed control, any required changes or modifications can be done by updating the microprogram in control memory. A hardwired control for the basic computer is presented in this section. A microprogrammed control unit for a similar computer is presented in Chap. 7.

control unit

The block diagram of the control unit is shown in Fig. 5-6. It consists of two decoders, a sequence counter, and a number of control logic gates. An instruction read from memory is placed in the instruction register (*IR*). The position of this register in the common bus system is indicated in Fig. 5-4. The instruction register is shown again in Fig. 5-6, where it is divided into three parts: the *I* bit, the operation code, and bits 0 through 11. The operation code in bits 12 through 14 are decoded with a 3×8 decoder. The eight outputs of the decoder are designated by the symbols D_0 through D_7. The subscripted decimal number is equivalent to the binary value of the corresponding opera-tion code. Bit 15 of the instruction is transferred to a flip-flop designated by the symbol *I*. Bits 0 through 11 are applied to the control logic gates. The 4-bit sequence counter can count in binary from 0 through 15. The outputs of the

timing signals

counter are decoded into 16 timing signals T_0 through T_{15}. The internal logic of the control gates will be derived later when we consider the design of the computer in detail.

The sequence counter *SC* can be incremented or cleared synchronously (see the counter of Fig. 2-11). Most of the time, the counter is incremented to provide the sequence of timing signals out of the 4×16 decoder. Once in awhile, the counter is cleared to 0, causing the next active timing signal to be T_0. As an example, consider the case where *SC* is incremented to provide timing signals T_0, T_1, T_2, T_3, and T_4 in sequence. At time T_4, *SC* is cleared to 0 if decoder output D_3 is active. This is expressed symbolically by the statement

$$D_3 T_4: \quad SC \leftarrow 0$$

The timing diagram of Fig. 5-7 shows the time relationship of the control signals. The sequence counter *SC* responds to the positive transition of the clock. Initially, the CLR input of *SC* is active. The first positive transition of the

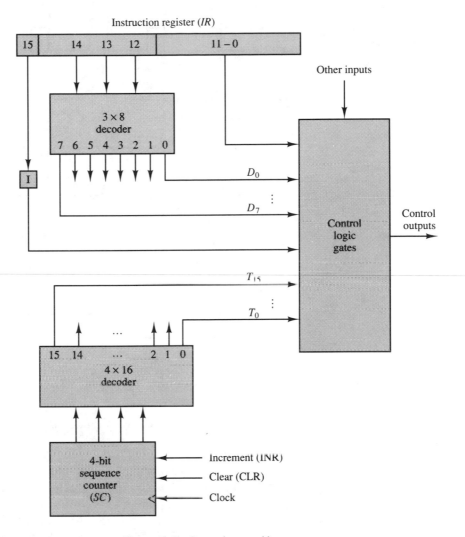

Figure 5-6 Control unit of basic computer.

clock clears *SC* to 0, which in turn activates the timing signal T_0 out of the decoder. T_0 is active during one clock cycle. The positive clock transition labeled T_0 in the diagram will trigger only those registers whose control inputs are connected to timing signal T_0. *SC* is incremented with every positive clock transition, unless its CLR input is active. This produces the sequence of timing signals T_0, T_1, T_2, T_3, T_4, and so on, as shown in the diagram. (Note the relationship between the timing signal and its corresponding positive clock transition.) If *SC* is not cleared, the timing signals will continue with T_5, T_6, up to T_{15} and back to T_0.

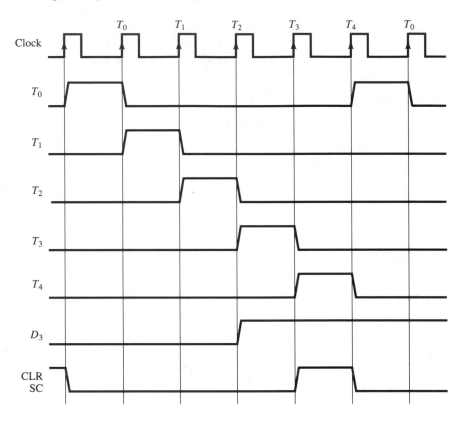

Figure 5-7 Example of control timing signals.

The last three waveforms in Fig. 5-7 show how SC is cleared when $D_3T_4 = 1$. Output D_3 from the operation decoder becomes active at the end of timing signal T_2. When timing signal T_4 becomes active, the output of the AND gate that implements the control function D_3T_4 becomes active. This signal is applied to the CLR input of SC. On the next positive clock transition (the one marked T_4 in the diagram) the counter is cleared to 0. This causes the timing signal T_0 to become active instead of T_5 that would have been active if SC were incremented instead of cleared.

A memory read or write cycle will be initiated with the rising edge of a timing signal. It will be assumed that a memory cycle time is less than the clock cycle time. According to this assumption, a memory read or write cycle initiated by a timing signal will be completed by the time the next clock goes through its positive transition. The clock transition will then be used to load the memory word into a register. This timing relationship is not valid in many computers because the memory cycle time is usually longer than the processor clock cycle. In such a case it is necessary to provide wait cycles in the processor until the memory word is available. To facilitate the presentation, we will assume that a wait period is not necessary in the basic computer.

To fully comprehend the operation of the computer, it is crucial that one understands the timing relationship between the clock transition and the timing signals. For example, the register transfer statement

$$T_0: \quad AR \leftarrow PC$$

specifies a transfer of the content of PC into AR if timing signal T_0 is active. T_0 is active during an entire clock cycle interval. During this time the content of PC is placed onto the bus (with $S_2S_1S_0 = 010$) and the LD (load) input of AR is enabled. The actual transfer does not occur until the end of the clock cycle when the clock goes through a positive transition. This same positive clock transition increments the sequence counter SC from 0000 to 0001. The next clock cycle has T_1 active and T_0 inactive.

5-5 Instruction Cycle

A program residing in the memory unit of the computer consists of a sequence of instructions. The program is executed in the computer by going through a cycle for each instruction. Each instruction cycle in turn is subdivided into a sequence of subcycles or phases. In the basic computer each instruction cycle consists of the following phases:

1. Fetch an instruction from memory.
2. Decode the instruction.
3. Read the effective address from memory if the instruction has an indirect address.
4. Execute the instruction.

Upon the completion of step 4, the control goes back to step 1 to fetch, decode, and execute the next instruction. This process continues indefinitely unless a HALT instruction is encountered.

Fetch and Decode

Initially, the program counter PC is loaded with the address of the first instruction in the program. The sequence counter SC is cleared to 0, providing a decoded timing signal T_0. After each clock pulse, SC is incremented by one, so that the timing signals go through a sequence T_0, T_1, T_2, and so on. The microoperations for the fetch and decode phases can be specified by the following register transfer statements.

T_0: $AR \leftarrow PC$
T_1: $IR \leftarrow M[AR]$, $PC \leftarrow PC + 1$
T_2: $D_0, \ldots, D_7 \leftarrow$ Decode $IR(12\text{–}14)$, $AR \leftarrow IR(0\text{–}11)$, $I \leftarrow IR(15)$

Since only AR is connected to the address inputs of memory, it is necessary to transfer the address from PC to AR during the clock transition associated with timing signal T_0. The instruction read from memory is then placed
in the instruction register IR with the clock transition associated with timing

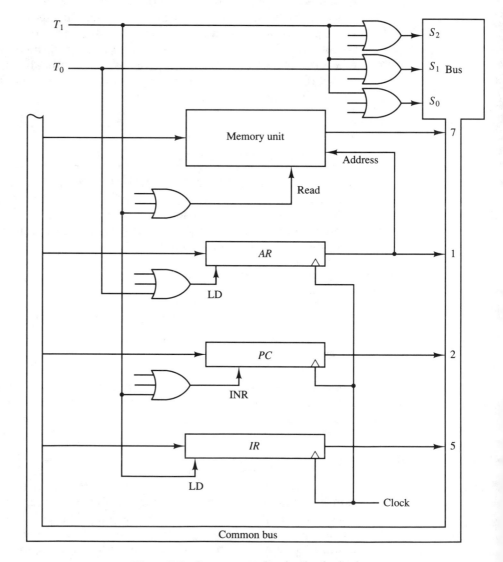

Figure 5-8 Register transfers for the fetch phase.

signal T_1. At the same time, PC is incremented by one to prepare it for the address of the next instruction in the program. At time T_2, the operation code in IR is decoded, the indirect bit is transferred to flip-flop I, and the address part of the instruction is transferred to AR. Note that SC is incremented after each clock pulse to produce the sequence T_0, T_1, and T_2.

Figure 5-8 shows how the first two register transfer statements are implemented in the bus system. To provide the data path for the transfer of PC to AR we must apply timing signal T_0 to achieve the following connection:

1. Place the content of PC onto the bus by making the bus selection inputs $S_2S_1S_0$ equal to 010.

2. Transfer the content of the bus to AR by enabling the LD input of AR.

The next clock transition initiates the transfer from PC to AR since $T_0 = 1$. In order to implement the second statement

$$T_1. \quad IR \leftarrow M[AR], \quad PC \leftarrow PC + 1$$

it is necessary to use timing signal T_1 to provide the following connections in the bus system.

1. Enable the read input of memory.

2. Place the content of memory onto the bus by making $S_2S_1S_0 = 111$.

3. Transfer the content of the bus to IR by enabling the LD input of IR.

4. Increment PC by enabling the INR input of PC.

The next clock transition initiates the read and increment operations since $T_1 = 1$.

Figure 5-8 duplicates a portion of the bus system and shows how T_0 and T_1 are connected to the control inputs of the registers, the memory, and the bus selection inputs. Multiple input OR gates are included in the diagram because there are other control functions that will initiate similar operations.

Determine the Type of Instruction

The timing signal that is active after the decoding is T_3. During time T_3, the control unit determines the type of instruction that was just read from memory. The flowchart of Fig. 5-9 presents an initial configuration for the instruction cycle and shows how the control determines the instruction type after the decoding. The three possible instruction types available in the basic computer are specified in Fig. 5-5.

Decoder output D_7 is equal to 1 if the operation code is equal to binary 111. From Fig. 5-5 we determine that if $D_7 = 1$, the instruction must be a

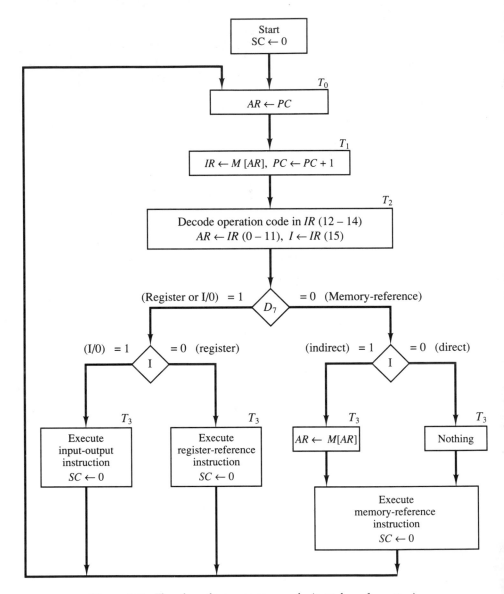

Figure 5-9 Flowchart for instruction cycle (initial configuration).

register-reference or input–output type. If $D_7 = 0$, the operation code must be one of the other seven values 000 through 110, specifying a memory-reference instruction. Control then inspects the value of the first bit of the instruction, which is now available in flip-flop I. If $D_7 = 0$ and $I = 1$, we have a memory-reference instruction with an indirect address. It is then necessary to read the

indirect address

effective address from memory. The microoperation for the indirect address condition can be symbolized by the register transfer statement

$$AR \leftarrow M[AR]$$

Initially, AR holds the address part of the instruction. This address is used during the memory read operation. The word at the address given by AR is read from memory and placed on the common bus. The LD input of AR is then enabled to receive the indirect address that resided in the 12 least significant bits of the memory word.

The three instruction types are subdivided into four separate paths. The selected operation is activated with the clock transition associated with timing signal T_3. This can be symbolized as follows:

$$
\begin{aligned}
&D_7'IT_3: && AR \leftarrow M[AR] \\
&D_7'I'T_3: && \text{Nothing} \\
&D_7 I'T_3: && \text{Execute a register-reference instruction} \\
&D_7 IT_3: && \text{Execute an input–output instruction}
\end{aligned}
$$

When a memory-reference instruction with $I = 0$ is encountered, it is not necessary to do anything since the effective address is already in AR. However, the sequence counter SC must be incremented when $D_7'T_3 = 1$, so that the execution of the memory-reference instruction can be continued with timing variable T_4. A register-reference or input–output instruction can be executed with the clock associated with timing signal T_3. After the instruction is executed, SC is cleared to 0 and control returns to the fetch phase with $T_0 = 1$.

Note that the sequence counter SC is either incremented or cleared to 0 with every positive clock transition. We will adopt the convention that if SC is incremented, we will not write the statement $SC \leftarrow SC + 1$, but it will be implied that the control goes to the next timing signal in sequence. When SC is to be cleared, we will include the statement $SC \leftarrow 0$.

The register transfers needed for the execution of the register-reference instructions are presented in this section. The memory-reference instructions are explained in the next section. The input–output instructions are included in Sec. 5-7.

Register-Reference Instructions

Register-reference instructions are recognized by the control when $D_7 = 1$ and $I = 0$. These instructions use bits 0 through 11 of the instruction code to specify one of 12 instructions. These 12 bits are available in $IR(0–11)$. They were also transferred to AR during time T_2.

The control functions and microoperations for the register-reference instructions are listed in Table 5-3. These instructions are executed with the clock transition associated with timing variable T_3. Each control function needs the Boolean relation $D_7I'T_3$, which we designate for convenience by the symbol r. The control function is distinguished by one of the bits in $IR(0-11)$. By assigning the symbol B_i to bit i of IR, all control functions can be simply denoted by rB_i. For example, the instruction CLA has the hexadecimal code 7800 (see Table 5-2), which gives the binary equivalent 0111 1000 0000 0000. The first bit is a zero and is equivalent to I'. The next three bits constitute the operation code and are recognized from decoder output D_7. Bit 11 in IR is 1 and is recognized from B_{11}. The control function that initiates the microoperation for this instruction is $D_7I'T_3B_{11} = rB_{11}$. The execution of a register-reference instruction is completed at time T_3. The sequence counter SC is cleared to 0 and the control goes back to fetch the next instruction with timing signal T_0.

The first seven register-reference instructions perform clear, complement, circular shift, and increment microoperations on the AC or E registers. The next four instructions cause a skip of the next instruction in sequence when a stated condition is satisfied. The skipping of the instruction is achieved by incrementing PC once again (in addition, it is being incremented during the fetch phase at time T_1). The condition control statements must be recognized as part of the control conditions. The AC is positive when the sign bit in $AC(15) = 0$; it is negative when $AC(15) = 1$. The content of AC is zero ($AC = 0$) if all the flip-flops of the register are zero. The HLT instruction clears a start–stop flip-flop S and stops the sequence counter from counting. To restore the operation of the computer, the start–stop flip-flop must be set manually.

TABLE 5-3 Execution of Register-Reference Instructions

$D_7I'T_3 = r$ (common to all register-reference instructions)
$IR(i) = B_i$ [bit in $IR(0-11)$ that specifies the operation]

	r:	$SC \leftarrow 0$	Clear SC
CLA	rB_{11}:	$AC \leftarrow 0$	Clear AC
CLE	rB_{10}:	$E \leftarrow 0$	Clear E
CMA	rB_9:	$AC \leftarrow \overline{AC}$	Complement AC
CME	rB_8:	$E \leftarrow \overline{E}$	Complement E
CIR	rB_7:	$AC \leftarrow \text{shr } AC, AC(15) \leftarrow E, E \leftarrow AC(0)$	Circulate right
CIL	rB_6:	$AC \leftarrow \text{shl } AC, AC(0) \leftarrow E, E \leftarrow AC(15)$	Circulate left
INC	rB_5:	$AC \leftarrow AC + 1$	Increment AC
SPA	rB_4:	If $(AC(15) = 0)$ then $(PC \leftarrow PC + 1)$	Skip if positive
SNA	rB_3:	If $(AC(15) = 1)$ then $(PC \leftarrow PC + 1)$	Skip if negative
SZA	rB_2:	If $(AC = 0)$ then $PC \leftarrow PC + 1$	Skip if AC zero
SZE	rB_1:	If $(E = 0)$ then $(PC \leftarrow PC + 1)$	Skip if E zero
HLT	rB_0:	$S \leftarrow 0$ (S is a start–stop flip-flop)	Halt computer

5-6 Memory-Reference Instructions

In order to specify the microoperations needed for the execution of each instruction, it is necessary that the function that they are intended to perform be defined precisely. Looking back to Table 5-2, where the instructions are listed, we find that some instructions have an ambiguous description. This is because the explanation of an instruction in words is usually lengthy, and not enough space is available in the table for such a lengthy explanation. We will now show that the function of the memory-reference instructions can be defined precisely by means of register transfer notation.

effective address

Table 5-4 lists the seven memory-reference instructions. The decoded output D_i for $i = 0, 1, 2, 3, 4, 5,$ and 6 from the operation decoder that belongs to each instruction is included in the table. The effective address of the instruction is in the address register AR and was placed there during timing signal T_2 when $I = 0$, or during timing signal T_3 when $I = 1$. The execution of the memory-reference instructions starts with timing signal T_4. The symbolic description of each instruction is specified in the table in terms of register transfer notation. The actual execution of the instruction in the bus system will require a sequence of microoperations. This is because data stored in memory cannot be processed directly. The data must be read from memory to a register where they can be operated on with logic circuits. We now explain the operation of each instruction and list the control functions and microoperations needed for their execution. A flowchart that summarizes all the microoperations is presented at the end of this section.

TABLE 5-4 Memory-Reference Instructions

Symbol	Operation decoder	Symbolic description
AND	D_0	$AC \leftarrow AC \wedge M[AR]$
ADD	D_1	$AC \leftarrow AC + M[AR], \quad E \leftarrow C_{out}$
LDA	D_2	$AC \leftarrow M[AR]$
STA	D_3	$M[AR] \leftarrow AC$
BUN	D_4	$PC \leftarrow AR$
BSA	D_5	$M[AR] \leftarrow PC, \quad PC \leftarrow AR + 1$
ISZ	D_6	$M[AR] \leftarrow M[AR] + 1,$
		If $M[AR] + 1 = 0$ then $PC \leftarrow PC + 1$

AND to AC

This is an instruction that performs the AND logic operation on pairs of bits in AC and the memory word specified by the effective address. The result of the operation is transferred to AC. The microoperations that execute this instruction are:

$$D_0T_4: \quad DR \leftarrow M[AR]$$
$$D_0T_5: \quad AC \leftarrow AC \land DR, \quad SC \leftarrow 0$$

The control function for this instruction uses the operation decoder D_0 since this output of the decoder is active when the instruction has an AND operation whose binary code value is 000. Two timing signals are needed to execute the instruction. The clock transition associated with timing signal T_4 transfers the operand from memory into DR. The clock transition associated with the next timing signal T_5 transfers to AC the result of the AND logic operation between the contents of DR and AC. The same clock transition clears SC to 0, transferring control to timing signal T_0 to start a new instruction cycle.

ADD to AC

This instruction adds the content of the memory word specified by the effective address to the value of AC. The sum is transferred into AC and the output carry C_{out} is transferred to the E (extended accumulator) flip-flop. The microoperations needed to execute this instruction are

$$D_1T_4: \quad DR \leftarrow M[AR]$$
$$D_1T_5: \quad AC \leftarrow AC + DR, \quad E \leftarrow C_{out}, \quad SC \leftarrow 0$$

The same two timing signals, T_4 and T_5, are used again but with operation decoder D_1 instead of D_0, which was used for the AND instruction. After the instruction is fetched from memory and decoded, only one output of the operation decoder will be active, and that output determines the sequence of microoperations that the control follows during the execution of a memory-reference instruction.

LDA: Load to AC

This instruction transfers the memory word specified by the effective address to AC. The microoperations needed to execute this instruction are

$$D_2T_4: \quad DR \leftarrow M[AR]$$
$$D_2T_5: \quad AC \leftarrow DR, \quad SC \leftarrow 0$$

Looking back at the bus system shown in Fig. 5-4 we note that there is no direct path from the bus into AC. The adder and logic circuit receive information from DR which can be transferred into AC. Therefore, it is necessary to read the memory word into DR first and then transfer the content of DR into AC. The reason for not connecting the bus to the inputs of AC is the delay encountered in the adder and logic circuit. It is assumed that the time it takes to read from memory and transfer the word through the bus as well as the adder and logic circuit is more than the time of one clock cycle. By not connecting the bus to the inputs of AC we can maintain one clock cycle per microoperation.

STA: Store AC

This instruction stores the content of AC into the memory word specified by the effective address. Since the output of AC is applied to the bus and the data input of memory is connected to the bus, we can execute this instruction with one microoperation:

$$D_3T_4: \quad M[AR] \leftarrow AC, \quad SC \leftarrow 0$$

BUN: Branch Unconditionally

This instruction transfers the program to the instruction specified by the effective address. Remember that PC holds the address of the instruction to be read from memory in the next instruction cycle. PC is incremented at time T_1 to prepare it for the address of the next instruction in the program sequence. The BUN instruction allows the programmer to specify an instruction out of sequence and we say that the program branches (or jumps) unconditionally. The instruction is executed with one microoperation:

$$D_4T_4: \quad PC \leftarrow AR, \quad SC \leftarrow 0$$

The effective address from AR is transferred through the common bus to PC. Resetting SC to 0 transfers control to T_0. The next instruction is then fetched and executed from the memory address given by the new value in PC.

BSA: Branch and Save Return Address

This instruction is useful for branching to a portion of the program called a subroutine or procedure. When executed, the BSA instruction stores the address of the next instruction in sequence (which is available in PC) into a memory location specified by the effective address. The effective address plus one is then transferred to PC to serve as the address of the first instruction in the subroutine. This operation was specified in Table 5-4 with the following register transfer:

$$M[AR] \leftarrow PC, \quad PC \leftarrow AR + 1$$

A numerical example that demonstrates how this instruction is used with a subroutine is shown in Fig. 5-10. The BSA instruction is assumed to be in memory at address 20. The *I* bit is 0 and the address part of the instruction has the binary equivalent of 135. After the fetch and decode phases, *PC* contains 21, which is the address of the next instruction in the program (referred to as the *return address*). *AR* holds the effective address 135. This is shown in part (a) of the figure. The BSA instruction performs the following numerical operation:

return address

$$M[135] \leftarrow 21, \quad PC \leftarrow 135 + 1 = 136$$

The result of this operation is shown in part (b) of the figure. The return address 21 is stored in memory location 135 and control continues with the subroutine program starting from address 136. The return to the original program (at address 21) is accomplished by means of an indirect BUN instruction placed at the end of the subroutine. When this instruction is executed, control goes to the indirect phase to read the effective address at location 135, where it finds the previously saved address 21. When the BUN instruction is executed, the effective address 21 is transferred to *PC*. The next instruction cycle finds *PC* with the value 21, so control continues to execute the instruction at the return address.

subroutine call

The BSA instruction performs the function usually referred to as a subroutine call. The indirect BUN instruction at the end of the subroutine performs the function referred to as a subroutine return. In most commercial computers, the return address associated with a subroutine is stored in either a processor

Figure 5-10 Example of BSA instruction execution.

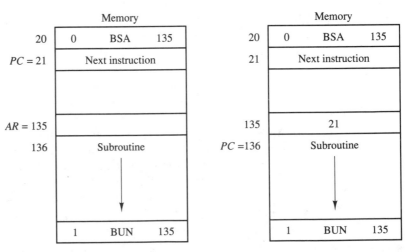

(a) Memory, *PC*, and *AR* at time T_4 (b) Memory and *PC* after execution

register or in a portion of memory called a stack. This is discussed in more detail in Sec. 8-7.

It is not possible to perform the operation of the BSA instruction in one clock cycle when we use the bus system of the basic computer. To use the memory and the bus properly, the BSA instruction must be executed with a sequence of two microoperations:

$$D_5T_4: \quad M[AR] \leftarrow PC, \quad AR \leftarrow AR + 1$$
$$D_5T_5: \quad PC \leftarrow AR, \quad SC \leftarrow 0$$

Timing signal T_4 initiates a memory write operation, places the content of PC onto the bus, and enables the INR input of AR. The memory write operation is completed and AR is incremented by the time the next clock transition occurs. The bus is used at T_5 to transfer the content of AR to PC.

ISZ: Increment and Skip if Zero

This instruction increments the word specified by the effective address, and if the incremented value is equal to 0, PC is incremented by 1. The programmer usually stores a negative number (in 2's complement) in the memory word. As this negative number is repeatedly incremented by one, it eventually reaches the value of zero. At that time PC is incremented by one in order to skip the next instruction in the program.

Since it is not possible to increment a word inside the memory, it is necessary to read the word into DR, increment DR, and store the word back into memory. This is done with the following sequence of microoperations:

$$D_6T_4: \quad DR \leftarrow M[AR]$$
$$D_6T_5: \quad DR \leftarrow DR + 1$$
$$D_6T_6: \quad M[AR] \leftarrow DR, \quad \text{if } (DR = 0) \text{ then } (PC \leftarrow PC + 1), \quad SC \leftarrow 0$$

Control Flowchart

A flowchart showing all microoperations for the execution of the seven memory-reference instructions is shown in Fig. 5-11. The control functions are indicated on top of each box. The microoperations that are performed during time T_4, T_5, or T_6 depend on the operation code value. This is indicated in the flowchart by six different paths, one of which the control takes after the instruction is decoded. The sequence counter SC is cleared to 0 with the last timing signal in each case. This causes a transfer of control to timing signal T_0 to start the next instruction cycle.

Note that we need only seven timing signals to execute the longest instruction (ISZ). The computer can be designed with a 3-bit sequence counter. The reason for using a 4-bit counter for SC is to provide additional timing signals for other instructions that are presented in the problems section.

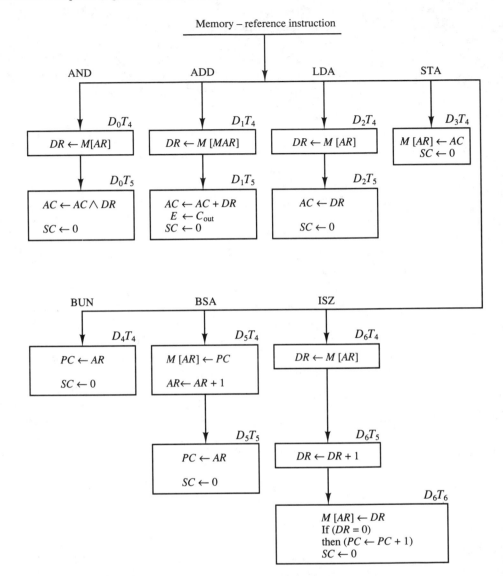

Figure 5-11 Flowchart for memory-reference instructions.

5-7 Input–Output and Interrupt

A computer can serve no useful purpose unless it communicates with the external environment. Instructions and data stored in memory must come from some input device. Computational results must be transmitted to the user through some output device. Commercial computers include many types of input and output devices. To demonstrate the most basic requirements for input and output communication, we will use as an illustration a terminal unit with a keyboard and printer. Input–output organization is dicsussed further in Chap. 11.

Input–Output Configuration

The terminal sends and receives serial information. Each quantity of information has eight bits of an alphanumeric code. The serial information from the keyboard is shifted into the input register INPR. The serial information for the printer is stored in the output register OUTR. These two registers communicate with a communication interface serially and with the AC in parallel. The input–output configuration is shown in Fig. 5-12. The transmitter interface receives serial information from the keyboard and transmits it to INPR. The receiver interface receives information from OUTR and sends it to the printer serially. The operation of the serial communication interface is explained in Sec. 11-3.

input register

The input register INPR consists of eight bits and holds an alphanumeric input information. The 1-bit input flag FGI is a control flip-flop. The flag bit is

Figure 5-12   Input-output configuration.

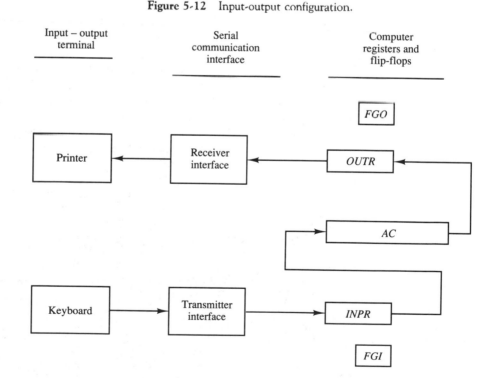

set to 1 when new information is available in the input device and is cleared to 0 when the information is accepted by the computer. The flag is needed to synchronize the timing rate difference between the input device and the computer. The process of information transfer is as follows. Initially, the input flag *FGI* is cleared to 0. When a key is struck in the keyboard, an 8-bit alphanumeric code is shifted into *INPR* and the input flag *FGI* is set to 1. As long as the flag is set, the information in *INPR* cannot be changed by striking another key. The computer checks the flag bit; if it is 1, the information from *INPR* is transferred in parallel into *AC* and *FGI* is cleared to 0. Once the flag is cleared, new information can be shifted into *INPR* by striking another key.

output register
The output register *OUTR* works similarly but the direction of information flow is reversed. Initially, the output flag *FGO* is set to 1. The computer checks the flag bit; if it is 1, the information from *AC* is transferred in parallel to *OUTR* and *FGO* is cleared to 0. The output device accepts the coded information, prints the corresponding character, and when the operation is completed, it sets *FGO* to 1. The computer does not load a new character into *OUTR* when *FGO* is 0 because this condition indicates that the output device is in the process of printing the character.

Input–Output Instructions

Input and output instructions are needed for transferring information to and from *AC* register, for checking the flag bits, and for controlling the interrupt facility. Input–output instructions have an operation code 1111 and are recognized by the control when $D_7 = 1$ and $I = 1$. The remaining bits of the instruction specify the particular operation. The control functions and microoperations for the input–output instructions are listed in Table 5-5. These instructions are executed with the clock transition associated with timing signal T_3. Each control function needs a Boolean relation D_7IT_3, which we designate for convenience by the symbol p. The control function is distinguished by one of the bits in $IR(6–11)$. By assigning the symbol B_i to bit i of IR, all control functions

TABLE 5-5 Input-Output Instructions

$D_7IT_3 = p$ (common to all input–output instructions)
$IR(i) = B_i$ [bit in $IR(6–11)$ that specifies the instruction]

	p:	$SC \leftarrow 0$	Clear SC
INP	pB_{11}:	$AC(0–7) \leftarrow INPR, \quad FGI \leftarrow 0$	Input character
OUT	pB_{10}:	$OUTR \leftarrow AC(0–7), \quad FGO \leftarrow 0$	Output character
SKI	pB_9:	If $(FGI = 1)$ then $(PC \leftarrow PC + 1)$	Skip on input flag
SKO	pB_8:	If $(FGO = 1)$ then $(PC \leftarrow PC + 1)$	Skip on output flag
ION	pB_7:	$IEN \leftarrow 1$	Interrupt enable on
IOF	pB_6:	$IEN \leftarrow 0$	Interrupt enable off

can be denoted by pB_i for i = 6 though 11. The sequence counter SC is cleared to 0 when $p = D_7IT_3 = 1$.

The INP instruction transfers the input information from $INPR$ into the eight low-order bits of AC and also clears the input flag to 0. The OUT instruction transfers the eight least significant bits of AC into the output register $OUTR$ and clears the output flag to 0. The next two instructions in Table 5-5 check the status of the flags and cause a skip of the next instruction if the flag is 1. The instruction that is skipped will normally be a branch instruction to return and check the flag again. The branch instruction is not skipped if the flag is 0. If the flag is 1, the branch instruction is skipped and an input or output instruction is executed. (Examples of input and output programs are given in Sec. 6-8.) The last two instructions set and clear an interrupt enable flip-flop IEN. The purpose of IEN is explained in conjunction with the interrupt operation.

Program Interrupt

The process of communication just described is referred to as programmed control transfer. The computer keeps checking the flag bit, and when it finds it set, it initiates an information transfer. The difference of information flow rate between the computer and that of the input–output device makes this type of transfer inefficient. To see why this is inefficient, consider a computer that can go through an instruction cycle in 1 μs. Assume that the input–output device can transfer information at a maximum rate of 10 characters per second. This is equivalent to one character every 100,000 μs. Two instructions are executed when the computer checks the flag bit and decides not to transfer the information. This means that at the maximum rate, the computer will check the flag 50,000 times between each transfer. The computer is wasting time while checking the flag instead of doing some other useful processing task.

An alternative to the programmed controlled procedure is to let the external device inform the computer when it is ready for the transfer. In the meantime the computer can be busy with other tasks. This type of transfer uses the interrupt facility. While the computer is running a program, it does not check the flags. However, when a flag is set, the computer is momentarily interrupted from proceeding with the current program and is informed of the fact that a flag has been set. The computer deviates momentarily from what it is doing to take care of the input or output transfer. It then returns to the current program to continue what it was doing before the interrupt.

The interrupt enable flip-flop IEN can be set and cleared with two instructions. When IEN is cleared to 0 (with the IOF instruction), the flags cannot interrupt the computer. When IEN is set to 1 (with the ION instruction), the computer can be interrupted. These two instructions provide the programmer with the capability of making a decision as to whether or not to use the interrupt facility.

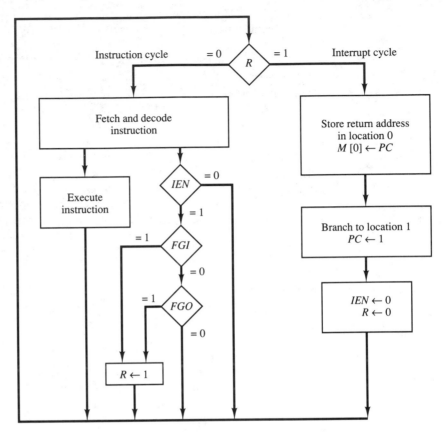

Figure 5-13   Flowchart for interrupt cycle.

The way that the interrupt is handled by the computer can be explained by means of the flowchart of Fig. 5-13. An interrupt flip-flop R is included in the computer. When $R = 0$, the computer goes through an instruction cycle. During the execute phase of the instruction cycle *IEN* is checked by the control. If it is 0, it indicates that the programmer does not want to use the interrupt, so control continues with the next instruction cycle. If *IEN* is 1, control checks the flag bits. If both flags are 0, it indicates that neither the input nor the output registers are ready for transfer of information. In this case, control continues with the next instruction cycle. If either flag is set to 1 while *IEN* = 1, flip-flop R is set to 1. At the end of the execute phase, control checks the value of R, and if it is equal to 1, it goes to an interrupt cycle instead of an instruction cycle.

interrupt cycle

The interrupt cycle is a hardware implementation of a branch and save return address operation. The return address available in *PC* is stored in a specific location where it can be found later when the program returns to the instruction at which it was interrupted. This location may be a processor register, a memory stack, or a specific memory location. Here we choose the memory location at address 0 as the place for storing the return address. Control then inserts address 1 into *PC* and clears *IEN* and *R* so that no more interruptions can occur until the interrupt request from the flag has been serviced.

An example that shows what happens during the interrupt cycle is shown in Fig. 5-14. Suppose that an interrupt occurs and *R* is set to 1 while the control is executing the instruction at address 255. At this time, the return address 256 is in *PC*. The programmer has previously placed an input–output service program in memory starting from address 1120 and a BUN 1120 instruction at address 1. This is shown in Fig. 5-14(a).

When control reaches timing signal T_0 and finds that $R = 1$, it proceeds with the interrupt cycle. The content of *PC* (256) is stored in memory location 0, *PC* is set to 1, and *R* is cleared to 0. At the beginning of the next instruction cycle, the instruction that is read from memory is in address 1 since this is the content of *PC*. The branch instruction at address 1 causes the program to transfer to the input–output service program at address 1120. This program checks the flags, determines which flag is set, and then transfers the required input or output information. Once this is done, the instruction ION is executed to set *IEN* to 1 (to enable further interrupts), and the program returns to the location where it was interrupted. This is shown in Fig. 5-14(b).

The instruction that returns the computer to the original place in the main program is a branch indirect instruction with an address part of 0. This instruction is placed at the end of the I/O service program. After this instruction is

Figure 5-14 Demonstration of the interrupt cycle.

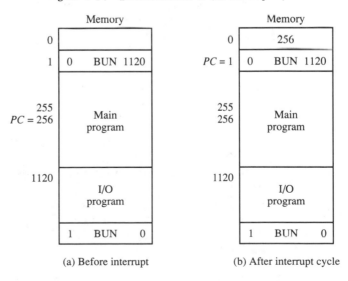

(a) Before interrupt   (b) After interrupt cycle

read from memory during the fetch phase, control goes to the indirect phase (because $I = 1$) to read the effective address. The effective address is in location 0 and is the return address that was stored there during the previous interrupt cycle. The execution of the indirect BUN instruction results in placing into PC the return address from location 0.

Interrupt Cycle

We are now ready to list the register transfer statements for the interrupt cycle. The interrupt cycle is initiated after the last execute phase if the interrupt flip-flop R is equal to 1. This flip-flop is set to 1 if $IEN = 1$ and either FGI or FGO are equal to 1. This can happen with any clock transition except when timing signals T_0, T_1, or T_2 are active. The condition for setting flip-flop R to 1 can be expressed with the following register transfer statement:

$$T_0'T_1'T_2'(IEN)(FGI + FGO): \quad R \leftarrow 1$$

The symbol $+$ between FGI and FGO in the control function designates a logic OR operation. This is ANDed with IEN and $T_0'T_1'T_2'$.

modified fetch phase   We now modify the fetch and decode phases of the instruction cycle. Instead of using only timing signals T_0, T_1, and T_2 (as shown in Fig. 5-9) we will AND the three timing signals with R' so that the fetch and decode phases will be recognized from the three control functions $R'T_0$, $R'T_1$, and $R'T_2$. The reason for this is that after the instruction is executed and SC is cleared to 0, the control will go through a fetch phase only if $R = 0$. Otherwise, if $R = 1$, the control will go through an interrupt cycle. The interrupt cycle stores the return address (available in PC) into memory location 0, branches to memory location 1, and clears IEN, R, and SC to 0. This can be done with the following sequence of microoperations:

$$
\begin{aligned}
RT_0: &\quad AR \leftarrow 0, \quad TR \leftarrow PC \\
RT_1: &\quad M[AR] \leftarrow TR, \quad PC \leftarrow 0 \\
RT_2: &\quad PC \leftarrow PC + 1, \quad IEN \leftarrow 0, \quad R \leftarrow 0, \quad SC \leftarrow 0
\end{aligned}
$$

During the first timing signal AR is cleared to 0, and the content of PC is transferred to the temporary register TR. With the second timing signal, the return address is stored in memory at location 0 and PC is cleared to 0. The third timing signal increments PC to 1, clears IEN and R, and control goes back to T_0 by clearing SC to 0. The beginning of the next instruction cycle has the condition $R'T_0$ and the content of PC is equal to 1. The control then goes through an instruction cycle that fetches and executes the BUN instruction in location 1.

5-8 Complete Computer Description

The final flowchart of the instruction cycle, including the interrupt cycle for the basic computer, is shown in Fig. 5-15. The interrupt flip-flop R may be set at any time during the indirect or execute phases. Control returns to timing signal T_0 after SC is cleared to 0. If $R = 1$, the computer goes through an interrupt cycle. If $R = 0$, the computer goes through an instruction cycle. If the instruction is one of the memory-reference instructions, the computer first checks if there is an indirect address and then continues to execute the decoded instruction according to the flowchart of Fig. 5-11. If the instruction is one of the register-reference instructions, it is executed with one of the microoperations listed in Table 5-3. If it is an input–output instruction, it is executed with one of the microoperations listed in Table 5-5.

Instead of using a flowchart, we can describe the operation of the computer with a list of register transfer statements. This is done by accumulating all the control functions and microoperations in one table. The entries in the table are taken from Figs. 5-11 and 5-15, and Tables 5-3 and 5-5.

The control functions and microoperations for the entire computer are summarized in Table 5-6. The register transfer statements in this table describe in a concise form the internal organization of the basic computer. They also give all the information necessary for the design of the logic circuits of the computer. The control functions and conditional control statements listed in the table formulate the Boolean functions for the gates in the control unit. The list of microoperations specifies the type of control inputs needed for the registers and memory. A register transfer language is useful not only for describing the internal organization of a digital system but also for specifying the logic circuits needed for its design.

5-9 Design of Basic Computer

The basic computer consists of the following hardware components:

1. A memory unit with 4096 words of 16 bits each
2. Nine registers: AR, PC, DR, AC, IR, TR, $OUTR$, $INPR$, and SC
3. Seven flip-flops: I, S, E, R, IEN, FGI, and FGO
4. Two decoders: a 3×8 operation decoder and a 4×16 timing decoder
5. A 16-bit common bus
6. Control logic gates
7. Adder and logic circuit connected to the input of AC

The memory unit is a standard component that can be obtained readily from a commercial source. The registers are of the type shown in Fig. 2-11 and

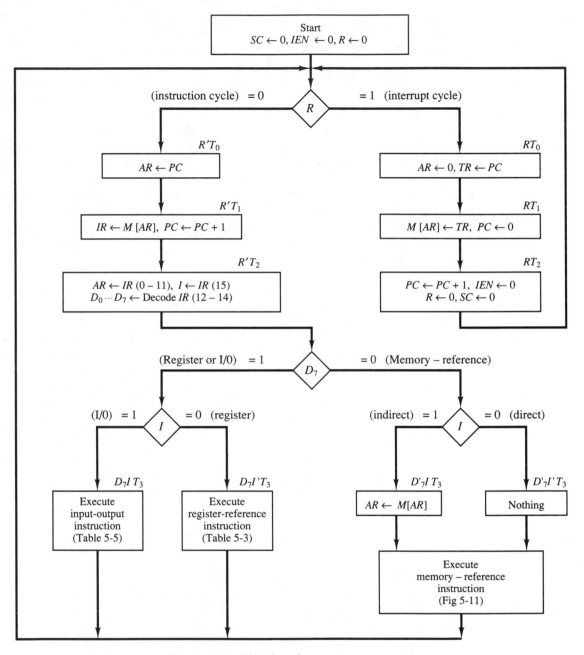

Figure 5-15 Flowchart for computer operation.

TABLE 5-6 Control Functions and Microoperations for the Basic Computer

Fetch	$R'T_0$:	$AR \leftarrow PC$
	$R'T_1$:	$IR \leftarrow M[AR], \quad PC \leftarrow PC + 1$
Decode	$R'T_2$:	$D_0, \ldots, D_7 \leftarrow$ Decode $IR(12-14)$,
		$AR \leftarrow IR(0-11), \quad I \leftarrow IR(15)$
Indirect	$D_7'IT_3$:	$AR \leftarrow M[AR]$
Interrupt:		
$T_0'T_1'T_2'(IEN)(FGI + FGO)$:		$R \leftarrow 1$
	RT_0:	$AR \leftarrow 0, \quad TR \leftarrow PC$
	RT_1:	$M[AR] \leftarrow TR, \quad PC \leftarrow 0$
	RT_2:	$PC \leftarrow PC + 1, \quad IEN \leftarrow 0, \quad R \leftarrow 0, \quad SC \leftarrow 0$
Memory-reference:		
AND	D_0T_4:	$DR \leftarrow M[AR]$
	D_0T_5:	$AC \leftarrow AC \wedge DR, \quad SC \leftarrow 0$
ADD	D_1T_4:	$DR \leftarrow M[AR]$
	D_1T_5:	$AC \leftarrow AC + DR, \quad E \leftarrow C_{out}, \quad SC \leftarrow 0$
LDA	D_2T_4:	$DR \leftarrow M[AR]$
	D_2T_5:	$AC \leftarrow DR, \quad SC \leftarrow 0$
STA	D_3T_4:	$M[AR] \leftarrow AC, \quad SC \leftarrow 0$
BUN	D_4T_4:	$PC \leftarrow AR, \quad SC \leftarrow 0$
BSA	D_5T_4:	$M[AR] \leftarrow PC, \quad AR \leftarrow AR + 1$
	D_5T_5:	$PC \leftarrow AR, \quad SC \leftarrow 0$
ISZ	D_6T_4:	$DR \leftarrow M[AR]$
	D_6T_5:	$DR \leftarrow DR + 1$
	D_6T_6:	$M[AR] \leftarrow DR, \quad$ if $(DR = 0)$ then $(PC \leftarrow PC + 1), \quad SC \leftarrow 0$
Register-reference:		
	$D_7I'T_3 = r$ (common to all register-reference instructions)	
	$IR(i) = B_i \ (i = 0, 1, 2, \ldots, 11)$	
	r:	$SC \leftarrow 0$
CLA	rB_{11}:	$AC \leftarrow 0$
CLE	rB_{10}:	$E \leftarrow 0$
CMA	rB_9:	$AC \leftarrow \overline{AC}$
CME	rB_8:	$E \leftarrow \overline{E}$
CIR	rB_7:	$AC \leftarrow$ shr $AC, \quad AC(15) \leftarrow E, \quad E \leftarrow AC(0)$
CIL	rB_6:	$AC \leftarrow$ shl $AC, \quad AC(0) \leftarrow E, \quad E \leftarrow AC(15)$
INC	rB_5:	$AC \leftarrow AC + 1$
SPA	rB_4:	If $(AC(15) = 0)$ then $(PC \leftarrow PC + 1)$
SNA	rB_3:	If $(AC(15) = 1)$ then $(PC \leftarrow PC + 1)$
SZA	rB_2:	If $(AC = 0)$ then $PC \leftarrow PC + 1$
SZE	rB_1:	If $(E = 0)$ then $(PC \leftarrow PC + 1)$
HLT	rB_0:	$S \leftarrow 0$
Input-output:		
	$D_7IT_3 = p$ (common to all input-output instructions)	
	$IR(i) = B_i \ (i = 6, 7, 8, 9, 10, 11)$	
	p:	$SC \leftarrow 0$
INP	pB_{11}:	$AC(0-7) \leftarrow INPR, \quad FGI \leftarrow 0$
OUT	pB_{10}:	$OUTR \leftarrow AC(0-7), \quad FGO \leftarrow 0$
SKI	pB_9:	If $(FGI = 1)$ then $(PC \leftarrow PC + 1)$
SKO	pB_8:	If $(FGO = 1)$ then $(PC \leftarrow PC + 1)$
ION	pB_7:	$IEN \leftarrow 1$
IOF	pB_6:	$IEN \leftarrow 0$

are similar to integrated circuit type 74163. The flip-flops can be either of the *D* or *JK* type, as described in Sec. 1-6. The two decoders are standard components similar to the ones presented in Sec. 2-2. The common bus system can be constructed with sixteen 8×1 multiplexers in a configuration similar to the one shown in Fig. 4-3. We are now going to show how to design the control logic gates. The next section deals with the design of the adder and logic circuit associated with *AC*.

Control Logic Gates

control unit   The block diagram of the control logic gates is shown in Fig. 5-6. The inputs to this circuit come from the two decoders, the *I* flip-flop, and bits 0 through 11 of *IR*. The other inputs to the control logic are: *AC* bits 0 through 15 to check if $AC = 0$ and to detect the sign bit in $AC(15)$; *DR* bits 0 through 15 to check if $DR = 0$; and the values of the seven flip-flops.

The outputs of the control logic circuit are:

1. Signals to control the inputs of the nine registers
2. Signals to control the read and write inputs of memory
3. Signals to set, clear, or complement the flip-flops
4. Signals for S_2, S_1, and S_0 to select a register for the bus
5. Signals to control the *AC* adder and logic circuit

The specifications for the various control signals can be obtained directly from the list of register transfer statements in Table 5-6.

Control of Registers and Memory

The registers of the computer connected to a common bus system are shown in Fig. 5-4. The control inputs of the registers are LD (load), INR (increment), and CLR (clear). Suppose that we want to derive the gate structure associated with the control inputs of *AR*. We scan Table 5-6 to find all the statements that change the content of *AR*:

$$R'T_0: \quad AR \leftarrow PC$$
$$R'T_2: \quad AR \leftarrow IR(0\text{--}11)$$
$$D_7'IT_3: \quad AR \leftarrow M[AR]$$
$$RT_0: \quad AR \leftarrow 0$$
$$D_5T_4: \quad AR \leftarrow AR + 1$$

The first three statements specify transfer of information from a register or memory to *AR*. The content of the source register or memory is placed on the bus and the content of the bus is transferred into AR by enabling its LD control input. The fourth statement clears AR to 0. The last statement increments AR by 1. The control functions can be combined into three Boolean expressions as follows:

$$LD(AR) = R'T_0 + R'T_2 + D_7'IT_3$$
$$CLR(AR) = RT_0$$
$$INR(AR) = D_5T_4$$

where $LD(AR)$ is the load input of AR, $CLR(AR)$ is the clear input of AR, and $INR(AR)$ is the increment input of AR. The control gate logic associated with AR is shown in Fig. 5-16.

In a similar fashion we can derive the control gates for the other registers as well as the logic needed to control the read and write inputs of memory. The logic gates associated with the read input of memory is derived by scanning Table 5-6 to find the statements that specify a read operation. The read operation is recognized from the symbol $\leftarrow M[AR]$.

$$Read = R'T_1 + D_7'IT_3 + (D_0 + D_1 + D_2 + D_6)T_4$$

The output of the logic gates that implement the Boolean expression above must be connected to the read input of memory.

Figure 5-16 Control gates associated with AR.

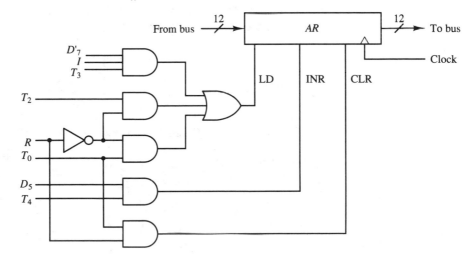

Control of Single Flip-flops

The control gates for the seven flip-flops can be determined in a similar manner. For example, Table 5-6 shows that *IEN* may change as a result of the two instructions ION and IOF.

$$pB_7: \quad IEN \leftarrow 1$$
$$pB_6: \quad IEN \leftarrow 0$$

where $p = D_7 IT_3$ and B_7 and B_6 are bits 7 and 6 of *IR*, respectively. Moreover, at the end of the interrupt cycle *IEN* is cleared to 0.

$$RT_2: \quad IEN \leftarrow 0$$

If we use a *JK* flip-flip for *IEN*, the control gate logic will be as shown in Fig. 5-17.

Control of Common Bus

The 16-bit common bus shown in Fig. 5-4 is controlled by the selection inputs S_2, S_1, and S_0. The decimal number shown with each bus input specifies the equivalent binary number that must be applied to the selection inputs in order to select the corresponding register. Table 5-7 specifies the binary numbers for $S_2 S_1 S_0$ that select each register. Each binary number is associated with a Boolean variable x_1 through x_7, corresponding to the gate structure that must be active in order to select the register or memory for the bus. For example, when $x_1 = 1$, the value of $S_2 S_1 S_0$ must be 001 and the output of *AR* will be selected for the bus. Table 5-7 is recognized as the truth table of a binary encoder. The placement of the encoder at the inputs of the bus selection logic is shown in Fig. 5-18. The Boolean functions for the encoder are

$$S_0 = x_1 + x_3 + x_5 + x_7$$
$$S_1 = x_2 + x_3 + x_6 + x_7$$
$$S_2 = x_4 + x_5 + x_6 + x_7$$

Figure 5-17   Control inputs for *IEN*.

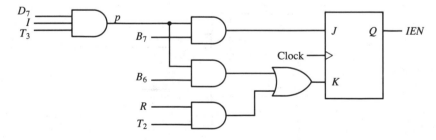

TABLE 5-7 Encoder for Bus Selection Circuit

		Inputs						Outputs		Register selected
x_1	x_2	x_3	x_4	x_5	x_6	x_7	S_2	S_1	S_0	for bus
0	0	0	0	0	0	0	0	0	0	None
1	0	0	0	0	0	0	0	0	1	AR
0	1	0	0	0	0	0	0	1	0	PC
0	0	1	0	0	0	0	0	1	1	DR
0	0	0	1	0	0	0	1	0	0	AC
0	0	0	0	1	0	0	1	0	1	IR
0	0	0	0	0	1	0	1	1	0	TR
0	0	0	0	0	0	1	1	1	1	Memory

To determine the logic for each encoder input, it is necessary to find the control functions that place the corresponding register onto the bus. For example, to find the logic that makes $x_1 - 1$, we scan all register transfer statements in Table 5-6 and extract those statements that have AR as a source.

$$D_4T_4: \quad PC \leftarrow AR$$
$$D_5T_5: \quad PC \leftarrow AR$$

Therefore, the Boolean function for x_1 is

$$x_1 = D_4T_4 + D_5T_5$$

The data output from memory are selected for the bus when $x_7 = 1$ and $S_2S_1S_0 = 111$. The gate logic that generates x_7 must also be applied to the read input of memory. Therefore, the Boolean function for x_7 is the same as the one derived previously for the read operation.

$$x_7 = R'T_1 + D_7'IT_3 + (D_0 + D_1 + D_2 + D_6)T_4$$

In a similar manner we can determine the gate logic for the other registers.

Figure 5-18   Encoder for bus selection inputs.

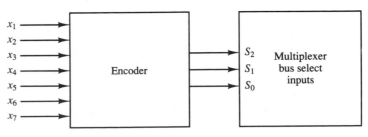

5-10 Design of Accumulator Logic

The circuits associated with the AC register are shown in Fig. 5-19. The adder and logic circuit has three sets of inputs. One set of 16 inputs comes from the outputs of AC. Another set of 16 inputs comes from the data register DR. A third set of eight inputs comes from the input register $INPR$. The outputs of the adder and logic circuit provide the data inputs for the register. In addition, it is necessary to include logic gates for controlling the LD, INR, and CLR in the register and for controlling the operation of the adder and logic circuit.

In order to design the logic associated with AC, it is necessary to go over the register transfer statements in Table 5-6 and extract all the statements that change the content of AC.

D_0T_5:	$AC \leftarrow AC \wedge DR$	AND with DR
D_1T_5:	$AC \leftarrow AC + DR$	Add with DR
D_2T_5:	$AC \leftarrow DR$	Transfer from DR
pB_{11}:	$AC(0\text{--}7) \leftarrow INPR$	Transfer from $INPR$
rB_9:	$AC \leftarrow \overline{AC}$	Complement
rB_7:	$AC \leftarrow \text{shr } AC, \quad AC(15) \leftarrow E$	Shift right
rB_6:	$AC \leftarrow \text{shl } AC, \quad AC(0) \leftarrow E$	Shift left
rB_{11}:	$AC \leftarrow 0$	Clear
rB_5:	$AC \leftarrow AC + 1$	Increment

From this list we can derive the control logic gates and the adder and logic circuit.

Figure 5-19 Circuits associated with AC.

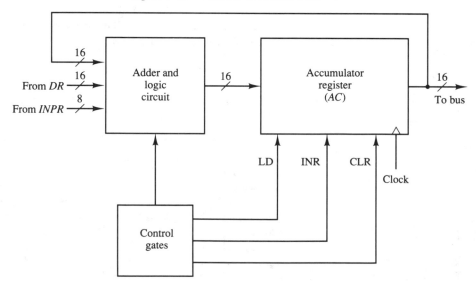

Control of *AC* Register

The gate structure that controls the LD, INR, and CLR inputs of *AC* is shown in Fig. 5-20. The gate configuration is derived from the control functions in the list above. The control function for the clear microoperation is rB_{11}, where $r = D_7I'T_3$ and $B_{11} = IR(11)$. The output of the AND gate that generates this control function is connected to the CLR input of the register. Similarly, the output of the gate that implements the increment microoperation is connected to the INR input of the register. The other seven microoperations are generated in the adder and logic circuit and are loaded into *AC* at the proper time. The outputs of the gates for each control function is marked with a symbolic name. These outputs are used in the design of the adder and logic circuit.

Figure 5-20   Gate structure for controlling the LD, INR, and CLR of AC.

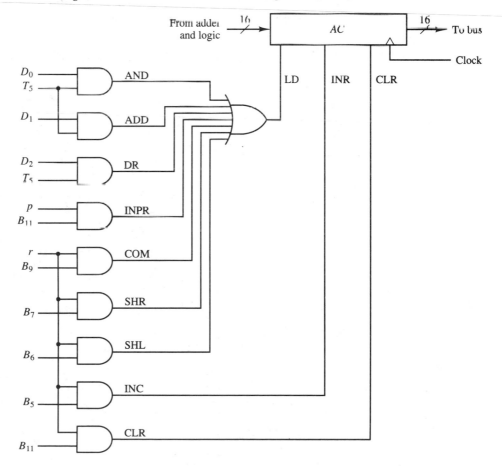

Adder and Logic Circuit

The adder and logic circuit can be subdivided into 16 stages, with each stage corresponding to one bit of AC. The internal construction of the register is as shown in Fig. 2-11. Looking back at that figure we note that each stage has a JK flip-flop, two OR gates, and two AND gates. The load (LD) input is connected to the inputs of the AND gates. Figure 5-21 shows one such AC register stage (with the OR gates removed). The input is labeled I_i and the output $AC(i)$. When the LD input is enabled, the 16 inputs I_i for $i = 0, 1, 2, \ldots, 15$ are transferred to AC (0–15).

adder and logic circuit

One stage of the adder and logic circuit consists of seven AND gates, one OR gate and a full-adder (FA), as shown in Fig. 5-21. The inputs of the gates with symbolic names come from the outputs of gates marked with the same symbolic name in Fig. 5-20. For example, the input marked ADD in Fig. 5-21 is connected to the output marked ADD in Fig. 5-20.

The AND operation is achieved by ANDing $AC(i)$ with the corresponding bit in the data register $DR(i)$. The ADD operation is obtained using a binary adder similar to the one shown in Fig. 4-6. One stage of the adder uses a

Figure 5-21   One stage of adder and logic circuit.

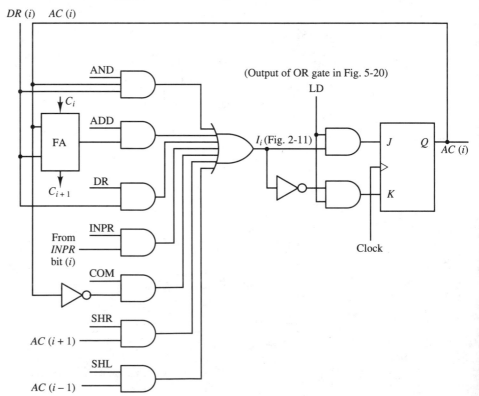

full-adder with the corresponding input and output carries. The transfer from *INPR* to *AC* is only for bits 0 through 7. The complement microoperation is obtained by inverting the bit value in *AC*. The shift-right operation transfers the bit from $AC(i + 1)$, and the shift-left operation transfers the bit from $AC(i - 1)$. The complete adder and logic circuit consists of 16 stages connected together.

═══════════════╡ PROBLEMS ╞═══════════════

5-1. A computer uses a memory unit with 256K words of 32 bits each. A binary instruction code is stored in one word of memory. The instruction has four parts: an indirect bit, an operation code, a register code part to specify one of 64 registers, and an address part.

 a. How many bits are there in the operation code, the register code part, and the address part?

 b. Draw the instruction word format and indicate the number of bits in each part.

 c. How many bits are there in the data and address inputs of the memory?

5-2. What is the difference between a direct and an indirect address instruction? How many references to memory are needed for each type of instruction to bring an operand into a processor register?

5-3. The following control inputs are active in the bus system shown in Fig. 5-4. For each case, specify the register transfer that will be executed during the next clock transition.

	S_2	S_1	S_0	LD of register	Memory	Adder
a.	1	1	1	IR	Read	—
b.	1	1	0	PC	—	—
c.	1	0	0	DR	Write	—
d.	0	0	0	AC	—	Add

5-4. The following register transfers are to be executed in the system of Fig. 5-4. For each transfer, specify: (1) the binary value that must be applied to bus select inputs S_2, S_1, and S_0; (2) the register whose LD control input must be active (if any); (3) a memory read or write operation (if needed); and (4) the operation in the adder and logic circuit (if any).

 a. $AR \leftarrow PC$
 b. $IR \leftarrow M[AR]$
 c. $M[AR] \leftarrow TR$
 d. $AC \leftarrow DR, DR \leftarrow AC$ (done simultaneously)

5-5. Explain why each of the following microoperations cannot be executed during a single clock pulse in the system shown in Fig. 5-4. Specify a sequence of microoperations that will perform the operation.

a. $IR \leftarrow M[PC]$

b. $AC \leftarrow AC + TR$

c. $DR \leftarrow DR + AC$ (AC does not change)

5-6.   Consider the instruction formats of the basic computer shown in Fig. 5-5 and the list of instructions given in Table 5-2. For each of the following 16-bit instructions, give the equivalent four-digit hexadecimal code and explain in your own words what it is that the instruction is going to perform.

a. 0001 0000 0010 0100

b. 1011 0001 0010 0100

c. 0111 0000 0010 0000

5-7.   What are the two instructions needed in the basic computer in order to set the E flip-flop to 1?

5-8.   Draw a timing diagram similar to Fig. 5-7 assuming that SC is cleared to 0 at time T_3 if control signal C_7 is active.

$$C_7T_3: \quad SC \leftarrow 0$$

C_7 is activated with the positive clock transition associated with T_1.

5-9.   The content of AC in the basic computer is hexadecimal A937 and the initial value of E is 1. Determine the contents of AC, E, PC, AR, and IR in hexadecimal after the execution of the CLA instruction. Repeat 11 more times, starting from each one of the register-reference instructions. The initial value of PC is hexadecimal 021.

5-10.   An instruction at address 021 in the basic computer has $I = 0$, an operation code of the AND instruction, and an address part equal to 083 (all numbers are in hexadecimal). The memory word at address 083 contains the operand B8F2 and the content of AC is A937. Go over the instruction cycle and determine the contents of the following registers at the end of the execute phase: PC, AR, DR, AC, and IR. Repeat the problem six more times starting with an operation code of another memory-reference instruction.

5-11.   Show the contents in hexadecimal of registers PC, AR, DR, IR, and SC of the basic computer when an ISZ indirect instruction is fetched from memory and executed. The initial content of PC is 7FF. The content of memory at address 7FF is EA9F. The content of memory at address A9F is 0C35. The content of memory at address C35 is FFFF. Give the answer in a table with five columns, one for each register and a row for each timing signal. Show the contents of the registers after the positive transition of each clock pulse.

5-12.   The content of PC in the basic computer is 3AF (all numbers are in hexadecimal). The content of AC is 7EC3. The content of memory at address 3AF is 932E. The content of memory at address 32E is 09AC. The content of memory at address 9AC is 8B9F.

a. What is the instruction that will be fetched and executed next?

b. Show the binary operation that will be performed in the AC when the instruction is executed.

c. Give the contents of registers PC, AR, DR, AC, and IR in hexadecimal and the values of E, I, and the sequence counter SC in binary at the end of the instruction cycle.

5-13. Assume that the first six memory-reference instructions in the basic computer listed in Table 5-4 are to be changed to the instructions specified in the following table. EA is the effective address that resides in AR during time T_4. Assume that the adder and logic circuit in Fig. 5-4 can perform the exclusive-OR operation $AC \leftarrow AC \oplus DR$. Assume further that the adder and logic circuit cannot perform subtraction directly. The subtraction must be done using the 2's complement of the subtrahend by complementing and incrementing AC. Give the sequence of register transfer statements needed to execute each of the listed instructions starting from timing T_4. Note that the value in AC should not change unless the instruction specifies a change in its content. You can use TR to store the content of AC temporary or you can exchange DR and AC.

Symbol	Opcode	Symbolic designation	Description in words
XOR	000	$AC \leftarrow AC \oplus M[EA]$	Exclusive-OR to AC
ADM	001	$M[EA] \leftarrow M[EA] + AC$	Add AC to memory
SUB	010	$AC \leftarrow AC - M[EA]$	Subtract memory from AC
XCH	011	$AC \leftarrow M[EA], \quad M[EA] \leftarrow AC$	Exchange AC and memory
SEQ	100	If $(M[EA] = AC)$ then $(PC \leftarrow PC + 1)$	Skip on equal
BPA	101	If $(AC > 0)$ then $(PC \leftarrow EA)$	Branch if AC positive and non-zero

5-14. Make the following changes to the basic computer.
1. Add a register to the bus system CTR (count register) to be selected with $S_2S_1S_0 = 000$.
2. Replace the ISZ instruction with an instruction that loads a number into CTR.

LDC Address $CTR \leftarrow M[Address]$

3. Add a register reference instruction ICSZ: Increment CTR and skip next instruction if zero. Discuss the advantage of this change.

5-15. The memory unit of the basic computer shown in Fig. 5-3 is to be changed to a 65,536 × 16 memory, requiring an address of 16 bits. The instruction format of a memory-reference instruction shown in Fig. 5-5(a) remains the same for $I = 1$ (indirect address) with the address part of the instruction residing in positions 0 through 11. But when $I = 0$ (direct address), the address of the instruction is given by the 16 bits in the next word following the instruction. Modify the microoperations during time T_2, T_3, (and T_4 if necessary) to conform with this configuration.

5-16. A computer uses a memory of 65,536 words with eight bits in each word. It has the following registers: PC, AR, TR (16 bits each), and AC, DR, IR (eight bits each). A memory-reference instruction consists of three words: an 8-bit operation-code (one word) and a 16-bit address (in the next two words). All operands are eight bits. There is no indirect bit.

    a. Draw a block diagram of the computer showing the memory and registers as in Fig. 5-3. (Do not use a common bus).

    b. Draw a diagram showing the placement in memory of a typical three-word instruction and the corresponding 8-bit operand.

    c. List the sequence of microoperations for fetching a memory reference instruction and then placing the operand in DR. Start from timing signal T_0.

5-17. A digital computer has a memory unit with a capacity of 16,384 words, 40 bits per word. The instruction code format consists of six bits for the operation part and 14 bits for the address part (no indirect mode bit). Two instructions are packed in one memory word, and a 40-bit instruction register IR is available in the control unit. Formulate a procedure for fetching and executing instructions for this computer.

5-18. An output program resides in memory starting from address 2300. It is executed after the computer recognizes an interrupt when FGO becomes a 1 (while $IEN = 1$).

    a. What instruction must be placed at address 1?

    b. What must be the last two instructions of the output program?

5-19. The register transfer statements for a register R and the memory in a computer are as follows (the X's are control functions that occur at random):

$$X_3' X_1: \quad R \leftarrow M[AR] \qquad \text{Read memory word into } R$$
$$X_1' X_2: \quad R \leftarrow AC \qquad\quad \text{Transfer } AC \text{ to } R$$
$$X_1' X_3: \quad M[AR] \leftarrow R \qquad \text{Write } R \text{ to memory}$$

The memory has data inputs, data outputs, address inputs, and control inputs to read and write as in Fig. 2-12. Draw the hardware implementation of R and the memory in block diagram form. Show how the control functions X_1 through X_3 select the load control input of R, the select inputs of multiplexers that you include in the diagram, and the read and write inputs of the memory.

5-20. The operations to be performed with a flip-flop F (not used in the basic computer) are specified by the following register transfer statements:

$$xT_3: \quad F \leftarrow 1 \qquad \text{Set } F \text{ to } 1$$
$$yT_1: \quad F \leftarrow 0 \qquad \text{Clear } F \text{ to } 0$$
$$zT_2: \quad F \leftarrow \bar{F} \qquad \text{Complement } F$$
$$wT_5: \quad F \leftarrow G \qquad \text{Transfer value of } G \text{ to } F$$

Otherwise, the content of F must not change. Draw the logic diagram showing the connections of the gates that form the control functions and the inputs of flip-flop F. Use a JK flip-flop and minimize the number of gates.

5-21. Derive the control gates associated with the program counter *PC* in the basic computer.

5-22. Derive the control gates for the write input of the memory in the basic computer.

5-23. Show the complete logic of the interrupt flip-flops *R* in the basic computer. Use a *JK* flip-flop and minimize the number of gates.

5-24. Derive the Boolean logic expression for x_2 (see Table 5-7). Show that x_2 can be generated with one AND gate and one OR gate.

5-25. Derive the Boolean expression for the gate structure that clears the sequence counter *SC* to 0. Draw the logic diagram of the gates and show how the output is connected to the INR and CLR inputs of *SC* (see Fig. 5-6). Minimize the number of gates.

REFERENCES

1. Bell, C. G., J. C. Mudge, and J. E. McNamara, Computer Engineering. Bedford, MA: Digital Press, 1980.

2. Booth, T. L., *Introduction to Computer Engineering*, 3rd ed. New York: John Wiley, 1984.

3. Gibson, G. A., *Computer Systems Concepts and Design*. Englewood Cliffs, NJ: Prentice Hall, 1991.

4. Gray, N. A. B., *Introduction to Computer Systems*. Englewood Cliffs, NJ: Prentice Hall, 1987.

5. Hill, F. J., and G. R. Peterson, *Digital Systems: Hardware Organization and Design*, 3rd ed. New York: John Wiley, 1987.

6. Lewin, M. H. *Logic Design and Computer Organization*. Reading, MA: Addison-Wesley, 1983.

7. Mano, M. M., *Computer Engineering: Hardware Design*. Englewood Cliffs, NJ: Prentice Hall, 1988.

8. Patterson, D. A. and J. L. Hennessy, *Computer Architecture: A Quantitative Approach*. San Mateo, CA: Morgan Kaufmann Publishers, 1990.

9. Prosser, F. P., and D. E. Winkel, *The Art of Digital Design*, 2nd ed. Englewood Cliffs, NJ: Prentice Hall, 1987.

10. Shiva, S. G., *Computer Design and Architecture*, 2nd ed. New York: HarperCollins Publishers, 1991.

CHAPTER SIX

Programming
the Basic Computer

IN THIS CHAPTER

6-1   Introduction

A total computer system includes both *hardware* and *software*. Hardware consists of the physical components and all associated equipment. Software refers to the programs that are written for the computer. It is possible to be familiar with various aspects of computer software without being concerned with details of how the computer hardware operates. It is also possible to design parts of the hardware without a knowledge of its software capabilities. However, those concerned with computer architecture should have a knowledge of both hardware and software because the two branches influence each other.

Writing a program for a computer consists of specifying, directly or indirectly, a sequence of machine instructions. Machine instructions inside the computer form a binary pattern which is difficult, if not impossible, for people to work with and understand. It is preferable to write programs with the more familiar symbols of the alphanumeric character set. As a consequence, there is a need for translating user-oriented symbolic programs into binary programs recognized by the hardware.

A program written by a user may be either dependent or independent of the physical computer that runs his program. For example, a program written in standard Fortran is machine independent because most computers provide a translator program that converts the standard Fortran program to the binary code of the computer available in the particular installation. But the translator program itself is machine dependent because it must translate the Fortran program to the binary code recognized by the hardware of the particular computer used.

This chapter introduces some elementary programming concepts and shows their relation to the hardware representation of instructions. The first part presents the basic operation and structure of a program that translates a user's symbolic program into an equivalent binary program. The discussion emphasizes the important concepts of the translator rather than the details of actually producing the program itself. The usefulness of various machine instructions is then demonstrated by means of several basic programming examples.

instruction set

The instruction set of the basic computer, whose hardware organization was explored in Chap. 5, is used in this chapter to illustrate many of the techniques commonly used to program a computer. In this way it is possible to explore the relationship between a program and the hardware operations that execute the instructions.

The 25 instructions of the basic computer are repeated in Table 6-1 to provide an easy reference for the programming examples that follow. Each instruction is assigned a three-letter symbol to facilitate writing symbolic programs. The first seven instructions are memory-reference instructions and the other 18 are register-reference and input–output instructions. A memory-reference instruction has three parts: a mode bit, an operation code of three bits, and a 12-bit address. The first hexadecimal digit of a memory-reference instruction includes the mode bit and the operation code. The other three digits specify the address. In an indirect address instruction the mode bit is 1 and the first hexadecimal digit ranges in value from 8 to E. In a direct mode, the range is from 0 to 6. The other 18 instructions have a 16-bit operation code. The code for each instruction is listed as a four-digit hexadecimal number. The first digit of a register-reference instruction is always 7. The first digit of an input–output instruction is always F. The symbol m used in the description column denotes the effective address. The letter M refers to the memory word (operand) found at the effective address.

6-2 Machine Language

A program is a list of instructions or statements for directing the computer to perform a required data-processing task. There are various types of programming languages that one may *write* for a computer, but the computer can *execute* programs only when they are represented internally in binary form. Programs

TABLE 6-1 Computer Instructions

Symbol	Hexadecimal code	Description
AND	0 or 8	AND M to AC
ADD	1 or 9	Add M to AC, carry to E
LDA	2 or A	Load AC from M
STA	3 or B	Store AC in M
BUN	4 or C	Branch unconditionally to m
BSA	5 or D	Save return address in m and branch to $m + 1$
ISZ	6 or E	Increment M and skip if zero
CLA	7800	Clear AC
CLE	7400	Clear E
CMA	7200	Complement AC
CME	7100	Complement E
CIR	7080	Circulate right E and AC
CIL	7040	Circulate left E and AC
INC	7020	Increment AC
SPA	7010	Skip if AC is positive
SNA	7008	Skip if AC is negative
SZA	7004	Skip if AC is zero
SZE	7002	Skip if E is zero
HLT	7001	Halt computer
INP	F800	Input information and clear flag
OUT	F400	Output information and clear flag
SKI	F200	Skip if input flag is on
SKO	F100	Skip if output flag is on
ION	F080	Turn interrupt on
IOF	F040	Turn interrupt off

written in any other language must be translated to the binary representation of instructions before they can be executed by the computer. Programs written for a computer may be in one of the following categories:

1. *Binary code*. This is a sequence of instructions and operands in binary that list the exact representation of instructions as they appear in computer memory.

2. *Octal or hexadecimal code*. This is an equivalent translation of the binary code to octal or hexadecimal representation.

3. *Symbolic code*. The user employs symbols (letters, numerals, or special characters) for the operation part, the address part, and other parts of the instruction code. Each symbolic instruction can be translated into one binary coded instruction. This translation is done by a special program called an *assembler*. Because an assembler translates the sym-

assembly language

bols, this type of symbolic program is referred to as an *assembly language* program.

4. *High-level programming languages*. These are special languages developed to reflect the procedures used in the solution of a problem rather than be concerned with the computer hardware behavior. An example of a high-level programming language is *Fortran*. It employs problem-oriented symbols and formats. The program is written in a sequence of statements in a form that people prefer to think in when solving a problem. However, each statement must be translated into a sequence of binary instructions before the program can be executed in a computer. The program that translates a high-level language program to binary is called a *compiler*.

machine language

Strictly speaking, a *machine language* program is a binary program of category 1. Because of the simple equivalency between binary and octal or hexadecimal representation, it is customary to refer to category 2 as machine language. Because of the one-to-one relationship between a symbolic instruction and its binary equivalent, an assembly language is considered to be a machine-level language.

We now use the basic computer to illustrate the relation between binary and assembly languages. Consider the binary program listed in Table 6-2. The first column gives the memory location (in binary) of each instruction or operand. The second column lists the binary content of these memory locations. (The *location* is the address of the memory word where the instruction is stored. It is important to differentiate it from the address part of the instruction itself.) The program can be stored in the indicated portion of memory, and then executed by the computer starting from address 0. The hardware of the computer will execute these instructions and perform the intended task. However, a person looking at this program will have a difficult time understanding what is to be achieved when this program is executed. Nevertheless, the computer hardware recognizes *only* this type of instruction code.

TABLE 6-2 Binary Program to Add Two Numbers

Location	Instruction code
0	0010 0000 0000 0100
1	0001 0000 0000 0101
10	0011 0000 0000 0110
11	0111 0000 0000 0001
100	0000 0000 0101 0011
101	1111 1111 1110 1001
110	0000 0000 0000 0000

TABLE 6-3 Hexadecimal Program to Add Two Numbers

Location	Instruction
000	2004
001	1005
002	3006
003	7001
004	0053
005	FFE9
006	0000

Writing 16 bits for each instruction is tedious because there are too many digits. We can reduce the number of digits per instruction if we write the octal equivalent of the binary code. This will require six digits per instruction. On the other hand, we can reduce each instruction to four digits if we write the *hexadecimal code* equivalent hexadecimal code as shown in Table 6-3. The hexadecimal representation is convenient to use; however, one must realize that each hexadecimal digit must be converted to its equivalent 4-bit number when the program is entered into the computer. The advantage of writing binary programs in equivalent octal or hexadecimal form should be evident from this example.

The program in Table 6-4 uses the symbolic names of instructions (listed in Table 6-1) instead of their binary or hexadecimal equivalent. The address parts of memory-reference instructions, as well as operands, remain in their hexadecimal value. Note that location 005 has a negative operand because the sign bit in the leftmost position is 1. The inclusion of a column for comments provides some means for explaining the function of each instruction. Symbolic programs are easier to handle, and as a consequence, it is preferable to write programs with symbols. These symbols can be converted to their binary code equivalent to produce the binary program.

We can go one step further and replace each hexadecimal address by a

TABLE 6-4 Program with Symbolic Operation Codes

Location	Instruction	Comments
000	LDA 004	Load first operand into *AC*
001	ADD 005	Add second operand to *AC*
002	STA 006	Store sum in location 006
003	HLT	Halt computer
004	0053	First operand
005	FFE9	Second operand (negative)
006	0000	Store sum here

TABLE 6-5 Assembly Language Program to Add Two Numbers

	ORG 0	/Origin of program is location 0
	LDA A	/Load operand from location A
	ADD B	/Add operand from location B
	STA C	/Store sum in location C
	HLT	/Halt computer
A,	DEC 83	/Decimal operand
B,	DEC −23	/Decimal operand
C,	DEC 0	/Sum stored in location C
	END	/End of symbolic program

symbolic address and each hexadecimal operand by a decimal operand. This is convenient because one usually does not know exactly the numeric memory location of operands while writing a program. If the operands are placed in memory following the instructions, and if the length of the program is not known in advance, the numerical location of operands is not known until the end of the program is reached. In addition, decimal numbers are more familiar than their hexadecimal equivalents.

The program in Table 6-5 is the assembly-language program for adding two numbers. The symbol ORG followed by a number is not a machine instruction. Its purpose is to specify an *origin*, that is, the memory location of the next instruction below it. The next three lines have symbolic addresses. Their value is specified by their being present as a label in the first column. Decimal operands are specified following the symbol DEC. The numbers may be positive or negative, but if negative, they must be converted to binary in the signed-2's complement representation. The last line has the symbol END indicating the end of the program. The symbols ORG, DEC, and END, called *pseudoinstructions*, are defined in the next section. Note that all comments are preceded by a slash.

The equivalent Fortran program for adding two integer numbers is listed in Table 6-6. The two values for A and B may be specified by an input statement or by a data statement. The arithmetic operation for the two numbers is specified by one simple statement. The translation of this Fortran program into a binary program consists of assigning three memory locations, one each for the augend, addend, and sum, and then deriving the sequence of binary

TABLE 6-6 Fortran Program to Add Two Numbers

```
INTEGER A, B, C
DATA A,83  B,−23
C = A + B
END
```

instructions that form the sum. Thus a compiler program translates the symbols of the Fortran program into the binary values listed in the program of Table 6-2.

6-3 Assembly Language

A programming language is defined by a set of rules. Users must conform with all format rules of the language if they want their programs to be translated correctly. Almost every commercial computer has its own particular assembly language. The rules for writing assembly language programs are documented and published in manuals which are usually available from the computer manufacturer.

The basic unit of an assembly language program is a line of code. The specific language is defined by a set of rules that specify the symbols that can be used and how they may be combined to form a line of code. We will now formulate the rules of an assembly language for writing symbolic programs for the basic computer.

Rules of the Language

Each line of an assembly language program is arranged in three columns called fields. The fields specify the following information.

1. The *label* field may be empty or it may specify a symbolic address.
2. The *instruction* field specifies a machine instruction or a pseudoinstruction.
3. The *comment* field may be empty or it may include a comment.

symbolic address A symbolic address consists of one, two, or three, but not more than three alphanumeric characters. The first character must be a letter; the next two may be letters or numerals. The symbol can be chosen arbitrarily by the programmer. A symbolic address in the label field is terminated by a comma so that it will be recognized as a label by the assembler.

The instruction field in an assembly language program may specify one of the following items:

1. A memory-reference instruction (MRI)
2. A register-reference or input–output instruction (non-MRI)
3. A pseudoinstruction with or without an operand

A memory-reference instruction occupies two or three symbols separated by spaces. The first must be a three-letter symbol defining an MRI operation code from Table 6-1. The second is a symbolic address. The third symbol, which may or may not be present, is the letter I. If I is missing, the line denotes a direct address instruction. The presence of the symbol I denotes an indirect address instruction.

A non-MRI is defined as an instruction that does not have an address part. A non-MRI is recognized in the instruction field of a program by any one of the three-letter symbols listed in Table 6-1 for the register-reference and input–output instructions.

The following is an illustration of the symbols that may be placed in the instruction field of a program.

```
CLA             non—MRI
ADD OPR         direct address MRI
ADD PTR I       indirect address MRI
```

The first three-letter symbol in each line must be one of the instruction symbols of the computer and must be listed in Table 6-1. A memory-reference instruction, such as ADD, must be followed by a symbolic address. The letter I may or may not be present.

A symbolic address in the instruction field specifies the memory location of an operand. This location must be defined somewhere in the program by appearing again as a label in the first column. To be able to translate an assembly language program to a binary program, it is absolutely necessary that each symbolic address that is mentioned in the instruction field *must* occur again in the label field.

pseudoinstruction   A pseudoinstruction is not a machine instruction but rather an instruction to the assembler giving information about some phase of the translation. Four pseudoinstructions that are recognized by the assembler are listed in Table 6-7. (Other assembly language programs recognize many more pseudoinstructions.) The ORG (origin) pseudoinstruction informs the assembler that the instruction or operand in the following line is to be placed in a memory location specified by the number next to ORG. It is possible to use ORG more than once in a program to specify more than one segment of memory. The END symbol

TABLE 6-7 Definition of Pseudoinstructions

Symbol	Information for the Assembler
ORG N	Hexadecimal number N is the memory location for the instruction or operand listed in the following line
END	Denotes the end of symbolic program
DEC N	Signed decimal number N to be converted to binary
HEX N	Hexadecimal number N to be converted to binary

is placed at the end of the program to inform the assembler that the program is terminated. The other two pseudoinstructions specify the radix of the operand and tell the assembler how to convert the listed number to a binary number.

The third field in a program is reserved for comments. A line of code may or may not have a comment, but if it has, it must be preceded by a slash for the assembler to recognize the beginning of a comment field. Comments are useful for explaining the program and are helpful in understanding the step-by-step procedure taken by the program. Comments are inserted for explanation purposes only and are neglected during the binary translation process.

An Example

The program of Table 6-8 is an example of an assembly language program. The first line has the pseudoinstruction ORG to define the origin of the program at memory location $(100)_{16}$. The next six lines define machine instructions, and the last four have pseudoinstructions. Three symbolic addresses have been used and each is listed in column 1 as a label and in column 2 as an address of a memory-reference instruction. Three of the pseudoinstructions specify operands, and the last one signifies the END of the program.

When the program is translated into binary code and executed by the computer it will perform a subtraction between two numbers. The subtraction is performed by adding the minuend to the 2's complement of the subtrahend. The subtrahend is a negative number. It is converted into a binary number in signed-2's complement representation because we dictate that all negative numbers be in their 2's complement form. When the 2's complement of the subtrahend is taken (by complementing and incrementing the AC), -23 converts to $+23$ and the difference is $83 + (2's$ complement of $-23) = 83 + 23 = 106$.

TABLE 6-8 Assembly Language Program to Subtract Two Numbers

	ORG 100	/Origin of program is location 100
	LDA SUB	/Load subtrahend to AC
	CMA	/Complement AC
	INC	/Increment AC
	ADD MIN	/Add minuend to AC
	STA DIF	/Store difference
	HLT	/Halt computer
MIN,	DEC 83	/Minuend
SUB,	DEC -23	/Subtrahend
DIF,	HEX 0	/Difference stored here
	END	/End of symbolic program

Translation to Binary

The translation of the symbolic program into binary is done by a special program called an *assembler*. The tasks performed by the assembler will be better understood if we first perform the translation on paper. The translation of the symbolic program of Table 6-8 into an equivalent binary code may be done by scanning the program and replacing the symbols by their machine code binary equivalent. Starting from the first line, we encounter an ORG pseudoinstruction. This tells us to start the binary program from hexadecimal location 100. The second line has two symbols. It must be a memory-reference instruction to be placed in location 100. Since the letter I is missing, the first bit of the instruction code must be 0. The symbolic name of the operation is LDA. Checking Table 6-1 we find that the first hexadecimal digit of the instruction should be 2. The binary value of the address part must be obtained from the address symbol SUB. We scan the label column and find this symbol in line 9. To determine its hexadecimal value we note that line 2 contains an instruction for location 100 and every other line specifies a machine instruction or an operand for sequential memory locations. Counting lines, we find that label SUB in line 9 corresponds to memory location 107. So the hexadecimal address of the instruction LDA must be 107. When the two parts of the instruction are assembled, we obtain the hexadecimal code 2107. The other lines representing machine instructions are translated in a similar fashion and their hexadecimal code is listed in Table 6-9.

Two lines in the symbolic program specify decimal operands with the pseudoinstruction DEC. A third specifies a zero by means of a HEX pseudoinstruction (DEC could be used as well). Decimal 83 is converted to binary and placed in location 106 in its hexadecimal equivalent. Decimal −23 is a negative number and must be converted into binary in signed-2's complement form.

TABLE 6-9 Listing of Translated Program of Table 6-8

Hexadecimal code		Symbolic program	
Location	Content		
			ORG 100
100	2107		LDA SUB
101	7200		CMA
102	7020		INC
103	1106		ADD MIN
104	3108		STA DIF
105	7001		HLT
106	0053	MIN,	DEC 83
107	FFE9	SUB,	DEC −23
108	0000	DIF,	HEX 0
			END

The hexadecimal equivalent of the binary number is placed in location 107. The END symbol signals the end of the symbolic program telling us that there are no more lines to translate.

address symbol table

The translation process can be simplified if we scan the entire symbolic program twice. No translation is done during the first scan. We merely assign a memory location to each machine instruction and operand. The location assignment will define the address value of labels and facilitate the translation process during the second scan. Thus in Table 6-9, we assign location 100 to the first instruction after ORG. We then assign sequential locations for each line of code that has a machine instruction or operand up to the end of the program. (ORG and END are not assigned a numerical location because they do not represent an instruction or an operand.) When the first scan is completed, we associate with each label its location number and form a table that defines the hexadecimal value of each symbolic address. For this program, the address symbol table is as follows:

Address symbol	Hexadecimal address
MIN	106
SUB	107
DIF	108

During the second scan of the symbolic program we refer to the address symbol table to determine the address value of a memory-reference instruction. For example, the line of code LDA SUB is translated during the second scan by getting the hexadecimal value of LDA from Table 6-1 and the hexadecimal value of SUB from the address-symbol table listed above. We then assemble the two parts into a four-digit hexadecimal instruction. The hexadecimal code can be easily converted to binary if we wish to know exactly how this program resides in computer memory.

When the translation from symbols to binary is done by an assembler program, the first scan is called the *first pass*, and the second is called the *second pass*.

6-4 The Assembler

An assembler is a program that accepts a symbolic language program and produces its binary machine language equivalent. The input symbolic program is called the *source program* and the resulting binary program is called the *object program*. The assembler is a program that operates on character strings and produces an equivalent binary interpretation.

Representation of Symbolic Program in Memory

Prior to starting the assembly process, the symbolic program must be stored in memory. The user types the symbolic program on a terminal. A loader program is used to input the characters of the symbolic program into memory. Since the program consists of symbols, its representation in memory must use an alphanumeric character code. In the basic computer, each character is represented by an 8-bit code. The high-order bit is always 0 and the other seven bits are as specified by ASCII. The hexadecimal equivalent of the character set is listed in Table 6-10. Each character is assigned two hexadecimal digits which can be easily converted to their equivalent 8-bit code. The last entry in the table does not print a character but is associated with the physical movement of the cursor in the terminal. The code for CR is produced when the return key is depressed. This causes the "carriage" to return to its initial position to start typing a new line. The assembler recognizes a CR code as the end of a line of code.

line of code   A line of code is stored in consecutive memory locations with two characters in each location. Two characters can be stored in each word since a memory word has a capacity of 16 bits. A label symbol is terminated with a comma. Operation and address symbols are terminated with a space and the end of the line is recognized by the CR code. For example, the following line of code:

```
PL3,    LDA SUB I
```

TABLE 6-10 Hexadecimal Character Code

Character	Code	Character	Code	Character	Code
A	41	Q	51	6	36
B	42	R	52	7	37
C	43	S	53	8	38
D	44	T	54	9	39
E	45	U	55	space	20
F	46	V	56	(	28
G	47	W	57	)	29
H	48	X	58	*	2A
I	49	Y	59	+	2B
J	4A	Z	5A	,	2C
K	4B	0	30	−	2D
L	4C	1	31	.	2E
M	4D	2	32	/	2F
N	4E	3	33	=	3D
O	4F	4	34	CR	0D (carriage
P	50	5	35		return)

TABLE 6-11 Computer Representation of the Line of Code: PL3, LDA SUB I

Memory word	Symbol	Hexadecimal code	Binary representation
1	P L	50 4C	0101 0000 0100 1100
2	3 ,	33 2C	0011 0011 0010 1100
3	L D	4C 44	0100 1100 0100 0100
4	A	41 20	0100 0001 0010 0000
5	S U	53 55	0101 0011 0101 0101
6	B	42 20	0100 0010 0010 0000
7	I CR	49 0D	0100 1001 0000 1101

is stored in seven consecutive memory locations, as shown in Table 6-11. The label PL3 occupies two words and is terminated by the code for comma (2C). The instruction field in the line of code may have one or more symbols. Each symbol is terminated by the code for space (20) except for the last symbol, which is terminated by the code of carriage return (0D). If the line of code has a comment, the assembler recognizes it by the code for a slash (2F). The assembler neglects all characters in the comment field and keeps checking for a CR code. When this code is encountered, it replaces the space code after the last symbol in the line of code.

The input for the assembler program is the user's symbolic language program in ASCII. This input is scanned by the assembler twice to produce the equivalent binary program. The binary program constitutes the output generated by the assembler. We will now describe briefly the major tasks that must be performed by the assembler during the translation process.

First Pass

location counter (LC)

A two-pass assembler scans the entire symbolic program twice. During the first pass, it generates a table that correlates all user-defined address symbols with their binary equivalent value. The binary translation is done during the second pass. To keep track of the location of instructions, the assembler uses a memory word called a *location counter* (abbreviated LC). The content of LC stores the value of the memory location assigned to the instruction or operand presently being processed. The ORG pseudoinstruction initializes the location counter to the value of the first location. Since instructions are stored in sequential locations, the content of LC is incremented by 1 after processing each line of code. To avoid ambiguity in case ORG is missing, the assembler sets the location counter to 0 initially.

The tasks performed by the assembler during the first pass are described in the flowchart of Fig. 6-1. LC is initially set to 0. A line of symbolic code is analyzed to determine if it has a label (by the presence of a comma). If the line

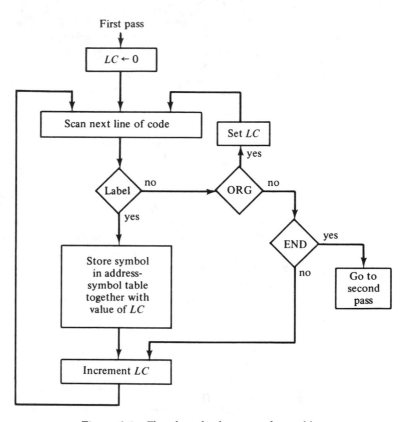

Figure 6-1 Flowchart for first pass of assembler.

of code has no label, the assembler checks the symbol in the instruction field. If it contains an ORG pseudoinstruction, the assembler sets LC to the number that follows ORG and goes back to process the next line. If the line has an END pseudoinstruction, the assembler terminates the first pass and goes to the second pass. (Note that a line with ORG or END should not have a label.) If the line of code contains a label, it is stored in the address symbol table together with its binary equivalent number specified by the content of LC. Nothing is stored in the table if no label is encountered. LC is then incremented by 1 and a new line of code is processed.

For the program of Table 6-8, the assembler generates the address symbol table listed in Table 6-12. Each label symbol is stored in two memory locations and is terminated by a comma. If the label contains less than three characters, the memory locations are filled with the code for space. The value found in LC while the line was processed is stored in the next sequential memory location. The program has three symbolic addresses: MIN, SUB, and DIF. These symbols represent 12-bit addresses equivalent to hexadecimal 106, 107, and 108,

TABLE 6-12 Address Symbol Table for Program in Table 6-8

Memory word	Symbol or (LC)*	Hexadecimal code	Binary representation
1	M I	4D 49	0100 1101 0100 1001
2	N ,	4E 2C	0100 1110 0010 1100
3	(LC)	01 06	0000 0001 0000 0110
4	S U	53 55	0101 0011 0101 0101
5	B ,	42 2C	0100 0010 0010 1100
6	(LC)	01 07	0000 0001 0000 0111
7	D I	44 49	0100 0100 0100 1001
8	F ,	46 2C	0100 0110 0010 1100
9	(LC)	01 08	0000 0001 0000 1000

* (LC) designates content of location counter.

respectively. The address symbol table occupies three words for each label symbol encountered and constitutes the output data that the assembler generates during the first pass.

Second Pass

table-lookup

Machine instructions are translated during the second pass by means of table-lookup procedures. A table-lookup procedure is a search of table entries to determine whether a specific item matches one of the items stored in the table. The assembler uses four tables. Any symbol that is encountered in the program must be available as an entry in one of these tables; otherwise, the symbol cannot be interpreted. We assign the following names to the four tables:

1. Pseudoinstruction table.
2. MRI table.
3. Non-MRI table.
4. Address symbol table.

The entries of the pseudoinstruction table are the four symbols ORG, END, DEC, and HEX. Each entry refers the assembler to a subroutine that processes the pseudoinstruction when encountered in the program. The MRI table contains the seven symbols of the memory-reference instructions and their 3-bit operation code equivalent. The non-MRI table contains the symbols for the 18 register-reference and input–output instructions and their 16-bit binary code equivalent. The address symbol table is generated during the first pass of the assembly process. The assembler searches these tables to find the symbol that it is currently processing in order to determine its binary value.

The tasks performed by the assembler during the second pass are described in the flowchart of Fig. 6-2. LC is initially set to 0. Lines of code are then analyzed one at a time. Labels are neglected during the second pass, so the assembler goes immediately to the instruction field and proceeds to check the first symbol encountered. It first checks the pseudoinstruction table. A match with ORG sends the assembler to a subroutine that sets LC to an initial value. A match with END terminates the translation process. An operand pseudoinstruction causes a conversion of the operand into binary. This operand is placed in the memory location specified by the content of LC. The location counter is then incremented by 1 and the assembler continues to analyze the next line of code.

If the symbol encountered is not a pseudoinstruction, the assembler refers to the MRI table. If the symbol is not found in this table, the assembler refers to the non-MRI table. A symbol found in the non-MRI table corresponds to a register reference or input–output instruction. The assembler stores the 16-bit instruction code into the memory word specified by LC. The location counter is incremented and a new line analyzed.

When a symbol is found in the MRI table, the assembler extracts its equivalent 3-bit code and inserts it in bits 2 through 4 of a word. A memory reference instruction is specified by two or three symbols. The second symbol is a symbolic address and the third, which may or may not be present, is the letter I. The symbolic address is converted to binary by searching the address symbol table. The first bit of the instruction is set to 0 or 1, depending on whether the letter I is absent or present. The three parts of the binary instruction code are assembled and then stored in the memory location specified by the content of LC. The location counter is incremented and the assembler continues to process the next line.

error diagnostics
One important task of an assembler is to check for possible errors in the symbolic program. This is called *error diagnostics*. One such error may be an invalid machine code symbol which is detected by its being absent in the MRI and non-MRI tables. The assembler cannot translate such a symbol because it does not know its binary equivalent value. In such a case, the assembler prints an error message to inform the programmer that his symbolic program has an error at a specific line of code. Another possible error may occur if the program has a symbolic address that did not appear also as a label. The assembler cannot translate the line of code properly because the binary equivalent of the symbol will not be found in the address symbol table generated during the first pass. Other errors may occur and a practical assembler should detect all such errors and print an error message for each.

It should be emphasized that a practical assembler is much more complicated than the one explained here. Most computers give the programmer more flexibility in writing assembly language programs. For example, the user may be allowed to use either a number or a symbol to specify an address. Many assemblers allow the user to specify an address by an arithmetic expression. Many more pseudoinstructions may be specified to facilitate the programming

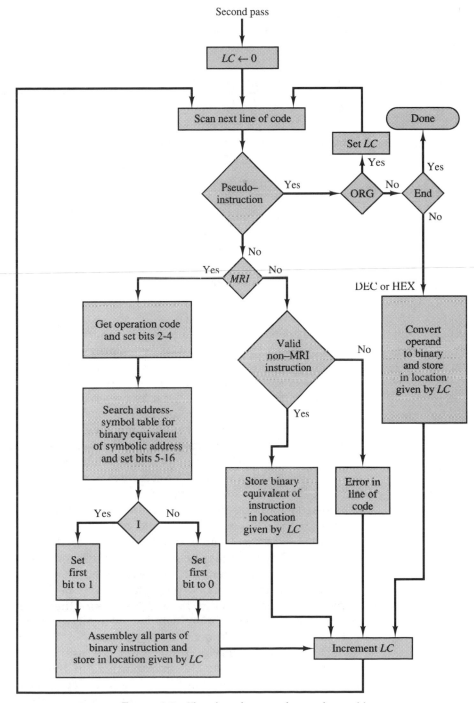

Figure 6-2 Flowchart for second pass of assembler.

task. As the assembly language becomes more sophisticated, the assembler becomes more complicated.

6-5   Program Loops

A program loop is a sequence of instructions that are executed many times, each time with a different set of data. Program loops are specified in Fortran by a DO statement. The following is an example of a Fortran program that forms the sum of 100 integer numbers.

```
      DIMENSION  A(100)
      INTEGER  SUM,  A
      SUM = 0
      DO  3  J = 1,  100
   3  SUM = SUM + A(J)
```

Statement number 3 is executed 100 times, each time with a different operand A(J) for $J = 1, 2, \ldots, 100$.

compiler

A system program that translates a program written in a high-level programming language such as the above to a machine language program is called a *compiler*. A compiler is a more complicated program than an assembler and requires knowledge of systems programming to fully understand its operation. Nevertheless, we can demonstrate the basic functions of a compiler by going through the process of translating the program above to an assembly language program. A compiler may use an assembly language as an intermediate step in the translation or may translate the program directly to binary.

The first statement in the Fortran program is a DIMENSION statement. This statement instructs the compiler to reserve 100 words of memory for 100 operands. The value of the operands is determined from an input statement (not listed in the program). The second statement informs the compiler that the numbers are integers. If they were of the *real* type, the compiler would have to reserve locations for floating-point numbers and generate instructions that perform the subsequent arithmetic with floating-point data. These two statements are nonexecutable and are similar to the pseudoinstructions in an assembly language. Suppose that the compiler reserves locations $(150)_{16}$ to $(1B3)_{16}$ for the 100 operands. These reserved memory words are listed in lines 19 to 118 in the translated program of Table 6-13. This is done by the ORG pseudoinstruction in line 18, which specifies the origin of the operands. The first and last operands are listed with a specific decimal number, although these values are not known during compilation. The compiler just reserves the data space in memory and the values are inserted later when an input data statement is executed. The line numbers in the symbolic program are for reference only and are not part of the translated symbolic program.

The indexing of the DO statement is translated into the instructions in

TABLE 6-13 Symbolic Program to Add 100 Numbers

Line			
1		ORG 100	/Origin of program is HEX 100
2		LDA ADS	/Load first address of operands
3		STA PTR	/Store in pointer
4		LDA NBR	/Load minus 100
5		STA CTR	/Store in counter
6		CLA	/Clear accumulator
7	LOP,	ADD PTR I	/Add an operand to AC
8		ISZ PTR	/Increment pointer
9		ISZ CTR	/Increment counter
10		BUN LOP	/Repeat loop again
11		STA SUM	/Store sum
12		HLT	/Halt
13	ADS,	HEX 150	/First address of operands
14	PTR,	HEX 0	/This location reserved for a pointer
15	NBR,	DEC 100	/Constant to initialized counter
16	CTR,	HEX 0	/This location reserved for a counter
17	SUM,	HEX 0	/Sum is stored here
18		ORG 150	/Origin of operands is HEX 150
19		DEC 75	/First operand
•			
•			
•			
118		DEC 23	/Last operand
119		END	/End of symbolic program

lines 2 through 5 and the constants in lines 13 through 16. The address of the first operand (150) is stored in location ADS in line 13. The number of times that Fortran statement number 3 must be executed is 100. So −100 is stored in location NBR. The compiler then generates the instructions in lines 2 through 5 to initialize the program loop. The address of the first operand is transferred to location PTR. This corresponds to setting A(J) to A(1). The number −100 is then transferred to location CTR. This location acts as a counter with its content incremented by one every time the program loop is executed. When the value of the counter reaches zero, the 100 operations will be completed and the program will exit from the loop.

Some compilers will translate the statement SUM = 0 into a machine instruction that initializes location SUM to zero. A reference to this location is then made every time Fortran statement number 3 is executed. A more intelligent compiler will realize that the sum can be formed in the accumulator and only the final result stored in location SUM. This compiler will produce an instruction in line 6 to clear the AC. It will also reserve a memory location symbolized by SUM (in line 17) for storing the value of this variable at the termination of the loop.

The program loop specified by the DO statement is translated to the sequence of instructions listed in lines 7 through 10. Line 7 specifies an indirect ADD instruction because it has the symbol I. The address of the current operand is stored in location PTR. When this location is addressed indirectly the computer takes the content of PTR to be the address of the operand. As a result, the operand in location 150 is added to the accumulator. Location PTR is then incremented with the ISZ instruction in line 8, so its value changes to the value of the address of the next sequential operand. Location CTR is incremented in line 9, and if it is not zero, the computer does not skip the next instruction. The next instruction is a branch (BUN) instruction to the beginning of the loop, so the computer returns to repeat the loop once again. When location CTR reaches zero (after the loop is executed 100 times), the next instruction is skipped and the computer executes the instructions in lines 11 and 12. The sum formed in the accumulator is stored in SUM and the computer halts. The halt instruction is inserted here for clarity; actually, the program will branch to a location where it will continue to execute the rest of the program or branch to the beginning of another program. Note that ISZ in line 8 is used merely to add 1 to the address pointer PTR. Since the address is a positive number, a skip will never occur.

pointer
counter

The program of Table 6-13 introduces the idea of a pointer and a counter which can be used, together with the indirect address operation, to form a program loop. The pointer points to the address of the current operand and the counter counts the number of times that the program loop is executed. In this example we use two memory locations for these functions. In computers with more than one processor register, it is possible to use one processor register as a pointer, another as a counter, and a third as an accumulator. When processor registers are used as pointers and counters they are called *index registers*. Index registers are discussed in Sec. 8-5.

6-6   Programming Arithmetic and Logic Operations

The number of instructions available in a computer may be a few hundred in a large system or a few dozen in a small one. Some computers perform a given operation with one machine instruction; others may require a large number of machine instructions to perform the same operation. As an illustration, consider the four basic arithmetic operations. Some computers have machine instructions to add, subtract, multiply, and divide. Others, such as the basic computer, have only one arithmetic instruction, such as ADD. Operations not included in the set of machine instructions must be implemented by a program.

We have shown in Table 6-8 a program for subtracting two numbers. Programs for the other arithmetic operations can be developed in a similar fashion.

Operations that are implemented in a computer with one machine instruction are said to be implemented by hardware. Operations implemented by a set of instructions that constitute a program are said to be implemented by software. Some computers provide an extensive set of hardware instructions designed to speed up common tasks. Others contain a smaller set of hardware instructions and depend more heavily on the software implementation of many operations. Hardware implementation is more costly because of the additional circuits needed to implement the operation. Software implementation results in long programs both in number of instructions and in execution time.

This section demonstrates the software implementation of a few arithmetic and logic operations. Programs can be developed for any arithmetic operation and not only for fixed-point binary data but for decimal and floating-point data as well. The hardware implementation of arithmetic operations is carried out in Chap. 10.

Multiplication Program

We now develop a program for multiplying two numbers. To simplify the program, we neglect the sign bit and assume positive numbers. We also assume that the two binary numbers have no more than eight significant bits so their product cannot exceed the word capacity of 16 bits. It is possible to modify the program to take care of the signs or use 16-bit numbers. However, the product may be up to 31 bits in length and will occupy two words of memory.

The program for multiplying two numbers is based on the procedure we use to multiply numbers with paper and pencil. As shown in the numerical example of Fig. 6-3, the multiplication process consists of checking the bits of the multiplier Y and adding the multiplicand X as many times as there are 1's in Y, provided that the value of X is shifted left from one line to the next. Since the computer can add only two numbers at a time, we reserve a memory location, denoted by P, to store intermediate sums. The intermediate sums are called partial products since they hold a partial product until all numbers are added. As shown in the numerical example under P, the partial product starts with zero. The multiplicand X is added to the content of P for each bit of the multiplier Y that is 1. The value of X is shifted left after checking each bit of the multiplier. The final value in P forms the product. The numerical example has numbers with four significant bits. When multiplied, the product contains eight significant bits. The computer can use numbers with eight significant bits to produce a product of up to 16 bits.

The flowchart of Fig. 6-3 shows the step-by-step procedure for program-

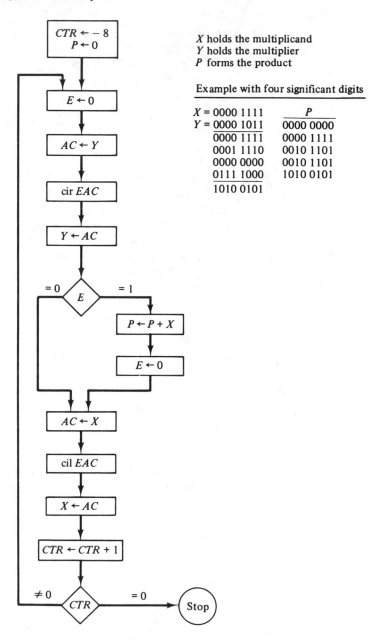

X holds the multiplicand
Y holds the multiplier
P forms the product

Example with four significant digits

X = 0000 1111	P
Y = 0000 1011	0000 0000
0000 1111	0000 1111
0001 1110	0010 1101
0000 0000	0010 1101
0111 1000	1010 0101
1010 0101	

Figure 6-3 Flowchart for multiplication program.

ming the multiplication operation. The program has a loop that is traversed eight times, once for each significant bit of the multiplier. Initially, location X holds the multiplicand and location Y holds the multiplier. A counter CTR is set to -8 and location P is cleared to zero.

The multiplier bit can be checked if it is transferred to the E register. This is done by clearing E, loading the value of Y into the AC, circulating right E and AC and storing the shifted number back into location Y. This bit stored in E is the low-order bit of the multiplier. We now check the value of E. If it is 1, the multiplicand X is added to the partial product P. If it is 0, the partial product does not change. We then shift the value of X once to the left by loading it into the AC and circulating left E and AC. The loop is repeated eight times by incrementing location CTR and checking when it reaches zero. When the counter reaches zero, the program exits from the loop with the product stored in location P.

The program in Table 6-14 lists the instructions for multiplying two unsigned numbers. The initialization is not listed but should be included when the program is loaded into the computer. The initialization consists of bringing the multiplicand and multiplier into locations X and Y, respectively; initializing the counter to -8; and initializing location P to zero. If these locations are not

TABLE 6-14 Program to Multiply Two Positive Numbers

	ORG 100	
LOP,	CLE	/Clear E
	LDA Y	/Load multiplier
	CIR	/Transfer multiplier bit to E
	STA Y	/Store shifted multiplier
	SZE	/Check if bit is zero
	BUN ONE	/Bit is one; go to ONE
	BUN ZRO	/Bit is zero; go to ZRO
ONE,	LDA X	/Load multiplicand
	ADD P	/Add to partial product
	STA P	/Store partial product
	CLE	/Clear E
ZRO,	LDA X	/Load multiplicand
	CIL	/Shift left
	STA X	/Store shifted multiplicand
	ISZ CTR	/Increment counter
	BUN LOP	/Counter not zero; repeat loop
	HLT	/Counter is zero; halt
CTR,	DEC -8	/This location serves as a counter
X,	HEX 000F	/Multiplicand stored here
Y,	HEX 000B	/Multiplier stored here
P,	HEX 0	/Product formed here
	END	

initialized, the program may run with incorrect data. The program itself is straightforward and follows the steps listed in the flowchart. The comments may help in following the step-by-step procedure.

This example has shown that if a computer does not have a machine instruction for a required operation, the operation can be programmed by a sequence of machine instructions. Thus we have demonstrated the software implementation of the multiplication operation. The corresponding hardware implementation is presented in Sec. 10-3.

Double-Precision Addition

When two 16-bit unsigned numbers are multiplied, the result is a 32-bit product that must be stored in two memory words. A number stored in two memory words is said to have double precision. When a partial product is computed, it is necessary that a double-precision number be added to the shifted multiplicand, which is also a double-precision number. For greater accuracy, the programmer may wish to employ double-precision numbers and perform arithmetic with operands that occupy two memory words. We now develop a program that adds two double-precision numbers.

One of the double-precision numbers is placed in two consecutive memory locations, AL and AH, with AL holding the 16 low-order bits. The other number is placed in BL and BH. The program is listed in Table 6-15. The two low-order portions are added and the carry transferred into E. The AC is cleared and the bit in E is circulated into the least significant position of the AC. The two high-order portions are then added to the carry and the double-precision sum is stored in CL and CH.

TABLE 6-15 Program to Add Two Double-Precision Numbers

	LDA AL	/Load A low
	ADD BL	/Add B low, carry in E
	STA CL	/Store in C low
	CLA	/Clear AC
	CIL	/Circulate to bring carry into $AC(16)$
	ADD AH	/Add A high and carry
	ADD BH	/Add B high
	STA CH	/Store in C high
	HLT	
AL,	—	/Location of operands
AH,	—	
BL,	—	
BH,	—	
CL,	—	
CH,	—	

Logic Operations

The basic computer has three machine instructions that perform logic operations: AND, CMA, and CLA. The LDA instruction may be considered as a logic operation that transfers a logic operand into the AC. In Sec. 4-5 we listed 16 different logic operations. All 16 logic operations can be implemented by software means because any logic function can be implemented using the AND and complement operations. For example, the OR operation is not available as a machine instruction in the basic computer. From DeMorgan's theorem we recognize the relation $x + y = (x'y')'$. The second expression contains only AND and complement operations. A program that forms the OR operation of two logic operands A and B is as follows:

```
LDA A      Load first operand A
CMA        Complement to get A̅
STA TMP    Store in a temporary location
LDA B      Load second operand B
CMA        Complement to get B̅
AND TMP    AND with A̅ to get A̅ ∧ B̅
CMA        Complement again to get A ∨ B
```

The other logic operations can be implemented by software in a similar fashion.

Shift Operations

The circular-shift operations are machine instructions in the basic computer. The other shifts of interest are the logical shifts and arithmetic shifts. These two shifts can be programmed with a small number of instructions.

The logical shift requires that zeros be added to the extreme positions. This is easily accomplished by clearing E and circulating the AC and E. Thus for a logical shift-right operation we need the two instructions

```
CLE
CIR
```

For a logical shift-left operation we need the two instructions

```
CLE
CIL
```

The arithmetic shifts depend on the type of representation of negative numbers. For the basic computer we have adopted the signed-2's complement representation. The rules for arithmetic shifts are listed in Sec. 4-6. For an arithmetic right-shift it is necessary that the sign bit in the leftmost position remain unchanged. But the sign bit itself is shifted into the high-order bit position of the number. The program for the arithmetic right-shift requires that we set E to the same value as the sign bit and circulate right, thus:

```
CLE   /Clear E to 0
SPA   /Skip if AC is positive; E remains 0
CME   /AC is negative; set E to 1
CIR   /Circulate E and AC
```

For arithmetic shift-left it is necessary that the added bit in the least significant position be 0. This is easily done by clearing E prior to the circulate-left operation. The sign bit must not change during this shift. With a circulate instruction, the sign bit moves into E. It is then necessary to compare the sign bit with the value of E after the operation. If the two values are equal, the arithmetic shift has been correctly implemented. If they are not equal, an overflow occurs. An overflow indicates that the unshifted number was too large. When multiplied by 2 (by means of the shift), the number so obtained exceeds the capacity of the AC.

6-7 Subroutines

Frequently, the same piece of code must be written over again in many different parts of a program. Instead of repeating the code every time it is needed, there is an obvious advantage if the common instructions are written only once. A set of common instructions that can be used in a program many times is called a *subroutine*. Each time that a subroutine is used in the main part of the program, a branch is executed to the beginning of the subroutine. After the subroutine has been executed, a branch is made back to the main program.

A subroutine consists of a self-contained sequence of instructions that carries out a given task. A branch can be made to the subroutine from any part of the main program. This poses the problem of how the subroutine knows which location to return to, since many different locations in the main program may make branches to the same subroutine. It is therefore necessary to store the return address somewhere in the computer for the subroutine to know where to return. Because branching to a subroutine and returning to the main program is such a common operation, all computers provide special instructions to facilitate subroutine entry and return.

In the basic computer, the link between the main program and a subroutine is the BSA instruction (branch and save return address). To explain how this instruction is used, let us write a subroutine that shifts the content of the accumulator four times to the left. Shifting a word four times is a useful operation for processing binary-coded decimal numbers or alphanumeric characters. Such an operation could have been included as a machine instruction in the computer. Since it is not included, a subroutine is formed to accomplish this task. The program of Table 6-16 starts by loading the value of X into the

TABLE 6-16 Program to Demonstrate the Use of Subroutines

Location			
		ORG 100	/Main program
100		LDA X	/Load X
101		BSA SH4	/Branch to subroutine
102		STA X	/Store shifted number
103		LDA Y	/Load Y
104		BSA SH4	/Branch to subroutine again
105		STA Y	/Store shifted number
106		HLT	
107	X,	HEX 1234	
108	Y,	HEX 4321	
			/Subroutine to shift left 4 times
109	SH4,	HEX 0	/Store return address here
10A		CIL	/Circulate left once
10B		CIL	
10C		CIL	
10D		CIL	/Circulate left fourth time
10E		AND MSK	/Set AC(13–16) to zero
10F		BUN SH4 I	/Return to main program
110	MSK,	HEX FFF0	/Mask operand
		END	

AC. The next instruction encountered is BSA SH4. The BSA instruction is in location 101. Subroutine SH4 must return to location 102 after it finishes its task. When the BSA instruction is executed, the control unit stores the return address 102 into the location defined by the symbolic address SH4 (which is 109). It also transfers the value of SH4 + 1 into the program counter. After this instruction is executed, memory location 109 contains the binary equivalent of hexadecimal 102 and the program counter contains the binary equivalent of hexadecimal 10A. This action has saved the return address and the subroutine is now executed starting from location 10A (since this is the content of PC in the next fetch cycle).

The computation in the subroutine circulates the content of AC four times to the left. In order to accomplish a logical shift operation, the four low-order bits must be set to zero. This is done by masking FFF0 with the content of AC. A mask operation is a logic AND operation that clears the bits of the AC where the mask operand is zero and leaves the bits of the AC unchanged where the mask operand bits are 1's.

The last instruction in the subroutine returns the computer to the main program. This is accomplished by the indirect branch instruction with an address symbol identical to the symbol used for the subroutine name. The address to which the computer branches is not SH4 but the value found in location SH4 because this is an indirect address instruction. What is found in location SH4 is the return address 102 which was previously stored there by the BSA instruction. The computer returns to execute the instruction in location 102. The main program continues by storing the shifted number into location X. A new number is then loaded into the AC from location Y, and another branch is made to the subroutine. This time location SH4 will contain the return address 105 since this is now the location of the next instruction after BSA. The new operand is shifted and the subroutine returns to the main program at location 105.

From this example we see that the first memory location of each subroutine serves as a link between the main program and the subroutine. The procedure for branching to a subroutine and returning to the main program is referred to as a subroutine *linkage*. The BSA instruction performs an operation commonly called subroutine *call*. The last instruction of the subroutine performs an operation commonly called subroutine *return*.

The procedure used in the basic computer for subroutine linkage is commonly found in computers with only one processor register. Many computers have multiple processor registers and some of them are assigned the name *index registers*. In such computers, an index register is usually employed to implement the subroutine linkage. A branch-to-subroutine instruction stores the return address in an index register. A return-from-subroutine instruction is effected by branching to the address presently stored in the index register.

Subroutine Parameters and Data Linkage

When a subroutine is called, the main program must transfer the data it wishes the subroutine to work with. In the previous example, the data were transferred through the accumulator. The operand was loaded into the AC prior to the branch. The subroutine shifted the number and left it there to be accepted by the main program. In general, it is necessary for the subroutine to have access to data from the calling program and to return results to that program. The accumulator can be used for a single input parameter and a single output parameter. In computers with multiple processor registers, more parameters can be transferred this way. Another way to transfer data to a subroutine is through the memory. Data are often placed in memory locations following the call. They can also be placed in a block of storage. The first address of the block is then placed in the memory location following the call. In any case, the return address always gives the link information for transferring data between the main program and the subroutine.

As an illustration, consider a subroutine that performs the logic OR operation. Two operands must be transferred to the subroutine and the subroutine must return the result of the operation. The accumulator can be used to transfer one operand and to receive the result. The other operand is inserted in the location following the BSA instruction. This is demonstrated in the program of Table 6-17. The first operand in location X is loaded into the *AC*. The second operand is stored in location 202 following the BSA instruction. After the branch, the first location in the subroutine holds the number 202. Note that in this case, 202 is not the return address but the address of the second operand. The subroutine starts performing the OR operation by complementing the first operand in the *AC* and storing it in a temporary location TMP. The second operand is loaded into the *AC* by an indirect instruction at location OR. Remember that location OR contains the number 202. When the instruction refers to it indirectly, the operand at location 202 is loaded into the *AC*. This operand is complemented and then ANDed with the operand stored in TMP. Complementing the result forms the OR operation.

The return from the subroutine must be manipulated so that the main program continues from location 203 where the next instruction is located. This is accomplished by incrementing location OR with the ISZ instruction. Now location OR holds the number 203 and an indirect BUN instruction causes a return to the proper place.

It is possible to have more than one operand following the BSA instruc-

TABLE 6-17 Program to Demonstrate Parameter Linkage

Location			
		ORG 200	
200		LDA X	/Load first operand into *AC*
201		BSA OR	/Branch to subroutine OR
202		HEX 3AF6	/Second operand stored here
203		STA Y	/Subroutine returns here
204		HLT	
205	X,	HEX 7B95	/First operand stored here
206	Y,	HEX 0	/Result stored here
207	OR,	HEX 0	/Subroutine OR
208		CMA	/Complement first operand
209		STA TMP	/Store in temporary location
20A		LDA OR I	/Load second operand
20B		CMA	/Complement second operand
20C		AND TMP	/AND complemented first operand
20D		CMA	/Complement again to get OR
20E		ISZ OR	/Increment return address
20F		BUN OR I	/Return to main program
210	TMP,	HEX 0	/Temporary storage
		END	

tion. The subroutine must increment the return address stored in its first location for each operand that it extracts from the calling program. Moreover, the calling program can reserve one or more locations for the subroutine to return results that are computed. The first location in the subroutine must be incremented for these locations as well, before the return. If there is a large amount of data to be transferred, the data can be placed in a block of storage and the address of the first item in the block is then used as the linking parameter.

A subroutine that moves a block of data starting at address 100 into a block starting with address 200 is listed in Table 6-18. The length of the block is 16 words. The first introduction is a branch to subroutine MVE. The first part of the subroutine transfers the three parameters 100, 200 and −16 from the main program and places them in its own storage location. The items are retrieved from their blocks by the use of two pointers. The counter ensures that only 16 items are moved. When the subroutine completes its operation, the data required is in the block starting from the location 200. The return to the main program is to the HLT instruction.

TABLE 6-18 Subroutine to Move a Block of Data

		/Main program
	BSA MVE	/Branch to subroutine
	HEX 100	/First address of source data
	HEX 200	/First address of destination data
	DEC −16	/Number of items to move
	HLT	
MVE,	HEX 0	/Subroutine MVE
	LDA MVE I	/Bring address of source
	STA PT1	/Store in first pointer
	ISZ MVE	/Increment return address
	LDA MVE I	/Bring address of destination
	STA PT2	/Store in second pointer
	ISZ MVE	/Increment return address
	LDA MVE I	/Bring number of items
	STA CTR	/Store in counter
	ISZ MVE	/Increment return address
LOP,	LDA PT1 I	/Load source item
	STA PT2 I	/Store in destination
	ISZ PT1	/Increment source pointer
	ISZ PT2	/Increment destination pointer
	ISZ CTR	/Increment counter
	BUN LOP	/Repeat 16 times
	BUN MVE I	/Return to main program
PT1,	—	
PT2,	—	
CTR,	—	

6-8   Input–Output Programming

Users of the computer write programs with symbols that are defined by the programming language employed. The symbols are strings of characters and each character is assigned an 8-bit code so that it can be stored in computer memory. A binary-coded character enters the computer when an INP (input) instruction is executed. A binary-coded character is transferred to the output device when an OUT (output) instruction is executed. The output device detects the binary code and types the corresponding character.

Table 6-19(a) lists the instructions needed to input a character and store it in memory. The SKI instruction checks the input flag to see if a character is available for transfer. The next instruction is skipped if the input flag bit is 1. The INP instruction transfers the binary-coded character into $AC(0–7)$. The character is then printed by means of the OUT instruction. A terminal unit that communicates directly with a computer does not print the character when a key is depressed. To type it, it is necessary to send an OUT instruction for the printer. In this way, the user is ensured that the correct transfer has occurred. If the SKI instruction finds the flag bit at 0, the next instruction in sequence is executed. This instruction is a branch to return and check the flag bit again. Because the input device is much slower than the computer, the two instructions in the loop will be executed many times before a character is transferred into the accumulator.

Table 6-19(b) lists the instructions needed to print a character initially stored in memory. The character is first loaded into the AC. The output flag is then checked. If it is 0, the computer remains in a two-instruction loop checking the flag bit. When the flag changes to 1, the character is transferred from the accumulator to the printer.

TABLE 6-19 Programs to Input and Output One Character

(a) Input a character:		
CIF,	SKI	/Check input flag
	BUN CIF	/Flag=0, branch to check again
	INP	/Flag=1, input character
	OUT	/Print character
	STA CHR	/Store character
	HLT	
CHR,	—	/Store character here
(b) Output one character:		
	LDA CHR	/Load character into AC
COF,	SKO	/Check output flag
	BUN COF	/Flag=0, branch to check again
	OUT	/Flag=1, output character
	HLT	
CHR,	HEX 0057	/Character is "W"

Character Manipulation

A computer is not just a calculator but also a symbol manipulator. The binary-coded characters that represent symbols can be manipulated by computer instructions to achieve various data-processing tasks. One such task may be to pack two characters in one word. This is convenient because each character occupies 8 bits and a memory word contains 16 bits. The program in Table 6-20 lists a subroutine named IN2 that inputs two characters and packs them into one 16-bit word. The packed word remains in the accumulator. Note that subroutine SH4 (Table 6-16) is called twice to shift the accumulator left eight times.

In the discussion of the assembler it was assumed that the symbolic program is stored in a section of memory which is sometimes called a *buffer*. The symbolic program being typed enters through the input device and is stored in consecutive memory locations in the buffer. The program listed in Table 6-21 can be used to input a symbolic program from the keyboard, pack two characters in one word, and store them in the buffer. The first address of the buffer is 500. The first double character is stored in location 500 and all characters are stored in sequential locations. The program uses a pointer for keeping track of the current empty location in the buffer. No counter is used in the program, so characters will be read as long as they are available or until the buffer reaches location 0 (after location FFFF). In a practical situation it may be necessary to limit the size of the buffer and a counter may be used for this purpose. Note that subroutine IN2 of Table 6-20 is called to input and pack the two characters.

In discussing the second pass of the assembler in Sec. 6-4 it was mentioned that one of the most common operations of an assembler is table lookup. This is an operation that searches a table to find out if it contains a given symbol. The search may be done by comparing the given symbol with each of the symbols stored in the table. The search terminates when a match occurs

TABLE 6-20 Subroutine to Input and Pack Two Characters

IN2,	—	/Subroutine entry
FST,	SKI	
	BUN FST	
	INP	/Input first character
	OUT	
	BSA SH4	/Shift left four times
	BSA SH4	/Shift left four more times
SCD,	SKI	
	BUN SCD	
	INP	/Input second character
	OUT	
	BUN IN2 I	/Return

TABLE 6-21 Program to Store Input Characters in a Buffer

	LDA ADS	/Load first address of buffer
	STA PTR	/Initialize pointer
LOP,	BSA IN2	/Go to subroutine IN2 (Table 6-20)
	STA PTR I	/Store double character word in buffer
	ISZ PTR	/Increment pointer
	BUN LOP	/Branch to input more characters
	HLT	
ADS,	HEX 500	/First address of buffer
PTR,	HEX 0	/Location for pointer

or if none of the symbols match. When a match occurs, the assembler retrieves the equivalent binary value. A program for comparing two words is listed in Table 6-22. The comparison is accomplished by forming the 2's complement of a word (as if it were a number) and arithmetically adding it to the second word. If the result is zero, the two words are equal and a match occurs. If the result is not zero, the words are not the same. This program can serve as a subroutine in a table-lookup program.

Program Interrupt

The running time of input and output programs is made up primarily of the time spent by the computer in waiting for the external device to set its flag. The waiting loop that checks the flag keeps the computer occupied with a task that wastes a large amount of time. This waiting time can be eliminated if the interrupt facility is used to notify the computer when a flag is set. The advantage of using the interrupt is that the information transfer is initiated upon request from the external device. In the meantime, the computer can be busy performing other useful tasks. Obviously, if no other program resides in memory, there is nothing for the computer to do, so it might as well check for

TABLE 6-22 Program to Compare Two Words

	LDA WD1	/Load first word
	CMA	
	INC	/Form 2's complement
	ADD WD2	/Add second word
	SZA	/Skip if *AC* is zero
	BUN UEQ	/Branch to "unequal" routine
	BUN EQL	/Branch to "equal" routine
WD1,	—	
WD2,	—	

the flags. The interrupt facility is useful in a multiprogram environment when two or more programs reside in memory at the same time.

Only one program can be executed at any given time even though two or more programs may reside in memory. The program currently being executed is referred to as the running program. The other programs are usually waiting for input or output data. The function of the interrupt facility is to take care of the data transfer of one (or more) program while another program is currently being executed. The running program must include an ION instruction to turn the interrupt on. If the interrupt facility is not used, the program must include an IOF instruction to turn it off. (The *start* switch of the computer should also turn the interrupt off.)

The interrupt facility allows the running program to proceed until the input or output device sets its ready flag. Whenever a flag is set to 1, the computer completes the execution of the instruction in progress and then acknowledges the interrupt. The result of this action is that the return address is stored in location 0. The instruction in location 1 is then performed; this initiates a service routine for the input or output transfer. The service routine can be stored anywhere in memory provided a branch to the start of the routine is stored in location 1. The service routine must have instructions to perform the following tasks:

1. Save contents of processor registers.
2. Check which flag is set.
3. Service the device whose flag is set.
4. Restore contents of processor registers.
5. Turn the interrupt facility on.
6. Return to the running program.

The contents of processor registers before the interrupt and after the return to the running program must be the same; otherwise, the running program may be in error. Since the service routine may use these registers, it is necessary to save their contents at the beginning of the routine and restore them at the end. The sequence by which the flags are checked dictates the priority assigned to each device. Even though two or more flags may be set at the same time, the devices nevertheless are serviced one at a time. The device with higher priority is serviced first followed by the one with lower priority.

The occurrence of an interrupt disables the facility from further interrupts. The service routine must turn the interrupt on before the return to the running program. This will enable further interrupts while the computer is executing the running program. The interrupt facility should not be turned on until after the return address is inserted into the program counter.

An example of a program that services an interrupt is listed in Table 6-23.

TABLE 6-23 Program to Service an Interrupt

Location			
0	ZRO,	—	/Return address stored here
1		BUN SRV	/Branch to service routine
100		CLA	/Portion of running program
101		ION	/Turn on interrupt facility
102		LDA X	
103		ADD Y	/Interrupt occurs here
104		STA Z	/Program returns here after interrupt
.		.	
.		.	
.			/Interrupt service routine
200	SRV,	STA SAC	/Store content of *AC*
		CIR	/Move *E* into *AC*(1)
		STA SE	/Store content of *E*
		SKI	/Check input flag
		BUN NXT	/Flag is off, check next flag
		INP	/Flag is on, input character
		OUT	/Print character
		STA PT1 I	/Store it in input buffer
		ISZ PT1	/Increment input pointer
	NXT,	SKO	/Check output flag
		BUN EXT	/Flag is off, exit
		LDA PT2 I	/Load character from output buffer
		OUT	/Output character
		ISZ PT2	/Increment output pointer
	EXT,	LDA SE	/Restore value of *AC*(1)
		CIL	/Shift it to *E*
		LDA SAC	/Restore content of *AC*
		ION	/Turn interrupt on
		BUN ZRO I	/Return to running program
	SAC,	—	/*AC* is stored here
	SE,	—	/*E* is stored here
	PT1,	—	/Pointer of input buffer
	PT2,	—	/Pointer of output buffer

Location 0 is reserved for the return address. Location 1 has a branch instruction to the beginning of the service routine SRV. The portion of the running program listed has an ION instruction that turns the interrupt on. Suppose that an interrupt occurs while the computer is executing the instruction in location 103. The interrupt cycle stores the binary equivalent of hexadecimal 104 in location 0 and branches to location 1. The branch instruction in location 1 sends the computer to the service routine SRV.

The service routine performs the six tasks mentioned above. The contents of AC and E are stored in special locations. (These are the only processor registers in the basic computer.) The flags are checked sequentially, the input flag first and the output flag second. If any or both flags are set, an item of data is transferred to or from the corresponding memory buffer. Before returning to the running program the previous contents of E and AC are restored and the interrupt facility is turned on. The last instruction causes a branch to the address stored in location 0. This is the return address stored there previously during the interrupt cycle. Hence the running program will continue from location 104, where it was interrupted.

A typical computer may have many more input and output devices connected to the interrupt facility. Furthermore, interrupt sources are not limited to input and output transfers. Interrupts can be used for other purposes, such as internal processing errors or special alarm conditions. Further discussion of interrupts and some advanced concepts concerning this important subject can be found in Sec. 11-5.

PROBLEMS

6-1. The following program is stored in the memory unit of the basic computer. Show the contents of the AC, PC, and IR (in hexadecimal), at the end, after each instruction is executed. All numbers listed below are in hexadecimal.

Location	Instruction
010	CLA
011	ADD 016
012	BUN 014
013	HLT
014	AND 017
015	BUN 013
016	C1A5
017	93C6

6-2. The following program is a list of instructions in hexadecimal code. The computer executes the instructions starting from address 100. What are the content of AC and the memory word at address 103 when the computer halts?

Location	Instruction
100	5103
101	7200
102	7001
103	0000
104	7800
105	7020
106	C103

6-3.   List the assembly language program (of the equivalent binary instructions) generated by a compiler from the following Fortran program. Assume integer variables.

```
SUM = 0
SUM = SUM + A + B
DIF = DIF - C
SUM = SUM + DIF
```

6-4.   Can the letter I be used as a symbolic address in the assembly language program defined for the basic computer? Justify the answer.

6-5.   What happens during the first pass of the assembler (Fig. 6-1) if the line of code that has a pseudoinstruction ORG or END also has a label? Modify the flowchart to include an error message if this occurs.

6-6.   A line of code in an assembly language program is as follows:

DEC −35

a. Show that four memory words are required to store the line of code and give their binary content.

b. Show that one memory word stores the binary translated code and give its binary content.

6-7.   a. Obtain the address symbol table generated for the program of Table 6-13 during the first pass of the assembler.

b. List the translated program in hexadecimal.

6-8.   The pseudoinstruction BSS N (block started by symbol) is sometimes employed to reserve N memory words for a group of operands. For example, the line of code

A,   BSS 10

informs the assembler that a block of 10 (decimal) locations is to be left free, starting from location A. This is similar to the Fortran statement DIMENSION A(10). Modify the flowchart of Fig. 6-1 to process this pseudoinstruction.

6-9. Modify the flowchart of Fig. 6-2 to include an error message when a symbolic address is not defined by a label.

6-10. Show how the MRI and non-MRI tables can be stored in memory.

6-11. List the assembly language program (of the equivalent binary instructions) generated by a compiler for the following IF statement:

$$IF(A - B) \; 10, \; 20, \; 30$$

The program branches to statement 10 if $A - B < 0$; to statement 20 if $A - B = 0$; and to statement 30 if $A - B > 0$.

6-12.
  a. Explain in words what the following program accomplishes when it is executed. What is the value of location CTR when the computer halts?
  b. List the address symbol table obtained during the first pass of the assembler.
  c. List the hexadecimal code of the translated program.

		ORG	100
100		CLE	
101		CLA	
102		STA	CTR
103		LDA	WRD
104		SZA	
105		BUN	ROT
106		BUN	STP
107	ROT,	CIL	
108		SZE	
109		BUN	AGN
10A		BUN	ROT
10B	AGN,	CLE	
10C		ISZ	CTR
10D		SZA	
10E		BUN	ROT
10F	STP,	HLT	
110	CTR,	HEX	0
111	WRD,	HEX	62C1
		END	

6-13. Write a program loop, using a pointer and a counter, that clears to 0 the contents of hexadecimal locations 500 through 5FF.

6-14. Write a program to multiply two positive numbers by a repeated addition method. For example, to multiply 5×4, the program evaluates the product by adding 5 four times, or $5 + 5 + 5 + 5$.

6-15. The multiplication program of Table 6-14 is not initialized. After the program is executed once, location CTR will be left with zero. Show that if the program is executed again starting from location 100, the loop will be traversed 65536 times. Add the needed instructions to initialize the program.

6-16. Write a program to multiply two unsigned positive numbers, each with 16 significant bits, to produce an unsigned double-precision product.

6-17. Write a program to multiply two signed numbers with negative numbers being initially in signed-2's complement representation. The product should be single-precision and signed-2's complement representation if negative.

6-18. Write a program to subtract two double-precision numbers.

6-19. Write a program that evaluates the logic exclusive-OR of two logic operands.

6-20. Write a program for the arithmetic shift-left operation. Branch to OVF if an overflow occurs.

6-21. Write a subroutine to subtract two numbers. In the calling program, the BSA instruction is followed by the subtrahend and minuend. The difference is returned to the main program in the third location following the BSA instruction.

6-22. Write a subroutine to complement each word in a block of data. In the calling program, the BSA instruction is followed by two parameters: the starting address of the block and the number of words in the block.

6-23. Write a subroutine to circulate E and AC four times to the right. If AC contains hexadecimal 079C and $E = 1$, what are the contents of AC and E after the subroutine is executed?

6-24. Write a program to accept input characters, pack two characters in one word and store them in consecutive locations in a memory buffer. The first address of the buffer is $(400)_{16}$. The size of the buffer is $(512)_{10}$ words. If the buffer overflows, the computer should halt.

6-25. Write a program to unpack two characters from location WRD and store them in bits 0 through 7 of locations CH1 and CH2. Bits 9 through 15 should contain zeros.

6-26. Obtain a flowchart for a program to check for a CR code (hexadecimal 0D) in a memory buffer. The buffer contains two characters per word. When the code for CR is encountered, the program transfers it to bits 0 through 7 of location LNE without disturbing bits 8 through 15.

6-27. Translate the service routine SRV from Table 6-23 to its equivalent hexadecimal code. Assume that the routine is stored starting from location 200.

6-28. Write an interrupt service routine that performs all the required functions but the input device is serviced only if a special location, MOD, contains all 1's. The output device is serviced only if location MOD contains all 0's.

REFERENCES

1. Booth, T. L., *Introduction to Computer Engineering*, 3rd ed. New York: John Wiley, 1984.

2. Gear, C. W., *Computer Organization and Programming*, 3rd ed. New York: McGraw-Hill, 1980.

3. Gibson, G. A., *Computer Systems Concepts and Design*. Englewood Cliffs, NJ: Prentice Hall, 1991.

4. Gray, N. A. B., *Introduction to Computer Systems*. Englewood Cliffs, NJ: Prentice Hall, 1987.

5. Levy, H. M., and R. H. Eckhouse, Jr., *Computer Programming and Architecture: The VAX-11*. Bedford, MA: Digital Press, 1980.

6. Lewin, M. H., *Logic Design and Computer Organization*. Reading, MA: Addison-Wesley, 1983.

7. Prosser, F. P., and D. E. Winkel, *The Art of Digital Design*, 2nd ed. Englewood Cliffs, NJ: Prentice Hall, 1987.

8. Shiva, S. G., *Computer Design and Architecture*, 2nd ed. New York: HarperCollins Publishers, 1991.

9. Tanenbaum, A. S., *Structured Computer Organization*, 3rd ed. Englewood Cliffs, NJ: Prentice Hall, 1990.

10. Wakerly, J. F., *Microcomputer Architecture and Programming*. New York: John Wiley, 1981.

CHAPTER SEVEN

Microprogrammed Control

IN THIS CHAPTER

7-1   Control Memory

The function of the control unit in a digital computer is to initiate sequences of microoperations. The number of different types of microoperations that are available in a given system is finite. The complexity of the digital system is derived from the number of sequences of microoperations that are performed. When the control signals are generated by hardware using conventional logic design techniques, the control unit is said to be *hardwired*. Microprogramming is a second alternative for designing the control unit of a digital computer. The principle of microprogramming is an elegant and systematic method for controlling the microoperation sequences in a digital computer.

The control function that specifies a microoperation is a binary variable. When it is in one binary state, the corresponding microoperation is executed. A control variable in the opposite binary state does not change the state of the registers in the system. The active state of a control variable may be either the 1 state or the 0 state, depending on the application. In a bus-organized system, the control signals that specify microoperations are groups of bits that select the paths in multiplexers, decoders, and arithmetic logic units.

The control unit initiates a series of sequential steps of microoperations. During any given time, certain microoperations are to be initiated, while others remain idle. The control variables at any given time can be represented by a string of 1's and 0's called a control word. As such, control words can be programmed to perform various operations on the components of the system. A control unit whose binary control variables are stored in memory is called

control word

microinstruction

microprogram

control memory

a *microprogrammed control unit*. Each word in control memory contains within it a *microinstruction*. The microinstruction specifies one or more microoperations for the system. A sequence of microinstructions constitutes a *microprogram*. Since alterations of the microprogram are not needed once the control unit is in operation, the control memory can be a read-only memory (ROM). The content of the words in ROM are fixed and cannot be altered by simple programming since no writing capability is available in the ROM. ROM words are made permanent during the hardware production of the unit. The use of a microprogram involves placing all control variables in words of ROM for use by the control unit through successive read operations. The content of the word in ROM at a given address specifies a microinstruction.

A more advanced development known as *dynamic* microprogramming permits a microprogram to be loaded initially from an auxiliary memory such as a magnetic disk. Control units that use dynamic microprogramming employ a writable control memory. This type of memory can be used for writing (to change the microprogram) but is used mostly for reading. A memory that is part of a control unit is referred to as a *control memory*.

A computer that employs a microprogrammed control unit will have two separate memories: a main memory and a control memory. The main memory is available to the user for storing the programs. The contents of main memory may alter when the data are manipulated and every time that the program is changed. The user's program in main memory consists of machine instructions and data. In contrast, the control memory holds a fixed microprogram that cannot be altered by the occasional user. The microprogram consists of microinstructions that specify various internal control signals for execution of register microoperations. Each machine instruction initiates a series of microinstructions in control memory. These microinstructions generate the microoperations to fetch the instruction from main memory; to evaluate the effective address, to execute the operation specified by the instruction, and to return control to the fetch phase in order to repeat the cycle for the next instruction.

The general configuration of a microprogrammed control unit is demonstrated in the block diagram of Fig. 7-1. The control memory is assumed to be a ROM, within which all control information is permanently stored. The

Figure 7-1   Microprogrammed control organization.

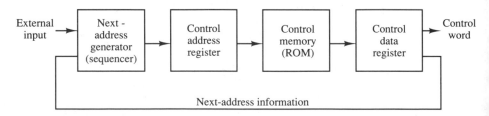

*control address
register*

control memory address register specifies the address of the microinstruction, and the control data register holds the microinstruction read from memory. The microinstruction contains a control word that specifies one or more microoperations for the data processor. Once these operations are executed, the control must determine the next address. The location of the next microinstruction may be the one next in sequence, or it may be located somewhere else in the control memory. For this reason it is necessary to use some bits of the present microinstruction to control the generation of the address of the next microinstruction. The next address may also be a function of external input conditions. While the microoperations are being executed, the next address is computed in the next address generator circuit and then transferred into the control address register to read the next microinstruction. Thus a microinstruction contains bits for initiating microoperations in the data processor part and bits that determine the address sequence for the control memory.

sequencer

The next address generator is sometimes called a microprogram *sequencer*, as it determines the address sequence that is read from control memory. The address of the next microinstruction can be specified in several ways, depending on the sequencer inputs. Typical functions of a microprogram sequencer are incrementing the control address register by one, loading into the control address register an address from control memory, transferring an external address, or loading an initial address to start the control operations.

pipeline register

The control data register holds the present microinstruction while the next address is computed and read from memory. The data register is sometimes called a *pipeline register*. It allows the execution of the microoperations specified by the control word simultaneously with the generation of the next microinstruction. This configuration requires a two-phase clock, with one clock applied to the address register and the other to the data register.

The system can operate without the control data register by applying a single-phase clock to the address register. The control word and next-address information are taken directly from the control memory. It must be realized that a ROM operates as a combinational circuit, with the address value as the input and the corresponding word as the output. The content of the specified word in ROM remains in the output wires as long as its address value remains in the address register. No read signal is needed as in a random-access memory. Each clock pulse will execute the microoperations specified by the control word and also transfer a new address to the control address register. In the example that follows we assume a single-phase clock and therefore we do not use a control data register. In this way the address register is the only component in the control system that receives clock pulses. The other two components: the sequencer and the control memory are combinational circuits and do not need a clock.

The main advantage of the microprogrammed control is the fact that once the hardware configuration is established, there should be no need for further hardware or wiring changes. If we want to establish a different control sequence for the system, all we need to do is specify a different set of microinstructions for control memory. The hardware configuration should not be changed for different operations; the only thing that must be changed is the microprogram residing in control memory.

hardwired control

It should be mentioned that most computers based on the reduced instruction set computer (RISC) architecture concept (see Sec. 8-8) use hardwired control rather than a control memory with a microprogram. An example of a hardwired control for a simple computer is presented in Sec. 5-4.

7-2 Address Sequencing

routine

Microinstructions are stored in control memory in groups, with each group specifying a *routine*. Each computer instruction has its own microprogram routine in control memory to generate the microoperations that execute the instruction. The hardware that controls the address sequencing of the control memory must be capable of sequencing the microinstructions within a routine and be able to branch from one routine to another. To appreciate the address sequencing in a microprogram control unit, let us enumerate the steps that the control must undergo during the execution of a single computer instruction.

An initial address is loaded into the control address register when power is turned on in the computer. This address is usually the address of the first microinstruction that activates the instruction fetch routine. The fetch routine may be sequenced by incrementing the control address register through the rest of its microinstructions. At the end of the fetch routine, the instruction is in the instruction register of the computer.

The control memory next must go through the routine that determines the effective address of the operand. A machine instruction may have bits that specify various addressing modes, such as indirect address and index registers. The effective address computation routine in control memory can be reached through a branch microinstruction, which is conditioned on the status of the mode bits of the instruction. When the effective address computation routine is completed, the address of the operand is available in the memory address register.

The next step is to generate the microoperations that execute the instruction fetched from memory. The microoperation steps to be generated in processor registers depend on the operation code part of the instruction. Each instruction has its own microprogram routine stored in a given location of control memory. The transformation from the instruction code bits to an address in control memory where the routine is located is referred to as a

mapping

mapping process. A mapping procedure is a rule that transforms the instruction code into a control memory address. Once the required routine is reached, the microinstructions that execute the instruction may be sequenced by incrementing the control address register, but sometimes the sequence of microoperations will depend on values of certain status bits in processor registers. Microprograms that employ subroutines will require an external register for storing the return address. Return addresses cannot be stored in ROM because the unit has no writing capability.

When the execution of the instruction is completed, control must return to the fetch routine. This is accomplished by executing an unconditional branch microinstruction to the first address of the fetch routine. In summary, the address sequencing capabilities required in a control memory are:

1. Incrementing of the control address register.
2. Unconditional branch or conditional branch, depending on status bit conditions.
3. A mapping process from the bits of the instruction to an address for control memory.
4. A facility for subroutine call and return.

Figure 7-2 shows a block diagram of a control memory and the associated hardware needed for selecting the next microinstruction address. The microinstruction in control memory contains a set of bits to initiate microoperations in computer registers and other bits to specify the method by which the next address is obtained. The diagram shows four different paths from which the control address register (CAR) receives the address. The incrementer increments the content of the control address register by one, to select the next microinstruction in sequence. Branching is achieved by specifying the branch address in one of the fields of the microinstruction. Conditional branching is obtained by using part of the microinstruction to select a specific status bit in order to determine its condition. An external address is transferred into control memory via a mapping logic circuit. The return address for a subroutine is stored in a special register whose value is then used when the microprogram wishes to return from the subroutine.

Conditional Branching

special bits

The branch logic of Fig. 7-2 provides decision-making capabilities in the control unit. The status conditions are special bits in the system that provide parameter information such as the carry-out of an adder, the sign bit of a number, the mode bits of an instruction, and input or output status conditions. Information in these bits can be tested and actions initiated based on their condition: whether their value is 1 or 0. The status bits, together with the field in the microinstruction that specifies a branch address, control the conditional branch decisions generated in the branch logic.

branch logic

The branch logic hardware may be implemented in a variety of ways. The simplest way is to test the specified condition and branch to the indicated address if the condition is met; otherwise, the address register is incremented.

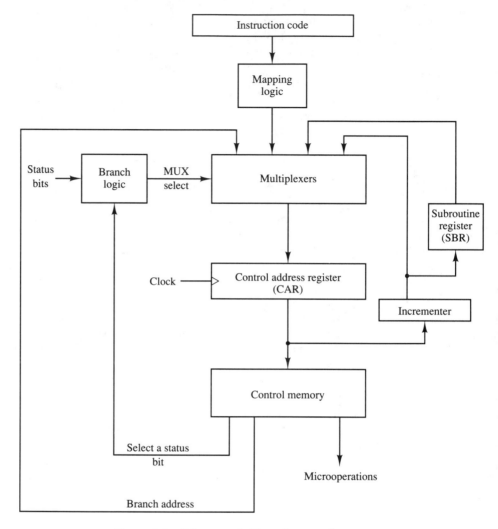

Figure 7-2 Selection of address for control memory.

This can be implemented with a multiplexer. Suppose that there are eight status bit conditions in the system. Three bits in the microinstruction are used to specify any one of eight status bit conditions. These three bits provide the selection variables for the multiplexer. If the selected status bit is in the 1 state, the output of the multiplexer is 1; otherwise, it is 0. A 1 output in the multiplexer generates a control signal to transfer the branch address from the microinstruction into the control address register. A 0 output in the multiplexer causes the address register to be incremented. In this configuration, the microprogram follows one of two possible paths, depending on the value of the selected status bit.

An unconditional branch microinstruction can be implemented by loading the branch address from control memory into the control address register. This can be accomplished by fixing the value of one status bit at the input of the multiplexer, so it is always equal to 1. A reference to this bit by the status bit select lines from control memory causes the branch address to be loaded into the control address register unconditionally.

Mapping of Instruction

A special type of branch exists when a microinstruction specifies a branch to the first word in control memory where a microprogram routine for an instruction is located. The status bits for this type of branch are the bits in the operation code part of the instruction. For example, a computer with a simple instruction format as shown in Fig. 7-3 has an operation code of four bits which can specify up to 16 distinct instructions. Assume further that the control memory has 128 words, requiring an address of seven bits. For each operation code there exists a microprogram routine in control memory that executes the instruction. One simple mapping process that converts the 4-bit operation code to a 7-bit address for control memory is shown in Fig. 7-3. This mapping consists of placing a 0 in the most significant bit of the address, transferring the four operation code bits, and clearing the two least significant bits of the control address register. This provides for each computer instruction a microprogram routine with a capacity of four microinstructions. If the routine needs more than four microinstructions, it can use addresses 1000000 through 1111111. If it uses fewer than four microinstructions, the unused memory locations would be available for other routines.

One can extend this concept to a more general mapping rule by using a ROM to specify the mapping function. In this configuration, the bits of the instruction specify the address of a mapping ROM. The contents of the mapping ROM give the bits for the control address register. In this way the microprogram routine that executes the instruction can be placed in any desired location in control memory. The mapping concept provides flexibility for adding instructions for control memory as the need arises.

Figure 7-3   Mapping from instruction code to microinstruction address.

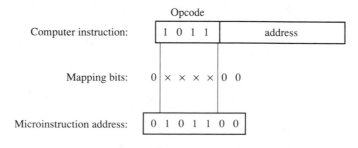

The mapping function is sometimes implemented by means of an integrated circuit called programmable logic device or PLD. A PLD is similar to ROM in concept except that it uses AND and OR gates with internal electronic fuses. The interconnection between inputs, AND gates, OR gates, and outputs can be programmed as in ROM. A mapping function that can be expressed in terms of Boolean expressions can be implemented conveniently with a PLD.

Subroutines

Subroutines are programs that are used by other routines to accomplish a particular task. A subroutine can be called from any point within the main body of the microprogram. Frequently, many microprograms contain identical sections of code. Microinstructions can be saved by employing subroutines that use common sections of microcode. For example, the sequence of microoperations needed to generate the effective address of the operand for an instruction is common to all memory reference instructions. This sequence could be a subroutine that is called from within many other routines to execute the effective address computation.

subroutine register

Microprograms that use subroutines must have a provision for storing the return address during a subroutine call and restoring the address during a subroutine return. This may be accomplished by placing the incremented output from the control address register into a subroutine register and branching to the beginning of the subroutine. The subroutine register can then become the source for transferring the address for the return to the main routine. The best way to structure a register file that stores addresses for subroutines is to organize the registers in a last-in, first-out (LIFO) stack. The use of a stack in subroutine calls and returns is explained in more detail in Sec. 8-7.

7-3 Microprogram Example

Once the configuration of a computer and its microprogrammed control unit is established, the designer's task is to generate the microcode for the control memory. This code generation is called microprogramming and is a process similar to conventional machine language programming. To appreciate this process, we present here a simple digital computer and show how it is microprogrammed. The computer used here is similar but not identical to the basic computer introduced in Chap. 5.

Computer Configuration

The block diagram of the computer is shown in Fig. 7-4. It consists of two memory units: a main memory for storing instructions and data, and a control memory for storing the microprogram. Four registers are associated with the processor unit and two with the control unit. The processor registers are

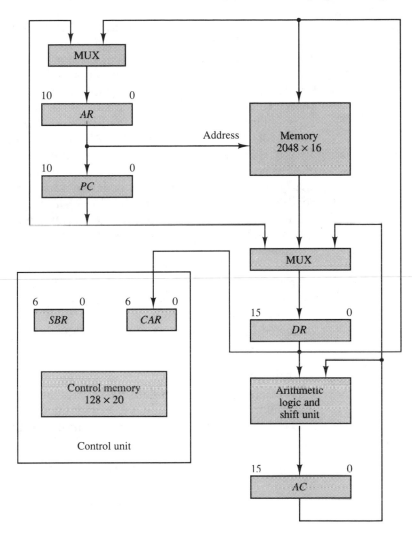

Figure 7-4 Computer hardware configuration.

program counter PC, address register AR, data register DR, and accumulator register AC. The function of these registers is similar to the basic computer introduced in Chap. 5 (see Fig. 5-3). The control unit has a control address register CAR and a subroutine register SBR. The control memory and its registers are organized as a microprogrammed control unit, as shown in Fig. 7-2.

The transfer of information among the registers in the processor is done through multiplexers rather than a common bus. DR can receive information from AC, PC, or memory. AR can receive information from PC or DR. PC can receive information only from AR. The arithmetic, logic, and shift unit performs microoperations with data from AC and DR and places the result in AC. Note that memory receives its address from AR. Input data written to memory come from DR, and data read from memory can go only to DR.

instruction format

The computer instruction format is depicted in Fig. 7-5(a). It consists of three fields: a 1-bit field for indirect addressing symbolized by I, a 4-bit operation code (opcode), and an 11-bit address field. Figure 7-5(b) lists four of the 16 possible memory-reference instructions. The ADD instruction adds the content of the operand found in the effective address to the content of AC. The BRANCH instruction causes a branch to the effective address if the operand in AC is negative. The program proceeds with the next consecutive instruction if AC is not negative. The AC is negative if its sign bit (the bit in the leftmost position of the register) is a 1. The STORE instruction transfers the content of AC into the memory word specified by the effective address. The EXCHANGE instruction swaps the data between AC and the memory word specified by the effective address.

It will be shown subsequently that each computer instruction must be microprogrammed. In order not to complicate the microprogramming example, only four instructions are considered here. It should be realized that 12 other instructions can be included and each instruction must be microprogrammed by the procedure outlined below.

Microinstruction Format

microinstruction format

The microinstruction format for the control memory is shown in Fig. 7-6. The 20 bits of the microinstruction are divided into four functional parts. The three fields F1, F2, and F3 specify microoperations for the computer. The CD field

Figure 7-5 Computer instructions.

15	14	11	10	0
I	Opcode		Address	

(a) Instruction format

Symbol	Opcode	Description
ADD	0000	$AC \leftarrow AC + M\,[EA]$
BRANCH	0001	If $(AC < 0)$ then $(PC \leftarrow EA)$
STORE	0010	$M\,[EA] \leftarrow AC$
EXCHANGE	0011	$AC \leftarrow M[EA],\ M[EA] \leftarrow AC$

EA is the effective address

(b) Four computer instructions

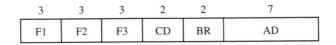

3	3	3	2	2	7
F1	F2	F3	CD	BR	AD

F1, F2, F3: Microoperation fields

CD: Condition for branching

BR: Branch field

AD: Address field

Figure 7-6 Microinstruction code format (20 bits).

selects status bit conditions. The BR field specifies the type of branch to be used. The AD field contains a branch address. The address field is seven bits wide, since the control memory has $128 = 2^7$ words.

microoperations
 The microoperations are subdivided into three fields of three bits each. The three bits in each field are encoded to specify seven distinct microoperations as listed in Table 7-1. This gives a total of 21 microoperations. No more than three microoperations can be chosen for a microinstruction, one from each field. If fewer than three microoperations are used, one or more of the fields will use the binary code 000 for no operation. As an illustration, a microinstruction can specify two simultaneous microoperations from F2 and F3 and none from F1.

$$DR \leftarrow M[AR] \quad \text{with F2} = 100$$

$$\text{and} \quad PC \leftarrow PC + 1 \quad \text{with F3} = 101$$

The nine bits of the microoperation fields will then be 000 100 101. It is important to realize that two or more conflicting microoperations cannot be specified simultaneously. For example, a microoperation field 010 001 000 has no meaning because it specifies the operations to clear AC to 0 and subtract DR from AC at the same time.

 Each microoperation in Table 7-1 is defined with a register transfer statement and is assigned a symbol for use in a symbolic microprogram. All transfer-type microoperations symbols use five letters. The first two letters designate the source register, the third letter is always a T, and the last two letters designate the destination register. For example, the microoperation that specifies the transfer $AC \leftarrow DR$ (F1 = 100) has the symbol DRTAC, which stands for a transfer from DR to AC.

condition field
 The CD (condition) field consists of two bits which are encoded to specify four status bit conditions as listed in Table 7-1. The first condition is always a 1, so that a reference to $CD = 00$ (or the symbol U) will always find the condition to be true. When this condition is used in conjunction with the BR (branch) field, it provides an unconditional branch operation. The indirect bit

TABLE 7-1 Symbols and Binary Code for Microinstruction Fields

F1	Microoperation	Symbol
000	None	NOP
001	$AC \leftarrow AC + DR$	ADD
010	$AC \leftarrow 0$	CLRAC
011	$AC \leftarrow AC + 1$	INCAC
100	$AC \leftarrow DR$	DRTAC
101	$AR \leftarrow DR(0{-}10)$	DRTAR
110	$AR \leftarrow PC$	PCTAR
111	$M[AR] \leftarrow DR$	WRITE

F2	Microoperation	Symbol
000	None	NOP
001	$AC \leftarrow AC - DR$	SUB
010	$AC \leftarrow AC \vee DR$	OR
011	$AC \leftarrow AC \wedge DR$	AND
100	$DR \leftarrow M[AR]$	READ
101	$DR \leftarrow AC$	ACTDR
110	$DR \leftarrow DR + 1$	INCDR
111	$DR(0{-}10) \leftarrow PC$	PCTDR

F3	Microoperation	Symbol
000	None	NOP
001	$AC \leftarrow AC \oplus DR$	XOR
010	$AC \leftarrow \overline{AC}$	COM
011	$AC \leftarrow \text{shl } AC$	SHL
100	$AC \leftarrow \text{shr } AC$	SHR
101	$PC \leftarrow PC + 1$	INCPC
110	$PC \leftarrow AR$	ARTPC
111	Reserved	

CD	Condition	Symbol	Comments
00	Always = 1	U	Unconditional branch
01	$DR(15)$	I	Indirect address bit
10	$AC(15)$	S	Sign bit of AC
11	$AC = 0$	Z	Zero value in AC

BR	Symbol	Function
00	JMP	$CAR \leftarrow AD$ if condition = 1
		$CAR \leftarrow CAR + 1$ if condition = 0
01	CALL	$CAR \leftarrow AD, SBR \leftarrow CAR + 1$ if condition = 1
		$CAR \leftarrow CAR + 1$ if condition = 0
10	RET	$CAR \leftarrow SBR$ (Return from subroutine)
11	MAP	$CAR(2{-}5) \leftarrow DR(11{-}14), CAR(0,1,6) \leftarrow 0$

I is available from bit 15 of *DR* after an instruction is read from memory. The sign bit of *AC* provides the next status bit. The zero value, symbolized by *Z*, is a binary variable whose value is equal to 1 if all the bits in *AC* are equal to zero. We will use the symbols U, I, S, and Z for the four status bits when we write microprograms in symbolic form.

branch field

The BR (branch) field consists of two bits. It is used, in conjunction with the address field AD, to choose the address of the next microinstruction. As shown in Table 7-1, when BR = 00, the control performs a jump (JMP) operation (which is similar to a branch), and when BR = 01, it performs a call to subroutine (CALL) operation. The two operations are identical except that a call microinstruction stores the return address in the subroutine register *SBR*. The jump and call operations depend on the value of the CD field. If the status bit condition specified in the CD field is equal to 1, the next address in the AD field is transferred to the control address register *CAR*. Otherwise, *CAR* is incremented by 1.

The return from subroutine is accomplished with a BR field equal to 10. This causes the transfer of the return address from *SBR* to *CAR*. The mapping from the operation code bits of the instruction to an address for *CAR* is accomplished when the BR field is equal to 11. This mapping is as depicted in Fig. 7-3. The bits of the operation code are in $DR(11-14)$ after an instruction is read from memory. Note that the last two conditions in the BR field are independent of the values in the CD and AD fields.

Symbolic Microinstructions

The symbols defined in Table 7-1 can be used to specify microinstructions in symbolic form. A symbolic microprogram can be translated into its binary equivalent by means of an assembler. A microprogram assembler is similar in concept to a conventional computer assembler as defined in Sec. 6-3. The simplest and most straightforward way to formulate an assembly language for a microprogram is to define symbols for each field of the microinstruction and to give users the capability for defining their own symbolic addresses.

Each line of the assembly language microprogram defines a symbolic microinstruction. Each symbolic microinstruction is divided into five fields: label, microoperations, CD, BR, and AD. The fields specify the following information.

1. The label field may be empty or it may specify a symbolic address. A label is terminated with a colon (:).
2. The microoperations field consists of one, two, or three symbols, separated by commas, from those defined in Table 7-1. There may be no more than one symbol from each F field. The NOP symbol is used when the microinstruction has no microoperations. This will be translated by the assembler to nine zeros.

address field

3. The CD field has one of the letters U, I, S, or Z.

4. The BR field contains one of the four symbols defined in Table 7-1.

5. The AD field specifies a value for the address field of the microinstruction in one of three possible ways:

    a. With a symbolic address, which must also appear as a label.

    b. With the symbol NEXT to designate the next address in sequence.

    c. When the BR field contains a RET or MAP symbol, the AD field is left empty and is converted to seven zeros by the assembler.

ORG

We will use also the pseudoinstruction ORG to define the origin, or first address, of a microprogram routine. Thus the symbol ORG 64 informs the assembler to place the next microinstruction in control memory at decimal address 64, which is equivalent to the binary address 1000000.

The Fetch Routine

The control memory has 128 words, and each word contains 20 bits. To microprogram the control memory, it is necessary to determine the bit values of each of the 128 words. The first 64 words (addresses 0 to 63) are to be occupied by the routines for the 16 instructions. The last 64 words may be used for any other purpose. A convenient starting location for the fetch routine is address 64. The microinstructions needed for the fetch routine are

$$AR \leftarrow PC$$

$$DR \leftarrow M[AR], \quad PC \leftarrow PC + 1$$

$$AR \leftarrow DR(0\text{--}10), \quad CAR(2\text{--}5) \leftarrow DR(11\text{--}14), \quad CAR(0,1,6) \leftarrow 0$$

The address of the instruction is transferred from PC to AR and the instruction is then read from memory into DR. Since no instruction register is available, the instruction code remains in DR. The address part is transferred to AR and then control is transferred to one of 16 routines by mapping the operation code part of the instruction from DR into CAR.

fetch and decode

The fetch routine needs three microinstructions, which are placed in control memory at addresses 64, 65, and 66. Using the assembly language conventions defined previously, we can write the symbolic microprogram for the fetch routine as follows:

```
        ORG 64
FETCH:  PCTAR          U   JMP   NEXT
        READ, INCPC    U   JMP   NEXT
        DRTAR          U   MAP
```

The translation of the symbolic microprogram to binary produces the following binary microprogram. The bit values are obtained from Table 7-1.

Binary Address	F1	F2	F3	CD	BR	AD
1000000	110	000	000	00	00	1000001
1000001	000	100	101	00	00	1000010
1000010	101	000	000	00	11	0000000

The three microinstructions that constitute the fetch routine have been listed in three different representations. The register transfer representation shows the internal register transfer operations that each microinstruction implements. The symbolic representation is useful for writing microprograms in an assembly language format. The binary representation is the actual internal content that must be stored in control memory. It is customary to write microprograms in symbolic form and then use an assembler program to obtain a translation to binary.

Symbolic Microprogram

The execution of the third (MAP) microinstruction in the fetch routine results in a branch to address 0xxxx00, where xxxx are the four bits of the operation code. For example, if the instruction is an ADD instruction whose operation code is 0000, the MAP microinstruction will transfer to *CAR* the address 0000000, which is the start address for the ADD routine in control memory. The first address for the BRANCH and STORE routines are 0 0001 00 (decimal 4) and 0 0010 00 (decimal 8), respectively. The first address for the other 13 routines are at address values 12, 16, 20, ..., 60. This gives four words in control memory for each routine.

In each routine we must provide microinstructions for evaluating the effective address and for executing the instruction. The indirect address mode is associated with all memory-reference instructions. A saving in the number of control memory words may be achieved if the microinstructions for the indirect address are stored as a subroutine. This subroutine, symbolized by INDRCT, is located right after the fetch routine, as shown in Table 7-2. The table also shows the symbolic microprogram for the fetch routine and the microinstruction routines that execute four computer instructions.

To see how the transfer and return from the indirect subroutine occurs, assume that the MAP microinstruction at the end of the fetch routine caused a branch to address 0, where the ADD routine is stored. The first microinstruction in the ADD routine calls subroutine INDRCT, conditioned on status bit *I*. If $I = 1$, a branch to INDRCT occurs and the return address (address 1 in this case) is stored in the subroutine register *SBR*. The INDRCT subroutine has two microinstructions:

```
INDRCT:    READ      U    JMP    NEXT
           DRTAR     U    RET
```

TABLE 7-2 Symbolic Microprogram (Partial)

Label	Microoperations	CD	BR	AD
	ORG 0			
ADD:	NOP	I	CALL	INDRCT
	READ	U	JMP	NEXT
	ADD	U	JMP	FETCH
	ORG 4			
BRANCH:	NOP	S	JMP	OVER
	NOP	U	JMP	FETCH
OVER:	NOP	I	CALL	INDRCT
	ARTPC	U	JMP	FETCH
	ORG 8			
STORE:	NOP	I	CALL	INDRCT
	ACTDR	U	JMP	NEXT
	WRITE	U	JMP	FETCH
	ORG 12			
EXCHANGE:	NOP	I	CALL	INDRCT
	READ	U	JMP	NEXT
	ACTDR, DRTAC	U	JMP	NEXT
	WRITE	U	JMP	FETCH
	ORG 64			
FETCH:	PCTAR	U	JMP	NEXT
	READ, INCPC	U	JMP	NEXT
	DRTAR	U	MAP	
INDRCT:	READ	U	JMP	NEXT
	DRTAR	U	RET	

Remember that an indirect address considers the address part of the instruction as the address where the effective address is stored rather than the address of the operand. Therefore, the memory has to be accessed to get the effective address, which is then transferred to AR. The return from subroutine (RET) transfers the address from SBR to CAR, thus returning to the second microinstruction of the ADD routine.

execution of instructions

The execution of the ADD instruction is carried out by the microinstructions at addresses 1 and 2. The first microinstruction reads the operand from memory into DR. The second microinstruction performs an add microoperation with the content of DR and AC and then jumps back to the beginning of the fetch routine.

The BRANCH instruction should cause a branch to the effective address if $AC < 0$. The AC will be less than zero if its sign is negative, which is detected from status bit S being a 1. The BRANCH routine in Table 7-2 starts by checking the value of S. If S is equal to 0, no branch occurs and the next microinstruction causes a jump back to the fetch routine without altering the content of PC. If S is equal to 1, the first JMP microinstruction transfers control to location OVER. The microinstruction at this location calls the INDRCT subroutine if $I = 1$. The effective address is then transferred from AR to PC and the microprogram jumps back to the fetch routine.

The STORE routine again uses the INDRCT subroutine if $I = 1$. The content of AC is transferred into DR. A memory write operation is initiated to store the content of DR in a location specified by the effective address in AR.

The EXCHANGE routine reads the operand from the effective address and places it in DR. The contents of DR and AC are interchanged in the third microinstruction. This interchange is possible when the registers are of the edge-triggered type (see Fig. 1-23). The original content of AC that is now in DR is stored back in memory.

Note that Table 7-2 contains a partial list of the microprogram. Only four out of 16 possible computer instructions have been microprogrammed. Also, control memory words at locations 69 to 127 have not been used. Instructions such as multiply, divide, and others that require a long sequence of microoperations will need more than four microinstructions for their execution. Control memory words 69 to 127 can be used for this purpose.

Binary Microprogram

The symbolic microprogram is a convenient form for writing microprograms in a way that people can read and understand. But this is not the way that the microprogram is stored in memory. The symbolic microprogram must be translated to binary either by means of an assembler program or by the user if the microprogram is simple enough as in this example.

The equivalent binary form of the microprogram is listed in Table 7-3. The addresses for control memory are given in both decimal and binary. The binary content of each microinstruction is derived from the symbols and their equivalent binary values as defined in Table 7-1.

Note that address 3 has no equivalent in the symbolic microprogram since the ADD routine has only three microinstructions at addresses 0, 1, and 2. The next routine starts at address 4. Even though address 3 is not used, some binary value must be specified for each word in control memory. We could have specified all 0's in the word since this location will never be used. However, if some unforeseen error occurs, or if a noise signal sets CAR to the value of 3, it will be wise to jump to address 64, which is the beginning of the fetch routine.

control memory

The binary microprogram listed in Table 7-3 specifies the word content of the control memory. When a ROM is used for the control memory, the

TABLE 7-3 Binary Microprogram for Control Memory (Partial)

Micro Routine	Address Decimal	Address Binary	F1	F2	F3	CD	BR	AD
ADD	0	0000000	000	000	000	01	01	1000011
	1	0000001	000	100	000	00	00	0000010
	2	0000010	001	000	000	00	00	1000000
	3	0000011	000	000	000	00	00	1000000
BRANCH	4	0000100	000	000	000	10	00	0000110
	5	0000101	000	000	000	00	00	1000000
	6	0000110	000	000	000	01	01	1000011
	7	0000111	000	000	110	00	00	1000000
STORE	8	0001000	000	000	000	01	01	1000011
	9	0001001	000	101	000	00	00	0001010
	10	0001010	111	000	000	00	00	1000000
	11	0001011	000	000	000	00	00	1000000
EXCHANGE	12	0001100	000	000	000	01	01	1000011
	13	0001101	001	000	000	00	00	0001110
	14	0001110	100	101	000	00	00	0001111
	15	0001111	111	000	000	00	00	1000000
FETCH	64	1000000	110	000	000	00	00	1000001
	65	1000001	000	100	101	00	00	1000010
	66	1000010	101	000	000	00	11	0000000
INDRCT	67	1000011	000	100	000	00	00	1000100
	68	1000100	101	000	000	00	10	0000000

microprogram binary list provides the truth table for fabricating the unit. This fabrication is a hardware process and consists of creating a mask for the ROM so as to produce the 1's and 0's for each word. The bits of ROM are fixed once the internal links are fused during the hardware production. The ROM is made of IC packages that can be removed if necessary and replaced by other packages. To modify the instruction set of the computer, it is necessary to generate a new microprogram and mask a new ROM. The old one can be removed and the new one inserted in its place.

If a writable control memory is employed, the ROM is replaced by a RAM. The advantage of employing a RAM for the control memory is that the microprogram can be altered simply by writing a new pattern of 1's and 0's without resorting to hardware procedures. A writable control memory possesses the flexibility of choosing the instruction set of a computer dynamically by changing the microprogram under processor control. However, most microprogrammed systems use a ROM for the control memory because it is cheaper and faster than a RAM and also to prevent the occasional user from changing the architecture of the system.

7-4 Design of Control Unit

The bits of the microinstruction are usually divided into fields, with each field defining a distinct, separate function. The various fields encountered in instruction formats provide control bits to initiate microoperations in the system, special bits to specify the way that the next address is to be evaluated, and an address field for branching. The number of control bits that initiate microoperations can be reduced by grouping mutually exclusive variables into fields and encoding the k bits in each field to provide 2^k microoperations. Each field requires a decoder to produce the corresponding control signals. This method reduces the size of the microinstruction bits but requires additional hardware external to the control memory. It also increases the delay time of the control signals because they must propagate through the decoding circuits.

The encoding of control bits was demonstrated in the programming example of the preceding section. The nine bits of the microoperation field are divided into three subfields of three bits each. The control memory output of each subfield must be decoded to provide the distinct microoperations. The outputs of the decoders are connected to the appropriate inputs in the processor unit.

decoding of F fields
Figure 7-7 shows the three decoders and some of the connections that must be made from their outputs. Each of the three fields of the microinstruction presently available in the output of control memory are decoded with a 3×8 decoder to provide eight outputs. Each of these outputs must be connected to the proper circuit to initiate the corresponding microoperation as specified in Table 7-1. For example, when $F1 = 101$ (binary 5), the next clock pulse transition transfers the content of $DR(0-10)$ to AR (symbolized by DRTAR in Table 7-1). Similarly, when $F1 = 110$ (binary 6) there is a transfer from PC to AR (symbolized by PCTAR). As shown in Fig. 7-7, outputs 5 and 6 of decoder $F1$ are connected to the load input of AR so that when either one of these outputs is active, information from the multiplexers is transferred to AR. The multiplexers select the information from DR when output 5 is active and from PC when output 5 is inactive. The transfer into AR occurs with a clock pulse transition only when output 5 or output 6 of the decoder are active. The other outputs of the decoders that initiate transfers between registers must be connected in a similar fashion.

arithmetic logic shift unit
The arithmetic logic shift unit can be designed as in Figs. 5-19 and 5-20. Instead of using gates to generate the control signals marked by the symbols AND, ADD, and DR in Fig. 5-19, these inputs will now come from the outputs of the decoders associated with the symbols AND, ADD, and DRTAC, respec-

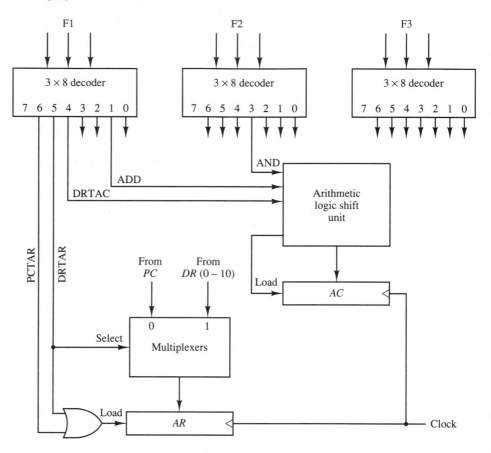

Figure 7-7 Decoding of microoperation fields.

tively, as shown in Fig. 7-7. The other outputs of the decoders that are associated with an *AC* operation must also be connected to the arithmetic logic shift unit in a similar fashion.

Microprogram Sequencer

The basic components of a microprogrammed control unit are the control memory and the circuits that select the next address. The address selection part is called a microprogram sequencer. A microprogram sequencer can be constructed with digital functions to suit a particular application. However, just as there are large ROM units available in integrated circuit packages, so are general-purpose sequencers suited for the construction of microprogram control units. To guarantee a wide range of acceptability, an integrated circuit sequencer must provide an internal organization that can be adapted to a wide range of applications.

The purpose of a microprogram sequencer is to present an address to the control memory so that a microinstruction may be read and executed. The next-address logic of the sequencer determines the specific address source to be loaded into the control address register. The choice of the address source is guided by the next-address information bits that the sequencer receives from the present microinstruction. Commercial sequencers include within the unit an internal register stack used for temporary storage of addresses during microprogram looping and subroutine calls. Some sequencers provide an output register which can function as the address register for the control memory.

To illustrate the internal structure of a typical microprogram sequencer we will show a particular unit that is suitable for use in the microprogram computer example developed in the preceding section. The block diagram of the microprogram sequencer is shown in Fig. 7-8. The control memory is included in the diagram to show the interaction between the sequencer and the memory attached to it. There are two multiplexers in the circuit. The first multiplexer selects an address from one of four sources and routes it into a control address register CAR. The second multiplexer tests the value of a selected status bit and the result of the test is applied to an input logic circuit. The output from CAR provides the address for the control memory. The content of CAR is incremented and applied to one of the multiplexer inputs and to the subroutine register SBR. The other three inputs to multiplexer number 1 come from the address field of the present microinstruction, from the output of SBR, and from an external source that maps the instruction. Although the diagram shows a single subroutine register, a typical sequencer will have a register stack about four to eight levels deep. In this way, a number of subroutines can be active at the same time. A push and pop operation, in conjunction with a stack pointer, stores and retrieves the return address during the call and return microinstructions.

The CD (condition) field of the microinstruction selectgs one of the status bits in the second multiplexer. If the bit selected is equal to 1, the T (test) variable is equal to 1; otherwise, it is equal to 0. The T value together with the two bits from the BR (branch) field go to an input logic circuit. The input logic in a particular sequencer will determine the type of operations that are available in the unit. Typical sequencer operations are: increment, branch or jump, call and return from subroutine, load an external address, push or pop the stack, and other address sequencing operations. With three inputs, the sequencer can provide up to eight address sequencing operations. Some commercial sequencers have three or four inputs in addition to the T input and thus provide a wider range of operations.

design of input logic   The input logic circuit in Fig. 7-8 has three inputs, I_0, I_1, and T, and three outputs, S_0, S_1, and L. Variables S_0 and S_1 select one of the source addresses for CAR. Variable L enables the load input in SBR. The binary values of the two selection variables determine the path in the multiplexer. For example, with $S_1 S_0 = 10$, multiplexer input number 2 is selected and establishes a transfer

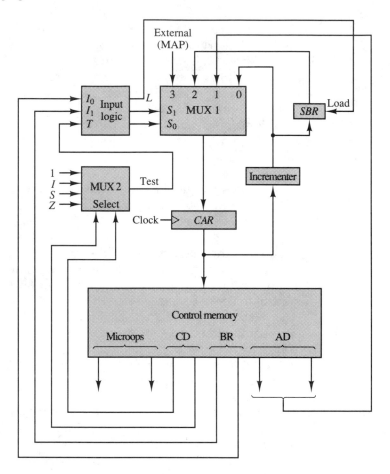

Figure 7-8 Microprogram sequencer for a control memory.

path from *SBR* to *CAR*. Note that each of the four inputs as well as the output of MUX 1 contains a 7-bit address.

The truth table for the input logic circuit is shown in Table 7-4. Inputs I_1 and I_0 are identical to the bit values in the BR field. The function listed in each entry was defined in Table 7-1. The bit values for S_1 and S_0 are determined from the stated function and the path in the multiplexer that establishes the required transfer. The subroutine register is loaded with the incremented value of *CAR* during a call microinstruction (BR = 01) provided that the status bit condition is satisfied ($T = 1$). The truth table can be used to obtain the simplified Boolean functions for the input logic circuit:

$$S_1 = I_1$$
$$S_0 = I_1 I_0 + I_1'T$$
$$L = I_1'I_0T$$

TABLE 7-4 Input Logic Truth Table for Microprogram Sequencer

BR Field	Input I_1 I_0 T	MUX 1 S_1 S_0	Load SBR L
0 0	0 0 0	0 0	0
0 0	0 0 1	0 1	0
0 1	0 1 0	0 0	0
0 1	0 1 1	0 1	1
1 0	1 0 ×	1 0	0
1 1	1 1 ×	1 1	0

The circuit can be constructed with three AND gates, an OR gate, and an inverter.

Note that the incrementer circuit in the sequencer of Fig. 7-8 is not a counter constructed with flip-flops but rather a combinational circuit constructed with gates. A combinational circuit incrementer can be designed by cascading a series of half-adder circuits (see Fig. 4-8). The output carry from one stage must be applied to the input of the next stage. One input in the first least significant stage must be equal to 1 to provide the increment-by-one operation.

PROBLEMS

7-1. What is the difference between a microprocessor and a microprogram? Is it possible to design a microprocessor without a microprogram? Are all microprogrammed computers also microprocessors?

7-2. Explain the difference between hardwired control and microprogrammed control. Is it possible to have a hardwired control associated with a control memory?

7-3. Define the following: (a) microoperation; (b) microinstruction; (c) microprogram; (d) microcode.

7-4. The microprogrammed control organization shown in Fig. 7-1 has the following propagation delay times. 40 ns to generate the next address, 10 ns to transfer the address into the control address register, 40 ns to access the control memory ROM, 10 ns to transfer the microinstruction into the control data register, and 40 ns to perform the required microoperations specified by the control word. What is the maximum clock frequency that the control can use? What would the clock frequency be if the control data register is not used?

7-5. The system shown in Fig. 7-2 uses a control memory of 1024 words of 32 bits each. The microinstruction has three fields as shown in the diagram. The microoperations field has 16 bits.
a. How many bits are there in the branch address field and the select field?

b. If there are 16 status bits in the system, how many bits of the branch logic are used to select a status bit?

c. How many bits are left to select an input for the multiplexers?

7-6. The control memory in Fig. 7-2 has 4096 words of 24 bits each.

a. How many bits are there in the control address register?

b. How many bits are there in each of the four inputs shown going into the multiplexers?

c. What are the number of inputs in each multiplexer and how many multiplexers are needed?

7-7. Using the mapping procedure described in Fig. 7-3, give the first microinstruction address for the following operation code: (a) 0010; (b) 1011; (c) 1111.

7-8. Formulate a mapping procedure that provides eight consecutive microinstructions for each routine. The operation code has six bits and the control memory has 2048 words.

7-9. Explain how the mapping from an instruction code to a microinstruction address can be done by means of a read-only memory. What is the advantage of this method compared to the one in Fig. 7-3?

7-10. Why do we need the two multiplexers in the computer hardware configuration shown in Fig. 7-4? Is there another way that information from multiple sources can be transferred to a common destination?

7-11. Using Table 7-1, give the 9-bit microoperation field for the following microoperations:

a. $AC \leftarrow AC + 1$, $DR \leftarrow DR + 1$

b. $PC \leftarrow PC + 1$, $DR \leftarrow M[AR]$

c. $DR \leftarrow AC$, $AC \leftarrow DR$

7-12. Using Table 7-1, convert the following symbolic microoperations to register transfer statements and to binary.

a. READ, INCPC

b. ACTDR, DRTAC

c. ARTPC, DRTAC, WRITE

7-13. Suppose that we change the ADD routine listed in Table 7-2 to the following two microinstructions.

```
ADD:    READ    I    CALL    INDR2
        ADD     U    JMP     FETCH
```

What should be subroutine INDR2?

7-14. The following is a symbolic microprogram for an instruction in the computer defined in Sec. 7-3.

```
ORG 40
NOP       S    JMP     FETCH
NOP       Z    JMP     FETCH
NOP       I    CALL    INDRCT
ARTPC     U    JMP     FETCH
```

a. Specify the operation performed when the instruction is executed.

b. Convert the four microinstructions into their equivalent binary form.

7-15. The computer of Sec. 7-3 has the following binary microprogram:

Address	Binary Microprogram
60	0 1 0 0 0 0 0 1 0 0 0 0 0 1 0 0 0 0 1 1
61	1 1 1 1 0 0 0 0 0 0 1 0 1 1 0 0 0 0 0 0
62	0 0 1 0 0 1 0 0 0 1 0 1 0 0 1 1 1 1 1 1
63	1 0 1 1 1 0 0 0 0 1 1 1 1 0 1 1 1 1 0 0

   a. Translate it to a symbolic microprogram as in Table 7-2. (FETCH is in address 64 and INDRCT in address 67.)
   b. List all the things that will be wrong when this microprogram is executed in the computer.

7-16. Add the following instructions to the computer of Sec 7-3 (*EA* is the effective address). Write the symbolic microprogram for each routine as in Table 7-2. (Note that *AC* must not change in value unless the instruction specifies a change in *AC*.)

Symbol	Opcode	Symbolic Function	Description
AND	0100	$AC \leftarrow AC \wedge M[EA]$	AND
SUB	0101	$AC \leftarrow AC - M[EA]$	Subtract
ADM	0110	$M[EA] \leftarrow M[EA] + AC$	Add to memory
BTCL	0111	$AC \leftarrow AC \wedge \overline{M[EA]}$	Bit clear
BZ	1000	If $(AC = 0)$ then $(PC \leftarrow EA)$	Branch if AC zero
SEQ	1001	If $(AC = M[EA])$ then $(PC \leftarrow PC + 1)$	Skip if equal
BPNZ	1010	If $(AC > 0)$ then $(PC \leftarrow EA)$	Branch if positive and nonzero

7-17. Write a symbolic microprogram routine for the ISZ (increment and skip if zero) instruction defined in Chap. 5 (Table 5-4). Use the microinstruction format of Sec. 7-3. Note that $DR = 0$ status condition is not available in the CD field of the computer defined in Sec. 7-3. However, you can exchange *AC* and *DR* and check if $AC = 0$ with the Z bit.

7-18. Write the symbolic microprogram routines for the BSA (branch and save address) instructions defined in Chap. 5 (Table 5-4). Use the microinstruction format of Sec. 7-3. Minimize the number of microinstructions.

7-19. Show how outputs 5 and 6 of decoder F3 in Fig. 7-7 are to be connected to the program counter *PC*.

7-20. Show how a 9-bit microoperation field in a microinstruction can be divided into subfields to specify 46 microoperations. How many microoperations can be specified in one microinstruction?

7-21. A computer has 16 registers, an ALU (arithmetic logic unit) with 32 operations, and a shifter with eight operations, all connected to a common bus system.
   a. Formulate a control word for a microoperation.
   b. Specify the number of bits in each field of the control word and give a general encoding scheme.
   c. Show the bits of the control word that specify the microoperation $R4 \leftarrow R5 + R6$.

7-22. Assume that the input logic of the microprogram sequencer of Fig. 7-8 has four inputs, I_2, I_1, I_0, T (test), and three outputs, S_1, S_0, and L. The operations that are performed in the unit are listed in the following table. Design the input logic circuit using a minimum number of gates.

I_2	I_1	I_0	Operation
0	0	0	Increment CAR if $T = 1$, jump to AD if $T = 0$
$\times$	0	1	Jump to AD unconditionally
1	0	0	Increment CAR unconditionally
0	1	0	Jump to AD if $T = 1$, increment CAR if $T = 0$
1	1	0	Call subroutine if $T = 1$, increment CAR if $T = 0$
0	1	1	Return from subroutine unconditionally
1	1	1	Map external address unconditionally

7-23. Design a 7-bit combinational circuit incrementer for the microprogram sequencer of Fig. 7-8 (see Fig. 4-8). Modify the incrementer by including a control input D. When $D = 0$, the circuit increments by one, but when $D = 1$, the circuit increments by two.

7-24. Insert an exclusive-OR gate between MUX 2 and the input logic of Fig. 7-8. One input to the gate comes from the test output of the multiplexer. The other input to the gate comes from a bit labeled P (for polarity) in the microinstruction from control memory. The output of the gate goes to the input T of the input logic. What does the polarity control P accomplish?

REFERENCES

1. Dasgupta, S., *Computer Architecture: A Modern Synthesis*. Vol. 1. New York: John Wiley, 1989.

2. Gorsline, G. W., *Computer Organization: Hardware/Software*, 2nd ed. Englewood Cliffs, NJ: Prentice Hall, 1986.

3. Hamacher, V. C., Z. G. Vranesic, and S. G. Zaky, *Computer Organization*, 3rd ed. New York: McGraw-Hill, 1990.

4. Hays, J. F., *Computer Architecture and Organization*, 2nd ed. New York: McGraw-Hill, 1988.

5. Langholz, G., J. Francioni, and A. Kandel, *Elements of Computer Organization.* Englewood Cliffs, NJ: Prentice Hall, 1989.

6. Lewin, M. H., *Logic Design and Computer Organization.* Reading, MA: Addison-Wesley, 1983.

7. Mano, M. M., *Computer Engineering: Hardware Design.* Englewood Cliffs, NJ: Prentice Hall, 1988.

8. Rafiquzzaman, M., and R. Chandra, *Modern Computer Architecture.* St Paul, MN: West Publishing, 1988.

9. Stallings, W., *Computer Organization and Architecture*, 2nd ed. New York: Macmillan, 1989.

10. Tanenbaum, A. S., *Structured Computer Organization*, 3rd ed. Englewood Cliffs, NJ: Prentice Hall, 1990.

11. Ward, S. A., and R. H. Halstead, Jr., *Computation Structures.* Cambridge, MA: MIT Press, 1990.

CHAPTER EIGHT

Central Processing Unit

IN THIS CHAPTER

8-1 Introduction

CPU

The part of the computer that performs the bulk of data-processing operations is called the central processing unit and is referred to as the CPU. The CPU is made up of three major parts, as shown in Fig. 8-1. The register set stores intermediate data used during the execution of the instructions. The arithmetic logic unit (ALU) performs the required microoperations for executing the instructions. The control unit supervises the transfer of information among the registers and instructs the ALU as to which operation to perform.

The CPU performs a variety of functions dictated by the type of instructions that are incorporated in the computer. Computer architecture is sometimes defined as the computer structure and behavior as seen by the programmer that uses machine language instructions. This includes the instruction formats, addressing modes, the instruction set, and the general organization of the CPU registers.

One boundary where the computer designer and the computer programmer see the same machine is the part of the CPU associated with the instruction set. From the designer's point of view, the computer instruction set provides the specifications for the design of the CPU. The design of a CPU is

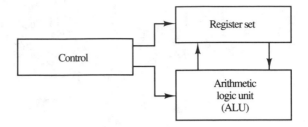

Figure 8-1   Major components of CPU.

a task that in large part involves choosing the hardware for implementing the machine instructions. The user who programs the computer in machine or assembly language must be aware of the register set, the memory structure, the type of data supported by the instructions, and the function that each instruction performs.

Design examples of simple CPUs are carried out in Chaps. 5 and 7. This chapter describes the organization and architecture of the CPU with an emphasis on the user's view of the computer. We briefly describe how the registers communicate with the ALU through buses and explain the operation of the memory stack. We then present the type of instruction formats available, the addressing modes used to retrieve data from memory, and typical instructions commonly incorporated in computers. The last section presents the concept of reduced instruction set computer (RISC).

8-2   General Register Organization

In the programming examples of Chap. 6, we have shown that memory locations are needed for storing pointers, counters, return addresses, temporary results, and partial products during multiplication. Having to refer to memory locations for such applications is time consuming because memory access is the most time-consuming operation in a computer. It is more convenient and more efficient to store these intermediate values in processor registers. When a large number of registers are included in the CPU, it is most efficient to connect them through a common bus system. The registers communicate with each other not only for direct data transfers, but also while performing various microoperations. Hence it is necessary to provide a common unit that can perform all the arithmetic, logic, and shift microoperations in the processor.

bus system

A bus organization for seven CPU registers is shown in Fig. 8-2. The output of each register is connected to two multiplexers (MUX) to form the two buses *A* and *B*. The selection lines in each multiplexer select one register or the input data for the particular bus. The *A* and *B* buses form the inputs to a

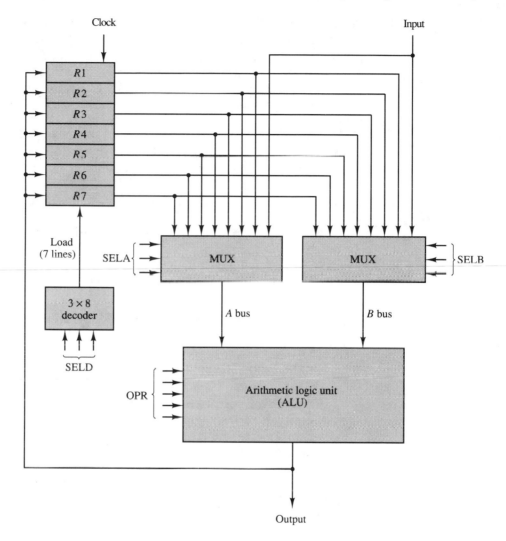

(a) Block diagram

(b) Control word

Figure 8-2   Register set with common ALU.

common arithmetic logic unit (ALU). The operation selected in the ALU determines the arithmetic or logic microoperation that is to be performed. The result of the microoperation is available for output data and also goes into the inputs of all the registers. The register that receives the information from the output bus is selected by a decoder. The decoder activates one of the register load inputs, thus providing a transfer path between the data in the output bus and the inputs of the selected destination register.

The control unit that operates the CPU bus system directs the information flow through the registers and ALU by selecting the various components in the system. For example, to perform the operation

$$R1 \leftarrow R2 + R3$$

the control must provide binary selection variables to the following selector inputs:

1. MUX A selector (SELA): to place the content of $R2$ into bus A.
2. MUX B selector (SELB): to place the content of $R3$ into bus B.
3. ALU operation selector (OPR): to provide the arithmetic addition $A + B$.
4. Decoder destination selector (SELD): to transfer the content of the output bus into $R1$.

The four control selection variables are generated in the control unit and must be available at the beginning of a clock cycle. The data from the two source registers propagate through the gates in the multiplexers and the ALU, to the output bus, and into the inputs of the destination register, all during the clock cycle interval. Then, when the next clock transition occurs, the binary information from the output bus is transferred into $R1$. To achieve a fast response time, the ALU is constructed with high-speed circuits. The buses are implemented with multiplexers or three-state gates, as shown in Sec. 4-3.

Control Word

control word

There are 14 binary selection inputs in the unit, and their combined value specifies a *control word*. The 14-bit control word is defined in Fig. 8-2(b). It consists of four fields. Three fields contain three bits each, and one field has five bits. The three bits of SELA select a source register for the A input of the ALU. The three bits of SELB select a register for the B input of the ALU. The three bits of SELD select a destination register using the decoder and its seven load outputs. The five bits of OPR select one of the operations in the ALU. The 14-bit control word when applied to the selection inputs specify a particular microoperation.

The encoding of the register selections is specified in Table 8-1. The 3-bit

TABLE 8-1 Encoding of Register Selection Fields

Binary Code	SELA	SELB	SELD
000	Input	Input	None
001	R1	R1	R1
010	R2	R2	R2
011	R3	R3	R3
100	R4	R4	R4
101	R5	R5	R5
110	R6	R6	R6
111	R7	R7	R7

binary code listed in the first column of the table specifies the binary code for each of the three fields. The register selected by fields SELA, SELB, and SELD is the one whose decimal number is equivalent to the binary number in the code. When SELA or SELB is 000, the corresponding multiplexer selects the external input data. When SELD = 000, no destination register is selected but the contents of the output bus are available in the external output.

ALU   The ALU provides arithmetic and logic operations. In addition, the CPU must provide shift operations. The shifter may be placed in the input of the ALU to provide a preshift capability, or at the output of the ALU to provide postshifting capability. In some cases, the shift operations are included with the ALU. An arithmetic logic and shift unit was designed in Sec. 4-7. The function table for this ALU is listed in Table 4-8. The encoding of the ALU operations for the CPU is taken from Sec. 4-7 and is specified in Table 8-2. The OPR field has five bits and each operation is designated with a symbolic name.

TABLE 8-2 Encoding of ALU Operations

OPR Select	Operation	Symbol
00000	Transfer A	TSFA
00001	Increment A	INCA
00010	Add $A + B$	ADD
00101	Subtract $A - B$	SUB
00110	Decrement A	DECA
01000	AND A and B	AND
01010	OR A and B	OR
01100	XOR A and B	XOR
01110	Complement A	COMA
10000	Shift right A	SHRA
11000	Shift left A	SHLA

Examples of Microoperations

A control word of 14 bits is needed to specify a microoperation in the CPU. The control word for a given microoperation can be derived from the selection variables. For example, the subtract microoperation given by the statement

$$R1 \leftarrow R2 - R3$$

specifies $R2$ for the A input of the ALU, $R3$ for the B input of the ALU, $R1$ for the destination register, and an ALU operation to subtract $A - B$. Thus the control word is specified by the four fields and the corresponding binary value for each field is obtained from the encoding listed in Tables 8-1 and 8-2. The binary control word for the subtract microoperation is 010 011 001 00101 and is obtained as follows:

Field:	SELA	SELB	SELD	OPR
Symbol:	R2	R3	R1	SUB
Control word:	010	011	001	00101

The control word for this microoperation and a few others are listed in Table 8-3.

The increment and transfer microoperations do not use the B input of the ALU. For these cases, the B field is marked with a dash. We assign 000 to any unused field when formulating the binary control word, although any other binary number may be used. To place the content of a register into the output terminals we place the content of the register into the A input of the ALU, but none of the registers are selected to accept the data. The ALU operation TSFA places the data from the register, through the ALU, into the output terminals. The direct transfer from input to output is accomplished with a control word

TABLE 8-3 Examples of Microoperations for the CPU

Microoperation	Symbolic Designation				Control Word
	SELA	SELB	SELD	OPR	
$R1 \leftarrow R2 - R3$	R2	R3	R1	SUB	010 011 001 00101
$R4 \leftarrow R4 \vee R5$	R4	R5	R4	OR	100 101 100 01010
$R6 \leftarrow R6 + 1$	R6	—	R6	INCA	110 000 110 00001
$R7 \leftarrow R1$	R1	—	R7	TSFA	001 000 111 00000
Output $\leftarrow R2$	R2	—	None	TSFA	010 000 000 00000
Output $\leftarrow$ Input	Input	—	None	TSFA	000 000 000 00000
$R4 \leftarrow$ shl $R4$	R4	—	R4	SHLA	100 000 100 11000
$R5 \leftarrow 0$	R5	R5	R5	XOR	101 101 101 01100

of all 0's (making the B field 000). A register can be cleared to 0 with an exclusive-OR operation. This is because $x \oplus x = 0$.

It is apparent from these examples that many other microoperations can be generated in the CPU. The most efficient way to generate control words with a large number of bits is to store them in a memory unit. A memory unit that stores control words is referred to as a control memory. By reading consecutive control words from memory, it is possible to initiate the desired sequence of microoperations for the CPU. This type of control is referred to as micropro-grammed control. A microprogrammed control unit is shown in Fig. 7-8. The binary control word for the CPU will come from the outputs of the control memory marked "micro-ops."

8-3 Stack Organization

LIFO

A useful feature that is included in the CPU of most computers is a stack or last-in, first-out (LIFO) list. A stack is a storage device that stores information in such a manner that the item stored last is the first item retrieved. The operation of a stack can be compared to a stack of trays. The last tray placed on top of the stack is the first to be taken off.

The stack in digital computers is essentially a memory unit with an address register that can count only (after an initial value is loaded into it). The

stack pointer

register that holds the address for the stack is called a stack pointer (*SP*) because its value always points at the top item in the stack. Contrary to a stack of trays where the tray itself may be taken out or inserted, the physical registers of a stack are always available for reading or writing. It is the content of the word that is inserted or deleted.

The two operations of a stack are the insertion and deletion of items. The operation of insertion is called *push* (or push-down) because it can be thought of as the result of pushing a new item on top. The operation of deletion is called *pop* (or pop-up) because it can be thought of as the result of removing one item so that the stack pops up. However, nothing is pushed or popped in a computer stack. These operations are simulated by incrementing or decrementing the stack pointer register.

Register Stack

A stack can be placed in a portion of a large memory or it can be organized as a collection of a finite number of memory words or registers. Figure 8-3 shows the organization of a 64-word register stack. The stack pointer register *SP* contains a binary number whose value is equal to the address of the word that is currently on top of the stack. Three items are placed in the stack: *A*, *B*, and *C*, in that order. Item *C* is on top of the stack so that the content of *SP* is now 3. To remove the top item, the stack is popped by reading the memory word

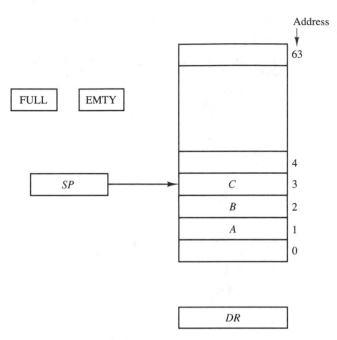

Figure 8-3   Block diagram of a 64-word stack.

at address 3 and decrementing the content of *SP*. Item *B* is now on top of the stack since *SP* holds address 2. To insert a new item, the stack is pushed by incrementing *SP* and writing a word in the next-higher location in the stack. Note that item *C* has been read out but not physically removed. This does not matter because when the stack is pushed, a new item is written in its place.

In a 64-word stack, the stack pointer contains 6 bits because $2^6 = 64$. Since *SP* has only six bits, it cannot exceed a number greater than 63 (111111 in binary). When 63 is incremented by 1, the result is 0 since $111111 + 1 = 1000000$ in binary, but *SP* can accommodate only the six least significant bits. Similarly, when 000000 is decremented by 1, the result is 111111. The one-bit register *FULL* is set to 1 when the stack is full, and the one-bit register *EMTY* is set to 1 when the stack is empty of items. *DR* is the data register that holds the binary data to be written into or read out of the stack.

Initially, *SP* is cleared to 0, *EMTY* is set to 1, and *FULL* is cleared to 0, so that *SP* points to the word at address 0 and the stack is marked empty and not full. If the stack is not full (if *FULL* = 0), a new item is inserted with a push operation. The push operation is implemented with the following sequence of microoperations:

push

$$SP \leftarrow SP + 1 \qquad \text{Increment stack pointer}$$
$$M[SP] \leftarrow DR \qquad \text{Write item on top of the stack}$$

If $(SP = 0)$ then $(FULL \leftarrow 1)$	Check if stack is full
$EMTY \leftarrow 0$	Mark the stack not empty

The stack pointer is incremented so that it points to the address of the next-higher word. A memory write operation inserts the word from DR into the top of the stack. Note that SP holds the address of the top of the stack and that $M[SP]$ denotes the memory word specified by the address presently available in SP. The first item stored in the stack is at address 1. The last item is stored at address 0. If SP reaches 0, the stack is full of items, so $FULL$ is set to 1. This condition is reached if the top item prior to the last push was in location 63 and, after incrementing SP, the last item is stored in location 0. Once an item is stored in location 0, there are no more empty registers in the stack. If an item is written in the stack, obviously the stack cannot be empty, so $EMTY$ is cleared to 0.

pop

A new item is deleted from the stack if the stack is not empty (if $EMTY = 0$). The pop operation consists of the following sequence of micro-operations:

$DR \leftarrow M[SP]$	Read item from the top of stack
$SP \leftarrow SP - 1$	Decrement stack pointer
If $(SP = 0)$ then $(EMTY \leftarrow 1)$	Check if stack is empty
$FULL \leftarrow 0$	Mark the stack not full

The top item is read from the stack into DR. The stack pointer is then decremented. If its value reaches zero, the stack is empty, so $EMTY$ is set to 1. This condition is reached if the item read was in location 1. Once this item is read out, SP is decremented and reaches the value 0, which is the initial value of SP. Note that if a pop operation reads the item from location 0 and then SP is decremented, SP changes to 111111, which is equivalent to decimal 63. In this configuration, the word in address 0 receives the last item in the stack. Note also that an erroneous operation will result if the stack is pushed when $FULL = 1$ or popped when $EMTY = 1$.

Memory Stack

A stack can exist as a stand-alone unit as in Fig. 8-3 or can be implemented in a random-access memory attached to a CPU. The implementation of a stack in the CPU is done by assigning a portion of memory to a stack operation and using a processor register as a stack pointer. Figure 8-4 shows a portion of computer memory partitioned into three segments: program, data, and stack. The program counter PC points at the address of the next instruction in the program. The address register AR points at an array of data. The stack pointer

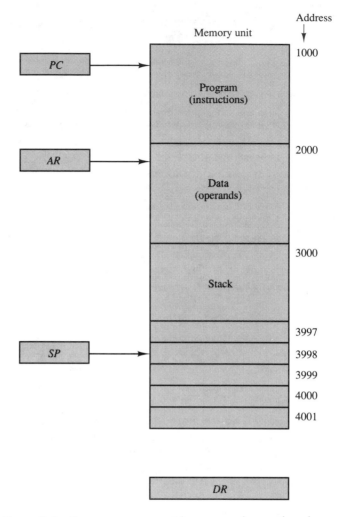

Figure 8-4 Computer memory with program, data, and stack segments.

SP points at the top of the stack. The three registers are connected to a common address bus, and either one can provide an address for memory. *PC* is used during the fetch phase to read an instruction. *AR* is used during the execute phase to read an operand. *SP* is used to push or pop items into or from the stack.

As shown in Fig. 8-4, the initial value of *SP* is 4001 and the stack grows with decreasing addresses. Thus the first item stored in the stack is at address 4000, the second item is stored at address 3999, and the last address that can be used for the stack is 3000. No provisions are available for stack limit checks.

We assume that the items in the stack communicate with a data register *DR*. A new item is inserted with the push operation as follows:

$$SP \leftarrow SP - 1$$

$$M[SP] \leftarrow DR$$

The stack pointer is decremented so that it points at the address of the next word. A memory write operation inserts the word from *DR* into the top of the stack. A new item is deleted with a pop operation as follows:

$$DR \leftarrow M[SP]$$

$$SP \leftarrow SP + 1$$

The top item is read from the stack into *DR*. The stack pointer is then incremented to point at the next item in the stack.

stack limits Most computers do not provide hardware to check for stack overflow (full stack) or underflow (empty stack). The stack limits can be checked by using two processor registers: one to hold the upper limit (3000 in this case), and the other to hold the lower limit (4001 in this case). After a push operation, *SP* is compared with the upper-limit register and after a pop operation, *SP* is compared with the lower-limit register.

The two microoperations needed for either the push or pop are (1) an access to memory through *SP*, and (2) updating *SP*. Which of the two microoperations is done first and whether *SP* is updated by incrementing or decrementing depends on the organization of the stack. In Fig. 8-4 the stack grows by *decreasing* the memory address. The stack may be constructed to grow by *increasing* the memory address as in Fig. 8-3 In such a case, *SP* is incremented for the push operation and decremented for the pop operation. A stack may be constructed so that *SP* points at the next *empty* location above the top of the stack. In this case the sequence of microoperations must be interchanged.

A stack pointer is loaded with an initial value. This initial value must be the bottom address of an assigned stack in memory. Henceforth, *SP* is automatically decremented or incremented with every push or pop operation. The advantage of a memory stack is that the CPU can refer to it without having to specify an address, since the address is always available and automatically updated in the stack pointer.

Reverse Polish Notation

A stack organization is very effective for evaluating arithmetic expressions. The common mathematical method of writing arithmetic expressions imposes difficulties when evaluated by a computer. The common arithmetic expressions are written in *infix notation*, with each operator written *between* the operands. Consider the simple arithmetic expression

$$A * B + C * D$$

The star (denoting multiplication) is placed between two operands A and B or C and D. The plus is between the two products. To evaluate this arithmetic expression it is necessary to compute the product $A * B$, store this product while computing $C * D$, and then sum the two products. From this example we see that to evaluate arithmetic expressions in infix notation it is necessary to scan back and forth along the expression to determine the next operation to be performed.

RPN

The Polish mathematician Lukasiewicz showed that arithmetic expressions can be represented in *prefix notation*. This representation, often referred to as *Polish notation*, places the operator before the operands. The *postfix notation*, referred to as *reverse Polish notation* (RPN), places the operator after the operands. The following examples demonstrate the three representations:

$$A + B \quad \text{Infix notation}$$

$$+AB \quad \text{Prefix or Polish notation}$$

$$AB+ \quad \text{Postfix or reverse Polish notation}$$

The reverse Polish notation is in a form suitable for stack manipulation. The expression

$$A * B + C * D$$

is written in reverse Polish notation as

$$AB * CD * +$$

and is evaluated as follows: Scan the expression from left to right. When an operator is reached, perform the operation with the two operands found on the left side of the operator. Remove the two operands and the operator and replace them by the number obtained from the result of the operation. Continue to scan the expression and repeat the procedure for every operator encountered until there are no more operators.

For the expression above we find the operator $*$ after A and B. We perform the operation $A * B$ and replace A, B, and $*$ by the product to obtain

$$(A * B) CD * +$$

where $(A * B)$ is a *single* quantity obtained from the product. The next operator is a $*$ and its previous two operands are C and D, so we perform $C * D$ and obtain an expression with two operands and one operator:

$$(A * B)(C * D) +$$

The next operator is $+$ and the two operands to be added are the two products, so we add the two quantities to obtain the result.

conversion to RPN   The conversion from infix notation to reverse Polish notation must take into consideration the operational hierarchy adopted for infix notation. This hierarchy dictates that we first perform all arithmetic inside inner parentheses, then inside outer parentheses, and do multiplication and division operations before addition and subtraction operations. Consider the expression

$$(A + B) * [C * (D + E) + F]$$

To evaluate the expression we must first perform the arithmetic inside the parentheses $(A + B)$ and $(D + E)$. Next we must calculate the expression inside the square brackets. The multiplication of $C * (D + E)$ must be done prior to the addition of F since multiplication has precedence over addition. The last operation is the multiplication of the two terms between the parentheses and brackets. The expression can be converted to reverse Polish notation, without the use of parentheses, by taking into consideration the operation hierarchy. The converted expression is

$$AB + DE + C * F + *$$

Proceeding from left to right, we first add A and B, then add D and E. At this point we are left with

$$(A + B)(D + E)C * F + *$$

where $(A + B)$ and $(D + E)$ are each a *single* number obtained from the sum. The two operands for the next $*$ are C and $(D+E)$. These two numbers are multiplied and the product added to F. The final $*$ causes the multiplication of the two terms.

Evaluation of Arithmetic Expressions

Reverse Polish notation, combined with a stack arrangement of registers, is the most efficient way known for evaluating arithmetic expressions. This procedure is employed in some electronic calculators and also in some computers. The stack is particularly useful for handling long, complex problems involving chain calculations. It is based on the fact that any arithmetic expression can be expressed in parentheses-free Polish notation.

The procedure consists of first converting the arithmetic expression into its equivalent reverse Polish notation. The operands are pushed into the stack in the order in which they appear. The initiation of an operation depends on whether we have a calculator or a computer. In a calculator, the operators are entered through the keyboard. In a computer, they must be initiated by instructions that contain an operation field (no address field is required). The following microoperations are executed with the stack when an operation is entered in a calculator or issued by the control in a computer: (1) the two topmost operands in the stack are used for the operation, and (2) the stack is popped and the result of the operation replaces the lower operand. By pushing the operands into the stack continuously and performing the operations as defined above, the expression is evaluated in the proper order and the final result remains on top of the stack.

The following numerical example may clarify this procedure. Consider the arithmetic expression

$$(3*4) + (5*6)$$

In reverse Polish notation, it is expressed as

$$34*56*+$$

stack operations   Now consider the stack operations shown in Fig. 8-5. Each box represents one stack operation and the arrow always points to the top of the stack. Scanning the expression from left to right, we encounter two operands. First the number 3 is pushed into the stack, then the number 4. The next symbol is the multiplication operator $*$. This causes a multiplication of the two topmost items in the stack. The stack is then popped and the product is placed on top of the stack, replacing the two original operands. Next we encounter the two operands 5 and 6, so they are pushed into the stack. The stack operation that results from the next $*$ replaces these two numbers by their product. The last operation causes an arithmetic addition of the two topmost numbers in the stack to produce the final result of 42.

Scientific calculators that employ an internal stack require that the user convert the arithmetic expressions into reverse Polish notation. Computers that use a stack-organized CPU provide a system program to perform the

Figure 8-5   Stack operations to evaluate 3 · 4 + 5 · 6.

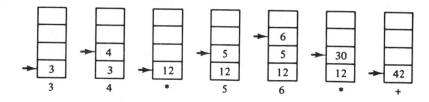

conversion for the user. Most compilers, irrespective of their CPU organization, convert all arithmetic expressions into Polish notation anyway because this is the most efficient method for translating arithmetic expressions into machine language instructions. So in essence, a stack-organized CPU may be more efficient in some applications than a CPU without a stack.

8-4 Instruction Formats

The physical and logical structure of computers is normally described in reference manuals provided with the system. Such manuals explain the internal construction of the CPU, including the processor registers available and their logical capabilities. They list all hardware-implemented instructions, specify their binary code format, and provide a precise definition of each instruction. A computer will usually have a variety of instruction code formats. It is the function of the control unit within the CPU to interpret each instruction code and provide the necessary control functions needed to process the instruction.

The format of an instruction is usually depicted in a rectangular box symbolizing the bits of the instruction as they appear in memory words or in a control register. The bits of the instruction are divided into groups called fields. The most common fields found in instruction formats are:

1. An operation code field that specifies the operation to be performed.
2. An address field that designates a memory address or a processor register.
3. A mode field that specifies the way the operand or the effective address is determined.

Other special fields are sometimes employed under certain circumstances, as for example a field that gives the number of shifts in a shift-type instruction.

The operation code field of an instruction is a group of bits that define various processor operations, such as add, subtract, complement, and shift. The most common operations available in computer instructions are enumerated and discussed in Sec. 8-6. The bits that define the mode field of an instruction code specify a variety of alternatives for choosing the operands from the given address. The various addressing modes that have been formulated for digital computers are presented in Sec. 8-5. In this section we are concerned with the address field of an instruction format and consider the effect of including multiple address fields in an instruction.

register address

Operations specified by computer instructions are executed on some data stored in memory or processor registers. Operands residing in memory are specified by their memory address. Operands residing in processor registers are specified with a register address. A register address is a binary number of k bits that defines one of 2^k registers in the CPU. Thus a CPU with 16 processor registers $R0$ through $R15$ will have a register address field of four bits. The binary number 0101, for example, will designate register $R5$.

Computers may have instructions of several different lengths containing varying number of addresses. The number of address fields in the instruction format of a computer depends on the internal organization of its registers. Most computers fall into one of three types of CPU organizations:

1. Single accumulator organization.
2. General register organization.
3. Stack organization.

An example of an accumulator-type organization is the basic computer presented in Chap. 5. All operations are performed with an implied accumulator register. The instruction format in this type of computer uses one address field. For example, the instruction that specifies an arithmetic addition is defined by an assembly language instruction as

        ADD   X

where X is the address of the operand. The ADD instruction in this case results in the operation $AC \leftarrow AC + M[X]$. AC is the accumulator register and $M[X]$ symbolizes the memory word located at address X.

An example of a general register type of organization was presented in Fig. 7-1. The instruction format in this type of computer needs three register address fields. Thus the instruction for an arithmetic addition may be written in an assembly language as

        ADD   R1, R2, R3

to denote the operation $R1 \leftarrow R2 + R3$. The number of address fields in the instruction can be reduced from three to two if the destination register is the same as one of the source registers. Thus the instruction

        ADD   R1, R2

would denote the operation $R1 \leftarrow R1 + R2$. Only register addresses for $R1$ and $R2$ need be specified in this instruction.

Computers with multiple processor registers use the move instruction with a mnemonic MOV to symbolize a transfer instruction. Thus the instruction

        MOV   R1, R2

denotes the transfer $R1 \leftarrow R2$ (or $R2 \leftarrow R1$, depending on the particular computer). Thus transfer-type instructions need two address fields to specify the source and the destination.

General register-type computers employ two or three address fields in their instruction format. Each address field may specify a processor register or a memory word. An instruction symbolized by

    ADD   R1, X

would specify the operation $R1 \leftarrow R1 + M[X]$. It has two address fields, one for register $R1$ and the other for the memory address X.

The stack-organized CPU was presented in Fig. 8-4. Computers with stack organization would have PUSH and POP instructions which require an address field. Thus the instruction

    PUSH   X

will push the word at address X to the top of the stack. The stack pointer is updated automatically. Operation-type instructions do not need an address field in stack-organized computers. This is because the operation is performed on the two items that are on top of the stack. The instruction

    ADD

in a stack computer consists of an operation code only with no address field. This operation has the effect of popping the two top numbers from the stack, adding the numbers, and pushing the sum into the stack. There is no need to specify operands with an address field since all operands are implied to be in the stack.

Most computers fall into one of the three types of organizations that have just been described. Some computers combine features from more than one organizational structure. For example, the Intel 8080 microprocessor has seven CPU registers, one of which is an accumulator register. As a consequence, the processor has some of the characteristics of a general register type and some of the characteristics of an accumulator type. All arithmetic and logic instructions, as well as the load and store instructions, use the accumulator register, so these instructions have only one address field. On the other hand, instructions that transfer data among the seven processor registers have a format that contains two register address fields. Moreover, the Intel 8080 processor has a stack pointer and instructions to push and pop from a memory stack. The processor, however, does not have the zero-address-type instructions which are characteristic of a stack-organized CPU.

To illustrate the influence of the number of addresses on computer programs, we will evaluate the arithmetic statement

$$X = (A + B) * (C + D)$$

using zero, one, two, or three address instructions. We will use the symbols ADD, SUB, MUL, and DIV for the four arithmetic operations; MOV for the transfer-type operation; and LOAD and STORE for transfers to and from memory and *AC* register. We will assume that the operands are in memory addresses *A*, *B*, *C*, and *D*, and the result must be stored in memory at address *X*.

Three-Address Instructions

Computers with three-address instruction formats can use each address field to specify either a processor register or a memory operand. The program in assembly language that evaluates $X = (A + B) * (C + D)$ is shown below, together with comments that explain the register transfer operation of each instruction.

```
ADD    R1, A, B     R1 ← M[A] + M[B]
ADD    R2, C, D     R2 ← M[C] + M[D]
MUL    X, R1, R2    M[X] ← R1 * R2
```

It is assumed that the computer has two processor registers, *R*1 and *R*2. The symbol *M*[*A*] denotes the operand at memory address symbolized by *A*.

The advantage of the three-address format is that it results in short programs when evaluating arithmetic expressions. The disadvantage is that the binary-coded instructions require too many bits to specify three addresses. An example of a commercial computer that uses three-address instructions is the Cyber 170. The instruction formats in the Cyber computer are restricted to either three register address fields or two register address fields and one memory address field.

Two-Address Instructions

Two-address instructions are the most common in commercial computers. Here again each address field can specify either a processor register or a memory word. The program to evaluate $X = (A + B) * (C + D)$ is as follows:

```
MOV    R1, A       R1 ← M[A]
ADD    R1, B       R1 ← R1 + M[B]
MOV    R2, C       R2 ← M[C]
ADD    R2, D       R2 ← R2 + M[D]
MUL    R1, R2      R1 ← R1 * R2
MOV    X, R1       M[X] ← R1
```

The MOV instruction moves or transfers the operands to and from memory and processor registers. The first symbol listed in an instruction is assumed to be both a source and the destination where the result of the operation is transferred.

One-Address Instructions

One-address instructions use an implied accumulator (*AC*) register for all data manipulation. For multiplication and division there is a need for a second register. However, here we will neglect the second register and assume that the *AC* contains the result of all operations. The program to evaluate $X = (A + B)*(C + D)$ is

```
LOAD    A    AC ← M[A]
ADD     B    AC ← AC + M[B]
STORE   T    M[T] ← AC
LOAD    C    AC ← M[C]
ADD     D    AC ← AC + M[D]
MUL     T    AC ← AC * M[T]
STORE   X    M[X] ← AC
```

All operations are done between the *AC* register and a memory operand. *T* is the address of a temporary memory location required for storing the intermediate result.

Zero-Address Instructions

A stack-organized computer does not use an address field for the instructions ADD and MUL. The PUSH and POP instructions, however, need an address field to specify the operand that communicates with the stack. The following program shows how $X = (A + B)*(C + D)$ will be written for a stack-organized computer. (*TOS* stands for top of stack.)

```
PUSH    A    TOS ← A
PUSH    B    TOS ← B
ADD          TOS ← (A + B)
PUSH    C    TOS ← C
PUSH    D    TOS ← D
ADD          TOS ← (C + D)
MUL          TOS ← (C + D) * (A + B)
POP     X    M[X] ← TOS
```

To evaluate arithmetic expressions in a stack computer, it is necessary to convert the expression into reverse Polish notation. The name "zero-address" is given to this type of computer because of the absence of an address field in the computational instructions.

RISC Instructions

The advantages of a reduced instruction set computer (RISC) architecture are explained in Sec. 8-8. The instruction set of a typical RISC processor is restricted to the use of load and store instructions when communicating between memory and CPU. All other instructions are executed within the registers of the CPU without referring to memory. A program for a RISC-type CPU consists of LOAD and STORE instructions that have one memory and one register address, and computational-type instructions that have three addresses with all three specifying processor registers. The following is a program to evaluate $X = (A + B) * (C + D)$.

```
LOAD    R1, A         R1 ← M[A]
LOAD    R2, B         R2 ← M[B]
LOAD    R3, C         R3 ← M[C]
LOAD    R4, D         R4 ← M[D]
ADD     R1, R1, R2    R1 ← R1 + R2
ADD     R3, R3, R2    R3 ← R3 + R4
MUL     R1, R1, R3    R1 ← R1 * R3
STORE   X, R1         M[X] ← R1
```

The load instructions transfer the operands from memory to CPU registers. The add and multiply operations are executed with data in the registers without accessing memory. The result of the computations is then stored in memory with a store instruction.

8-5 Addressing Modes

The operation field of an instruction specifies the operation to be performed. This operation must be executed on some data stored in computer registers or memory words. The way the operands are chosen during program execution is dependent on the addressing mode of the instruction. The addressing mode specifies a rule for interpreting or modifying the address field of the instruction before the operand is actually referenced. Computers use addressing mode techniques for the purpose of accommodating one or both of the following provisions:

1. To give programming versatility to the user by providing such facilities as pointers to memory, counters for loop control, indexing of data, and program relocation.
2. To reduce the number of bits in the addressing field of the instruction.

The availability of the addressing modes gives the experienced assembly language programmer flexibility for writing programs that are more efficient with respect to the number of instructions and execution time.

To understand the various addressing modes to be presented in this section, it is imperative that we understand the basic operation cycle of the computer. The control unit of a computer is designed to go through an instruction cycle that is divided into three major phases:

1. Fetch the instruction from memory.
2. Decode the instruction.
3. Execute the instruction.

program counter (PC)

There is one register in the computer called the program counter or *PC* that keeps track of the instructions in the program stored in memory. *PC* holds the address of the instruction to be executed next and is incremented each time an instruction is fetched from memory. The decoding done in step 2 determines the operation to be performed, the addressing mode of the instruction, and the location of the operands. The computer then executes the instruction and returns to step 1 to fetch the next instruction in sequence.

In some computers the addressing mode of the instruction is specified with a distinct binary code, just like the operation code is specified. Other computers use a single binary code that designates both the operation and the mode of the instruction. Instructions may be defined with a variety of addressing modes, and sometimes, two or more addressing modes are combined in one instruction.

mode field

An example of an instruction format with a distinct addressing mode field is shown in Fig. 8-6. The operation code specifies the operation to be performed. The mode field is used to locate the operands needed for the operation. There may or may not be an address field in the instruction. If there is an address field, it may designate a memory address or a processor register. Moreover, as discussed in the preceding section, the instruction may have more than one address field, and each address field may be associated with its own particular addressing mode.

Although most addressing modes modify the address field of the instruction, there are two modes that need no address field at all. These are the implied and immediate modes.

Implied Mode: In this mode the operands are specified implicitly in the definition of the instruction. For example, the instruction "complement accumulator" is an implied-mode instruction because the operand in the accumulator register is implied in the definition of the instruction. In fact, all register reference instructions that use an accumulator are implied-mode instructions.

Figure 8-6 Instruction format with mode field.

Opcode	Mode	Address

Zero-address instructions in a stack-organized computer are implied-mode instructions since the operands are implied to be on top of the stack.

Immediate Mode: In this mode the operand is specified in the instruction itself. In other words, an immediate-mode instruction has an operand field rather than an address field. The operand field contains the actual operand to be used in conjunction with the operation specified in the instruction. Immediate-mode instructions are useful for initializing registers to a constant value.

It was mentioned previously that the address field of an instruction may specify either a memory word or a processor register. When the address field specifies a processor register, the instruction is said to be in the register mode.

Register Mode: In this mode the operands are in registers that reside within the CPU. The particular register is selected from a register field in the instruction. A k-bit field can specify any one of 2^k registers.

Register Indirect Mode: In this mode the instruction specifies a register in the CPU whose contents give the address of the operand in memory. In other words, the selected register contains the address of the operand rather than the operand itself. Before using a register indirect mode instruction, the programmer must ensure that the memory address of the operand is placed in the processor register with a previous instruction. A reference to the register is then equivalent to specifying a memory address. The advantage of a register indirect mode instruction is that the address field of the instruction uses fewer bits to select a register than would have been required to specify a memory address directly.

Autoincrement or Autodecrement Mode: This is similar to the register indirect mode except that the register is incremented or decremented after (or before) its value is used to access memory. When the address stored in the register refers to a table of data in memory, it is necessary to increment or decrement the register after every access to the table. This can be achieved by using the increment or decrement instruction. However, because it is such a common requirement, some computers incorporate a special mode that automatically increments or decrements the content of the register after data access.

effective address

The address field of an instruction is used by the control unit in the CPU to obtain the operand from memory. Sometimes the value given in the address field is the address of the operand, but sometimes it is just an address from which the address of the operand is calculated. To differentiate among the various addressing modes it is necessary to distinguish between the address part of the instruction and the effective address used by the control when executing the instruction. The *effective address* is defined to be the memory address obtained from the computation dictated by the given addressing mode. The effective address is the address of the operand in a computational-type instruction. It is the address where control branches in response to a branch-type instruction. We have already defined two addressing modes in Chap. 5. They are summarized here for reference.

Direct Address Mode: In this mode the effective address is equal to the address part of the instruction. The operand resides in memory and its address is given directly by the address field of the instruction. In a branch-type instruction the address field specifies the actual branch address.

Indirect Address Mode: In this mode the address field of the instruction gives the address where the effective address is stored in memory. Control fetches the instruction from memory and uses its address part to access memory again to read the effective address. The indirect address mode is also explained in Sec. 5-1 in conjunction with Fig. 5-2.

A few addressing modes require that the address field of the instruction be added to the content of a specific register in the CPU. The effective address in these modes is obtained from the following computation:

effective address = address part of instruction + content of CPU register

The CPU register used in the computation may be the program counter, an index register, or a base register. In either case we have a different addressing mode which is used for a different application.

Relative Address Mode: In this mode the content of the program counter is added to the address part of the instruction in order to obtain the effective address. The address part of the instruction is usually a signed number (in 2's complement representation) which can be either positive or negative. When this number is added to the content of the program counter, the result produces an effective address whose position in memory is relative to the address of the next instruction. To clarify with an example, assume that the program counter contains the number 825 and the address part of the instruction contains the number 24. The instruction at location 825 is read from memory during the fetch phase and the program counter is then incremented by one to 826. The effective address computation for the relative address mode is 826 + 24 = 850. This is 24 memory locations forward from the address of the next instruction. Relative addressing is often used with branch-type instructions when the branch address is in the area surrounding the instruction word itself. It results in a shorter address field in the instruction format since the relative address can be specified with a smaller number of bits compared to the number of bits required to designate the entire memory address.

Indexed Addressing Mode: In this mode the content of an index register is added to the address part of the instruction to obtain the effective address. The index register is a special CPU register that contains an index value. The address field of the instruction defines the beginning address of a data array in memory. Each operand in the array is stored in memory relative to the beginning address. The distance between the beginning address and the address of the operand is the index value stored in the index register. Any operand in the array can be accessed with the same instruction provided that the index register contains the correct index value. The index register can be incremented to facilitate access to consecutive operands. Note that if an index-type instruction does not include an address field in its format, the instruction converts to the register indirect mode of operation.

Some computers dedicate one CPU register to function solely as an index register. This register is involved implicitly when the index-mode instruction is used. In computers with many processor registers, any one of the CPU registers can contain the index number. In such a case the register must be specified explicitly in a register field within the instruction format.

Base Register Addressing Mode: In this mode the content of a base register is added to the address part of the instruction to obtain the effective address. This is similar to the indexed addressing mode except that the register is now called a base register instead of an index register. The difference between the two modes is in the way they are used rather than in the way that they are computed. An index register is assumed to hold an index number that is relative to the address part of the instruction. A base register is assumed to hold a base address and the address field of the instruction gives a displacement relative to this base address. The base register addressing mode is used in computers to facilitate the relocation of programs in memory. When programs and data are moved from one segment of memory to another, as required in multiprogramming systems, the address values of instructions must reflect this change of position. With a base register, the displacement values of instructions do not have to change. Only the value of the base register requires updating to reflect the beginning of a new memory segment.

Numerical Example

To show the differences between the various modes, we will show the effect of the addressing modes on the instruction defined in Fig. 8-7. The two-word instruction at address 200 and 201 is a "load to AC" instruction with an address field equal to 500. The first word of the instruction specifies the operation code and mode, and the second word specifies the address part. PC has the value 200 for fetching this instruction. The content of processor register $R1$ is 400, and the content of an index register XR is 100. AC receives the operand after the instruction is executed. The figure lists a few pertinent addresses and shows the memory content at each of these addresses.

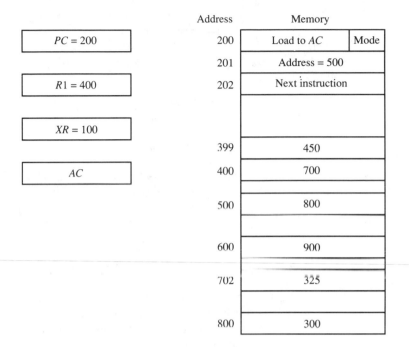

Figure 8-7 Numerical example for addressing modes.

The mode field of the instruction can specify any one of a number of modes. For each possible mode we calculate the effective address and the operand that must be loaded into AC. In the direct address mode the effective address is the address part of the instruction 500 and the operand to be loaded into AC is 800. In the immediate mode the second word of the instruction is taken as the operand rather than an address, so 500 is loaded into AC. (The effective address in this case is 201.) In the indirect mode the effective address is stored in memory at address 500. Therefore, the effective address is 800 and the operand is 300. In the relative mode the effective address is $500 + 202 = 702$ and the operand is 325. (Note that the value in PC after the fetch phase and during the execute phase is 202.) In the index mode the effective address is $XR + 500 = 100 + 500 = 600$ and the operand is 900. In the register mode the operand is in $R1$ and 400 is loaded into AC. (There is no effective address in this case.) In the register indirect mode the effective address is 400, equal to the content of $R1$ and the operand loaded into AC is 700. The autoincrement mode is the same as the register indirect mode except that $R1$ is incremented to 401 after the execution of the instruction. The autodecrement mode decrements $R1$ to 399 prior to the execution of the instruction. The operand loaded into AC is now 450. Table 8-4 lists the values of the effective address and the operand loaded into AC for the nine addressing modes.

TABLE 8-4 Tabular List of Numerical Example

Addressing Mode	Effective Address	Content of AC
Direct address	500	800
Immediate operand	201	500
Indirect address	800	300
Relative address	702	325
Indexed address	600	900
Register	—	400
Register indirect	400	700
Autoincrement	400	700
Autodecrement	399	450

8-6 Data Transfer and Manipulation

Computers provide an extensive set of instructions to give the user the flexibility to carry out various computational tasks. The instruction set of different computers differ from each other mostly in the way the operands are determined from the address and mode fields. The actual operations available in the instruction set are not very different from one computer to another. It so happens that the binary code assignments in the operation code field is different in different computers, even for the same operation. It may also happen that the symbolic name given to instructions in the assembly language notation is different in different computers, even for the same instruction. Nevertheless, *set of* *basic operations* there is a set of basic operations that most, if not all, computers include in their instruction repertoire. The basic set of operations available in a typical computer is the subject covered in this and the next section.

Most computer instructions can be classified into three categories:

1. Data transfer instructions
2. Data manipulation instructions
3. Program control instructions

Data transfer instructions cause transfer of data from one location to another without changing the binary information content. Data manipulation instructions are those that perform arithmetic, logic, and shift operations. Program control instructions provide decision-making capabilities and change the path taken by the program when executed in the computer. The instruction set of a particular computer determines the register transfer operations and control decisions that are available to the user.

Data Transfer Instructions

Data transfer instructions move data from one place in the computer to another without changing the data content. The most common transfers are between memory and processor registers, between processor registers and input or output, and between the processor registers themselves. Table 8-5 gives a list of eight data transfer instructions used in many computers. Accompanying each instruction is a mnemonic symbol. It must be realized that different computers use different mnemonics for the same instruction name.

The *load* instruction has been used mostly to designate a transfer from memory to a processor register, usually an accumulator. The *store* instruction designates a transfer from a processor register into memory. The *move* instruction has been used in computers with multiple CPU registers to designate a transfer from one register to another. It has also been used for data transfers between CPU registers and memory or between two memory words. The *exchange* instruction swaps information between two registers or a register and a memory word. The *input* and *output* instructions transfer data among processor registers and input or output terminals. The *push* and *pop* instructions transfer data between processor registers and a memory stack.

It must be realized that the instructions listed in Table 8-5, as well as in subsequent tables in this section, are often associated with a variety of addressing modes. Some assembly language conventions modify the mnemonic symbol to differentiate between the different addressing modes. For example, the mnemonic for *load immediate* becomes LDI. Other assembly language conventions use a special character to designate the addressing mode. For example, the immediate mode is recognized from a pound sign # placed before the operand. In any case, the important thing is to realize that each instruction can occur with a variety of addressing modes. As an example, consider the *load to accumulator* instruction when used with eight different addressing modes.

TABLE 8-5 Typical Data Transfer
Instructions

Name	Mnemonic
Load	LD
Store	ST
Move	MOV
Exchange	XCH
Input	IN
Output	OUT
Push	PUSH
Pop	POP

TABLE 8-6 Eight Addressing Modes for the Load Instruction

Mode	Assembly Convention	Register Transfer
Direct address	LD ADR	$AC \leftarrow M[ADR]$
Indirect address	LD @ADR	$AC \leftarrow M[M[ADR]]$
Relative address	LD $ADR	$AC \leftarrow M[PC + ADR]$
Immediate operand	LD #NBR	$AC \leftarrow NBR$
Index addressing	LD ADR(X)	$AC \leftarrow M[ADR + XR]$
Register	LD R1	$AC \leftarrow R1$
Register indirect	LD (R1)	$AC \leftarrow M[R1]$
Autoincrement	LD (R1)+	$AC \leftarrow M[R1], R1 \leftarrow R1 + 1$

Table 8-6 shows the recommended assembly language convention and the actual transfer accomplished in each case. *ADR* stands for an address, *NBR* is a number or operand, *X* is an index register, *R1* is a processor register, and *AC* is the accumulator register. The @ character symbolizes an indirect address. The $ character before an address makes the address relative to the program counter *PC*. The # character precedes the operand in an immediate-mode instruction. An indexed mode instruction is recognized by a register that is placed in parentheses after the symbolic address. The register mode is symbolized by giving the name of a processor register. In the register indirect mode, the name of the register that holds the memory address is enclosed in parentheses. The autoincrement mode is distinguished from the register indirect mode by placing a plus after the parenthesized register. The autodecrement mode would use a minus instead. To be able to write assembly language programs for a computer, it is necessary to know the type of instructions available and also to be familiar with the addressing modes used in the particular computer.

Data Manipulation Instructions

Data manipulation instructions perform operations on data and provide the computational capabilities for the computer. The data manipulation instructions in a typical computer are usually divided into three basic types:

1. Arithmetic instructions
2. Logical and bit manipulation instructions
3. Shift instructions

A list of data manipulation instructions will look very much like the list of microoperations given in Chap. 4. It must be realized, however, that each instruction when executed in the computer must go through the fetch phase to read its binary code value from memory. The operands must also be brought into processor registers according to the rules of the instruction addressing mode. The last step is to execute the instruction in the processor. This last step is implemented by means of microoperations as explained in Chap. 4 or through an ALU and shifter as shown in Fig. 8-2. Some of the arithmetic instructions need special circuits for their implementation.

Arithmetic Instructions

The four basic arithmetic operations are addition, subtraction, multiplication, and division. Most computers provide instructions for all four operations. Some small computers have only addition and possibly subtraction instructions. The multiplication and division must then be generated by means of software subroutines. The four basic arithmetic operations are sufficient for formulating solutions to scientific problems when expressed in terms of numerical analysis methods.

A list of typical arithmetic instructions is given in Table 8-7. The increment instruction adds 1 to the value stored in a register or memory word. One common characteristic of the increment operations when executed in processor registers is that a binary number of all 1's when incremented produces a result of all 0's. The decrement instruction subtracts 1 from a value stored in a register or memory word. A number with all 0's, when decremented, produces a number with all 1's.

data type

The add, subtract, multiply, and divide instructions may be available for different types of data. The data type assumed to be in processor registers during the execution of these arithmetic operations is included in the definition of the operation code. An arithmetic instruction may specify fixed-point or floating-point data, binary or decimal data, single-precision or double-precision data. The various data types are presented in Chap. 3.

It is not uncommon to find computers with three or more add instruc-

TABLE 8-7 Typical Arithmetic Instructions

Name	Mnemonic
Increment	INC
Decrement	DEC
Add	ADD
Subtract	SUB
Multiply	MUL
Divide	DIV
Add with carry	ADDC
Subtract with borrow	SUBB
Negate (2's complement)	NEG

tions: one for binary integers, one for floating-point operands, and one for decimal operands. The mnemonics for three add instructions that specify different data types are shown below.

```
ADDI    Add two binary integer numbers
ADDF    Add two floating-point numbers
ADDD    Add two decimal numbers in BCD
```

Algorithms for integer, floating-point, and decimal arithmetic operations are developed in Chap. 10.

The number of bits in any register is of finite length and therefore the results of arithmetic operations are of finite precision. Some computers provide hardware double-precision operations where the length of each operand is taken to be the length of two memory words. Most small computers provide special instructions to facilitate double-precision arithmetic. A special carry flip-flop is used to store the carry from an operation. The instruction "add with carry" performs the addition on two operands plus the value of the carry from the previous computation. Similarly, the "subtract with borrow" instruction subtracts two words and a borrow which may have resulted from a previous subtract operation. The negate instruction forms the 2's complement of a number, effectively reversing the sign of an integer when represented in the signed-2's complement form.

Logical and Bit Manipulation Instructions

Logical instructions perform binary operations on strings of bits stored in registers. They are useful for manipulating individual bits or a group of bits that represent binary-coded information. The logical instructions consider each bit of the operand separately and treat it as a Boolean variable. By proper application of the logical instructions it is possible to change bit values, to clear a group of bits, or to insert new bit values into operands stored in registers or memory words.

Some typical logical and bit manipulation instructions are listed in Table 8-8. The clear instruction causes the specified operand to be replaced by 0's. The complement instruction produces the 1's complement by inverting all the bits of the operand. The AND, OR, and XOR instructions produce the corresponding logical operations on individual bits of the operands. Although they perform Boolean operations, when used in computer instructions, the logical instructions should be considered as performing bit manipulation operations. There are three bit manipulation operations possible: a selected bit can be cleared to 0, or can be set to 1, or can be complemented. The three logical instructions are usually applied to do just that.

clear selected bits   The AND instruction is used to clear a bit or a selected group of bits of an operand. For any Boolean variable x, the relationships $x \cdot 0 = 0$ and $x \cdot 1 = x$ dictate that a binary variable ANDed with a 0 produces a 0; but the variable

TABLE 8-8 Typical Logical and Bit Manipulation Instructions

Name	Mnemonic
Clear	CLR
Complement	COM
AND	AND
OR	OR
Exclusive-OR	XOR
Clear carry	CLRC
Set carry	SETC
Complement carry	COMC
Enable interrupt	EI
Disable interrupt	DI

does not change in value when ANDed with a 1. Therefore, the AND instruction can be used to clear bits of an operand selectively by ANDing the operand with another operand that has 0's in the bit positions that must be cleared. The AND instruction is also called a *mask* because it masks or inserts 0's in a selected portion of an operand.

set selected bits
  The OR instruction is used to set a bit or a selected group of bits of an operand. For any Boolean variable x, the relationships $x + 1 = 1$ and $x + 0 = x$ dictate that a binary variable ORed with a 1 produces a 1; but the variable does not change when ORed with a 0. Therefore, the OR instruction can be used to selectively set bits of an operand by ORing it with another operand with 1's in the bit positions that must be set to 1.

complement selected bits
  Similarly, the XOR instruction is used to selectively complement bits of an operand. This is because of the Boolean relationships $x \oplus 1 = x'$ and $x \oplus 0 = x$. Thus a binary variable is complemented when XORed with a 1 but does not change in value when XORed with a 0. Numerical examples showing the three logic operations are given in Sec. 4-5.

  A few other bit manipulation instructions are included in Table 8-8. Individual bits such as a carry can be cleared, set, or complemented with appropriate instructions. Another example is a flip-flop that controls the interrupt facility and is either enabled or disabled by means of bit manipulation instructions.

Shift Instructions

Instructions to shift the content of an operand are quite useful and are often provided in several variations. Shifts are operations in which the bits of a word are moved to the left or right. The bit shifted in at the end of the word determines the type of shift used. Shift instructions may specify either logical shifts, arithmetic shifts, or rotate-type operations. In either case the shift may be to the right or to the left.

Table 8-9 lists four types of shift instructions. The logical shift inserts 0 to the end bit position. The end position is the leftmost bit for shift right and the rightmost bit position for the shift left. Arithmetic shifts usually conform with the rules for signed-2's complement numbers. These rules are given in Sec. 4-6. The arithmetic shift-right instruction must preserve the sign bit in the leftmost position. The sign bit is shifted to the right together with the rest of the number, but the sign bit itself remains unchanged. This is a shift-right operation with the end bit remaining the same. The arithmetic shift-left instruction inserts 0 to the end position and is identical to the logical shift-left instruction. For this reason many computers do not provide a distinct arithmetic shift-left instruction when the logical shift-left instruction is already available.

The rotate instructions produce a circular shift. Bits shifted out at one end of the word are not lost as in a logical shift but are circulated back into the other end. The rotate through carry instruction treats a carry bit as an extension of the register whose word is being rotated. Thus a rotate-left through carry instruction transfers the carry bit into the rightmost bit position of the register, transfers the leftmost bit position into the carry, and at the same time, shifts the entire register to the left.

Some computers have a multiple-field format for the shift instructions. One field contains the operation code and the others specify the type of shift and the number of times that an operand is to be shifted. A possible instruction code format of a shift instruction may include five fields as follows:

```
OP   REG   TYPE   RL   COUNT
```

Here OP is the operation code field; REG is a register address that specifies the location of the operand; TYPE is a 2-bit field specifying the four different types of shifts; RL is a 1-bit field specifying a shift right or left; and COUNT is a k-bit field specifying up to $2^k - 1$ shifts. With such a format, it is possible to specify the type of shift, the direction, and the number of shifts, all in one instruction.

TABLE 8-9 Typical Shift Instructions

Name	Mnemonic
Logical shift right	SHR
Logical shift left	SHL
Arithmetic shift right	SHRA
Arithmetic shift left	SHLA
Rotate right	ROR
Rotate left	ROL
Rotate right through carry	RORC
Rotate left through carry	ROLC

8-7 Program Control

Instructions are always stored in successive memory locations. When processed in the CPU, the instructions are fetched from consecutive memory locations and executed. Each time an instruction is fetched from memory, the program counter is incremented so that it contains the address of the next instruction in sequence. After the execution of a data transfer or data manipulation instruction, control returns to the fetch cycle with the program counter containing the address of the instruction next in sequence. On the other hand, a program control type of instruction, when executed, may change the address value in the program counter and cause the flow of control to be altered. In other words, program control instructions specify conditions for altering the content of the program counter, while data transfer and manipulation instructions specify conditions for data-processing operations. The change in value of the program counter as a result of the execution of a program control instruction causes a break in the sequence of instruction execution. This is an important feature in digital computers, as it provides control over the flow of program execution and a capability for branching to different program segments.

Some typical program control instructions are listed in Table 8-10. The branch and jump instructions are used interchangeably to mean the same thing, but sometimes they are used to denote different addressing modes. The branch is usually a one-address instruction. It is written in assembly language as BR ADR, where ADR is a symbolic name for an address. When executed, the branch instruction causes a transfer of the value of ADR into the program counter. Since the program counter contains the address of the instruction to be executed, the next instruction will come from location ADR.

Branch and jump instructions may be conditional or unconditional. An unconditional branch instruction causes a branch to the specified address without any conditions. The conditional branch instruction specifies a condition such as branch if positive or branch if zero. If the condition is met, the program counter is loaded with the branch address and the next instruction is taken

TABLE 8-10 Typical Program Control Instructions

Name	Mnemonic
Branch	BR
Jump	JMP
Skip	SKP
Call	CALL
Return	RET
Compare (by subtraction)	CMP
Test (by ANDing)	TST

from this address. If the condition is not met, the program counter is not changed and the next instruction is taken from the next location in sequence.

The skip instruction does not need an address field and is therefore a zero-address instruction. A conditional skip instruction will skip the next instruction if the condition is met. This is accomplished by incrementing the program counter during the execute phase in addition to its being incremented during the fetch phase. If the condition is not met, control proceeds with the next instruction in sequence where the programmer inserts an unconditional branch instruction. Thus a skip-branch pair of instructions causes a branch if the condition is not met, while a single conditional branch instruction causes a branch if the condition is met.

The call and return instructions are used in conjunction with subroutines. Their performance and implementation are discussed later in this section. The compare and test instructions do not change the program sequence directly. They are listed in Table 8-10 because of their application in setting conditions for subsequent conditional branch instructions. The compare instruction performs a subtraction between two operands, but the result of the operation is not retained. However, certain status bit conditions are set as a result of the operation. Similarly, the test instruction performs the logical AND of two operands and updates certain status bits without retaining the result or changing the operands. The status bits of interest are the carry bit, the sign bit, a zero indication, and an overflow condition. The generation of these status bits will be discussed first and then we will show how they are used in conditional branch instructions.

Status Bit Conditions

It is sometimes convenient to supplement the ALU circuit in the CPU with a status register where status bit conditions can be stored for further analysis. Status bits are also called *condition-code* bits or *flag* bits. Figure 8-8 shows the block diagram of an 8-bit ALU with a 4-bit status register. The four status bits are symbolized by C, S, Z, and V. The bits are set or cleared as a result of an operation performed in the ALU.

1. Bit C (carry) is set to 1 if the end carry C_8 is 1. It is cleared to 0 if the carry is 0.

2. Bit S (sign) is set to 1 if the highest-order bit F_7 is 1. It is set to 0 if the bit is 0.

3. Bit Z (zero) is set to 1 if the output of the ALU contains all 0's. It is cleared to 0 otherwise. In other words, $Z = 1$ if the output is zero and $Z = 0$ if the output is not zero.

4. Bit V (overflow) is set to 1 if the exclusive-OR of the last two carries is equal to 1, and cleared to 0 otherwise. This is the condition for an

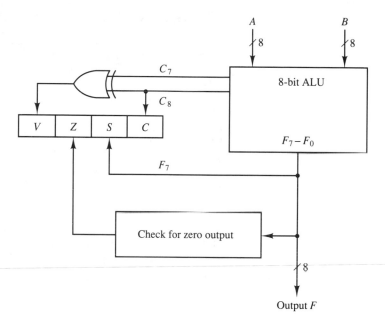

Figure 8-8 Status register bits.

overflow when negative numbers are in 2's complement (see Sec. 3-3). For the 8-bit ALU, $V = 1$ if the output is greater than $+127$ or less than -128.

The status bits can be checked after an ALU operation to determine certain relationships that exist between the values of A and B. If bit V is set after the addition of two signed numbers, it indicates an overflow condition. If Z is set after an exclusive-OR operation, it indicates that $A = B$. This is so because $x \oplus x = 0$, and the exclusive-OR of two equal operands gives an all-0's result which sets the Z bit. A single bit in A can be checked to determine if it is 0 or 1 by masking all bits except the bit in question and then checking the Z status bit. For example, let $A = 101x1100$, where x is the bit to be checked. The AND operation of A with $B = 00010000$ produces a result $000x0000$. If $x = 0$, the Z status bit is set, but if $x = 1$, the Z bit is cleared since the result is not zero. The AND operation can be generated with the TEST instruction listed in Table 8-10 if the original content of A must be preserved.

Conditional Branch Instructions

Table 8-11 gives a list of the most common branch instructions. Each mnemonic is constructed with the letter B (for branch) and an abbreviation of the condition name. When the opposite condition state is used, the letter N (for no) is

TABLE 8-11 Conditional Branch Instructions

Mnemonic	Branch condition	Tested condition
BZ	Branch if zero	$Z = 1$
BNZ	Branch if not zero	$Z = 0$
BC	Branch if carry	$C = 1$
BNC	Branch if no carry	$C = 0$
BP	Branch if plus	$S = 0$
BM	Branch if minus	$S = 1$
BV	Branch if overflow	$V = 1$
BNV	Branch if no overflow	$V = 0$
	Unsigned compare conditions $(A - B)$	
BHI	Branch if higher	$A > B$
BHE	Branch if higher or equal	$A \geq B$
BLO	Branch if lower	$A < B$
BLOE	Branch if lower or equal	$A \leq B$
BE	Branch if equal	$A = B$
BNE	Branch if not equal	$A \neq B$
	Signed compare conditions $(A - B)$	
BGT	Branch if greater than	$A > B$
BGE	Branch if greater or equal	$A \geq B$
BLT	Branch if less than	$A < B$
BLE	Branch if less or equal	$A \leq B$
BE	Branch if equal	$A = B$
BNE	Branch if not equal	$A \neq B$

inserted to define the 0 state. Thus BC is Branch on Carry, and BNC is Branch on No Carry. If the stated condition is true, program control is transferred to the address specified by the instruction. If not, control continues with the instruction that follows. The conditional instructions can be associated also with the jump, skip, call, or return type of program control instructions.

The zero status bit is used for testing if the result of an ALU operation is equal to zero or not. The carry bit is used to check if there is a carry out of the most significant bit position of the ALU. It is also used in conjunction with the rotate instructions to check the bit shifted from the end position of a register into the carry position. The sign bit reflects the state of the most significant bit of the output from the ALU. $S = 0$ denotes a positive sign and $S = 1$, a negative sign. Therefore, a branch on plus checks for a sign bit of 0 and a branch on minus checks for a sign bit of 1. It must be realized, however, that these two conditional branch instructions can be used to check the value of the most significant bit whether it represents a sign or not. The overflow bit is used in conjunction with arithmetic operations done on signed numbers in 2's complement representation.

As stated previously, the compare instruction performs a subtraction of two operands, say $A - B$. The result of the operation is not transferred into a destination register, but the status bits are affected. The status register provides information about the relative magnitude of A and B. Some computers provide conditional branch instructions that can be applied right after the execution of a compare instruction. The specific conditions to be tested depend on whether the two numbers A and B are considered to be unsigned or signed numbers. Table 8-11 gives a list of such conditional branch instructions. Note that we use the words higher and lower to denote the relations between unsigned numbers, and greater and less than for signed numbers. The relative magnitude shown under the tested condition column in the table seems to be the same for unsigned and signed numbers. However, this is not the case since each must be considered separately as explained in the following numerical example.

numerical example   Consider an 8-bit ALU as shown in Fig. 8-8. The largest unsigned number that can be accommodated in 8 bits is 255. The range of signed numbers is between $+127$ and -128. The subtraction of two numbers is the same whether they are unsigned or in signed-2's complement representation (see Chap. 3). Let $A = 11110000$ and $B = 00010100$. To perform $A - B$, the ALU takes the 2's complement of B and adds it to A.

$$
\begin{array}{rl}
A: & 11110000 \\
\overline{B} + 1: & +11101100 \\
\hline
A - B: & 11011100 \qquad C - 1 \quad S - 1 \quad V = 0 \quad Z = 0
\end{array}
$$

The compare instruction updates the status bits as shown. $C = 1$ because there is a carry out of the last stage. $S = 1$ because the leftmost bit is 1. $V = 0$ because the last two carries are both equal to 1, and $Z = 0$ because the result is not equal to 0.

If we assume unsigned numbers, the decimal equivalent of A is 240 and that of B is 20. The subtraction in decimal is $240 - 20 = 220$. The binary result 11011100 is indeed the equivalent of decimal 220. Since $240 > 20$, we have that $A > B$ and $A \neq B$. These two relations can also be derived from the fact that status bit C is equal to 1 and bit Z is equal to 0. The instructions that will cause a branch after this comparison are BHI (branch if higher), BHE (branch if higher or equal), and BNE (branch if not equal).

If we assume signed numbers, the decimal equivalent of A is -16. This is because the sign of A is negative and 11110000 is the 2's complement of 00010000, which is the decimal equivalent of $+16$. The decimal equivalent of B is $+20$. The subtraction in decimal is $(-16) - (+20) = -36$. The binary result 11011100 (the 2's complement of 00100100) is indeed the equivalent of decimal -36. Since $(-16) < (+20)$ we have that $A < B$ and $A \neq B$. These two relations can also be derived from the fact that status bits $S = 1$ (negative), $V = 0$ (no overflow), and $Z = 0$ (not zero). The instructions that will cause a branch after this comparison are BLT (branch if less than), BLE (branch if less or equal), and BNE (branch if not equal).

It should be noted that the instruction BNE and BNZ (branch if not zero) are identical. Similarly, the two instructions BE (branch if equal) and BZ (branch if zero) are also identical. Each is repeated three times in Table 8-11 for the purpose of clarity and completeness.

It should be obvious from the example that the relative magnitude of two unsigned numbers can be determined (after a compare instruction) from the values of status bits C and Z (see Prob. 8-26). The relative magnitude of two signed numbers can be determined from the values of S, V, and Z (see Prob. 8-27).

Some computers consider the C bit to be a borrow bit after a subtraction operation $A - B$. A borrow does not occur if $A \geq B$, but a bit must be borrowed from the next most significant position if $A < B$. The condition for a borrow is the complement of the carry obtained when the subtraction is done by taking the 2's complement of B. For this reason, a processor that considers the C bit to be a borrow after a subtraction will complement the C bit after adding the 2's complement of the subtrahend and denote this bit a borrow.

Subroutine Call and Return

A subroutine is a self-contained sequence of instructions that performs a given computational task. During the execution of a program, a subroutine may be called to perform its function many times at various points in the main program. Each time a subroutine is called, a branch is executed to the beginning of the subroutine to start executing its set of instructions. After the subroutine has been executed, a branch is made back to the main program.

The instruction that transfers program control to a subroutine is known by different names. The most common names used are *call subroutine*, *jump to subroutine*, *branch to subroutine*, or *branch and save address*. A call subroutine instruction consists of an operation code together with an address that specifies the beginning of the subroutine. The instruction is executed by performing two operations: (1) the address of the next instruction available in the program counter (the return address) is stored in a temporary location so the subroutine knows where to return, and (2) control is transferred to the beginning of the subroutine. The last instruction of every subroutine, commonly called *return from subroutine*, transfers the return address from the temporary location into the program counter. This results in a transfer of program control to the instruction whose address was originally stored in the temporary location.

Different computers use a different temporary location for storing the return address. Some store the return address in the first memory location of the subroutine, some store it in a fixed location in memory, some store it in a processor register, and some store it in a memory stack. The most efficient way is to store the return address in a memory stack. The advantage of using a stack for the return address is that when a succession of subroutines is called, the sequential return addresses can be pushed into the stack. The return from subroutine instruction causes the stack to pop and the contents of the top of the stack are transferred to the program counter. In this way, the return is always to the program that last called a subroutine. A subroutine call is implemented with the following microoperations:

$SP \leftarrow SP - 1$ Decrement stack pointer

$M[SP] \leftarrow PC$ Push content of PC onto the stack

$PC \leftarrow$ effective address   Transfer control to the subroutine

If another subroutine is called by the current subroutine, the new return address is pushed into the stack, and so on. The instruction that returns from the last subroutine is implemented by the microoperations:

$PC \leftarrow M[SP]$ Pop stack and transfer to PC

$SP \leftarrow SP + 1$ Increment stack pointer

By using a subroutine stack, all return addresses are automatically stored by the hardware in one unit. The programmer does not have to be concerned or remember where the return address was stored.

A *recursive subroutine* is a subroutine that calls itself. If only one register or memory location is used to store the return address, and the recursive subroutine calls itself, it destroys the previous return address. This is undesirable because vital information is destroyed. This problem can be solved if different storage locations are employed for each use of the subroutine while another lighter-level use is still active. When a stack is used, each return address can be pushed into the stack without destroying any previous values. This solves the problem of recursive subroutines because the next subroutine to exit is always the last subroutine that was called.

Program Interrupt

The concept of program interrupt is used to handle a variety of problems that arise out of normal program sequence. Program interrupt refers to the transfer of program control from a currently running program to another service program as a result of an external or internal generated request. Control returns to the original program after the service program is executed.

The interrupt procedure is, in principle, quite similar to a subroutine call except for three variations: (1) The interrupt is usually initiated by an internal or external signal rather than from the execution of an instruction (except for software interrupt as explained later); (2) the address of the interrupt service program is determined by the hardware rather than from the address field of an instruction; and (3) an interrupt procedure usually stores all the information necessary to define the state of the CPU rather than storing only the program counter. These three procedural concepts are clarified further below.

After a program has been interrupted and the service routine been executed, the CPU must return to exactly the same state that it was when the interrupt occurred. Only if this happens will the interrupted program be able to resume exactly as if nothing had happened. The state of the CPU at the end of the execute cycle (when the interrupt is recognized) is determined from:

1. The content of the program counter

2. The content of all processor registers

3. The content of certain status conditions

program status word

supervisor mode

The collection of all status bit conditions in the CPU is sometimes called a *program status word* or PSW. The PSW is stored in a separate hardware register and contains the status information that characterizes the state of the CPU. Typically, it includes the status bits from the last ALU operation and it specifies the interrupts that are allowed to occur and whether the CPU is operating in a supervisor or user mode. Many computers have a resident operating system that controls and supervises all other programs in the computer. When the CPU is executing a program that is part of the operating system, it is said to be in the supervisor or system mode. Certain instructions are privileged and can be executed in this mode only. The CPU is normally in the user mode when executing user programs. The mode that the CPU is operating at any given time is determined from special status bits in the PSW.

Some computers store only the program counter when responding to an interrupt. The service program must then include instructions to store status and register content before these resources are used. Only a few computers store both program counter and all status and register content in response to an interrupt. Most computers just store the program counter and the PSW. In some cases, there exist two sets of processor registers within the computer, one for each CPU mode. In this way, when the program switches from the user to the supervisor mode (or vice versa) in response to an interrupt, it is not necessary to store the contents of processor registers as each mode uses its own set of registers.

The hardware procedure for processing an interrupt is very similar to the execution of a subroutine call instruction. The state of the CPU is pushed into a memory stack and the beginning address of the service routine is transferred to the program counter. The beginning address of the service routine is determined by the hardware rather than the address field of an instruction. Some computers assign one memory location where interrupts are always transferred. The service routine must then determine what caused the interrupt and proceed to service it. Some computers assign a memory location for each possible interrupt. Sometimes, the hardware interrupt provides its own address that directs the CPU to the desired service routine. In any case, the CPU must possess some form of hardware procedure for selecting a branch address for servicing the interrupt.

The CPU does not respond to an interrupt until the end of an instruction execution. Just before going to the next fetch phase, control checks for any interrupt signals. If an interrupt is pending, control goes to a hardware interrupt cycle. During this cycle, the contents of PC and PSW are pushed onto the stack. The branch address for the particular interrupt is then transferred to PC and a new PSW is loaded into the status register. The service program can now be executed starting from the branch address and having a CPU mode as specified in the new PSW.

The last instruction in the service program is a *return from interrupt* instruction. When this instruction is executed, the stack is popped to retrieve the old PSW and the return address. The PSW is transferred to the status register and the return address to the program counter. Thus the CPU state is restored and the original program can continue executing.

Types of Interrupts

There are three major types of interrupts that cause a break in the normal execution of a program. They can be classified as:

1. External interrupts
2. Internal interrupts
3. Software interrupts

External interrupts come from input–output (I/O) devices, from a timing device, from a circuit monitoring the power supply, or from any other external source. Examples that cause external interrupts are I/O device requesting transfer of data, I/O device finished transfer of data, elapsed time of an event, or power failure. Timeout interrupt may result from a program that is in an endless loop and thus exceeded its time allocation. Power failure interrupt may have as its service routine a program that transfers the complete state of the CPU into a nondestructive memory in the few milliseconds before power ceases.

Internal interrupts arise from illegal or erroneous use of an instruction or data. Internal interrupts are also called *traps*. Examples of interrupts caused by internal error conditions are register overflow, attempt to divide by zero, an invalid operation code, stack overflow, and protection violation. These error conditions usually occur as a result of a premature termination of the instruction execution. The service program that processes the internal interrupt determines the corrective measure to be taken.

The difference between internal and external interrupts is that the internal interrupt is initiated by some exceptional condition caused by the program itself rather than by an external event. Internal interrupts are synchronous with the program while external interrupts are asynchronous. If the program is rerun, the internal interrupts will occur in the same place each time. External interrupts depend on external conditions that are independent of the program being executed at the time.

software interrupt

External and internal interrupts are initiated from signals that occur in the hardware of the CPU. A software interrupt is initiated by executing an instruction. Software interrupt is a special call instruction that behaves like an interrupt rather than a subroutine call. It can be used by the programmer to initiate an interrupt procedure at any desired point in the program. The most common use of software interrupt is associated with a supervisor call instruction. This instruction provides means for switching from a CPU user mode to the supervisor mode. Certain operations in the computer may be assigned to the supervisor mode only, as for example, a complex input or output transfer procedure. A program written by a user must run in the user mode. When an input or output transfer is required, the supervisor mode is requested by means of a supervisor call instruction. This instruction causes a software interrupt that stores the old CPU state and brings in a new PSW that belongs to the supervisor mode. The calling program must pass information to the operating system in order to specify the particular task requested.

8-8 Reduced Instruction Set Computer (RISC)

An important aspect of computer architecture is the design of the instruction set for the processor. The instruction set chosen for a particular computer determines the way that machine language programs are constructed. Early computers had small and simple instruction sets, forced mainly by the need to minimize the hardware used to implement them. As digital hardware became cheaper with the advent of integrated circuits, computer instructions tended to increase both in number and complexity. Many computers have instruction sets that include more than 100 and sometimes even more than 200 instructions. These computers also employ a variety of data types and a large number of addressing modes. The trend into computer hardware complexity was influenced by various factors, such as upgrading existing models to provide more customer applications, adding instructions that facilitate the translation from high-level language into machine language programs, and striving to develop machines that move functions from software implementation into hardware implementation. A computer with a large number of instructions is classified as a *complex instruction set computer*, abbreviated CISC.

CISC

RISC

In the early 1980s, a number of computer designers recommended that computers use fewer instructions with simple constructs so they can be executed much faster within the CPU without having to use memory as often. This type of computer is classified as a *reduced instruction set computer* or RISC. In this section we introduce the major characteristics of CISC and RISC architectures and then present the instruction set and instruction format of a RISC processor.

CISC Characteristics

The design of an instruction set for a computer must take into consideration not only machine language constructs, but also the requirements imposed on the use of high-level programming languages. The translation from high-level to machine language programs is done by means of a compiler program. One reason for the trend to provide a complex instruction set is the desire to simplify the compilation and improve the overall computer performance. The task of a compiler is to generate a sequence of machine instructions for each high-level language statement. The task is simplified if there are machine instructions that implement the statements directly. The essential goal of a CISC architecture is to attempt to provide a single machine instruction for each statement that is written in a high-level language. Examples of CISC architectures are the Digital Equipment Corporation VAX computer and the IBM 370 computer.

Another characteristic of CISC architecture is the incorporation of variable-length instruction formats. Instructions that require register operands may be only two bytes in length, but instructions that need two memory addresses may need five bytes to include the entire instruction code. If the computer has 32-bit words (four bytes), the first instruction occupies half a word, while the second instruction needs one word in addition to one byte in the next word. Packing variable instruction formats in a fixed-length memory word requires special decoding circuits that count bytes within words and frame the instructions according to their byte length.

The instructions in a typical CISC processor provide direct manipulation of operands residing in memory. For example, an ADD instruction may specify one operand in memory through index addressing and a second operand in memory through a direct addressing. Another memory location may be included in the instruction to store the sum. This requires three memory references during execution of the instruction. Although CISC processors have instructions that use only processor registers, the availability of other modes of operations tend to simplify high-level language compilation. However, as more instructions and addressing modes are incorporated into a computer, the more hardware logic is needed to implement and support them, and this may cause the computations to slow down. In summary, the major characteristics of CISC architecture are:

1. A large number of instructions—typically from 100 to 250 instructions
2. Some instructions that perform specialized tasks and are used infrequently

3. A large variety of addressing modes—typically from 5 to 20 different modes

4. Variable-length instruction formats

5. Instructions that manipulate operands in memory

RISC Characteristics

The concept of RISC architecture involves an attempt to reduce execution time by simplifying the instruction set of the computer. The major characteristics of a RISC processor are:

1. Relatively few instructions

2. Relatively few addressing modes

3. Memory access limited to load and store instructions

4. All operations done within the registers of the CPU

5. Fixed-length, easily decoded instruction format

6. Single-cycle instruction execution

7. Hardwired rather than microprogrammed control

The small set of instructions of a typical RISC processor consists mostly of register-to-register operations, with only simple load and store operations for memory access. Thus each operand is brought into a processor register with a load instruction. All computations are done among the data stored in processor registers. Results are transferred to memory by means of store instructions. This architectural feature simplifies the instruction set and encourages the optimization of register manipulation. The use of only a few addressing modes results from the fact that almost all instructions have simple register addressing. Other addressing modes may be included, such as immediate operands and relative mode.

By using a relatively simple instruction format, the instruction length can be fixed and aligned on word boundaries. An important aspect of RISC instruction format is that it is easy to decode. Thus the operation code and register fields of the instruction code can be accessed simultaneously by the control. By simplifying the instructions and their format, it is possible to simplify the control logic. For faster operations, a hardwired control is preferable over a microprogrammed control. An example of hardwired control is presented in Chap. 5 in conjunction with the control unit of the basic computer. Examples of microprogrammed control are presented in Chap. 7.

A characteristic of RISC processors is their ability to execute one instruction per clock cycle. This is done by overlapping the fetch, decode, and execute phases of two or three instructions by using a procedure referred to as pipelining. A load or store instruction may require two clock cycles because access to memory takes more time than register operations. Efficient pipelining, as well as a few other characteristics, are sometimes attributed to RISC, although they may exist in non-RISC architectures as well. Other characteristics attributed to RISC architecture are:

1. A relatively large number of registers in the processor unit
2. Use of overlapped register windows to speed-up procedure call and return
3. Efficient instruction pipeline
4. Compiler support for efficient translation of high-level language programs into machine language programs

A large number of registers is useful for storing intermediate results and for optimizing operand references. The advantage of register storage as opposed to memory storage is that registers can transfer information to other registers much faster than the transfer of information to and from memory. Thus register-to-memory operations can be minimized by keeping the most frequent accessed operands in registers. Studies that show improved performance for RISC architecture do not differentiate between the effects of the reduced instruction set and the effects of a large register file. For this reason a large number of registers in the processing unit are sometimes associated with RISC processors. The use of overlapped register windows when transferring program control after a procedure call is explained below. Instruction pipeline in RISC is presented in Sec. 9-5 after we explain the concept of pipelining.

pipelining

Overlapped Register Windows

Procedure call and return occurs quite often in high-level programming languages. When translated into machine language, a procedure call produces a sequence of instructions that save register values, pass parameters needed for the procedure, and then calls a subroutine to execute the body of the procedure. After a procedure return, the program restores the old register values, passes results to the calling program, and returns from the subroutine. Saving and restoring registers and passing of parameters and results involve time-consuming operations. Some computers provide multiple-register banks, and each procedure is allocated its own bank of registers. This eliminates the need for saving and restoring register values. Some computers use the memory stack to store the parameters that are needed by the procedure, but this requires a memory access every time the stack is accessed.

A characteristic of some RISC processors is their use of *overlapped register windows* to provide the passing of parameters and avoid the need for saving and restoring register values. Each procedure call results in the allocation of a new window consisting of a set of registers from the register file for use by the new procedure. Each procedure call activates a new register window by incrementing a pointer, while the return statement decrements the pointer and causes the activation of the previous window. Windows for adjacent procedures have overlapping registers that are shared to provide the passing of parameters and results.

The concept of overlapped register windows is illustrated in Fig. 8-9. The system has a total of 74 registers. Registers $R0$ through $R9$ are global registers that hold parameters shared by all procedures. The other 64 registers are divided into four windows to accommodate procedures A, B, C, and D. Each register window consists of 10 local registers and two sets of six registers common to adjacent windows. Local registers are used for local variables. Common registers are used for exchange of parameters and results between adjacent procedures. The common overlapped registers permit parameters to be passed without the actual movement of data. Only one register window is activated at any given time with a pointer indicating the active window. Each procedure call activates a new register window by incrementing the pointer. The high registers of the calling procedure overlap the low registers of the called procedure, and therefore the parameters automatically transfer from calling to called procedure.

As an example, suppose that procedure A calls procedure B. Registers $R26$ through $R31$ are common to both procedures, and therefore procedure A stores the parameters for procedure B in these registers. Procedure B uses local registers $R32$ through $R41$ for local variable storage. If procedure B calls procedure C, it will pass the parameters through registers $R42$ through $R47$. When procedure B is ready to return at the end of its computation, the program stores results of the computation in registers $R26$ through $R31$ and transfers back to the register window of procedure A. Note that registers $R10$ through $R15$ are common to procedures A and D because the four windows have a circular organization with A being adjacent to D.

As mentioned previously, the 10 global registers $R0$ through $R9$ are available to all procedures. Each procedure in Fig. 8-9 has available a total of 32 registers while it is active. This includes 10 global registers, 10 local registers, six low overlapping registers, and six high overlapping registers. Other fixed-size register window schemes are possible, and each may differ in the size of the register window and the size of the total register file. In general, the organization of register windows will have the following relationships:

number of global registers = G
number of local registers in each window = L
number of registers common to two windows = C
number of windows = W

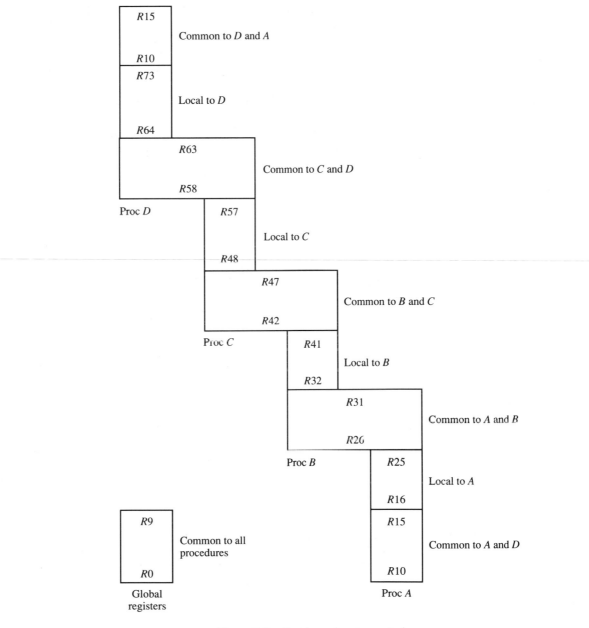

Figure 8-9   Overlapped register windows.

The number of registers available for each window is calculated as follows:

$$\text{window size} = L + 2C + G$$

The total number of registers needed in the processor is

$$\text{register file} = (L + C)W + G$$

In the example of Fig. 8-9 we have $G = 10$, $L = 10$, $C = 6$, and $W = 4$. The window size is $10 + 12 + 10 = 32$ registers, and the register file consists of $(10 + 6) \times 4 + 10 = 74$ registers.

Berkeley RISC I

One of the first projects intended to show the advantages of RISC architecture was conducted at the University of California, Berkeley. The Berkeley RISC I is a 32-bit integrated circuit CPU. It supports 32-bit addresses and either 8-, 16-, or 32-bit data. It has a 32-bit instruction format and a total of 31 instructions. There are three basic addressing modes: register addressing, immediate operand, and relative to PC addressing for branch instructions. It has a register file of 138 registers arranged into 10 global registers and 8 windows of 32 registers in each. The 32 registers in each window have an organization similar to the one shown in Fig. 8-9. Since only one set of 32 registers in a window is

Figure 8-10   Berkeley RISC I instruction formats.

31	24	23	19	18	14	13	12		5	4	0
Opcode		Rd		Rs		0		Not used		S2	
8		5		5		1		8		5	

(a) Register mode: (S2 specifies a register)

31	24	23	19	18	14	13	12		0
Opcode		Rd		Rs		1		S2	
8		5		5		1		13	

(b) Register–immediate mode: (S2 specifies an operand)

31	24	23	19	18		0
Opcode		COND		Y	
8		5		19	

(c) PC relative mode:

accessed at any given time, the instruction format can specify a processor register with a register field of five bits.

Figure 8-10 shows the 32-bit instruction formats used for register-to-register instructions and memory access instructions. Seven of the bits in the operation code specify an operation, and the eighth bit indicates whether to update the status bits after an ALU operation. For register-to-register instructions, the 5-bit Rd field selects one of the 32 registers as a destination for the result of the operation. The operation is performed with the data specified in fields Rs and S2. Rs is one of the source registers. If bit 13 of the instruction is 0, the low-order 5 bits of S2 specify another source register. If bit 13 of the instruction is 1, S2 specifies a sign-extended 13-bit constant. Thus the instruction has a three-address format, but the second source may be either a register or an immediate operand. Memory access instructions use Rs to specify a 32-bit address in a register and S2 to specify an offset. Register $R0$ contains all 0's, so it can be used in any field to specify a zero quantity. The third instruction format combines the last three fields to form a 19-bit relative address Y and is used primarily with the jump and call instructions. The COND field replaces the Rd field for jump instructions and is used to specify one of 16 possible branch conditions.

The 31 instructions of RISC I are listed in Table 8-12. They have been grouped into three categories. Data manipulation instructions perform arithmetic, logic, and shift operations. The symbols under the opcode and operands columns are used when writing assembly language programs. The register transfer and description columns explain the instruction in register transfer notation and in words. Note that all instructions have three operands. The second source S2 can be either a register or an immediate operand, symbolized by the number sign #. Consider, for example, the ADD instruction and how it can be used to perform a variety of operations.

ADD R22,R21,R23	$R23 \leftarrow R22 + R21$
ADD R22,#150,R23	$R23 \leftarrow R22 + 150$
ADD R0,R21,R22	$R22 \leftarrow R21$ (Move)
ADD R0,#150,R22	$R22 \leftarrow 150$ (Load immediate)
ADD R22,#1,R22	$R22 \leftarrow R22 + 1$ (Increment)

By using register $R0$, which always contains 0's, it is possible to transfer the contents of one register or a constant into another register. The increment operation is accomplished by adding a constant 1 to a register.

The data transfer instructions consist of six load instructions, three store instructions, and two instructions that transfer the program status word PSW. The register that holds PSW contains the status of the CPU and includes the program counter, the status bits from the ALU, pointers used in conjunction with the register windows, and other information that determines the state of the CPU.

TABLE 8-12 Instruction Set of Berkeley RISC I

Opcode	Operands	Register Transfer	Description
Data manipulation instructions			
ADD	Rs,S2,Rd	$Rd \leftarrow Rs + S2$	Integer add
ADDC	Rs,S2,Rd	$Rd \leftarrow Rs + S2 + carry$	Add with carry
SUB	Rs,S2,Rd	$Rd \leftarrow Rs - S2$	Integer subtract
SUBC	Rs,S2,Rd	$Rd \leftarrow Rs - S2 - carry$	Subtract with carry
SUBR	Rs,S2,Rd	$Rd \leftarrow S2 - Rs$	Subtract reverse
SUBCR	Rs,S2,Rd	$Rd \leftarrow S2 - Rs - carry$	Subtract with carry
AND	Rs,S2,Rd	$Rd \leftarrow Rs \wedge S2$	AND
OR	Rs,S2,Rd	$Rd \leftarrow Rs \vee S2$	OR
XOR	Rs,S2,Rd	$Rd \leftarrow Rs \oplus S2$	Exclusive-OR
SLL	Rs,S2,Rd	$Rd \leftarrow Rs$ shifted by $S2$	Shift-left
SRL	Rs,S2,Rd	$Rd \leftarrow Rs$ shifted by $S2$	Shift-right logical
SRA	Rs,S2,Rd	$Rd \leftarrow Rs$ shifted by $S2$	Shift-right arithmetic
Data transfer instructions			
LDL	(Rs)S2,Rd	$Rd \leftarrow M[Rs + S2]$	Load long
LDSU	(Rs)S2,Rd	$Rd \leftarrow M[Rs + S2]$	Load short unsigned
LDSS	(Rs)S2,Rd	$Rd \leftarrow M[Rs + S2]$	Load short signed
LDBU	(Rs)S2,Rd	$Rd \leftarrow M[Rs + S2]$	Load byte unsigned
LDBS	(Rs)S2,Rd	$Rd \leftarrow M[Rs + S2]$	Load byte signed
LDHI	Rd,Y	$Rd \leftarrow Y$	Load immediate high
STL	Rd,(Rs)S2	$M[Rs + S2] \leftarrow Rd$	Store long
STS	Rd,(Rs)S2	$M[Rs + S2] \leftarrow Rd$	Store short
STB	Rd,(Rs)S2	$M[Rs + S2] \leftarrow Rd$	Store byte
GETPSW	Rd	$Rd \leftarrow PSW$	Load status word
PUTPSW	Rd	$PSW \leftarrow Rd$	Set status word
Program control instructions			
JMP	COND, S2(Rs)	$PC \leftarrow Rs + S2$	Conditional jump
JMPR	COND,Y	$PC \leftarrow PC + Y$	Jump relative
CALL	Rd,S2(Rs)	$Rd \leftarrow PC$ $PC \leftarrow Rs + S2$ $CWP \leftarrow CWP - 1$	Call subroutine and change window
CALLR	Rd,Y	$Rd \leftarrow PC$ $PC \leftarrow PC + Y$ $CWP \leftarrow CWP - 1$	Call relative and change window
RET	Rd,S2	$PC \leftarrow Rd + S2$ $CWP - CWP + 1$	Return and change window
CALLINT	Rd	$Rd \leftarrow PC$ $CWP \leftarrow CWP - 1$	Disable interrupts
RETINT	Rd,S2	$PC \leftarrow Rd + S2$ $CWP \leftarrow CWP + 1$	Enable interrupts
GTLPC	Rd	$Rd \leftarrow PC$	Get last PC

The load and store instructions move data between a register and memory. The load instructions accommodate signed or unsigned data of eight bits (byte) or 16 bits (short word). The long-word instructions operate on 32-bit data. Although there appears to be a register plus displacement addressing mode in data transfer instructions, register indirect addressing and direct addressing is also possible. The following are examples of load long instructions with different addressing modes.

$$\text{LDL (R22)\#150,R5} \qquad R5 \leftarrow M[R22] + 150$$
$$\text{LDL (R22)\#0,R5} \qquad R5 \leftarrow M[R22]$$
$$\text{LDL (R0)\#500,R5} \qquad R5 \leftarrow M[500]$$

The effective address in the first instruction is evaluated from the contents of register $R22$ plus a displacement of 150. The second instruction uses a 0 displacement, which reduces it to a register indirect mode. The third instruction uses all 0's from register $R0$ to produce a direct address type of instruction.

The program control instructions operate with the program counter PC to control the program sequence. There are two jump and two call instructions. One uses an index plus displacement addressing; the second uses a relative to PC mode with the 19-bit Y value as the relative address. The call and return instructions use a 3-bit CWP (current window pointer) register which points to the currently active register window. Every time the program calls a new procedure, CWP is decremented by one to point to the next-lower register window. After a return instruction CWP is incremented by one to return to the previous register window.

PROBLEMS

8-1. A bus-organized CPU similar to Fig. 8-2 has 16 registers with 32 bits in each, an ALU, and a destination decoder.
    a. How many multiplexers are there in the A bus, and what is the size of each multiplexer?
    b. How many selection inputs are needed for MUX A and MUX B?
    c. How many inputs and outputs are there in the decoder?
    d. How many inputs and outputs are there in the ALU for data, including input and output carries?
    e. Formulate a control word for the system assuming that the ALU has 35 operations.

8-2. The bus system of Fig. 8-2 has the following propagation delay times: 30 ns for the signals to propagate through the multiplexers, 80 ns to perform the ADD operation in the ALU, 20 ns delay in the destination decoder, and 10 ns to clock the data into the destination register. What is the minimum cycle time that can be used for the clock?

8-3.   Specify the control word that must be applied to the processor of Fig. 8-2 to implement the following microoperations.
a. $R1 \leftarrow R2 + R3$
b. $R4 \leftarrow R4$
c. $R5 \leftarrow R5 - 1$
d. $R6 \leftarrow \text{shl } R1$
e. $R7 \leftarrow \text{input}$

8-4.   Determine the microoperations that will be executed in the processor of Fig. 8-2 when the following 14-bit control words are applied.
a. 00101001100101
b. 00000000000000
c. 01001001001100
d. 00000100000010
e. 11110001110000

8-5.   Let $SP = 000000$ in the stack of Fig. 8-3. How many items are there in the stack if:
a. FULL = 1 and EMTY = 0?
b. FULL = 0 and EMTY = 1?

8-6.   A stack is organized such that SP always points at the next empty location on the stack. This means that SP can be initialized to 4000 in Fig. 8-4 and the first item in the stack is stored in location 4000. List the microoperations for the push and pop operations.

8-7.   Convert the following arithmetic expressions from infix to reverse Polish notation.
a. $A * B + C * D + E * F$
b. $A * B + A * (B * D + C * E)$
c. $A + B * [C * D + E * (F + G)]$
d. $\dfrac{A * [B + C * (D + E)]}{F * (G + H)}$

8-8.   Convert the following arithmetic expressions from reverse Polish notation to infix notation.
a. $A \ B \ C \ D \ E + * - /$
b. $A \ B \ C \ D \ E * / - +$
c. $A \ B \ C * / \ D - E \ F / +$
d. $A \ B \ C \ D \ E \ F \ G + * + * + *$

8-9.   Convert the following numerical arithmetic expression into reverse Polish notation and show the stack operations for evaluating the numerical result.

$$(3 + 4)[10(2 + 6) + 8]$$

8-10.   A first-in, first-out (FIFO) has a memory organization that stores information in such a manner that the item that is stored first is the first item that is retrieved. Show how a FIFO memory operates with three counters. A write counter WC holds the address for writing into memory. A read counter RC holds the address for reading from memory. An available storage counter ASC indicates the number of words stored in FIFO. ASC is incremented for every word stored and decremented for every item that is retrieved.

8-11.   A computer has 32-bit instructions and 12-bit addresses. If there are 250 two-address instructions, how many one-address instructions can be formulated?

8-12.   Write a program to evaluate the arithmetic statement:

$$X = \frac{A - B + C*(D*E - F)}{G + H*K}$$

    a. Using a general register computer with three address instructions.
    b. Using a general register computer with two address instructions.
    c. Using an accumulator type computer with one address instructions.
    d. Using a stack organized computer with zero-address operation instructions.

8-13.   The memory unit of a computer has 256K words of 32 bits each. The computer has an instruction format with four fields: an operation code field, a mode field to specify one of seven addressing modes, a register address field to specify one of 60 processor registers, and a memory address. Specify the instruction format and the number of bits in each field if the in instruction is in one memory word.

8-14.   A two-word instruction is stored in memory at an address designated by the symbol W. The address field of the instruction (stored at W + 1) is designated by the symbol Y. The operand used during the execution of the instruction is stored at an address symbolized by Z. An index register contains the value X. State how Z is calculated from the other addresses if the addressing mode of the instruction is
    a. direct
    b. indirect
    c. relative
    d. indexed

8-15.   A relative mode branch type of instruction is stored in memory at an address equivalent to decimal 750. The branch is made to an address equivalent to decimal 500.
    a. What should be the value of the relative address field of the instruction (in decimal)?
    b. Determine the relative address value in binary using 12 bits. (Why must the number be in 2's complement?)
    c. Determine the binary value in PC after the fetch phase and calculate the binary value of 500. Then show that the binary value in PC plus the relative address calculated in part (b) is equal to the binary value of 500.

8-16.   How many times does the control unit refer to memory when it fetches and executes an indirect addressing mode instruction if the instruction is (a) a computational type requiring an operand from memory; (b) a branch type.

8-17.   What must the address field of an indexed addressing mode instruction be to make it the same as a register indirect mode instruction?

8-18.   An instruction is stored at location 300 with its address field at location 301. The address field has the value 400. A processor register R1 contains the number 200. Evaluate the effective address if the addressing mode of the instruction is (a) direct; (b) immediate; (c) relative; (d) register indirect; (e) index with $R1$ as the index register.

8-19. Assuming an 8-bit computer, show the multiple precision addition of the two 32-bit unsigned numbers listed below using the add with carry instruction. Each byte is expressed as a two-digit hexadecimal number.

$$(6E\ C3\ 56\ 7A) + (13\ 55\ 6B\ 8F)$$

8-20. Perform the logic AND, OR, and XOR with the two binary strings 10011100 and 10101010.

8-21. Given the 16-bit value 1001101011001101. What operation must be performed in order to:
a. clear to 0 the first eight bits?
b. set to 1 the last eight bits?
c. complement the middle eight bits?

8-22. An 8-bit register contains the value 01111011 and the carry bit is equal to 1. Perform the eight shift operations given by the instructions listed in Table 8-9. Each time, start from the initial value given above.

8-23. Represent the following signed numbers in binary using eight bits. $+83$; -83; $+68$; -68.
a. Perform the addition $(-83) + (+68)$ in binary and interpret the result obtained.
b. Perform the subtraction $(-68) - (+83)$ in binary and indicate if there is an overflow.
c. Shift binary -68 once to the right and give the value of the shifted number in decimal.
d. Shift binary -83 once to the left and indicate if there is an overflow.

8-24. Show that the circuit labeled "check for zero output" in Fig. 8-8 is an 8-bit NOR gate.

8-25. An 8-bit computer has a register R. Determine the values of status bits C, S, Z, and V (Fig. 8-8) after each of the following instructions. The initial value of register R in each case is hexadecimal 72. The numbers below are also in hexadecimal.
a. Add immediate operand C6 to R.
b. Add immediate operand 1E to R.
c. Subtract immediate operand 9A from R.
d. AND immediate operand 8D to R.
e. Exclusive-OR R with R.

8-26. Two unsigned numbers A and B are compared by subtracting $A - B$. The carry status bit is considered as a borrow bit after a compare instruction in most commercial computers, so that $C = 1$ if $A < B$. Show that the relative magnitude of A and B can be determined from inspection of status bits C and Z as specified in the table for Problem 8-26. (See also Table 8-11.)

8-27. Two signed numbers A and B represented in signed-2's complement form are compared by subtracting $A - B$. Status bits S, Z, and V are set or cleared depending on the result of the operation. (Note that there is a sign reversal

Table for Problem 8-26

Relation	Condition of Status Bits
$A > B$	$C = 0$ and $Z = 0$
$A \geq B$	$C = 0$
$A < B$	$C = 1$
$A \leq B$	$C = 1$ or $Z = 1$
$A = B$	$Z = 1$
$A \neq B$	$Z = 0$

if an overflow occurs.) Show that the relative magnitude of A and B can be determined from inspection of the status bits as specified below. (See also Table 8-11.)

Table for Problem 8-27

Relation	Condition of Status Bits
$A > B$	$(S \oplus V) = 0$ and $Z = 0$
$A \geq B$	$(S \oplus V) = 0$
$A < B$	$(S \oplus V) = 1$
$A \leq B$	$(S \oplus V) = 1$ or $Z = 1$
$A = B$	$Z = 1$
$A \neq B$	$Z = 0$

8-28.   It is necessary to design a digital circuit with four inputs C, S, Z, and V and 10 outputs, one for each of the branch conditions listed in Probs. 8-26 and 8-27. (The equal and unequal conditions are common to both tables.) Draw the logic diagram of the circuit using two OR gates, one XOR gate, and five inverters.

8-29.   Consider the two 8-bit numbers $A = 01000001$ and $B = 10000100$.
   a. Give the decimal equivalent of each number assuming that (1) they are unsigned, and (2) they are signed.
   b. Add the two binary numbers and interpret the sum assuming that the numbers are (1) unsigned, and (2) signed.
   c. Determine the values of the C, Z, S, and V status bits after the addition.
   d. List the conditional branch instructions from Table 8-11 that will have a true condition.

8-30.   The program in a computer compares two unsigned numbers A and B by performing a subtraction $A - B$ and updating the status bits. Let $A = 01000001$ and $B = 10000100$.
   a. Evaluate the difference and interpret the binary result.
   b. Determine the values of status bits C (borrow) and Z.
   c. List the conditional branch instructions from Table 8-11 that will have a true condition.

8-31.   The program in a computer compares two signed numbers A and B by performing the subtraction $A - B$ and updating the status bits. Let $A = 01000001$ and $B = 10000100$.

a. Evaluate the difference and interpret the binary result.

b. Determine the value of status bits S, Z, and V.

c. List the conditional branch instructions from Table 8-11 that will have a true condition.

8-32.   The content of the top of a memory stack is 5320. The content of the stack pointer SP is 3560. A two-word call subroutine instruction is located in memory at address 1120 followed by the address field of 6720 at location 1121. What are the content of PC, SP, and the top of the stack:

a. Before the call instruction is fetched from memory?

b. After the call instruction is executed?

c. After the return from subroutine?

8-33.   What are the basic differences between a branch instruction, a call subroutine instruction, and program interrupt?

8-34.   Give five examples of external interrupts and five examples of internal interrupts. What is the difference between a software interrupt and a subroutine call?

8-35.   A computer responds to an interrupt request signal by pushing onto the stack the contents of PC and the current PSW (program status word). It then reads a new PSW from memory from a location given by an interrupt address symbolized by IAD. The first address of the service program is taken from memory at location IAD + 1.

a. List the sequence of microoperations for the interrupt cycle.

b. List the sequence of microoperations for the return from interrupt instruction.

8-36.   Examples of computers with variable instruction formats are IBM 370, VAX 11, and Intel 386. Compare the variable instruction formats of one of these computers with the fixed-length instruction format used in RISC I.

8-37.   Three computers use register windows with the following characteristics. Determine the window size and the total number of registers in each computer.

	Computer 1	Computer 2	Computer 3
Global registers	10	8	16
Local registers	10	8	16
Common registers	6	8	16
Number of windows	8	4	16

8-38.   Give an example of a RISC I instructions that will perform the following operations.

a. Decrement a register

b. Complement a register

c. Negate a register

    d. Clear a register to 0

    e. Divide a signed number by 4

    f. No operation

8-39. Write the RISC I instructions in assembly language that will cause a jump to address 3200 if the Z (zero) status bit is equal to 1.

    a. Using immediate mode

    b. Using a relative address mode (assume that $PC = 3400$)

REFERENCES

1. Gear, C. W., *Computer Organization and Programming*, 3rd ed. New York: McGraw-Hill, 1980.

2. Gorsline, G. W., *Computer Organization: Hardware/Software*, 2nd ed. Englewood Cliffs, NJ: Prentice Hall, 1986.

3. Gray, N. A. B., *Introduction to Computer Systems*. Englewood Cliffs, NJ: Prentice Hall, 1987.

4. Hamacher, V. C., Z. G. Vranesic, and S. G. Zaky, *Computer Organization*, 3rd ed. New York: McGraw-Hill, 1990.

5. Hays, J. F., *Computer Architecture and Organization*, 2nd ed. New York: McGraw-Hill, 1988.

6. Langholz, G., J. Francioni, and A. Kandel, *Elements of Computer Organization*. Englewood Cliffs, NJ: Prentice Hall, 1989.

7. Levy, H. M., and R. H. Eckhouse, Jr., *Computer Programming and Architecture: The VAX-11*. Bedford, MA: Digital Press, 1980.

8. Lippiatt, A. G., and G. L. Wright, *The Architecture of Small Computer Systems*, 2nd ed. Englewood Cliffs, NJ: Prentice Hall, 1985.

9. Mano, M. M., *Computer Engineering: Hardware Design*. Englewood Cliffs, NJ: Prentice Hall, 1988.

10. Murray, W. D., *Computer and Digital System Architecture*. Englewood Cliffs, NJ: Prentice Hall, 1990.

11. Patterson, D. A., and J. L. Hennessy, *Computer Architecture: A Quantitative Approach*. San Mateo, CA: Morgan Kaufmann Publishers, 1990.

12. Patterson, D. A., and C. H. Sequin, "A VLSI RISC." *IEEE Computer*, September 1982, pp. 8–22.

13. Pollard, L. H., *Computer Design and Architecture*. Englewood Cliffs, NJ: Prentice Hall, 1990.

14. Rafiquzzaman, M., and R. Chandra, *Modern Computer Architecture*. St. Paul, MN: West Publishers, 1988.

15. Siewiorek, D., C. G. Bell, and A. Newell, *Computer Structures: Principles and Examples*. New York: McGraw-Hill, 1982.

16. Stallings, W., *Computer Organization and Architecture*, 2nd ed. New York: Macmillan, 1989.

17. Tanenbaum, A. S., *Structured Computer Organization*, 3rd ed. Englewood Cliffs, NJ: Prentice Hall, 1990.

18. Tomek, I., *Introduction to Computer Organization*. Rockville, MD: Computer Science Press, 1981.

19. Toy, W., and B. Zee, *Computer Hardware/Software Architecture*. Englewood Cliffs, NJ: Prentice Hall, 1986.

20. Ward, S. A., and R. H. Halstead, Jr., *Computation Structures*. Cambridge, MA: MIT Press, 1990.

CHAPTER NINE

Pipeline and Vector Processing

IN THIS CHAPTER

9-1   Parallel Processing

Parallel processing is a term used to denote a large class of techniques that are used to provide simultaneous data-processing tasks for the purpose of increasing the computational speed of a computer system. Instead of processing each instruction sequentially as in a conventional computer, a parallel processing system is able to perform concurrent data processing to achieve faster execution time. For example, while an instruction is being executed in the ALU, the next instruction can be read from memory. The system may have two or more ALUs and be able to execute two or more instructions at the same time. Furthermore, the system may have two or more processors operating concurrently. The purpose of parallel processing is to speed up the computer processing capability and increase its throughput, that is, the amount of processing that can be accomplished during a given interval of time. The amount of hardware increases with parallel processing, and with it, the cost of the system increases. However, technological developments have reduced hardware costs to the point where parallel processing techniques are economically feasible.

throughput

Parallel processing can be viewed from various levels of complexity. At the lowest level, we distinguish between parallel and serial operations by the type of registers used. Shift registers operate in serial fashion one bit at a time, while registers with parallel load operate with all the bits of the word simulta-neously. Parallel processing at a higher level of complexity can be achieved by having a multiplicity of functional units that perform identical or different operations simultaneously. Parallel processing is established by distributing the data among the multiple functional units. For example, the arithmetic, logic, and shift operations can be separated into three units and the operands diverted to each unit under the supervision of a control unit.

multiple functional units

Figure 9-1 shows one possible way of separating the execution unit into eight functional units operating in parallel. The operands in the registers are applied to one of the units depending on the operation specified by the instruc-

Figure 9-1   Processor with multiple functional units.

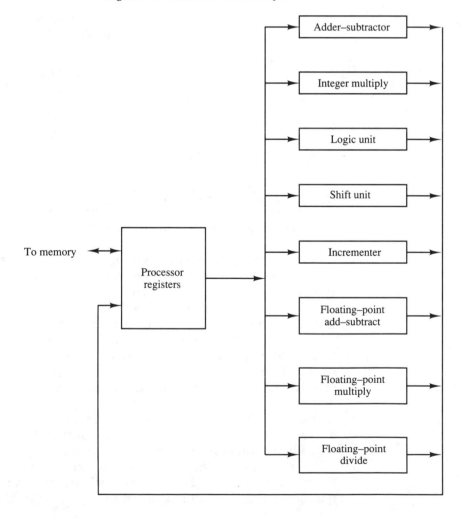

tion associated with the operands. The operation performed in each functional unit is indicated in each block of the diagram. The adder and integer multiplier perform the arithmetic operations with integer numbers. The floating-point operations are separated into three circuits operating in parallel. The logic, shift, and increment operations can be performed concurrently on different data. All units are independent of each other, so one number can be shifted while another number is being incremented. A multifunctional organization is usually associated with a complex control unit to coordinate all the activities among the various components.

There are a variety of ways that parallel processing can be classified. It can be considered from the internal organization of the processors, from the interconnection structure between processors, or from the flow of information through the system. One classification introduced by M. J. Flynn considers the organization of a computer system by the number of instructions and data items that are manipulated simultaneously. The normal operation of a computer is to fetch instructions from memory and execute them in the processor. The sequence of instructions read from memory constitutes an *instruction stream*. The operations performed on the data in the processor constitutes a *data stream*. Parallel processing may occur in the instruction stream, in the data stream, or in both. Flynn's classification divides computers into four major groups as follows:

Single instruction stream, single data stream (SISD)

Single instruction stream, multiple data stream (SIMD)

Multiple instruction stream, single data stream (MISD)

Multiple instruction stream, multiple data stream (MIMD)

SISD represents the organization of a single computer containing a control unit, a processor unit, and a memory unit. Instructions are executed sequentially and the system may or may not have internal parallel processing capabilities. Parallel processing in this case may be achieved by means of multiple functional units or by pipeline processing.

SIMD   SIMD represents an organization that includes many processing units under the supervision of a common control unit. All processors receive the same instruction from the control unit but operate on different items of data. The shared memory unit must contain multiple modules so that it can communicate with all the processors simultaneously. MISD structure is only of theoretical interest since no practical system has been constructed using this organization. MIMD organization refers to a computer system capable of

MIMD   processing several programs at the same time. Most multiprocessor and multicomputer systems can be classified in this category.

Flynn's classification depends on the distinction between the performance of the control unit and the data-processing unit. It emphasizes the behavioral characteristics of the computer system rather than its operational and structural interconnections. One type of parallel processing that does not fit Flynn's classification is pipelining. The only two categories used from this classification are SIMD array processors discussed in Sec. 9-7, and MIMD multiprocessors presented in Chap. 13.

In this chapter we consider parallel processing under the following main topics:

1. Pipeline processing
2. Vector processing
3. Array processors

Pipeline processing is an implementation technique where arithmetic suboperations or the phases of a computer instruction cycle overlap in execution. Vector processing deals with computations involving large vectors and matrices. Array processors perform computations on large arrays of data.

9-2   Pipelining

Pipelining is a technique of decomposing a sequential process into suboperations, with each subprocess being executed in a special dedicated segment that operates concurrently with all other segments. A pipeline can be visualized as a collection of processing segments through which binary information flows. Each segment performs partial processing dictated by the way the task is partitioned. The result obtained from the computation in each segment is transferred to the next segment in the pipeline. The final result is obtained after the data have passed through all segments. The name "pipeline" implies a flow of information analogous to an industrial assembly line. It is characteristic of pipelines that several computations can be in progress in distinct segments at the same time. The overlapping of computation is made possible by associating a register with each segment in the pipeline. The registers provide isolation between each segment so that each can operate on distinct data simultaneously.

Perhaps the simplest way of viewing the pipeline structure is to imagine that each segment consists of an input register followed by a combinational circuit. The register holds the data and the combinational circuit performs the suboperation in the particular segment. The output of the combinational circuit in a given segment is applied to the input register of the next segment. A clock is applied to all registers after enough time has elapsed to perform all segment activity. In this way the information flows through the pipeline one step at a time.

an example   The pipeline organization will be demonstrated by means of a simple example. Suppose that we want to perform the combined multiply and add operations with a stream of numbers.

$$A_i * B_i + C_i \qquad \text{for } i = 1, 2, 3, \ldots, 7$$

Each suboperation is to be implemented in a segment within a pipeline. Each segment has one or two registers and a combinational circuit as shown in Fig. 9-2. $R1$ through $R5$ are registers that receive new data with every clock pulse. The multiplier and adder are combinational circuits. The suboperations performed in each segment of the pipeline are as follows:

$$R1 \leftarrow A_i, \quad R2 \leftarrow B_i \qquad \text{Input } A_i \text{ and } B_i$$
$$R3 \leftarrow R1 * R2, \quad R4 \leftarrow C_i \qquad \text{Multiply and input } C_i$$
$$R5 \leftarrow R3 + R4 \qquad \text{Add } C_i \text{ to product}$$

The five registers are loaded with new data every clock pulse. The effect of each clock is shown in Table 9-1. The first clock pulse transfers A_1 and B_1 into $R1$ and

Figure 9-2   Example of pipeline processing.

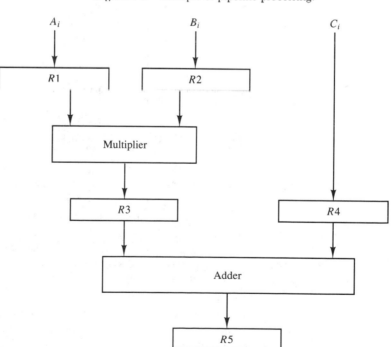

TABLE 9-1 Content of Registers in Pipeline Example

Clock Pulse Number	Segment 1		Segment 2		Segment 3
	$R1$	$R2$	$R3$	$R4$	$R5$
1	A_1	B_1	—	—	—
2	A_2	B_2	$A_1 * B_1$	C_1	—
3	A_3	B_3	$A_2 * B_2$	C_2	$A_1 * B_1 + C_1$
4	A_4	B_4	$A_3 * B_3$	C_3	$A_2 * B_2 + C_2$
5	A_5	B_5	$A_4 * B_4$	C_4	$A_3 * B_3 + C_3$
6	A_6	B_6	$A_5 * B_5$	C_5	$A_4 * B_4 + C_4$
7	A_7	B_7	$A_6 * B_6$	C_6	$A_5 * B_5 + C_5$
8	—	—	$A_7 * B_7$	C_7	$A_6 * B_6 + C_6$
9	—	—	—	—	$A_7 * B_7 + C_7$

$R2$. The second clock pulse transfers the product of $R1$ and $R2$ into $R3$ and C_1 into $R4$. The same clock pulse transfers A_2 and B_2 into $R1$ and $R2$. The third clock pulse operates on all three segments simultaneously. It places A_3 and B_3 into $R1$ and $R2$, transfers the product of $R1$ and $R2$ into $R3$, transfers C_2 into $R4$, and places the sum of $R3$ and $R4$ into $R5$. It takes three clock pulses to fill up the pipe and retrieve the first output from $R5$. From there on, each clock produces a new output and moves the data one step down the pipeline. This happens as long as new input data flow into the system. When no more input data are available, the clock must continue until the last output emerges out of the pipeline.

General Considerations

Any operation that can be decomposed into a sequence of suboperations of about the same complexity can be implemented by a pipeline processor. The technique is efficient for those applications that need to repeat the same task many times with different sets of data. The general structure of a four-segment pipeline is illustrated in Fig. 9-3. The operands pass through all four segments in a fixed sequence. Each segment consists of a combinational circuit S_i that performs a suboperation over the data stream flowing through the pipe. The segments are separated by registers R_i that hold the intermediate results between the stages. Information flows between adjacent stages under the control of a common clock applied to all the registers simultaneously. We

task

define a *task* as the total operation performed going through all the segments in the pipeline.

space-time diagram

The behavior of a pipeline can be illustrated with a *space-time* diagram. This is a diagram that shows the segment utilization as a function of time. The space-time diagram of a four-segment pipeline is demonstrated in Fig. 9-4. The horizontal axis displays the time in clock cycles and the vertical axis gives the

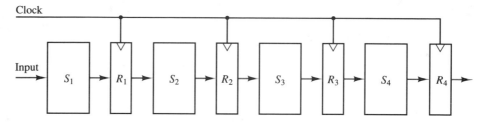

Figure 9-3 Four-segment pipeline.

segment number. The diagram shows six tasks T_1 through T_6 executed in four segments. Initially, task T_1 is handled by segment 1. After the first clock, segment 2 is busy with T_1, while segment 1 is busy with task T_2. Continuing in this manner, the first task T_1 is completed after the fourth clock cycle. From then on, the pipe completes a task every clock cycle. No matter how many segments there are in the system, once the pipeline is full, it takes only one clock period to obtain an output.

Now consider the case where a k-segment pipeline with a clock cycle time t_p is used to execute n tasks. The first task T_1 requires a time equal to kt_p to complete its operation since there are k segments in the pipe. The remaining $n - 1$ tasks emerge from the pipe at the rate of one task per clock cycle and they will be completed after a time equal to $(n - 1)t_p$. Therefore, to complete n tasks using a k-segment pipeline requires $k + (n - 1)$ clock cycles. For example, the diagram of Fig. 9-4 shows four segments and six tasks. The time required to complete all the operations is $4 + (6 - 1) = 9$ clock cycles, as indicated in the diagram.

Next consider a nonpipeline unit that performs the same operation and takes a time equal to t_n to complete each task. The total time required for n tasks is nt_n. The *speedup* of a pipeline processing over an equivalent nonpipeline processing is defined by the ratio

$$S = \frac{nt_n}{(k + n - 1)t_p}$$

Figure 9-4 Space-time diagram for pipeline.

Segment:	1	2	3	4	5	6	7	8	9
1	T_1	T_2	T_3	T_4	T_5	T_6			
2		T_1	T_2	T_3	T_4	T_5	T_6		
3			T_1	T_2	T_3	T_4	T_5	T_6	
4				T_1	T_2	T_3	T_4	T_5	T_6

Clock cycles

As the number of tasks increases, n becomes much larger than $k - 1$, and $k + n - 1$ approaches the value of n. Under this condition, the speedup becomes

$$S = \frac{t_n}{t_p}$$

If we assume that the time it takes to process a task is the same in the pipeline and nonpipeline circuits, we will have $t_n = kt_p$. Including this assumption, the speedup reduces to

$$S = \frac{kt_p}{t_p} = k$$

This shows that the theoretical maximum speedup that a pipeline can provide is k, where k is the number of segments in the pipeline.

To clarify the meaning of the speedup ratio, consider the following numerical example. Let the time it takes to process a suboperation in each segment be equal to $t_p = 20$ ns. Assume that the pipeline has $k = 4$ segments and executes $n = 100$ tasks in sequence. The pipeline system will take $(k + n - 1)t_p = (4 + 99) \times 20 = 2060$ ns to complete. Assuming that $t_n = kt_p = 4 \times 20 = 80$ ns, a nonpipeline system requires $nkt_p = 100 \times 80 = 8000$ ns to complete the 100 tasks. The speedup ratio is equal to 8000/2060 = 3.88. As the number of tasks increases, the speedup will approach 4, which is equal to the number of segments in the pipeline. If we assume that $t_n = 60$ ns, the speedup becomes 60/20 = 3.

To duplicate the theoretical speed advantage of a pipeline process by means of multiple functional units, it is necessary to construct k identical units that will be operating in parallel. The implication is that a k-segment pipeline processor can be expected to equal the performance of k copies of an equivalent nonpipeline circuit under equal operating conditions. This is illustrated in Fig. 9-5, where four identical circuits are connected in parallel. Each P circuit performs the same task of an equivalent pipeline circuit. Instead of operating with the input data in sequence as in a pipeline, the parallel circuits accept four input data items simultaneously and perform four tasks at the same time. As far as the speed of operation is concerned, this is equivalent to a four segment pipeline. Note that the four-unit circuit of Fig. 9-5 constitutes a single-instruction multiple-data (SIMD) organization since the same instruction is used to operate on multiple data in parallel.

There are various reasons why the pipeline cannot operate at its maximum theoretical rate. Different segments may take different times to complete their suboperation. The clock cycle must be chosen to equal the time delay of the segment with the maximum propagation time. This causes all other segments to waste time while waiting for the next clock. Moreover, it is not always

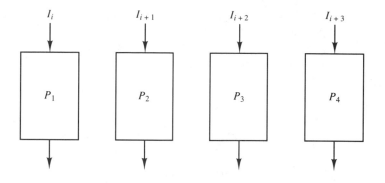

Figure 9-5   Multiple functional units in parallel.

correct to assume that a nonpipe circuit has the same time delay as that of an equivalent pipeline circuit. Many of the intermediate registers will not be needed in a single unit circuit, which can usually be constructed entirely as a combinational circuit. Nevertheless, the pipeline technique provides a faster operation over a purely serial sequence even though the maximum theoretical speed is never fully achieved.

There are two areas of computer design where the pipeline organization is applicable. An *arithmetic pipeline* divides an arithmetic operation into suboperations for execution in the pipeline segments. An *instruction pipeline* operates on a stream of instructions by overlapping the fetch, decode, and execute phases of the instruction cycle. The two types of pipelines are explained in the following sections.

9-3   Arithmetic Pipeline

Pipeline arithmetic units are usually found in very high speed computers. They are used to implement floating-point operations, multiplication of fixed-point numbers, and similar computations encountered in scientific problems. A pipeline multiplier is essentially an array multiplier as described in Fig. 10-10, with special adders designed to minimize the carry propagation time through the partial products. Floating-point operations are easily decomposed into suboperations as demonstrated in Sec. 10-5. We will now show an example of a pipeline unit for floating-point addition and subtraction.

The inputs to the floating-point adder pipeline are two normalized floating-point binary numbers.

$$X = A \times 2^a$$
$$Y = B \times 2^b$$

A and *B* are two fractions that represent the mantissas and *a* and *b* are the exponents. The floating-point addition and subtraction can be performed in four segments, as shown in Fig. 9-6. The registers labeled *R* are placed between the segments to store intermediate results. The suboperations that are performed in the four segments are:

1. Compare the exponents.
2. Align the mantissas.
3. Add or subtract the mantissas.
4. Normalize the result.

This follows the procedure outlined in the flowchart of Fig. 10-15 but with some variations that are used to reduce the execution time of the suboperations. The exponents are compared by subtracting them to determine their difference. The larger exponent is chosen as the exponent of the result. The exponent difference determines how many times the mantissa associated with the smaller exponent must be shifted to the right. This produces an alignment of the two mantissas. It should be noted that the shift must be designed as a combinational circuit to reduce the shift time. The two mantissas are added or subtracted in segment 3. The result is normalized in segment 4. When an overflow occurs, the mantissa of the sum or difference is shifted right and the exponent incremented by one. If an underflow occurs, the number of leading zeros in the mantissa determines the number of left shifts in the mantissa and the number that must be subtracted from the exponent.

The following numerical example may clarify the suboperations performed in each segment. For simplicity, we use decimal numbers, although Fig. 9-6 refers to binary numbers. Consider the two normalized floating-point numbers:

$$X = 0.9504 \times 10^3$$

$$Y = 0.8200 \times 10^2$$

The two exponents are subtracted in the first segment to obtain $3 - 2 = 1$. The larger exponent 3 is chosen as the exponent of the result. The next segment shifts the mantissa of *Y* to the right to obtain

$$X = 0.9504 \times 10^3$$

$$Y = 0.0820 \times 10^3$$

This aligns the two mantissas under the same exponent. The addition of the two mantissas in segment 3 produces the sum

$$Z = 1.0324 \times 10^3$$

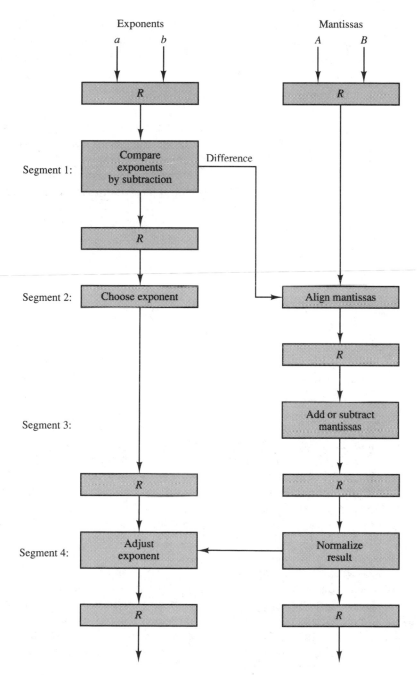

Figure 9-6 Pipeline for floating-point addition and subtraction.

The sum is adjusted by normalizing the result so that it has a fraction with a nonzero first digit. This is done by shifting the mantissa once to the right and incrementing the exponent by one to obtain the normalized sum.

$$Z = 0.10324 \times 10^4$$

The comparator, shifter, adder-subtractor, incrementer, and decrementer in the floating-point pipeline are implemented with combinational circuits. Suppose that the time delays of the four segments are $t_1 = 60$ ns, $t_2 = 70$ ns, $t_3 = 100$ ns, $t_4 = 80$ ns, and the interface registers have a delay of $t_r = 10$ ns. The clock cycle is chosen to be $t_p = t_3 + t_r = 110$ ns. An equivalent nonpipeline floating-point adder-subtractor will have a delay time $t_n = t_1 + t_2 + t_3 + t_4 + t_r = 320$ ns. In this case the pipelined adder has a speedup of 320/110 = 2.9 over the nonpipelined adder.

9-4   Instruction Pipeline

Pipeline processing can occur not only in the data stream but in the instruction stream as well. An instruction pipeline reads consecutive instructions from memory while previous instructions are being executed in other segments. This causes the instruction fetch and execute phases to overlap and perform simultaneous operations. One possible digression associated with such a scheme is that an instruction may cause a branch out of sequence. In that case the pipeline must be emptied and all the instructions that have been read from memory after the branch instruction must be discarded.

Consider a computer with an instruction fetch unit and an instruction execution unit designed to provide a two-segment pipeline. The instruction fetch segment can be implemented by means of a first-in, first-out (FIFO) buffer. This is a type of unit that forms a queue rather than a stack. Whenever the execution unit is not using memory, the control increments the program counter and uses its address value to read consecutive instructions from memory. The instructions are inserted into the FIFO buffer so that they can be executed on a first-in, first-out basis. Thus an instruction stream can be placed in a queue, waiting for decoding and processing by the execution segment. The instruction stream queuing mechanism provides an efficient way for reducing the average access time to memory for reading instructions. Whenever there is space in the FIFO buffer, the control unit initiates the next instruction fetch phase. The buffer acts as a queue from which control then extracts the instructions for the execution unit.

instruction cycle   Computers with complex instructions require other phases in addition to the fetch and execute to process an instruction completely. In the most general case, the computer needs to process each instruction with the following sequence of steps.

1. Fetch the instruction from memory.
2. Decode the instruction.
3. Calculate the effective address.
4. Fetch the operands from memory.
5. Execute the instruction.
6. Store the result in the proper place.

There are certain difficulties that will prevent the instruction pipeline from operating at its maximum rate. Different segments may take different times to operate on the incoming information. Some segments are skipped for certain operations. For example, a register mode instruction does not need an effective address calculation. Two or more segments may require memory access at the same time, causing one segment to wait until another is finished with the memory. Memory access conflicts are sometimes resolved by using two memory buses for accessing instructions and data in separate modules. In this way, an instruction word and a data word can be read simultaneously from two different modules.

The design of an instruction pipeline will be most efficient if the instruction cycle is divided into segments of equal duration. The time that each step takes to fulfill its function depends on the instruction and the way it is executed.

Example: Four-Segment Instruction Pipeline

Assume that the decoding of the instruction can be combined with the calculation of the effective address into one segment. Assume further that most of the instructions place the result into a processor register so that the instruction execution and storing of the result can be combined into one segment. This reduces the instruction pipeline into four segments.

Figure 9-7 shows how the instruction cycle in the CPU can be processed with a four-segment pipeline. While an instruction is being executed in segment 4, the next instruction in sequence is busy fetching an operand from memory in segment 3. The effective address may be calculated in a separate arithmetic circuit for the third instruction, and whenever the memory is available, the fourth and all subsequent instructions can be fetched and placed in an instruction FIFO. Thus up to four suboperations in the instruction cycle can overlap and up to four different instructions can be in progress of being processed at the same time.

Once in a while, an instruction in the sequence may be a program control type that causes a branch out of normal sequence. In that case the pending operations in the last two segments are completed and all information stored in the instruction buffer is deleted. The pipeline then restarts from the new address stored in the program counter. Similarly, an interrupt request, when acknowledged, will cause the pipeline to empty and start again from a new address value.

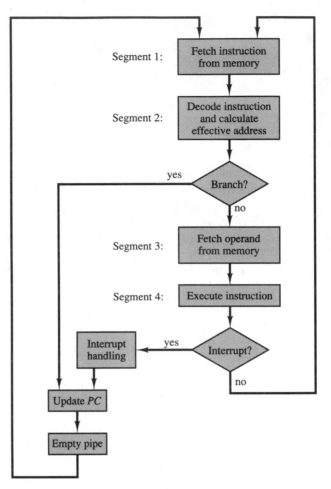

Figure 9-7   Four-segment CPU pipeline.

Figure 9-8 shows the operation of the instruction pipeline. The time in the horizontal axis is divided into steps of equal duration. The four segments are represented in the diagram with an abbreviated symbol.

1. FI is the segment that fetches an instruction.
2. DA is the segment that decodes the instruction and calculates the effective address.
3. FO is the segment that fetches the operand.
4. EX is the segment that executes the instruction.

It is assumed that the processor has separate instruction and data memories so that the operation in FI and FO can proceed at the same time. In the absence

Step:		1	2	3	4	5	6	7	8	9	10	11	12	13
Instruction:	1	FI	DA	FO	EX									
	2		FI	DA	FO	EX								
(Branch)	3			FI	DA	FO	EX							
	4				FI	–	–	FI	DA	FO	EX			
	5					–	–	–	FI	DA	FO	EX		
	6									FI	DA	FO	EX	
	7										FI	DA	FO	EX

Figure 9-8 Timing of instruction pipeline.

of a branch instruction, each segment operates on different instructions. Thus, in step 4, instruction 1 is being executed in segment EX; the operand for instruction 2 is being fetched in segment FO; instruction 3 is being decoded in segment DA; and instruction 4 is being fetched from memory in segment FI.

Assume now that instruction 3 is a branch instruction. As soon as this instruction is decoded in segment DA in step 4, the transfer from FI to DA of the other instructions is halted until the branch instruction is executed in step 6. If the branch is taken, a new instruction is fetched in step 7. If the branch is not taken, the instruction fetched previously in step 4 can be used. The pipeline then continues until a new branch instruction is encountered.

Another delay may occur in the pipeline if the EX segment needs to store the result of the operation in the data memory while the FO segment needs to fetch an operand. In that case, segment FO must wait until segment EX has finished its operation.

pipeline conflicts   In general, there are three major difficulties that cause the instruction pipeline to deviate from its normal operation.

1. *Resource conflicts* caused by access to memory by two segments at the same time. Most of these conflicts can be resolved by using separate instruction and data memories.

2. *Data dependency* conflicts arise when an instruction depends on the result of a previous instruction, but this result is not yet available.

3. *Branch difficulties* arise from branch and other instructions that change the value of *PC*.

Data Dependency

A difficulty that may caused a degradation of performance in an instruction pipeline is due to possible collision of data or address. A collision occurs when an instruction cannot proceed because previous instructions did not complete certain operations. A data dependency occurs when an instruction needs data that are not yet available. For example, an instruction in the FO segment may need to fetch an operand that is being generated at the same time by the previous instruction in segment EX. Therefore, the second instruction must wait for data to become available by the first instruction. Similarly, an address dependency may occur when an operand address cannot be calculated because the information needed by the addressing mode is not available. For example, an instruction with register indirect mode cannot proceed to fetch the operand if the previous instruction is loading the address into the register. Therefore, the operand access to memory must be delayed until the required address is available. Pipelined computers deal with such conflicts between data dependencies in a variety of ways.

hardware interlocks

The most straightforward method is to insert *hardware interlocks*. An interlock is a circuit that detects instructions whose source operands are destinations of instructions farther up in the pipeline. Detection of this situation causes the instruction whose source is not available to be delayed by enough clock cycles to resolve the conflict. This approach maintains the program sequence by using hardware to insert the required delays.

operand forwarding

Another technique called *operand forwarding* uses special hardware to detect a conflict and then avoid it by routing the data through special paths between pipeline segments. For example, instead of transferring an ALU result into a destination register, the hardware checks the destination operand, and if it is needed as a source in the next instruction, it passes the result directly into the ALU input, bypassing the register file. This method requires additional hardware paths through multiplexers as well as the circuit that detects the conflict.

A procedure employed in some computers is to give the responsibility for solving data conflicts problems to the compiler that translates the high-level programming language into a machine language program. The compiler for such computers is designed to detect a data conflict and reorder the instructions as necessary to delay the loading of the conflicting data by inserting *delayed load*

no-operation instructions. This method is referred to as *delayed load*. An example of delayed load is presented in the next section.

Handling of Branch Instructions

One of the major problems in operating an instruction pipeline is the occurrence of branch instructions. A branch instruction can be conditional or unconditional. An unconditional branch always alters the sequential program flow by loading the program counter with the target address. In a conditional branch, the control selects the target instruction if the condition is satisfied or the next sequential instruction if the condition is not satisfied. As mentioned previously, the branch instruction breaks the normal sequence of the instruction stream, causing difficulties in the operation of the instruction pipeline.

Pipelined computers employ various hardware techniques to minimize the performance degradation caused by instruction branching.

prefetch target instruction

One way of handling a conditional branch is to prefetch the target instruction in addition to the instruction following the branch. Both are saved until the branch is executed. If the branch condition is successful, the pipeline continues from the branch target instruction. An extension of this procedure is to continue fetching instructions from both places until the branch decision is made. At that time control chooses the instruction stream of the correct program flow.

branch target buffer

Another possibility is the use of a *branch target buffer* or BTB. The BTB is an associative memory (see Sec. 12-4) included in the fetch segment of the pipeline. Each entry in the BTB consists of the address of a previously executed branch instruction and the target instruction for that branch. It also stores the next few instructions after the branch target instruction. When the pipeline decodes a branch instruction, it searches the associative memory BTB for the address of the instruction. If it is in the BTB, the instruction is available directly and prefetch continues from the new path. If the instruction is not in the BTB, the pipeline shifts to a new instruction stream and stores the target instruction in the BTB. The advantage of this scheme is that branch instructions that have occurred previously are readily available in the pipeline without interruption.

loop buffer

A variation of the BTB is the *loop buffer*. This is a small very high speed register file maintained by the instruction fetch segment of the pipeline. When a program loop is detected in the program, it is stored in the loop buffer in its entirety, including all branches. The program loop can be executed directly without having to access memory until the loop mode is removed by the final branching out.

branch prediction

Another procedure that some computers use is *branch prediction*. A pipeline with branch prediction uses some additional logic to guess the outcome of a conditional branch instruction before it is executed. The pipeline then begins prefetching the instruction stream from the predicted path. A correct prediction eliminates the wasted time caused by branch penalties.

delayed branch

A procedure employed in most RISC processors is the *delayed branch*. In this procedure, the compiler detects the branch instructions and rearranges the machine language code sequence by inserting useful instructions that keep the pipeline operating without interruptions. An example of delayed branch is the insertion of a no-operation instruction after a branch instruction. This causes the computer to fetch the target instruction during the execution of the no-operation instruction, allowing a continuous flow of the pipeline. An example of delayed branch is presented in the next section.

9-5 RISC Pipeline

The reduced instruction set computer (RISC) was introduced in Sec. 8-8. Among the characteristics attributed to RISC is its ability to use an efficient instruction pipeline. The simplicity of the instruction set can be utilized to implement an instruction pipeline using a small number of suboperations, with each being executed in one clock cycle. Because of the fixed-length instruction format, the decoding of the operation can occur at the same time as the register selection. All data manipulation instructions have register-to-register operations. Since all operands are in registers, there is no need for calculating an effective address or fetching of operands from memory. Therefore, the instruction pipeline can be implemented with two or three segments. One segment fetches the instruction from program memory, and the other segment executes the instruction in the ALU. A third segment may be used to store the result of the ALU operation in a destination register.

The data transfer instructions in RISC are limited to load and store instructions. These instructions use register indirect addressing. They usually need three or four stages in the pipeline. To prevent conflicts between a memory access to fetch an instruction and to load or store an operand, most RISC machines use two separate buses with two memories: one for storing the instructions and the other for storing the data. The two memories can sometime operate at the same speed as the CPU clock and are referred to as cache memories (see Sec. 12-6).

As mentioned in Sec. 8-8, one of the major advantages of RISC is its ability to execute instructions at the rate of one per clock cycle. It is not possible to expect that every instruction be fetched from memory and executed in one clock cycle. What is done, in effect, is to start each instruction with each clock cycle and to pipeline the processor to achieve the goal of single-cycle instruction execution. The advantage of RISC over CISC (complex instruction set computer) is that RISC can achieve pipeline segments, requiring just one clock cycle, while CISC uses many segments in its pipeline, with the longest segment requiring two or more clock cycles.

single-cycle instruction execution

compiler support

Another characteristic of RISC is the support given by the compiler that translates the high-level language program into machine language program. Instead of designing hardware to handle the difficulties associated with data conflicts and branch penalties, RISC processors rely on the efficiency of the compiler to detect and minimize the delays encountered with these problems. The following examples show how a compiler can optimize the machine language program to compensate for pipeline conflicts.

Example: Three-Segment Instruction Pipeline

A typical set of instructions for a RISC processor are listed in Table 8-12. We see from this table that there are three types of instructions. The data manipulation instructions operate on data in processor registers. The data transfer instructions are load and store instructions that use an effective address obtained from the addition of the contents of two registers or a register and a displacement constant provided in the instruction. The program control instructions use register values and a constant to evaluate the branch address, which is transferred to a register or the program counter PC.

Now consider the hardware operation for such a computer. The control section fetches the instruction from program memory into an instruction register. The instruction is decoded at the same time that the registers needed for the execution of the instruction are selected. The processor unit consists of a number of registers and an arithmetic logic unit (ALU) that performs the necessary arithmetic, logic, and shift operations. A data memory is used to load or store the data from a selected register in the register file. The instruction cycle can be divided into three suboperations and implemented in three segments:

I: Instruction fetch

A: ALU operation

E: Execute instruction

The I segment fetches the instruction from program memory. The instruction is decoded and an ALU operation is performed in the A segment. The ALU is used for three different functions, depending on the decoded instruction. It performs an operation for a data manipulation instruction, it evaluates the effective address for a load or store instruction, or it calculates the branch address for a program control instruction. The E segment directs the output of the ALU to one of three destinations, depending on the decoded instruction. It transfers the result of the ALU operation into a destination register in the register file, it transfers the effective address to a data memory for loading or storing, or it transfers the branch address to the program counter.

Delayed Load

Consider now the operation of the following four instructions:

1. LOAD: $R1 \leftarrow M[\text{address 1}]$
2. LOAD: $R2 \leftarrow M[\text{address 2}]$
3. ADD: $R3 \leftarrow R1 + R2$
4. STORE: $M[\text{address 3}] \leftarrow R3$

If the three-segment pipeline proceeds without interruptions, there will be a data conflict in instruction 3 because the operand in $R2$ is not yet available in the A segment. This can be seen from the timing of the pipeline shown in Fig. 9-9(a). The E segment in clock cycle 4 is in a process of placing the memory data into $R2$. The A segment in clock cycle 4 is using the data from $R2$, but the value in $R2$ will not be the correct value since it has not yet been transferred from memory. It is up to the compiler to make sure that the instruction following the load instruction uses the data fetched from memory. If the compiler cannot find a useful instruction to put after the load, it inserts a no-op (no-operation) instruction. This is a type of instruction that is fetched from

Clock cycles:	1	2	3	4	5	6
1. Load $R1$	I	A	E			
2. Load $R2$		I	A	E		
3. Add $R1 + R2$			I	A	E	
4. Store $R3$				I	A	E

(a) Pipeline timing with data conflict

Clock cycle:	1	2	3	4	5	6	7
1. Load $R1$	I	A	E				
2. Load $R2$		I	A	E			
3. No-operation			I	A	E		
4. Add $R1 + R2$				I	A	E	
5. Store $R3$					I	A	E

(b) Pipeline timing with delayed load

Figure 9-9   Three-segment pipeline timing.

memory but has no operation, thus wasting a clock cycle. This concept of delaying the use of the data loaded from memory is referred to as *delayed load*.

Figure 9-9(b) shows the same program with a no-op instruction inserted after the load to $R2$ instruction. The data is loaded into $R2$ in clock cycle 4. The add instruction uses the value of $R2$ in step 5. Thus the no-op instruction is used to advance one clock cycle in order to compensate for the data conflict in the pipeline. (Note that no operation is performed in segment A during clock cycle 4 or segment E during clock cycle 5.) The advantage of the delayed load approach is that the data dependency is taken care of by the compiler rather than the hardware. This results in a simpler hardware segment since the segment does not have to check if the content of the register being accessed is currently valid or not.

Delayed Branch

It was shown in Fig. 9-8 that a branch instruction delays the pipeline operation until the instruction at the branch address is fetched. Several techniques for reducing branch penalties were discussed in the preceding section. The method used in most RISC processors is to rely on the compiler to redefine the branches so that they take effect at the proper time in the pipeline. This method is referred to as *delayed branch*.

The compiler for a processor that uses delayed branches is designed to analyze the instructions before and after the branch and rearrange the program sequence by inserting useful instructions in the delay steps. For example, the compiler can determine that the program dependencies allow one or more instructions preceding the branch to be moved into the delay steps after the branch. These instructions are then fetched from memory and executed through the pipeline while the branch instruction is being executed in other segments. The effect is the same as if the instructions were executed in their original order, except that the branch delay is removed. It is up to the compiler to find useful instructions to put after the branch instruction. Failing that, the compiler can insert no-op instructions.

An example of delayed branch is shown in Fig. 9-10. The program for this example consists of five instructions:

Load from memory to $R1$

Increment $R2$

Add $R3$ to $R4$

Subtract $R5$ from $R6$

Branch to address X

In Fig. 9-10(a) the compiler inserts two no-op instructions after the branch. The branch address X is transferred to PC in clock cycle 7. The fetching of the instruction at X is delayed by two clock cycles by the no-op instructions. The instruction at X starts the fetch phase at clock cycle 8 after the program counter PC has been updated.

The program in Fig. 9-10(b) is rearranged by placing the add and subtract instructions after the branch instruction instead of before as in the original program. Inspection of the pipeline timing shows that PC is updated to the value of X in clock cycle 5, but the add and subtract instructions are fetched from memory and executed in the proper sequence. In other words, if the load instruction is at address 101 and X is equal to 350, the branch instruction is fetched from address 103. The add instruction is fetched from address 104 and executed in clock cycle 6. The subtract instruction is fetched from address 105 and executed in clock cycle 7. Since the value of X is transferred to PC with clock cycle 5 in the E segment, the instruction fetched from memory at clock cycle 6 is from address 350, which is the instruction at the branch address.

9-6 Vector Processing

There is a class of computational problems that are beyond the capabilities of a conventional computer. These problems are characterized by the fact that they require a vast number of computations that will take a conventional computer days or even weeks to complete. In many science and engineering

Clock cycles:	1	2	3	4	5	6	7	8	9	10
1. Load	I	A	E							
2. Increment		I	A	E						
3. Add			I	A	E					
4. Subtract				I	A	E				
5. Branch to X					I	A	E			
6. No-operation						I	A	E		
7. No-operation							I	A	E	
8. Instruction in X								I	A	E

(a) Using no-operation instructions

Clock cycles:	1	2	3	4	5	6	7	8
1. Load	I	A	E					
2. Increment		I	A	E				
3. Branch to X			I	A	E			
4. Add				I	A	E		
5. Subtract					I	A	E	
6. Instruction in X						I	A	E

(b) Rearranging the instructions

Figure 9-10   Example of delayed branch.

applications, the problems can be formulated in terms of vectors and matrices that lend themselves to vector processing.

applications

Computers with vector processing capabilities are in demand in specialized applications. The following are representative application areas where vector processing is of the utmost importance.

Long-range weather forecasting
Petroleum explorations
Seismic data analysis
Medical diagnosis
Aerodynamics and space flight simulations

Artificial intelligence and expert systems

Mapping the human genome

Image processing

Without sophisticated computers, many of the required computations cannot be completed within a reasonable amount of time. To achieve the required level of high performance it is necessary to utilize the fastest and most reliable hardware and apply innovative procedures from vector and parallel processing techniques.

Vector Operations

Many scientific problems require arithmetic operations on large arrays of numbers. These numbers are usually formulated as vectors and matrices of floating-point numbers. A vector is an ordered set of a one-dimensional array of data items. A vector V of length n is represented as a row vector by $V = [V_1 \ V_2 \ V_3 \ \cdots \ V_n]$. It may be represented as a column vector if the data items are listed in a column. A conventional sequential computer is capable of processing operands one at a time. Consequently, operations on vectors must be broken down into single computations with subscripted variables. The element V_i of vector V is written as $V(I)$ and the index I refers to a memory address or register where the number is stored. To examine the difference between a conventional scalar processor and a vector processor, consider the following Fortran DO loop:

```
       DO 20 I = 1, 100
   20   C(I) = B(I) + A(I)
```

This is a program for adding two vectors A and B of length 100 to produce a vector C. This is implemented in machine language by the following sequence of operations.

```
       Initialize I = 0
   20   Read A(I)
       Read B(I)
       Store C(I) = A(I) + B(I)
       Increment I = I + 1
       If I ≤ 100 go to 20
       Continue
```

This constitutes a program loop that reads a pair of operands from arrays A and B and performs a floating-point addition. The loop control variable is then updated and the steps repeat 100 times.

A computer capable of vector processing eliminates the overhead associated with the time it takes to fetch and execute the instructions in the program loop. It allows operations to be specified with a single vector instruction of the form

$$C(1:100) = A(1:100) + B(1:100)$$

The vector instruction includes the initial address of the operands, the length of the vectors, and the operation to be performed, all in one composite instruction. The addition is done with a pipelined floating-point adder similar to the one shown in Fig. 9-6.

A possible instruction format for a vector instruction is shown in Fig. 9-11. This is essentially a three-address instruction with three fields specifying the base address of the operands and an additional field that gives the length of the data items in the vectors. This assumes that the vector operands reside in memory. It is also possible to design the processor with a large number of registers and store all operands in registers prior to the addition operation. In that case the base address and length in the vector instruction specify a group of CPU registers.

Matrix Multiplication

Matrix multiplication is one of the most computational intensive operations performed in computers with vector processors. The multiplication of two $n \times n$ matrices consists of n^2 inner products or n^3 multiply–add operations. An $n \times m$ matrix of numbers has n rows and m columns and may be considered as constituting a set of n row vectors or a set of m column vectors. Consider, for example, the multiplication of two 3×3 matrices A and B.

$$\begin{bmatrix} a_{11} & a_{12} & a_{13} \\ a_{21} & a_{22} & a_{23} \\ a_{31} & a_{32} & a_{33} \end{bmatrix} \times \begin{bmatrix} b_{11} & b_{12} & b_{13} \\ b_{21} & b_{22} & b_{23} \\ b_{31} & b_{32} & b_{33} \end{bmatrix} = \begin{bmatrix} c_{11} & c_{12} & c_{13} \\ c_{21} & c_{22} & c_{23} \\ c_{31} & c_{32} & c_{33} \end{bmatrix}$$

The product matrix C is a 3×3 matrix whose elements are related to the elements of A and B by the inner product:

$$c_{ij} = \sum_{k=1}^{3} a_{ik} \times b_{kj}$$

For example, the number in the first row and first column of matrix C is calculated by letting $i = 1, j = 1$, to obtain

$$c_{11} = a_{11} b_{11} + a_{12} b_{21} + a_{13} b_{31}$$

Figure 9-11   Instruction format for vector processor.

Operation code	Base address source 1	Base address source 2	Base address destination	Vector length

This requires three multiplications and (after initializing c_{11} to 0) three additions. The total number of multiplications or additions required to compute the matrix product is $9 \times 3 = 27$. If we consider the linked multiply–add operation $c + a \times b$ as a cumulative operation, the product of two $n \times n$ matrices requires n^3 multiply–add operations. The computation consists of n^2 inner products, with each inner product requiring n multiply–add operations, assuming that c is initialized to zero before computing each element in the product matrix.

In general, the inner product consists of the sum of k product terms of the form

$$C = A_1 B_1 + A_2 B_2 + A_3 B_3 + A_4 B_4 + \cdots + A_k B_k$$

In a typical application k may be equal to 100 or even 1000. The inner product calculation on a pipeline vector processor is shown in Fig. 9-12. The values of A and B are either in memory or in processor registers. The floating-point multiplier pipeline and the floating-point adder pipeline are assumed to have four segments each. All segment registers in the multiplier and adder are initialized to 0. Therefore, the output of the adder is 0 for the first eight cycles until both pipes are full. A_i and B_i pairs are brought in and multiplied at a rate of one pair per cycle. After the first four cycles, the products begin to be added to the output of the adder. During the next four cycles 0 is added to the products entering the adder pipeline. At the end of the eighth cycle, the first four products $A_1 B_1$ through $A_4 B_4$ are in the four adder segments, and the next four products, $A_5 B_5$ through $A_8 B_8$, are in the multiplier segments. At the beginning of the ninth cycle, the output of the adder is $A_1 B_1$ and the output of the multiplier is $A_5 B_5$. Thus the ninth cycle starts the addition $A_1 B_1 + A_5 B_5$ in the adder pipeline. The tenth cycle starts the addition $A_2 B_2 + A_6 B_6$, and so on. This pattern breaks down the summation into four sections as follows:

$$C = A_1 B_1 + A_5 B_5 + A_9 B_9 + A_{13} B_{13} + \cdots$$
$$+ A_2 B_2 + A_6 B_6 + A_{10} B_{10} + A_{14} B_{14} + \cdots$$
$$+ A_3 B_3 + A_7 B_7 + A_{11} B_{11} + A_{15} B_{15} + \cdots$$
$$+ A_4 B_4 + A_8 B_8 + A_{12} B_{12} + A_{16} B_{16} + \cdots$$

Figure 9-12   Pipeline for calculating an inner product.

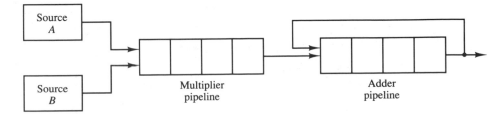

When there are no more product terms to be added, the system inserts four zeros into the multiplier pipeline. The adder pipeline will then have one partial product in each of its four segments, corresponding to the four sums listed in the four rows in the above equation. The four partial sums are then added to form the final sum.

Memory Interleaving

Pipeline and vector processors often require simultaneous access to memory from two or more sources. An instruction pipeline may require the fetching of an instruction and an operand at the same time from two different segments. Similarly, an arithmetic pipeline usually requires two or more operands to enter the pipeline at the same time. Instead of using two memory buses for simultaneous access, the memory can be partitioned into a number of modules connected to a common memory address and data buses. A memory module is a memory array together with its own address and data registers. Figure 9-13 shows a memory unit with four modules. Each memory array has its own address register AR and data register DR. The address registers receive information from a common address bus and the data registers communicate with a bidirectional data bus. The two least significant bits of the address can be used to distinguish between the four modules. The modular system permits one module to initiate a memory access while other modules are in the process of reading or writing a word and each module can honor a memory request independent of the state of the other modules.

Figure 9-13 Multiple module memory organization.

Address bus

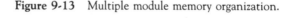
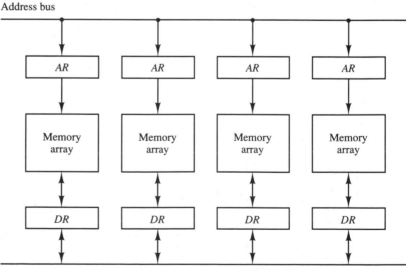

Data bus

The advantage of a modular memory is that it allows the use of a technique called *interleaving*. In an interleaved memory, different sets of addresses are assigned to different memory modules. For example, in a two-module memory system, the even addresses may be in one module and the odd addresses in the other. When the number of modules is a power of 2, the least significant bits of the address select a memory module and the remaining bits designate the specific location to be accessed within the selected module.

A modular memory is useful in systems with pipeline and vector processing. A vector processor that uses an n-way interleaved memory can fetch n operands from n different modules. By staggering the memory access, the effective memory cycle time can be reduced by a factor close to the number of modules. A CPU with instruction pipeline can take advantage of multiple memory modules so that each segment in the pipeline can access memory independent of memory access from other segments.

Supercomputers

A commercial computer with vector instructions and pipelined floating-point arithmetic operations is referred to as a *supercomputer*. Supercomputers are very powerful, high-performance machines used mostly for scientific computations. To speed up the operation, the components are packed tightly together to minimize the distance that the electronic signals have to travel. Supercomputers also use special techniques for removing the heat from circuits to prevent them from burning up because of their close proximity.

The instruction set of supercomputers contains the standard data transfer, data manipulation, and program control instructions of conventional computers. This is augmented by instructions that process vectors and combinations of scalars and vectors. A supercomputer is a computer system best known for its high computational speed, fast and large memory systems, and the extensive use of parallel processing. It is equipped with multiple functional units and each unit has its own pipeline configuration. Although the supercomputer is capable of general-purpose applications found in all other computers, it is specifically optimized for the type of numerical calculations involving vectors and matrices of floating-point numbers.

Supercomputers are not suitable for normal everyday processing of a typical computer installation. They are limited in their use to a number of scientific applications, such as numerical weather forecasting, seismic wave analysis, and space research. They have limited use and limited market because of their high price.

A measure used to evaluate computers in their ability to perform a given number of floating-point operations per second is referred to as *flops*. The term *megaflops* is used to denote million flops and *gigaflops* to denote billion flops. A typical supercomputer has a basic cycle time of 4 to 20 ns. If the processor can calculate a floating-point operation through a pipeline each cycle time, it will have the ability to perform 50 to 250 megaflops. This rate would be sustained from the time the first answer is produced and does not include the initial setup time of the pipeline.

The first supercomputer developed in 1976 is the Cray-1 supercomputer. It uses vector processing with 12 distinct functional units in parallel. Each functional unit is segmented to process the incoming data through a pipeline. All the functional units can operate concurrently with operands stored in the large number of registers (over 150) in the CPU. A floating-point operation can be performed on two sets of 64-bit operands during one clock cycle of 12.5 ns. This gives a rate of 80 megaflops during the time that the data are processed through the pipeline. It has a memory capacity of 4 million 64-bit words. The memory is divided into 16 banks, with each bank having a 50-ns access time. This means that when all 16 banks are accessed simultaneously, the memory transfer rate is 320 million words per second. Cray research extended its supercomputer to a multiprocessor configuration called Cray X-MP and Cray Y-MP. The new Cray-2 supercomputer is 12 times more powerful than the Cray-1 in vector processing mode.

Another early model supercomputer is the Fujitsu VP-200. It has a scalar processor and a vector processor that can operate concurrently. Like the Cray supercomputers, a large number of registers and multiple functional units are used to enable register-to-register vector operations. There are four execution pipelines in the vector processor, and when operating simultaneously, they can achieve up to 300 megaflops. The main memory has 32 million words connected to the vector registers through load and store pipelines. The VP-200 has 83 vector instructions and 195 scalar instructions. The newer VP-2600 uses a clock cycle of 3.2 ns and claims a peak performance of 5 gigaflops.

9-7   Array Processors

An array processor is a processor that performs computations on large arrays of data. The term is used to refer to two different types of processors. An *attached array processor* is an auxiliary processor attached to a general-purpose computer. It is intended to improve the performance of the host computer in specific numerical computation tasks. An *SIMD array processor* is a processor that has a single-instruction multiple-data organization. It manipulates vector instructions by means of multiple functional units responding to a common instruction. Although both types of array processors manipulate vectors, their internal organization is different.

Attached Array Processor
An attached array processor is designed as a peripheral for a conventional host computer, and its purpose is to enhance the performance of the computer by providing vector processing for complex scientific applications. It achieves

high performance by means of parallel processing with multiple functional units. It includes an arithmetic unit containing one or more pipelined floating-point adders and multipliers. The array processor can be programmed by the user to accommodate a variety of complex arithmetic problems.

Figure 9-14 shows the interconnection of an attached array processor to a host computer. The host computer is a general-purpose commercial computer and the attached processor is a back-end machine driven by the host computer. The array processor is connected through an input–output controller to the computer and the computer treats it like an external interface. The data for the attached processor are transferred from main memory to a local memory through a high-speed bus. The general-purpose computer without the attached processor serves the users that need conventional data processing. The system with the attached processor satisfies the needs for complex arithmetic applications.

Some manufacturers of attached array processors offer a model that can be connected to a variety of different host computers. For example, when attached to a VAX 11 computer, the FSP-164/MAX from Floating-Point Systems increases the computing power of the VAX to 100 megaflops. The objective of the attached array processor is to provide vector manipulation capabilities to a conventional computer at a fraction of the cost of supercomputers.

SIMD Array Processor

An SIMD array processor is a computer with multiple processing units operating in parallel. The processing units are synchronized to perform the same operation under the control of a common control unit, thus providing a single instruction stream, multiple data stream (SIMD) organization. A general block diagram of an array processor is shown in Fig. 9-15. It contains a set of identical processing elements (PEs), each having a local memory M. Each processor element includes an ALU, a floating-point arithmetic unit, and working registers. The master control unit controls the operations in the processor elements. The main memory is used for storage of the program. The function of the master control unit is to decode the instructions and determine how the instruction is to be executed. Scalar and program control instructions are

Figure 9-14 Attached array processor with host computer.

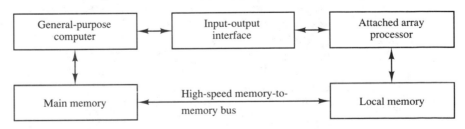

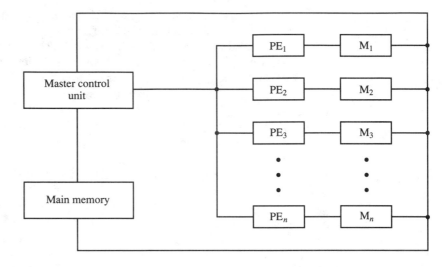

Figure 9-15 SIMD array processor organization.

directly executed within the master control unit. Vector instructions are broadcast to all PEs simultaneously. Each PE uses operands stored in its local memory. Vector operands are distributed to the local memories prior to the parallel execution of the instruction.

Consider, for example, the vector addition $C = A + B$. The master control unit first stores the ith components a_i and b_i of A and B in local memory M_i for $i = 1, 2, 3, \ldots, n$. It then broadcasts the floating-point add instruction $c_i = a_i + b_i$ to all PEs, causing the addition to take place simultaneously. The components of c_i are stored in fixed locations in each local memory. This produces the desired vector sum in one add cycle.

Masking schemes are used to control the status of each PE during the execution of vector instructions. Each PE has a flag that is set when the PE is active and reset when the PE is inactive. This ensures that only those PEs that need to participate are active during the execution of the instruction. For example, suppose that the array processor contains a set of 64 PEs. If a vector length of less than 64 data items is to be processed, the control unit selects the proper number of PEs to be active. Vectors of greater length than 64 must be divided into 64-word portions by the control unit.

The best known SIMD array processor is the ILLIAC IV computer developed at the University of Illinois and manufactured by the Burroughs Corp. This computer is no longer in operation. SIMD processors are highly specialized computers. They are suited primarily for numerical problems that can be expressed in vector or matrix form. However, they are not very efficient in other types of computations or in dealing with conventional data-processing programs.

PROBLEMS

9-1.   In certain scientific computations it is necessary to perform the arithmetic operation $(A_i + B_i)(C_i + D_i)$ with a stream of numbers. Specify a pipeline configuration to carry out this task. List the contents of all registers in the pipeline for $i = 1$ through 6.

9-2.   Draw a space-time diagram for a six-segment pipeline showing the time it takes to process eight tasks.

9-3.   Determine the number of clock cycles that it takes to process 200 tasks in a six-segment pipeline.

9-4.   A nonpipeline system takes 50 ns to process a task. The same task can be processed in a six-segment pipeline with a clock cycle of 10 ns. Determine the speedup ratio of the pipeline for 100 tasks. What is the maximum speedup that can be achieved?

9-5.   The pipeline of Fig. 9-2 has the following propagation times: 40 ns for the operands to be read from memory into registers $R1$ and $R2$, 45 ns for the signal to propagate through the multiplier, 5 ns for the transfer into $R3$, and 15 ns to add the two numbers into $R5$.
   a. What is the minimum clock cycle time that can be used?
   b. A nonpipeline system can perform the same operation by removing $R3$ and $R4$. How long will it take to multiply and add the operands without using the pipeline?
   c. Calculate the speedup of the pipeline for 10 tasks and again for 100 tasks.
   d. What is the maximum speedup that can be achieved?

9-6.   It is necessary to design a pipeline for a fixed-point multiplier that multiplies two 8-bit binary integers. Each segment consists of a number of AND gates and a binary adder similar to an array multiplier as shown in Fig. 10-10.
   a. How many AND gates are there in each segment, and what size of adder is needed?
   b. How many segments are there in the pipeline?
   c. If the propagation delay in each segment is 30 ns, what is the average time that it takes to multiply two fixed-point numbers in the pipeline?

9-7.   The time delay of the four segments in the pipeline of Fig. 9-6 are as follows: $t_1 = 50$ ns, $t_2 = 30$ ns, $t_3 = 95$ ns, and $t_4 = 45$ ns. The interface registers delay time $t_r = 5$ ns.
   a. How long would it take to add 100 pairs of numbers in the pipeline?
   b. How can we reduce the total time to about one-half of the time calculated in part (a)?

9-8.   How would you use the floating-point pipeline adder of Fig. 9-6 to add 100 floating-point numbers $X_1 + X_2 + X_3 + \cdots + X_{100}$?

9-9.   Formulate a six-segment instruction pipeline for a computer. Specify the operations to be performed in each segment.

9-10.   Explain four possible hardware schemes that can be used in an instruction pipeline in order to minimize the performance degradation caused by instruction branching.

9-11. Consider the four instructions in the following program. Suppose that the first instruction starts from step 1 in the pipeline used in Fig. 9-8. Specify what operations are performed in the four segments during step 4.

```
Load      R1 ← M[312]
ADD       R2 ← R2 + M[313]
INC       R3 ← R3 + 1
STORE     M[314] ← R3
```

9-12. Give an example of a program that will cause data conflict in the three-segment pipeline of Sec. 9-5.

9-13. Give an example that uses delayed load with the three-segment pipeline of Sec. 9-5.

9-14. Give an example of a program that will cause a branch penalty in the three-segment pipeline of Sec. 9-5.

9-15. Give an example that uses delayed branch with the three-segment pipeline of Sec. 9-5.

9-16. Consider the multiplication of two 40×40 matrices using a vector processor.
   a. How many product terms are there in each inner product, and how many inner products must be evaluated?
   b. How many multiply–add operations are needed to calculate the product matrix?

9-17. How many clock cycles does it take to process an inner product in the pipeline of Fig. 9-12 when used to evaluate the product of two 60×60 matrices? How many inner products are there, and how many clock cycles does it take to evaluate the product matrix?

9-18. Assign addresses to an array of data of 1024 words to be stored in the memory described in Fig. 9-13.

9-19. A weather forecasting computation requires 250 billion floating-point operations. The problem is processed in a supercomputer that can perform 100 megaflops. How long will it take to do these calculations?

9-20. Consider a computer with four floating-point pipeline processors. Suppose that each processor uses a cycle time of 40 ns. How long will it take to perform 400 floating-point operations? Is there a difference if the same 400 operations are carried out using a single pipeline processor with a cycle time of 10 ns?

REFERENCES

1. Dasgupta, S., *Computer Architecture: A Modern Synthesis*, Vol. 2. New York: John Wiley, 1989.

2. DeCegama, A. L., *Parallel Processing Architecture and VLSI Hardware*. Englewood Cliffs, NJ: Prentice Hall, 1989.

3. Gibson, G. A., *Computer Systems Concepts and Design*. Englewood Cliffs, NJ: Prentice Hall, 1991.

4. Hays, J. F., *Computer Architecture and Organization*, 2nd ed. New York: McGraw-Hill, 1988.

5. Hwang, K., and F. A. Briggs, *Computer Architecture and Parallel Processing*. New York: McGraw-Hill, 1984.

6. Kain, R., *Computer Architecture: Software and Hardware*. Vol. 2. Englewood Cliffs, NJ: Prentice Hall, 1989.

7. Lee, J. K. F., and A. J. Smith, "Branch Prediction Strategies and Branch Target Buffer Design." *Computer*, Vol. 17, No. 1 (January 1984), pp. 6–22.

8. Lilja, D. J., "Reducing the Branch Penalties in Pipeline Processors." *Computer*, Vol. 21, No. 7 (July 1988), pp. 47–55.

9. Patterson, D. A., and J. L. Hennessy, *Computer Architecture: A Quantitative Approach*. San Mateo, CA: Morgan Kaufmann Publishers, 1990.

10. Pollard, L. H., *Computer Design and Architecture*. Englewood Cliffs, NJ: Prentice Hall, 1990.

11. Stone, H. S., *High-Performance Computer Architecture*, 2nd ed. Reading, MA: Addison-Wesley, 1990.

12. Tabak, D., *Multiprocessors*. Englewood Cliffs, NJ: Prentice Hall, 1990.

CHAPTER TEN

Computer Arithmetic

IN THIS CHAPTER

10-1   Introduction

Arithmetic instructions in digital computers manipulate data to produce results necessary for the solution of computational problems. These instructions perform arithmetic calculations and are responsible for the bulk of activity involved in processing data in a computer. The four basic arithmetic operations are addition, subtraction, multiplication, and division. From these four basic operations, it is possible to formulate other arithmetic functions and solve scientific problems by means of numerical analysis methods.

An arithmetic processor is the part of a processor unit that executes arithmetic operations. The data type assumed to reside in processor registers during the execution of an arithmetic instruction is specified in the definition of the instruction. An arithmetic instruction may specify binary or decimal data, and in each case the data may be in fixed-point or floating-point form. Fixed-point numbers may represent integers or fractions. Negative numbers may be in signed-magnitude or signed-complement representation. The arithmetic processor is very simple if only a binary fixed-point *add* instruction is included. It would be more complicated if it includes all four arithmetic operations for binary and decimal data in fixed-point and floating-point representation.

At an early age we are taught how to perform the basic arithmetic operations in signed-magnitude representation. This knowledge is valuable when the operations are to be implemented by hardware. However, the designer must be thoroughly familiar with the sequence of steps to be followed in order to carry out the operation and achieve a correct result. The solution to any problem that is stated by a finite number of well-defined procedural steps is called an *algorithm*. An algorithm was stated in Sec. 3-3 for the addition of two fixed-point binary numbers when negative numbers are in signed-2's complement representation. This is a simple algorithm since all it needs for its implementation is a parallel binary adder. When negative numbers are in signed-magnitude representation, the algorithm is slightly more complicated and its implementation requires circuits to add and subtract, and to compare the signs and the magnitudes of the numbers. Usually, an algorithm will contain a number of procedural steps which are dependent on results of previous steps. A convenient method for presenting algorithms is a flowchart. The computational steps are specified in the flowchart inside rectangular boxes. The decision steps are indicated inside diamond-shaped boxes from which two or more alternate paths emerge.

algorithm

In this chapter we develop the various arithmetic algorithms and show the procedure for implementing them with digital hardware. We consider addition, subtraction, multiplication, and division for the following types of data:

1. Fixed-point binary data in signed-magnitude representation
2. Fixed-point binary data in signed-2's complement representation
3. Floating-point binary data
4. Binary-coded decimal (BCD) data

10-2   Addition and Subtraction

As stated in Sec. 3-3, there are three ways of representing negative fixed-point binary numbers: signed-magnitude, signed-1's complement, or signed-2's complement. Most computers use the signed-2's complement representation when performing arithmetic operations with integers. For floating-point operations, most computers use the signed-magnitude representation for the mantissa. In this section we develop the addition and subtraction algorithms for data represented in signed-magnitude and again for data represented in signed-2's complement.

It is important to realize that the adopted representation for negative numbers refers to the representation of numbers in the registers before and after the execution of the arithmetic operation. It does not mean that complement arithmetic may not be used in an intermediate step. For example, it is convenient to employ complement arithmetic when performing a subtraction operation with numbers in signed-magnitude representation. As long as the initial minuend and subtrahend, as well as the final difference, are in signed-magnitude form the fact that complements have been used in an intermediate step does not alter the fact that the representation is in signed-magnitude.

Addition and Subtraction with Signed-Magnitude Data

The representation of numbers in signed-magnitude is familiar because it is used in everyday arithmetic calculations. The procedure for adding or subtracting two signed binary numbers with paper and pencil is simple and straightforward. A review of this procedure will be helpful for deriving the hardware algorithm.

magnitude

We designate the magnitude of the two numbers by A and B. When the signed numbers are added or subtracted, we find that there are eight different conditions to consider, depending on the sign of the numbers and the operation performed. These conditions are listed in the first column of Table 10-1. The other columns in the table show the actual operation to be performed with the *magnitude* of the numbers. The last column is needed to prevent a negative zero. In other words, when two equal numbers are subtracted, the result should be $+0$ not -0.

The algorithms for addition and subtraction are derived from the table and can be stated as follows (the words inside parentheses should be used for the subtraction algorithm):

addition (subtraction) algorithm

Addition (subtraction) algorithm: when the signs of A and B are identical (different), add the two magnitudes and attach the sign of A to the result. When the signs of A and B are different (identical), compare the magnitudes and

TABLE 10-1 Addition and Subtraction of Signed-Magnitude Numbers

Operation	Add Magnitudes	Subtract Magnitudes		
		When $A > B$	When $A < B$	When $A = B$
$(+A) + (+B)$	$+(A + B)$			
$(+A) + (-B)$		$+(A - B)$	$-(B - A)$	$+(A - B)$
$(-A) + (+B)$		$-(A - B)$	$+(B - A)$	$+(A - B)$
$(-A) + (-B)$	$-(A + B)$			
$(+A) - (+B)$		$+(A - B)$	$-(B - A)$	$+(A - B)$
$(+A) - (-B)$	$+(A + B)$			
$(-A) - (+B)$	$-(A + B)$			
$(-A) - (-B)$		$-(A - B)$	$+(B - A)$	$+(A - B)$

subtract the smaller number from the larger. Choose the sign of the result to be the same as A if $A > B$ or the complement of the sign of A if $A < B$. If the two magnitudes are equal, subtract B from A and make the sign of the result positive.

The two algorithms are similar except for the sign comparison. The procedure to be followed for identical signs in the addition algorithm is the same as for different signs in the subtraction algorithm, and vice versa.

Hardware Implementation

To implement the two arithmetic operations with hardware, it is first necessary that the two numbers be stored in registers. Let A and B be two registers that hold the magnitudes of the numbers, and A_s and B_s be two flip-flops that hold the corresponding signs. The result of the operation may be transferred to a third register: however, a saving is achieved if the result is transferred into A and A_s. Thus A and A_s together form an accumulator register.

Consider now the hardware implementation of the algorithms above. First, a parallel-adder is needed to perform the microoperation $A + B$. Second, a comparator circuit is needed to establish if $A > B$, $A = B$, or $A < B$. Third, two parallel-subtractor circuits are needed to perform the microoperations $A - B$ and $B - A$. The sign relationship can be determined from an exclusive-OR gate with A_s and B_s as inputs.

This procedure requires a magnitude comparator, an adder, and two subtractors. However, a different procedure can be found that requires less equipment. First, we know that subtraction can be accomplished by means of complement and add. Second, the result of a comparison can be determined from the end carry after the subtraction. Careful investigation of the alternatives reveals that the use of 2's complement for subtraction and comparison is an efficient procedure that requires only an adder and a complementer.

Figure 10-1 shows a block diagram of the hardware for implementing the addition and subtraction operations. It consists of registers A and B and sign flip-flops A_s and B_s. Subtraction is done by adding A to the 2's complement of B. The output carry is transferred to flip-flop E, where it can be checked to determine the relative magnitudes of the two numbers. The add-overflow flip-flop AVF holds the overflow bit when A and B are added. The A register provides other microoperations that may be needed when we specify the sequence of steps in the algorithm.

The addition of A plus B is done through the parallel adder. The S (sum) output of the adder is applied to the input of the A register. The complementer provides an output of B or the complement of B depending on the state of the mode control M. The complementer consists of exclusive-OR gates and the parallel adder consists of full-adder circuits as shown in Fig. 4-7 in Chap. 4. The M signal is also applied to the input carry of the adder. When $M = 0$, the output of B is transferred to the adder, the input carry is 0, and the output of

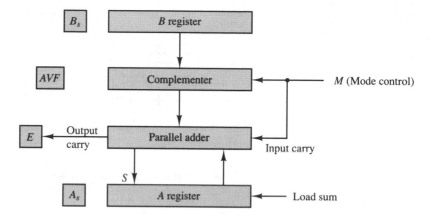

Figure 10-1   Hardware for signed-magnitude addition and subtraction.

the adder is equal to the sum $A + B$. When $M = 1$, the 1's complement of B is applied to the adder, the input carry is 1, and output $S = A + \overline{B} + 1$. This is equal to A plus the 2's complement of B, which is equivalent to the subtraction $A - B$.

Hardware Algorithm

The flowchart for the hardware algorithm is presented in Fig. 10-2. The two signs A_s and B_s are compared by an exclusive-OR gate. If the output of the gate is 0, the signs are identical; if it is 1, the signs are different. For an *add* operation, identical signs dictate that the magnitudes be added. For a *subtract* operation, different signs dictate that the magnitudes be added. The magnitudes are added with a microoperation $EA \leftarrow A + B$, where EA is a register that combines E and A. The carry in E after the addition constitutes an overflow if it is equal to 1. The value of E is transferred into the add-overflow flip-flop AVF.

The two magnitudes are subtracted if the signs are different for an *add* operation or identical for a *subtract* operation. The magnitudes are subtracted by adding A to the 2's complement of B. No overflow can occur if the numbers are subtracted so AVF is cleared to 0. A 1 in E indicates that $A \geq B$ and the number in A is the correct result. If this number is zero, the sign A_s must be made positive to avoid a negative zero. A 0 in E indicates that $A < B$. For this case it is necessary to take the 2's complement of the value in A. This operation can be done with one microoperation $A \leftarrow \overline{A} + 1$. However, we assume that the A register has circuits for microoperations *complement* and *increment*, so the 2's complement is obtained from these two microoperations. In other paths of the flowchart, the sign of the result is the same as the sign of A, so no change in A_s is required. However, when $A < B$, the sign of the result is the complement of the original sign of A. It is then necessary to complement A_s to obtain

complement and increment

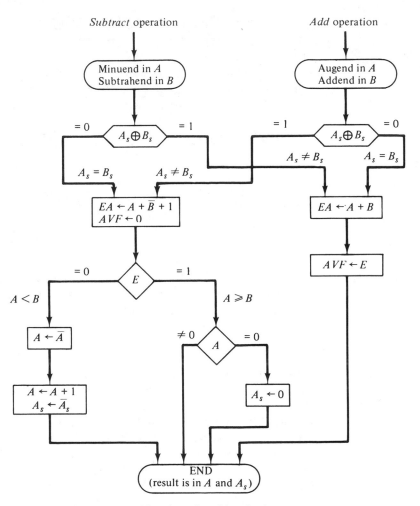

Figure 10-2 Flowchart for add and subtract operations.

the correct sign. The final result is found in register A and its sign in A_s. The value in AVF provides an overflow indication. The final value of E is immaterial.

Addition and Subtraction with Signed-2's Complement Data

The signed-2's complement representation of numbers together with arithmetic algorithms for addition and subtraction are introduced in Sec. 3-3. They are summarized here for easy reference. The leftmost bit of a binary number represents the sign bit: 0 for positive and 1 for negative. If the sign bit is 1, the entire number is represented in 2's complement form. Thus +33 is represented as 00100001 and −33 as 11011111. Note that 11011111 is the 2's complement of 00100001, and vice versa.

The addition of two numbers in signed-2's complement form consists of adding the numbers with the sign bits treated the same as the other bits of the number. A carry-out of the sign-bit position is discarded. The subtraction consists of first taking the 2's complement of the subtrahend and then adding it to the minuend.

When two numbers of n digits each are added and the sum occupies $n + 1$ digits, we say that an overflow occurred. The effect of an overflow on the sum of two signed-2's complement numbers is discussed in Sec. 3-3. An overflow can be detected by inspecting the last two carries out of the addition. When the two carries are applied to an exclusive-OR gate, the overflow is detected when the output of the gate is equal to 1.

The register configuration for the hardware implementation is shown in Fig. 10-3. This is the same configuration as in Fig. 10-1 except that the sign bits are not separated from the rest of the registers. We name the A register AC (accumulator) and the B register BR. The leftmost bit in AC and BR represent the sign bits of the numbers. The two sign bits are added or subtracted together with the other bits in the complementer and parallel adder. The overflow flip-flop V is set to 1 if there is an overflow. The output carry in this case is discarded.

The algorithm for adding and subtracting two binary numbers in signed-2's complement representation is shown in the flowchart of Fig. 10-4. The sum is obtained by adding the contents of AC and BR (including their sign bits). The overflow bit V is set to 1 if the exclusive-OR of the last two carries is 1, and it is cleared to 0 otherwise. The subtraction operation is accomplished by adding the content of AC to the 2's complement of BR. Taking the 2's complement of BR has the effect of changing a positive number to negative, and vice versa. An overflow must be checked during this operation because the two numbers added could have the same sign. The programmer must realize that if an overflow occurs, there will be an erroneous result in the AC register.

Figure 10-3 Hardware for signed-2's complement addition and subtraction.

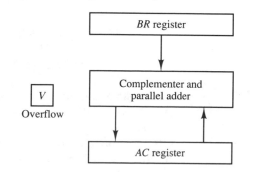

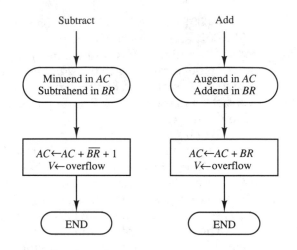

Figure 10-4 Algorithm for adding and subtracting numbers in signed-2's complement representation.

Comparing this algorithm with its signed-magnitude counterpart, we note that it is much simpler to add and subtract numbers if negative numbers are maintained in signed-2's complement representation. For this reason most computers adopt this representation over the more familiar signed-magnitude.

10-3 Multiplication Algorithms

Multiplication of two fixed-point binary numbers in signed-magnitude representation is done with paper and pencil by a process of successive shift and add operations. This process is best illustrated with a numerical example.

$$
\begin{array}{rll}
23 & 10111 & \text{Multiplicand} \\
\underline{19} & \underline{\times\ 10011} & \text{Multiplier} \\
 & 10111 & \\
 & 10111 & \\
 & 00000 & + \\
 & 00000 & \\
 & \underline{10111\quad\ } & \\
437 & 110110101 & \text{Product}
\end{array}
$$

The process consists of looking at successive bits of the multiplier, least significant bit first. If the multiplier bit is a 1, the multiplicand is copied down; otherwise, zeros are copied down. The numbers copied down in successive lines are shifted one position to the left from the previous number. Finally, the numbers are added and their sum forms the product.

The sign of the product is determined from the signs of the multiplicand and multiplier. If they are alike, the sign of the product is positive. If they are unlike, the sign of the product is negative.

Hardware Implementation for Signed-Magnitude Data

When multiplication is implemented in a digital computer, it is convenient to change the process slightly. First, instead of providing registers to store and add simultaneously as many binary numbers as there are bits in the multiplier, it is convenient to provide an adder for the summation of only two binary numbers and successively accumulate the partial products in a register. Second, instead of shifting the multiplicand to the left, the partial product is shifted to the right, which results in leaving the partial product and the multiplicand in the required relative positions. Third, when the corresponding bit of the multiplier is 0, there is no need to add all zeros to the partial product since it will not alter its value.

The hardware for multiplication consists of the equipment shown in Fig. 10-1 plus two more registers. These registers together with registers A and B are shown in Fig. 10-5. The multiplier is stored in the Q register and its sign in Q_s. The sequence counter SC is initially set to a number equal to the number of bits in the multiplier. The counter is decremented by 1 after forming each partial product. When the content of the counter reaches zero, the product is formed and the process stops.

Initially, the multiplicand is in register B and the multiplier in Q. The sum of A and B forms a partial product which is transferred to the EA register. Both partial product and multiplier are shifted to the right. This shift will be denoted by the statement shr EAQ to designate the right shift depicted in Fig. 10-5. The

Figure 10-5 Hardware for multiply operation.

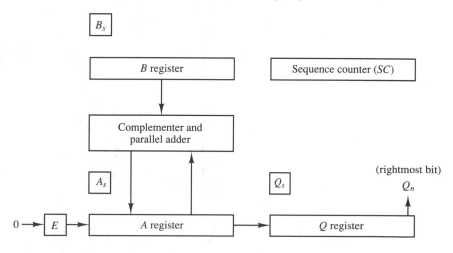

least significant bit of *A* is shifted into the most significant position of *Q*, the bit from *E* is shifted into the most significant position of *A*, and 0 is shifted into *E*. After the shift, one bit of the partial product is shifted into *Q*, pushing the multiplier bits one position to the right. In this manner, the rightmost flip-flop in register *Q*, designated by Q_n, will hold the bit of the multiplier, which must be inspected next.

Hardware Algorithm

Figure 10-6 is a flowchart of the hardware multiply algorithm. Initially, the multiplicand is in *B* and the multiplier in *Q*. Their corresponding signs are in B_s and Q_s, respectively. The signs are compared, and both *A* and *Q* are set to

Figure 10-6   Flowchart for multiply operation.

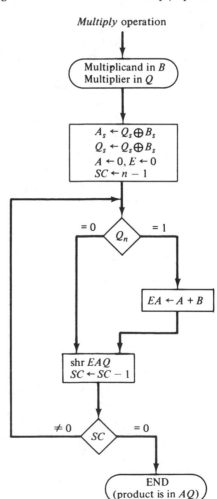

correspond to the sign of the product since a double-length product will be stored in registers A and Q. Registers A and E are cleared and the sequence counter SC is set to a number equal to the number of bits of the multiplier. We are assuming here that operands are transferred to registers from a memory unit that has words of n bits. Since an operand must be stored with its sign, one bit of the word will be occupied by the sign and the magnitude will consist of $n - 1$ bits.

After the initialization, the low-order bit of the multiplier in Q_n is tested. If it is a 1, the multiplicand in B is added to the present partial product in A. If it is a 0, nothing is done. Register EAQ is then shifted once to the right to form the new partial product. The sequence counter is decremented by 1 and its new value checked. If it is not equal to zero, the process is repeated and a new partial product is formed. The process stops when $SC = 0$. Note that the partial product formed in A is shifted into Q one bit at a time and eventually replaces the multiplier. The final product is available in both A and Q, with A holding the most significant bits and Q holding the least significant bits.

The previous numerical example is repeated in Table 10-2 to clarify the hardware multiplication process. The procedure follows the steps outlined in the flowchart.

Booth Multiplication Algorithm

Booth algorithm gives a procedure for multiplying binary integers in signed-2's complement representation. It operates on the fact that strings of 0's in the multiplier require no addition but just shifting, and a string of 1's in the multiplier from bit weight 2^k to weight 2^m can be treated as $2^{k+1} - 2^m$. For example, the binary number 001110 (+14) has a string of 1's from 2^3 to 2^1

TABLE 10-2 Numerical Example for Binary Multiplier

Multiplicand $B = 10111$	E	A	Q	SC
Multiplier in Q	0	00000	10011	101
$Q_n = 1$; add B		10111		
First partial product	0	10111		
Shift right EAQ	0	01011	11001	100
$Q_n = 1$; add B		10111		
Second partial product	1	00010		
Shift right EAQ	0	10001	01100	011
$Q_n = 0$; shift right EAQ	0	01000	10110	010
$Q_n = 0$; shift right EAQ	0	00100	01011	001
$Q_n = 1$; add B		10111		
Fifth partial product	0	11011		
Shift right EAQ	0	01101	10101	000
Final product in $AQ = 0110110101$				

($k = 3, m = 1$). The number can be represented as $2^{k+1} - 2^m = 2^4 - 2^1 = 16 - 2 = 14$. Therefore, the multiplication $M \times 14$, where M is the multiplicand and 14 the multiplier, can be done as $M \times 2^4 - M \times 2^1$. Thus the product can be obtained by shifting the binary multiplicand M four times to the left and subtracting M shifted left once.

As in all multiplication schemes, Booth algorithm requires examination of the multiplier bits and shifting of the partial product. Prior to the shifting, the multiplicand may be added to the partial product, subtracted from the partial product, or left unchanged according to the following rules:

1. The multiplicand is subtracted from the partial product upon encountering the first least significant 1 in a string of 1's in the multiplier.

2. The multiplicand is added to the partial product upon encountering the first 0 (provided that there was a previous 1) in a string of 0's in the multiplier.

3. The partial product does not change when the multiplier bit is identical to the previous multiplier bit.

The algorithm works for positive or negative multipliers in 2's complement representation. This is because a negative multiplier ends with a string of 1's and the last operation will be a subtraction of the appropriate weight. For example, a multiplier equal to -14 is represented in 2's complement as 110010 and is treated as $-2^4 + 2^2 - 2^1 = -14$.

The hardware implementation of Booth algorithm requires the register configuration shown in Fig. 10-7. This is similar to Fig. 10-5 except that the sign bits are not separated from the rest of the registers. To show this difference, we rename registers A, B, and Q, as AC, BR, and QR, respectively. Q_n designates the least significant bit of the multiplier in register QR. An extra flip-flop Q_{n+1} is appended to QR to facilitate a double bit inspection of the multiplier. The flowchart for Booth algorithm is shown in Fig. 10-8. AC and the appended

Figure 10-7 Hardware for Booth algorithm.

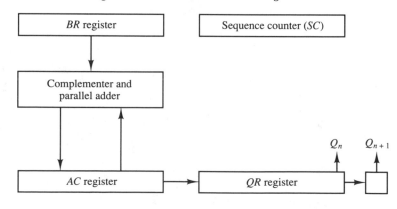

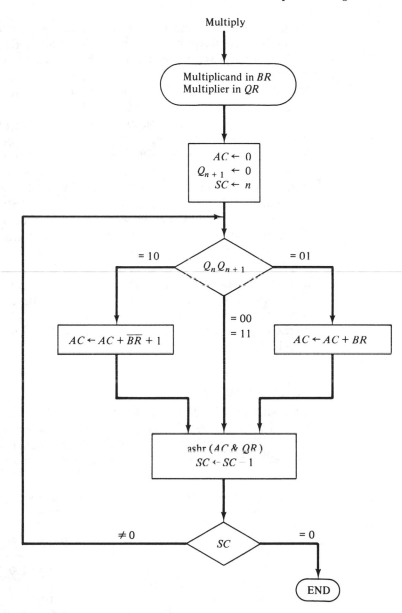

Figure 10-8 Booth algorithm for multiplication of signed-2's complement numbers.

bit Q_{n+1} are initially cleared to 0 and the sequence counter SC is set to a number n equal to the number of bits in the multiplier. The two bits of the multiplier in Q_n and Q_{n+1} are inspected. If the two bits are equal to 10, it means that the first 1 in a string of 1's has been encountered. This requires a subtraction of the multiplicand from the partial product in AC. If the two bits are equal to 01, it means that the first 0 in a string of 0's has been encountered. This requires the addition of the multiplicand to the partial product in AC. When the two bits are equal, the partial product does not change. An overflow cannot occur because the addition and subtraction of the multiplicand follow each other. As a consequence, the two numbers that are added always have opposite signs, a condition that excludes an overflow. The next step is to shift right the partial product and the multiplier (including bit Q_{n+1}). This is an arithmetic shift right (ashr) operation which shifts AC and QR to the right and leaves the sign bit in AC unchanged (see Sec. 4-6). The sequence counter is decremented and the computational loop is repeated n times.

A numerical example of Booth algorithm is shown in Table 10-3 for $n = 5$. It shows the step-by-step multiplication of $(-9) \times (-13) = +117$. Note that the multiplier in QR is negative and that the multiplicand in BR is also negative. The 10-bit product appears in AC and QR and is positive. The final value of Q_{n+1} is the original sign bit of the multiplier and should not be taken as part of the product.

Array Multiplier

Checking the bits of the multiplier one at a time and forming partial products is a sequential operation that requires a sequence of add and shift microoperations. The multiplication of two binary numbers can be done with one microoperation by means of a combinational circuit that forms the product bits all

TABLE 10-3 Example of Multiplication with Booth Algorithm

$Q_n\ Q_{n+1}$	$BR = 10111$ $\overline{BR} + 1 = 01001$	AC	QR	Q_{n+1}	SC
	Initial	00000	10011	0	101
1 0	Subtract BR	01001			
		01001			
	ashr	00100	11001	1	100
1 1	ashr	00010	01100	1	011
0 1	Add BR	10111			
		11001			
	ashr	11100	10110	0	010
0 0	ashr	11110	01011	0	001
1 0	Subtract BR	01001			
		00111			
	ashr	00011	10101	1	000

at once. This is a fast way of multiplying two numbers since all it takes is the time for the signals to propagate through the gates that form the multiplication array. However, an array multiplier requires a large number of gates, and for this reason it was not economical until the development of integrated circuits.

To see how an array multiplier can be implemented with a combinational circuit, consider the multiplication of two 2-bit numbers as shown in Fig. 10-9. The multiplicand bits are b_1 and b_0, the multiplier bits are a_1 and a_0, and the product is $c_3 c_2 c_1 c_0$. The first partial product is formed by multiplying a_0 by $b_1 b_0$. The multiplication of two bits such as a_0 and b_0 produces a 1 if both bits are 1; otherwise, it produces a 0. This is identical to an AND operation and can be implemented with an AND gate. As shown in the diagram, the first partial product is formed by means of two AND gates. The second partial product is formed by multiplying a_1 by $b_1 b_0$ and is shifted one position to the left. The two partial products are added with two half-adder (HA) circuits. Usually, there are more bits in the partial products and it will be necessary to use full-adders to produce the sum. Note that the least significant bit of the product does not have to go through an adder since it is formed by the output of the first AND gate.

A combinational circuit binary multiplier with more bits can be constructed in a similar fashion. A bit of the multiplier is ANDed with each bit of the multiplicand in as many levels as there are bits in the multiplier. The binary output in each level of AND gates is added in parallel with the partial product of the previous level to form a new partial product. The last level produces the product. For j multiplier bits and k multiplicand bits we need $j \times k$ AND gates and $(j - 1)$ k-bit adders to produce a product of $j + k$ bits.

As a second example, consider a multiplier circuit that multiplies a binary number of four bits with a number of three bits. Let the multiplicand be

Figure 10-9 2-bit by 2-bit array multiplier.

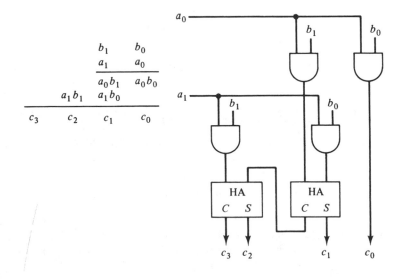

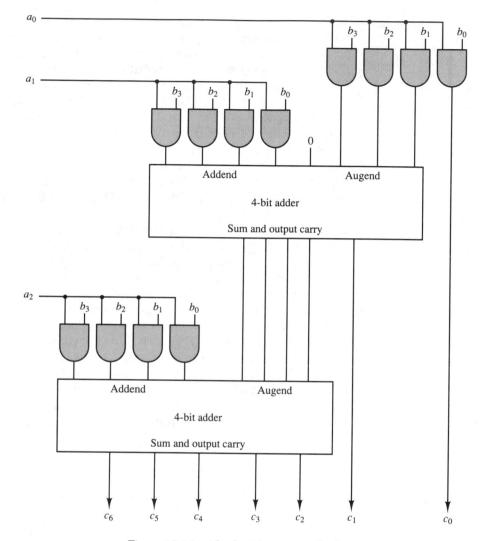

Figure 10-10 4-bit by 3-bit array multiplier.

represented by $b_3 b_2 b_1 b_0$ and the multiplier by $a_2 a_1 a_0$. Since $k = 4$ and $j = 3$, we need 12 AND gates and two 4-bit adders to produce a product of seven bits. The logic diagram of the multiplier is shown in Fig. 10-10.

10-4 Division Algorithms

Division of two fixed-point binary numbers in signed-magnitude representation is done with paper and pencil by a process of successive compare, shift, and subtract operations. Binary division is simpler than decimal division because the quotient digits are either 0 or 1 and there is no need to estimate how many times the dividend or partial remainder fits into the divisor. The division process is illustrated by a numerical example in Fig. 10-11. The divisor B consists of five bits and the dividend A, of ten bits. The five most significant bits of the dividend are compared with the divisor. Since the 5-bit number is smaller than B, we try again by taking the six most significant bits of A and compare this number with B. The 6-bit number is greater than B, so we place a 1 for the quotient bit in the sixth position above the dividend. The divisor is then shifted once to the right and subtracted from the dividend. The difference

partial remainder

is called a *partial remainder* because the division could have stopped here to obtain a quotient of 1 and a remainder equal to the partial remainder. The process is continued by comparing a partial remainder with the divisor. If the partial remainder is greater than or equal to the divisor, the quotient bit is equal to 1. The divisor is then shifted right and subtracted from the partial remainder. If the partial remainder is smaller than the divisor, the quotient bit is 0 and no subtraction is needed. The divisor is shifted once to the right in any case. Note that the result gives both a quotient and a remainder.

Hardware Implementation for Signed-Magnitude Data

When the division is implemented in a digital computer, it is convenient to change the process slightly. Instead of shifting the divisor to the right, the dividend, or partial remainder, is shifted to the left, thus leaving the two numbers in the required relative position. Subtraction may be achieved by adding A to the 2's complement of B. The information about the relative magnitudes is then available from the end-carry.

The hardware for implementing the division operation is identical to that required for multiplication and consists of the components shown in Fig. 10-5. Register EAQ is now shifted to the left with 0 inserted into Q_n and the previous value of E lost. The numerical example is repeated in Fig. 10-12 to clarify the

Figure 10-11 Example of binary division.

```
Divisor:              11010      Quotient = Q
B = 10001     )0111000000        Dividend = A
                 01110           5 bits of A < B, quotient has 5 bits
                 011100          6 bits of A ≥ B
                -10001           Shift right B and subtract; enter 1 in Q

               -010110           7 bits of remainder ≥ B
               --10001           Shift right B and subtract; enter 1 in Q

               --001010          Remainder < B; enter 0 in Q; shift right B
               ---010100         Remainder ≥ B
               ----10001         Shift right B and subtract; enter 1 in Q

               ----000110        Remainder < B; enter 0 in Q
               -----00110        Final remainder
```

Divisor $B = 10001,$ $\qquad\qquad \bar{B} + 1 = 01111$

	E	A	Q	SC
Dividend:		01110	00000	5
shl EAQ	0	11100	00000	
add $\bar{B} + 1$		01111		
$E = 1$	1	01011		
Set $Q_n = 1$	1	01011	00001	4
shl EAQ	0	10110	00010	
Add $\bar{B} + 1$		01111		
$E = 1$	1	00101		
Set $Q_n = 1$	1	00101	00011	3
shl EAQ	0	01010	00110	
Add $\bar{B} + 1$		01111		
$E = 0$; leave $Q_n = 0$	0	11001	00110	
Add B		10001		
				2
Restore remainder	1	01010		
shl EAQ	0	10100	01100	
Add $\bar{B} + 1$		01111		
$E = 1$	1	00011		
Set $Q_n = 1$	1	00011	01101	1
shl EAQ	0	00110	11010	
Add $\bar{B} + 1$		01111		
$E = 0$; leave $Q_n = 0$	0	10101	11010	
Add B		10001		
Restore remainder	1	00110	11010	0
Neglect E				
Remainder in A:		00110		
Quotient in Q:			11010	

Figure 10-12 Example of binary division with digital hardware.

proposed division process. The divisor is stored in the B register and the double-length dividend is stored in registers A and Q. The dividend is shifted to the left and the divisor is subtracted by adding its 2's complement value. The information about the relative magnitude is available in E. If $E = 1$, it signifies that $A \geq B$. A quotient bit 1 is inserted into Q_n and the partial remainder is shifted to the left to repeat the process. If $E = 0$, it signifies that $A < B$ so the quotient in Q_n remains a 0 (inserted during the shift). The value of B is then added to restore the partial remainder in A to its previous value. The partial remainder is shifted to the left and the process is repeated again until all five quotient bits are formed. Note that while the partial remainder is shifted left, the quotient bits are shifted also and after five shifts, the quotient is in Q and the final remainder is in A.

Before showing the algorithm in flowchart form, we have to consider the sign of the result and a possible overflow condition. The sign of the quotient is determined from the signs of the dividend and the divisor. If the two signs are alike, the sign of the quotient is plus. If they are unalike, the sign is minus. The sign of the remainder is the same as the sign of the dividend.

Divide Overflow

The division operation may result in a quotient with an overflow. This is not a problem when working with paper and pencil but is critical when the operation is implemented with hardware. This is because the length of registers is finite and will not hold a number that exceeds the standard length. To see this, consider a system that has 5-bit registers. We use one register to hold the divisor and two registers to hold the dividend. From the example of Fig. 10-11 we note that the quotient will consist of six bits if the five most significant bits of the dividend constitute a number greater than the divisor. The quotient is to be stored in a standard 5-bit register, so the overflow bit will require one more flip-flop for storing the sixth bit. This divide-overflow condition must be avoided in normal computer operations because the entire quotient will be too long for transfer into a memory unit that has words of standard length, that is, the same as the length of registers. Provisions to ensure that this condition is detected must be included in either the hardware or the software of the computer, or in a combination of the two.

When the dividend is twice as long as the divisor, the condition for overflow can be stated as follows: A divide-overflow condition occurs if the high-order half bits of the dividend constitute a number greater than or equal to the divisor. Another problem associated with division is the fact that a division by zero must be avoided. The divide-overflow condition takes care of this condition as well. This occurs because any dividend will be greater than or equal to a divisor which is equal to zero. Overflow condition is usually detected when a special flip-flop is set. We will call it a divide-overflow flip-flop and label it DVF.

The occurrence of a divide overflow can be handled in a variety of ways. In some computers it is the responsibility of the programmers to check if DVF is set after each divide instruction. They then can branch to a subroutine that takes a corrective measure such as rescaling the data to avoid overflow. In some older computers, the occurrence of a divide overflow stopped the computer and this condition was referred to as a *divide stop*. Stopping the operation of the computer is not recommended because it is time consuming. The procedure in most computers is to provide an interrupt request when DVF is set. The interrupt causes the computer to suspend the current program and branch to a service routine to take a corrective measure. The most common corrective measure is to remove the program and type an error message explaining the reason why the program could not be completed. It is then the responsibility of the user who wrote the program to rescale the data or take any other corrective measure. The best way to avoid a divide overflow is to use floating-point data. We will see in Sec. 10-5 that a divide overflow can be handled very simply if numbers are in floating-point representation.

Hardware Algorithm

The hardware divide algorithm is shown in the flowchart of Fig. 10-13. The dividend is in A and Q and the divisor in B. The sign of the result is transferred into Q_s to be part of the quotient. A constant is set into the sequence counter SC to specify the number of bits in the quotient. As in multiplication, we assume that operands are transferred to registers from a memory unit that has

Figure 10-13 Flowchart for divide operation.

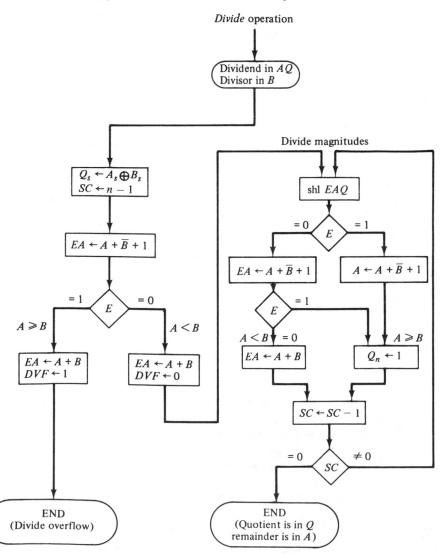

words of n bits. Since an operand must be stored with its sign, one bit of the word will be occupied by the sign and the magnitude will consist of $n-1$ bits.

A divide-overflow condition is tested by subtracting the divisor in B from half of the bits of the dividend stored in A. If $A \geq B$, the divide-overflow flip-flop DVF is set and the operation is terminated prematurely. If $A < B$, no divide overflow occurs so the value of the dividend is restored by adding B to A.

The division of the magnitudes starts by shifting the dividend in AQ to the left with the high-order bit shifted into E. If the bit shifted into E is 1, we know that $EA > B$ because EA consists of a 1 followed by $n-1$ bits while B consists of only $n-1$ bits. In this case, B must be subtracted from EA and 1 inserted into Q_n for the quotient bit. Since register A is missing the high-order bit of the dividend (which is in E), its value is $EA - 2^{n-1}$. Adding to this value the 2's complement of B results in

$$(EA - 2^{n-1}) + (2^{n-1} - B) = EA - B$$

The carry from this addition is not transferred to E if we want E to remain a 1.

If the shift-left operation inserts a 0 into E, the divisor is subtracted by adding its 2's complement value and the carry is transferred into E. If $E = 1$, it signifies that $A \geq B$; therefore, Q_n is set to 1. If $E = 0$, it signifies that $A < B$ and the original number is restored by adding B to A. In the latter case we leave a 0 in Q_n (0 was inserted during the shift).

This process is repeated again with register A holding the partial remainder. After $n - 1$ times, the quotient magnitude is formed in register Q and the remainder is found in register A. The quotient sign is in Q_s and the sign of the remainder in A_s is the same as the original sign of the dividend.

Other Algorithms

restoring method

The hardware method just described is called the *restoring method*. The reason for this name is that the partial remainder is restored by adding the divisor to the negative difference. Two other methods are available for dividing numbers, the *comparison* method and the *nonrestoring* method. In the comparison method

comparison and nonrestoring method

A and B are compared *prior* to the subtraction operation. Then if $A \geq B$, B is subtracted from A. If $A < B$ nothing is done. The partial remainder is shifted left and the numbers are compared again. The comparison can be determined prior to the subtraction by inspecting the end-carry out of the parallel-adder prior to its transfer to register E.

In the nonrestoring method, B is not added if the difference is negative but instead, the negative difference is shifted left and then B is added. To see why this is possible consider the case when $A < B$. From the flowchart in Fig. 9-11 we note that the operations performed are $A - B + B$; that is, B is subtracted and then added to restore A. The next time around the loop, this number is shifted left (or multiplied by 2) and B subtracted again. This gives $2(A - B + B) - B = 2A - B$. This result is obtained in the nonrestoring method by leaving $A - B$ as is. The next time around the loop, the number is shifted left and B *added* to give $2(A - B) + B = 2A - B$, which is the same as before. Thus, in the nonrestoring method, B is subtracted if the previous value of Q_n was a 1, but B is added if the previous value of Q_n was a 0 and no restoring of the partial remainder is required. This process saves the step of adding the divisor if A is less than B, but it requires special control logic to remember the previous result. The first time the dividend is shifted, B must be subtracted. Also, if the last bit of the quotient is 0, the partial remainder must be restored to obtain the correct final remainder.

10-5 Floating-Point Arithmetic Operations

Many high-level programming languages have a facility for specifying floating-point numbers. The most common way is to specify them by a *real* declaration statement as opposed to fixed-point numbers, which are specified by an *integer* declaration statement. Any computer that has a compiler for such high-level programming language must have a provision for handling floating-point arithmetic operations. The operations are quite often included in the internal hardware. If no hardware is available for the operations, the compiler must be designed with a package of floating-point software subroutines. Although the hardware method is more expensive, it is so much more efficient than the software method that floating-point hardware is included in most computers and is omitted only in very small ones.

integer declaration statement

Basic Considerations

Floating-point representation of data was introduced in Sec. 3-4. A floating-point number in computer registers consists of two parts: a mantissa m and an exponent e. The two parts represent a number obtained from multiplying m times a radix r raised to the value of e; thus

$$m \times r^e$$

The mantissa may be a fraction or an integer. The location of the radix point and the value of the radix r are assumed and are not included in the registers. For example, assume a fraction representation and a radix 10. The decimal number 537.25 is represented in a register with $m = 53725$ and $e = 3$ and is interpreted to represent the floating-point number

$$.53725 \times 10^3$$

A floating-point number is normalized if the most significant digit of the mantissa is nonzero. In this way the mantissa contains the maximum possible number of significant digits. A zero cannot be normalized because it does not have a nonzero digit. It is represented in floating-point by all 0's in the mantissa and exponent.

Floating-point representation increases the range of numbers that can be accommodated in a given register. Consider a computer with 48-bit words. Since one bit must be reserved for the sign, the range of fixed-point integer numbers will be $\pm(2^{47} - 1)$, which is approximately $\pm10^{14}$. The 48 bits can be used to represent a floating-point number with 36 bits for the mantissa and 12 bits for the exponent. Assuming fraction representation for the mantissa and taking the two sign bits into consideration, the range of numbers that can be accommodated is

$$\pm(1 - 2^{-35}) \times 2^{2047}$$

This number is derived from a fraction that contains 35 1's, an exponent of 11 bits (excluding its sign), and the fact that $2^{11} - 1 = 2047$. The largest number that can be accommodated is approximately 10^{615}, which is a very large number. The mantissa can accommodate 35 bits (excluding the sign) and if considered as an integer it can store a number as large as $(2^{35} - 1)$. This is approximately equal to 10^{10}, which is equivalent to a decimal number of 10 digits.

Computers with shorter word lengths use two or more words to represent a floating-point number. An 8-bit microcomputer may use four words to represent one floating-point number. One word of 8 bits is reserved for the exponent and the 24 bits of the other three words are used for the mantissa.

Arithmetic operations with floating-point numbers are more complicated than with fixed-point numbers and their execution takes longer and requires more complex hardware. Adding or subtracting two numbers requires first an alignment of the radix point since the exponent parts must be made equal before adding or subtracting the mantissas. The alignment is done by shifting one mantissa while its exponent is adjusted until it is equal to the other exponent. Consider the sum of the following floating-point numbers:

$$.5372400 \times 10^2$$

$$+ .1580000 \times 10^{-1}$$

It is necessary that the two exponents be equal before the mantissas can be added. We can either shift the first number three positions to the left, or shift the second number three positions to the right. When the mantissas are stored in registers, shifting to the left causes a loss of most significant digits. Shifting to the right causes a loss of least significant digits. The second method is preferable because it only reduces the accuracy, while the first method may cause an error. The usual alignment procedure is to shift the mantissa that has the smaller exponent to the right by a number of places equal to the difference between the exponents. After this is done, the mantissas can be added:

$$
\begin{array}{r}
.5372400 \times 10^2 \\
+.0001580 \times 10^2 \\
\hline
.5373980 \times 10^2
\end{array}
$$

When two normalized mantissas are added, the sum may contain an overflow digit. An overflow can be corrected easily by shifting the sum once to the right and incrementing the exponent. When two numbers are subtracted, the result may contain most significant zeros as shown in the following example:

$$
\begin{array}{r}
.56780 \times 10^5 \\
-.56430 \times 10^5 \\
\hline
.00350 \times 10^5
\end{array}
$$

A floating-point number that has a 0 in the most significant position of the mantissa is said to have an *underflow*. To normalize a number that contains an underflow, it is necessary to shift the mantissa to the left and decrement the exponent until a nonzero digit appears in the first position. In the example above, it is necessary to shift left twice to obtain $.35000 \times 10^3$. In most computers, a normalization procedure is performed after each operation to ensure that all results are in a normalized form.

Floating-point multiplication and division do not require an alignment of the mantissas. The product can be formed by multiplying the two mantissas and adding the exponents. Division is accomplished by dividing the mantissas and subtracting the exponents.

The operations performed with the mantissas are the same as in fixed-point numbers, so the two can share the same registers and circuits. The operations performed with the exponents are compare and increment (for aligning the mantissas), add and subtract (for multiplication and division), and decrement (to normalize the result). The exponent may be represented in any one of the three representations: signed-magnitude, signed-2's complement, or signed-1's complement.

A fourth representation employed in many computers is known as a *biased* exponent. In this representation, the sign bit is removed from being a separate entity. The bias is a positive number that is added to each exponent as the floating-point number is formed, so that internally all exponents are positive. The following example may clarify this type of representation. Consider an exponent that ranges from -50 to 49. Internally, it is represented by two digits (without a sign) by adding to it a bias of 50. The exponent register contains the number $e + 50$, where e is the actual exponent. This way, the exponents are represented in registers as positive numbers in the range of 00 to 99. Positive exponents in registers have the range of numbers from 99 to 50. The subtraction of 50 gives the positive values from 49 to 0. Negative exponents are represented in registers in the range from 49 to 00. The subtraction of 50 gives the negative values in the range of −1 to −50.

The advantage of biased exponents is that they contain only positive numbers. It is then simpler to compare their relative magnitude without being concerned with their signs. As a consequence, a magnitude comparator can be used to compare their relative magnitude during the alignment of the mantissa. Another advantage is that the smallest possible biased exponent contains all zeros. The floating-point representation of zero is then a zero mantissa and the smallest possible exponent.

In the examples above, we used decimal numbers to demonstrate some of the concepts that must be understood when dealing with floating-point numbers. Obviously, the same concepts apply to binary numbers as well. The algorithms developed in this section are for binary numbers. Decimal computer arithmetic is discussed in the next section.

Register Configuration

The register configuration for floating-point operations is quite similar to the layout for fixed-point operations. As a general rule, the same registers and adder used for fixed-point arithmetic are used for processing the mantissas. The difference lies in the way the exponents are handled.

The register organization for floating-point operations is shown in Fig. 10-14. There are three registers, BR, AC, and QR. Each register is subdivided into two parts. The mantissa part has the same uppercase letter symbols as in fixed-point representation. The exponent part uses the corresponding lower-case letter symbol.

It is assumed that each floating-point number has a mantissa in signed-magnitude representation and a biased exponent. Thus the AC has a mantissa

Figure 10-14   Registers for floating-point arithmetic operations.

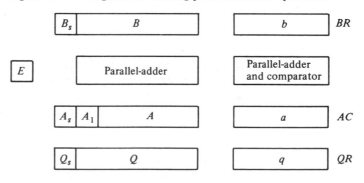

whose sign is in A_s and a magnitude that is in A. The exponent is in the part of the register denoted by the lowercase letter symbol a. The diagram shows explicitly the most significant bit of A, labeled by A_1. The bit in this position must be a 1 for the number to be normalized. Note that the symbol AC represents the entire register, that is, the concatenation of A_s, A, and a.

Similarly, register BR is subdivided into B_s, B, and b, and QR into Q_s, Q, and q. A parallel-adder adds the two mantissas and transfers the sum into A and the carry into E. A separate parallel-adder is used for the exponents. Since the exponents are biased, they do not have a distinct sign bit but are represented as a biased positive quantity. It is assumed that the floating-point numbers are so large that the chance of an exponent overflow is very remote, and for this reason the exponent overflow will be neglected. The exponents are also connected to a magnitude comparator that provides three binary outputs to indicate their relative magnitude.

The number in the mantissa will be taken as a *fraction*, so the binary point is assumed to reside to the left of the magnitude part. Integer representation for floating-point causes certain scaling problems during multiplication and division. To avoid these problems, we adopt a fraction representation.

The numbers in the registers are assumed to be initially normalized. After each arithmetic operation, the result will be normalized. Thus all floating-point operands coming from and going to the memory unit are always normalized.

Addition and Subtraction

During addition or subtraction, the two floating-point operands are in AC and BR. The sum or difference is formed in the AC. The algorithm can be divided into four consecutive parts:

1. Check for zeros.
2. Align the mantissas.
3. Add or subtract the mantissas.
4. Normalize the result.

A floating-point number that is zero cannot be normalized. If this number is used during the computation, the result may also be zero. Instead of checking for zeros during the normalization process we check for zeros at the beginning and terminate the process if necessary. The alignment of the mantissas must be carried out prior to their operation. After the mantissas are added or subtracted, the result may be unnormalized. The normalization procedure ensures that the result is normalized prior to its transfer to memory.

The flowchart for adding or subtracting two floating-point binary numbers is shown in Fig. 10-15. If BR is equal to zero, the operation is terminated, with the value in the AC being the result. If AC is equal to zero, we transfer

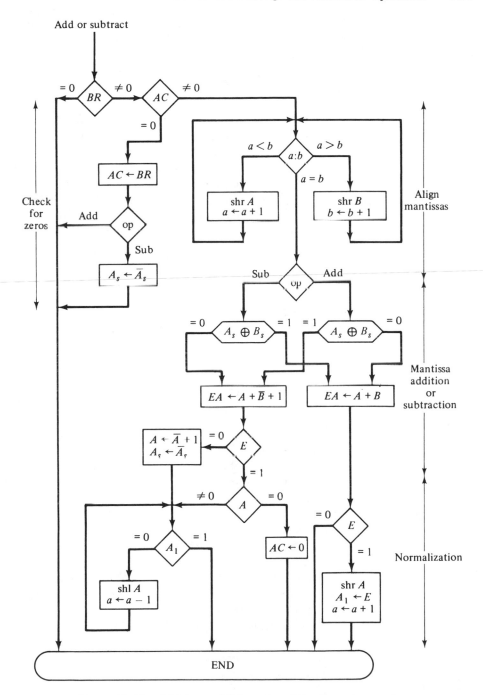

Figure 10-15 Addition and subtraction of floating-point numbers.

the content of BR into AC and also complement its sign if the numbers are to be subtracted. If neither number is equal to zero, we proceed to align the mantissas.

The magnitude comparator attached to exponents a and b provides three outputs that indicate their relative magnitude. If the two exponents are equal, we go to perform the arithmetic operation. If the exponents are not equal, the mantissa having the smaller exponent is shifted to the right and its exponent incremented. This process is repeated until the two exponents are equal.

The addition and subtraction of the two mantissas is identical to the fixed-point addition and subtraction algorithm presented in Fig. 10-2. The magnitude part is added or subtracted depending on the operation and the signs of the two mantissas. If an overflow occurs when the magnitudes are added, it is transferred into flip-flop E. If E is equal to 1, the bit is transferred into A_1 and all other bits of A are shifted right. The exponent must be incremented to maintain the correct number. No underflow may occur in this case because the original mantissa that was not shifted during the alignment was already in a normalized position.

If the magnitudes were subtracted, the result may be zero or may have an underflow. If the mantissa is zero, the entire floating-point number in the AC is made zero. Otherwise, the mantissa must have at least one bit that is equal to 1. The mantissa has an underflow if the most significant bit in position A_1 is 0. In that case, the mantissa is shifted left and the exponent decremented. The bit in A_1 is checked again and the process is repeated until it is equal to 1. When $A_1 = 1$, the mantissa is normalized and the operation is completed.

Multiplication

The multiplication of two floating-point numbers requires that we multiply the mantissas and add the exponents. No comparison of exponents or alignment of mantissas is necessary. The multiplication of the mantissas is performed in the same way as in fixed-point to provide a double-precision product. The double-precision answer is used in fixed-point numbers to increase the accuracy of the product. In floating-point, the range of a single-precision mantissa combined with the exponent is usually accurate enough so that only single-precision numbers are maintained. Thus the half most significant bits of the mantissa product and the exponent will be taken together to form a single-precision floating-point product.

The multiplication algorithm can be subdivided into four parts:

1. Check for zeros.
2. Add the exponents.
3. Multiply the mantissas.
4. Normalize the product.

Steps 2 and 3 can be done simultaneously if separate adders are available for the mantissas and exponents.

The flowchart for floating-point multiplication is shown in Fig. 10-16. The two operands are checked to determine if they contain a zero. If either operand is equal to zero, the product in the AC is set to zero and the operation is

Figure 10-16   Multiplication of floating-point numbers.

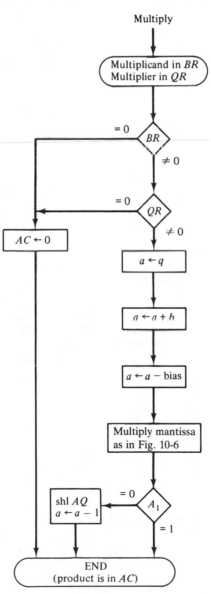

terminated. If neither of the operands is equal to zero, the process continues with the exponent addition.

The exponent of the multiplier is in q and the adder is between exponents a and b. It is necessary to transfer the exponents from q to a, add the two exponents, and transfer the sum into a. Since both exponents are biased by the addition of a constant, the exponent sum will have double this bias. The correct biased exponent for the product is obtained by subtracting the bias number from the sum.

The multiplication of the mantissas is done as in the fixed-point case with the product residing in A and Q. Overflow cannot occur during multiplication, so there is no need to check for it.

The product may have an underflow, so the most significant bit in A is checked. If it is a 1, the product is already normalized. If it is a 0, the mantissa in AQ is shifted left and the exponent decremented. Note that only one normalization shift is necessary. The multiplier and multiplicand were originally normalized and contained fractions. The smallest normalized operand is 0.1, so the smallest possible product is 0.01. Therefore, only one leading zero may occur.

Although the low-order half of the mantissa is in Q, we do not use it for the floating-point product. Only the value in the AC is taken as the product.

Division

Floating-point division requires that the exponents be subtracted and the mantissas divided. The mantissa division is done as in fixed-point except that the dividend has a single-precision mantissa that is placed in the AC. Remember that the mantissa dividend is a fraction and not an integer. For integer representation, a single-precision dividend must be placed in register Q and register A must be cleared. The zeros in A are to the left of the binary point and have no significance. In fraction representation, a single-precision dividend is placed in register A and register Q is cleared. The zeros in Q are to the right of the binary point and have no significance.

The check for divide-overflow is the same as in fixed-point representation. However, with floating-point numbers the divide-overflow imposes no problems. If the dividend is greater than or equal to the divisor, the dividend fraction is shifted to the right and its exponent incremented by 1. For normalized operands this is a sufficient operation to ensure that no mantissa divide-overflow will occur. The operation above is referred to as a *dividend alignment*.

dividend alignment

The division of two normalized floating-point numbers will always result in a normalized quotient provided that a dividend alignment is carried out before the division. Therefore, unlike the other operations, the quotient obtained after the division does not require a normalization.

The division algorithm can be subdivided into five parts:

1. Check for zeros.
2. Initialize registers and evaluate the sign.

3. Align the dividend.
4. Subtract the exponents.
5. Divide the mantissas.

The flowchart for floating-point division is shown in Fig. 10-17. The two operands are checked for zero. If the divisor is zero, it indicates an attempt to divide by zero, which is an illegal operation. The operation is terminated with an error message. An alternative procedure would be to set the quotient in QR to the most positive number possible (if the dividend is positive) or to the most negative possible (if the dividend is negative). If the dividend in AC is zero, the quotient in QR is made zero and the operation terminates.

If the operands are not zero, we proceed to determine the sign of the quotient and store it in Q_s. The sign of the dividend in A_s is left unchanged to be the sign of the remainder. The Q register is cleared and the sequence counter SC is set to a number equal to the number of bits in the quotient.

The dividend alignment is similar to the divide-overflow check in the fixed-point operation. The proper alignment requires that the fraction dividend be smaller than the divisor. The two fractions are compared by a subtraction test. The carry in E determines their relative magnitude. The dividend fraction is restored to its original value by adding the divisor. If $A \geq B$, it is necessary to shift A once to the right and increment the dividend exponent. Since both operands are normalized, this alignment ensures that $A < B$.

Next, the divisor exponent is subtracted from the dividend exponent. Since both exponents were originally biased, the subtraction operation gives the difference without the bias. The bias is then added and the result transferred into q because the quotient is formed in QR.

The magnitudes of the mantissas are divided as in the fixed-point case. After the operation, the mantissa quotient resides in Q and the remainder in A. The floating-point quotient is already normalized and resides in QR. The exponent of the remainder should be the same as the exponent of the dividend. The binary point for the remainder mantissa lies $(n - 1)$ positions to the left of A_1. The remainder can be converted to a normalized fraction by subtracting $n - 1$ from the dividend exponent and by shift and decrement until the bit in A_1 is equal to 1. This is not shown in the flow chart and is left as an exercise.

10-6 Decimal Arithmetic Unit

The user of a computer prepares data with decimal numbers and receives results in decimal form. A CPU with an arithmetic logic unit can perform arithmetic microoperations with binary data. To perform arithmetic operations with decimal data, it is necessary to convert the input decimal numbers to binary, to perform all calculations with binary numbers, and to convert the results into decimal. This may be an efficient method in applications requiring a large number of calculations and a relatively smaller amount of input and

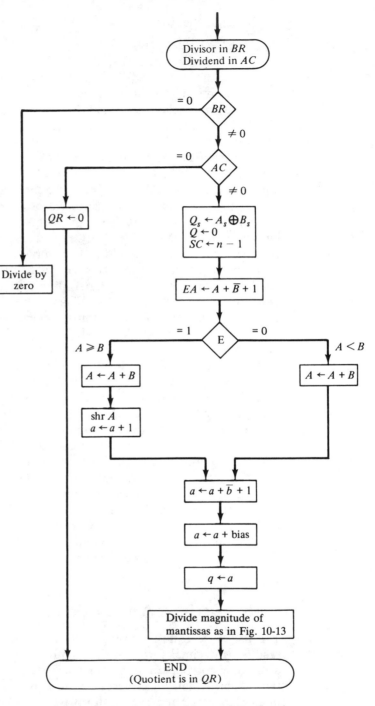

Figure 10-17 Division of floating-point numbers.

output data. When the application calls for a large amount of input–output and a relatively smaller number of arithmetic calculations, it becomes convenient to do the internal arithmetic directly with the decimal numbers. Computers capable of performing decimal arithmetic must store the decimal data in binary-coded form. The decimal numbers are then applied to a decimal arithmetic unit capable of executing decimal arithmetic microoperations.

Electronic calculators invariably use an internal decimal arithmetic unit since inputs and outputs are frequent. There does not seem to be a reason for converting the keyboard input numbers to binary and again converting the displayed results to decimal, since this process requires special circuits and also takes a longer time to execute. Many computers have hardware for arithmetic calculations with both binary and decimal data. Users can specify by pro-grammed instructions whether they want the computer to perform calculations with binary or decimal data.

A decimal arithmetic unit is a digital function that performs decimal microoperations. It can add or subtract decimal numbers, usually by forming the 9's or 10's complement of the subtrahend. The unit accepts coded decimal numbers and generates results in the same adopted binary code. A single-stage decimal arithmetic unit consists of nine binary input variables and five binary output variables, since a minimum of four bits is required to represent each coded decimal digit. Each stage must have four inputs for the augend digit, four inputs for the addend digit, and an input-carry. The outputs include four terminals for the sum digit and one for the output-carry. Of course, there is a wide variety of possible circuit configurations dependent on the code used to represent the decimal digits.

BCD Adder

Consider the arithmetic addition of two decimal digits in BCD, together with a possible carry from a previous stage. Since each input digit does not exceed 9, the output sum cannot be greater than $9 + 9 + 1 = 19$, the 1 in the sum being an input-carry. Suppose that we apply two BCD digits to a 4-bit binary adder. The adder will form the sum in *binary* and produce a result that may range from 0 to 19. These binary numbers are listed in Table 10-4 and are labeled by symbols K, Z_8, Z_4, Z_2, and Z_1. K is the carry and the subscripts under the letter Z represent the weights 8, 4, 2, and 1 that can be assigned to the four bits in the BCD code. The first column in the table lists the binary sums as they appear in the outputs of a 4-bit *binary* adder. The output sum of two *decimal* numbers must be represented in BCD and should appear in the form listed in the second column of the table. The problem is to find a simple rule by which the binary number in the first column can be converted to the correct BCD digit representation of the number in the second column.

In examining the contents of the table, it is apparent that when the binary sum is equal to or less than 1001, the corresponding BCD number is identical

TABLE 10-4 Derivation of BCD Adder

Binary Sum					BCD Sum					
K	Z_8	Z_4	Z_2	Z_1	C	S_8	S_4	S_2	S_1	Decimal
0	0	0	0	0	0	0	0	0	0	0
0	0	0	0	1	0	0	0	0	1	1
0	0	0	1	0	0	0	0	1	0	2
0	0	0	1	1	0	0	0	1	1	3
0	0	1	0	0	0	0	1	0	0	4
0	0	1	0	1	0	0	1	0	1	5
0	0	1	1	0	0	0	1	1	0	6
0	0	1	1	1	0	0	1	1	1	7
0	1	0	0	0	0	1	0	0	0	8
0	1	0	0	1	0	1	0	0	1	9
0	1	0	1	0	1	0	0	0	0	10
0	1	0	1	1	1	0	0	0	1	11
0	1	1	0	0	1	0	0	1	0	12
0	1	1	0	1	1	0	0	1	1	13
0	1	1	1	0	1	0	1	0	0	14
0	1	1	1	1	1	0	1	0	1	15
1	0	0	0	0	1	0	1	1	0	16
1	0	0	0	1	1	0	1	1	1	17
1	0	0	1	0	1	1	0	0	0	18
1	0	0	1	1	1	1	0	0	1	19

and therefore no conversion is needed. When the binary sum is greater than 1001, we obtain a nonvalid BCD representation. The addition of binary 6 (0110) to the binary sum converts it to the correct BCD representation and also produces an output-carry as required.

One method of adding decimal numbers in BCD would be to employ one 4-bit binary adder and perform the arithmetic operation one digit at a time. The low-order pair of BCD digits is first added to produce a binary sum. If the result is equal or greater than 1010, it is corrected by adding 0110 to the binary sum. This second operation will automatically produce an output-carry for the next pair of significant digits. The next higher-order pair of digits, together with the input-carry, is then added to produce their binary sum. If this result is equal to or greater than 1010, it is corrected by adding 0110. The procedure is repeated until all decimal digits are added.

The logic circuit that detects the necessary correction can be derived from the table entries. It is obvious that a correction is needed when the binary sum has an output carry $K = 1$. The other six combinations from 1010 to 1111 that need a correction have a 1 in position Z_8. To distinguish them from binary 1000 and 1001 which also have a 1 in position Z_8, we specify further that either Z_4

or Z_2 must have a 1. The condition for a correction and an output-carry can be expressed by the Boolean function

$$C = K + Z_8 Z_4 + Z_8 Z_2$$

When $C = 1$, it is necessary to add 0110 to the binary sum and provide an output-carry for the next stage.

A BCD adder is a circuit that adds two BCD digits in parallel and produces a sum digit also in BCD. A BCD adder must include the correction logic in its internal construction. To add 0110 to the binary sum, we use a second 4-bit binary adder as shown in Fig. 10-18. The two decimal digits, together with the input-carry, are first added in the top 4-bit binary adder to produce the binary sum. When the output-carry is equal to 0, nothing is added to the binary sum. When it is equal to 1, binary 0110 is added to the binary sum through the bottom 4-bit binary adder. The output-carry generated from the bottom binary adder may be ignored, since it supplies information already available in the output-carry terminal.

Figure 10-18   Block diagram of BCD adder.

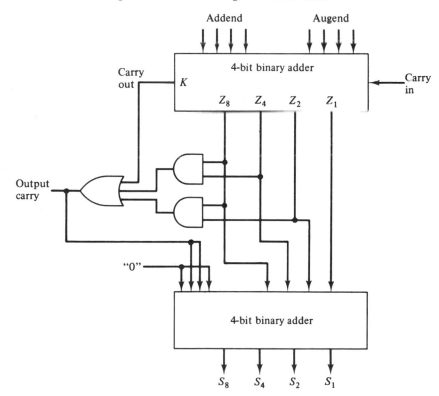

A decimal parallel-adder that adds n decimal digits needs n BCD adder stages with the output-carry from one stage connected to the input-carry of the next-higher-order stage. To achieve shorter propagation delays, BCD adders include the necessary circuits for carry look-ahead. Furthermore, the adder circuit for the correction does not need all four full-adders, and this circuit can be optimized.

BCD Subtraction

A straight subtraction of two decimal numbers will require a subtractor circuit that will be somewhat different from a BCD adder. It is more economical to perform the subtraction by taking the 9's or 10's complement of the subtrahend and adding it to the minuend. Since the BCD is not a self-complementing code, the 9's complement cannot be obtained by complementing each bit in the code. It must be formed by a circuit that subtracts each BCD digit from 9.

The 9's complement of a decimal digit represented in BCD may be obtained by complementing the bits in the coded representation of the digit provided a correction is included. There are two possible correction methods. In the first method, binary 1010 (decimal 10) is added to each complemented digit and the carry discarded after each addition. In the second method, binary 0110 (decimal 6) is added before the digit is complemented. As a numerical illustration, the 9's complement of BCD 0111 (decimal 7) is computed by first complementing each bit to obtain 1000. Adding binary 1010 and discarding the carry, we obtain 0010 (decimal 2). By the second method, we add 0110 to 0111 to obtain 1101. Complementing each bit, we obtain the required result of 0010. Complementing each bit of a 4-bit binary number N is identical to the subtraction of the number from 1111 (decimal 15). Adding the binary equivalent of decimal 10 gives $15 - N + 10 = 9 - N + 16$. But 16 signifies the carry that is discarded, so the result is $9 - N$ as required. Adding the binary equivalent of decimal 6 and then complementing gives $15 - (N + 6) = 9 - N$ as required.

The 9's complement of a BCD digit can also be obtained through a combinational circuit. When this circuit is attached to a BCD adder, the result is a BCD adder/subtractor. Let the subtrahend (or addend) digit be denoted by the four binary variables B_8, B_4, B_2, and B_1. Let M be a mode bit that controls the add/subtract operation. When $M = 0$, the two digits are added; when $M = 1$, the digits are subtracted. Let the binary variables x_8, x_4, x_2, and x_1 be the outputs of the 9's complementer circuit. By an examination of the truth table for the circuit, it may be observed (see Prob. 10-30) that B_1 should always be complemented; B_2 is always the same in the 9's complement as in the original digit; x_4 is 1 when the exclusive-OR of B_2 and B_4 is 1; and x_8 is 1 when $B_8 B_4 B_2 = 000$. The Boolean functions for the 9's complementer circuit are

$$x_1 = B_1 M' + B_1' M$$

$$x_2 = B_2$$

$$x_4 = B_4 M' + (B_4' B_2 + B_4 B_2')M$$

$$x_8 = B_8 M' + B_8' B_4' B_2' M$$

From these equations we see that $x = B$ when $M = 0$. When $M = 1$, the x outputs produce the 9's complement of B.

One stage of a decimal arithmetic unit that can add or subtract two BCD digits is shown in Fig. 10-19. It consists of a BCD adder and a 9's complementer. The mode M controls the operation of the unit. With $M = 0$, the S outputs form the sum of A and B. With $M = 1$, the S outputs form the sum of A plus the 9's complement of B. For numbers with n decimal digits we need n such stages. The output carry C_{i+1} from one stage must be connected to the input carry C_i of the next-higher-order stage. The best way to subtract the two decimal numbers is to let $M = 1$ and apply a 1 to the input carry C_1 of the first stage. The outputs will form the sum of A plus the 10's complement of B, which is equivalent to a subtraction operation if the carry-out of the last stage is discarded.

10-7 Decimal Arithmetic Operations

The algorithms for arithmetic operations with decimal data are similar to the algorithms for the corresponding operations with binary data. In fact, except for a slight modification in the multiplication and division algorithms, the same

Figure 10-19 One stage of a decimal arithmetic unit.

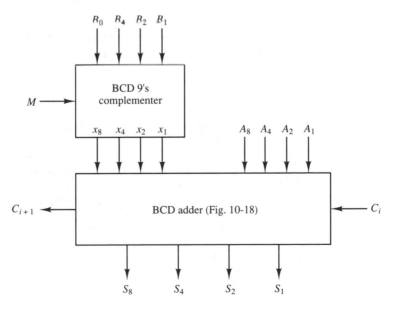

flowcharts can be used for both types of data provided that we interpret the microoperation symbols properly. Decimal numbers in BCD are stored in computer registers in groups of four bits. Each 4-bit group represents a decimal digit and must be taken as a unit when performing decimal microoperations.

For convenience, we will use the same symbols for binary and decimal arithmetic microoperations but give them a different interpretation. As shown in Table 10-5, a bar over the register letter symbol denotes the 9's complement of the decimal number stored in the register. Adding 1 to the 9's complement produces the 10's complement. Thus, for decimal numbers, the symbol $A \leftarrow A + \overline{B} + 1$ denotes a transfer of the decimal sum formed by adding the original content A to the 10's complement of B. The use of identical symbols for the 9's complement and the 1's complement may be confusing if both types of data are employed in the same system. If this is the case, it may be better to adopt a different symbol for the 9's complement. If only one type of data is being considered, the symbol would apply to the type of data used.

Incrementing or decrementing a register is the same for binary and decimal except for the number of states that the register is allowed to have. A binary counter goes through 16 states, from 0000 to 1111, when incremented. A decimal counter goes through 10 states from 0000 to 1001 and back to 0000, since 9 is the last count. Similarly, a binary counter sequences from 1111 to 0000 when decremented. A decimal counter goes from 1001 to 0000.

A decimal shift right or left is preceded by the letter d to indicate a shift over the four bits that hold the decimal digits. As a numerical illustration consider a register A holding decimal 7860 in BCD. The bit pattern of the 12 flip-flops is

$$0111 \quad 1000 \quad 0110 \quad 0000$$

The microoperation *dshr A* shifts the decimal number one digit to the right to give 0786. This shift is over the four bits and changes the content of the register into

$$0000 \quad 0111 \quad 1000 \quad 0110$$

TABLE 10-5 Decimal Arithmetic Microoperation Symbols

Symbolic Designation	Description
$A \leftarrow A + B$	Add decimal numbers and transfer sum into A
$\overline{B}$	9's complement of B
$A \leftarrow A + \overline{B} + 1$	Content of A plus 10's complement of B into A
$Q_L \leftarrow Q_L + 1$	Increment BCD number in Q_L
dshr A	Decimal shift-right register A
dshl A	Decimal shift-left register A

Addition and Subtraction

The algorithm for addition and subtraction of binary signed-magnitude numbers applies also to decimal signed-magnitude numbers provided that we interpret the microoperation symbols in the proper manner. Similarly, the algorithm for binary signed-2's complement numbers applies to decimal signed-10's complement numbers. The binary data must employ a binary adder and a complementer. The decimal data must employ a decimal arithmetic unit capable of adding two BCD numbers and forming the 9's complement of the subtrahend as shown in Fig. 10-19.

Decimal data can be added in three different ways, as shown in Fig. 10-20. The parallel method uses a decimal arithmetic unit composed of as many BCD adders as there are digits in the number. The sum is formed in parallel and requires only one microoperation. In the digit-serial bit-parallel method, the digits are applied to a single BCD adder serially, while the bits of each coded digit are transferred in parallel. The sum is formed by shifting the decimal numbers through the BCD adder one at a time. For k decimal digits, this configuration requires k microoperations, one for each decimal shift. In the all serial adder, the bits are shifted one at a time through a full-adder. The binary sum formed after four shifts must be corrected into a valid BCD digit. This correction, discussed in Sec. 10-6, consists of checking the binary sum. If it is greater than or equal to 1010, the binary sum is corrected by adding to it 0110 and generating a carry for the next pair of digits.

The parallel method is fast but requires a large number of adders. The digit-serial bit-parallel method requires only one BCD adder, which is shared by all the digits. It is slower than the parallel method because of the time required to shift the digits. The all serial method requires a minimum amount of equipment but is very slow.

Multiplication

The multiplication of fixed-point decimal numbers is similar to binary except for the way the partial products are formed. A decimal multiplier has digits that range in value from 0 to 9, whereas a binary multiplier has only 0 and 1 digits. In the binary case, the multiplicand is added to the partial product if the multiplier bit is 1. In the decimal case, the multiplicand must be multiplied by the digit multiplier and the result added to the partial product. This operation can be accomplished by adding the multiplicand to the partial product a number of times equal to the value of the multiplier digit.

The registers organization for the decimal multiplication is shown in Fig. 10-21. We are assuming here four-digit numbers, with each digit occupying four bits, for a total of 16 bits for each number. There are three registers, A, B, and Q, each having a corresponding sign flip-flop A_s, B_s, and Q_s.

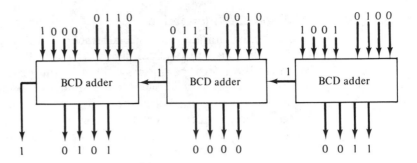

(a) Parallel decimal addition: 624 + 879 = 1503

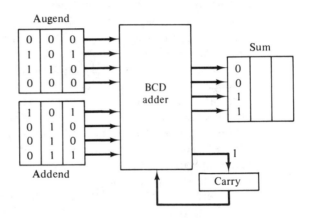

(b) Digit-serial, bit-parallel decimal addition

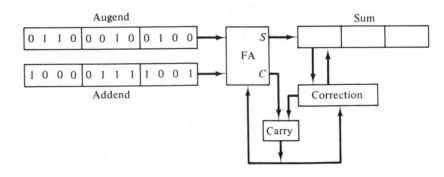

(c) All serial decimal addition

Figure 10-20 Three ways of adding decimal numbers.

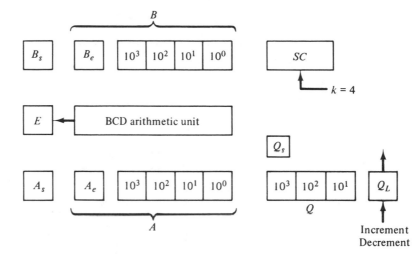

Figure 10-21   Registers for decimal arithmetic multiplication and division.

Registers A and B have four more bits designated by A_e and B_e that provide an extension of one more digit to the registers. The BCD arithmetic unit adds the five digits in parallel and places the sum in the five-digit A register. The end-carry goes to flip-flop E. The purpose of digit A_e is to accommodate an overflow while adding the multiplicand to the partial product during multiplication. The purpose of digit B_e is to form the 9's complement of the divisor when subtracted from the partial remainder during the division operation. The least significant digit in register Q is denoted by Q_L. This digit can be incremented or decremented.

A decimal operand coming from memory consists of 17 bits. One bit (the sign) is transferred to B_s and the magnitude of the operand is placed in the lower 16 bits of B. Both B_e and A_e are cleared initially. The result of the operation is also 17 bits long and does not use the A_e part of the A register.

The decimal multiplication algorithm is shown in Fig. 10-22. Initially, the entire A register and B_e are cleared and the sequence counter SC is set to a number k equal to the number of digits in the multiplier. The low-order digit of the multiplier in Q_L is checked. If it is not equal to 0, the multiplicand in B is added to the partial product in A once and Q_L is decremented. Q_L is checked again and the process is repeated until it is equal to 0. In this way, the multiplicand in B is added to the partial product a number of times equal to the multiplier digit. Any temporary overflow digit will reside in A_e and can range in value from 0 to 9.

Next, the partial product and the multiplier are shifted once to the right. This places zero in A_e and transfers the next multiplier quotient into Q_L. The process is then repeated k times to form a double-length product in AQ.

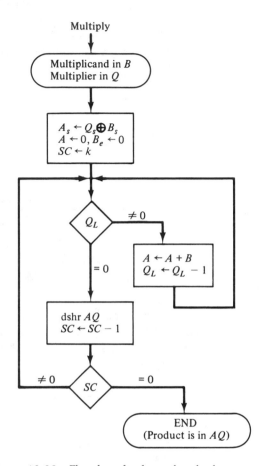

Figure 10-22   Flowchart for decimal multiplication.

Division

Decimal division is similar to binary division except of course that the quotient digits may have any of the 10 values from 0 to 9. In the restoring division method, the divisor is subtracted from the dividend or partial remainder as many times as necessary until a negative remainder results. The correct remainder is then restored by adding the divisor. The digit in the quotient reflects the number of subtractions up to but excluding the one that caused the negative difference.

The decimal division algorithm is shown in Fig. 10-23. It is similar to the algorithm with binary data except for the way the quotient bits are formed. The dividend (or partial remainder) is shifted to the left, with its most significant digit placed in A_e. The divisor is then subtracted by adding its 10's complement value. Since B_e is initially cleared, its complement value is 9 as required. The carry in E determines the relative magnitude of A and B. If $E = 0$, it signifies

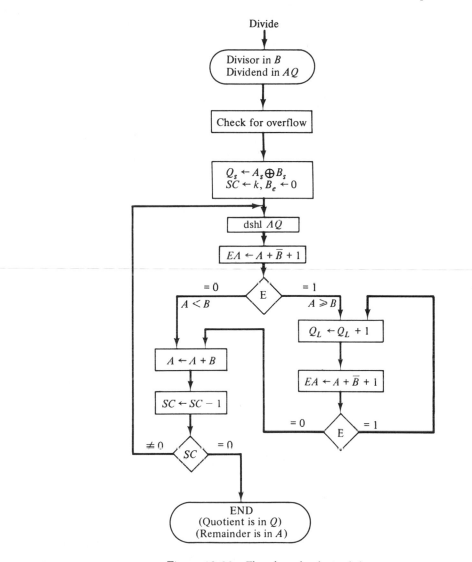

Figure 10-23 Flowchart for decimal division.

that $A < B$. In this case the divisor is added to restore the partial remainder and Q_L stays at 0 (inserted there during the shift). If $E = 1$, it signifies that $A \geq B$. The quotient digit in Q_L is incremented once and the divisor subtracted again. This process is repeated until the subtraction results in a negative difference which is recognized by E being 0. When this occurs, the quotient digit is not incremented but the divisor is added to restore the positive remainder. In this way, the quotient digit is made equal to the number of times that the partial remainder "goes" into the divisor.

The partial remainder and the quotient bits are shifted once to the left and the process is repeated k times to form k quotient digits. The remainder is then found in register A and the quotient is in register Q. The value of E is neglected.

Floating-Point Operations

Decimal floating-point arithmetic operations follow the same procedures as binary operations. The algorithms in Sec. 10-5 can be adopted for decimal data provided that the microoperation symbols are interpreted correctly. The multiplication and division of the mantissas must be done by the methods described above.

═══════════════ **PROBLEMS** ═══════════════

10-1.   The complementer shown in Fig. 10-1 is not needed if instead of performing $A + \bar{B} + 1$ we perform $B + \bar{A}$ (B plus the 1's complement of A). Derive an algorithm in flowchart form for addition and subtraction of fixed-point binary numbers in signed-magnitude representation with the magnitudes subtracted by the two microoperations $A \leftarrow \bar{A}$ and $EA \leftarrow A + B$.

10-2.   Mark each individual path in the flowchart of Fig. 10-2 by a number and then indicate the overall path that the algorithm takes when the following signed-magnitude numbers are computed. In each case give the value of AVF. The leftmost bit in the following numbers represents the sign bit.
   a. 0 101101 + 0 011111
   b. 1 011111 + 1 101101
   c. 0 101101 − 0 011111
   d. 0 101101 − 0 101101
   e. 1 011111 − 0 101101

10-3.   Perform the arithmetic operations below with binary numbers and with negative numbers in signed-2's complement representation. Use seven bits to accommodate each number together with its sign. In each case, determine if there is an overflow by checking the carries into and out of the sign bit position.
   a. (+35) + (+40)
   b. (−35) + (−40)
   c. (−35) − (+40)

10-4.   Consider the binary numbers when they are in signed-2's complement representation. Each number has n bits: one for the sign and $k = n - 1$ for the magnitude. A negative number $-X$ is represented as $2^k + (2^k - X)$, where the first 2^k designates the sign bit and $(2^k - X)$ is the 2's complement of X. A positive number is represented as $0 + X$, where the 0 designates the sign bit, and X, the k-bit magnitude. Using these generalized symbols, prove that the sum $(\pm X) + (\pm Y)$ can be formed by adding the numbers including their sign bits and discarding the carry-out of the sign-bit position. In other words, prove the algorithm for adding two binary numbers in signed-2's complement representation.

10-5.   Formulate a hardware procedure for detecting an overflow by comparing the sign of the sum with the signs of the augend and addend. The numbers are in signed-2's complement representation.

10-6.   **a.** Perform the operation $(-9) + (-6) = -15$ with binary numbers in signed-1's complement representation using only five bits to represent each number (including the sign). Show that the overflow detection procedure of checking the inequality of the last two carries fails in this case.

b. Suggest a modified procedure for detecting an overflow when signed-1's complement numbers are used.

10-7.   Derive an algorithm in flowchart form for adding and subtracting two fixed-point binary numbers when negative numbers are in signed-1's complement representation.

10-8.   Prove that the multiplication of two n-digit numbers in base r gives a product no more than $2n$ digits in length. Show that this statement implies that no overflow can occur in the multiplication operation.

10-9.   Show the contents of registers E, A, Q, and SC (as in Table 10-2) during the process of multiplication of two binary numbers, 11111 (multiplicand) and 10101 (multiplier). The signs are not included.

10-10.   Show the contents of registers E, A, Q, and SC (as in Fig. 10-12) during the process of division of (a) 10100011 by 1011; (b) 00001111 by 0011. (Use a dividend of eight bits.)

10-11.   Show that adding B after the operation $A + \bar{B} + 1$ restores the original value of A. What should be done with the end carry?

10-12.   Why should the sign of the remainder after a division be the same as the sign of the dividend?

10-13.   Design an array multiplier that multiplies two 4-bit numbers. Use AND gates and binary adders.

10-14.   Show the step-by-step multiplication process using Booth algorithm (as in Table 10-3) when the following binary numbers are multiplied. Assume 5-bit registers that hold signed numbers. The multiplicand in both cases is +15.
a. $(+15) \times (+13)$
b. $(+15) \times (-13)$

10-15.   Derive an algorithm in flowchart form for the nonrestoring method of fixed-point binary division.

10-16.   Derive an algorithm for evaluating the square root of a binary fixed-point number.

10-17.   A binary floating-point number has seven bits for a biased exponent. The constant used for the bias is 64.
a. List the biased representation of all exponents from -64 to $+63$.

b. Show that a 7-bit magnitude comparator can be used to compare the relative magnitude of the two exponents.

c. Show that after the addition of two biased exponents it is necessary to subtract 64 in order to have a biased exponents sum. How would you subtract 64 by adding its 2's complement value?

d. Show that after the subtraction of two biased exponents it is necessary to add 64 in order to have a biased exponent difference.

10-18. Derive an algorithm in flowchart form for the comparison of two signed binary numbers when negative numbers are in signed-2's complement representation:

a. By means of a subtraction operation with the signed-2's complement numbers.

b. By scanning and comparing pairs of bits from left to right.

10-19. Repeat Prob. 10-18 for signed-magnitude binary numbers.

10-20. Let n be the number of bits of the mantissa in a binary floating-point number. When the mantissas are aligned during the addition or subtraction, the exponent difference may be greater than $n - 1$. If this occurs, the mantissa with the smaller exponent is shifted entirely out of the register. Modify the mantissa alignment in Fig. 10-15 by including a sequence counter SC that counts the number of shifts. If the number of shifts is greater than $n - 1$, the larger number is then used to determine the result.

10-21. The procedure for aligning mantissas during addition or subtraction of floating-point numbers can be stated as follows: Subtract the smaller exponent from the larger and shift right the mantissa having the smaller exponent a number of places equal to the difference between the exponents. The exponent of the sum (or difference) is equal to the larger exponents. Without using a magnitude comparator, assuming biased exponents, and taking into account that only the AC can be shifted, derive an algorithm in flowchart form for aligning the mantissas and placing the larger exponent in the AC.

10-22. Show that there can be no mantissa overflow after a multiplication operation.

10-23. Show that the division of two normalized floating-point numbers with fractional mantissas will always result in a normalized quotient provided a dividend alignment is carried out prior to the division operation.

10-24. Extend the flowchart of Fig. 10-17 to provide a normalized floating-point remainder in the AC. The mantissa should be a fraction.

10-25. The algorithms for the floating-point arithmetic operations in Sec. 10-5 neglect the possibility of exponent overflow or underflow.

a. Go over the three flowcharts and find where an exponent overflow may occur.

b. Repeat (a) for exponent underflow. An exponent underflow occurs if the exponent is more negative than the smallest number that can be accommodated in the register.

c. Show how an exponent overflow or underflow can be detected by the hardware.

10-26. If we assume integer representation for the mantissa of floating-point numbers, we encounter certain scaling problems during multiplication and division. Let the number of bits in the magnitude part of the mantissa be $(n - 1)$. For integer representation:

a. Show that if a single-precision product is used, $(n - 1)$ must be added to the exponent product in the AC.

b. Show that if a single-precision mantissa dividend is used, $(n - 1)$ must be subtracted from the exponent dividend when Q is cleared.

10-27. Show the hardware to be used for the addition and subtraction of two decimal numbers in signed-magnitude representation. Indicate how an overflow is detected.

10-28. Show that $673 - 356$ can be computed by adding 673 to the 10's complement of 356 and discarding the end carry. Draw the block diagram of a three-stage decimal arithmetic unit and show how this operation is implemented. List all input bits and output bits of the unit.

10-29. Show that the lower 4-bit binary adder in Fig. 10-1 can be replaced by one full-adder and two half-adders.

10-30. Using combinational circuit design techniques, derive the Boolean functions for the BCD 9's complementer of Fig. 10-19. Draw the logic diagram.

10-31. It is necessary to design an adder for two decimal digits represented in the excess-3 code (Table 3-6). Show that the correction after adding two digits with a 4-bit binary adder is as follows:

a. The output carry is equal to the uncorrected carry.

b. If output carry = 1, add 0011.

c. If output carry = 0, add 1101 and ignore the carry from this addition. Show that the excess-3 adder can be constructed with seven full-adders and two inverters.

10-32. Derive the circuit for a 9's complementer when decimal digits are represented in the excess-3 code (Table 3-6). A mode control input determines whether the digit is complemented or not. What is the advantage of using this code over BCD?

10-33. Show the hardware to be used for the addition and subtraction of two decimal numbers with negative numbers in signed-10's complement representation. Indicate how an overflow is detected. Derive the flowchart algorithm and try a few numbers to convince yourself that the algorithm produces correct results.

10-34. Show the content of registers A, B, Q, and SC during the decimal multiplication (Fig. 10-22) of (a) 470×152 and (b) 999×199. Assume three-digit registers and take the second number as the multiplier.

10-35. Show the content of registers A, E, Q, and SC during the decimal division (Fig. 10-23) of 1680/32. Assume two-digit registers.

10-36. Show that subregister A_e in Fig. 10-21 is zero at the termination of (a) the decimal multiplication as specified in Fig. 10-22, and (b) the decimal division as specified in Fig. 10-23.

10-37. Change the floating-point arithmetic algorithms in Sec. 10-5 from binary to decimal data. In a table, list how each microoperation symbol should be interpreted.

REFERENCES

1. Blaauw, G., *Digital Systems Implementation*. Englewood Cliffs, NJ: Prentice Hall, 1976.

2. Cavanagh, J. J. F., *Digital Computer Arithmetic*. New York: McGraw-Hill, 1984.

3. Hamacher, V. C., Z. G. Vranesic, and S. G. Zaky, *Computer Organization*, 3rd ed. New York: McGraw-Hill, 1990.

4. Hays, J. F., *Computer Architecture and Organization*, 2nd ed. New York: McGraw-Hill, 1988.

5. Hill, F. J., and G. R. Peterson, *Digital Systems: Hardware Organization and Design*, 3rd ed. New York: John Wiley, 1987.

6. Hwang, K., *Computer Arithmetic*. New York: John Wiley, 1979.

7. Kulisch, V. W., and W. L. Miranker, *Computer Arithmetic in Theory and Practice*. New York: Academic Press, 1980.

8. Schmid, H., *Decimal Arithmetic*. New York: John Wiley, 1979.

CHAPTER ELEVEN

Input–Output Organization

IN THIS CHAPTER

11-1   Peripheral Devices

I/O

The input–output subsystem of a computer, referred to as I/O, provides an efficient mode of communication between the central system and the outside environment. Programs and data must be entered into computer memory for processing and results obtained from computations must be recorded or displayed for the user. A computer serves no useful purpose without the ability to receive information from an outside source and to transmit results in a meaningful form.

The most familiar means of entering information into a computer is through a typewriter-like keyboard that allows a person to enter alphanumeric information directly. Every time a key is depressed, the terminal sends a binary coded character to the computer. The fastest possible speed for entering information this way depends on the person's typing speed. On the other hand, the central processing unit is an extremely fast device capable of performing operations at very high speed. When input information is transferred to the processor via a slow keyboard, the processor will be idle most of the time while waiting for the information to arrive. To use a computer efficiently, a large amount of programs and data must be prepared in advance and transmitted into a storage medium such as magnetic tapes or disks. The information in the disk is then transferred into computer memory at a rapid rate. Results of programs are also transferred into a high-speed storage, such as disks, from which they can be transferred later into a printer to provide a printed output of results.

peripheral

Devices that are under the direct control of the computer are said to be connected on-line. These devices are designed to read information into or out of the memory unit upon command from the CPU and are considered to be part of the total computer system. Input or output devices attached to the computer are also called *peripherals*. Among the most common peripherals are keyboards, display units, and printers. Peripherals that provide auxiliary storage for the system are magnetic disks and tapes. Peripherals are electromechanical and electromagnetic devices of some complexity. Only a very brief discussion of their function will be given here without going into detail of their internal construction.

monitor and keyboard

Video monitors are the most commonly used peripherals. They consist of a keyboard as the input device and a display unit as the output device. There are different types of video monitors, but the most popular use a cathode ray tube (CRT). The CRT contains an electronic gun that sends an electronic beam to a phosphorescent screen in front of the tube. The beam can be deflected horizontally and vertically. To produce a pattern on the screen, a grid inside the CRT receives a variable voltage that causes the beam to hit the screen and make it glow at selected spots. Horizontal and vertical signals deflect the beam and make it sweep across the tube, causing the visual pattern to appear on the screen. A characteristic feature of display devices is a cursor that marks the position in the screen where the next character will be inserted. The cursor can be moved to any position in the screen, to a single character, the beginning of a word, or to any line. Edit keys add or delete information based on the cursor position. The display terminal can operate in a single-character mode where all characters entered on the screen through the keyboard are transmitted to the computer simultaneously. In the block mode, the edited text is first stored in a local memory inside the terminal. The text is transferred to the computer as a block of data.

printer

Printers provide a permanent record on paper of computer output data or text. There are three basic types of character printers: daisywheel, dot matrix, and laser printers. The daisywheel printer contains a wheel with the characters placed along the circumference. To print a character, the wheel rotates to the proper position and an energized magnet then presses the letter against the ribbon. The dot matrix printer contains a set of dots along the printing mechanism. For example, a 5×7 dot matrix printer that prints 80 characters per line has seven horizontal lines, each consisting of $5 \times 80 = 400$ dots. Each dot can be printed or not, depending on the specific characters that are printed on the line. The laser printer uses a rotating photographic drum that is used to imprint the character images. The pattern is then transferred onto paper in the same manner as a copying machine.

magnetic tape

Magnetic tapes are used mostly for storing files of data: for example, a company's payroll record. Access is sequential and consists of records that can be accessed one after another as the tape moves along a stationary read–write mechanism. It is one of the cheapest and slowest methods for storage and has the advantage that tapes can be removed when not in use. Magnetic disks have

magnetic disk

high-speed rotational surfaces coated with magnetic material. Access is achieved by moving a read–write mechanism to a track in the magnetized surface. Disks are used mostly for bulk storage of programs and data. Tapes and disks are discussed further in Sec. 12-1 in conjunction with their role as auxiliary memory.

Other input and output devices encountered in computer systems are digital incremental plotters, optical and magnetic character readers, analog-to-digital converters, and various data acquisition equipment. Not all input comes from people, and not all output is intended for people. Computers are used to control various processes in real time, such as machine tooling, assembly line procedures, and chemical and industrial processes. For such applications, a method must be provided for sensing status conditions in the process and sending control signals to the process being controlled.

The input–output organization of a computer is a function of the size of the computer and the devices connected to it. The difference between a small and a large system is mostly dependent on the amount of hardware the computer has available for communicating with peripheral units and the number of peripherals connected to the system. Since each peripheral behaves differently from any other, it would be prohibitive to dwell on the detailed interconnections needed between the computer and each peripheral. Certain techniques common to most peripherals are presented in this chapter.

ASCII Alphanumeric Characters

Input and output devices that communicate with people and the computer are usually involved in the transfer of alphanumeric information to and from the device and the computer. The standard binary code for the alphanumeric

ASCII

characters is ASCII (American Standard Code for Information Interchange). It uses seven bits to code 128 characters as shown in Table 11-1. The seven bits of the code are designated by b_1 through b_7, with b_7 being the most significant bit. The letter A, for example, is represented in ASCII as 1000001 (column 100, row 0001). The ASCII code contains 94 characters that can be printed and 34 nonprinting characters used for various control functions. The printing characters consist of the 26 uppercase letters A through Z, the 26 lowercase letters, the 10 numerals 0 through 9, and 32 special printable characters such as %, *, and $.

The 34 control characters are designated in the ASCII table with abbrevi-

TABLE 11-1 American Standard Code for Information Interchange (ASCII)

$b_4 b_3 b_2 b_1$	$b_7 b_6 b_5$							
	000	001	010	011	100	101	110	111
0000	NUL	DLE	SP	0	@	P	`	p
0001	SOH	DC1	!	1	A	Q	a	q
0010	STX	DC2	"	2	B	R	b	r
0011	ETX	DC3	#	3	C	S	c	s
0100	EOT	DC4	$	4	D	T	d	t
0101	ENQ	NAK	%	5	E	U	e	u
0110	ACK	SYN	&	6	F	V	f	v
0111	BEL	ETB	'	7	G	W	g	w
1000	BS	CAN	(	8	H	X	h	x
1001	HT	EM	)	9	I	Y	i	y
1010	LF	SUB	*	:	J	Z	j	z
1011	VT	ESC	+	;	K	[	k	{
1100	FF	FS	,	<	L	\	l	|
1101	CR	GS	–	=	M	]	m	}
1110	SO	RS	.	>	N	∧	n	~
1111	SI	US	/	?	O	—	o	DEL

Control characters

NUL	Null	DLE	Data link escape
SOH	Start of heading	DC1	Device control 1
STX	Start of text	DC2	Device control 2
ETX	End of text	DC3	Device control 3
EOT	End of transmission	DC4	Device control 4
ENQ	Enquiry	NAK	Negative acknowledge
ACK	Acknowledge	SYN	Synchronous idle
BEL	Bell	ETB	End of transmission block
BS	Backspace	CAN	Cancel
HT	Horizontal tab	EM	End of medium
LF	Line feed	SUB	Substitute
VT	Vertical tab	ESC	Escape
FF	Form feed	FS	File separator
CR	Carriage return	GS	Group separator
SO	Shift out	RS	Record separator
SI	Shift in	US	Unit separator
SP	Space	DEL	Delete

ated names. They are listed again below the table with their functional names. The control characters are used for routing data and arranging the printed text into a prescribed format. There are three types of control characters: format effectors, information separators, and communication control characters. Format effectors are characters that control the layout of printing. They include the familiar typewriter controls, such as backspace (BS), horizontal tabulation (HT), and carriage return (CR). Information separators are used to separate the data into divisions like paragraphs and pages. They include characters such as record separator (RS) and file separator (FS). The communication control characters are useful during the transmission of text between remote terminals. Examples of communication control characters are STX (start of text) and ETX (end of text), which are used to frame a text message when transmitted through a communication medium.

byte

ASCII is a 7-bit code, but most computers manipulate an 8-bit quantity as a single unit called a *byte*. Therefore, ASCII characters most often are stored one per byte. The extra bit is sometimes used for other purposes, depending on the application. For example, some printers recognize 8-bit ASCII characters with the most significant bit set to 0. Additional 128 8-bit characters with the most significant bit set to 1 are used for other symbols, such as the Greek alphabet or italic type font. When used in data communication, the eighth bit may be employed to indicate the parity of the binary-coded character.

11-2   Input–Output Interface

Input–output interface provides a method for transferring information between internal storage and external I/O devices. Peripherals connected to a computer need special communication links for interfacing them with the central processing unit. The purpose of the communication link is to resolve the differences that exist between the central computer and each peripheral. The major differences are:

1. Peripherals are electromechanical and electromagnetic devices and their manner of operation is different from the operation of the CPU and memory, which are electronic devices. Therefore, a conversion of signal values may be required.

2. The data transfer rate of peripherals is usually slower than the transfer rate of the CPU, and consequently, a synchronization mechanism may be needed.

3. Data codes and formats in peripherals differ from the word format in the CPU and memory.

4. The operating modes of peripherals are different from each other and each must be controlled so as not to disturb the operation of other peripherals connected to the CPU.

interface

To resolve these differences, computer systems include special hardware components between the CPU and peripherals to supervise and synchronize all input and output transfers. These components are called *interface* units because they interface between the processor bus and the peripheral device.

In addition, each device may have its own controller that supervises the operations of the particular mechanism in the peripheral.

I/O Bus and Interface Modules

A typical communication link between the processor and several peripherals is shown in Fig. 11-1. The I/O bus consists of data lines, address lines, and control lines. The magnetic disk, printer, and terminal are employed in practically any general-purpose computer. The magnetic tape is used in some computers for backup storage. Each peripheral device has associated with it an interface unit. Each interface decodes the address and control received from the I/O bus, interprets them for the peripheral, and provides signals for the peripheral controller. It also synchronizes the data flow and supervises the transfer between peripheral and processor. Each peripheral has its own controller that operates the particular electromechanical device. For example, the printer controller controls the paper motion, the print timing, and the selection of printing characters. A controller may be housed separately or may be physically integrated with the peripheral.

The I/O bus from the processor is attached to all peripheral interfaces. To communicate with a particular device, the processor places a device address on the address lines. Each interface attached to the I/O bus contains an address decoder that monitors the address lines. When the interface detects its own address, it activates the path between the bus lines and the device that it controls. All peripherals whose address does not correspond to the address in the bus are disabled by their interface.

At the same time that the address is made available in the address lines, the processor provides a function code in the control lines. The interface

Figure 11-1 Connection of I/O bus to input-output devices.

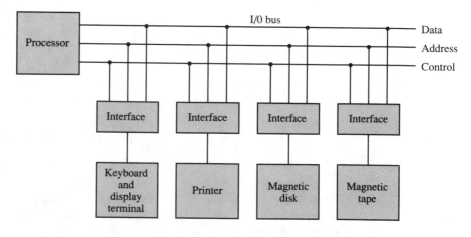

I/O command

selected responds to the function code and proceeds to execute it. The function code is referred to as an I/O command and is in essence an instruction that is executed in the interface and its attached peripheral unit. The interpretation of the command depends on the peripheral that the processor is addressing. There are four types of commands that an interface may receive. They are classified as control, status, data output, and data input.

control command

A *control command* is issued to activate the peripheral and to inform it what to do. For example, a magnetic tape unit may be instructed to backspace the tape by one record, to rewind the tape, or to start the tape moving in the forward direction. The particular control command issued depends on the peripheral, and each peripheral receives its own distinguished sequence of control commands, depending on its mode of operation.

status

A *status command* is used to test various status conditions in the interface and the peripheral. For example, the computer may wish to check the status of the peripheral before a transfer is initiated. During the transfer, one or more errors may occur which are detected by the interface. These errors are designated by setting bits in a status register that the processor can read at certain intervals.

output data

A *data output command* causes the interface to respond by transferring data from the bus into one of its registers. Consider an example with a tape unit. The computer starts the tape moving by issuing a control command. The processor then monitors the status of the tape by means of a status command. When the tape is in the correct position, the processor issues a data output command. The interface responds to the address and command and transfers the information from the data lines in the bus to its buffer register. The interface then communicates with the tape controller and sends the data to be stored on tape.

input data

The *data input command* is the opposite of the data output. In this case the interface receives an item of data from the peripheral and places it in its buffer register. The processor checks if data are available by means of a status command and then issues a data input command. The interface places the data on the data lines, where they are accepted by the processor.

I/O versus Memory Bus

In addition to communicating with I/O, the processor must communicate with the memory unit. Like the I/O bus, the memory bus contains data, address, and read/write control lines. There are three ways that computer buses can be used to communicate with memory and I/O:

1. Use two separate buses, one for memory and the other for I/O.
2. Use one common bus for both memory and I/O but have separate control lines for each.
3. Use one common bus for memory and I/O with common control lines.

IOP

In the first method, the computer has independent sets of data, address, and control buses, one for accessing memory and the other for I/O. This is done in computers that provide a separate I/O processor (IOP) in addition to the central processing unit (CPU). The memory communicates with both the CPU and the IOP through a memory bus. The IOP communicates also with the input and output devices through a separate I/O bus with its own address, data and control lines. The purpose of the IOP is to provide an independent pathway for the transfer of information between external devices and internal memory. The I/O processor is sometimes called a data channel. In Sec. 11-7 we discuss the function of the IOP in more detail.

Isolated versus Memory-Mapped I/O

Many computers use one common bus to transfer information between memory or I/O and the CPU. The distinction between a memory transfer and I/O transfer is made through separate read and write lines. The CPU specifies whether the address on the address lines is for a memory word or for an interface register by enabling one of two possible read or write lines. The *I/O read* and *I/O write* control lines are enabled during an I/O transfer. The *memory read* and *memory write* control lines are enabled during a memory transfer. This configuration isolates all I/O interface addresses from the addresses assigned to memory and is referred to as the *isolated I/O method* for assigning addresses in a common bus.

isolated I/O

In the isolated I/O configuration, the CPU has distinct input and output instructions, and each of these instructions is associated with the address of an interface register. When the CPU fetches and decodes the operation code of an input or output instruction, it places the address associated with the instruction into the common address lines. At the same time, it enables the I/O read (for input) or I/O write (for output) control line. This informs the external components that are attached to the common bus that the address in the address lines is for an interface register and not for a memory word. On the other hand, when the CPU is fetching an instruction or an operand from memory, it places the memory address on the address lines and enables the memory read or memory write control line. This informs the external components that the address is for a memory word and not for an I/O interface.

memory-mapped

The isolated I/O method isolates memory and I/O addresses so that memory address values are not affected by interface address assignment since each has its own address space. The other alternative is to use the same address space for both memory and I/O. This is the case in computers that employ only one set of read and write signals and do not distinguish between memory and I/O addresses. This configuration is referred to as *memory-mapped I/O*. The computer treats an interface register as being part of the memory system. The assigned addresses for interface registers cannot be used for memory words, which reduces the memory address range available.

In a memory-mapped I/O organization there are no specific input or output instructions. The CPU can manipulate I/O data residing in interface registers with the same instructions that are used to manipulate memory words. Each interface is organized as a set of registers that respond to read and write requests in the normal address space. Typically, a segment of the total address space is reserved for interface registers, but in general, they can be located at any address as long as there is not also a memory word that responds to the same address.

Computers with memory-mapped I/O can use memory-type instructions to access I/O data. It allows the computer to use the same instructions for either input–output transfers or for memory transfers. The advantage is that the load and store instructions used for reading and writing from memory can be used to input and output data from I/O registers. In a typical computer, there are more memory-reference instructions than I/O instructions. With memory-mapped I/O all instructions that refer to memory are also available for I/O.

Example of I/O Interface

I/O port

An example of an I/O interface unit is shown in block diagram form in Fig. 11-2. It consists of two data registers called *ports*, a control register, a status register, bus buffers, and timing and control circuits. The interface communicates with the CPU through the data bus. The chip select and register select inputs determine the address assigned to the interface. The I/O read and write are two control lines that specify an input or output, respectively. The four registers communicate directly with the I/O device attached to the interface.

The I/O data to and from the device can be transferred into either port A or port B. The interface may operate with an output device or with an input device, or with a device that requires both input and output. If the interface is connected to a printer, it will only output data, and if it services a character reader, it will only input data. A magnetic disk unit transfers data in both directions but not at the same time, so the interface can use bidirectional lines. A command is passed to the I/O device by sending a word to the appropriate interface register. In a system like this, the function code in the I/O bus is not needed because control is sent to the control register, status information is received from the status register, and data are transferred to and from ports A and B registers. Thus the transfer of data, control, and status information is always via the common data bus. The distinction between data, control, or status information is determined from the particular interface register with which the CPU communicates.

The control register receives control information from the CPU. By loading appropriate bits into the control register, the interface and the I/O device attached to it can be placed in a variety of operating modes. For example, port A may be defined as an input port and port B as an output port. A magnetic tape unit may be instructed to rewind the tape or to start the tape moving in

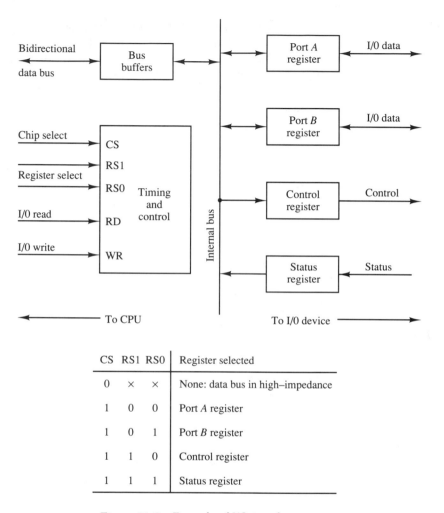

Figure 11-2 Example of I/O interface unit.

CS	RS1	RS0	Register selected
0	×	×	None: data bus in high–impedance
1	0	0	Port A register
1	0	1	Port B register
1	1	0	Control register
1	1	1	Status register

the forward direction. The bits in the status register are used for status conditions and for recording errors that may occur during the data transfer. For example, a status bit may indicate that port A has received a new data item from the I/O device. Another bit in the status register may indicate that a parity error has occurred during the transfer.

The interface registers communicate with the CPU through the bidirectional data bus. The address bus selects the interface unit through the chip select and the two register select inputs. A circuit must be provided externally (usually, a decoder) to detect the address assigned to the interface registers. This circuit enables the chip select (CS) input when the interface is selected by the address bus. The two register select inputs RS1 and RS0 are usually connected to the two least significant lines of the address bus. These two inputs select one of the four registers in the interface as specified in the table accompanying the diagram. The content of the selected register is transfer into the CPU via the data bus when the I/O read signal is enabled. The CPU transfers binary information into the selected register via the data bus when the I/O write input is enabled.

11-3   Asynchronous Data Transfer

The internal operations in a digital system are synchronized by means of clock pulses supplied by a common pulse generator. Clock pulses are applied to all registers within a unit and all data transfers among internal registers occur simultaneously during the occurrence of a clock pulse. Two units, such as a CPU and an I/O interface, are designed independently of each other. If the registers in the interface share a common clock with the CPU registers, the transfer between the two units is said to be synchronous. In most cases, the internal timing in each unit is independent from the other in that each uses its own private clock for internal registers. In that case, the two units are said to be asynchronous to each other. This approach is widely used in most computer systems.

strobe

Asynchronous data transfer between two independent units requires that control signals be transmitted between the communicating units to indicate the time at which data is being transmitted. One way of achieving this is by means of a *strobe* pulse supplied by one of the units to indicate to the other unit when the transfer has to occur. Another method commonly used is to accompany each data item being transferred with a control signal that indicates the presence of data in the bus. The unit receiving the data item responds with another control signal to acknowledge receipt of the data. This type of agreement between two independent units is referred to as *handshaking*.

handshaking

The strobe pulse method and the handshaking method of asynchronous data transfer are not restricted to I/O transfers. In fact, they are used extensively on numerous occasions requiring the transfer of data between two independent units. In the general case we consider the transmitting unit as the source and the receiving unit as the destination. For example, the CPU is the source unit during an output or a write transfer and it is the destination unit during an input or a read transfer. It is customary to specify the asynchronous transfer between two independent units by means of a timing diagram that shows the timing relationship that must exist between the control signals and the data in the buses. The sequence of control during an asynchronous transfer depends on whether the transfer is initiated by the source or by the destination unit.

timing diagram

Strobe Control

The strobe control method of asynchronous data transfer employs a single control line to time each transfer. The strobe may be activated by either the source or the destination unit. Figure 11-3(a) shows a source-initiated transfer.

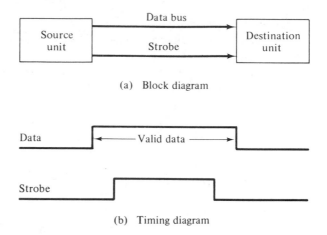

(a) Block diagram

(b) Timing diagram

Figure 11-3 Source-initiated strobe for data transfer.

The data bus carries the binary information from source unit to the destination unit. Typically, the bus has multiple lines to transfer an entire byte or word. The strobe is a single line that informs the destination unit when a valid data word is available in the bus.

As shown in the timing diagram of Fig. 11-3(b), the source unit first places the data on the data bus. After a brief delay to ensure that the data settle to a steady value, the source activates the strobe pulse. The information on the data bus and the strobe signal remain in the active state for a sufficient time period to allow the destination unit to receive the data. Often, the destination unit uses the falling edge of the strobe pulse to transfer the contents of the data bus into one of its internal registers. The source removes the data from the bus a brief period after it disables its strobe pulse. Actually, the source does not have to change the information in the data bus. The fact that the strobe signal is disabled indicates that the data bus does not contain valid data. New valid data will be available only after the strobe is enabled again.

Figure 11-4 shows a data transfer initiated by the destination unit. In this case the destination unit activates the strobe pulse, informing the source to provide the data. The source unit responds by placing the requested binary information on the data bus. The data must be valid and remain in the bus long enough for the destination unit to accept it. The falling edge of the strobe pulse can be used again to trigger a destination register. The destination unit then disables the strobe. The source removes the data from the bus after a predetermined time interval.

In many computers the strobe pulse is actually controlled by the clock pulses in the CPU. The CPU is always in control of the buses and informs the external units how to transfer data. For example, the strobe of Fig. 11-3 could be a memory-write control signal from the CPU to a memory unit. The source, being the CPU, places a word on the data bus and informs the memory unit,

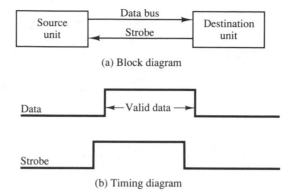

(a) Block diagram

(b) Timing diagram

Figure 11-4 Destination-initiated strobe for data transfer.

which is the destination, that this is a write operation. Similarly, the strobe of Fig. 11-4 could be a memory-read control signal from the CPU to a memory unit. The destination, the CPU, initiates the read operation to inform the memory, which is the source, to place a selected word into the data bus.

The transfer of data between the CPU and an interface unit is similar to the strobe transfer just described. Data transfer between an interface and an I/O device is commonly controlled by a set of handshaking lines.

Handshaking

The disadvantage of the strobe method is that the source unit that initiates the transfer has no way of knowing whether the destination unit has actually received the data item that was placed in the bus. Similarly, a destination unit that initiates the transfer has no way of knowing whether the source unit has actually placed the data on the bus. The handshake method solves this problem by introducing a second control signal that provides a reply to the unit that *two-wire control* initiates the transfer. The basic principle of the two-wire handshaking method of data transfer is as follows. One control line is in the same direction as the data flow in the bus from the source to the destination. It is used by the source unit to inform the destination unit whether there are valid data in the bus. The other control line is in the other direction from the destination to the source. It is used by the destination unit to inform the source whether it can accept data. The sequence of control during the transfer depends on the unit that initiates the transfer.

Figure 11-5 shows the data transfer procedure when initiated by the source. The two handshaking lines are *data valid*, which is generated by the source unit, and *data accepted*, generated by the destination unit. The timing diagram shows the exchange of signals between the two units. The sequence of events listed in part (c) shows the four possible states that the system can

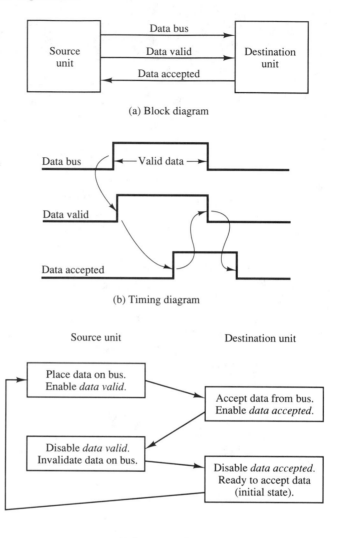

(a) Block diagram

(b) Timing diagram

(c) Sequence of events

Figure 11-5 Source-initiated transfer using handshaking.

be at any given time. The source unit initiates the transfer by placing the data on the bus and enabling its *data valid* signal. The *data accepted* signal is activated by the destination unit after it accepts the data from the bus. The source unit then disables its *data valid* signal, which invalidates the data on the bus. The destination unit then disables its *data accepted* signal and the system goes into its initial state. The source does not send the next data item until after the destination unit shows its readiness to accept new data by disabling its *data accepted* signal. This scheme allows arbitrary delays from one state to the next and permits each unit to respond at its own data transfer rate. The rate of transfer is determined by the slowest unit.

The destination-initiated transfer using handshaking lines is shown in Fig. 11-6. Note that the name of the signal generated by the destination unit has been changed to *ready for data* to reflect its new meaning. The source unit in this case does not place data on the bus until after it receives the *ready for data* signal from the destination unit. From there on, the handshaking procedure follows the same pattern as in the source-initiated case. Note that the

Figure 11-6 Destination-initiated transfer using handshaking.

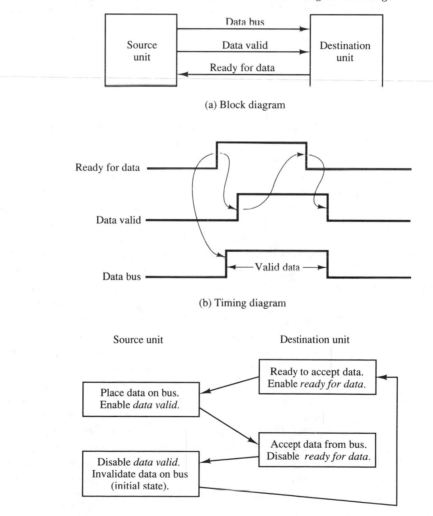

(a) Block diagram

(b) Timing diagram

(c) Sequence of events

sequence of events in both cases would be identical if we consider the *ready for data* signal as the complement of *data accepted*. In fact, the only difference between the source-initiated and the destination-initiated transfer is in their choice of initial state.

The handshaking scheme provides a high degree of flexibility and reliability because the successful completion of a data transfer relies on active participation by both units. If one unit is faulty, the data transfer will not be completed. Such an error can be detected by means of a *timeout* mechanism, which produces an alarm if the data transfer is not completed within a predetermined time. The timeout is implemented by means of an internal clock that starts counting time when the unit enables one of its handshaking control signals. If the return handshake signal does not respond within a given time period, the unit assumes that an error has occurred. The timeout signal can be used to interrupt the processor and hence execute a service routine that takes appropriate error recovery action.

timeout

Asynchronous Serial Transfer

The transfer of data between two units may be done in parallel or serial. In parallel data transmission, each bit of the message has its own path and the total message is transmitted at the same time. This means that an *n*-bit message must be transmitted through *n* separate conductor paths. In serial data transmission, each bit in the message is sent in sequence one at a time. This method requires the use of one pair of conductors or one conductor and a common ground. Parallel transmission is faster but requires many wires. It is used for short distances and where speed is important. Serial transmission is slower but is less expensive since it requires only one pair of conductors.

Serial transmission can be synchronous or asynchronous. In synchronous transmission, the two units share a common clock frequency and bits are transmitted continuously at the rate dictated by the clock pulses. In long-distant serial transmission, each unit is driven by a separate clock of the same frequency. Synchronization signals are transmitted periodically between the two units to keep their clocks in step with each other. In asynchronous transmission, binary information is sent only when it is available and the line remains idle when there is no information to be transmitted. This is in contrast to synchronous transmission, where bits must be transmitted continuously to keep the clock frequency in both units synchronized with each other. Synchronous serial transmission is discussed further in Sec. 11-8.

A serial asynchronous data transmission technique used in many interactive terminals employs special bits that are inserted at both ends of the character code. With this technique, each character consists of three parts: a start bit, the character bits, and stop bits. The convention is that the transmitter rests

synchronous

asynchronous

start bit

at the 1-state when no characters are transmitted. The first bit, called the start bit, is always a 0 and is used to indicate the beginning of a character. The last bit called the stop bit is always a 1. An example of this format is shown in Fig. 11-7.

A transmitted character can be detected by the receiver from knowledge of the transmission rules:

1. When a character is not being sent, the line is kept in the 1-state.
2. The initiation of a character transmission is detected from the start bit, which is always 0.
3. The character bits always follow the start bit.
4. After the last bit of the character is transmitted, a stop bit is detected when the line returns to the 1-state for at least one bit time.

stop bit

Using these rules, the receiver can detect the start bit when the line goes from 1 to 0. A clock in the receiver examines the line at proper bit times. The receiver knows the transfer rate of the bits and the number of character bits to accept. After the character bits are transmitted, one or two stop bits are sent. The stop bits are always in the 1-state and frame the end of the character to signify the idle or wait state.

At the end of the character the line is held at the 1-state for a period of at least one or two bit times so that both the transmitter and receiver can resynchronize. The length of time that the line stays in this state depends on the amount of time required for the equipment to resynchronize. Some older electromechanical terminals use two stop bits, but newer terminals use one stop bit. The line remains in the 1-state until another character is transmitted. The stop time ensures that a new character will not follow for one or two bit times.

As an illustration, consider the serial transmission of a terminal whose transfer rate is 10 characters per second. Each transmitted character consists

Figure 11-7   Asynchronous serial transmission.

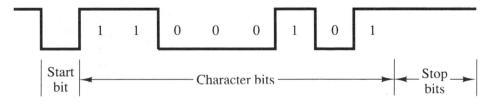

of a start bit, eight information bits, and two stop bits, for a total of 11 bits. Ten characters per second means that each character takes 0.1 s for transfer. Since there are 11 bits to be transmitted, it follows that the bit time is 9.09 ms. The *baud rate* is defined as the rate at which serial information is transmitted and is equivalent to the data transfer in bits per second. Ten characters per second with an 11-bit format has a transfer rate of 110 baud.

baud rate

The terminal has a keyboard and a printer. Every time a key is depressed, the terminal sends 11 bits serially along a wire. To print a character in the printer, an 11-bit message must be received along another wire. The terminal interface consists of a transmitter and a receiver. The transmitter accepts an 8-bit character from the computer and proceeds to send a serial 11-bit message into the printer line. The receiver accepts a serial 11-bit message from the keyboard line and forwards the 8-bit character code into the computer. Integrated circuits are available which are specifically designed to provide the interface between computer and similar interactive terminals. Such a circuit is called an *asynchronous communication interface* or a *universal asynchronous receiver-transmitter* (UART).

Asynchronous Communication Interface

The block diagram of an asynchronous communication interface is shown in Fig. 11-8. It functions as both a transmitter and a receiver. The interface is initialized for a particular mode of transfer by means of a control byte that is loaded into its control register. The transmitter register accepts a data byte from the CPU through the data bus. This byte is transferred to a shift register for serial transmission. The receiver portion receives serial information into another shift register, and when a complete data byte is accumulated, it is transferred to the receiver register. The CPU can select the receiver register to read the byte through the data bus. The bits in the status register are used for input and output flags and for recording certain errors that may occur during the transmission. The CPU can read the status register to check the status of the flag bits and to determine if any errors have occurred. The chip select and the read and write control lines communicate with the CPU. The chip select (CS) input is used to select the interface through the address bus. The register select (RS) is associated with the read (RD) and write (WR) controls. Two registers are write-only and two are read-only. The register selected is a function of the RS value and the RD and WR status, as listed in the table accompanying the diagram.

The operation of the asynchronous communication interface is initialized by the CPU by sending a byte to the control register. The initialization procedure places the interface in a specific mode of operation as it defines certain parameters such as the baud rate to use, how many bits are in each character, whether to generate and check parity, and how many stop bits are appended to each character. Two bits in the status register are used as flags. One bit is

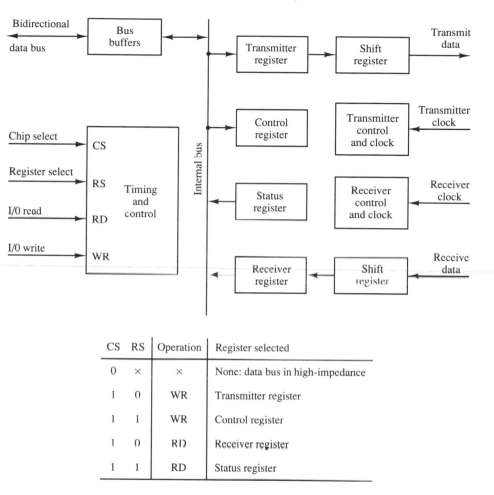

CS	RS	Operation	Register selected
0	×	×	None: data bus in high-impedance
1	0	WR	Transmitter register
1	1	WR	Control register
1	0	RD	Receiver register
1	1	RD	Status register

Figure 11-8 Block diagram of a typical asynchronous communication interface.

transmitter

used to indicate whether the transmitter register is empty and another bit is used to indicate whether the receiver register is full.

The operation of the transmitter portion of the interface is as follows. The CPU reads the status register and checks the flag to see if the transmitter register is empty. If it is empty, the CPU transfers a character to the transmitter register and the interface clears the flag to mark the register full. The first bit in the transmitter shift register is set to 0 to generate a start bit. The character is transferred in parallel from the transmitter register to the shift register and the appropriate number of stop bits are appended into the shift register. The transmitter register is then marked empty. The character can now be transmitted one bit at a time by shifting the data in the shift register at the specified baud rate. The CPU can transfer another character to the transmitter register after checking the flag in the status register. The interface is said to be *double buffered* because a new character can be loaded as soon as the previous one starts transmission.

receiver

The operation of the receiver portion of the interface is similar. The receive data input is in the 1-state when the line is idle. The receiver control monitors the receive-data line for a 0 signal to detect the occurrence of a start bit. Once a start bit has been detected, the incoming bits of the character are shifted into the shift register at the prescribed baud rate. After receiving the data bits, the interface checks for the parity and stop bits. The character without the start and stop bits is then transferred in parallel from the shift register to the receiver register. The flag in the status register is set to indicate that the receiver register is full. The CPU reads the status register and checks the flag, and if set, it reads the data from the receiver register.

The interface checks for any possible errors during transmission and sets appropriate bits in the status register. The CPU can read the status register at any time to check if any errors have occurred. Three possible errors that the interface checks during transmission are parity error, framing error, and over-run error. Parity error occurs if the number of 1's in the received data is not the correct parity. A framing error occurs if the right number of stop bits is not detected at the end of the received character. An overrun error occurs if the CPU does not read the character from the receiver register before the next one becomes available in the shift register. Overrun error results in a loss of characters in the received data stream.

First-In, First-Out Buffer

FIFO

A first-in, first-out (FIFO) buffer is a memory unit that stores information in such a manner that the item first in is the item first out. A FIFO buffer comes with separate input and output terminals. The important feature of this buffer is that it can input data and output data at two different rates and the output data are always in the same order in which the data entered the buffer. When placed between two units, the FIFO can accept data from the source unit at one rate of transfer and deliver the data to the destination unit at another rate. If the source unit is slower than the destination unit, the buffer can be filled with data at a slow rate and later emptied at the higher rate. If the source is faster than the destination, the FIFO is useful for those cases where the source data arrive in bursts that fill out the buffer but the time between bursts is long enough for the destination unit to empty some or all the information from the buffer. Thus a FIFO buffer can be useful in some applications when data are transferred asynchronously. It piles up data as they come in and gives them away in the same order when the data are needed.

The logic diagram of a typical 4×4 FIFO buffer is shown in Fig. 11-9. It consists of four 4-bit registers RI, $I = 1, 2, 3, 4$, and a control register with

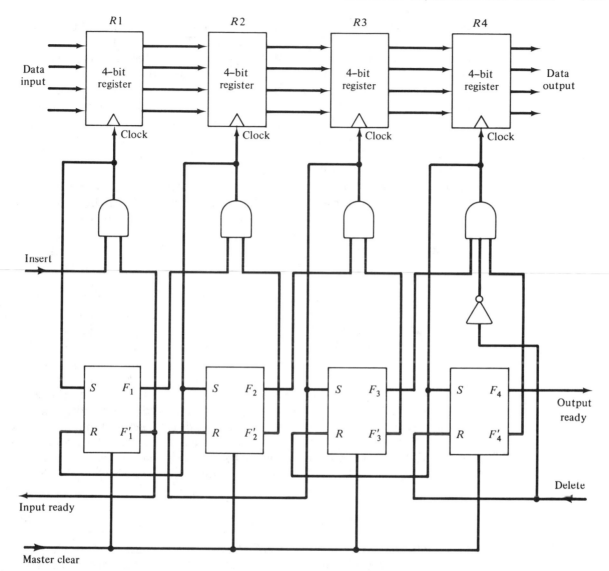

Figure 11-9   Circuit diagram of 4 × 4 FIFO buffer.

flip-flops F_i, $i = 1, 2, 3, 4$, one for each register. The FIFO can store four words of four bits each. The number of bits per word can be increased by increasing the number of bits in each register and the number of words can be increased by increasing the number of registers.

A flip-flop F_i in the control register that is set to 1 indicates that a 4-bit data word is stored in the corresponding register RI. A 0 in F_i indicates that the corresponding register does not contain valid data. The control register directs the movement of data through the registers. Whenever the F_i bit of the control register is set ($F_i = 1$) and the F_{i+1} bit is reset ($F'_{i+1} = 1$), a clock is generated causing register $R(I + 1)$ to accept the data from register RI. The same clock transition sets F_{i+1} to 1 and resets F_i to 0. This causes the control flag to move one position to the right together with the data. Data in the registers move down the FIFO toward the output as long as there are empty locations ahead of it. This ripple-through operation stops when the data reach a register RI with the next flip-flop F_{i+1} being set to 1, or at the last register $R4$. An overall master clear is used to initialize all control register flip-flops to 0.

Data are inserted into the buffer provided that the *input ready* signal is enabled. This occurs when the first control flip-flop F_1 is reset, indicating that register $R1$ is empty. Data are loaded from the input lines by enabling the clock in $R1$ through the *insert* control line. The same clock sets F_1, which disables the *input ready* control, indicating that the FIFO is now busy and unable to accept more data. The ripple-through process begins provided that $R2$ is empty. The data in $R1$ are transferred into $R2$ and F_1 is cleared. This enables the *input ready* line, indicating that the inputs are now available for another data word. If the FIFO is full, F_1 remains set and the *input ready* line stays in the 0 state. Note that the two control lines *input ready* and *insert* constitute a destination-initiated pair of handshake lines.

The data falling through the registers stack up at the output end. The *output ready* control line is enabled when the last control flip-flop F_4 is set, indicating that there are valid data in the output register $R4$. The output data from $R4$ are accepted by a destination unit, which then enables the *delete* control signal. This resets F_4, causing *output ready* to disable, indicating that the data on the output are no longer valid. Only after the *delete* signal goes back to 0 can the data from $R3$ move into $R4$. If the FIFO is empty, there will be no data in $R3$ and F_4 will remain in the reset state. Note that the two control lines *output ready* and *delete* constitute a source-initiated pair of handshake lines.

11-4 Modes of Transfer

Binary information received from an external device is usually stored in memory for later processing. Information transferred from the central computer into an external device originates in the memory unit. The CPU merely executes the I/O instructions and may accept the data temporarily, but the ultimate source or destination is the memory unit. Data transfer between the central computer and I/O devices may be handled in a variety of modes. Some modes use the CPU as an intermediate path; others transfer the data directly to and from the memory unit. Data transfer to and from peripherals may be handled in one of three possible modes:

1. Programmed I/O
2. Interrupt-initiated I/O
3. Direct memory access (DMA)

programmed I/O

Programmed I/O operations are the result of I/O instructions written in the computer program. Each data item transfer is initiated by an instruction in the program. Usually, the transfer is to and from a CPU register and peripheral. Other instructions are needed to transfer the data to and from CPU and memory. Transferring data under program control requires constant monitoring of the peripheral by the CPU. Once a data transfer is initiated, the CPU is required to monitor the interface to see when a transfer can again be made. It is up to the programmed instructions executed in the CPU to keep close tabs on everything that is taking place in the interface unit and the I/O device.

interrupt

In the programmed I/O method, the CPU stays in a program loop until the I/O unit indicates that it is ready for data transfer. This is a time-consuming process since it keeps the processor busy needlessly. It can be avoided by using an interrupt facility and special commands to inform the interface to issue an interrupt request signal when the data are available from the device. In the meantime the CPU can proceed to execute another program. The interface meanwhile keeps monitoring the device. When the interface determines that the device is ready for data transfer, it generates an interrupt request to the computer. Upon detecting the external interrupt signal, the CPU momentarily stops the task it is processing, branches to a service program to process the I/O transfer, and then returns to the task it was originally performing.

DMA

Transfer of data under programmed I/O is between CPU and peripheral. In direct memory access (DMA), the interface transfers data into and out of the memory unit through the memory bus. The CPU initiates the transfer by supplying the interface with the starting address and the number of words needed to be transferred and then proceeds to execute other tasks. When the transfer is made, the DMA requests memory cycles through the memory bus. When the request is granted by the memory controller, the DMA transfers the data directly into memory. The CPU merely delays its memory access operation to allow the direct memory I/O transfer. Since peripheral speed is usually slower than processor speed, I/O-memory transfers are infrequent compared to processor access to memory. DMA transfer is discussed in more detail in Sec. 11-6.

IOP

Many computers combine the interface logic with the requirements for direct memory access into one unit and call it an I/O processor (IOP). The IOP can handle many peripherals through a DMA and interrupt facility. In such a system, the computer is divided into three separate modules: the memory unit, the CPU, and the IOP. I/O processors are presented in Sec. 11-7.

Example of Programmed I/O

In the programmed I/O method, the I/O device does not have direct access to memory. A transfer from an I/O device to memory requires the execution of several instructions by the CPU, including an input instruction to transfer the data from the device to the CPU and a store instruction to transfer the data from the CPU to memory. Other instructions may be needed to verify that the data are available from the device and to count the numbers of words transferred.

An example of data transfer from an I/O device through an interface into the CPU is shown in Fig. 11-10. The device transfers bytes of data one at a time as they are available. When a byte of data is available, the device places it in the I/O bus and enables its data valid line. The interface accepts the byte into its data register and enables the data accepted line. The interface sets a bit in the status register that we will refer to as an *F* or "flag" bit. The device can now disable the data valid line, but it will not transfer another byte until the data accepted line is disabled by the interface. This is according to the handshaking procedure established in Fig. 11-5.

A program is written for the computer to check the flag in the status register to determine if a byte has been placed in the data register by the I/O device. This is done by reading the status register into a CPU register and checking the value of the flag bit. If the flag is equal to 1, the CPU reads the data from the data register. The flag bit is then cleared to 0 by either the CPU or the interface, depending on how the interface circuits are designed. Once the flag is cleared, the interface disables the data accepted line and the device can then transfer the next data byte.

A flowchart of the program that must be written for the CPU is shown in Fig. 11-11. It is assumed that the device is sending a sequence of bytes that must be stored in memory. The transfer of each byte requires three instructions:

1. Read the status register.
2. Check the status of the flag bit and branch to step 1 if not set or to step 3 if set.
3. Read the data register.

Each byte is read into a CPU register and then transferred to memory with a store instruction. A common I/O programming task is to transfer a block of words from an I/O device and store them in a memory buffer. A program that

Figure 11-10   Data transfer from I/O device to CPU.

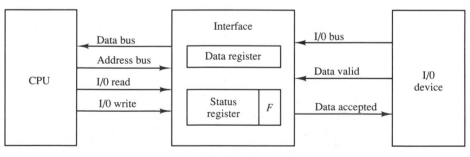

F = Flag bit

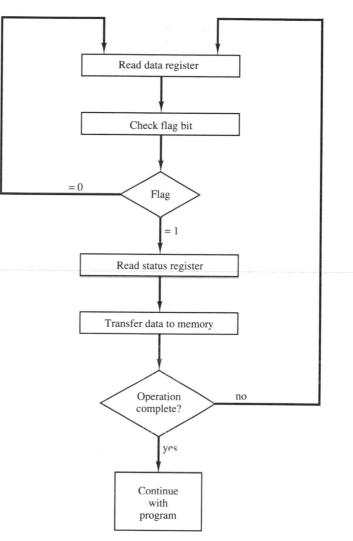

Figure 11-11   Flowchart for CPU program to input data.

stores input characters in a memory buffer using the instructions defined in Chap. 6 is listed in Table 6-21.

The programmed I/O method is particularly useful in small low-speed computers or in systems that are dedicated to monitor a device continuously. The difference in information transfer rate between the CPU and the I/O device makes this type of transfer inefficient. To see why this is inefficient, consider a typical computer that can execute the two instructions that read the status register and check the flag in 1 μs. Assume that the input device transfers its data at an average rate of 100 bytes per second. This is equivalent to one byte every 10,000 μs. This means that the CPU will check the flag 10,000 times between each transfer. The CPU is wasting time while checking the flag instead of doing some other useful processing task.

Interrupt-Initiated I/O

An alternative to the CPU constantly monitoring the flag is to let the interface inform the computer when it is ready to transfer data. This mode of transfer uses the interrupt facility. While the CPU is running a program, it does not check the flag. However, when the flag is set, the computer is momentarily interrupted from proceeding with the current program and is informed of the fact that the flag has been set. The CPU deviates from what it is doing to take care of the input or output transfer. After the transfer is completed, the computer returns to the previous program to continue what it was doing before the interrupt.

The CPU responds to the interrupt signal by storing the return address from the program counter into a memory stack and then control branches to a service routine that processes the required I/O transfer. The way that the processor chooses the branch address of the service routine varies from one unit to another. In principle, there are two methods for accomplishing this. One is called *vectored interrupt* and the other, *nonvectored interrupt*. In a nonvectored interrupt, the branch address is assigned to a fixed location in memory. In a vectored interrupt, the source that interrupts supplies the branch informa-

vectored interrupt

tion to the computer. This information is called the *interrupt vector*. In some computers the interrupt vector is the first address of the I/O service routine. In other computers the interrupt vector is an address that points to a location in memory where the beginning address of the I/O service routine is stored. A system with vectored interrupt is demonstrated in Sec. 11-5.

Software Considerations

The previous discussion was concerned with the basic hardware needed to interface I/O devices to a computer system. A computer must also have software routines for controlling peripherals and for transfer of data between the

I/O routines

processor and peripherals. I/O routines must issue control commands to activate the peripheral and to check the device status to determine when it is ready for data transfer. Once ready, information is transferred item by item until all the data are transferred. In some cases, a control command is then given to execute a device function such as stop tape or print characters. Error checking and other useful steps often accompany the transfers. In interrupt-controlled transfers, the I/O software must issue commands to the peripheral to interrupt when ready and to service the interrupt when it occurs. In DMA transfer, the I/O software must initiate the DMA channel to start its operation.

Software control of input–output equipment is a complex undertaking. For this reason I/O routines for standard peripherals are provided by the manufacturer as part of the computer system. They are usually included within the operating system. Most operating systems are supplied with a variety of I/O programs to support the particular line of peripherals offered for the computer. I/O routines are usually available as operating system procedures and the user refers to the established routines to specify the type of transfer required without going into detailed machine language programs.

11-5 Priority Interrupt

Data transfer between the CPU and an I/O device is initiated by the CPU. However, the CPU cannot start the transfer unless the device is ready to communicate with the CPU. The readiness of the device can be determined from an interrupt signal. The CPU responds to the interrupt request by storing the return address from PC into a memory stack and then the program branches to a service routine that processes the required transfer. As discussed in Sec. 8-7, some processors also push the current PSW (program status word) onto the stack and load a new PSW for the service routine. We neglect the PSW here in order not to complicate the discussion of I/O interrupts.

In a typical application a number of I/O devices are attached to the computer, with each device being able to originate an interrupt request. The first task of the interrupt system is to identify the source of the interrupt. There is also the possibility that several sources will request service simultaneously. In this case the system must also decide which device to service first.

priority interrupt

A priority interrupt is a system that establishes a priority over the various sources to determine which condition is to be serviced first when two or more requests arrive simultaneously. The system may also determine which conditions are permitted to interrupt the computer while another interrupt is being serviced. Higher-priority interrupt levels are assigned to requests which, if delayed or interrupted, could have serious consequences. Devices with high-speed transfers such as magnetic disks are given high priority, and slow devices such as keyboards receive low priority. When two devices interrupt the computer at the same time, the computer services the device, with the higher priority first.

polling

Establishing the priority of simultaneous interrupts can be done by software or hardware. A polling procedure is used to identify the highest-priority source by software means. In this method there is one common branch address for all interrupts. The program that takes care of interrupts begins at the branch address and polls the interrupt sources in sequence. The order in which they are tested determines the priority of each interrupt. The highest-priority source is tested first, and if its interrupt signal is on, control branches to a service routine for this source. Otherwise, the next-lower-priority source is tested, and so on. Thus the initial service routine for all interrupts consists of a program that tests the interrupt sources in sequence and branches to one of many possible service routines. The particular service routine reached belongs to the highest-priority device among all devices that interrupted the computer. The disadvantage of the software method is that if there are many interrupts, the time required to poll them can exceed the time available to service the I/O device. In this situation a hardware priority-interrupt unit can be used to speed up the operation.

A hardware priority-interrupt unit functions as an overall manager in an interrupt system environment. It accepts interrupt requests from many sources, determines which of the incoming requests has the highest priority, and issues an interrupt request to the computer based on this determination. To speed up the operation, each interrupt source has its own interrupt vector to access its own service routine directly. Thus no polling is required because all the decisions are established by the hardware priority-interrupt unit. The hardware priority function can be established by either a serial or a parallel connection of interrupt lines. The serial connection is also known as the daisy-chaining method.

Daisy-Chaining Priority

The daisy-chaining method of establishing priority consists of a serial connection of all devices that request an interrupt. The device with the highest priority is placed in the first position, followed by lower-priority devices up to the device with the lowest priority, which is placed last in the chain. This method of connection between three devices and the CPU is shown in Fig. 11-12. The interrupt request line is common to all devices and forms a wired logic connection. If any device has its interrupt signal in the low-level state, the interrupt line goes to the low-level state and enables the interrupt input in the CPU. When no interrupts are pending, the interrupt line stays in the high-level state and no interrupts are recognized by the CPU. This is equivalent to a negative-logic OR operation. The CPU responds to an interrupt request by enabling the interrupt acknowledge line. This signal is received by device 1 at its *PI* (priority in) input. The acknowledge signal passes on to the next device through the *PO* (priority out) output only if device 1 is not requesting an interrupt. If device 1 has a pending interrupt, it blocks the acknowledge signal from the next device by placing a 0 in the *PO* output. It then proceeds to insert its own interrupt *vector address (VAD)* vector address (VAD) into the data bus for the CPU to use during the interrupt cycle.

A device with a 0 in its *PI* input generates a 0 in its *PO* output to inform the next-lower-priority device that the acknowledge signal has been blocked. A device that is requesting an interrupt and has a 1 in its *PI* input will intercept the acknowledge signal by placing a 0 in its *PO* output. If the device does not have pending interrupts, it transmits the acknowledge signal to the next device

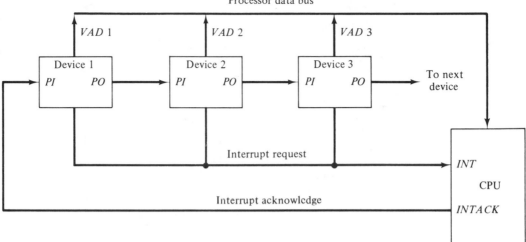

Figure 11-12 Daisy-chain priority interrupt.

by placing a 1 in its *PO* output. Thus the device with *PI* = 1 and *PO* = 0 is the one with the highest priority that is requesting an interrupt, and this device places its VAD on the data bus. The daisy chain arrangement gives the highest priority to the device that receives the interrupt acknowledge signal from the CPU. The farther the device is from the first position, the lower is its priority.

Figure 11-13 shows the internal logic that must be included within each device when connected in the daisy-chaining scheme. The device sets its *RF* flip-flop when it wants to interrupt the CPU. The output of the *RF* flip-flop goes through an open-collector inverter, a circuit that provides the wired logic for the common interrupt line. If *PI* = 0, both *PO* and the enable line to VAD are equal to 0, irrespective of the value of *RF*. If *PI* = 1 and *RF* = 0, then *PO* = 1 and the vector address is disabled. This condition passes the acknowledge signal to the next device through *PO*. The device is active when *PI* = 1 and *RF* = 1. This condition places a 0 in *PO* and enables the vector address for the data bus. It is assumed that each device has its own distinct vector address. The *RF* flip-flop is reset after a sufficient delay to ensure that the CPU has received the vector address.

Parallel Priority Interrupt

The parallel priority interrupt method uses a register whose bits are set separately by the interrupt signal from each device. Priority is established according to the position of the bits in the register. In addition to the interrupt register, the circuit may include a mask register whose purpose is to control the status of each interrupt request. The mask register can be programmed to disable

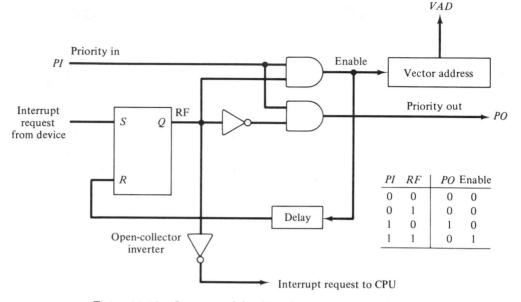

Figure 11-13 One stage of the daisy-chain priority arrangement.

lower-priority interrupts while a higher-priority device is being serviced. It can also provide a facility that allows a high-priority device to interrupt the CPU while a lower-priority device is being serviced.

priority logic
The priority logic for a system of four interrupt sources is shown in Fig. 11-14. It consists of an interrupt register whose individual bits are set by external conditions and cleared by program instructions. The magnetic disk, being a high-speed device, is given the highest priority. The printer has the next priority, followed by a character reader and a keyboard. The mask register has the same number of bits as the interrupt register. By means of program instructions, it is possible to set or reset any bit in the mask register. Each interrupt bit and its corresponding mask bit are applied to an AND gate to produce the four inputs to a priority encoder. In this way an interrupt is recognized only if its corresponding mask bit is set to 1 by the program. The priority encoder generates two bits of the vector address, which is transferred to the CPU.

Another output from the encoder sets an interrupt status flip-flop *IST* when an interrupt that is not masked occurs. The interrupt enable flip-flop *IEN* can be set or cleared by the program to provide an overall control over the interrupt system. The outputs of *IST* ANDed with *IEN* provide a common interrupt signal for the CPU. The interrupt acknowledge INTACK signal from the CPU enables the bus buffers in the output register and a vector address VAD is placed into the data bus. We will now explain the priority encoder circuit and then discuss the interaction between the priority interrupt controller and the CPU.

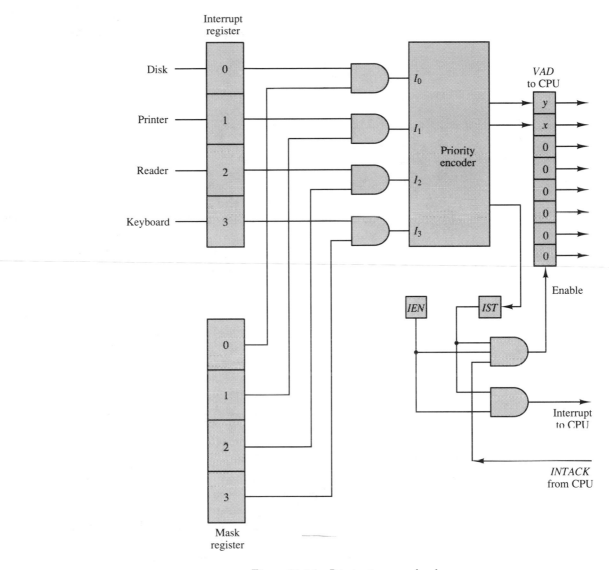

Figure 11-14 Priority interrupt hardware.

Priority Encoder

The priority encoder is a circuit that implements the priority function. The logic of the priority encoder is such that if two or more inputs arrive at the same time, the input having the highest priority will take precedence. The truth table of a four-input priority encoder is given in Table 11-2. The ×'s in the table designate don't-care conditions. Input I_0 has the highest priority; so regardless of the values of other inputs, when this input is 1, the output generates an output $xy = 00$. I_1 has the next priority level. The output is 01 if $I_1 = 1$ provided

TABLE 11-2 Priority Encoder Truth Table

Inputs				Outputs			
I_0	I_1	I_2	I_3	x	y	IST	Boolean functions
1	×	×	×	0	0	1	
0	1	×	×	0	1	1	$x = I_0'I_1'$
0	0	1	×	1	0	1	$y = I_0'I_1 + I_0'I_2'$
0	0	0	1	1	1	1	$(IST) = I_0 + I_1 + I_2 + I_3$
0	0	0	0	×	×	0	

that $I_0 = 0$, regardless of the values of the other two lower-priority inputs. The output for I_2 is generated only if higher-priority inputs are 0, and so on down the priority level. The interrupt status IST is set only when one or more inputs are equal to 1. If all inputs are 0, IST is cleared to 0 and the other outputs of the encoder are not used, so they are marked with don't-care conditions. This is because the vector address is not transferred to the CPU when $IST = 0$. The Boolean functions listed in the table specify the internal logic of the encoder. Usually, a computer will have more than four interrupt sources. A priority encoder with eight inputs, for example, will generate an output of three bits.

The output of the priority encoder is used to form part of the vector address for each interrupt source. The other bits of the vector address can be assigned any value. For example, the vector address can be formed by appending six zeros to the x and y outputs of the encoder. With this choice the interrupt vectors for the four I/O devices are assigned binary numbers 0, 1, 2, and 3.

Interrupt Cycle

The interrupt enable flip-flop IEN shown in Fig. 11-14 can be set or cleared by program instructions. When IEN is cleared, the interrupt request coming from IST is neglected by the CPU. The program-controlled IEN bit allows the programmer to choose whether to use the interrupt facility. If an instruction to clear IEN has been inserted in the program, it means that the user does not want his program to be interrupted. An instruction to set IEN indicates that the interrupt facility will be used while the current program is running. Most computers include internal hardware that clears IEN to 0 every time an interrupt is acknowledged by the processor.

At the end of each instruction cycle the CPU checks IEN and the interrupt signal from IST. If either is equal to 0, control continues with the next instruction. If both IEN and IST are equal to 1, the CPU goes to an interrupt cycle. During the interrupt cycle the CPU performs the following sequence of microoperations:

$$SP \leftarrow SP - 1 \quad \text{Decrement stack pointer}$$

$$M[SP] \leftarrow PC \quad \text{Push } PC \text{ into stack}$$

> $INTACK \leftarrow 1$ Enable interrupt acknowledge
>
> $PC \leftarrow VAD$ Transfer vector address to PC
>
> $IEN \leftarrow 0$ Disable further interrupts
>
> Go to fetch next instruction

The CPU pushes the return address from PC into the stack. It then acknowledges the interrupt by enabling the $INTACK$ line. The priority interrupt unit responds by placing a unique interrupt vector into the CPU data bus. The CPU transfers the vector address into PC and clears IEN prior to going to the next fetch phase. The instruction read from memory during the next fetch phase will be the one located at the vector address.

Software Routines

A priority interrupt system is a combination of hardware and software techniques. So far we have discussed the hardware aspects of a priority interrupt system. The computer must also have software routines for servicing the interrupt requests and for controlling the interrupt hardware registers. Figure 11-15 shows the programs that must reside in memory for handling the

Figure 11-15 Programs stored in memory for servicing interrupts.

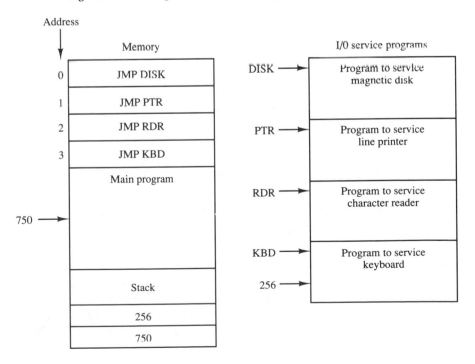

service program

interrupt system. Each device has its own service program that can be reached through a jump (JMP) instruction stored at the assigned vector address. The symbolic name of each routine represents the starting address of the service program. The stack shown in the diagram is used for storing the return address after each interrupt.

To illustrate with a specific example assume that the keyboard sets its interrupt bit while the CPU is executing the instruction in location 749 of the main program. At the end of the instruction cycle, the computer goes to an interrupt cycle. It stores the return address 750 in the stack and then accepts the vector address 00000011 from the bus and transfers it to *PC*. The instruction in location 3 is executed next, resulting in transfer of control to the KBD routine. Now suppose that the disk sets its interrupt bit when the CPU is executing the instruction at address 255 in the KBD program. Address 256 is pushed into the stack and control is transferred to the DISK service program. The last instruction in each routine is a return from interrupt instruction. When the disk service program is completed, the return instruction pops the stack and places 256 into *PC*. This returns control to the KBD routine to continue servicing the keyboard. At the end of the KBD program, the last instruction pops the stack and returns control to the main program at address 750. Thus, a higher-priority device can interrupt a lower-priority device. It is assumed that the time spent in servicing the high-priority interrupt is short compared to the transfer rate of the low-priority device so that no loss of information takes place.

Initial and Final Operations

Each interrupt service routine must have an initial and final set of operations for controlling the registers in the hardware interrupt system. Remember that the interrupt enable *IEN* is cleared at the end of an interrupt cycle. This flip-flop must be set again to enable higher-priority interrupt requests, but not before lower-priority interrupts are disabled. The initial sequence of each interrupt service routine must have instructions to control the interrupt hardware in the following manner:

1. Clear lower-level mask register bits.
2. Clear interrupt status bit *IST*.
3. Save contents of processor registers.
4. Set interrupt enable bit *IEN*.
5. Proceed with service routine.

The lower-level mask register bits (including the bit of the source that interrupted) are cleared to prevent these conditions from enabling the interrupt. Although lower-priority interrupt sources are assigned to higher-numbered bits in the mask register, priority can be changed if desired since the programmer can use any bit configuration for the mask register. The interrupt status bit must be cleared so it can be set again when a higher-priority interrupt occurs. The contents of processor registers are saved because they may be needed by the program that has been interrupted after control returns to it. The interrupt enable *IEN* is then set to allow other (higher-priority) interrupts and the computer proceeds to service the interrupt request.

The final sequence in each interrupt service routine must have instructions to control the interrupt hardware in the following manner:

1. Clear interrupt enable bit *IEN*.
2. Restore contents of processor registers.
3. Clear the bit in the interrupt register belonging to the source that has been serviced.
4. Set lower-level priority bits in the mask register.
5. Restore return address into *PC* and set *IEN*.

The bit in the interrupt register belonging to the source of the interrupt must be cleared so that it will be available again for the source to interrupt. The lower-priority bits in the mask register (including the bit of the source being interrupted) are set so they can enable the interrupt. The return to the interrupted program is accomplished by restoring the return address to *PC*. Note that the hardware must be designed so that no interrupts occur while executing steps 2 through 5; otherwise, the return address may be lost and the information in the mask and processor registers may be ambiguous if an interrupt is acknowledged while executing the operations in these steps. For this reason *IEN* is initially cleared and then set after the return address is transferred into *PC*.

The initial and final operations listed above are referred to as *overhead* operations or *housekeeping* chores. They are not part of the service program proper but are essential for processing interrupts. All overhead operations can be implemented by software. This is done by inserting the proper instructions at the beginning and at the end of each service routine. Some of the overhead operations can be done automatically by the hardware. The contents of processor registers can be pushed into a stack by the hardware before branching to the service routine. Other initial and final operations can be assigned to the hardware. In this way, it is possible to reduce the time between receipt of an interrupt and the execution of the instructions that service the interrupt source.

11-6 Direct Memory Access (DMA)

The transfer of data between a fast storage device such as magnetic disk and memory is often limited by the speed of the CPU. Removing the CPU from the path and letting the peripheral device manage the memory buses directly would improve the speed of transfer. This transfer technique is called direct memory access (DMA). During DMA transfer, the CPU is idle and has no control of the memory buses. A DMA controller takes over the buses to manage the transfer directly between the I/O device and memory.

The CPU may be placed in an idle state in a variety of ways. One common method extensively used in microprocessors is to disable the buses through special control signals. Figure 11-16 shows two control signals in the CPU that facilitate the DMA transfer. The *bus request* (*BR*) input is used by the DMA controller to request the CPU to relinquish control of the buses. When this input is active, the CPU terminates the execution of the current instruction and places the address bus, the data bus, and the read and write lines into a high-impedance state. The high-impedance state behaves like an open circuit, which means that the output is disconnected and does not have a logic significance (see Sec. 4-3). The CPU activates the *bus grant* (*BG*) output to inform the external DMA that the buses are in the high-impedance state. The DMA that originated the bus request can now take control of the buses to conduct memory transfers without processor intervention. When the DMA terminates the transfer, it disables the bus request line. The CPU disables the bus grant, takes control of the buses, and returns to its normal operation.

When the DMA takes control of the bus system, it communicates directly with the memory. The transfer can be made in several ways. In DMA *burst transfer*, a block sequence consisting of a number of memory words is transferred in a continuous burst while the DMA controller is master of the memory buses. This mode of transfer is needed for fast devices such as magnetic disks, where data transmission cannot be stopped or slowed down until an entire block is transferred. An alternative technique called *cycle stealing* allows the DMA controller to transfer one data word at a time, after which it must return control of the buses to the CPU. The CPU merely delays its operation for one memory cycle to allow the direct memory I/O transfer to "steal" one memory cycle.

DMA Controller

The DMA controller needs the usual circuits of an interface to communicate with the CPU and I/O device. In addition, it needs an address register, a word count register, and a set of address lines. The address register and address lines

bus request

bus grant

burst transfer

cycle stealing

Figure 11-16 CPU bus signals for DMA transfer.

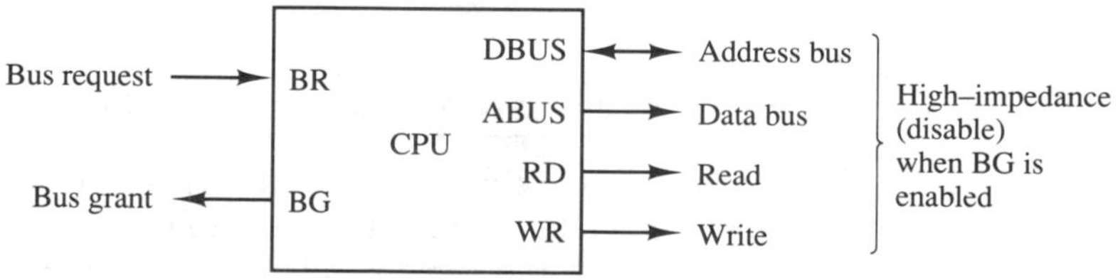

are used for direct communication with the memory. The word count register specifies the number of words that must be transferred. The data transfer may be done directly between the device and memory under control of the DMA.

Figure 11-17 shows the block diagram of a typical DMA controller. The unit communicates with the CPU via the data bus and control lines. The registers in the DMA are selected by the CPU through the address bus by enabling the *DS* (DMA select) and *RS* (register select) inputs. The *RD* (read) and *WR* (write) inputs are bidirectional. When the *BG* (bus grant) input is 0, the CPU can communicate with the DMA registers through the data bus to read from or write to the DMA registers. When *BG* = 1, the CPU has relinquished the buses and the DMA can communicate directly with the memory by specifying an address in the address bus and activating the *RD* or *WR* control. The DMA communicates with the external peripheral through the request and acknowledge lines by using a prescribed handshaking procedure.

The DMA controller has three registers: an address register, a word count register, and a control register. The address register contains an address to specify the desired location in memory. The address bits go through bus buffers into the address bus. The address register is incremented after each word that is transferred to memory. The word count register holds the number of words to be transferred. This register is decremented by one after each word transfer and internally tested for zero. The control register specifies the mode of transfer. All registers in the DMA appear to the CPU as I/O interface registers. Thus the CPU can read from or write into the DMA registers under program control via the data bus.

Figure 11-17 Block diagram of DMA controller.

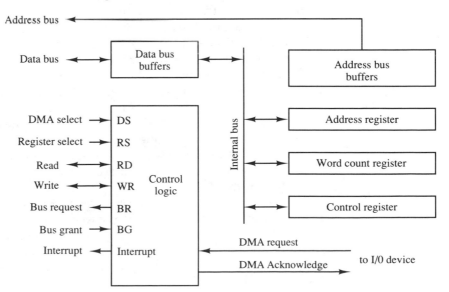

The DMA is first initialized by the CPU. After that, the DMA starts and continues to transfer data between memory and peripheral unit until an entire block is transferred. The initialization process is essentially a program consisting of I/O instructions that include the address for selecting particular DMA registers. The CPU initializes the DMA by sending the following information through the data bus:

1. The starting address of the memory block where data are available (for read) or where data are to be stored (for write)
2. The word count, which is the number of words in the memory block
3. Control to specify the mode of transfer such as read or write
4. A control to start the DMA transfer

The starting address is stored in the address register. The word count is stored in the word count register, and the control information in the control register. Once the DMA is initialized, the CPU stops communicating with the DMA unless it receives an interrupt signal or if it wants to check how many words have been transferred.

DMA Transfer

The position of the DMA controller among the other components in a computer system is illustrated in Fig. 11-18. The CPU communicates with the DMA through the address and data buses as with any interface unit. The DMA has its own address, which activates the *DS* and *RS* lines. The CPU initializes the DMA through the data bus. Once the DMA receives the start control command, it can start the transfer between the peripheral device and the memory.

When the peripheral device sends a DMA request, the DMA controller activates the *BR* line, informing the CPU to relinquish the buses. The CPU responds with its *BG* line, informing the DMA that its buses are disabled. The DMA then puts the current value of its address register into the address bus, initiates the *RD* or *WR* signal, and sends a DMA acknowledge to the peripheral device. Note that the *RD* and *WR* lines in the DMA controller are bidirectional. The direction of transfer depends on the status of the *BG* line. When *BG* = 0, the *RD* and *WR* are input lines allowing the CPU to communicate with the internal DMA registers. When *BG* = 1, the *RD* and *WR* are output lines from the DMA controller to the random-access memory to specify the read or write operation for the data.

When the peripheral device receives a DMA acknowledge, it puts a word in the data bus (for write) or receives a word from the data bus (for read). Thus the DMA controls the read or write operations and supplies the address for the memory. The peripheral unit can then communicate with memory through the data bus for direct transfer between the two units while the CPU is momentarily disabled.

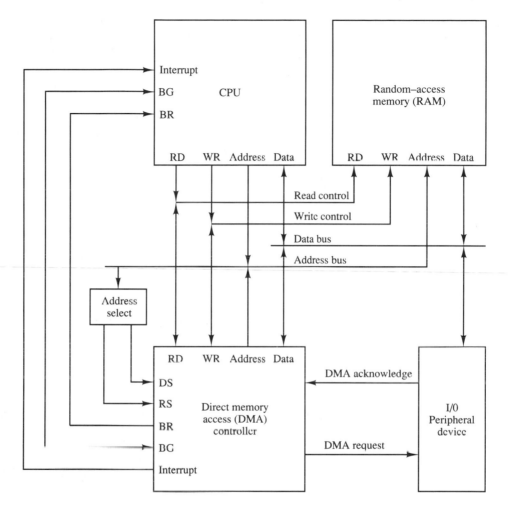

Figure 11-18   DMA transfer in a computer system.

For each word that is transferred, the DMA increments its address register and decrements its word count register. If the word count does not reach zero, the DMA checks the request line coming from the peripheral. For a high-speed device, the line will be active as soon as the previous transfer is completed. A second transfer is then initiated, and the process continues until the entire block is transferred. If the peripheral speed is slower, the DMA request line may come somewhat later. In this case the DMA disables the bus request line so that the CPU can continue to execute its program. When the peripheral requests a transfer, the DMA requests the buses again.

If the word count register reaches zero, the DMA stops any further transfer and removes its bus request. It also informs the CPU of the termination by means of an interrupt. When the CPU responds to the interrupt, it reads the content of the word count register. The zero value of this register indicates that all the words were transferred successfully. The CPU can read this register at any time to check the number of words already transferred.

A DMA controller may have more than one channel. In this case, each channel has a request and acknowledge pair of control signals which are connected to separate peripheral devices. Each channel also has its own address register and word count register within the DMA controller. A priority among the channels may be established so that channels with high priority are serviced before channels with lower priority.

DMA transfer is very useful in many applications. It is used for fast transfer of information between magnetic disks and memory. It is also useful for updating the display in an interactive terminal. Typically, an image of the screen display of the terminal is kept in memory which can be updated under program control. The contents of the memory can be transferred to the screen periodically by means of DMA transfer.

11-7 Input–Output Processor (IOP)

Instead of having each interface communicate with the CPU, a computer may incorporate one or more external processors and assign them the task of communicating directly with all I/O devices. An input–output processor (IOP) may be classified as a processor with direct memory access capability that communicates with I/O devices. In this configuration, the computer system can be divided into a memory unit, and a number of processors comprised of the CPU and one or more IOPs. Each IOP takes care of input and output tasks, relieving the CPU from the housekeeping chores involved in I/O transfers. A processor that communicates with remote terminals over telephone and other communication media in a serial fashion is called a data communication processor (DCP).

I/O processing

The IOP is similar to a CPU except that it is designed to handle the details of I/O processing. Unlike the DMA controller that must be set up entirely by the CPU, the IOP can fetch and execute its own instructions. IOP instructions are specifically designed to facilitate I/O transfers. In addition, the IOP can perform other processing tasks, such as arithmetic, logic, branching, and code translation.

The block diagram of a computer with two processors is shown in Fig. 11-19. The memory unit occupies a central position and can communicate with each processor by means of direct memory access. The CPU is responsible for processing data needed in the solution of computational tasks. The IOP provides a path for transfer of data between various peripheral devices and the memory unit. The CPU is usually assigned the task of initiating the I/O program. From then on the IOP operates independent of the CPU and continues to transfer data from external devices and memory.

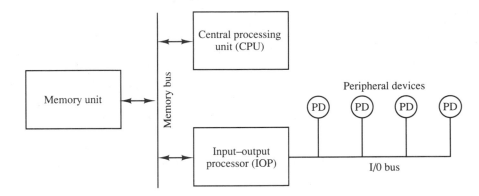

Figure 11-19   Block diagram of a computer with I/O processor.

The data formats of peripheral devices differ from memory and CPU data formats. The IOP must structure data words from many different sources. For example, it may be necessary to take four bytes from an input device and pack them into one 32-bit word before the transfer to memory. Data are gathered in the IOP at the device rate and bit capacity while the CPU is executing its own program. After the input data are assembled into a memory word, they are transferred from IOP directly into memory by "stealing" one memory cycle from the CPU. Similarly, an output word transferred from memory to the IOP is directed from the IOP to the output device at the device rate and bit capacity.

The communication between the IOP and the devices attached to it is similar to the program control method of transfer. Communication with the memory is similar to the direct memory access method. The way by which the CPU and IOP communicate depends on the level of sophistication included in the system. In very-large-scale computers, each processor is independent of all others and any one processor can initiate an operation. In most computer systems, the CPU is the master while the IOP is a slave processor. The CPU is assigned the task of initiating all operations, but I/O instructions are executed in the IOP. CPU instructions provide operations to start an I/O transfer and also to test I/O status conditions needed for making decisions on various I/O activities. The IOP, in turn, typically asks for CPU attention by means of an interrupt. It also responds to CPU requests by placing a status word in a prescribed location in memory to be examined later by a CPU program. When an I/O operation is desired, the CPU informs the IOP where to find the I/O program and then leaves the transfer details to the IOP.

commands

Instructions that are read from memory by an IOP are sometimes called *commands*, to distinguish them from instructions that are read by the CPU. Otherwise, an instruction and a command have similar functions. Commands are prepared by experienced programmers and are stored in memory. The command words constitute the program for the IOP. The CPU informs the IOP where to find the commands in memory when it is time to execute the I/O program.

CPU–IOP Communication

The communication between CPU and IOP may take different forms, depending on the particular computer considered. In most cases the memory unit acts as a message center where each processor leaves information for the other. To appreciate the operation of a typical IOP, we will illustrate by a specific example the method by which the CPU and IOP communicate. This is a simplified example that omits many operating details in order to provide an overview of basic concepts.

The sequence of operations may be carried out as shown in the flowchart of Fig. 11-20. The CPU sends an instruction to test the IOP path. The IOP

Figure 11-20 CPU-IOP communication.

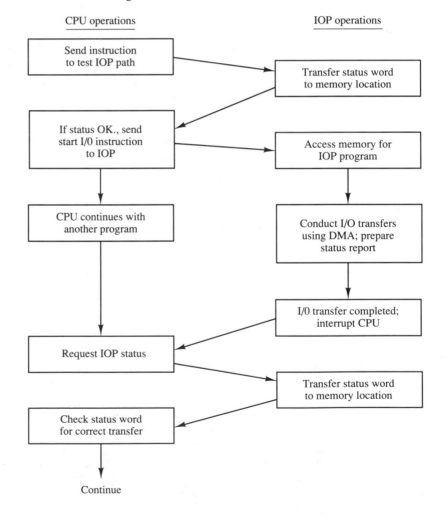

CPU operations

Send instruction to test IOP path

Transfer status word to memory location

If status OK., send start I/0 instruction to IOP

IOP operations

Access memory for IOP program

CPU continues with another program

Conduct I/O transfers using DMA; prepare status report

I/0 transfer completed; interrupt CPU

Request IOP status

Transfer status word to memory location

Check status word for correct transfer

Continue

responds by inserting a status word in memory for the CPU to check. The bits of the status word indicate the condition of the IOP and I/O device, such as IOP overload condition, device busy with another transfer, or device ready for I/O transfer. The CPU refers to the status word in memory to decide what to do next. If all is in order, the CPU sends the instruction to start I/O transfer. The memory address received with this instruction tells the IOP where to find its program.

The CPU can now continue with another program while the IOP is busy with the I/O program. Both programs refer to memory by means of DMA transfer. When the IOP terminates the execution of its program, it sends an interrupt request to the CPU. The CPU responds to the interrupt by issuing an instruction to read the status from the IOP. The IOP responds by placing the contents of its status report into a specified memory location. The status word indicates whether the transfer has been completed or if any errors occurred during the transfer. From inspection of the bits in the status word, the CPU determines if the I/O operation was completed satisfactorily without errors.

The IOP takes care of all data transfers between several I/O units and the memory while the CPU is processing another program. The IOP and CPU are competing for the use of memory, so the number of devices that can be in operation is limited by the access time of the memory. It is not possible to saturate the memory by I/O devices in most systems, as the speed of most devices is much slower than the CPU. However, some very fast units, such as magnetic disks, can use an appreciable number of the available memory cycles. In that case, the speed of the CPU may deteriorate because it will often have to wait for the IOP to conduct memory transfers.

IBM 370 I/O Channel

The I/O processor in the IBM 370 computer is called a *channel*. A typical computer system configuration includes a number of channels with each channel attached to one or more I/O devices. There are three types of channels: multiplexer, selector, and block-multiplexer. The multiplexer channel can be connected to a number of slow- and medium-speed devices and is capable of operating with a number of I/O devices simultaneously. The selector channel is designed to handle one I/O operation at a time and is normally used to control one high-speed device. The block-multiplexer channel combines the features of both the multiplexer and selector channels. It provides a connection to a number of high-speed devices, but all I/O transfers are conducted with an entire block of data as compared to a multiplexer channel, which can transfer only one byte at a time.

The CPU communicates directly with the channels through dedicated control lines and indirectly through reserved storage areas in memory. Figure 11-21 shows the word formats associated with the channel operation.

Operation code	Channel address	Device address

(a) I/O instruction format

Key	Address	Status	Count

(b) Channel status word format

Command code	Data address	Flags	Count

(c) Channel command word format

Figure 11-21   IBM 370 I/O related word formats.

The I/O instruction format has three fields: operation code, channel address, and device address. The computer system may have a number of channels, and each is assigned an address. Similarly, each channel may be connected to several devices and each device is assigned an address. The operation code specifies one of eight I/O instructions: start I/O, start I/O fast release, test I/O, clear I/O, halt I/O, halt device, test channel, and store channel identification. The addressed channel responds to each of the I/O instructions and executes it. It also sets one of four condition codes in a processor register called PSW (processor status word). The CPU can check the condition code in the PSW to determine the result of the I/O operation. The meaning of the four condition codes is different for each I/O instruction. But, in general, they specify whether the channel or the device is busy, whether or not it is operational, whether interruptions are pending, if the I/O operation had started successfully, and whether a status word was stored in memory by the channel.

The format of the channel status word is shown in Fig. 11-21(b). It is always stored in location 64 in memory. The key field is a protection mechanism used to prevent unauthorized access by one user to information that belongs to another user or to the operating system. The address field in the status word gives the address of the last command word used by the channel. The count field gives the residual count when the transfer was terminated. The count field will show zero if the transfer was completed successfully. The status field identifies the conditions in the device and the channel and any errors that occurred during the transfer.

The difference between the start I/O and start I/O fast release instructions is that the latter requires less CPU time for its execution. When the channel receives one of these two instructions, it refers to memory location 72 for the address of the first channel command word (CCW). The format of the channel command word is shown in Fig. 11-21(c). The data address field specifies the first address of a memory buffer and the count field gives the number of bytes involved in the transfer. The command field specifies an I/O operation and the flag bits provide additional information for the channel. The command field corresponds to an operation code that specifies one of six basic types of I/O operations:

1. *Write*. Transfer data from memory to I/O device.
2. *Read*. Transfer data from I/O device to memory.
3. *Read backwards*. Read magnetic tape with tape moving backward.
4. *Control*. Used to initiate an operation not involving transfer of data, such as rewinding of tape or positioning a disk-access mechanism.
5. *Sense*. Informs the channel to transfer its channel status word to memory location 64.
6. *Transfer in channel*. Used instead of a jump instruction. Here the data address field specifies the address of the next command word to be executed by the channel.

An example of a channel program is shown in Table 11-3. It consists of three command words. The first causes a transfer into a magnetic tape of 60 bytes from memory starting at address 4000. The next two command words perform a similar function with a different portion of memory and byte count. The six flags in each control word specify certain interrelations between the command words. The first flag is set to 1 in the first command word to specify "data chaining." It results in combining the 60 bytes from the first command word with the 20 bytes of its successor into one record of 80 bytes. The 80 bytes are written on tape without any separation or gaps even though two memory sections were used. The second flag is set to 1 in the second command word to specify "command chaining." It informs the channel that the next command word will use the same I/O device, in this case, the tape. The channel informs the tape unit to start inserting a record gap on the tape and proceeds to read the next command word from memory. The 40 bytes of the third command

TABLE 11-3 IBM-370 Channel Program Example

Command	Address	Flags	Count
Write tape	4000	100000	60
Write tape	6000	010000	20
Write tape	3000	000000	40

word are then written on tape as a separate record. When all the flags are equal to zero, it signifies the end of I/O operations for the particular I/O device.

A memory map showing all pertinent information for I/O processing is illustrated in Fig. 11-22. The operation begins when the CPU program encounters a start I/O instruction. The IOP then goes to memory location 72 to obtain a channel address word. This word contains the starting address of the I/O channel program. The channel then proceeds to execute the program specified by the channel command words. The channel constructs a status word during

Figure 11-22 Location of information in memory for I/O operations in the IBM 370.

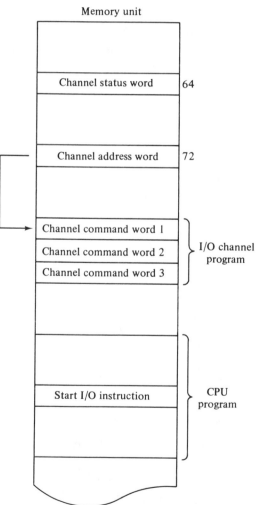

the transfer and stores it in location 64. Upon interruption, the CPU can refer to memory location 64 for the status word.

Intel 8089 IOP

The Intel 8089 I/O processor is contained in a 40-pin integrated circuit package. Within the 8089 are two independent units called *channels*. Each channel combines the general characteristics of a processor unit with those of a direct memory access controller. The 8089 is designed to function as an IOP in a microcomputer system where the Intel 8086 microprocessor is used as the CPU. The 8086 CPU initiates an I/O operation by building a message in memory that describes the function to be performed. The 8089 IOP reads the message from memory, carries out the operation, and notifies the CPU when it has finished.

In contrast to the IBM 370 channel, which has only six basic I/O commands, the 8089 IOP has 50 basic instructions that can operate on individual bits, on bytes, or 16-bit words. The IOP can execute programs in a manner similar to a CPU except that the instruction set is specifically chosen to provide efficient input–output processing. The instruction set includes general data transfer instructions, basic arithmetic and logic operations, conditional and unconditional branch operations, and subroutine call and return capabilities. The set also includes special instructions to initiate DMA transfers and issue an interrupt request to the CPU. It provides efficient data transfer between any two components attached to the system bus, such as I/O to memory, memory to memory, or I/O to I/O.

A microcomputer system using the Intel 8086/8089 pair of integrated circuits is shown in Fig. 11-23. The 8086 functions as the CPU and the 8089 as the IOP. The two units share a common memory through a bus controller connected to a system bus, which is called a "multibus" by Intel. The IOP uses a local bus to communicate with various interface units connected to I/O devices. The CPU communicates with the IOP by enabling the *channel attention* line. The *select* line is used by the CPU to select one of two channels in the 8089. The IOP gets the attention of the CPU by sending an interrupt request.

The CPU and IOP communicate with each other by writing messages for one another in system memory. The CPU prepares the message area and signals the IOP by enabling the channel attention line. The IOP reads the message, performs the required I/O functions, and executes the appropriate channel program. When the channel has completed its program, it issues an interrupt request to the CPU.

The communication scheme consists of program sections called "blocks," which are stored in memory as shown in Fig. 11-24. Each block contains control and parameter information as well as an address pointer to its successor block. The address of the control block is passed to each IOP channel during initialization. The busy flag indicates whether the IOP is busy or ready to perform

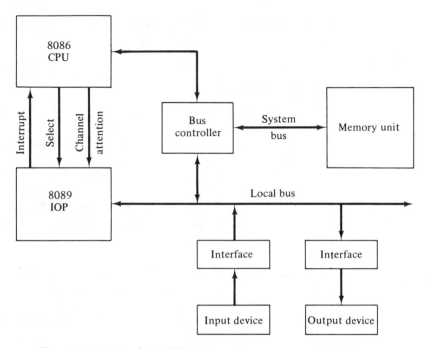

Figure 11-23   Intel 8086/8089 microcomputer system block diagram.

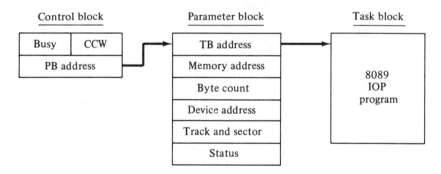

Figure 11-24   Location of information in memory for I/O operations in the Intel 8086/8089 microcomputer system.

a new I/O operation. The CCW (channel command word) is specified by the CPU to indicate the type of operation required from the IOP. The CCW in the 8089 does not have the same meaning as the command word in the IBM channel. The CCW here is more like an I/O instruction that specifies an operation for the IOP, such as start operation, suspend operation, resume operation, and halt I/O program. The parameter block contains variable data that the IOP program must use in carrying out its task. The task block contains the actual program to be executed in the IOP.

The CPU and IOP work together through the control and parameter blocks. The CPU obtains use of the shared memory after checking the busy flag to ensure that the IOP is available. The CPU then fills in the information in the parameter block and writes a "start operation" command in the CCW. After the communication blocks have been set up, the CPU enables the channel attention signal to inform the IOP to start its I/O operation. The CPU then continues with another program. The IOP responds to the channel attention signal by placing the address of the control block into its program counter. The IOP refers to the control block and sets the busy flag. It then checks the operation in the CCW. The PB (parameter block) address and TB (task block) address are then transferred into internal IOP registers. The IOP starts executing the program in the task block using the information in the parameter block. The entries in the parameter block depend on the I/O device. The parameters listed in Fig. 11-24 are suitable for data transfer to or from a magnetic disk. The memory address specifies the beginning address of a memory buffer. The byte count gives the number of bytes to be transferred. The device address specifies the particular I/O device to be used. The track and sector numbers locate the data on the disk. When the I/O operation is completed, the IOP stores its status bits in the status word location of the parameter block and interrupts the CPU. The CPU can refer to the status word to check if the transfer has been completed satisfactorily.

11-8   Serial Communication

A data communication processor is an I/O processor that distributes and collects data from many remote terminals connected through telephone and other communication lines. It is a specialized I/O processor designed to communicate directly with data communication networks. A communication network may consist of any of a wide variety of devices, such as printers, interactive display devices, digital sensors, or a remote computing facility. With the use of a data communication processor, the computer can service fragments of each network demand in an interspersed manner and thus have the apparent behavior of serving many users at once. In this way the computer is able to operate efficiently in a time-sharing environment.

data communication processor

The most striking difference between an I/O processor and a data communication processor is in the way the processor communicates with the I/O devices. An I/O processor communicates with the peripherals through a common I/O bus that is comprised of many data and control lines. All peripherals share the common bus and use it to transfer information to and from the I/O processor. A data communication processor communicates with each terminal through a single pair of wires. Both data and control information are transferred in a serial fashion with the result that the transfer rate is much slower. The task of the data communication processor is to transmit and collect digital information to and from each terminal, determine if the information is data or control and respond to all requests according to predetermined established procedures. The processor, obviously, must also communicate with the CPU and memory in the same manner as any I/O processor.

The way that remote terminals are connected to a data communication processor is via telephone lines or other public or private communication facilities. Since telephone lines were originally designed for voice communication and computers communicate in terms of digital signals, some form of conversion must be used. The converters are called *data sets*, *acoustic couplers*,

modem

or *modems* (from "modulator-demodulator"). A modem converts digital signals into audio tones to be transmitted over telephone lines and also converts audio tones from the line to digital signals for machine use. Various modulation schemes as well as different grades of communication media and transmission speeds are used. A communication line may be connected to a synchronous or asynchronous interface, depending on the transmission method of the remote terminal. An asynchronous interface receives serial data with start and stop bits in each character as shown in Fig. 11-7. This type of interface is similar to the asynchronous communication interface unit presented in Fig. 11-8.

Synchronous transmission does not use start-stop bits to frame characters and therefore makes more efficient use of the communication link. High-speed devices use synchronous transmission to realize this efficiency. The modems used in synchronous transmission have internal clocks that are set to the frequency that bits are being transmitted in the communication line. For proper operation, it is required that the clocks in the transmitter and receiver modems remain synchronized at all times. The communication line, however, contains only the data bits from which the clock information must be extracted. Frequency synchronization is achieved by the receiving modem from the signal transitions that occur in the received data. Any frequency shift that may occur between the transmitter and receiver clocks is continuously adjusted by maintaining the receiver clock at the frequency of the incoming bit stream. The modem transfers the received data together with the clock to the interface unit. The interface or terminal on the transmitter side also uses the clock information from its modem. In this way, the same bit rate is maintained in both transmitter and receiver.

Contrary to asynchronous transmission, where each character can be sent separately with its own start and stop bits, synchronous transmission must send a continuous message in order to maintain synchronism. The message consists of a group of bits transmitted sequentially as a block of data. The entire block is transmitted with special control characters at the beginning and end of the block. The control characters at the beginning of the block supply the information needed to separate the incoming bits into individual characters.

One of the functions of the data communication processor is to check for transmission errors. An error can be detected by checking the parity in each character received. Another procedure used in asynchronous terminals involving a human operator is to *echo* the character. The character transmitted from the keyboard to the computer is recognized by the processor and retransmitted to the terminal printer. The operator would realize that an error occurred during transmission if the character printed is not the same as the character whose key he has struck.

block transfer

In synchronous transmission, where an entire block of characters is transmitted, each character has a parity bit for the receiver to check. After the entire block is sent, the transmitter sends one more character that constitutes a parity over the length of the message. This character is called a longitudinal redundancy check (LRC) and is the accumulation of the exclusive-OR of all transmitted characters. The receiving station calculates the LRC as it receives characters and compares it with the transmitted LRC. The calculated and received LRC should be equal for error-free messages. If the receiver finds an error in the transmitted block, it informs the sender to retransmit the same block once again. Another method used for checking errors in transmission is

CRC

the cyclic redundancy check (CRC). This is a polynomial code obtained from the message bits by passing them through a feedback shift register containing a number of exclusive-OR gates. This type of code is suitable for detecting burst errors occurring in the communication channel.

Data can be transmitted between two points in three different modes: simplex, half-duplex, or full-duplex. A *simplex* line carries information in one direction only. This mode is seldom used in data communication because the receiver cannot communicate with the transmitter to indicate the occurrence of errors. Examples of simplex transmission are radio and television broadcasting.

A *half-duplex* transmission system is one that is capable of transmitting in both directions but data can be transmitted in only one direction at a time. A pair of wires is needed for this mode. A common situation is for one modem to act as the transmitter and the other as the receiver. When transmission in one direction is completed, the role of the modems is reversed to enable transmission in the reverse direction. The time required to switch a half-duplex line from one direction to the other is called the turnaround time.

full-duplex

A *full-duplex* transmission can send and receive data in both directions simultaneously. This can be achieved by means of a four-wire link, with a different pair of wires dedicated to each direction of transmission. Alternatively, a two-wire circuit can support full-duplex communication if the frequency spectrum is subdivided into two nonoverlapping frequency bands to create separate receive and transmit channels in the same physical pair of wires.

protocol

The communication lines, modems, and other equipment used in the transmission of information between two or more stations is called a *data link*. The orderly transfer of information in a data link is accomplished by means of a *protocol*. A data link control protocol is a set of rules that are followed by interconnecting computers and terminals to ensure the orderly transfer of information. The purpose of a data link protocol is to establish and terminate a connection between two stations, to identify the sender and receiver, to ensure that all messages are passed correctly without errors, and to handle all control functions involved in a sequence of data transfers. Protocols are divided into two major categories according to the message-framing technique used. These are character-oriented protocol and bit-oriented protocol.

Character-Oriented Protocol

The character-oriented protocol is based on the binary code of a character set. The code most commonly used is ASCII (American Standard Code for Information Interchange). It is a 7-bit code with an eighth bit used for parity. The code has 128 characters, of which 95 are graphic characters and 33 are control characters. The graphic characters include the upper- and lowercase letters, the ten numerals, and a variety of special symbols. A list of the ASCII characters can be found in Table 11-1. The control characters are used for the purpose of routing data, arranging the test in a desired format, and for the layout of the printed page. The characters that control the transmission are called *communication control* characters. These characters are listed in Table 11-4. Each character has a 7-bit code and is referred to by a three-letter symbol. The role of each character in the control of data transmission is stated briefly in the function column of the table.

SYN character   The SYN character serves as synchronizing agent between the transmitter and receiver. When the 7-bit ASCII code is used with an odd-parity bit in the most significant position, the assigned SYN character has the 8-bit code 00010110 which has the property that, upon circular shifting, it repeats itself only after a full 8-bit cycle. When the transmitter starts sending 8-bit characters, it sends a few characters first and then sends the actual message. The initial continuous string of bits accepted by the receiver is checked for a SYN character. In other words, with each clock pulse, the receiver checks the last eight bits

TABLE 11-4 ASCII Communication Control Characters

Code	Symbol	Meaning	Function
0010110	SYN	Synchronous idle	Establishes synchronism
0000001	SOH	Start of heading	Heading of block message
0000010	STX	Start of text	Precedes block of text
0000011	ETX	End of text	Terminates block of text
0000100	EOT	End of transmission	Concludes transmission
0000110	ACK	Acknowledge	Affirmative acknowledgement
0010101	NAK	Negative acknowledge	Negative acknowledgement
0000101	ENQ	Inquiry	Inquire if terminal is on
0010111	ETB	End of transmission block	End of block of data
0010000	DLE	Data link escape	Special control character

received. If they do not match the bits of the SYN character, the receiver accepts the next bit, rejects the previous high-order bit, and again checks the last eight bits received for a SYN character. This is repeated after each clock pulse and bit received until a SYN character is recognized. Once a SYN character is detected, the receiver has framed a character. From here on the receiver counts every eight bits and accepts them as a single character. Usually, the receiver checks two consecutive SYN characters to remove any doubt that the first did not occur as a result of a noise signal on the line. Moreover, when the transmitter is idle and does not have any message characters to send, it sends a continuous string of SYN characters. The receiver recognizes these characters as a condition for synchronizing the line and goes into a synchronous idle state. In this state, the two units maintain bit and character synchronism even though no meaningful information is communicated.

Messages are transmitted through the data link with an established format consisting of a header field, a text field, and an error-checking field. A typical message format for a character-oriented protocol is shown in Fig. 11-25. The two SYN characters assure proper synchronization at the start of the message. Following the SYN characters is the header, which starts with an SOH (start of heading) character. The header consists of address and control information. The STX character terminates the header and signifies the beginning of the text transmission. The text portion of the message is variable in length and may contain any ASCII characters except the communication control characters. The text field is terminated with the ETX character. The last field is a block check character (BCC) used for error checking. It is usually either a longitudinal redundancy check (LRC) or a cyclic redundancy check (CRC).

The receiver accepts the message and calculates its own BCC. If the BCC transmitted does not agree with the BCC calculated by the receiver, the receiver responds with a negative acknowledge (NAK) character. The message is then retransmitted and checked again. Retransmission will be typically attempted several times before it is assumed that the line is faulty. When the transmitted BCC matches the one calculated by the receiver, the response is a positive acknowledgment using the ACK character.

Transmission Example

In order to appreciate the function of a data communication processor, let us illustrate by a specific example the method by which a terminal and the processor communicate. The communication with the memory unit and CPU is similar to any I/O processor.

Figure 11-25 Typical message format for character-oriented protocol.

SYN	SYN	SOH	Header	STX	Text	ETX	BCC

A typical message that might be sent from a terminal to the processor is listed in Table 11-5. A look at this message reveals that there are a number of control characters used for message formation. Each character, including the control characters, is transmitted serially as an 8-bit binary code which consists of the 7-bit ASCII code plus an odd parity bit in the eighth most significant position. The two SYN characters are used to synchronize the receiver and transmitter. The heading starts with the SOH character and continues with two characters that specify the address of the terminal. In this particular example, the address is T4, but in general it can have any set of two or more graphic characters. The STX character terminates the heading and signifies the beginning of the text transmission. The text data of concern here is "request balance of account number 1234." The individual characters for this message are not listed in the table because they will take too much space. It must be realized, however, that each character in the message has an 8-bit code and that each bit is transmitted serially. The ETX control character signifies the termination of the text characters. The next character following ETX is a longitudinal redundancy check (LRC). Each bit in this character is a parity bit calculated from all the bits in the same column in the code section of the table.

The data communication processor receives this message and proceeds to analyze it. It recognizes terminal T4 and stores the text associated with the message. While receiving the characters, the processor checks the parity in each character and also computes the longitudinal parity. The computed LRC is compared with the LRC character received. If the two match, a positive acknowledgment (ACK) is sent back to the terminal. If a mismatch exists, a

TABLE 11-5 Typical Transmission from a Terminal to Processor

Code	Symbol	Comments
0001 0110	SYN	First sync character
0001 0110	SYN	Second sync character
0000 0001	SOH	Start of heading
0101 0100	T	Address of terminal is T4
0011 0100	4	
0000 0010	STX	Start of text transmission
0101 0010		
0100 0101	request	Text sent is a request to respond with the balance of
·	balance	account number 1234
·	of account	
·	No. 1234	
1011 0011		
0011 0100		
1000 0011	ETX	End of text transmission
0111 0000	LRC	Longitudinal parity character

negative acknowledgment (NAK) is returned to the terminal, which would initiate a retransmission of the same block. If the processor finds the message without errors, it transfers the message into memory and interrupts the CPU. When the CPU acknowledges the interrupt, it analyzes the message and prepares a text message for responding to the request. The CPU sends an instruction to the data communication processor to send the message to the terminal.

A typical response from processor to terminal is listed in Table 11-6. After two SYN characters, the processor acknowledges the previous message with an ACK character. The line continues to idle with SYN character waiting for the response to come. The message received from the CPU is arranged in the proper format by the processor by inserting the required control characters before and after the text. The message has the heading SOH and the address of the terminal T4. The text message informs the terminal that the balance is $100. An LRC character is computed and sent to the terminal. If the terminal responds with a NAK character, the processor retransmits the message.

While the processor is taking care of this terminal it is busy processing other terminals as well. Since the characters are received in a serial fashion, it takes a certain amount of time to receive and collect an 8-bit character. During this time the processor is multiplexing all other communication lines and

TABLE 11-6 Typical Transmission from Processor to Terminal

Code	Symbol	Comments
0001 0110	SYN	First sync character
0001 0110	SYN	Second sync character
1000 0110	ACK	Processor acknowledges previous message
0001 0110	SYN	Line is idling
.	.	
.	.	
.	.	
0001 0110	SYN	Line is idling
0000 0001	SOH	Start of heading
0101 0100	T	Address of terminal is T4
0011 0100	4	
0000 0010	STX	Start of text transmission
1100 0010		
1100 0001	balance	Text sent is a response from the computer giving the
.	is	balance of account
.	$100.00	
.		
.		
1011 0000		
1000 0011	ETX	End of text transmission
1101 0101	LRC	Longitudinal parity character

services each one in turn. The speed of most remote terminals is extremely slow compared to the processor speed. This property allows multiplexing of many users to achieve greater efficiency in a time-sharing system. This also allows many users to operate simultaneously while each is being sampled at speeds comparable to normal human response.

Data Transparency

The character-oriented protocol was originally developed to communicate with keyboard, printer, and display devices that use alphanumeric characters exclusively. As the data communication field expanded, it became necessary to transmit binary information which is not ASCII text. This happens, for example, when two remote computers send programs and data to each other over a communication channel. An arbitrary bit pattern in the text message becomes a problem in the character-oriented protocol. This is because any 8-bit pattern belonging to a communication control character will be interpreted erroneously by the receiver. For example, if the binary data in the text portion of the message has the 8-bit pattern 10000011, the receiver will interpret this as an ETX character and assume that it reached the end of the text field. When the text portion of the message is variable in length and contains bits that are to be treated without reference to any particular code, it is said to contain transparent data. This feature requires that the character recognition logic of the receiver be turned off so that data patterns in the text field are not accidentally interpreted as communication control information.

DLE character   Data transparency is achieved in character-oriented protocols by inserting a DLE (data link escape) character before each communication control character. Thus, the start of heading is detected from the double character DLE SOH, and the text field is terminated with the double character DLE ETX. If the DLE bit pattern 00010000 occurs in the text portion of the message, the transmitter inserts another DLE bit pattern following it. The receiver removes all DLE characters and then checks the next 8-bit pattern. If it is another DLE bit pattern, the receiver considers it as part of the text and continues to receive text. Otherwise, the receiver takes the following 8-bit pattern to be a communication control character.

The achievement of data transparency by means of the DLE character is inefficient and somewhat complicated to implement. Therefore, other protocols have been developed to make the transmission of transparent data more efficient. One protocol used by Digital Equipment Corporation employs a byte count field that gives the number of bytes in the message that follows. The receiver must then count the number of bytes received to reach the end of the text field. The protocol that has been mostly used to solve the transparency problem (and other problems associated with the character-oriented protocol) is the bit-oriented protocol.

Bit-Oriented Protocol

The bit-oriented protocol does not use characters in its control field and is independent of any particular code. It allows the transmission of serial bit stream of any length without the implication of character boundaries. Messages are organized in a specific format called a frame. In addition to the information field, a frame contains address, control, and error-checking fields. The frame boundaries are determined from a special 8-bit number called a flag. Examples of bit-oriented protocols are SDLC (synchronous data link control) used by IBM, HDLC (high-level data link control) adopted by the International Standards Organization, and ADCCP (advanced data communication control procedure) adopted by the American National Standards Institute.

Any data communication link involves at least two participating stations. The station that has responsibility for the data link and issues the commands to control the link is called the primary station. The other station is a secondary station. Bit-oriented protocols assume the presence of one primary station and one or more secondary stations. All communication on the data link is from the primary station to one or more secondary stations, or from a secondary station to the primary station.

8-bit flag

The frame format for the bit-oriented protocol is shown in Fig. 11-26. A frame starts with the 8-bit flag 01111110 followed by an address and control sequence. The information field is not restricted in format or content and can be of any length. The frame check field is a CRC (cyclic redundancy check) sequence used for detecting errors in transmission. The ending flag indicates to the receiving station that the 16 bits just received constitute the CRC bits. The ending frame can be followed by another frame, another flag, or a sequence of consecutive 1's. When two frames follow each other, the intervening flag is simultaneously the ending flag of the first frame and the beginning flag of the next frame. If no information is exchanged, the transmitter sends a series of flags to keep the line in the active state. The line is said to be in the idle state with the occurrence of 15 or more consecutive 1's. Frames with certain control messages are sent without an information field. A frame must have a minimum of 32 bits between two flags to accommodate the address, control, and frame check fields. The maximum length depends on the condition of the communication channel and its ability to transmit long messages error-free.

zero insertion

To prevent a flag from occurring in the middle of a frame, the bit-oriented protocol uses a method called *zero insertion*. This requires that a 0 be inserted

Figure 11-26 Frame format for bit-oriented protocol.

Flag 01111110	Address 8 bits	Control 8 bits	Information any number of bits	Frame check 16 bits	Flag 01111110

by the transmitting station after any succession of five continuous 1's. The receiver always removes a 0 that follows a succession of five 1's. Thus the bit pattern 0111111 is transmitted as 01111101 and restored by the receiver to its original value by removal of the 0 following the five 1's. As a consequence, no pattern of 01111110 is ever transmitted between the beginning and ending flags.

Following the flag is the address field, which is used by the primary station to designate the secondary station address. When a secondary station transmits a frame, the address tells the primary station which secondary station originated the frame. An address field of eight bits can specify up to 256 addresses. Some bit-oriented protocols permit the use of an extended address field. To do this, the least significant bit of an address byte is set to 0 if another address byte follows. A 1 in the least significant bit of a byte is used to recognize the last address byte.

control field
Following the address field is the control field. The control field comes in three different formats, as shown in Fig. 11-27. The information transfer format is used for ordinary data transmission. Each frame transmitted in this format contains send and receive counts. A station that transmits sequenced frames counts and numbers each frame. This count is given by the send count N_s. A station receiving sequenced frames counts each error-free frame that it receives. This count is given by the receive count N_r. The N_r count advances when a frame is checked and found to be without errors. The receiver confirms accepted numbered information frames by returning its N_r count to the transmitting station.

The P/F bit is used by the primary station to poll a secondary station to

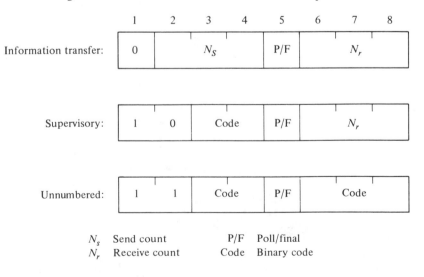

Figure 11-27 Control field format in bit-oriented protocol.

	1	2	3	4	5	6	7	8

Information transfer:

0		N_S		P/F		N_r	

Supervisory:

1	0	Code		P/F		N_r	

Unnumbered:

1	1	Code		P/F		Code	

N_s Send count   P/F Poll/final
N_r Receive count   Code Binary code

request that it initiate transmission. It is used by the secondary station to indicate the final transmitted frame. Thus the P/F field is called P (poll) when the primary station is transmitting but is designated as F (final) when a secondary station is transmitting. Each frame sent to the secondary station from the primary station has a P bit set to 0. When the primary station is finished and ready for the secondary station to respond, the P bit is set to 1. The secondary station then responds with a number of frames in which the F bit is set to 0. When the secondary station sends the last frame, it sets the F bit to 1. Therefore, the P/F bit is used to determine when data transmission from a station is finished.

The supervisory format of the control field is recognized from the first two bits being 1 and 0. The next two bits indicate the type of command. This follows by a P/F bit and a receive sequence frame count. The frames of the supervisory format do not carry an information field. They are used to assist in the transfer of information in that they confirm the acceptance of preceding frames carrying information, convey ready or busy conditions, and report frame numbering errors.

The unnumbered format is recognized from the first two bits being 11. The five code bits available in this format can specify up to 32 commands and responses. The primary station uses the control field to specify a command for a secondary station. The secondary station uses the control field to transmit a response to the primary station. Unnumbered-format frames are employed for initialization of link functions, reporting procedural errors, placing stations in a disconnected mode, and other data link control operations.

PROBLEMS

11-1. The addresses assigned to the four registers of the I/O interface of Fig. 11-2 are equal to the binary equivalent of 12, 13, 14, and 15. Show the external circuit that must be connected between an 8-bit I/O address from the CPU and the CS, $RS1$, and $RS0$ inputs of the interface.

11-2. Six interface units of the type shown in Fig. 11-2 are connected to a CPU that uses an I/O address of eight bits. Each one of the six chip select (CS) inputs is connected to a different address line. Thus the high-order address line is connected to the CS input of the first interface unit and the sixth address line is connected to the CS input of the sixth interface unit. The two low-order address lines are connected to the $RS1$ and $RS0$ of all six interface units. Determine the 8-bit address of each register in each interface.

11-3. List four peripheral devices that produce an acceptable output for a person to understand.

11-4. Write your full name in ASCII using eight bits per character with the leftmost bit always 0. Include a space between names and a period after a middle initial.

11-5.   What is the difference between isolated I/O and memory-mapped I/O? What are the advantages and disadvantages of each?

11-6.   Indicate whether the following constitute a control, status, or data transfer commands.
a. Skip next instruction if flag is set.
b. Seek a given record on a magnetic disk.
c. Check if I/O device is ready.
d. Move printer paper to beginning of next page.
e. Read interface status register.

11-7.   A commercial interface unit uses different names for the handshake lines associated with the transfer of data from the I/O device into the interface unit. The interface input handshake line is labeled *STB* (strobe), and the interface output handshake line is labeled *IBF* (input buffer full). A low-level signal on *STB* loads data from the I/O bus into the interface data register. A high-level signal on *IBF* indicates that the data item has been accepted by the interface. *IBF* goes low after an I/O read signal from the CPU when it reads the contents of the data register.
a. Draw a block diagram showing the CPU, the interface, and the I/O device together with the pertinent interconnections among the three units.
b. Draw a timing diagram for the handshaking transfer.
c. Obtain a sequence-of-events flowchart for the transfer from the device to the interface and from the interface to the CPU.

11-8.   A CPU with a 20-MHz clock is connected to a memory unit whose access time is 40 ns. Formulate a read and write timing diagrams using a READ strobe and a WRITE strobe. Include the address in the timing diagram.

11-9.   The asynchronous communication interface shown in Fig. 11-8 is connected between a CPU and a printer. Draw a flowchart that describes the sequence of operations in the transmitter portion of the interface when the CPU sends characters to be printed.

11-10.   Give at least six status conditions for the setting of individual bits in the status register of an asynchronous communication interface.

11-11.   How many bits are there in the transmitter shift register of Fig. 11-8 when the interface is attached to a terminal that needs one stop bit? List the bits in the shift register when the letter W is transmitted using ASCII with even parity.

11-12.   How many characters per second can be transmitted over a 1200-baud line in each of the following modes? (Assume a character code of eight bits.)
a. Synchronous serial transmission.
b. Asynchronous serial transmission with two stop bits.
c. Asynchronous serial transmission with one stop bit.

11-13.   Information is inserted into a FIFO buffer at a rate of m bytes per second. The information is deleted at a rate of n byte per second. The maximum capacity of the buffer is k bytes.
a. How long does it take for an empty buffer to fill up when $m > n$?
b. How long does it take for a full buffer to empty when $m < n$?
c. Is the FIFO buffer needed if $m = n$?

11-14. The bits in the control register of the FIFO shown in Fig. 11-9 are $F_1 F_2 F_3 F_4 = 0011$. Give the sequence of internal operations when an item is deleted from the FIFO and then a new item is inserted.

11-15. What are the values of input ready and output ready and control bits F_1 through F_4 in Fig. 11-9 when:
   a. The buffer is empty?
   b. The buffer is full?
   c. The buffer contains two data items?

11-16. Show a block diagram similar to Fig. 11-10 for the data transfer from a CPU to an interface and then to an I/O device. Determine a procedure for setting and clearing the flag bit.

11-17. Using the configuration established in Prob. 11-16, obtain a flowchart (similar to Fig. 11-11) for the CPU program to output data.

11-18. What is the basic advantage of using interrupt-initiated data transfer over transfer under program control without an interrupt?

11-19. In most computers an interrupt is recognized only after the execution of the instruction. Consider the possibility of acknowledging the interrupt at any time during the execution of the instruction. Discuss the difficulty that may arise.

11-20. What happens in the daisy-chain priority interrupt shown in Fig. 11-12 when device 1 requests an interrupt after device 2 has sent an interrupt request to the CPU but before the CPU responds with the interrupt acknowledge?

11-21. Consider a computer without priority interrupt hardware. Any one of many sources can interrupt the computer, and any interrupt request results in storing the return address and branching to a common interrupt routine. Explain how a priority can be established in the interrupt service program.

11-22. Using combinational circuit design techniques, derive the Boolean expressions listed in Table 11-2 for the priority encoder. Draw the logic diagram of the circuit.

11-23. Design a parallel priority interrupt hardware for a system with eight interrupt sources.

11-24. Obtain the truth table of an 8×3 priority encoder. Assume that the three outputs xyz from the priority encoder are used to provide a vector address of the form $101xyz00$. List the eight vector addresses starting from the one with the highest priority.

11-25. What should be done in Fig. 11-14 to make the four VAD values equal to the binary equivalent of 76, 77, 78, and 79?

11-26. What programming steps are required to check when a source interrupts the computer while it is still being serviced by a previous interrupt request from the same source?

11-27. Why are the read and write control lines in a DMA controller bidirectional? Under what condition and for what purpose are they used as inputs? Under what condition and for what purpose are they used as outputs?

11-28. It is necessary to transfer 256 words from a magnetic disk to a memory section starting from address 1230. The transfer is by means of DMA as shown in Fig. 11-18.

a. Give the initial values that the CPU must transfer to the DMA controller.

b. Give the step-by-step account of the actions taken during the input of the first two words.

11-29. A DMA controller transfers 16-bit words to memory using cycle stealing. The words are assembled from a device that transmits characters at a rate of 2400 characters per second. The CPU is fetching and executing instructions at an average rate of 1 million instructions per second. By how much will the CPU be slowed down because of the DMA transfer?

11-30. Why does DMA have priority over the CPU when both request a memory transfer?

11-31. Draw a flowchart similar to the one in Fig. 11-20 that describes the CPU–I/O channel communication in the IBM 370.

11-32. The address of a terminal connected to a data communication processor consists of two letters of the alphabet or a letter followed by one of the 10 numerals. How many different addresses can be formulated.

11-33. List a possible line procedure and the character sequence for the communication between a data communication processor and a remote terminal. The processor inquires if the terminal is operative. The terminal responds with yes or no. If the response is yes, the processor sends a block of text.

11-34. A data communication link employs the character-controlled protocol with data transparency using the DLE character. The text message that the transmitter sends between STX and ETX is as follows:

DLE STX DLE DLE ETX DLE DLE ETX DLE ETX

What is the binary value of the transparent text data?

11-35. What is the minimum number of bits that a frame must have in the bit-oriented protocol?

11-36. Show how the zero insertion works in the bit-oriented protocol when a zero followed by the 10 bits that represent the binary equivalent of 1023 are transmitted.

REFERENCES

1. Gorsline, G. W., *Computer Organization: Hardware/Software*, 2nd ed. Englewood Cliffs, NJ: Prentice Hall, 1986.

2. Hays, J. F., *Computer Architecture and Organization*, 2nd ed. New York: McGraw-Hill, 1988.

3. Hill, F. J., and G. R. Peterson, *Digital Systems: Hardware Organization and Design*, 3rd ed. New York: John Wiley, 1987.

4. Hwang, K., and F. A. Briggs, *Computer Architecture and Parallel Processing*. New York: McGraw-Hill, 1984.

5. Lippiatt, A. G., and G. L. Wright, *The Architecture of Small Computer Systems*, 2nd ed. Englewood Cliffs, NJ: Prentice Hall, 1985.

6. Patterson, D. A., and J. L. Hennessy, *Computer Architecture: A Quantitative Approach*. San Mateo, CA: Morgan Kaufmann Publishers, 1990.

7. Pollard, L. H., *Computer Design and Architecture*. Englewood Cliffs, NJ: Prentice Hall, 1990.

8. Rafiquzzaman, M., and R. Chandra, *Modern Computer Architecture*. St. Paul, MN: West Publishing, 1988.

9. Toy, W., and B. Zee, *Computer Hardware/Software Architecture*. Englewood Cliffs, NJ: Prentice Hall, 1986.

10. Wakerly, J. F., *Microcomputer Architecture and Programming*. New York: John Wiley, 1981.

11. Ward, S. A., and R. H. Halstead, Jr., *Computation Structures*. Cambridge, MA: MIT Press, 1990.

CHAPTER TWELVE

Memory Organization

IN THIS CHAPTER

12-1   Memory Hierarchy

The memory unit is an essential component in any digital computer since it is needed for storing programs and data. A very small computer with a limited application may be able to fulfill its intended task without the need of additional storage capacity. Most general-purpose computers would run more efficiently if they were equipped with additional storage beyond the capacity of the main memory. There is just not enough space in one memory unit to accommodate all the programs used in a typical computer. Moreover, most computer users accumulate and continue to accumulate large amounts of data-processing software. Not all accumulated information is needed by the processor at the same time. Therefore, it is more economical to use low-cost storage devices to serve as a backup for storing the information that is not currently used by the CPU. The memory unit that communicates directly with the CPU is called the *main memory*. Devices that provide backup storage are *auxiliary memory*   called *auxiliary memory*. The most common auxiliary memory devices used in computer systems are magnetic disks and tapes. They are used for storing system programs, large data files, and other backup information. Only programs and data currently needed by the processor reside in main memory. All other information is stored in auxiliary memory and transferred to main memory when needed.

The total memory capacity of a computer can be visualized as being a hierarchy of components. The memory hierarchy system consists of all storage devices employed in a computer system from the slow but high-capacity auxiliary memory to a relatively faster main memory, to an even smaller and faster cache memory accessible to the high-speed processing logic. Figure 12-1 illustrates the components in a typical memory hierarchy. At the bottom of the hierarchy are the relatively slow magnetic tapes used to store removable files. Next are the magnetic disks used as backup storage. The main memory occupies a central position by being able to communicate directly with the CPU and with auxiliary memory devices through an I/O processor. When programs not residing in main memory are needed by the CPU, they are brought in from auxiliary memory. Programs not currently needed in main memory are transferred into auxiliary memory to provide space for currently used programs and data.

cache memory

A special very-high-speed memory called a *cache* is sometimes used to increase the speed of processing by making current programs and data available to the CPU at a rapid rate. The cache memory is employed in computer systems to compensate for the speed differential between main memory access time and processor logic. CPU logic is usually faster than main memory access time, with the result that processing speed is limited primarily by the speed of main memory. A technique used to compensate for the mismatch in operating speeds is to employ an extremely fast, small cache between the CPU and main memory whose access time is close to processor logic clock cycle time. The cache is used for storing segments of programs currently being executed in the CPU and temporary data frequently needed in the present calculations.

Figure 12-1   Memory hierarchy in a computer system.

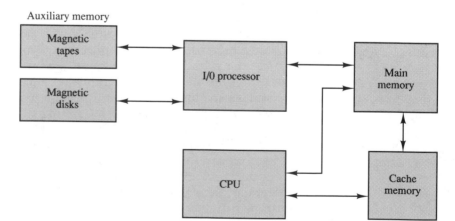

By making programs and data available at a rapid rate, it is possible to increase the performance rate of the computer.

While the I/O processor manages data transfers between auxiliary memory and main memory, the cache organization is concerned with the transfer of information between main memory and CPU. Thus each is involved with a different level in the memory hierarchy system. The reason for having two or three levels of memory hierarchy is economics. As the storage capacity of the memory increases, the cost per bit for storing binary information decreases and the access time of the memory becomes longer. The auxiliary memory has a large storage capacity, is relatively inexpensive, but has low access speed compared to main memory. The cache memory is very small, relatively expensive, and has very high access speed. Thus as the memory access speed increases, so does its relative cost. The overall goal of using a memory hierarchy is to obtain the highest-possible average access speed while minimizing the total cost of the entire memory system.

Auxiliary and cache memories are used for different purposes. The cache holds those parts of the program and data that are most heavily used, while the auxiliary memory holds those parts that are not presently used by the CPU. Moreover, the CPU has direct access to both cache and main memory but not to auxiliary memory. The transfer from auxiliary to main memory is usually done by means of direct memory access of large blocks of data. The typical access time ratio between cache and main memory is about 1 to 7. For example, a typical cache memory may have an access time of 100 ns, while main memory access time may be 700 ns. Auxiliary memory average access time is usually 1000 times that of main memory. Block size in auxiliary memory typically ranges from 256 to 2048 words, while cache block size is typically from 1 to 16 words.

multiprogramming

Many operating systems are designed to enable the CPU to process a number of independent programs concurrently. This concept, called *multiprogramming*, refers to the existence of two or more programs in different parts of the memory hierarchy at the same time. In this way it is possible to keep all parts of the computer busy by working with several programs in sequence. For example, suppose that a program is being executed in the CPU and an I/O transfer is required. The CPU initiates the I/O processor to start executing the transfer. This leaves the CPU free to execute another program. In a multiprogramming system, when one program is waiting for input or output transfer, there is another program ready to utilize the CPU.

With multiprogramming the need arises for running partial programs, for varying the amount of main memory in use by a given program, and for moving programs around the memory hierarchy. Computer programs are sometimes too long to be accommodated in the total space available in main memory. Moreover, a computer system uses many programs and all the programs cannot reside in main memory at all times. A program with its data normally resides in auxiliary memory. When the program or a segment of the program is to be executed, it is transferred to main memory to be executed by the CPU. Thus one may think of auxiliary memory as containing the totality of information stored in a computer system. It is the task of the operating system to maintain in main memory a portion of this information that is currently active. The part of the computer system that supervises the flow of information between auxiliary memory and main memory is called the *memory management system*. The hardware for a memory management system is presented in Sec. 12-7.

12-2   Main Memory

random-access memory (RAM)

The main memory is the central storage unit in a computer system. It is a relatively large and fast memory used to store programs and data during the computer operation. The principal technology used for the main memory is based on semiconductor integrated circuits. Integrated circuit RAM chips are available in two possible operating modes, *static* and *dynamic*. The static RAM consists essentially of internal flip-flops that store the binary information. The stored information remains valid as long as power is applied to the unit. The dynamic RAM stores the binary information in the form of electric charges that are applied to capacitors. The capacitors are provided inside the chip by MOS transistors. The stored charge on the capacitors tend to discharge with time and the capacitors must be periodically recharged by refreshing the dynamic memory. Refreshing is done by cycling through the words every few milliseconds to restore the decaying charge. The dynamic RAM offers reduced power consumption and larger storage capacity in a single memory chip. The static RAM is easier to use and has shorter read and write cycles.

read-only memory (ROM)

Most of the main memory in a general-purpose computer is made up of RAM integrated circuit chips, but a portion of the memory may be constructed with ROM chips. Originally, RAM was used to refer to a random-access memory, but now it is used to designate a read/write memory to distinguish it from a read-only memory, although ROM is also random access. RAM is used for storing the bulk of the programs and data that are subject to change. ROM is used for storing programs that are permanently resident in the computer and for tables of constants that do not change in value once the production of the computer is completed.

bootstrap loader

Among other things, the ROM portion of main memory is needed for storing an initial program called a *bootstrap loader*. The bootstrap loader is a program whose function is to start the computer software operating when power is turned on. Since RAM is volatile, its contents are destroyed when power is turned off. The contents of ROM remain unchanged after power is

computer startup

turned off and on again. The startup of a computer consists of turning the power on and starting the execution of an initial program. Thus when power is turned on, the hardware of the computer sets the program counter to the first address of the bootstrap loader. The bootstrap program loads a portion of the operating system from disk to main memory and control is then transferred to the operating system, which prepares the computer for general use.

RAM and ROM chips are available in a variety of sizes. If the memory needed for the computer is larger than the capacity of one chip, it is necessary to combine a number of chips to form the required memory size. To demonstrate the chip interconnection, we will show an example of a 1024 × 8 memory constructed with 128 × 8 RAM chips and 512 × 8 ROM chips.

RAM and ROM Chips

bidirectional bus

A RAM chip is better suited for communication with the CPU if it has one or more control inputs that select the chip only when needed. Another common feature is a bidirectional data bus that allows the transfer of data either from memory to CPU during a read operation, or from CPU to memory during a write operation. A bidirectional bus can be constructed with three-state buffers. A three state buffer output can be placed in one of three possible states: a signal equivalent to logic 1, a signal equivalent to logic 0, or a high-impedance state. The logic 1 and 0 are normal digital signals. The high-impedance state behaves like an open circuit, which means that the output does not carry a signal and has no logic significance.

The block diagram of a RAM chip is shown in Fig. 12-2. The capacity of the memory is 128 words of eight bits (one byte) per word. This requires a 7-bit

Figure 12-2 Typical RAM chip.

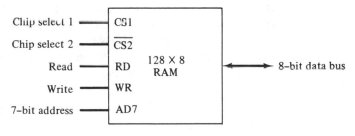

Chip select 1 —→ CS1
Chip select 2 —→ $\overline{CS2}$
Read —→ RD   128 × 8
                RAM   ←→ 8–bit data bus
Write —→ WR
7–bit address —→ AD7

(a) Block diagram

CS1	$\overline{CS2}$	RD	WR	Memory function	State of data bus
0	0	×	×	Inhibit	High-impedance
0	1	×	×	Inhibit	High-impedance
1	0	0	0	Inhibit	High-impedance
1	0	0	1	Write	Input data to RAM
1	0	1	×	Read	Output data from RAM
1	1	×	×	Inhibit	High-impedance

(b) Function table

address and an 8-bit bidirectional data bus. The read and write inputs specify the memory operation and the two chips select (CS) control inputs are for enabling the chip only when it is selected by the microprocessor. The availability of more than one control input to select the chip facilitates the decoding of the address lines when multiple chips are used in the microcomputer. The read and write inputs are sometimes combined into one line labeled R/W. When the chip is selected, the two binary states in this line specify the two operations of read or write.

The function table listed in Fig. 12-2(b) specifies the operation of the RAM chip. The unit is in operation only when CS1 = 1 and $\overline{CS2}$ = 0. The bar on top of the second select variable indicates that this input is enabled when it is equal to 0. If the chip select inputs are not enabled, or if they are enabled but the read or write inputs are not enabled, the memory is inhibited and its data bus is in a high-impedance state. When CS1 = 1 and $\overline{CS2}$ = 0, the memory can be placed in a write or read mode. When the WR input is enabled, the memory stores a byte from the data bus into a location specified by the address input lines. When the RD input is enabled, the content of the selected byte is placed into the data bus. The RD and WR signals control the memory operation as well as the bus buffers associated with the bidirectional data bus.

A ROM chip is organized externally in a similar manner. However, since a ROM can only read, the data bus can only be in an output mode. The block diagram of a ROM chip is shown in Fig. 12-3. For the same-size chip, it is possible to have more bits of ROM than of RAM, because the internal binary cells in ROM occupy less space than in RAM. For this reason, the diagram specifies a 512-byte ROM, while the RAM has only 128 bytes.

The nine address lines in the ROM chip specify any one of the 512 bytes stored in it. The two chip select inputs must be CS1 = 1 and $\overline{CS2}$ = 0 for the unit to operate. Otherwise, the data bus is in a high-impedance state. There is no need for a read or write control because the unit can only read. Thus when the chip is enabled by the two select inputs, the byte selected by the address lines appears on the data bus.

Memory Address Map

The designer of a computer system must calculate the amount of memory required for the particular application and assign it to either RAM or ROM. The interconnection between memory and processor is then established from knowledge of the size of memory needed and the type of RAM and ROM chips available. The addressing of memory can be established by means of a table that specifies the memory address assigned to each chip. The table, called a *memory address map*, is a pictorial representation of assigned address space for each chip in the system.

To demonstrate with a particular example, assume that a computer system needs 512 bytes of RAM and 512 bytes of ROM. The RAM and ROM chips

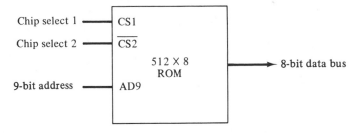

Figure 12-3 Typical ROM chip.

to be used are specified in Figs. 12-2 and 12-3. The memory address map for this configuration is shown in Table 12-1. The component column specifies whether a RAM or a ROM chip is used. The hexadecimal address column assigns a range of hexadecimal equivalent addresses for each chip. The address bus lines are listed in the third column. Although there are 16 lines in the address bus, the table shows only 10 lines because the other 6 are not used in this example and are assumed to be zero. The small x's under the address bus lines designate those lines that must be connected to the address inputs in each chip. The RAM chips have 128 bytes and need seven address lines. The ROM chip has 512 bytes and needs 9 address lines. The x's are always assigned to the low-order bus lines: lines 1 through 7 for the RAM and lines 1 through 9 for the ROM. It is now necessary to distinguish between four RAM chips by assigning to each a different address. For this particular example we choose bus lines 8 and 9 to represent four distinct binary combinations. Note that any other pair of unused bus lines can be chosen for this purpose. The table clearly shows that the nine low-order bus lines constitute a memory space for RAM equal to $2^9 = 512$ bytes. The distinction between a RAM and ROM address is done with another bus line. Here we choose line 10 for this purpose. When line 10 is 0, the CPU selects a RAM, and when this line is equal to 1, it selects the ROM.

The equivalent hexadecimal address for each chip is obtained from the information under the address bus assignment. The address bus lines are

TABLE 12-1 Memory Address Map for Microprocomputer

Component	Hexadecimal address	Address bus									
		10	9	8	7	6	5	4	3	2	1
RAM 1	0000–007F	0	0	0	x	x	x	x	x	x	x
RAM 2	0080–00FF	0	0	1	x	x	x	x	x	x	x
RAM 3	0100–017F	0	1	0	x	x	x	x	x	x	x
RAM 4	0180–01FF	0	1	1	x	x	x	x	x	x	x
ROM	0200–03FF	1	x	x	x	x	x	x	x	x	x

subdivided into groups of four bits each so that each group can be represented with a hexadecimal digit. The first hexadecimal digit represents lines 13 to 16 and is always 0. The next hexadecimal digit represents lines 9 to 12, but lines 11 and 12 are always 0. The range of hexadecimal addresses for each component is determined from the x's associated with it. These x's represent a binary number that can range from an all-0's to an all-1's value.

Memory Connection to CPU

RAM and ROM chips are connected to a CPU through the data and address buses. The low-order lines in the address bus select the byte within the chips and other lines in the address bus select a particular chip through its chip select inputs. The connection of memory chips to the CPU is shown in Fig. 12-4. This configuration gives a memory capacity of 512 bytes of RAM and 512 bytes of ROM. It implements the memory map of Table 12-1. Each RAM receives the seven low-order bits of the address bus to select one of 128 possible bytes. The particular RAM chip selected is determined from lines 8 and 9 in the address bus. This is done through a 2 × 4 decoder whose outputs go to the CS1 inputs in each RAM chip. Thus, when address lines 8 and 9 are equal to 00, the first RAM chip is selected. When 01, the second RAM chip is selected, and so on. The RD and WR outputs from the microprocessor are applied to the inputs of each RAM chip.

The selection between RAM and ROM is achieved through bus line 10. The RAMs are selected when the bit in this line is 0, and the ROM when the bit is 1. The other chip select input in the ROM is connected to the RD control line for the ROM chip to be enabled only during a read operation. Address bus lines 1 to 9 are applied to the input address of ROM without going through the decoder. This assigns addresses 0 to 511 to RAM and 512 to 1023 to ROM. The data bus of the ROM has only an output capability, whereas the data bus connected to the RAMs can transfer information in both directions.

The example just shown gives an indication of the interconnection complexity that can exist between memory chips and the CPU. The more chips that are connected, the more external decoders are required for selection among the chips. The designer must establish a memory map that assigns addresses to the various chips from which the required connections are determined.

12-3 Auxiliary Memory

The most common auxiliary memory devices used in computer systems are magnetic disks and tapes. Other components used, but not as frequently, are magnetic drums, magnetic bubble memory, and optical disks. To understand fully the physical mechanism of auxiliary memory devices one must have a knowledge of magnetics, electronics, and electromechanical systems. Al-

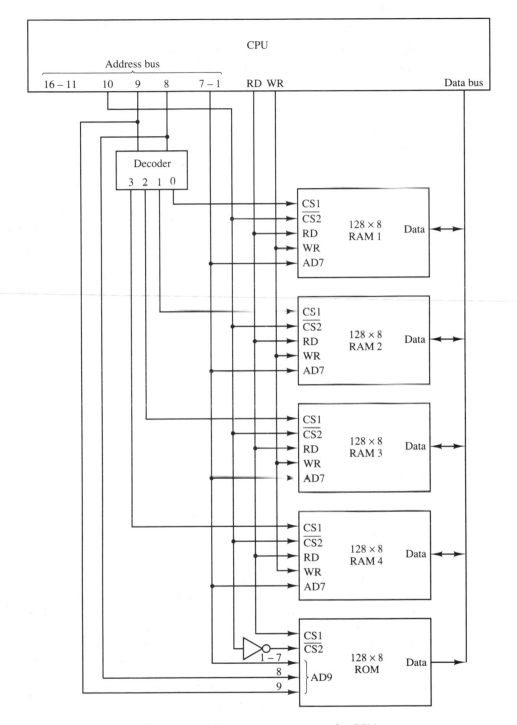

Figure 12-4 Memory connection to the CPU.

453

though the physical properties of these storage devices can be quite complex, their logical properties can be characterized and compared by a few parameters. The important characteristics of any device are its access mode, access time, transfer rate, capacity, and cost.

The average time required to reach a storage location in memory and obtain its contents is called the access time. In electromechanical devices with moving parts such as disks and tapes, the access time consists of a *seek* time required to position the read-write head to a location and a *transfer* time required to transfer data to or from the device. Because the seek time is usually much longer than the transfer time, auxiliary storage is organized in records or blocks. A record is a specified number of characters or words. Reading or writing is always done on entire records. The transfer rate is the number of characters or words that the device can transfer per second, after it has been positioned at the beginning of the record.

Magnetic drums and disks are quite similar in operation. Both consist of high-speed rotating surfaces coated with a magnetic recording medium. The rotating surface of the drum is a cylinder and that of the disk, a round flat plate. The recording surface rotates at uniform speed and is not started or stopped during access operations. Bits are recorded as magnetic spots on the surface as it passes a stationary mechanism called a *write head*. Stored bits are detected by a change in magnetic field produced by a recorded spot on the surface as it passes through a *read head*. The amount of surface available for recording in a disk is greater than in a drum of equal physical size. Therefore, more information can be stored on a disk than on a drum of comparable size. For this reason, disks have replaced drums in more recent computers.

Magnetic Disks

A magnetic disk is a circular plate constructed of metal or plastic coated with magnetized material. Often both sides of the disk are used and several disks may be stacked on one spindle with read/write heads available on each surface. All disks rotate together at high speed and are not stopped or started for access purposes. Bits are stored in the magnetized surface in spots along concentric circles called tracks. The tracks are commonly divided into sections called sectors. In most systems, the minimum quantity of information which can be transferred is a sector. The subdivision of one disk surface into tracks and sectors is shown in Fig. 12-5.

Some units use a single read/write head for each disk surface. In this type of unit, the track address bits are used by a mechanical assembly to move the head into the specified track position before reading or writing. In other disk systems, separate read/write heads are provided for each track in each surface. The address bits can then select a particular track electronically through a decoder circuit. This type of unit is more expensive and is found only in very large computer systems.

Permanent timing tracks are used in disks to synchronize the bits and

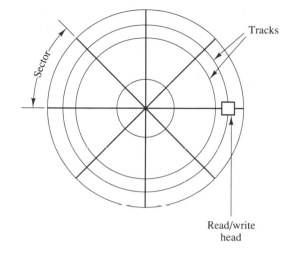

Figure 12-5 Magnetic disk.

recognize the sectors. A disk system is addressed by address bits that specify the disk number, the disk surface, the sector number and the track within the sector. After the read/write heads are positioned in the specified track, the system has to wait until the rotating disk reaches the specified sector under the read/write head. Information transfer is very fast once the beginning of a sector has been reached. Disks may have multiple heads and simultaneous transfer of bits from several tracks at the same time.

A track in a given sector near the circumference is longer than a track near the center of the disk. If bits are recorded with equal density, some tracks will contain more recorded bits than others. To make all the records in a sector of equal length, some disks use a variable recording density with higher density on tracks near the center than on tracks near the circumference. This equalizes the number of bits on all tracks of a given sector.

Disks that are permanently attached to the unit assembly and cannot be removed by the occasional user are called *hard disks*. A disk drive with removable disks is called a *floppy disk*. The disks used with a floppy disk drive are small removable disks made of plastic coated with magnetic recording material. There are two sizes commonly used, with diameters of 5.25 and 3.5 inches. The 3.5-inch disks are smaller and can store more data than can the 5.25-inch disks. Floppy disks are extensively used in personal computers as a medium for distributing software to computer users.

Magnetic Tape

A magnetic tape transport consists of the electrical, mechanical, and electronic components to provide the parts and control mechanism for a magnetic-tape unit. The tape itself is a strip of plastic coated with a magnetic recording medium. Bits are recorded as magnetic spots on the tape along several tracks. Usually, seven or nine bits are recorded simultaneously to form a character together with a parity bit. Read/write heads are mounted one in each track so that data can be recorded and read as a sequence of characters.

Magnetic tape units can be stopped, started to move forward or in reverse, or can be rewound. However, they cannot be started or stopped fast enough between individual characters. For this reason, information is recorded in blocks referred to as records. Gaps of unrecorded tape are inserted between records where the tape can be stopped. The tape starts moving while in a gap and attains its constant speed by the time it reaches the next record. Each record on tape has an identification bit pattern at the beginning and end. By reading the bit pattern at the beginning, the tape control identifies the record number. By reading the bit pattern at the end of the record, the control recognizes the beginning of a gap. A tape unit is addressed by specifying the record number and the number of characters in the record. Records may be of fixed or variable length.

12-4   Associative Memory

Many data-processing applications require the search of items in a table stored in memory. An assembler program searches the symbol address table in order to extract the symbol's binary equivalent. An account number may be searched in a file to determine the holder's name and account status. The established way to search a table is to store all items where they can be addressed in sequence. The search procedure is a strategy for choosing a sequence of addresses, reading the content of memory at each address, and comparing the information read with the item being searched until a match occurs. The number of accesses to memory depends on the location of the item and the efficiency of the search algorithm. Many search algorithms have been developed to minimize the number of accesses while searching for an item in a random or sequential access memory.

The time required to find an item stored in memory can be reduced considerably if stored data can be identified for access by the content of the data itself rather than by an address. A memory unit accessed by content is called an *associative memory* or *content addressable memory* (CAM). This type of memory is accessed simultaneously and in parallel on the basis of data content rather than by specific address or location. When a word is written in an associative memory, no address is given. The memory is capable of finding an empty unused location to store the word. When a word is to be read from an associative memory, the content of the word, or part of the word, is specified. The memory locates all words which match the specified content and marks them for reading.

Because of its organization, the associative memory is uniquely suited to do parallel searches by data association. Moreover, searches can be done on

content addressable memory

an entire word or on a specific field within a word. An associative memory is more expensive than a random access memory because each cell must have storage capability as well as logic circuits for matching its content with an external argument. For this reason, associative memories are used in applications where the search time is very critical and must be very short.

Hardware Organization

The block diagram of an associative memory is shown in Fig. 12-6. It consists of a memory array and logic for m words with n bits per word. The argument register A and key register K each have n bits, one for each bit of a word. The match register M has m bits, one for each memory word. Each word in memory is compared in parallel with the content of the argument register. The words that match the bits of the argument register set a corresponding bit in the match register. After the matching process, those bits in the match register that have been set indicate the fact that their corresponding words have been matched. Reading is accomplished by a sequential access to memory for those words whose corresponding bits in the match register have been set.

The key register provides a mask for choosing a particular field or key in the argument word. The entire argument is compared with each memory word if the key register contains all 1's. Otherwise, only those bits in the argument that have 1's in their corresponding position of the key register are compared. Thus the key provides a mask or identifying piece of information which

Figure 12-6   Block diagram of associative memory.

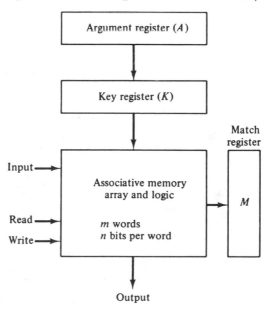

specifies how the reference to memory is made. To illustrate with a numerical example, suppose that the argument register A and the key register K have the bit configuration shown below. Only the three leftmost bits of A are compared with memory words because K has 1's in these positions.

A	101 111100	
K	111 000000	
Word 1	100 111100	no match
Word 2	101 000001	match

Word 2 matches the unmasked argument field because the three leftmost bits of the argument and the word are equal.

The relation between the memory array and external registers in an associative memory is shown in Fig. 12-7. The cells in the array are marked by the letter C with two subcripts. The first subscript gives the word number and the second specifies the bit position in the word. Thus cell C_{ij} is the cell for bit j in word i. A bit A_j in the argument register is compared with all the bits in column j of the array provided that $K_j = 1$. This is done for all columns $j = 1, 2, \ldots, n$. If a match occurs between all the unmasked bits of the argument and the bits in word i, the corresponding bit M_i in the match register is set to 1. If one or more unmasked bits of the argument and the word do not match, M_i is cleared to 0.

Figure 12-7   Associative memory of m word, n cells per word.

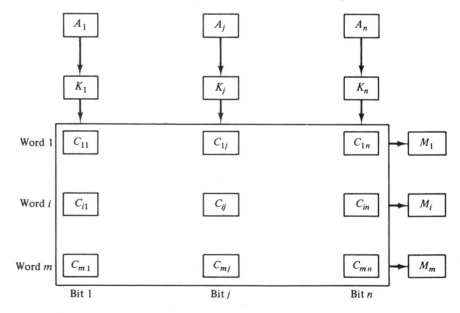

The internal organization of a typical cell C_{ij} is shown in Fig. 12-8. It consists of a flip-flop storage element F_{ij} and the circuits for reading, writing, and matching the cell. The input bit is transferred into the storage cell during a write operation. The bit stored is read out during a read operation. The match logic compares the content of the storage cell with the corresponding unmasked bit of the argument and provides an output for the decision logic that sets the bit in M_i.

Match Logic

The match logic for each word can be derived from the comparison algorithm for two binary numbers. First, we *neglect* the key bits and compare the argument in A with the bits stored in the cells of the words. Word i is equal to the argument in A if $A_j = F_{ij}$ for $j = 1, 2, \ldots, n$. Two bits are equal if they are both 1 or both 0. The equality of two bits can be expressed logically by the Boolean function

$$x_j = A_j F_{ij} + A_j' F_{ij}'$$

where $x_j = 1$ if the pair of bits in position j are equal; otherwise, $x_j = 0$.

For a word i to be equal to the argument in A we must have all x_j variables equal to 1. This is the condition for setting the corresponding match bit M_i to 1. The Boolean function for this condition is

$$M_i = x_1 x_2 x_3 \cdots x_n$$

and constitutes the AND operation of all pairs of matched bits in a word.

Figure 12-8 One cell of associative memory.

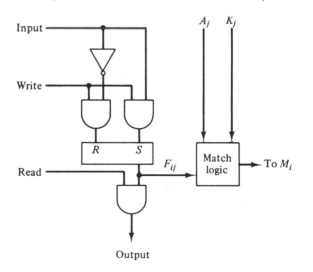

We now include the key bit K_j in the comparison logic. The requirement is that if $K_j = 0$, the corresponding bits of A_j and F_{ij} need no comparison. Only when $K_j = 1$ must they be compared. This requirement is achieved by ORing each term with K_j', thus:

$$x_j + K_j' = \begin{cases} x_j & \text{if } K_j = 1 \\ 1 & \text{if } K_j = 0 \end{cases}$$

When $K_j = 1$, we have $K_j' = 0$ and $x_j + 0 = x_j$. When $K_j = 0$, then $K_j' = 1$ and $x_j + 1 = 1$. A term $(x_j + K_j')$ will be in the 1 state if its pair of bits is not compared. This is necessary because each term is ANDed with all other terms so that an output of 1 will have no effect. The comparison of the bits has an effect only when $K_j = 1$.

The match logic for word i in an associative memory can now be expressed by the following Boolean function:

$$M_i = (x_1 + K_1')(x_2 + K_2')(x_3 + K_3') \cdots (x_n + K_n')$$

Each term in the expression will be equal to 1 if its corresponding $K_j = 0$. If $K_j = 1$, the term will be either 0 or 1 depending on the value of x_j. A match will occur and M_i will be equal to 1 if all terms are equal to 1.

If we substitute the original definition of x_j, the Boolean function above can be expressed as follows:

$$M_i = \prod_{j=1}^{n} (A_j F_{ij} + A_j' F_{ij}' + K_j')$$

where Π is a product symbol designating the AND operation of all n terms. We need m such functions, one for each word $i = 1, 2, 3, \ldots, m$.

The circuit for matching one word is shown in Fig. 12-9. Each cell requires two AND gates and one OR gate. The inverters for A_j and K_j are needed once for each column and are used for all bits in the column. The output of all OR gates in the cells of the same word go to the input of a common AND gate to generate the match signal for M_i. M_i will be logic 1 if a match occurs and 0 if no match occurs. Note that if the key register contains all 0's, output M_i will be a 1 irrespective of the value of A or the word. This occurrence must be avoided during normal operation.

Read Operation

If more than one word in memory matches the unmasked argument field, all the matched words will have 1's in the corresponding bit position of the match register. It is then necessary to scan the bits of the match register one at a time. The matched words are read in sequence by applying a read signal to each word line whose corresponding M_i bit is a 1.

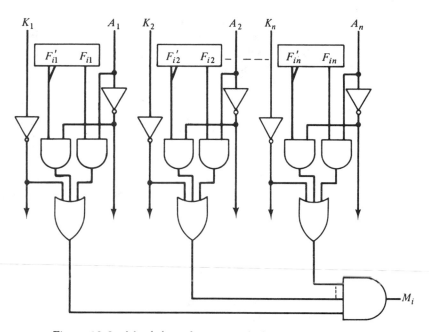

Figure 12-9 Match logic for one word of associative memory.

In most applications, the associative memory stores a table with no two identical items under a given key. In this case, only one word may match the unmasked argument field. By connecting output M_i directly to the read line in the same word position (instead of the M register), the content of the matched word will be presented automatically at the output lines and no special read command signal is needed. Furthermore, if we exclude words having a zero content, an all-zero output will indicate that no match occurred and that the searched item is not available in memory.

Write Operation

An associative memory must have a write capability for storing the information to be searched. Writing in an associative memory can take different forms, depending on the application. If the entire memory is loaded with new information at once prior to a search operation then the writing can be done by addressing each location in sequence. This will make the device a random-access memory for writing and a content addressable memory for reading. The advantage here is that the address for input can be decoded as in a random-access memory. Thus instead of having m address lines, one for each word in memory, the number of address lines can be reduced by the decoder to d lines, where $m = 2^d$.

If unwanted words have to be deleted and new words inserted one at a time, there is a need for a special register to distinguish between active and inactive words. This register, sometimes called a *tag register*, would have as many bits as there are words in the memory. For every active word stored in memory, the corresponding bit in the tag register is set to 1. A word is deleted from memory by clearing its tag bit to 0. Words are stored in memory by scanning the tag register until the first 0 bit is encountered. This gives the first available inactive word and a position for writing a new word. After the new word is stored in memory it is made active by setting its tag bit to 1. An unwanted word when deleted from memory can be cleared to all 0's if this value is used to specify an empty location. Moreover, the words that have a tag bit of 0 must be masked (together with the K_j bits) with the argument word so that only active words are compared.

12-5 Cache Memory

Analysis of a large number of typical programs has shown that the references to memory at any given interval of time tend to be confined within a few localized areas in memory. This phenomenon is known as the property of *locality of reference*. The reason for this property may be understood considering that a typical computer program flows in a straight-line fashion with program loops and subroutine calls encountered frequently. When a program loop is executed, the CPU repeatedly refers to the set of instructions in memory that constitute the loop. Every time a given subroutine is called, its set of instructions are fetched from memory. Thus loops and subroutines tend to localize the references to memory for fetching instructions. To a lesser degree, memory references to data also tend to be localized. Table-lookup procedures repeatedly refer to that portion in memory where the table is stored. Iterative procedures refer to common memory locations and array of numbers are confined within a local portion of memory. The result of all these observations is the locality of reference property, which states that over a short interval of time, the addresses generated by a typical program refer to a few localized areas of memory repeatedly, while the remainder of memory is accessed relatively infrequently.

If the active portions of the program and data are placed in a fast small memory, the average memory access time can be reduced, thus reducing the total execution time of the program. Such a fast small memory is referred to as a *cache memory*. It is placed between the CPU and main memory as illustrated in Fig. 12-1. The cache memory access time is less than the access time of main memory by a factor of 5 to 10. The cache is the fastest component in the memory hierarchy and approaches the speed of CPU components.

The fundamental idea of cache organization is that by keeping the most frequently accessed instructions and data in the fast cache memory, the average memory access time will approach the access time of the cache. Although the cache is only a small fraction of the size of main memory, a large fraction of memory requests will be found in the fast cache memory because of the locality of reference property of programs.

The basic operation of the cache is as follows. When the CPU needs to access memory, the cache is examined. If the word is found in the cache, it is read from the fast memory. If the word addressed by the CPU is not found in the cache, the main memory is accessed to read the word. A block of words containing the one just accessed is then transferred from main memory to cache memory. The block size may vary from one word (the one just accessed) to about 16 words adjacent to the one just accessed. In this manner, some data are transferred to cache so that future references to memory find the required words in the fast cache memory.

hit ratio

The performance of cache memory is frequently measured in terms of a quantity called *hit ratio*. When the CPU refers to memory and finds the word in cache, it is said to produce a *hit*. If the word is not found in cache, it is in main memory and it counts as a *miss*. The ratio of the number of hits divided by the total CPU references to memory (hits plus misses) is the hit ratio. The hit ratio is best measured experimentally by running representative programs in the computer and measuring the number of hits and misses during a given interval of time. Hit ratios of 0.9 and higher have been reported. This high ratio verifies the validity of the locality of reference property.

The average memory access time of a computer system can be improved considerably by use of a cache. If the hit ratio is high enough so that most of the time the CPU accesses the cache instead of main memory, the average access time is closer to the access time of the fast cache memory. For example, a computer with cache access time of 100 ns, a main memory access time of 1000 ns, and a hit ratio of 0.9 produces an average access time of 200 ns. This is a considerable improvement over a similar computer without a cache memory, whose access time is 1000 ns.

mapping

The basic characteristic of cache memory is its fast access time. Therefore, very little or no time must be wasted when searching for words in the cache. The transformation of data from main memory to cache memory is referred to as a *mapping* process. Three types of mapping procedures are of practical interest when considering the organization of cache memory:

1. Associative mapping
2. Direct mapping
3. Set-associative mapping

To help in the discussion of these three mapping procedures we will use a specific example of a memory organization as shown in Fig. 12-10. The main memory can store 32K words of 12 bits each. The cache is capable of storing 512 of these words at any given time. For every word stored in cache, there is

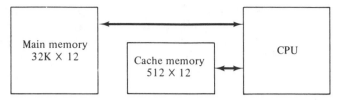

Figure 12-10 Example of cache memory.

a duplicate copy in main memory. The CPU communicates with both memories. It first sends a 15-bit address to cache. If there is a hit, the CPU accepts the 12-bit data from cache. If there is a miss, the CPU reads the word from main memory and the word is then transferred to cache.

Associative Mapping

The fastest and most flexible cache organization uses an associative memory. This organization is illustrated in Fig. 12-11. The associative memory stores both the address and content (data) of the memory word. This permits any location in cache to store any word from main memory. The diagram shows three words presently stored in the cache. The address value of 15 bits is shown as a five-digit octal number and its corresponding 12-bit word is shown as a four-digit octal number. A CPU address of 15 bits is placed in the argument register and the associative memory is searched for a matching address. If the

Figure 12-11 Associative mapping cache (all numbers in octal).

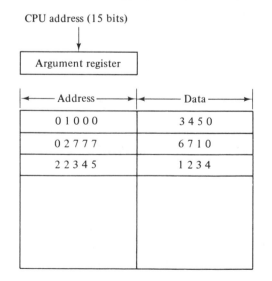

CPU address (15 bits)

Argument register

Address	Data
0 1 0 0 0	3 4 5 0
0 2 7 7 7	6 7 1 0
2 2 3 4 5	1 2 3 4

address is found, the corresponding 12-bit data is read and sent to the CPU. If no match occurs, the main memory is accessed for the word. The address–data pair is then transferred to the associative cache memory. If the cache is full, an address–data pair must be displaced to make room for a pair that is needed and not presently in the cache. The decision as to what pair is replaced is determined from the replacement algorithm that the designer chooses for the cache. A simple procedure is to replace cells of the cache in round-robin order whenever a new word is requested from main memory. This constitutes a first-in first-out (FIFO) replacement policy.

Direct Mapping

tag field

Associative memories are expensive compared to random-access memories because of the added logic associated with each cell. The possibility of using a random-access memory for the cache is investigated in Fig. 12-12. The CPU address of 15 bits is divided into two fields. The nine least significant bits constitute the *index* field and the remaining six bits form the *tag* field. The figure shows that main memory needs an address that includes both the tag and the index bits. The number of bits in the index field is equal to the number of address bits required to access the cache memory.

In the general case, there are 2^k words in cache memory and 2^n words in main memory. The n-bit memory address is divided into two fields: k bits for the index field and $n - k$ bits for the tag field. The direct mapping cache organization uses the n-bit address to access the main memory and the k-bit index to access the cache. The internal organization of the words in the cache memory is as shown in Fig. 12-13(b). Each word in cache consists of the data word and its associated tag. When a new word is first brought into the cache, the tag bits are stored alongside the data bits. When the CPU generates a memory request, the index field is used for the address to access the cache. The

Figure 12-12 Addressing relationships between main and cache memories.

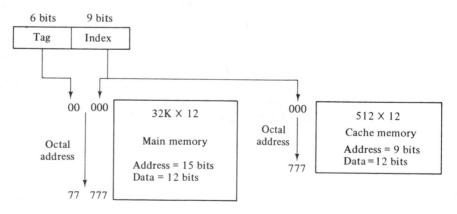

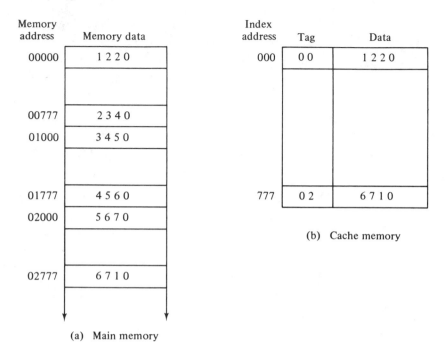

(a) Main memory

Figure 12-13 Direct mapping cache organization.

tag field of the CPU address is compared with the tag in the word read from the cache. If the two tags match, there is a hit and the desired data word is in cache. If there is no match, there is a miss and the required word is read from main memory. It is then stored in the cache together with the new tag, replacing the previous value. The disadvantage of direct mapping is that the hit ratio can drop considerably if two or more words whose addresses have the same index but different tags are accessed repeatedly. However, this possibility is minimized by the fact that such words are relatively far apart in the address range (multiples of 512 locations in this example.)

To see how the direct-mapping organization operates, consider the numerical example shown in Fig. 12-13. The word at address zero is presently stored in the cache (index = 000, tag = 00, data = 1220). Suppose that the CPU now wants to access the word at address 02000. The index address is 000, so it is used to access the cache. The two tags are then compared. The cache tag is 00 but the address tag is 02, which does not produce a match. Therefore, the main memory is accessed and the data word 5670 is transferred to the CPU. The cache word at index address 000 is then replaced with a tag of 02 and data of 5670.

The direct-mapping example just described uses a block size of one word. The same organization but using a block size of 8 words is shown in Fig. 12-14.

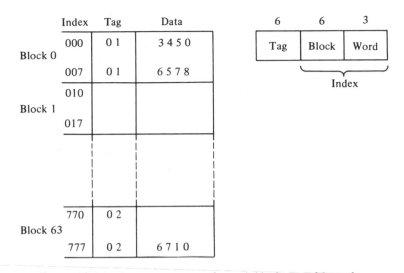

Figure 12-14 Direct mapping cache with block size of 8 words.

The index field is now divided into two parts: the block field and the word field. In a 512-word cache there are 64 blocks of 8 words each, since $64 \times 8 = 512$. The block number is specified with a 6-bit field and the word within the block is specified with a 3-bit field. The tag field stored within the cache is common to all eight words of the same block. Every time a miss occurs, an entire block of eight words must be transferred from main memory to cache memory. Although this takes extra time, the hit ratio will most likely improve with a larger block size because of the sequential nature of computer programs.

Set-Associative Mapping

It was mentioned previously that the disadvantage of direct mapping is that two words with the same index in their address but with different tag values cannot reside in cache memory at the same time. A third type of cache organization, called set-associative mapping, is an improvement over the direct-mapping organization in that each word of cache can store two or more words of memory under the same index address. Each data word is stored together with its tag and the number of tag–data items in one word of cache is said to form a set. An example of a set-associative cache organization for a set size of two is shown in Fig. 12-15. Each index address refers to two data words and their associated tags. Each tag requires six bits and each data word has 12 bits, so the word length is $2(6 + 12) = 36$ bits. An index address of nine bits can accommodate 512 words. Thus the size of cache memory is 512×36. It can accommodate 1024 words of main memory since each word of cache contains two data words. In general, a set-associative cache of set size k will accommodate k words of main memory in each word of cache.

Index	Tag	Data	Tag	Data
000	0 1	3 4 5 0	0 2	5 6 7 0
777	0 2	6 7 1 0	0 0	2 3 4 0

Figure 12-15 Two-way set-associative mapping cache.

The octal numbers listed in Fig. 12-15 are with reference to the main memory contents illustrated in Fig. 12-13(a). The words stored at addresses 01000 and 02000 of main memory are stored in cache memory at index address 000. Similarly, the words at addresses 02777 and 00777 are stored in cache at index address 777. When the CPU generates a memory request, the index value of the address is used to access the cache. The tag field of the CPU address is then compared with both tags in the cache to determine if a match occurs. The comparison logic is done by an associative search of the tags in the set similar to an associative memory search: thus the name "set-associative." The hit ratio will improve as the set size increases because more words with the same index but different tags can reside in cache. However, an increase in the set size increases the number of bits in words of cache and requires more complex comparison logic.

replacement algorithms

When a miss occurs in a set-associative cache and the set is full, it is necessary to replace one of the tag-data items with a new value. The most common replacement algorithms used are: random replacement, first-in, first-out (FIFO), and least recently used (LRU). With the random replacement policy the control chooses one tag–data item for replacement at random. The FIFO procedure selects for replacement the item that has been in the set the longest. The LRU algorithm selects for replacement the item that has been least recently used by the CPU. Both FIFO and LRU can be implemented by adding a few extra bits in each word of cache.

Writing into Cache

An important aspect of cache organization is concerned with memory write requests. When the CPU finds a word in cache during a read operation, the main memory is not involved in the transfer. However, if the operation is a write, there are two ways that the system can proceed.

write-through

The simplest and most commonly used procedure is to update main memory with every memory write operation, with cache memory being updated in parallel if it contains the word at the specified address. This is called the *write-through* method. This method has the advantage that main memory always contains the same data as the cache. This characteristic is important in systems with direct memory access transfers. It ensures that the data residing in main memory are valid at all times so that an I/O device communicating through DMA would receive the most recent updated data.

write-back

The second procedure is called the *write-back* method. In this method only the cache location is updated during a write operation. The location is then marked by a flag so that later when the word is removed from the cache it is copied into main memory. The reason for the write-back method is that during the time a word resides in the cache, it may be updated several times; however, as long as the word remains in the cache, it does not matter whether the copy in main memory is out of date, since requests from the word are filled from the cache. It is only when the word is displaced from the cache that an accurate copy need be rewritten into main memory. Analytical results indicate that the number of memory writes in a typical program ranges between 10 and 30 percent of the total references to memory.

Cache Initialization

One more aspect of cache organization that must be taken into consideration is the problem of initialization. The cache is initialized when power is applied to the computer or when the main memory is loaded with a complete set of programs from auxiliary memory. After initialization the cache is considered to be empty, but in effect it contains some nonvalid data. It is customary to include with each word in cache a *valid bit* to indicate whether or not the word contains valid data.

valid bit

The cache is initialized by clearing all the valid bits to 0. The valid bit of a particular cache word is set to 1 the first time this word is loaded from main memory and stays set unless the cache has to be initialized again. The introduction of the valid bit means that a word in cache is not replaced by another word unless the valid bit is set to 1 and a mismatch of tags occurs. If the valid bit happens to be 0, the new word automatically replaces the invalid data. Thus the initialization condition has the effect of forcing misses from the cache until it fills with valid data.

12-6 Virtual Memory

In a memory hierarchy system, programs and data are first stored in auxiliary memory. Portions of a program or data are brought into main memory as they are needed by the CPU. *Virtual memory* is a concept used in some large computer systems that permit the user to construct programs as though a large memory space were available, equal to the totality of auxiliary memory. Each address that is referenced by the CPU goes through an address mapping from the so-called virtual address to a physical address in main memory. Virtual memory is used to give programmers the illusion that they have a very large memory at their disposal, even though the computer actually has a relatively small main memory. A virtual memory system provides a mechanism for translating program-generated addresses into correct main memory locations. This is done dynamically, while programs are being executed in the CPU. The translation or mapping is handled automatically by the hardware by means of a mapping table.

Address Space and Memory Space

address space
memory space

An address used by a programmer will be called a *virtual address*, and the set of such addresses the *address space*. An address in main memory is called a *location* or *physical address*. The set of such locations is called the *memory space*. Thus the address space is the set of addresses generated by programs as they reference instructions and data; the memory space consists of the actual main memory locations directly addressable for processing. In most computers the address and memory spaces are identical. The address space is allowed to be larger than the memory space in computers with virtual memory.

As an illustration, consider a computer with a main-memory capacity of 32K words (K = 1024). Fifteen bits are needed to specify a physical address in memory since $32K = 2^{15}$. Suppose that the computer has available auxiliary memory for storing $2^{20} = 1024K$ words. Thus auxiliary memory has a capacity for storing information equivalent to the capacity of 32 main memories. Denoting the address space by N and the memory space by M, we then have for this example $N = 1024K$ and $M = 32K$.

In a multiprogram computer system, programs and data are transferred to and from auxiliary memory and main memory based on demands imposed by the CPU. Suppose that program 1 is currently being executed in the CPU. Program 1 and a portion of its associated data are moved from auxiliary memory into main memory as shown in Fig. 12-16. Portions of programs and data need not be in contiguous locations in memory since information is being moved in and out, and empty spaces may be available in scattered locations in memory.

In a virtual memory system, programmers are told that they have the total address space at their disposal. Moreover, the address field of the instruction code has a sufficient number of bits to specify all virtual addresses. In our example, the address field of an instruction code will consist of 20 bits but physical memory addresses must be specified with only 15 bits. Thus CPU will reference instructions and data with a 20-bit address, but the information at this address must be taken from physical memory because access to auxiliary storage for individual words will be prohibitively long. (Remember that for

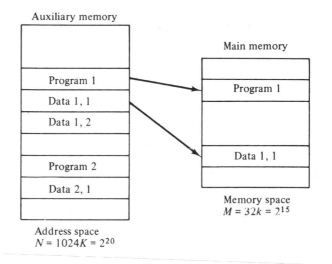

Figure 12-16 Relation between address and memory space in a virtual memory system.

efficient transfers, auxiliary storage moves an entire record to the main memory.) A table is then needed, as shown in Fig. 12-17, to map a virtual address of 20 bits to a physical address of 15 bits. The mapping is a dynamic operation, which means that every address is translated immediately as a word is referenced by CPU.

The mapping table may be stored in a separate memory as shown in Fig. 12-17 or in main memory. In the first case, an additional memory unit is required as well as one extra memory access time. In the second case, the table

Figure 12-17 Memory table for mapping a virtual address.

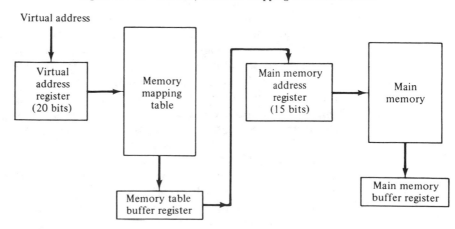

takes space from main memory and two accesses to memory are required with the program running at half speed. A third alternative is to use an associative memory as explained below.

Address Mapping Using Pages

The table implementation of the address mapping is simplified if the information in the address space and the memory space are each divided into groups of fixed size. The physical memory is broken down into groups of equal size *pages and blocks* called *blocks*, which may range from 64 to 4096 words each. The term *page* refers to groups of address space of the same size. For example, if a page or block consists of 1K words, then, using the previous example, address space is divided into 1024 pages and main memory is divided into 32 blocks. Although both a page and a block are split into groups of 1K words, a page refers to the organization of address space, while a block refers to the organization of memory space. The programs are also considered to be split into pages. Portions of programs are moved from auxiliary memory to main memory in *page frame* records equal to the size of a page. The term "page frame" is sometimes used to denote a block.

Consider a computer with an address space of 8K and a memory space of 4K. If we split each into groups of 1K words we obtain eight pages and four blocks as shown in Fig. 12-18. At any given time, up to four pages of address space may reside in main memory in any one of the four blocks.

The mapping from address space to memory space is facilitated if each virtual address is considered to be represented by two numbers: a page number address and a line within the page. In a computer with 2^p words per page, p bits are used to specify a line address and the remaining high-order bits of the virtual address specify the page number. In the example of Fig. 12-18, a virtual address has 13 bits. Since each page consists of $2^{10} = 1024$ words, the high-order three bits of a virtual address will specify one of the eight pages and the low-order 10 bits give the line address within the page. Note that the line address in address space and memory space is the same; the only mapping required is from a page number to a block number.

The organization of the memory mapping table in a paged system is shown in Fig. 12-19. The memory-page table consists of eight words, one for each page. The address in the page table denotes the page number and the content of the word gives the block number where that page is stored in main memory. The table shows that pages 1, 2, 5, and 6 are now available in main memory in blocks 3, 0, 1, and 2, respectively. A presence bit in each location indicates whether the page has been transferred from auxiliary memory into main memory. A 0 in the presence bit indicates that this page is not available in main memory. The CPU references a word in memory with a virtual address of 13 bits. The three high-order bits of the virtual address specify a page number and also an address for the memory-page table. The content of the

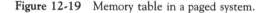

Figure 12-18 Address space and memory space split into groups of 1K words.

word in the memory page table at the page number address is read out into the memory table buffer register. If the presence bit is a 1, the block number thus read is transferred to the two high-order bits of the main memory address register. The line number from the virtual address is transferred into the 10 low-order bits of the memory address register. A read signal to main memory

Figure 12-19 Memory table in a paged system.

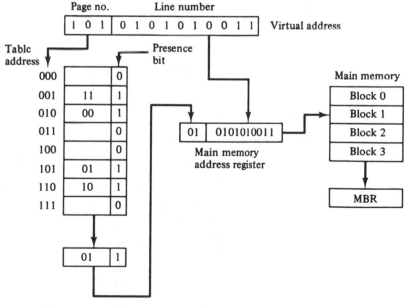

transfers the content of the word to the main memory buffer register ready to be used by the CPU. If the presence bit in the word read from the page table is 0, it signifies that the content of the word referenced by the virtual address does not reside in main memory. A call to the operating system is then generated to fetch the required page from auxiliary memory and place it into main memory before resuming computation.

Associative Memory Page Table

A random-access memory page table is inefficient with respect to storage utilization. In the example of Fig. 12-19 we observe that eight words of memory are needed, one for each page, but at least four words will always be marked empty because main memory cannot accommodate more than four blocks. In general, a system with n pages and m blocks would require a memory-page table of n locations of which up to m blocks will be marked with block numbers and all others will be empty. As a second numerical example, consider an address space of 1024K words and memory space of 32K words. If each page or block contains 1K words, the number of pages is 1024 and the number of blocks 32. The capacity of the memory-page table must be 1024 words and only 32 locations may have a presence bit equal to 1. At any given time, at least 992 locations will be empty and not in use.

A more efficient way to organize the page table would be to construct it with a number of words equal to the number of blocks in main memory. In this way the size of the memory is reduced and each location is fully utilized. This method can be implemented by means of an associative memory with each word in memory containing a page number together with its corresponding

Figure 12-20   An associative memory page table.

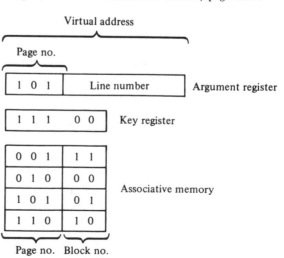

block number. The page field in each word is compared with the page number in the virtual address. If a match occurs, the word is read from memory and its corresponding block number is extracted.

Consider again the case of eight pages and four blocks as in the example of Fig. 12-19. We replace the random access memory-page table with an associative memory of four words as shown in Fig. 12-20. Each entry in the associative memory array consists of two fields. The first three bits specify a field for storing the page number. The last two bits constitute a field for storing the block number. The virtual address is placed in the argument register. The page number bits in the argument register are compared with all page numbers in the page field of the associative memory. If the page number is found, the 5-bit word is read out from memory. The corresponding block number, being in the same word, is transferred to the main memory address register. If no match occurs, a call to the operating system is generated to bring the required page from auxiliary memory.

Page Replacement

A virtual memory system is a combination of hardware and software techniques. The memory management software system handles all the software operations for the efficient utilization of memory space. It must decide (1) which page in main memory ought to be removed to make room for a new page, (2) when a new page is to be transferred from auxiliary memory to main memory, and (3) where the page is to be placed in main memory. The hardware mapping mechanism and the memory management software together constitute the architecture of a virtual memory.

page fault

When a program starts execution, one or more pages are transferred into main memory and the page table is set to indicate their position. The program is executed from main memory until it attempts to reference a page that is still in auxiliary memory. This condition is called *page fault*. When page fault occurs, the execution of the present program is suspended until the required page is brought into main memory. Since loading a page from auxiliary memory to main memory is basically an I/O operation, the operating system assigns this task to the I/O processor. In the meantime, control is transferred to the next program in memory that is waiting to be processed in the CPU. Later, when the memory block has been assigned and the transfer completed, the original program can resume its operation.

When a page fault occurs in a virtual memory system, it signifies that the page referenced by the CPU is not in main memory. A new page is then transferred from auxiliary memory to main memory. If main memory is full, it would be necessary to remove a page from a memory block to make room for the new page. The policy for choosing pages to remove is determined from the replacement algorithm that is used. The goal of a replacement policy is to try to remove the page least likely to be referenced in the immediate future.

Two of the most common replacement algorithms used are the *first-in*,

FIFO

first-out (FIFO) and the *least recently used* (LRU). The FIFO algorithm selects for replacement the page that has been in memory the longest time. Each time a page is loaded into memory, its identification number is pushed into a FIFO stack. FIFO will be full whenever memory has no more empty blocks. When a new page must be loaded, the page least recently brought in is removed. The page to be removed is easily determined because its identification number is at the top of the FIFO stack. The FIFO replacement policy has the advantage of being easy to implement. It has the disadvantage that under certain circumstances pages are removed and loaded from memory too frequently.

LRU

The LRU policy is more difficult to implement but has been more attractive on the assumption that the least recently used page is a better candidate for removal than the least recently loaded page as in FIFO. The LRU algorithm can be implemented by associating a counter with every page that is in main memory. When a page is referenced, its associated counter is set to zero. At fixed intervals of time, the counters associated with all pages presently in memory are incremented by 1. The least recently used page is the page with the highest count. The counters are often called *aging registers*, as their count indicates their age, that is, how long ago their associated pages have been referenced.

12-7   Memory Management Hardware

In a multiprogramming environment where many programs reside in memory it becomes necessary to move programs and data around the memory, to vary the amount of memory in use by a given program, and to prevent a program from changing other programs. The demands on computer memory brought about by multiprogramming have created the need for a memory management system. A memory management system is a collection of hardware and software procedures for managing the various programs residing in memory. The memory management software is part of an overall operating system available in many computers. Here we are concerned with the hardware unit associated with the memory management system.

The basic components of a memory management unit are:

1. A facility for dynamic storage relocation that maps logical memory references into physical memory addresses

2. A provision for sharing common programs stored in memory by different users

3. Protection of information against unauthorized access between users and preventing users from changing operating system functions

The dynamic storage relocation hardware is a mapping process similar to the paging system described in Sec. 12-6. The fixed page size used in the virtual memory system causes certain difficulties with respect to program size and the logical structure of programs. It is more convenient to divide programs and data into logical parts called segments. A *segment* is a set of logically related instructions or data elements associated with a given name. Segments may be generated by the programmer or by the operating system. Examples of segments are a subroutine, an array of data, a table of symbols, or a user's program.

segment

The sharing of common programs is an integral part of a multiprogramming system. For example, several users wishing to compile their Fortran programs should be able to share a single copy of the compiler rather than each user having a separate copy in memory. Other system programs residing in memory are also shared by all users in a multiprogramming system without having to produce multiple copies.

The third issue in multiprogramming is protecting one program from unwanted interaction with another. An example of unwanted interaction is one user's unauthorized copying of another user's program. Another aspect of protection is concerned with preventing the occasional user from performing operating system functions and thereby interrupting the orderly sequence of operations in a computer installation. The secrecy of certain programs must be kept from unauthorized personnel to prevent abuses in the confidential activities of an organization.

logical address

The address generated by a segmented program is called a *logical address*. This is similar to a virtual address except that logical address space is associated with variable-length segments rather than fixed-length pages. The logical address may be larger than the physical memory address as in virtual memory, but it may also be equal, and sometimes even smaller than the length of the physical memory address. In addition to relocation information, each segment has protection information associated with it. Shared programs are placed in a unique segment in each user's logical address space so that a single physical copy can be shared. The function of the memory management unit is to map logical addresses into physical addresses similar to the virtual memory mapping concept.

Segmented-Page Mapping

It was already mentioned that the property of logical space is that it uses variable-length segments. The length of each segment is allowed to grow and contract according to the needs of the program being executed. One way of specifying the length of a segment is by associating with it a number of equal-size pages. To see how this is done, consider the logical address shown in Fig. 12-21. The logical address is partitioned into three fields. The segment field specifies a segment number. The page field specifies the page within the segment and the word field gives the specific word within the page. A page field of k bits can specify up to 2^k pages. A segment number may be associated

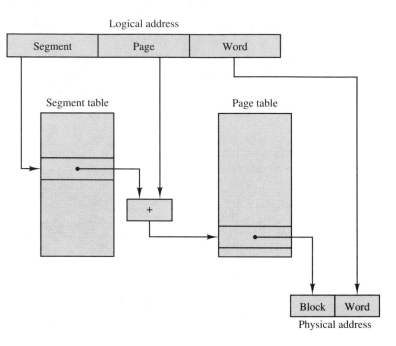

(a) Logical to physical address mapping

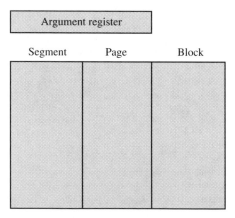

(b) Associative memory translation look-aside buffer (TLB)

Figure 12-21   Mapping in segmented-page memory management unit.

with just one page or with as many as 2^k pages. Thus the length of a segment would vary according to the number of pages that are assigned to it.

The mapping of the logical address into a physical address is done by means of two tables, as shown in Fig. 12-21(a). The segment number of the logical address specifies the address for the segment table. The entry in the segment table is a pointer address for a page table base. The page table base is added to the page number given in the logical address. The sum produces a pointer address to an entry in the page table. The value found in the page table provides the block number in physical memory. The concatenation of the block field with the word field produces the final physical mapped address.

The two mapping tables may be stored in two separate small memories or in main memory. In either case, a memory reference from the CPU will require three accesses to memory: one from the segment table, one from the page table, and the third from main memory. This would slow the system significantly when compared to a conventional system that requires only one reference to memory. To avoid this speed penalty, a fast associative memory is used to hold the most recently referenced table entries. (This type of memory is sometimes called a *translation lookaside buffer*, abbreviated TLB.) The first time a given block is referenced, its value together with the corresponding segment and page numbers are entered into the associative memory as shown in Fig. 12-21(b). Thus the mapping process is first attempted by associative search with the given segment and page numbers. If it succeeds, the mapping delay is only that of the associative memory. If no match occurs, the slower table mapping of Fig. 12-21(a) is used and the result transformed into the associative memory for future reference.

Numerical Example

A numerical example may clarify the operation of the memory management unit. Consider the 20-bit logical address specified in Fig. 12-22(a). The 4-bit segment number specifies one of 16 possible segments. The 8-bit page number can specify up to 256 pages, and the 8-bit word field implies a page size of 256 words. This configuration allows each segment to have any number of pages up to 256. The smallest possible segment will have one page or 256 words. The largest possible segment will have 256 pages, for a total of $256 \times 256 = 64K$ words.

The physical memory shown in Fig. 12-22(b) consists of 2^{20} words of 32 bits each. The 20-bit address is divided into two fields: a 12-bit block number and an 8-bit word number. Thus, physical memory is divided into 4096 blocks of 256 words each. A page in a logical address has a corresponding block in physical memory. Note that both the logical and physical address have 20 bits. In the absence of a memory management unit, the 20-bit address from the CPU can be used to access physical memory directly.

Consider a program loaded into memory that requires five pages. The operating system may assign to this program segment 6 and pages 0 through 4, as shown in Fig. 12-23(a). The total logical address range for the program is from hexadecimal 60000 to 604FF. When the program is loaded into physical memory, it is distributed among five blocks in physical memory where the operating system finds empty spaces. The correspondence between each memory block and logical page number is then entered in a table as shown in

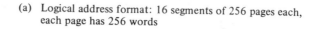

(a) Logical address format: 16 segments of 256 pages each,
each page has 256 words

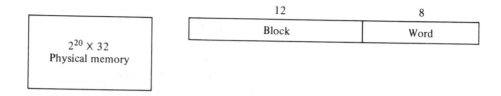

(b) Physical address format: 4096 blocks of 256 words each,
each word has 32 bits

Figure 12-22   An example of logical and physical addresses.

Fig. 12-23(b). The information from this table is entered in the segment and page tables as shown in Fig. 12-24(a).

Now consider the specific logical address given in Fig. 12-24. The 20-bit address is listed as a five-digit hexadecimal number. It refers to word number 7E of page 2 in segment 6. The base of segment 6 in the page table is at address 35. Segment 6 has associated with it five pages, as shown in the page table at addresses 35 through 39. Page 2 of segment 6 is at address $35 + 2 = 37$. The physical memory block is found in the page table to be 019. Word 7E in block 19 gives the 20-bit physical address 0197E. Note that page 0 of segment 6 maps into block 12 and page 1 maps into block 0. The associative memory in Fig.

Figure 12-23   Example of logical and physical memory address assignment.

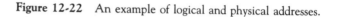

Hexadecimal address	Page number
60000	Page 0
60100	Page 1
60200	Page 2
60300	Page 3
60400 604FF	Page 4

Segment	Page	Block
6	00	012
6	01	000
6	02	019
6	03	053
6	04	A61

(a) Logical address assignment

(b) Segment-page versus memory block assignment

Logical address (in haxadecimal)

6	02	7E

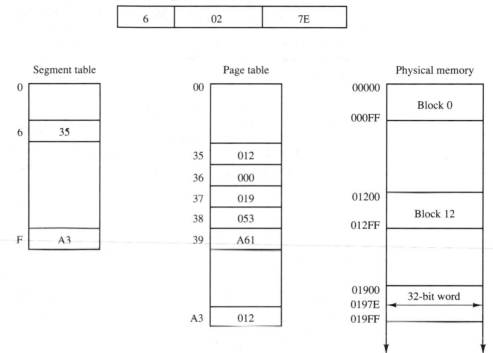

(a) Segment and page table mapping

Segment	Page	Block
6	02	019
6	04	A61

(b) Associative memory (TLB)

Figure 12-24 Logical to physical memory mapping example (all numbers are in hexadecimal).

12-24(b) shows that pages 2 and 4 of segment 6 have been referenced previously and therefore their corresponding block numbers are stored in the associative memory.

From this example it should be evident that the memory management system can assign any number of pages to each segment. Each logical page can be mapped into any block in physical memory. Pages can move to different blocks in memory depending on memory space requirements. The only updating required is the change of the block number in the page table. Segments can grow or shrink independently without affecting each other. Different segments can use the same block of memory if it is required to share a program by many users. For example, block number 12 in physical memory can be assigned a second logical address F0000 through F00FF. This specifies segment number 15 and page 0, which maps to block 12 as shown in Fig. 12-24(a).

Memory Protection

Memory protection can be assigned to the physical address or the logical address. The protection of memory through the physical address can be done by assigning to each block in memory a number of protection bits that indicate the type of access allowed to its corresponding block. Every time a page is moved from one block to another it would be necessary to update the block protection bits. A much better place to apply protection is in the logical address space rather than the physical address space. This can be done by including protection information within the segment table or segment register of the memory management hardware.

The content of each entry in the segment table or a segment register is called a descriptor. A typical descriptor would contain, in addition to a base address field, one or two additional fields for protection purposes. A typical format for a segment descriptor is shown in Fig. 12-25. The base address field gives the base of the page table address in a segmented-page organization or the block base address in a segment register organization. This is the address used in mapping from a logical to the physical address. The length field gives the segment size by specifying the maximum number of pages assigned to the segment. The length field is compared against the page number in the logical address. A size violation occurs if the page number falls outside the segment length boundary. Thus a given program and its data cannot access memory not assigned to it by the operating system.

The protection field in a segment descriptor specifies the access rights available to the particular segment. In a segmented-page organization, each

Figure 12-25 Format of a typical segment descriptor.

Base address	Length	Protection

entry in the page table may have its own protection field to describe the access rights of each page. The protection information is set into the descriptor by the master control program of the operating system. Some of the access rights of interest that are used for protecting the programs residing in memory are:

1. Full read and write privileges
2. Read only (write protection)
3. Execute only (program protection)
4. System only (operating system protection)

Full read and write privileges are given to a program when it is executing its own instructions. Write protection is useful for sharing system programs such as utility programs and other library routines. These system programs are stored in an area of memory where they can be shared by many users. They can be read by all programs, but no writing is allowed. This protects them from being changed by other programs.

The execute-only condition protects programs from being copied. It restricts the segment to be referenced only during the instruction fetch phase but not during the execute phase. Thus it allows the users to execute the segment program instructions but prevents them from reading the instructions as data for the purpose of copying their content.

Portions of the operating system will reside in memory at any given time. These system programs must be protected by making them inaccessible to unauthorized users. The operating system protection condition is placed in the descriptors of all operating system programs to prevent the occasional user from accessing operating system segments.

PROBLEMS

12-1.
    a. How many 128 × 8 RAM chips are needed to provide a memory capacity of 2048 bytes?
    b. How many lines of the address bus must be used to access 2048 bytes of memory? How many of these lines will be common to all chips?
    c. How many lines must be decoded for chip select? Specify the size of the decoders.

12-2. A computer uses RAM chips of 1024 × 1 capacity.
    a. How many chips are needed, and how should their address lines be connected to provide a memory capacity of 1024 bytes?
    b. How many chips are needed to provide a memory capacity of 16K bytes? Explain in words how the chips are to be connected to the address bus.

12-3. A ROM chip of 1024 × 8 bits has four select inputs and operates from a 5-volt power supply. How many pins are needed for the IC package? Draw a block diagram and label all input and output terminals in the ROM.

12-4. Extend the memory system of Fig. 12-4 to 4096 bytes of RAM and 4096 bytes of ROM. List the memory-address map and indicate what size decoders are needed.

12-5. A computer employs RAM chips of 256×8 and ROM chips of 1024×8. The computer system needs 2K bytes of RAM, 4K bytes of ROM, and four interface units, each with four registers. A memory-mapped I/O configuration is used. The two highest-order bits of the address bus are assigned 00 for RAM, 01 for ROM, and 10 for interface registers.
a. How many RAM and ROM chips are needed?
b. Draw a memory-address map for the system.
c. Give the address range in hexadecimal for RAM, ROM, and interface.

12-6. An 8-bit computer has a 16-bit address bus. The first 15 lines of the address are used to select a bank of 32K bytes of memory. The high-order bit of the address is used to select a register which receives the contents of the data bus. Explain how this configuration can be used to extend the memory capacity of the system to eight banks of 32K bytes each, for a total of 256K bytes of memory.

12-7. A magnetic disk system has the following parameters:

T_s = average time to position the magnetic head over a track

R = rotation speed of disk in revolutions per second

N_t = number of bits per track

N_s = number of bits per sector

Calculate the average time T_a that it will take to read one sector.

12-8. What is the transfer rate of an eight-track magnetic tape whose speed is 120 inches per second and whose density is 1600 bits per inch?

12-9. Obtain the complement function for the match logic of one word in an associative memory. In other words, show that M_i' is the sum of exclusive-OR functions. Draw the logic diagram for M_i' and terminate it with an inverter to obtain M_i.

12-10. Obtain the Boolean function for the match logic of one word in an associative memory taking into consideration a tag bit that indicates whether the word is active or inactive.

12-11. What additional logic is required to give a no-match result for a word in an associative memory when all key bits are zeros?

12-12. **a.** Draw the logic diagram of all the cells of one word in an associative memory. Include the read and write logic of Fig. 12-8 and the match logic of Fig. 12-9.
b. Draw the logic diagram of all cells along one vertical column (column j) in an associative memory. Include a common output line for all bits in the same column.

     c. From the diagrams in (a) and (b) show that if output M_i is connected to the *read* line of the same word, then the matched word will be read out, provided that only one word matches the masked argument.

12-13. Describe in words and by means of a block diagram how multiple matched words can be read out from an associative memory.

12-14. Derive the logic of one cell and of an entire word for an associative memory that has an output indicator when the unmasked argument is greater than (but not equal to) the word in the associative memory.

12-15. A two-way set associative cache memory uses blocks of four words. The cache can accommodate a total of 2048 words from main memory. The main memory size is 128K $\times$ 32.
     a. Formulate all pertinent information required to construct the cache memory.
     b. What is the size of the cache memory?

12-16. The access time of a cache memory is 100 ns and that of main memory 1000 ns. It is estimated that 80 percent of the memory requests are for read and the remaining 20 percent for write. The hit ratio for read accesses only is 0.9. A write-through procedure is used.
     a. What is the average access time of the system considering only memory read cycles?
     b. What is the average access time of the system for both read and write requests?
     c. What is the hit ratio taking into consideration the write cycles?

12-17. A four-way set-associative cache memory has four words in each set. A replacement procedure based on the least recently used (LRU) algorithm is implemented by means of 2-bit counters associated with each word in the set. A value in the range 0 to 3 is thus recorded for each word. When a hit occurs, the counter associated with the referenced word is set to 0, those counters with values originally lower than the referenced one are incremented by 1, and all others remain unchanged. If a miss occurs, the word with counter value 3 is removed, the new word is put in its place, and its counter is set to 0. The other three counters are incremented by 1. Show that this procedure works for the following sequence of word reference: A, B, C, D, B, E, D, A, C, E, C, E. (Start with A, B, C, D as the initial four words, with word A being the least recently used.)

12-18. A digital computer has a memory unit of 64K $\times$ 16 and a cache memory of 1K words. The cache uses direct mapping with a block size of four words.
     a. How many bits are there in the tag, index, block, and word fields of the address format?
     b. How many bits are there in each word of cache, and how are they divided into functions? Include a valid bit.
     c. How many blocks can the cache accommodate?

12-19. An address space is specified by 24 bits and the corresponding memory space by 16 bits.
     a. How many words are there in the address space?
     b. How many words are there in the memory space?

c. If a page consists of 2K words, how many pages and blocks are there in the system?

12-20. A virtual memory has a page size of 1K words. There are eight pages and four blocks. The associative memory page table contains the following entries:

Page	Block
0	3
1	1
4	2
6	0

Make a list of all virtual addresses (in decimal) that will cause a page fault if used by the CPU.

12-21. A virtual memory system has an address space of 8K words, a memory space of 4K words, and page and block sizes of 1K words (see Fig. 12-18). The following page reference changes occur during a given time interval. (Only page changes are listed. If the same page is referenced again, it is not listed twice.)

$$4 \quad 2 \quad 0 \quad 1 \quad 2 \quad 6 \quad 1 \quad 4 \quad 0 \quad 1 \quad 0 \quad 2 \quad 3 \quad 5 \quad 7$$

Determine the four pages that are resident in main memory after each page reference change if the replacement algorithm used is (a) FIFO; (b) LRU.

12-22. Determine the two logical addresses from Fig. 12-24(a) that will access physical memory at hexadecimal address 012AF.

12-23. The logical address space in a computer system consists of 128 segments. Each segment can have up to 32 pages of 4K words in each. Physical memory consists of 4K blocks of 4K words in each. Formulate the logical and physical address formats.

12-24. Give the binary number of the logical address formulated in Prob. 12-23 for segment 36 and word number 2000 in page 15.

REFERENCES

1. Baer, J. L., *Computer Systems Architecture*. Potomac, MD: Computer Science Press, 1980.

2. Dasgupta, S., *Computer Architecture: A Modern Synthesis*, Vol. 1. New York: John Wiley, 1989.

3. Gibson, G. A., *Computer Systems Concepts and Design*. Englewood Cliffs, NJ: Prentice Hall, 1991.

4. Hamacher, V. C., Z. G. Vranesic, and S. G. Zaky, *Computer Organization*, 3rd ed. New York: McGraw-Hill, 1990.

5. Hwang, K., and F. A. Briggs, *Computer Architecture and Parallel Processing*. New York: McGraw-Hill, 1984.

6. Kain, R., *Computer Architecture: Software and Hardware*, Vol. 1. Englewood Cliffs, NJ: Prentice Hall, 1989.

7. Langholz, G., J. Francioni, and A. Kandel, *Elements of Computer Organization*. Englewood Cliffs, NJ: Prentice Hall, 1989.

8. Murray, W. D., *Computer and Digital System Architecture*. Englewood Cliffs, NJ: Prentice Hall, 1990.

9. Patterson, D. A., and J. L. Hennessy, *Computer Architecture: A Quantitative Approach*. San Mateo, CA: Morgan Kaufmann Publishers, 1990.

10. Pollard, L. H., *Computer Design and Architecture*. Englewood Cliffs, NJ: Prentice Hall, 1990.

11. Stone, H. S. (ed.), *Introduction to Computer Architecture*, 2nd ed. Chicago: Science Research Associates, 1980.

CHAPTER THIRTEEN

Multiprocessors

IN THIS CHAPTER

13-1   Characteristics of Multiprocessors

A multiprocessor system is an interconnection of two or more CPUs with memory and input–output equipment. The term "processor" in *multiprocessor* can mean either a central processing unit (CPU) or an input–output processor (IOP). However, a system with a single CPU and one or more IOPs is usually not included in the definition of a multiprocessor system unless the IOP has computational facilities comparable to a CPU. As it is most commonly defined, a multiprocessor system implies the existence of multiple CPUs, although usually there will be one or more IOPs as well. As mentioned in Sec. 9-1, multiprocessors are classified as multiple instruction stream, multiple data stream (MIMD) systems.

MIMD

There are some similarities between multiprocessor and multicomputer systems since both support concurrent operations. However, there exists an important distinction between a system with multiple computers and a system with multiple processors. Computers are interconnected with each other by means of communication lines to form a *computer network*. The network consists of several autonomous computers that may or may not communicate with each other. A multiprocessor system is controlled by one operating system that provides interaction between processors and all the components of the system cooperate in the solution of a problem.

microprocessor

VLSI

Although some large-scale computers include two or more CPUs in their overall system, it is the emergence of the microprocessor that has been the major motivation for multiprocessor systems. The fact that microprocessors take very little physical space and are very inexpensive brings about the feasibility of interconnecting a large number of microprocessors into one composite system. Very-large-scale integrated circuit technology has reduced the cost of computer components to such a low level that the concept of applying multiple processors to meet system performance requirements has become an attractive design possibility.

Multiprocessing improves the reliability of the system so that a failure or error in one part has a limited effect on the rest of the system. If a fault causes one processor to fail, a second processor can be assigned to perform the functions of the disabled processor. The system as a whole can continue to function correctly with perhaps some loss in efficiency.

The benefit derived from a multiprocessor organization is an improved system performance. The system derives its high performance from the fact that computations can proceed in parallel in one of two ways.

1. Multiple independent jobs can be made to operate in parallel.
2. A single job can be partitioned into multiple parallel tasks.

An overall function can be partitioned into a number of tasks that each processor can handle individually. System tasks may be allocated to special-purpose processors whose design is optimized to perform certain types of processing efficiently. An example is a computer system where one processor performs the computations for an industrial process control while others monitor and control the various parameters, such as temperature and flow rate. Another example is a computer where one processor performs high-speed floating-point mathematical computations and another takes care of routine data-processing tasks.

Multiprocessing can improve performance by decomposing a program into parallel executable tasks. This can be achieved in one of two ways. The user can explicitly declare that certain tasks of the program be executed in parallel. This must be done prior to loading the program by specifying the parallel executable segments. Most multiprocessor manufacturers provide an operating system with programming language constructs suitable for specifying parallel processing. The other, more efficient way is to provide a compiler with multiprocessor software that can automatically detect parallelism in a user's program. The compiler checks for *data dependency* in the program. If a program depends on data generated in another part, the part yielding the needed data must be executed first. However, two parts of a program that do not use data generated by each can run concurrently. The parallelizing compiler checks the entire program to detect any possible data dependencies. These that have no data dependency are then considered for concurrent scheduling on different processors.

Multiprocessors are classified by the way their memory is organized. A multiprocessor system with common shared memory is classified as a *shared-memory* or *tightly coupled multiprocessor*. This does not preclude each processor from having its own local memory. In fact, most commercial tightly coupled multiprocessors provide a cache memory with each CPU. In addition, there is a global common memory that all CPUs can access. Information can therefore be shared among the CPUs by placing it in the common global memory.

tightly coupled

An alternative model of microprocessor is the *distributed-memory* or *loosely coupled* system. Each processor element in a loosely coupled system has its own private local memory. The processors are tied together by a switching scheme designed to route information from one processor to another through a message-passing scheme. The processors relay program and data to other processors in packets. A packet consists of an address, the data content, and some error detection code. The packets are addressed to a specific processor or taken by the first available processor, depending on the communication system used. Loosely coupled systems are most efficient when the interaction between tasks is minimal, whereas tightly coupled systems can tolerate a higher degree of interaction between tasks.

loosely coupled

13-2 Interconnection Structures

The components that form a multiprocessor system are CPUs, IOPs connected to input–output devices, and a memory unit that may be partitioned into a number of separate modules. The interconnection between the components can have different physical configurations, depending on the number of transfer paths that are available between the processors and memory in a shared memory system or among the processing elements in a loosely coupled system. There are several physical forms available for establishing an interconnection network. Some of these schemes are presented in this section:

1. Time-shared common bus
2. Multiport memory
3. Crossbar switch
4. Multistage switching network
5. Hypercube system

Time-Shared Common Bus

A common-bus multiprocessor system consists of a number of processors connected through a common path to a memory unit. A time-shared common bus for five processors is shown in Fig. 13-1. Only one processor can communicate with the memory or another processor at any given time. Transfer

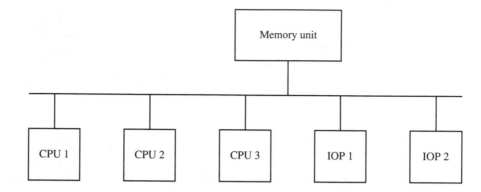

Figure 13-1 Time-shared common bus organization.

operations are conducted by the processor that is in control of the bus at the time. Any other processor wishing to initiate a transfer must first determine the availability status of the bus, and only after the bus becomes available can the processor address the destination unit to initiate the transfer. A command is issued to inform the destination unit what operation is to be performed. The receiving unit recognizes its address in the bus and responds to the control signals from the sender, after which the transfer is initiated. The system may exhibit transfer conflicts since one common bus is shared by all processors. These conflicts must be resolved by incorporating a bus controller that establishes priorities among the requesting units.

A single common-bus system is restricted to one transfer at a time. This means that when one processor is communicating with the memory, all other processors are either busy with internal operations or must be idle waiting for the bus. As a consequence, the total overall transfer rate within the system is limited by the speed of the single path. The processors in the system can be kept busy more often through the implementation of two or more independent buses to permit multiple simultaneous bus transfers. However, this increases the system cost and complexity.

A more economical implementation of a dual bus structure is depicted in Fig. 13-2. Here we have a number of local buses each connected to its own local memory and to one or more processors. Each local bus may be connected to a CPU, an IOP, or any combination of processors. A system bus controller links each local bus to a common system bus. The I/O devices connected to the local IOP, as well as the local memory, are available to the local processor. The memory connected to the common system bus is shared by all processors. If an IOP is connected directly to the system bus, the I/O devices attached to it may be made available to all processors. Only one processor can communicate

shared memory

with the shared memory and other common resources through the system bus at any given time. The other processors are kept busy communicating with their local memory and I/O devices. Part of the local memory may be designed

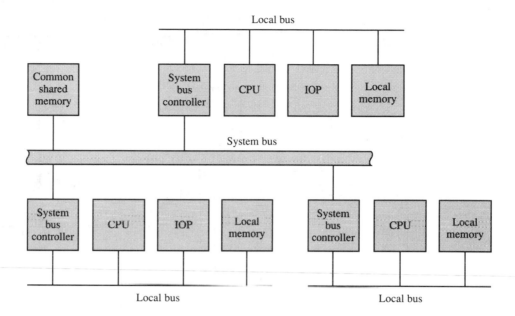

Figure 13-2 System bus structure for multiprocessors.

as a cache memory attached to the CPU (see Sec. 12-6). In this way, the average access time of the local memory can be made to approach the cycle time of the CPU to which it is attached.

Multiport Memory

A multiport memory system employs separate buses between each memory module and each CPU. This is shown in Fig. 13-3 for four CPUs and four memory modules (MMs). Each processor bus is connected to each memory module. A processor bus consists of the address, data, and control lines required to communicate with memory. The memory module is said to have four ports and each port accommodates one of the buses. The module must have internal control logic to determine which port will have access to memory at any given time. Memory access conflicts are resolved by assigning fixed priorities to each memory port. The priority for memory access associated with each processor may be established by the physical port position that its bus occupies in each module. Thus CPU 1 will have priority over CPU 2, CPU 2 will have priority over CPU 3, and CPU 4 will have the lowest priority.

The advantage of the multiport memory organization is the high transfer rate that can be achieved because of the multiple paths between processors and memory. The disadvantage is that it requires expensive memory control logic and a large number of cables and connectors. As a consequence, this intercon-

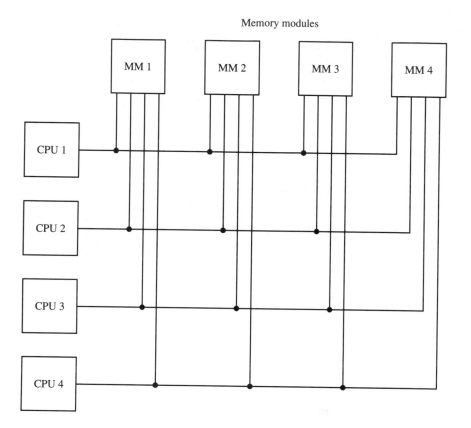

Figure 13-3 Multiport memory organization.

nection structure is usually appropriate for systems with a small number of processors.

Crossbar Switch

The crossbar switch organization consists of a number of crosspoints that are placed at intersections between processor buses and memory module paths. Figure 13-4 shows a crossbar switch interconnection between four CPUs and four memory modules. The small square in each crosspoint is a switch that determines the path from a processor to a memory module. Each switch point has control logic to set up the transfer path between a processor and memory. It examines the address that is placed in the bus to determine whether its particular module is being addressed. It also resolves multiple requests for access to the same memory module on a predetermined priority basis.

Figure 13-5 shows the functional design of a crossbar switch connected to one memory module. The circuit consists of multiplexers that select the data,

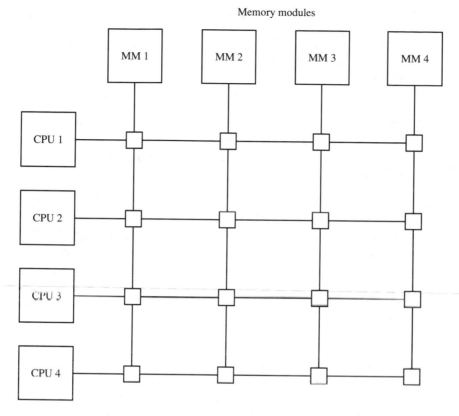

Memory modules

Figure 13-4 Crossbar switch.

Figure 13-5 Block diagram of crossbar switch.

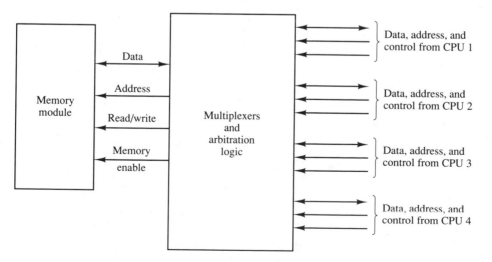

address, and control from one CPU for communication with the memory module. Priority levels are established by the arbitration logic to select one CPU when two or more CPUs attempt to access the same memory. The multiplexers are controlled with the binary code that is generated by a priority encoder within the arbitration logic.

A crossbar switch organization supports simultaneous transfers from all memory modules because there is a separate path associated with each module. However, the hardware required to implement the switch can become quite large and complex.

Multistage Switching Network

interchange switch

The basic component of a multistage network is a two-input, two-output interchange switch. As shown in Fig. 13-6, the 2 × 2 switch has two inputs, labeled *A* and *B*, and two outputs, labeled 0 and 1. There are control signals (not shown) associated with the switch that establish the interconnection between the input and output terminals. The switch has the capability of connecting input *A* to either of the outputs. Terminal *B* of the switch behaves in a similar fashion. The switch also has the capability to arbitrate between conflicting requests. If inputs *A* and *B* both request the same output terminal, only one of them will be connected; the other will be blocked.

Using the 2 × 2 switch as a building block, it is possible to build a multistage network to control the communication between a number of sources and destinations. To see how this is done, consider the binary tree shown in Fig. 13-7. The two processors P_1 and P_2 are connected through switches to eight memory modules marked in binary from 000 through 111. The path from a source to a destination is determined from the binary bits of the destination

Figure 13-6   Operation of a 2 × 2 interchange switch.

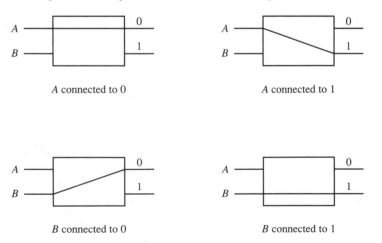

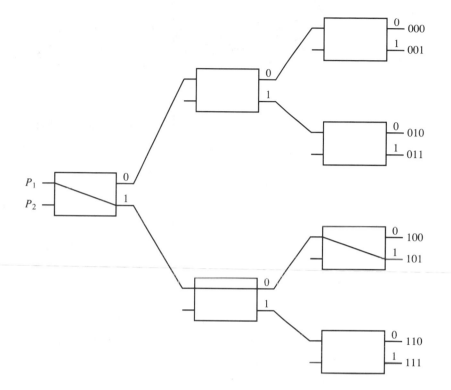

Figure 13-7 Binary tree with 2 × 2 switches.

number. The first bit of the destination number determines the switch output in the first level. The second bit specifies the output of the switch in the second level, and the third bit specifies the output of the switch in the third level. For example, to connect P_1 to memory 101, it is necessary to form a path from P_1 to output 1 in the first-level switch, output 0 in the second-level switch, and output 1 in the third-level switch. It is clear that either P_1 or P_2 can be connected to any one of the eight memories. Certain request patterns, however, cannot be satisfied simultaneously. For example, if P_1 is connected to one of the destinations 000 through 011, P_2 can be connected to only one of the destinations 100 through 111.

Many different topologies have been proposed for multistage switching networks to control processor–memory communication in a tightly coupled multiprocessor system or to control the communication between the processing elements in a loosely coupled system. One such topology is the omega *omega network* switching network shown in Fig. 13-8. In this configuration, there is exactly one path from each source to any particular destination. Some request patterns, however, cannot be connected simultaneously. For example, any two sources cannot be connected simultaneously to destinations 000 and 001.

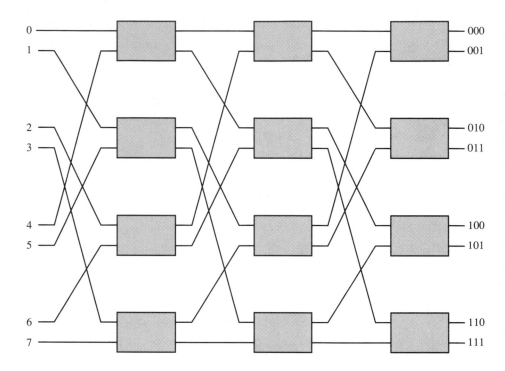

Figure 13-8 8 × 8 omega switching network.

A particular request is initiated in the switching network by the source, which sends a 3-bit pattern representing the destination number. As the binary pattern moves through the network, each level examines a different bit to determine the 2 × 2 switch setting. Level 1 inspects the most significant bit, level 2 inspects the middle bit, and level 3 inspects the least significant bit. When the request arrives on either input of the 2 × 2 switch, it is routed to the upper output if the specified bit is 0 or to the lower output if the bit is 1.

In a tightly coupled multiprocessor system, the source is a processor and the destination is a memory module. The first pass through the network sets up the path. Succeeding passes are used to transfer the address into memory and then transfer the data in either direction, depending on whether the request is a read or a write. In a loosely coupled multiprocessor system, both the source and destination are processing elements. After the path is established, the source processor transfers a message to the destination processor.

Hypercube Interconnection

The hypercube or binary n-cube multiprocessor structure is a loosely coupled system composed of $N = 2^n$ processors interconnected in an n-dimensional binary cube. Each processor forms a *node* of the cube. Although it is customary to refer to each node as having a processor, in effect it contains not only a CPU but also local memory and I/O interface. Each processor has direct communication paths to n other neighbor processors. These paths correspond to the *edges* of the cube. There are 2^n distinct n-bit binary addresses that can be assigned to the processors. Each processor address differs from that of each of its n neighbors by exactly one bit position.

Figure 13-9 shows the hypercube structure for $n = 1, 2$, and 3. A one-cube structure has $n = 1$ and $2^n = 2$. It contains two processors interconnected by a single path. A two-cube structure has $n = 2$ and $2^n = 4$. It contains four nodes interconnected as a square. A three-cube structure has eight nodes interconnected as a cube. An n-cube structure has 2^n nodes with a processor residing in each node. Each node is assigned a binary address in such a way that the addresses of two neighbors differ in exactly one bit position. For example, the three neighbors of the node with address 100 in a three-cube structure are 000, 110, and 101. Each of these binary numbers differs from address 100 by one bit value.

Routing messages through an n-cube structure may take from one to n links from a source node to a destination node. For example, in a three-cube structure, node 000 can communicate directly with node 001. It must cross at least two links to communicate with 011 (from 000 to 001 to 011 or from 000 to 010 to 011). It is necessary to go through at least three links to communicate from node 000 to node 111. A routing procedure can be developed by computing the exclusive-OR of the source node address with the destination node address. The resulting binary value will have 1 bits corresponding to the axes on which the two nodes differ. The message is then sent along any one of the axes. For example, in a three-cube structure, a message at 010 going to 001 produces an exclusive-OR of the two addresses equal to 011. The message can be sent along the second axis to 000 and then through the third axis to 001.

Figure 13-9   Hypercube structures for $n = 1, 2, 3$.

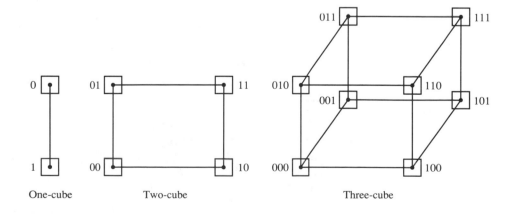

One-cube   Two-cube   Three-cube

A representative of the hypercube architecture is the Intel iPSC computer complex. It consists of 128 ($n = 7$) microcomputers connected through communication channels. Each node consists of a CPU, a floating-point processor, local memory, and serial communication interface units. The individual nodes operate independently on data stored in local memory according to resident programs. The data and programs to each node come through a message-passing system from other nodes or from a cube manager. Application programs are developed and compiled on the cube manager and then downloaded to the individual nodes. Computations are distributed through the system and executed concurrently.

13-3   Interprocessor Arbitration

Computer systems contain a number of buses at various levels to facilitate the transfer of information between components. The CPU contains a number of internal buses for transferring information between processor registers and ALU. A memory bus consists of lines for transferring data, address, and read/write information. An I/O bus is used to transfer information to and from input and output devices. A bus that connects major components in a multi-processor system, such as CPUs, IOPs, and memory, is called a *system bus*. The physical circuits of a system bus are contained in a number of identical printed circuit boards. Each board in the system belongs to a particular module. The board consists of circuits connected in parallel through connectors. Each pin of each circuit connector is connected by a wire to the corresponding pin of all other connectors in other boards. Thus any board can be plugged into a slot in the backplane that forms the system bus.

system bus

The processors in a shared memory multiprocessor system request access to common memory or other common resources through the system bus. If no other processor is currently utilizing the bus, the requesting processor may be granted access immediately. However, the requesting processor must wait if another processor is currently utilizing the system bus. Furthermore, other processors may request the system bus at the same time. Arbitration must then be performed to resolve this multiple contention for the shared resources. The arbitration logic would be part of the system bus controller placed between the local bus and the system bus as shown in Fig. 13-2.

System Bus

A typical system bus consists of approximately 100 signal lines. These lines are divided into three functional groups: data, address, and control. In addition, there are power distribution lines that supply power to the components. For example, the IEEE standard 796 multibus system has 16 data lines, 24 address lines, 26 control lines, and 20 power lines, for a total of 86 lines.

The data lines provide a path for the transfer of data between processors and common memory. The number of data lines is usually a multiple of 8, with 16 and 32 being most common. The address lines are used to identify a memory address or any other source or destination, such as input or output ports. The number of address lines determines the maximum possible memory capacity in the system. For example, an address of 24 lines can access up to 2^{24} (16 mega) words of memory. The data and address lines are terminated with three-state buffers (see Fig. 4-5). The address buffers are unidirectional from processor to memory. The data lines are bidirectional (see Fig. 12-3), allowing the transfer of data in either direction.

synchronous bus

Data transfers over the system bus may be synchronous or asynchronous. In a synchronous bus, each data item is transferred during a time slice known in advance to both source and destination units. Synchronization is achieved by driving both units from a common clock source. An alternative procedure is to have separate clocks of approximately the same frequency in each unit. Synchronization signals are transmitted periodically in order to keep all clocks

asynchronous bus

in the system in step with each other. In an asynchronous bus, each data item being transferred is accompanied by handshaking control signals (see Fig. 11-9) to indicate when the data are transferred from the source and received by the destination.

The control lines provide signals for controlling the information transfer between units. Timing signals indicate the validity of data and address information. Command signals specify operations to be performed. Typical control lines include transfer signals such as memory read and write, acknowledge of a transfer, interrupt requests, bus control signals such as bus request and bus grant, and signals for arbitration procedures.

Table 13-1 lists the 86 lines that are available in the IEEE standard 796 multibus. It includes 16 data lines and 24 address lines. All signals in the multibus are active or enabled in the low-level state. The data transfer control signals include memory read and write as well as I/O read and write. Consequently, the address lines can be used to address separate memory and I/O spaces. The memory or I/O responds with a transfer acknowledge signal when the transfer is completed. Each processor attached to the multibus has up to eight interrupt request outputs and one interrupt acknowledge input line. They are usually applied to a priority interrupt controller similar to the one described in Fig. 11-21. The miscellaneous control signals provide timing and initialization capabilities. In particular, the bus lock signal is essential for multiprocessor applications. This processor-activated signal serves to prevent other processors from getting hold of the bus while executing a test and set instruction. This instruction is needed for proper processor synchronization (see Sec. 13-4).

The six bus arbitration signals are used for interprocessor arbitration. These signals will be explained later after a discussion of the serial and parallel arbitration procedures.

TABLE 13-1 IEEE Standard 796 Multibus Signals

	Signal name
Data and address	
Data lines (16 lines)	DATA0–DATA15
Address lines (24 lines)	ADRS0–ADRS23
Data transfer	
Memory read	MRDC
Memory write	MWTC
IO read	IORC
IO write	IOWC
Transfer acknowledge	TACK
Interrupt control	
Interrupt request (8 lines)	INT0–INT7
Interrupt acknowledge	INTA
Miscellaneous control	
Master clock	CCLK
System initialization	INIT
Byte high enable	BHEN
Memory inhibit (2 lines)	INH1–INH2
Bus lock	LOCK
Bus arbitration	
Bus request	BREQ
Common bus request	CBRQ
Bus busy	BUSY
Bus clock	BCLK
Bus priority in	BPRN
Bus priority out	BPRO
Power and ground (20 lines)	

Reprinted with permission of the IEEE.

Serial Arbitration Procedure

Arbitration procedures service all processor requests on the basis of established priorities. A hardware bus priority resolving technique can be established by means of a serial or parallel connection of the units requesting control of the system bus. The serial priority resolving technique is obtained from a daisy-chain connection of bus arbitration circuits similar to the priority interrupt logic presented in Sec. 11-5. The processors connected to the system bus are assigned priority according to their position along the priority control line. The device closest to the priority line is assigned the highest priority. When multiple devices concurrently request the use of the bus, the device with the highest priority is granted access to it.

Figure 13-10 shows the daisy-chain connection of four arbiters. It is assumed that each processor has its own bus arbiter logic with priority-in and priority-out lines. The priority out (PO) of each arbiter is connected to the

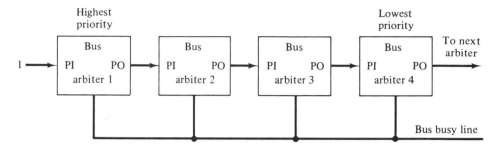

Figure 13-10   Serial (daisy-chain) arbitration.

priority in (*PI*) of the next-lower-priority arbiter. The *PI* of the highest-priority unit is maintained at a logic 1 value. The highest-priority unit in the system will always receive access to the system bus when it requests it. The *PO* output for a particular arbiter is equal to 1 if its *PI* input is equal to 1 and the processor associated with the arbiter logic is not requesting control of the bus. This is the way that priority is passed to the next unit in the chain. If the processor requests control of the bus and the corresponding arbiter finds its *PI* input equal to 1, it sets its *PO* output to 0. Lower-priority arbiters receive a 0 in *PI* and generate a 0 in *PO*. Thus the processor whose arbiter has a *PI* = 1 and *PO* = 0 is the one that is given control of the system bus.

A processor may be in the middle of a bus operation when a higher-priority processor requests the bus. The lower-priority processor must complete its bus operation before it relinquishes control of the bus. The bus busy line shown in Fig. 13-10 provides a mechanism for an orderly transfer of control. The busy line comes from open-collector circuits in each unit and provides a wired-OR logic connection. When an arbiter receives control of the bus (because its *PI* = 1 and *PO* = 0) it examines the busy line. If the line is inactive, it means that no other processor is using the bus. The arbiter activates the busy line and its processor takes control of the bus. However, if the arbiter finds the busy line active, it means that another processor is currently using the bus. The arbiter keeps examining the busy line while the lower-priority processor that lost control of the bus completes its operation. When the bus busy line returns to its inactive state, the higher-priority arbiter enables the busy line, and its corresponding processor can then conduct the required bus transfers.

Parallel Arbitration Logic

The parallel bus arbitration technique uses an external priority encoder and a decoder as shown in Fig. 13-11. Each bus arbiter in the parallel scheme has a bus request output line and a bus acknowledge input line. Each arbiter enables the request line when its processor is requesting access to the system

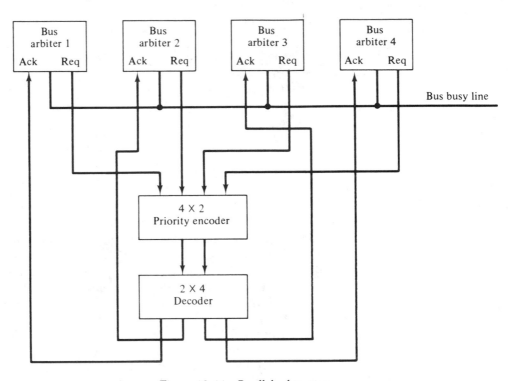

Figure 13-11 Parallel arbitration.

bus. The processor takes control of the bus if its acknowledge input line is enabled. The bus busy line provides an orderly transfer of control, as in the daisy-chaining case.

Figure 13-11 shows the request lines from four arbiters going into a 4×2 priority encoder. The output of the encoder generates a 2-bit code which represents the highest-priority unit among those requesting the bus. The truth table of the priority encoder can be found in Table 11-2 (Sec. 11-5). The 2-bit code from the encoder output drives a 2×4 decoder which enables the proper acknowledge line to grant bus access to the highest-priority unit.

We can now explain the function of the bus arbitration signals listed in Table 13-1. The bus priority-in BPRN and bus priority-out BPRO are used for a daisy-chain connection of bus arbitration circuits. The bus busy signal BUSY is an open-collector output used to instruct all arbiters when the bus is busy conducting a transfer. The common bus request CBRQ is also an open-collector output that serves to instruct the arbiter if there are any other arbiters of lower-priority requesting use of the system bus. The signals used to construct a parallel arbitration procedure are bus request BREQ and priority-in BPRN, corresponding to the request and acknowledge signals in Fig. 13-11. The bus clock BCLK is used to synchronize all bus transactions.

Dynamic Arbitration Algorithms

The two bus arbitration procedures just described use a static priority algorithm since the priority of each device is fixed by the way it is connected to the bus. In contrast, a dynamic priority algorithm gives the system the capability for changing the priority of the devices while the system is in operation. We now discuss a few arbitration procedures that use dynamic priority algorithms.

time slice

The *time slice* algorithm allocates a fixed-length time slice of bus time that is offered sequentially to each processor, in round-robin fashion. The service given to each system component with this scheme is independent of its location along the bus. No preference is given to any particular device since each is allotted the same amount of time to communicate with the bus.

polling

In a bus system that uses *polling*, the bus grant signal is replaced by a set of lines called poll lines which are connected to all units. These lines are used by the bus controller to define an address for each device connected to the bus. The bus controller sequences through the addresses in a prescribed manner. When a processor that requires access recognizes its address, it activates the bus busy line and then accesses the bus. After a number of bus cycles, the polling process continues by choosing a different processor. The polling sequence is normally programmable, and as a result, the selection priority can be altered under program control.

LRU

The *least recently used* (LRU) algorithm gives the highest priority to the requesting device that has not used the bus for the longest interval. The priorities are adjusted after a number of bus cycles according to the LRU algorithm. With this procedure, no processor is favored over any other since the priorities are dynamically changed to give every device an opportunity to access the bus.

FIFO

In the *first-come, first-serve* scheme, requests are served in the order received. To implement this algorithm, the bus controller establishes a queue arranged according to the time that the bus requests arrive. Each processor must wait for its turn to use the bus on a first-in, first-out (FIFO) basis.

rotating daisy-chain

The *rotating daisy-chain* procedure is a dynamic extension of the daisy-chain algorithm. In this scheme there is no central bus controller, and the priority line is connected from the priority-out of the last device back to the priority-in of the first device in a closed loop. This is similar to the connections shown in Fig. 13-10 except that the *PO* output of arbiter 4 is connected to the *PI* input of arbiter 1. Whichever device has access to the bus serves as a bus controller for the following arbitration. Each arbiter priority for a given bus cycle is determined by its position along the bus priority line from the arbiter whose processor is currently controlling the bus. Once an arbiter releases the bus, it has the lowest priority.

13-4 Interprocessor Communication and Synchronization

The various processors in a multiprocessor system must be provided with a facility for communicating with each other. A communication path can be established through common input–output channels. In a shared memory multiprocessor system, the most common procedure is to set aside a portion of memory that is accessible to all processors. The primary use of the common memory is to act as a message center similar to a mailbox, where each processor can leave messages for other processors and pick up messages intended for it.

The sending processor structures a request, a message, or a procedure, and places it in the memory mailbox. Status bits residing in common memory are generally used to indicate the condition of the mailbox, whether it has meaningful information, and for which processor it is intended. The receiving processor can check the mailbox periodically to determine if there are valid messages for it. The response time of this procedure can be time consuming since a processor will recognize a request only when polling messages. A more efficient procedure is for the sending processor to alert the receiving processor directly by means of an interrupt signal. This can be accomplished through a software-initiated interprocessor interrupt by means of an instruction in the program of one processor which when executed produces an external interrupt condition in a second processor. This alerts the interrupted processor of the fact that a new message was inserted by the interrupting processor.

In addition to shared memory, a multiprocessor system may have other shared resources. For example, a magnetic disk storage unit connected to an IOP may be available to all CPUs. This provides a facility for sharing of system programs stored in the disk. A communication path between two CPUs can be established through a link between two IOPs associated with two different CPUs. This type of link allows each CPU to treat the other as an I/O device so that messages can be transferred through the I/O path.

To prevent conflicting use of shared resources by several processors there must be a provision for assigning resources to processors. This task is given to the operating system. There are three organizations that have been used in the design of operating system for multiprocessors: master-slave configuration, separate operating system, and distributed operating system.

In a master-slave mode, one processor, designated the master, always executes the operating system functions. The remaining processors, denoted as slaves, do not perform operating system functions. If a slave processor needs an operating system service, it must request it by interrupting the master and waiting until the current program can be interrupted.

In the separate operating system organization, each processor can execute the operating system routines it needs. This organization is more suitable for loosely coupled systems where every processor may have its own copy of the entire operating system.

In the distributed operating system organization, the operating system routines are distributed among the available processors. However, each particular operating system function is assigned to only one processor at a time. This type of organization is also referred to as a floating operating system since the routines float from one processor to another and the execution of the routines may be assigned to different processors at different times.

In a loosely coupled multiprocessor system the memory is distributed among the processors and there is no shared memory for passing information. The communication between processors is by means of message passing through I/O channels. The communication is initiated by one processor calling a procedure that resides in the memory of the processor with which it wishes to communicate. When the sending processor and receiving processor name each other as a source and destination, a channel of communication is established. A message is then sent with a header and various data objects used to communicate between nodes. There may be a number of possible paths available to send the message between any two nodes. The operating system in each node contains routing information indicating the alternative paths that can be used to send a message to other nodes. The communication efficiency of the interprocessor network depends on the communication routing protocol, processor speed, data link speed, and the topology of the network.

Interprocessor Synchronization

The instruction set of a multiprocessor contains basic instructions that are used to implement communication and synchronization between cooperating processes. Communication refers to the exchange of data between different processes. For example, parameters passed to a procedure in a different processor constitute interprocessor communication. Synchronization refers to the special case where the data used to communicate between processors is control information. Synchronization is needed to enforce the correct sequence of processes and to ensure mutually exclusive access to shared writable data.

Multiprocessor systems usually include various mechanisms to deal with the synchronization of resources. Low-level primitives are implemented directly by the hardware. These primitives are the basic mechanisms that enforce mutual exclusion for more complex mechanisms implemented in software. A number of hardware mechanisms for mutual exclusion have been developed. One of the most popular methods is through the use of a binary semaphore.

Mutual Exclusion with a Semaphore

A properly functioning multiprocessor system must provide a mechanism that will guarantee orderly access to shared memory and other shared resources. This is necessary to protect data from being changed simultaneously by two or more processors. This mechanism has been termed *mutual exclusion*. Mutual exclusion must be provided in a multiprocessor system to enable one processor to exclude or lock out access to a shared resource by other processors when *critical section* it is in a *critical section*. A critical section is a program sequence that, once begun, must complete execution before another processor accesses the same shared resource.

A binary variable called a *semaphore* is often used to indicate whether or not a processor is executing a critical section. A semaphore is a software-controlled flag that is stored in a memory location that all processors can access. When the semaphore is equal to 1, it means that a processor is executing a critical program, so that the shared memory is not available to other processors. When the semaphore is equal to 0, the shared memory is available to any requesting processor. Processors that share the same memory segment agree by convention not to use the memory segment unless the semaphore is equal to 0, indicating that memory is available. They also agree to set the semaphore to 1 when they are executing a critical section and to clear it to 0 when they are finished.

Testing and setting the semaphore is itself a critical operation and must be performed as a single indivisible operation. If it is not, two or more processors may test the semaphore simultaneously and then each set it, allowing them to enter a critical section at the same time. This action would allow simultaneous execution of critical section, which can result in erroneous initialization of control parameters and a loss of essential information.

A semaphore can be initialized by means of a test and set instruction in *hardware lock* conjunction with a hardware *lock* mechanism. A hardware lock is a processor-generated signal that serves to prevent other processors from using the system bus as long as the signal is active. The test-and-set instruction tests and sets a semaphore and activates the lock mechanism during the time that the instruction is being executed. This prevents other processors from changing the semaphore between the time that the processor is testing it and the time that it is setting it. Assume that the semaphore is a bit in the least significant position of a memory word whose address is symbolized by SEM. Let the mnemonic TSL designate the "test and set while locked" operation. The instruction

        TSL   SEM

will be executed in two memory cycles (the first to read and the second to write) without interference as follows:

$$R \leftarrow M[SEM] \qquad \text{Test semaphore}$$
$$M[SEM] \leftarrow 1 \qquad \text{Set semaphore}$$

The semaphore is tested by transferring its value to a processor register R and then it is set to 1. The value in R determines what to do next. If the processor finds that $R = 1$, it knows that the semaphore was originally set. (The fact that it is set again does not change the semaphore value.) That means that another processor is executing a critical section, so the processor that checked the semaphore does not access the shared memory. If $R = 0$, it means that the common memory (or the shared resource that the semaphore represents) is available. The semaphore is set to 1 to prevent other processors from accessing memory. The processor can now execute the critical section. The last instruction in the program must clear location SEM to zero to release the shared resource to other processors.

Note that the lock signal must be active during the execution of the test-and-set instruction. It does not have to be active once the semaphore is set. Thus the lock mechanism prevents other processors from accessing memory while the semaphore is being set. The semaphore itself, when set, prevents other processors from accessing shared memory while one processor is executing a critical section.

13-5 Cache Coherence

The operation of cache memory is explained in Sec. 12-6. The primary advantage of cache is its ability to reduce the average access time in uniprocessors. When the processor finds a word in cache during a read operation, the main memory is not involved in the transfer. If the operation is to write, there are two commonly used procedures to update memory. In the *write-through* policy, both cache and main memory are updated with every write operation. In the *write-back* policy, only the cache is updated and the location is marked so that it can be copied later into main memory.

In a shared memory multiprocessor system, all the processors share a common memory. In addition, each processor may have a local memory, part or all of which may be a cache. The compelling reason for having separate caches for each processor is to reduce the average access time in each processor. The same information may reside in a number of copies in some caches and main memory. To ensure the ability of the system to execute memory operations correctly, the multiple copies must be kept identical. This requirement imposes a *cache coherence* problem. A memory scheme is *coherent* if the value returned on a load instruction is always the value given by the latest store instruction with the same address. Without a proper solution to the cache coherence problem, caching cannot be used in bus-oriented multiprocessors with two or more processors.

Conditions for Incoherence
Cache coherence problems exist in multiprocessors with private caches because of the need to share writable data. Read-only data can safely be replicated

without cache coherence enforcement mechanisms. To illustrate the problem, consider the three-processor configuration with private caches shown in Fig. 13-12. Sometime during the operation an element X from main memory is loaded into the three processors, P_1, P_2, and P_3. As a consequence, it is also copied into the private caches of the three processors. For simplicity, we assume that X contains the value of 52. The load on X to the three processors results in consistent copies in the caches and main memory.

If one of the processors performs a store to X, the copies of X in the caches become inconsistent. A load by the other processors will not return the latest value. Depending on the memory update policy used in the cache, the main memory may also be inconsistent with respect to the cache. This is shown in Fig. 13-13. A store to X (of the value of 120) into the cache of processor P_1 updates memory to the new value in a write-through policy. A write-through policy maintains consistency between memory and the originating cache, but the other two caches are inconsistent since they still hold the old value. In a write-back policy, main memory is not updated at the time of the store. The copies in the other two caches and main memory are inconsistent. Memory is updated eventually when the modified data in the cache are copied back into memory.

Another configuration that may cause consistency problems is a direct memory access (DMA) activity in conjunction with an IOP connected to the system bus. In the case of input, the DMA may modify locations in main memory that also reside in cache without updating the cache. During a DMA output, memory locations may be read before they are updated from the cache when using a write-back policy. I/O-based memory incoherence can be overcome by making the IOP a participant in the cache coherent solution that is adopted in the system.

Solutions to the Cache Coherence Problem

Various schemes have been proposed to solve the cache coherence problem in shared memory multiprocessors. We discuss some of these schemes briefly here. See references 3 and 10 for more detailed discussions.

A simple scheme is to disallow private caches for each processor and have a shared cache memory associated with main memory. Every data access is made to the shared cache. This method violates the principle of closeness of CPU to cache and increases the average memory access time. In effect, this scheme solves the problem by avoiding it.

For performance considerations it is desirable to attach a private cache to each processor. One scheme that has been used allows only nonshared and read-only data to be stored in caches. Such items are called *cachable*. *Shared writable data are noncachable.* The compiler must tag data as either cachable or noncachable, and the system hardware makes sure that only cachable data are stored in caches. The noncachable data remain in main memory. This method

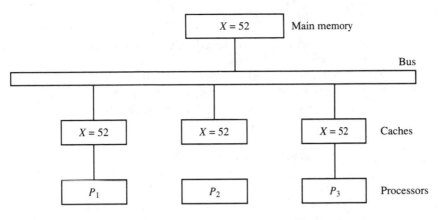

Figure 13-12 Cache configuration after a load on X.

Figure 13-13 Cache configuration after a store to X by processor P_1.

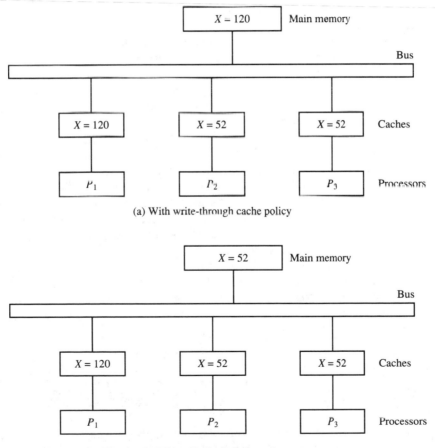

(a) With write-through cache policy

(b) With write-back cache policy

restricts the type of data stored in caches and introduces an extra software overhead that may degrade performance.

A scheme that allows writable data to exist in at least one cache is a method that employs a *centralized global table* in its compiler. The status of memory blocks is stored in the central global table. Each block is identified as *read-only* (RO) or *read and write* (RW). All caches can have copies of blocks identified as RO. Only one cache can have a copy of an RW block. Thus if the data are updated in the cache with an RW block, the other caches are not affected because they do not have a copy of this block.

The cache coherence problem can be solved by means of a combination of software and hardware or by means of hardware-only schemes. The two methods mentioned previously use software-based procedures that require the ability to tag information in order to disable caching of shared writable data. Hardware-only solutions are handled by the hardware automatically and have the advantage of higher speed and program transparency. In the hardware solution, the cache controller is specially designed to allow it to monitor all bus requests from CPUs and IOPs. All caches attached to the bus constantly monitor the network for possible write operations. Depending on the method used, they must then either update or invalidate their own cache copies when a match is detected. The bus controller that monitors this action is referred to as a *snoopy cache controller*. This is basically a hardware unit designed to maintain a bus-watching mechanism over all the caches attached to the bus.

snoopy cache controller

Various schemes have been proposed to solve the cache coherence problem by means of snoopy cache protocol. The simplest method is to adopt a write-through policy and use the following procedure. All the snoopy controllers watch the bus for memory store operations. When a word in a cache is updated by writing into it, the corresponding location in main memory is also updated. The local snoopy controllers in all other caches check their memory to determine if they have a copy of the word that has been overwritten. If a copy exists in a remote cache, that location is marked invalid. Because all caches snoop on all bus writes, whenever a word is written, the net effect is to update it in the original cache and main memory and remove it from all other caches. If at some future time a processor accesses the invalid item from its cache, the response is equivalent to a cache miss, and the updated item is transferred from main memory. In this way, inconsistent versions are prevented.

PROBLEMS

13-1.   Discuss the difference between tightly coupled multiprocessors and loosely coupled multiprocessors from the viewpoint of hardware organization and programming techniques.

13-2. What is the purpose of the system bus controller shown in Fig. 13-2? Explain how the system can be designed to distinguish between references to local memory and references to common shared memory.

13-3. How many switch points are there in a crossbar switch network that connects p processors to m memory modules?

13-4. The 8×8 omega switching network of Fig. 13-8 has three stages with four switches in each stage, for a total of 12 switches. How many stages and switches per stage are needed in an $n \times n$ omega switching network?

13-5. Suppose that the wire breaks between the switch in the first row, second column and the switch in the second row, third column in the omega switching network of Fig. 13-8. What paths will be disconnected?

13-6. Construct a diagram for a 4×4 omega switching network. Show the switch setting required to connect input 3 to output 1.

13-7. Three types of switches are used to design a multistage interconnection network: an interchange switch with two inputs and two outputs as in Fig. 13-6, an arbitration switch with two inputs and one output, and a distribution switch with one input and two outputs.
  a. Show how the arbitration and distribution switches operate.
  b. Using arbitration and interchange switches, construct an 8×4 network with a unique path between any source and any destination.
  c. Using distribution and interchange switches, construct a 4×8 network with a unique path between any source and any destination.

13-8. Draw a diagram showing the structure of a four-dimensional hypercube network. List all the paths available from node 7 to node 9 that use the minimum number of intermediate nodes.

13-9. Draw a logic diagram using gates and flip-flops showing the circuit of one bus arbiter stage in the daisy-chain arbitration scheme of Fig. 13-10.

13-10. The bus controlled by the parallel arbitration logic shown in Fig. 13-11 is initially idle. Devices 2 and 3 then request the bus at the same time. Specify the input and output binary values in the encoder and decoder and determine which bus arbiter is acknowledged.

13-11. Show how the arbitration logic of Fig. 13-10 can be modified to provide a rotating daisy-chain arbitration procedure. Explain how the priority is determined once the bus line is disabled.

13-12. Consider a bus topology in which two processors communicate through a buffer in shared memory. When one processor wishes to communicate with the other processor it puts the information in the memory buffer and sets a flag. Periodically, the other processor checks the flags to determine if it has information to receive. What can be done to ensure proper synchronization and to minimize the time between sending and receiving the information?

13-13. Describe the following terminology associated with multiprocessors. (a) mutual exclusion; (b) critical section; (c) hardware lock; (d) semaphore; (e) test-and-set instruction.

13-14. What is cache coherence, and why is it important in shared-memory multiprocessor systems? How can the problem be resolved with a snoopy cache controller?

REFERENCES

1. Dasgupta, S., *Computer Architecture: A Modern Synthesis*, Vol. 2. New York: John Wiley, 1989.

2. DeCegama, A. L., *Parallel Processing Architecture and VLSI Hardware*. Englewood Cliffs, NJ: Prentice Hall, 1989.

3. Dubois, M., C. Scheurich, and F. A. Briggs, "Synchronization, Coherence, and Event Ordering in Multiprocessors." *IEEE Computer*, Vol. 21, No. 2 (February 1988), pp. 9–21.

4. Gibson, G. A., *Computer Systems Concepts and Design*. Englewood Cliffs, NJ: Prentice Hall, 1991.

5. Gorsline, G. W., *Computer Organization: Hardware/Software*, 2nd ed. Englewood Cliffs, NJ: Prentice Hall, 1986.

6. Hays, J. F., *Computer Architecture and Organization*, 2nd ed. New York: McGraw-Hill, 1988.

7. Hwang, K., and F. A. Briggs, *Computer Architecture and Parallel Processing*. New York: McGraw-Hill, 1984.

8. Kain, R., *Computer Architecture: Software and Hardware*, Vol. 2. Englewood Cliffs, NJ: Prentice Hall, 1989.

9. Langholz, G., J. Francioni, and A. Kandel, *Elements of Computer Organization*. Englewood Cliffs, NJ: Prentice Hall, 1989.

10. Stenstrom, P., "A Survey of Cache Coherence Schemes for Multiprocessors." *IEEE Computer*, Vol. 23, No. 6 (June 1990), pp. 12–24.

11. Stone, H. S., *High-Performance Computer Architecture*. 2nd ed. Reading, MA: Addison-Wesley, 1990.

12. Tabak, D., *Multiprocessors*. Englewood Cliffs, NJ: Prentice Hall, 1990.

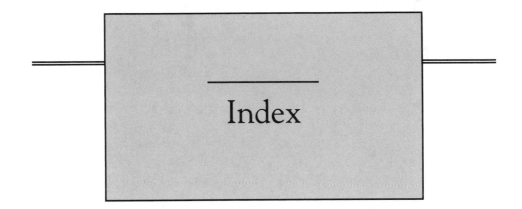

Index

Z